GOOD REASONING MATTERS!

FIFTH EDITION

GOOD REASONING MATTERS!

A Constructive Approach to Critical Thinking

Leo A. Groarke
Christopher W. Tindale

OXFORD
UNIVERSITY PRESS

OXFORD
UNIVERSITY PRESS

Oxford University Press is a department of the University of Oxford.
It furthers the University's objective of excellence in research, scholarship,
and education by publishing worldwide. Oxford is a registered trade mark of
Oxford University Press in the UK and in certain other countries.

Published in Canada by
Oxford University Press
8 Sampson Mews, Suite 204,
Don Mills, Ontario M3C 0H5 Canada

www.oupcanada.com

First Edition published in 1989
Second Edition published in 1997
Third Edition published in 2004
Fourth Edition published in 2008

Library and Archives Canada Cataloguing in Publication

Groarke, Leo
Good reasoning matters! : a constructive approach to critical
thinking / Leo A. Groarke & Christopher W. Tindale. — 5th ed.

Includes index.
First ed. by J. Frederick Little, Leo Groarke and Christopher Tindale.
ISBN 978–0–19–544575–6

1. Reasoning—Textbooks. 2. Critical thinking—Textbooks.
I. Tindale, Christopher W. (Christopher William) II. Title.

BC177.L58 2012   168   C2012-904069-X

Cover image: Tim Ridley/Dorling Kindersley/Getty Images

Printed and bound in Canada

3   4   5   —   19   18   17

CONTENTS

PREFACE

A Note to the Student

What is right or wrong
I don't know who to believe in
My soul sings a different song
I am right and you are wrong
I am right and you are wrong
I am right and you are wrong
No one's right and no one's wrong

—Creed, "In America"

We are all inundated by the messages we see, hear, and read in social media, on the Internet, television, and radio, in magazines and books, on bumper stickers and billboards.

Our sources of information and the myriad of messages they convey compete for our attention, soliciting our support. Debates rage, arguments and counter-arguments are offered, and advertisements tell us we should buy this and do that. We are pushed to take a stand, but the influx of contradictory messages is confusing.

How should we decide who is right, what is acceptable, and even what ideas or points of view we should spend our time, energy, and money exploring?

This book is designed to help you improve your reasoning so that you can reach your own conclusions about whatever topics you choose to study and address. We hope that you will emerge a reasoner who is proficient at assessing the arguments you encounter and able to construct convincing arguments of your own.

The thinking skills you will develop can be applied to all aspects of your life. They are particularly important in a democracy. Because in an age when "attack ads" are becoming more and more prevalent, its success depends on the ability of citizens to see through such irrelevancies and make significant political decisions about complex social and economic issues.

Many people think they are good at reasoning because they like to argue and are willing to defend a position "to the bitter end." But there is more to reasoning. A good arguer must know:

- what counts as a good reason for a claim;
- when claims are relevant to an argument and when they are not;
- what conclusions reasonably follow from different kinds of evidence;

- the difference between sufficient and insufficient evidence; and
- the expectations that attend different contexts and different audiences.

The key to success is not memorizing the principles of good reasoning but repeatedly applying them in practice.

You can develop your critical skills by doing the exercises in this book—and by making a concerted effort to employ a critical attitude in other contexts: in talking with friends, in reading the newspaper, in writing essays for your other courses, and so on. On the website associated with this text (www.oup.com/GoodReasoning5e) you will find many more exercises, quizzes, and review questions that will help in this endeavour.

When you apply your reasoning skills elsewhere, keep in mind that reasoning is rarely final and definitive. Many claims, issues, views, and arguments are open to differing interpretations. In preparing the examples in this book, we have made an effort to consider all reasonable points of view. We have done the same in the answers to selected (starred) exercises that are available on the course site.

But you may disagree with one of our analyses. When this happens, discuss your point of view with your instructor or another student. Because an exchange of opinion is essential to good reasoning, and good reasoning matters, your willingness to discuss your point of view with others will help you put into practice the principles we champion in this text.

A Note to the Instructor

Continued innovations in informal logic, critical thinking, the study of rhetoric, and communication studies have made informal logic, argumentation theory, and critical thinking among the most significant areas of pedagogy and inquiry to emerge in the last two decades. Our approach is one among many of value. We believe that it continues to provide an introduction to argument that features aspects of argument missing from many other texts.

In preparing the fifth edition we have benefitted enormously from the feedback of those who have used previous editions, including reviewers for the press. This has led to a significant revision with a number of important changes.

The most substantial of these have involved a reworking of the early chapters to introduce students to the fundamentals of argument before we turn to the complex issues that arise when one tries to interpret natural language arguments. This should make the material we cover easier to digest for students new to the study of argument. In keeping with this, we introduce the basic notions of argument with examples of simple argument, and provide many more examples (and many more exercises) with simple arguments before trying to apply these principles to complex and extended arguments.

Also, in response to requests by instructors, we have moved the formal logic chapters to appendices and dropped altogether the second chapter on syllogisms. This makes it easy to teach the course without them, but it also allows instructors to include sections on propositional logic and syllogisms (especially Venn diagrams) if they are inclined to do so. From the reviews we have received, instructors remain divided on the utility of formal logic in a critical thinking text, so the appendices seem the best way to satisfy all users.

As you will see as you peruse the chapters, we have added more exercises and many new (and recent) examples to make the book as current as possible. At the same time, we continue to retain those examples that work well and are particularly effective in illustrating points.

Finally, we have made a number of specific changes and additions requested by readers and reviewers where these made sense to us. In all decisions of this nature, our aim has been to produce a book that is current and attractive to array of instructors who have slightly different approaches and preferences in terms of what to include and what to exclude from a course on critical thinking.

We point out, though, that our approach continues to retain the central features that we believe makes it distinctive among a wealth of texts in the field. We continue, for example, to pay a great deal of attention to the construction (and not just the analysis) of arguments. Everyone agrees that teaching argumentation/critical thinking must include teaching the skills for evaluating arguments. We would add that the ability to construct good arguments is as important a skill (or set of skills), and we have designed our text with this in mind. The account of argumentative essay writing in the final chapter is an attempt to pull together the different issues that arise in the construction of good arguments in a way that will be relevant to virtually every college and university student, regardless of their discipline.

In teaching the difference between good and bad argument, we have emphasized argument schemes rather than the identification and assessment of fallacies. We believe that something can be learned from the latter approach, and we continue to benefit from the insights it makes possible, but we find it an unduly negative way to teach students how to reason. It fosters a negative attitude in students, who come to believe that logic is a tool for finding fault with almost every argument and arguer. While we do not avoid talk of fallacies, the emphasis is on good reasoning.

We use schemes as a recipe for good argument that can guide both the evaluation of arguments and their construction. Our interest in this approach has been fuelled by the conclusion that many types of argument that have been treated as fallacies constitute good argument schemes if they are used properly (a conclusion that is also evident in the scholarship). In most cases, the counter-side of a traditional fallacy is a legitimate argument scheme, i.e. an identifiable set of conditions and structure that define some proper form of argument. In helping to expand and deepen students' ability to construct good arguments, this text emphasizes these schemes.

An argument scheme like "appeal to authority" is, therefore, presented in a manner designed to show students how to compose good arguments by authority. Our emphasis on argument schemes of this sort gives the text a constructive, positive tone. Even when students are required to assess other people's arguments, we think that our approach encourages a thorough analysis and avoids the hasty application of a fallacy label.

As in earlier editions of this text, we continue to pay significant attention to the rhetorical features of argument. Audience has traditionally been ignored in logic books, but it is difficult to reconcile a failure to consider audiences with the reality of ordinary arguments, which are directed at audiences and constructed with them in mind. We therefore stress both the specific and the "universal" audience for arguments—that is, not only the specific audience to which an argument is directed but also the "universal audience," which can help us establish general standards of good reasoning.

Like earlier editions, this edition of *Good Reasoning Matters!* benefits from continuing research on the theory and pedagogy of argument. The aspects of this text reflecting developments in the field include a broad account of argument that encompasses a discussion of argumentative communication, visual (and other non-verbal) forms of argument, and an attempt to recognize the dialectical aspects of argument.

In spite of the introduction of many new contemporary examples, we have not hesitated to use historical examples when we think they can make a valuable contribution to the discussion in the book. We believe it is important to introduce students to a wide range of arguments that will encourage them to consider views and perspectives they might not be otherwise exposed to.

Another change to this edition has been to move the "Answers to Selected Exercises" from the back of the book to the companion website. This saves space in the text, and should make a small impact on the cost. But it will also encourage more students to go to the site and make use of the aids provided there. As always with our suggested answers, we encourage instructors (and students) to challenge and suggest alternatives to our analyses.

The website for the text (www.oup.com/GoodReasoning5e) includes many more examples of argument, an explanation of our approach to the different topics we discuss, teaching hints and suggestions, suggested answers to starred examples, and suggestions for further reading that correspond to each chapter of the book. The material for instructors is password-protected and not available to students.

Instructors who would like to comment on the text or the website should feel free to contact either author:

Leo A. Groarke (groarke@uwindsor.ca)
Christopher W. Tindale (ctindale@uwindsor.ca)

ACKNOWLEDGEMENTS

The authors would like to thank everyone who contributed to the completion of this edition. This includes instructors who have used previous versions of the book and passed along suggestions for improvement, as well as several reviewers and anonymous reviewers, whose comments have helped strengthen some aspects of the text; these include the following:

- Geoff Bowe, Thompson Rivers University
- Leslie Burkholder, University of British Columbia
- Megan Delehanty, University of Calgary
- Ahmad Rahmanian, University of New Brunswick
- Adam Rawlings, Trent University
- Janelle Ritchot, University of Manitoba.

We are particularly grateful to Leslie Burkholder, Hans V. Hansen, and David Hitchcock and his students for detailed remarks and suggestions for improving the text.

We have also benefitted from the interest and industry of Dina D'Andrea, Beverly Hamilton, and Laura Nicola. They each made a valuable contribution to the book and made its completion that much easier. And we would again like to thank our editors at Oxford for their continued enthusiasm for the project. As always, we alone remain responsible for any errors in the text.

We continue to benefit from research in this burgeoning field, and we hope improvements to this edition reflect this. It is always a pleasure to be able to draw so readily on scholarship that continues to advance our understanding of argumentation.

Leo A. Groarke
Christopher W. Tindale

For our colleagues in argumentation theory
at the University of Windsor

MAKING ROOM FOR ARGUMENT

> The basic unit of reasoning is the **argument**. In this chapter we introduce its elements and situate them within the contexts in which arguments occur. You should emerge with an understanding of the following key concepts:
>
> ▶ arguments
> ▶ premises and conclusions
> ▶ arguers
> ▶ systems of belief
> ▶ specific and universal audiences
> ▶ proponents and opponents.

Forty years after it produced the work that made it famous, the British comedy troupe Monty Python is a hit on YouTube. One of its classic skits is *The Argument Clinic*. It begins with an eager man telling a receptionist that he'd "like to have an argument." She directs him to "room 12" where, after a misadventure in a "room for abuse," he opens the door, smiles at the man behind the desk, and asks: "Is this the right room for an argument?"

If you think this odd, you're right. Usually, the expression "room for argument" is a way of saying that something is open to debate. But not in Monty Python, where a "room for argument" is an office you go to when you want to have an argument. If this sounds like your own office, then you may be a lawyer, a graduate student, or a professor. In real life, there are many offices, and many other rooms, for argument. The latter include debating halls, court rooms, legislative assemblies, seminar rooms, and our own homes. One finds other important places for argument in the physical and virtual spaces that make up books, scientific journals, newspapers, magazines, television shows, advertisements, websites, Facebook pages, and the condensed messages contained in Twitter tweets.

This is a book about arguments that inhabit these and other spaces. To make room for the discussion that will follow—and to show you why you should take it seriously (to provide you with an argument to this effect)—we need to begin by examining the meaning of "argument" and its role in our lives.

Why Make Room for Argument?

EAGER YOUNG MAN: Is this the right room for an argument?
MAN AT THE DESK: I've told you once.
EAGER YOUNG MAN: No you haven't.
MAN AT THE DESK: Yes I have.
EAGER YOUNG MAN: When?
MAN AT THE DESK: Just now.
EAGER YOUNG MAN: No you didn't.
MAN AT THE DESK: Yes I did.
EAGER YOUNG MAN: Didn't.
MAN AT THE DESK: Did.

What follows is a series of the same denials and insistences from each man, until the one looking for an argument gives up in exasperation and observes that what they are doing is not arguing but just contradicting each other.

In ordinary language the word "argument" can mean contradiction or, more generally, "disagreement." In these cases, the paradigm example of an argument is a *vehement* disagreement: a harangue, a quarrel, a yelling match. In this sense, the two men in Monty Python's argument clinic *are* arguing. Arguments like this are a significant, sometimes painful reality. But they are not the kinds of argument that are the subject of this book.

Those who study "argumentation" (philosophers, psychologists, logicians, rhetoricians, dialecticians, communication theorists, and others) typically understand an "argument" as an attempt to provide evidence or *reasons* for some point of view. Disagreement often leads to argument in this sense, for it raises the question whether there are reasons to favour our point of view, or the views of those with whom we disagree. So conceived, arguments help us judge the evidence for and against different points of view. This is why they play such an important role in helping us decide what views we should accept and reject.

The subjects of our arguments are many and varied. They include metaphysical questions about the world and our place within it. The recent discovery of many Earth-like planets has sparked much debate and argument. Are the scientific calculations that this discovery depends on reliable? Do they make plausible the claim that we are not alone in the universe? What implications are there for our religious beliefs and our place in the cosmos? What moral and political obligations do we have if we do find a planet inhabited by other forms of life? An argument about the latter underlies the story narrated in the Hollywood film *Avatar*, the most financially successful movie of all time.

Other arguments are rooted in moral, political, and social issues. Does freedom of religion include the right to polygamous marriage? Are gay, lesbian, and other kinds of couples (sisters, brothers) who live together entitled to the benefits the government grants to traditionally married couples? Is the website WikiLeaks justly criticized for releasing thousands of secret government documents? Does it threaten our security, or does it champion the cause of open, honest and transparent government? Are those who have tried to halt its operations—and take its founder, Julian Assange, to court—guilty of censorship? More generally, is it true, as some have suggested, that our new world of email, cell phone technology, instant video, Skype and the World Wide Web undermine censorship in a way that will usher in new democracies and grass roots political engagement?

Another important source of argument is the economy. Much has been made of the failure of economists to predict the global financial crisis instigated by the collapse of the American housing market. Some argue that this is evidence that shows that the assumptions embedded in classical economics are flawed. Others attempt to extrapolate from recent problems, using them as evidence for predictions about the global economy, as the effects of the financial crisis reverberate around the world. Politicians of different stripes offer arguments in support of and against the proposition that policies of economic stimulus are the way to deal with crises of this sort. Proponents of radically different kinds of reform debate what should be done for the provinces, states, cities and individuals who have been saddled with debts they cannot manage. Governments ponder the question whether a new economic reality requires a new approach to pensions, wages, and poverty.

Other arguments play a central role in our private and professional lives, providing the evidence we rely on when we decide what university or college is right for us, what car we should buy, and where we should live. We consider the arguments of our friends, bloggers, and book and movie reviewers when we decide what to read and what to see. We engage with the books and movies we consume actively, arguing about them and the perspectives they suggest. You should not be shy in demanding reasons for our own claim that a book like the present one can help you decide what beliefs to accept and reject.

We might easily expand our list of topics for argument. The important point is that it demonstrates the pervasive role that arguments play in our lives. This is one reason for taking a book about arguments seriously. But the prevalence of argument does not, by itself, show that you should buy this book or study argument. If argumentation was easily understood, constructed, and assessed, you might not need a book or a course on argument. Studying argument is a good idea because argument is a difficult and complex subject. This is reflected in the fact that errors in judgement and reasoning, and the faulty arguments that result, are commonplace.

We think that you will see this for yourself as you work through the many real life examples we have included in this book. In the meantime, it is worth noting that psychological research has uncovered many biases that interfere with ordinary reasoning. Among other things, it suggests that we tend to be overconfident in our judgements and our reasoning, a bias that is called the "overconfidence effect."

Consider the results of a set of studies by Dunning, Griffin, Milojkovic, and Ross (*Journal of Personality and Social Psychology*, Vol. 58, No. 4, 1990, pp. 610–621) that examined the impact of overconfidence on social prediction: "We compared people's expectations of success in predicting the actions of their peers with their actual performance, and our findings seem unambiguous and consistent. People proved to be markedly overconfident in general. Moreover, they proved to be most overconfident precisely when they were most confident. . . ." In one of their studies, the researchers found that students significantly overestimated the accuracy of their predictions about the behaviour of roommates with whom they had extensive day-to-day contact.

The overconfidence effect suggests that we think too highly of our understanding of the situations in which we find ourselves. **Confirmation bias** suggests that we favour arguments that confirm the biases and beliefs we already have, ignoring or dismissing evidence that contradicts them. Lord, Ross, and Lepper (*Journal of Personality and Social Psychology*, Vol. 37, No. 11, 1979, pp. 2098–2109) presented students with opinions on capital punishment with two studies, one confirming and one disconfirming their existing beliefs about the deterrent effect of capital punishment. Though there was no reason to favour one study over the other, they found that the students clearly favoured the study that supported their pre-existing views. In discussing the study that provided evidence against the deterrent effect of the death penalty, an opponent of capital punishment wrote that "No strong evidence to contradict the researchers has been presented." In response to the same study, a proponent of capital punishment dismissed the findings, writing that "The research didn't cover a long enough period of time."

The over confidence effect and confirmation bias suggest that we are too confident of our beliefs, and tend to dismiss the evidence that might change them. A host of other biases that have been studied raise questions about most people's ability to objectively assess the evidence for and against particular points of view. Among other things, there is evidence that we accept or reject some perspectives, not because of the reasons for accepting (or rejecting) them, but because of the way they are "framed" (in a way that emphasizes losses rather than gains, for example).

A bias called "the halo effect" occurs when people assume, as they often do, that people with good looks (or other positive attributes) are intelligent, pleasant, moral, and so on. More generally, the evidence suggests that people have a natural tendency to depend on simplistic stereotypes (about Americans, Canadians, the Chinese, the French, "foreigners," men with beards, professional women, welfare recipients, and so on) when making decisions and forming opinions.

In many cases, we are not even aware of biases that interfere with our assessment of the evidence at our disposal. In a famous set of experiments by Nisbett and Wilson (*Psychological Review*, Vol. 84, No. 3, 1977, pp. 231–259), an experimenter conducted a "consumer study" in which he laid out four pairs of pantyhose and asked consumers to pick the pair that they preferred. All four pairs were identical, but consumers were significantly more likely to select whatever pair was placed furthest to the right. For some reason, it seems that people (in our culture), seem to have a strong preference for the right-most object in a series.

It would be interesting to speculate on the reason for this (Is it because most people are right-handed? Is it because we read from left to right?) but the important point is that the people considering the pantyhose did not know that this was why they favoured it. When asked, they explained their preference by saying something about the strength or the sheerness or some other quality of the pantyhose. When the experimenter explicitly suggested that the position might have been a contributing factor, the subjects rejected this as peculiar.

There is a great deal that might be said about such biases and the reasons we incline toward them. For that kind of theorizing we recommend a course in cognitive psychology. In this book, it is enough to say that there are all sorts of ways in which these biases influence, and sometimes undermine, attempts to argue, even in scientific and theoretical contexts. In the course of our lives, the issues that this raises are exacerbated by many conscious and unconscious attempts to exploit these biases in argument. In marketing, politics and law courts, they often inform successful advertisements, political campaigns, and appeals to a judge or jury. In many cases, poor arguments successfully convince an audience of a particular point of view, not because they present compelling evidence for the perspective they propound, but because they illegitimately play upon our biases.

Consider the vodka advertisement we have recreated on the next page. It is an attempt to encourage us to drink a particular brand of vodka. We will discuss the mechanics of visual messages in Chapter 6. For the moment, it is enough to note that the crux of the image's meaning is the transformation that occurs when the content of a huge bottle of vodka splashes from the sky and transforms the slow and sleepy life of the village below into the activity and excitement in the urban metropolis it becomes. It is not easy to capture exactly the content of the image in a sentence, but we might roughly summarize it as the claim that "You should drink our vodka because it will transform your sleepy life into one of bustling activity and excitement."

When we summarize the message of the advertisement in this way, we can see it as an attempt at argument: as an attempt to provide a *reason* for drinking the brand of vodka highlighted in the advertisement. What is the reason? It is the claim that doing so will turn your sleepy life into one of bustling excitement. When the message is conveyed in this way, the lameness of the argument becomes apparent. Why should we accept that the consumption of vodka of any brand will transform one's life—literally or figuratively—from the life one experiences in a sleepy village to what one expects in an exciting urban centre like Toronto or New York? And yet the advertisement may still be effective. It may convince people to buy the vodka in question, not because it provides a compelling reason to do so, but because it is fun, playful, vivid, eye-catching, imaginative, and creative (some would point to its sexual overtones). It is a creative tour de force, especially when viewed in colour.

The study of argument is one way to minimize the influences that may interfere with the careful weighing of evidence for and against particular claims that are put to us. In the case of the vodka advertisement, assessing its strength as an argument can show us that it fails to provide convincing evidence for the proposal that we should buy the vodka in question. Thus, skill at assessing argument is one way to counter the many influences that conspire against our ability to reason well. More generally, the biases we must contend with underscore the importance of learning to reason well. Coupled with the prevalence of argument in all facets of our lives, this makes argument an important topic that you will do well to take seriously.

Image created by Dana Scott, © Leo Groarke

Illustration 1.1 "Transform your sleepy life"

EXERCISE 1A*

1. List four potential topics for argument.

2. Name an argumentative topic you have heard discussed, read about or seen on television or the World Wide Web in the last two days. Summarize an argument on the topic: i.e. explain what reasons might be provided in favour of, or in opposition to, a

*In this and other exercise sets, answers to starred questions are provided in the "Selected Answers" section of the course website.

relevant point of view. What is the claim the proposed argument tries to establish? What reasons does it provide in support of it?

3.* Summarize the argument we have provided in claiming that this is a book you should take seriously.

2 Defining Argument

We can illustrate the elements of argument with an example of the kind of argument adduced in a Sherlock Holmes detective story. It begins with a claim, usually unexpected. Suppose the claim is:

The crime was committed by someone in the house.

In answer to protests from his partner, Doctor Watson, Holmes inevitably backs his claim with reasons that support it. Reasons like:

(1) The living room window is open, but there are no footprints outside, even though the ground is soft after yesterday's rain.
(2) The clasp on the box was not broken but opened with the key that was hidden behind the clock.
(3) The dog did not bark.

These three reasons make up Holmes's argument. They provide evidence for the claim that the crime was an "inside job."

In keeping with this example, we define an *argument* as *a set of reasons offered in support of a claim*. The reasons may be presented orally, in a written text, or by means of photographs, symbols, and other non-verbal means (we discuss the latter in Chapter 3). They provide the evidence that is supposed to back the claim in question. The claim for which the reasons are given in support is called the argument's *conclusion*. The reasons are called its *premises*.

The simplest arguments have only one premise. In *The Argument Clinic* Monty Python's man looking for an argument presents one when he denies that an argument can be the same as a contradiction, retorting, "No it can't. An argument is a connected series of statements intended to establish a definite proposition."

Monty Python's man looking for an argument presents one himself when he denies that an argument can be the same as a contradiction, In support of this claim he defines "argument" as a series of connected statements that are intended to establish a further statement.

This one-premise argument can be summarized as follows:

Premise: An argument is a connected series of statements intended to establish a definite proposition.
Conclusion: It can't be the same as a contradiction.

In the Holmes example, the conclusion is supported by three premises—the three statements we have labelled (1), (2), and (3). Other arguments may have any number of premises. A complex extended argument, which might be the subject of a book or speech or film, might contain hundreds of premises arranged in sub-arguments that establish different parts of the case made for the principal conclusion.

Some Real-Life Examples

We take our first examples of real arguments from two Easter articles in a southern Ontario newspaper (*The Record*, 7 April 2007, p. A15). In "Quest for the Real Jesus Continues," the author describes the early followers of Jesus as people who "stood up to be counted among those who had witnessed that God returned Jesus from the dead." He continues:

> Could this just be an opinion, a hallucination, or a legend? Unlikely. There were too many eye-witnesses. The resurrection didn't happen in a dark corner, it didn't happen in a private place. It was a public event.

This is a paradigm example of an argument. The conclusion is the claim that "It is unlikely that the resurrection of Jesus was just an opinion, a hallucination, or a legend." The premise is that "There were too many eye-witnesses—the resurrection didn't happen in a dark corner or a private place, it was a public event." The argument offers the premise as evidence for the conclusion.

In a second article, "Christianity endures scrutiny and questioning" (*The Record*, 7 April 2007) another author discusses what she sees as the popularity of movies and media coverage that offend and question Christian beliefs. She notes that she is a Christian, but still welcomes such coverage:

> Regardless of what I think about the motivation to attack the fundamental beliefs of over two billion Christians around the world, I do want to thank the people who do just that. Why? Because each time Christianity is questioned, it causes churches and individual Christians to study deeper and pray for those who are seeking to know the truth about Jesus. It helps Christians to wake up and pay attention to what others are saying about their faith—even if it is wild speculation and hearsay that is stretched thin.

In this case, the argument might be summarized as follows:

Conclusion:	"Whatever the motivation of those who attack the fundamental beliefs of Christians, this is a good thing (something to be thankful for)."
First Premise:	"Each time Christianity is questioned, it causes churches and individual Christians to study deeper and pray for those who are seeking to know the truth about Jesus."
Second Premise:	"It helps Christians to wake up and pay attention to what others are saying about their faith—even if it is wild speculation and hearsay that is stretched thin."

Are these examples of *good* argument? That is a question we will put aside for now. Suffice it to say that assessing arguments is a two step process. The first step is identifying the components of an argument. The second is evaluating them. In this chapter, our focus is the first of these two steps.

EXERCISE 1B

1. Each of the following passages presents a simple argument. In each case, identify the premise(s) and conclusion.

   (i)* A clear increase in earthquakes and other natural catastrophes creates a compelling case for curbing our thirst for fossil fuels.

   (ii) Referendums bring out the worst impulses in a population. California's referendums have seriously weakened the educational system, and the Swiss have outlawed the building of mosques.

   (iii)* Feral cats are a major problem for urban centres. They carry disease, they fight, and they destroy wildlife.

   (iv) [From *The Windsor Star*, Editorial: "A One-term President?" by Toby Harnden, 17 September 2010, p. 8] "Obama is the first black American president, an established author, multimillionaire and acclaimed figure beyond American shores. It seems unlikely that he will decide not to run in 2012."

   (v)* [Adapted from a Letter to the Editor, *Popular Science*, March 2011, p. 12] In "Flapper Fashion" you state, "Last August . . . marked the first time a human-powered aircraft achieved sustained flight." No. Paul MacCready and Peter Lissman of AeroVironment, Inc. built the *Gossamer Condor*, which in 1977 won the Kremer Priveze for the first human-powered aircraft capable of controlled sustained flight.

   (vi) [From a CBC television report on the destruction of a house in Escondido, California, which was burned to the ground by authorities, November 2010] "A bomb squad concluded that it was too risky to send technicians into the house, because clothing and dishes were stacked next to volatile chemicals, and any knock against them could trigger an explosion."

   (vii) [From a discussion of a show on civil war drawings at the Virginia Museum of Fine Arts, in *American Artist: Drawing*, Winter 2011] The exhibition will be a boon to scholars and the public alike, as it gives viewers a chance to see how artists acted as eyewitnesses to history.

2. Explain the simple argument in each of the following by identifying the conclusion and reason(s) given.

   (i) [From "Small business statistics on Canadian small business & the economy," http://sbinfocanada.about.com, accessed 29 April 2012]
   Small businesses are major contributors to the job market. Small businesses account for over two thirds of employment in five industries: the (non-institutional) health care sector (89 per cent), the construction industry (76 per cent), other

services (73 per cent), accommodation and food (67 per cent), and forestry (67 per cent). According to Statistics Canada's Survey of Employment, Payrolls and Hours (SEPH), on average in 2007, SMEs employed just over 6.8 million, or 64 per cent, of private sector employees covered by SEPH.

(ii) [From an article in *The Atlantic* magazine, October 2010, on the Junior Eurovision Song Contest, p. 30] Countries on the Continent's geographic and political periphery have started to see the junior circuit as a vehicle for mainstream acceptance—cultural, economic, and even strategic. Seven of the 14 countries that will compete at Minsk are ex-Soviet republics. Malta, Cyprus, Serbia, Croatia, and Macedonia are also regular contenders. Georgian President Mikheil Saakashvili, who desperately wants his country admitted to NATO and the European Union, dispatched his wife to Rotterdam in 2007 to attend Georgia's debut performance. Ukraine's president and prime minister both attended last year's festivities in Kiev.

(iii) [From "Health News" in *More* magazine, February/March 2011, p. 30]
"If you've been diagnosed with metabolic bone disease, you need to be tested for celiac disease," says Terry Moore, a gastroenterologist at St Michael's Hospital in Toronto. The reason? Osteoporosis is a known complication of celiac disease, an under-diagnosed intestinal disorder where the immune system goes on attack mode in the presence of wheat, barley or rye gluten, damaging the intestinal lining and preventing the absorption of key nutrients and minerals such as calcium.

(iv) [From an article in the same source as (iii)]
"Legumes don't get any respect," says Fall River, NS, registered dietitian and author Mary Sue Waisman. This is a shame, given that they offer cheap, filling, high-protein and high-fibre ways to avoid spikes in your blood sugar and are packed with folate, which some studies have linked to lowered blood pressure and depression risk in women.

3. Write a short paragraph that contains a simple argument for some conclusion. Identify your argument's premises and conclusion.

3   Arguers and Systems of Belief

Arguments are communicative acts (what are sometimes called "speech acts"), that are used in attempts to establish some point of view. In the communication this implies, the first party to an argument is the arguer who presents the argument. Usually this is an individual, but it could be a group of people or a corporate body of some sort—a company, a branch of government, or some other organization. When we construct arguments, we ourselves are arguers.

An arguer uses an argument to try and establish (or reinforce) a point of view with reasons that support it. These arguments are rooted in a system or "web" of belief. Some aspects of this system may be determined by our sex, race, and nationality. Others may reflect our education, our career, the organizations we join, and our personal reflections. The system may change over time. Many people retain the religious beliefs they grew up with; others reject or change their perspective in a way that has a dramatic effect on their world view. Because our various convictions and beliefs are integrated, it can be difficult to separate them and their origins. Together, they circumscribe our self-identity, constitute our personal perspective, and give rise to the various opinions we subscribe to. Our strongest opinions are the embryos from which our arguments typically develop.

Deeply held beliefs may influence our arguments in ways that are evident in the assumptions behind our reasoning and the consequences that follow from it. Consider the following excerpt from a famous essay by George Grant which appeared as "The case against abortion" (*Today Magazine*, 3 November 1981, pp. 12–13). In arguing against abortions for convenience, Grant introduces the following consideration into the debate (p. 13):

> Mankind's greatest political achievement has been to limit ruthlessness by a system of legal rights. The individual was guarded against the abuses of arbitrary power, whether by state or by other individuals. Building this system required the courage of many. *It was fundamentally based on the assumption that human beings are more than just accidental blobs of matter. They have an eternal destiny and therefore the right to rights.* But the large-scale destruction of human beings by abortion questions that view.

We have italicized the two sentences relevant to the present discussion. Our system of legal rights, Grant maintains, is "based on the assumption that human beings are more than accidental blobs of matter." This "more" is that human beings have a "right to rights" because they "have an eternal destiny." This implies a number of important propositions: that we are planned, that our existence is intentional, and that there is something eternal or immortal about us, presumably as individuals. All this makes us created rather than "accidental blobs."

But created by whom? Though no mention is made of "God," belief in a deity (a creator) is implied. In drawing out this meaning, we have moved beyond what Grant explicitly stated, but reasonably so. It shows that Grant's reasoning is grounded in a religious commitment: that he believes we are part of a divine plan. In a case like this, an element of our belief system can have a key influence on our arguments. It is important that we identify these influences as we go about attempting to convince others of our conclusions, for they may miss our point or reject our premises in view of these elements. In the case at hand, Grant's argument needs to be reinforced because his premises are unlikely to be accepted by people who do not share his religious point of view.

We cannot remove an arguer's belief system in order to prevent its influence, nor is it necessary or advisable to try to do so. But it is important to guard against its unconscious or illegitimate influence. In our own case, this requires self-evaluation. We need to ask ourselves what assumptions underlie our claims and make sure that these assumptions are defensible in an argument. Just because we believe something strongly, we cannot assume that others will, or that the next argument we see supporting it will be good. Even when the conclusion of an argument is true, the argument and premises offered for it may be weak. One of the best ways to strengthen a position is by pointing out the flaws in **weak arguments** for it, and by showing how those flaws might be remedied or avoided. Scrutinizing our arguments and assumptions will help us build a stronger system of belief.

In the case of other arguers, our scrutiny of their arguments may lead us to ask which beliefs and influences lead to the views that they propound. Beyond sex, race, religion, and nationality, this may entail reflections on their educational background, their political views, and their economic and social standing. Such reflections can provide a profile of an arguer's belief system that helps us understand why the arguer reasons in a particular way.

In some cases, the strength of arguments crucially depends on the credibility of the arguer—on their *ethos*, a Greek term that designates one's character and trustworthiness. In Chapter 12, we consider a whole family of arguments—called **ethotic arguments**—in which the assessment of the arguer plays a central role. Assessing the perspective and the credibility of arguers, ourselves included, is important in the process of learning to argue well.

EXERCISE 1C

1. Consider your own belief system, and construct a profile of its major features.

2. Pick someone who has a different system of belief than you do (blogs are a good source for this). Provide a profile of the belief system's major features. How does your subject's belief system differ from your own?

3. The following are quotations relevant to arguments. In each case, construct a profile of the writer by explaining some of the beliefs that can be attributed to them.

    (i)* [From *Skeptic* magazine, "What is Naturopathy," Vol. 16, No. 2, 2011, p. 4] Naturopathy arose in a pre-scientific environment, then lost popularity as scientific medicine developed effective treatments during the 20th century. It had a resurgence in the 1970s as part of the trend of so-called "alternative" medicine. It is currently taught in six schools in the U.S. and licensed in 15 states."

    (ii) [From the mission statement for the *Journal of Cosmology*] Most scientific journals are aimed at specific, narrowly defined areas of research; tailored to those specialists who devote their lives to learning more and more about less and less. The alternative, we are told, is to learn less and less about more and more, and thus "generalists" and interdisciplinary journals are rare indeed, for how many wish to discover how little they know? The interdisciplinary *Journal of Cosmology* is devoted to the study of "cosmology" and is dedicated to those men and women of rare genius and curiosity who wish to understand more and more about more and more: The study of existence in its totality.

    (iii)*[From "Judgment day: How Arnold Schwarzenegger might just have saved California," *The Atlantic*, October 2010, p. 28] Previously, California's gerrymandered districts rewarded loyalty to entrenched partisan factions. As a result, few Republicans would ever vote for a tax hike and almost no Democrat would take on the unions. Redistricting will recast many legislative districts, making them significantly less Democratic or Republican. And candidates running in a wide-open primary will have to rely on a broader base of contributors. The power of the unions, the shock jocks, the anti-taxers, will all be diluted.

(iv) [From *Popular Science*, March 2011, p. 100] Rick Tumlinson, the co-founder of the Space Frontier Foundation, a growing group of entrepreneurs who hope to use private enterprise to succeed where they believe a risk-averse and direction-less NASA has failed, maintains that we will settle the new frontier only when there is a compelling profit motive for it. He lists space tourism, extraterrestrial mining, and the beaming of solar energy from space back to Earth as the best financial reasons to leave the planet. "We achieve permanent human settlements when people are making money," he says. "No bucks, no Buck Rogers."

(v) [In 2011, a serious injury to a Montreal player hit by a player from the Boston Bruins ignited a controversy over violence in ice hockey. The following argument is adapted from a related *Globe and Mail* article "Hockey loving dad believes it's time for a change," by Roy MacGregor, 11 March 2011, who wrote about Dave Sasson, a well-known Quebec hockey enthusiast who won a court battle that repealed a law banning street hockey] This year discussions with NHL general managers will be preoccupied with the problem of concussions. This is the outcome of a 2011 that no one could have imagined: a year that has seen the NHL's greatest star, Sidney Crosby, sidelined with a concussion. There have been more than seventy players who have had to take time off because of concussions, gang fights on the ice, a 10-game suspension for one offender, advertisers questioning their sponsorship, and a commissioner who refuses to take the issue seriously. Dave Sasson is right to call for an overhaul of the culture of the game we all enjoyed as we grew up.

(vi) [An excerpt from another column on the same controversy, entitled "Face it, hockey fans live for brutality," by Cathal Kelly of the *Toronto Star*, 11 March 2011]
What separates the NHL from other sports is full contact at high speeds and institutionalized fist fighting. That's it. Take cultural context out of the mix, and that's why Canadians watch hockey. Because it's fast and tough.

Asking people to mind their elbows at all times and pull out of hits on the boards isn't a little thing. It's a fundamental shift. It's mucking around with the basics. . . .The NHL understands this, but can't verbalize it in any way that won't get them crucified by opportunistic politicians and the usual set of hand-wringers who didn't like the game in the first place. . . .

No, players don't care; and fans care even less. How do we know? Because they continue to watch the game—in fact, TV ratings on both sides of the border are up. . . .

The NFL, which takes in grown men and spits out invalids, is turning over money like a Mexican drug cartel. The Ultimate Fighting Championship is sport's fastest comer overall. Pastoral pursuits like baseball and, increasingly, basketball are losing traction with young fans.

Elegance is out. Brutality is the growth industry.

4 Audiences

Arguers create arguments to convince an audience—someone or some group of people—of their conclusion. This makes audiences the second party to an argument. Sometimes we are our own audience. Sherlock Holmes probably acts as his own audience as he develops an argument in his mind. When he is satisfied, he addresses another audience—usually his partner, Watson. Sometimes, later in the story, he presents the argument to yet another audience, i.e. those who have hired him to solve the case he has resolved.

Poor reasoners tend to assume that whatever evidence convinces them of some conclusion will convince other audiences. When two people (say, Holmes and Watson) share similar systems of belief and points of view, this may be a reasonable assumption. But it is misleading in broader contexts in which we interact and argue with audiences who do not share our point of view. In these cases, it is egocentric to believe that our own convictions and beliefs are characteristic of the audience we address. The opposite should be expected, given that arguments are a means we use to convince people who have *different* points of view that they should share our conclusions.

Some Historical Examples

The role of audiences in argument is readily apparent if we look at historical examples of argument, for they were designed to appeal to audiences with attitudes, beliefs, and concerns other than our own.

Consider, to take a telling example, the content of cigarette advertisements in the following 1940s advertisement. It strikes us as peculiar, even bizarre, but many of these advertisements advocated for their brands by touting their medical benefits. In an advertisement for Philip Morris (which Morris refused to let us reproduce here), one reads that medical authorities—distinguished doctors and an authoritative medical journal—relying on clinical scientific studies concluded that Philip Morris was better for you than rival cigarettes. We would summarize the central argument in the advertisement as:

> **Premise:** Medical authorities know that Philip Morris is scientifically proven to be less irritating to the nose and throat.
>
> **Conclusion:** One should purchase (and smoke) America's "finest" cigarette, Philip Morris.

The premise in this argument is itself a conclusion of a sub-argument which features the premise: "Distinguished doctors, in clinical tests of men and women smokers—reported in an authoritative medical journal—found that substantially every case of irritation of nose and throat due to smoking cleared up completely, or definitely improved when smokers changed to Philip Morris."

The closest analogue to these statements today may be an attempt to market a "Vitamin E enhanced" cigarette by German Tobacco Group under the brand name

S.A.L.E. It features "an improved and soothing flavour" and is said to minimize the "irritation" that occurs when using conventional cigarettes. Though these claims might be compared to the Philip Morris's 1940 claim that its cigarettes were less irritating than other brands, there has been no attempt to promote smoking S.A.L.E. with appeals to scientific and medical authorities. At a time when health authorities have almost universally concluded that smoking is injurious to one's health, this is because no audience would accept an argument for a brand of cigarette that appeals to the findings of "distinguished doctors" and "medical authorities."

In the world in which we live, this is why the Philip Morris argument we have quoted has little impact. Instead of convincing contemporary audiences that they should smoke Philip Morris it is used by anti-smoking advocates as evidence for a very different conclusion: that cigarette companies and their advertisements should not be trusted. Partly in answer to these criticisms, Philip Morris, which still manufactures and sells cigarettes, has attempted to establish credibility in a way that makes more sense to contemporary audiences. To this end, its website www.philipmorrisusa.com emphasizes the *responsible* use of tobacco, and the ethics and integrity of its approach to sales. Philip Morris now promotes a *reduction* in the underage use of tobacco; provides advice on smoking cessation; and promotes itself as a company that "invests in our communities," "reduces our environmental impact," and "operates with compliance and integrity."

In the present context, the important point is that the difference between Philip Morris's approach to its public presence today and in the 1940s is attributable to the audience being addressed in each case. The 1940s advertisement we have quoted contains another feature that illustrates the significance of audience in a slogan that was printed alongside of it: 'Buy more war bonds." This was a common tag during World War II, when advertisers were concerned to address a population which was preoccupied with the war effort. This tendency is taken even further in an advertisement for Nestlé's chocolate bars in *Life* (11 November 1943) which advertises them under the title "U.S. troops fight on chocolate diet," emphasizing the fact that the American army included a Nestlé chocolate bar in its standard emergency rations.

Other historical advertisements illustrate the ways in which arguments assume and are directed to audiences with particular systems of belief. The Campbell Soup advertisement reproduced in Illustration 1.2—"A FEATHER in Mrs. Canada's Cap"—was addressed to women who read the magazine *Star Weekly* in the 1950s. It suggests that they should buy Campbell's Cream of Mushroom soup (*conclusion*) because it is "unusual and especially good" (*premise*), but emphasizes a different consideration which acts as the principle premise in the argument: i.e. the claim that it will win them praise and make a good impression on their families—and in this way be a "feather" in their "cap." Underlying the advertisement is the assumption that women are homemakers whose identity and satisfaction is tied to their ability to perform housework in ways that will earn the approval of their families. This reflects the view of women at the time (a view shared by the women who are the audience to whom the advertisement is directed), but one that is profoundly out of step with the attitudes, beliefs, and aspirations of popular audiences today.

Illustration 1.2   "A Feather in Mrs. Canada's Cap!"

We can highlight these differences by comparing the *Star Weekly* advertisement to advertisements today, which reject the view of women's identity that Campbell's soup appeals to. This does not mean that they always do so in a way that is not open to debate. The brand Wonderbra is known for an advertising campaign that offers a very different view of women's identity, emphasizing looks and sex appeal. One of their advertisements (which they would not give us permission to reproduce here) makes fun of the view of women in the 1950s advertisement we have looked at. It is a waist up photo of a voluptuous supermodel wearing only her Wonderbra, with the caption "I can't cook. Who cares?" The implied answer is that no one cares—because she is an alluring woman. Considered as an argument, the advertisement suggests that women should purchase Wonderbra (*conclusion*) because it will help them look sexy (*premise*). This rejects the view of women's identity highlighted in the 1950s advertisement, but it embraces a contemporary view which many would find equally offensive because it places so much emphasis on good looks and sexual appeal.

The image in the advertisement reproduced in Illustration 1.3 imitates another Wonderbra advertisement from the same campaign. The Wonderbra advertisement in question presents another supermodel in only her bra, with the caption "Regardez-moi dans les yeux. . . . J'ai dit les yeux. . . ." ("Look me in the eyes. . . . I said the eyes. . . ."). The point is that it is difficult not to stare at her chest adorned with her Wonderbra. Here again, the emphasis is on sexuality and good looks. In contrast, the advertisement we have reproduced (below) mimics that Wonderbra image, but in this case the model (Tanja Kiewitz) is a disabled woman with a missing limb. Inserted underneath the new image, the caption highlights our tendency to focus on her deformed limb rather than her good looks. CAP48, a Belgian group dedicated to disability awareness, used the advertisement to raise questions about our tendency to identify disabled people with their disabilities. It very successfully sparked a broad discussion of images of disabled in the media (for a sample, see the National Center on Disability and Journalism discussion at: http://ncdj.org/blog/2010/10/25/sizing-up-disability-in-the-media/).

One finds a more explicit rejection of the view of women one finds in the Wonderbra advertisements and the 1950s Campbell Soup advertisement in the cartoon from the *New Yorker* we have reproduced in Illustration 1.4. As in the first Wonderbra advertisement, the woman pictured—who is presented as a professional woman—frankly declares that she can't cook, but suggests that this doesn't matter for a very different reason: because she "can pay." One might see in this an implicit argument to the effect that cooking doesn't matter anymore, because a woman can establish her worth by being a professional and earning a good salary. In the present context, the three illustrations we have provided reflect different assumptions that appeal to different audiences who make different assumptions about the identity of women. The two contemporary examples explicitly reject the historical example we began with, but do so in different ways, appealing to different values: in the one case emphasizing good looks, in the other professional accomplishment.

REGARDEZ-MOI DANS LES YEUX…
…J'AI DIT LES YEUX.

POUR QUE LE HANDICAP NE SOIT PLUS UN HANDICAP. 000-0000037-37.

Illustration 1.3   "Regardez-moi. dans les yeux . . ."

"I can't cook, but I can pay."

© Bruce Eric Kaplan/The New Yorker Collection/www.cartoonbank.com

Illustration 1.4   "I can't cook, but I can pay"

Different Kinds of Audience

The historical advertisements we have noted try to convince an audience at a particular historical moment that they should buy a particular product. They strike us as odd because we do not share the belief system of the intended audience. You can be sure that future audiences will find our own arguments and advertisements peculiar because they will assume some other, yet to be determined, system of beliefs and values.

In constructing an argument, an effective arguer considers the audience to be addressed. A *specific audience* shares some set of beliefs and commitments. If you want to successfully address such an audience, you need to recognize the beliefs that characterize its members and respond to them. This may mean that you use different variations of an argument when you address the different audiences made up of professional women; sports fans; property owners; renters; stay at home husbands; young people; seniors; automobile drivers; conservatives; atheists; Catholics; gay rights activists; attendees at a scientific conference; and so on. In each case, your argument will be most effective if you make an effort to respond to *their* convictions and concerns.

In gauging an audience's receptivity to a conclusion we want to propound, we distinguish three types of specific audience: audiences that are *sympathetic* to what we are arguing; those that do not accept our position but are *open* to considering it; and audiences that are *hostile* to it. Needless to say, a hostile audience is the hardest to convince, for it subscribes to attitudes and beliefs that are in some way opposed to the perspective we are defending. At the same time, this is the most important audience to argue with, for it is the audience that, more than any other, needs a *reason* to be convinced.

Consider an example. An audience made of people with a college or university education will probably be a sympathetic audience when one is arguing for the maintenance and support of post-secondary education. In addressing them, we can probably assume the value of a higher education. This is something they should have witnessed and experienced for themselves. The extent of their sympathy is likely to reduce the degree of evidence required to convince them of the importance of government funding, more scholarships, or lower tuition fees.

In contrast, more evidence will be required when one addresses an audience that is sceptical of post-secondary education. In this case, one might found one's argument on some other aspect of an audience's system of belief. One might, for example, begin with the premise that we need a flourishing economy and argue that a post-secondary education provides benefits for all, including those without a college or university education. Given this premise one could go on to argue that we should support higher education on the basis of the further claim that a strong economy depends on the innovation and creativity which higher education fosters, providing evidence for this.

Whenever one addresses a specific audience, the best argumentative strategy is to try and demonstrate that one's conclusion follows from some aspect of *the audience's own perspective*. This means meeting such an audience where they are, understanding the thinking on their side, and leading them from it to the conclusion one proposes. In extreme cases, this might mean that one needs to begin by arguing for a fundamental change in their system of belief.

The need to pay attention to a specific audience's system(s) of belief does not mean that one is entitled to exploit its sensitivities. In many cases, an audience's sympathy for a particular cause or position interferes with its critical assessment of the evidence for and against a particular conclusion. While many arguers exploit these inclinations, sometimes purposely so, this produces weak arguments that will not hold up to scrutiny when one is faced with a broader audience.

It is important to recognize specific audiences in many instances. When assessing someone else's arguments, the fact that they are directed toward a specific audience will be a relevant factor in what we expect of the argument. At times, we will focus on specific audiences, but they are not the primary focus of this book. If one develops a good argument that is addressed to a specific audience, then one should also be able to defend it in front of a broader audience that includes reasonable people who have different points of view. In theoretical discussions of argument, the audience that includes *all* reasonable people is commonly referred to as the *universal* audience. Arguments that attempt to satisfy this audience must meet the most stringent standards for good arguments, standards that are explored in this text.

The nature (and even the existence) of the universal audience has been the subject of much discussion. For our purposes, it is enough to say that we will, in most cases, assume a broad audience that includes people with many different points of view. This is the sort of audience that you would have to assume if you were arguing in a newspaper, in a political debate, or to specialists that embrace competing points of view. Even when you argue to convince a specific audience—a situation in which you must strive to understand their beliefs, the assumptions behind their perspective, and the particular knowledge they have—remember that you should be able to defend your perspective in front of a broader audience with many different (and contrary) points of view. Being able to satisfy both specific and universal audiences is an important way to test your arguments and your conclusions.

1.* The following is a comment adapted from a letter to the editor that discusses legislation that would ban strikes by public employees. It contains an argument. What are the premises and conclusion? How has the writer failed to address their intended audience (the general readers of a newspaper)? What audience would be more appropriate for this particular argument?

> Bill 179 should be stopped. Not only does it take away the right to strike, it takes away the right to collective bargaining, through which both the employer and employee mutually agree to the terms and conditions under which they [employees] will work. As anyone who follows the news will know, the Pope has repeatedly stated that man has the right to demand what he feels is just compensation of his labours, including the right to strike.

2. Construct audience profiles for each of the following:

> **Example:** professional women
> Professional women are likely to be well-educated, to be strongly committed to equal rights for women, to value advancement in their profession, and to be sensitive to the issues that confront women in such careers.

a)* university students
b) Native North Americans
c)* sports fans
d) citizens of industrialized countries
e) pet owners
f) labour union members
g) farmers
h) media people

3. List the features you would include in the belief system of the universal audience.

4. In each of the following cases, identify the premises and conclusion in the argument, and discuss the audience to which it is addressed. Does it address the views of the specific and the universal audience?

(i) [From a letter to the *National Post* newspaper, 10 December 2007] No amount of studies will change the fact that parallel private health care systems are splendidly efficient. One need look no further than the systems in place in Sweden, Switzerland and Japan. All these countries deliver timely health care, with comparable or better outcomes than we have in Canada and at a lower cost.

(ii) [The following comes from a report on the Air France disaster in May 2009. "The riddle of flight AF447," The *Independent* newspaper, 10 June 2009] Airline disasters are meat and drink to conspiracy theorists. Several alternative explanations still exist for the Concorde disaster in Paris in 2000 and the terrorist bombing of a Pan Am jumbo plane over Lockerbie Scotland in 1988. The confusion and misinformation surrounding Flight AF447 will inevitably lead to similarly fevered speculation.

(iii) [From a Letter to the Editor, *The Globe and Mail*, Saturday, 1 September 2007, p. A20] "I am a carnivore," Jonathan Zimmerman twice proclaims in Why Is It A More Serious Crime To Kill A Dog Than Hit A Woman? (Aug. 29). If he thinks he's using the word effectively in its core sense, he's setting himself apart from the species, Homo Sapiens, to which I and most Globe readers belong. . . . True carnivores inflict cruelty and death on other creatures only out of necessity, unlike human beings.

(iv) [Jan Techau, head of the Alfred von Oppenheim Center for European Studies at the German Council on Foreign Relations, was one of a number of European leaders to comment in *Der Spiegel Online International* (11 May 2008) on the success of Barack Obama in the November 2008 American Presidential election] The manner in which the future American administration will treat its European counterparts will be all-important for constructive relations during the next four years. Europeans do not expect to find agreement on all policy issues with the U.S. Far from it—Europe itself finds it soberingly difficult to generate much-needed pan-EU unity, even on urgent policy issues. But Europeans expect to be treated without condescension and as nominally equal counterparts, even if it is true that the power imbalance between themselves and the U.S. is sometimes strikingly evident. In other words: a return to normal and established ways of diplomacy is much anticipated—and much needed. The new president could score easy points and make a huge difference by exercising old-fashioned, respectful leadership.

(v) [From the *National Post*, 8 December 2007. If you are unfamiliar with the Latimer case some quick research online will bring you the relevant details] Your letter writers claim there was a "miscarriage of justice" for Robert Latimer. I don't think so—Robert Latimer gassed his daughter to death. The words seem stark on the page, but they are true. He murdered her.

5. We have provided examples of argument that illustrate different views of women assumed by different audiences. Find two examples of argument (historical or contemporary) that illustrate different views of men and their identity. Discuss and contrast the views in question, and the audiences they appeal to.

5   Opponents and Proponents

The role of audiences in argument underscores the point that the presentation of an argument is not an isolated event, but a response to some issue, controversy, or difference of opinion. In many cases, it is a response to an argument that defends a contrary point of view. When you present your own argument, someone may respond by criticizing your reasoning, by requesting some kind of clarification, or by expounding an opposing argument. The give and take that this implies might be compared to a game of chess or some other game in which we move and counter-move in response to the moves of our **opponents**. In the case of argument, this process of exchange is called "dialectic."

We have already noted one instance of dialectic in our discussion of Philip Morris' 1940s advertisement. One might see this advertisement and others like it, as the first move in an exchange that produces criticisms from anti-smoking groups. In answer to these criticisms, Philip Morris has positioned itself differently. Its website www. philipmorrisusa.com makes the move and counter-move explicit, noting that "There are those who believe that a company that makes a dangerous and addictive product cannot be responsible," answering that "We believe that responsibility is defined not only by the products a company makes but also by the action it takes." Needless to say, the opponents of tobacco sales will themselves have a response to make to this answer to their concerns.

The dialectical exchange between proponents and opponents of particular points of view is a key dynamic in the history of ideas, where arguments and counter-arguments may shape debates that span centuries. An example rooted in the philosophy of Plato and Aristotle is the work of the Islamic philosopher, al-Ghazali, which is a critique of the views of Islamic thinkers who propound Platonic and Aristotelian points of views, most notably Ibn Sina (called Avicenna in the West). In answer to their views, al-Ghazali published a book entitled *The Incoherence of the Philosophers* (the *Tahāfut al-Falāsifa*) in which he becomes their opponent, criticizing key aspects of their arguments. The next step in the dialectic is evident in the work of another important Islamic philosopher, Ibn Rushd (known in the West as Averroes), who answers al-Ghazali in a work called *The Incoherence of the Incoherence*. The move and counter-move that characterizes these exchanges continues in the work of other philosophers who criticize Ibn Rushd, others who criticize them, and so on.

In situations which are explicitly designed to deal with arguments, the role of proponents and opponents is often formalized. In a court of criminal law, the prosecution propounds a case against the person accused of criminal activity. The defence acts as their opponent, criticising the prosecution's arguments and conclusion. In other processes of this sort, someone may be appointed as a "devil's advocate"—a role that makes them responsible for testing the arguments others propound. The term itself originates in the process of beatification which was once utilized in the Catholic church (the process by which someone is canonized and becomes a saint). Until Pope John Paul II changed the process in 1983, a devil's advocate was appointed to oppose (and in this way test) the arguments forwarded for the proposition that someone should be canonized.

Such processes underscore the role that opponents play in the development of argument, for their sceptical criticisms are an important way to test our reasoning. By definition, opponents are opposed to our arguments, but we still have an obligation to treat them fairly—in the same way that we have an obligation not to cheat competitors who oppose us in a game. Even when opponents are not included in our immediate audience, we are still obligated to develop our arguments in a way that tries to anticipate and answer their objections. If we are arguing for a public medicare system, this means that we should take seriously the objections to our arguments proposed by those who are opposed to publicly supported health care. If we are arguing against the use of animals in medical experiments, we should consider and respond to the views of those who think that it is justified because it is necessary for the development of new medicine.

A commitment to pay attention to the arguments of opponents forces us to take objections to our views seriously. In Judaism, a rabbi meeting with someone who wishes to convert must make three genuine attempts to persuade them that it is *not* a good idea. This is a powerful variant of the principle that one should take objections to one's conclusions seriously. It takes very seriously the idea that one is not ready to make a decision or hold a belief until one is certain enough not to be persuaded by objections to it. This is an ideal that we should aspire to in constructing arguments. Doing so will make our own arguments—and the conclusions they advocate—more compelling.

EXERCISE   1E

1.* Identify the arguments in the following excerpts from the lead article in the New Hampshire *Rockingham News* ("Dog-Fight Leader Gets Prison," 30 August 2002), which recounted the case of a man tried for cruelty to animals after he trained pit bull terriers to fight in matches, which he staged. For each excerpt, identify the premises and the conclusion of the argument, the specific audience, and the opponents of the view expressed.

    a) Judge Gillian Abrahamson said that the actions of the man who trained the dogs and staged the fights were disturbing because he had "inflicted such pain and torture on helpless animals for fun and profit."

    b) She held that the severity of the 37 counts of "Exhibition of Fighting Animals" justified a sentence in a state prison rather than a county jail.

    c) The attorney for the defendant asserted that the sentence handed down by Judge Abrahamson did not fit the crime because it was "unprecedented in its length."

    d) A coordinator for the Humane Society of the United States New England Regional Office supported the prison sentence, claiming that "the minor penalties associated with misdemeanour convictions are not a sufficient deterrent."

    e) They were not sufficient, she claimed, because "dog fighting yields such large profits for participants [that dog fighters] merely absorb these fines as part of the cost of doing business."

2.* A discussion of the dog-trainer's case above might easily evolve in a way that considers many related issues. Given that it is wrong to be cruel to animals, why is it permissible to kill them and eat them? Isn't killing animals a form of cruelty? Identify the position you would propound on the question whether it is permissible to eat animals. Construct a short argument responding to the views of your opponents in this context. Identify the premise and conclusion in your argument, and explain how it responds to the views of your opponents.

3. Someone defending dog fights might argue that we permit boxing, so we should permit dog fighting. Should these two sports be treated similarly? Why or why not? Construct an argument (with no more than three premises) for a conclusion one way or the other. Construct another argument that you would attribute to those who hold an opposing point of view. Construct a third argument that responds to these opponents.

4. Do you think that animals should be used in scientific experiments? Write a short (one paragraph) argument that supports your view. Imagine that your audience is the general public. Explain one way in which you might adapt your argument to take into account the position of your opponents.

5. Go to a newspaper or web blog and find an argument. Identify the arguer, the audience to which the argument is addressed, and the argument's opponents.

6 Summary

This chapter has introduced the basic ideas essential for a study of argument. We have considered the nature of arguments and how to recognize them. We have also looked at the other components of an argumentative situation: arguers and audiences. Both of these need to be understood in terms of the belief systems that comprise and motivate them. We have also considered different kinds of audience and what to expect with respect to each. Importantly, we have discussed specific and universal audiences, as well as the difference between opponents and proponents.

MAJOR EXERCISE 1M

1.* What is the argument in the following advertisement from *Family*, which features a large photo of a baby, accompanied by text? Who is the intended audience? How can you tell?

> YOU'RE THE ONE WHO HAS PROMISED TO PROTECT HER. PROTECT HER SCALP FROM IRRITATION WITH NEW IMPROVED JOHNSON'S BABY SHAMPOO, THE ONLY ONE CLINICALLY PROVEN HYPOALLERGENIC.

2. You are in the process of buying a new house. You must decide between three different options: (a) you buy a deluxe condominium on Lakeshore Boulevard; (b) you buy a modest bungalow on Northfield Road; (c) you decide to give up on the house and move into a downtown apartment. Option A will let you live the lifestyle you will most enjoy; option B will save you a significant amount of money; option C will place you within walking distance of a good grade school for your children. Pick an option and write an argument for it that is addressed to (a) your spouse; (b) your children; (c) your parents.

3. What is the argument in the following cartoon? Clearly identify the premise and conclusion.

By permission of Mike Luckovich and Creators Syndicate, Inc.

Illustration 1.5   "I'm txting while drvng"

4. The following graph is entitled "Gender Equality Equals Mexico." Summarize the implied argument.

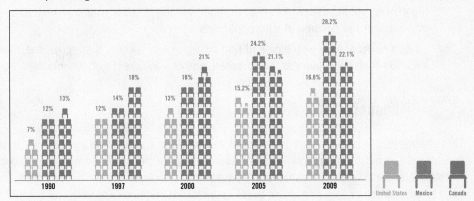

Graph 1.1   "Gender Equality Equals Mexico": Proportion of seats held by women in national parliaments (%)

Source: www.data.worldbank.org/indicator/SG.GEN.PARL.ZS/countries/MX-CA-US?display=default

5. For each of the following, discuss as many ideas from this chapter as the examples allow. Identify premises and conclusions; discuss the audiences involved with the beliefs that are assumed; and identify proponents and opponents.

    i)   [From an article entitled "Amazing Claims for Chlorophyll" posted on a website called *Quackwatch: Your Guide to Quackery, Health Fraud, and Intelligent Decisions*] What about deodorizing properties? Despite the sales hype, in products sold to the public, it doesn't have any. According to John C. Kephart, who performed studies at the laboratories of The National Chlorophyll and Chemical Company about 20 years ago, "No deodorant effect can possibly occur from the quantities of chlorophyll put in products such as gum, foot powder, cough drops, etc. To be effective, large doses must be given internally" (*Journal of Ecological Botany*, Vol. 9, No. 3, 1955).

    ii) [From a letter to *The Atlantic*, October 2010, in response to an article criticizing teachers and teachers' unions, pp. 21–22] Mr. Brooks's essay no more qualifies as a powerful idea than Senator Infhofe's observations about snow in Washington, D.C., qualify as a challenge to the facts of climate change.

         Mr. Brooks cites not one single fact to confirm his view that there has been "an absolute change in the correlation of forces" in relations between organized teachers and the communities they serve. He mentions only two proper names (one of which is General Patton) and provides not one quote in support of his argument.

    iii) [From "Health News" in *More* magazine, February/March 2011, p. 30] "There are so many changes that occur in women's lives from 40 to 60," says Marianna Golts, a psychiatrist at Toronto's Mount Sinai Hospital. "The stress of work, menopausal symptoms, aging parents, having kids or kids leaving—all these factors can contribute to your depression risk." . . . The safeguard is maintenance. "It's so important for women to put their needs first, get adequate sleep, exercise and have a life outside of family and work—all the normal things that usually get pushed aside at this point in a woman's life."

iv) [From *The Windsor Star*, p. A7, Opinion: "Keep phones out of class," by Cory Matchett, 24 September 2010] "The school board thinks it would be good for students and allow them to take notes on their phones. I think this is outrageous. I am a student at the university and have seen first-hand that many students just sit there and text all class. . . The world is far too complicated these days and the only way we are going to move in the right direction is by simplifying things. In my opinion, all you need to do well in school is paper, a pen and, most importantly, your mind."

v) [From *The Windsor Star*, Letters to the Editor, "Support for arts lacking in Windsor," by Mary Vasyliw, Monday, 7 March 2011, p. A7] "I would ask that every family with young children go out and actively support [the arts] before they are gone. Not only does it enrich the children's lives but brings many benefits to this city. To be a truly great city, there has to be a mixture of cultural and sporting activities for people of all ages."

vi) [From *More Magazine*, March 2011, pp. 52–53:] Singing can also nurture the body. A 2000 American study found that choral singing helps the immune system. The study measured the levels of immunoglobulin A and cortisol immediately after singing in a choir and after listening to choral music. The choir members had much higher levels of the immune-boosting chemicals right after singing

6. Connect each concept with its corresponding definition:

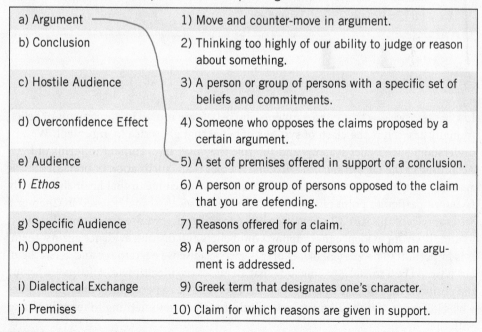

a) Argument	1) Move and counter-move in argument.
b) Conclusion	2) Thinking too highly of our ability to judge or reason about something.
c) Hostile Audience	3) A person or group of persons with a specific set of beliefs and commitments.
d) Overconfidence Effect	4) Someone who opposes the claims proposed by a certain argument.
e) Audience	5) A set of premises offered in support of a conclusion.
f) *Ethos*	6) A person or group of persons opposed to the claim that you are defending.
g) Specific Audience	7) Reasons offered for a claim.
h) Opponent	8) A person or a group of persons to whom an argument is addressed.
i) Dialectical Exchange	9) Greek term that designates one's character.
j) Premises	10) Claim for which reasons are given in support.

Table 1.1

For more online exercises, review questions, and quizzes related to the material in this chapter, please go to www.oupcanada.com/GoodReasoning5e

2

BIAS: READING BETWEEN THE LINES

Chapter 1 introduced arguments. In this chapter we discuss the differences in perspective that give rise to them. Because these differences can be hidden in the assumptions that lie behind an argument, you will often need to "read between the lines" to recognize them. Once they are recognized, we must decide whether an arguer's perspective has in any way interfered with good argument. To help you make such judgements, we highlight:

- ▶ bias and perspective
- ▶ vested interest
- ▶ conflict of interest
- ▶ slanting by omission and distortion.

1   Bias

In Chapter 1 we saw that our arguments and beliefs are rooted in our systems of belief. In many cases, it is the clash of systems of belief that gives rise to argument. We can understand such belief systems and the role they play in argument in terms of **bias**. According to the *Oxford English Dictionary*, a bias is an "inclination or prejudice for or against." When we say that an arguer has a bias, we often mean that he or she unfairly favours a particular point of view. The cognitive biases that we discussed in Chapter 1 are examples of this sort. Confirmation bias occurs because we are, for example, inclined to unduly favour evidence that supports our beliefs and dismiss evidence against them. It is important to be wary of biases of this sort because we need to try and avoid them, but it would be a mistake to conclude that all biases are illegitimate. All arguers favour the positions they believe in and argue for. Everyone has a perspective and this implies a bias in favour of it. It is a mistake to think that there is something inherently wrong with this.

All of us rely on our commitments and beliefs when we formulate our opinions. Problems arise only when our inclinations illegitimately influence the way we support our claims or interfere with our ability to listen to the reasons that others advance. In such cases, we may be said to have *illegitimate biases*. Good reasoners work hard to maintain a perspective that is not characterized by biases of this sort.

We need to be wary of illegitimate biases, especially our own, for all of us have a natural tendency to favour some positions over others. Many of the studies discussed in Chapter 1 suggested the extent to which reasoning can be influenced by our beliefs and by those things we would *like* to believe. In a broad review of the psychological literature on "motivated reasoning," Ziva Kunda cites many studies that provide "considerable evidence" that people try to arrive at those conclusions "they want to arrive at" (*Psychological Bulletin*, Vol. 108, No. 3, 1990, pp. 480–498).

One of the studies Kunda mentions concludes that smokers are less likely than non-smokers to be persuaded by the scientific evidence against smoking. In another study, a group of women were asked to read an article that argued that caffeine was bad for women. Women in the group who normally drank caffeinated beverages were much more skeptical of the article than the women who did not. In a third study, subjects who were given negative results after an intelligence test showed a marked tendency to agree with arguments that maintained that such tests were not reliable. In studies such as these, a person's judgement of an issue seems to be determined not by a careful review of the quality of the arguments, but by the individual's desire to preserve his or her beliefs or to believe a particular conclusion.

Though such forces make illegitimate biases a common feature of everyday argument, we must be careful when we charge someone with biases of this sort, for such charges are often made unfairly. Consider the following letter to the *National Post* (31 October 1998), written in response to an editorial cartoon that suggested that a doctor who performed abortions was murdered by a pro-life advocate:

> As a long-time pro-lifer, I was saddened by your cartoon. I have no idea about the identity of the cruel person who killed Dr Slepian, but I do know that he or she is not pro-life. For pro-lifers, there is no difference between an unborn child and a baby, child, teen, adult or older person.

This arguer probably overstates her conclusion when she says that she "knows" that the murderer was not pro-life, but her argument is still clear. It can be summarized as follows.

> For pro-lifers, there is no difference between an unborn child and a baby, child, teen, adult, or older person (*premise*), so the cruel person who killed Dr Slepian is not pro-life (*conclusion*).

This is an argument by a pro-life advocate who is defending pro-life advocates against the suggestion that one of them was responsible for the murder of Dr Slepian. Given that the arguer is so clearly committed to the pro-life perspective, you might wonder whether we should dismiss the argument as biased.

We think the question may be clearer if we rephrase it to ask whether this is a case in which an arguer's strong commitment to the position she defends creates an illegitimate bias that interferes with her judgement or her reasoning. We can find no reason to think so. The arguer is open about her commitments, and there is no obvious way in which they distort her views, her arguments, or her depiction of opposing points of view. We may disagree with her perspective, but she presents her argument in a way that leaves us free to evaluate it in an open-minded way.

Illegitimate biases can arise when arguers present arguments that do not fairly represent their own views or the views of their opponents. In such cases, arguers present issues in a way that favours a particular perspective. Usually this perspective is rooted in their own convictions, but there are cases in which arguments are biased because they reflect perspectives that originate not in the arguer but in arguments, articles, reports, and other material they rely on. Whatever their origin, and whether or not the arguer is aware of them, illegitimate biases lead to arguments that minimize, ignore, or dismiss evidence that invites a conclusion other than the one proposed.

In the final analysis, the question of whether a particular argument reflects illegitimate biases must be answered by carefully assessing the extent to which the arguer has fairly and accurately presented their own and their opponents' points of view. Because someone with an illegitimate bias will usually misrepresent the views of their opponents, the attempt to identify these views can help us determine whether we are dealing with a case of problematic bias.

As we write this chapter, one of the most successful business people in the world, Conrad Black, is facing the prospect of spending more time in an American jail, having been convicted of fraud in 2007. He had been granted bail, but a court decision in July 2011 required to him to return to jail in September 2011. His original trial in Chicago attracted media attention from around the world, and he has been widely criticized in the press. In spite of this, some of his supporters have been vocal. The Ad Hoc Committee for Conrad Black website (at www.supportlordblack.com) is complete with the latest news and buttons allowing people to send in messages of support. One supporter, for example, is quoted saying: "No, I don't know Conrad Black, never met him. No, I have made no examination of the evidence against him. Nor do I need to in order to assert his innocence."

This is the kind of case in which we might reasonably wonder whether arguments are biased. This is not because we presuppose any conclusion about what Black did or didn't do. Rather, our concern is that some of those who are proud to call themselves "supporters'" of Conrad Black are obviously predisposed to defend him and reject evidence against him. While this does not mean that you should jump to the conclusion that the arguments on the website are illegitimately biased, you should be aware of the possibility that this is so and treat arguments coming from such a source with care. To establish any illegitimate bias in this case, you must carefully examine the arguments against a broad background that includes objective reports of the Conrad Black situation, as well as arguments of those who are critical of Black.

To confuse matters somewhat, the website mentioned has been revealed as a hoax. Set up by a satirical magazine, *Frank*, it had allegedly fooled even Black himself. (The website resembles the *Save Martha* website that supported business woman and media personality Martha Stewart during her similar indictment—we used it to illustrate these points on bias in an earlier edition of this text.) But it still serves our purposes insofar as other people, legitimate supporters, had also been fooled into submitting messages advocating Black's innocence.

Vested Interests

The danger of illegitimate bias is particularly strong in any situation in which an arguer has a **vested interest**. This occurs when someone will benefit in some significant form if arguers see issues in a particular way. In such circumstances, an arguer may be attracted to a conclusion for the wrong reason—because it benefits them—and not because there are convincing premises that show that it is true.

In the most obvious cases, an arguer's vested interest is financial. Patricia Bickers discusses a good example in an essay on the relationship between art and fashion that she published in *Art Monthly* ("Marriage à la mode," November 2002). For artists, the underlying issue is whether fashion design is an art form and whether art galleries and the art establishment should treat it as such. Bickers discusses specific cases that have been the cause of controversy—in particular, a show of Giorgio Armani designs sponsored by the Guggenheim Museum in New York. In debates about this show, the central issue was whether the Guggenheim genuinely judged Armani designs to be worthy of the label "art" or reached this conclusion because Armani offered a gift of $15 million dollars to the Guggenheim Museum. From the point of view of argumentation, the issue is whether those deciding to show Armani or some other artist or designer were influenced by an illegitimate bias founded on a vested interest. The vested interest was the $15 million they were able to procure for their museum.

According to Bickers,

> Armani was perceived by many commentators at the time not only to have bought himself a show at the Guggenheim but to have taken over from the curators . . . none of the famous suits were included, for instance, instead the emphasis was on the designer's more recent, more glamorous—and still available—designs. It is no secret that in most art retrospectives many of the works discreetly labeled . . . are in fact for sale. . . . The Armani show, however, seemed to suggest that the museum itself was for sale—or at least for hire.

The arguments that Bickers reports here suggest not only that the Guggenheim decision was a case of illegitimate bias but that Armani himself was illegitimately biased when he decided which of his designs he would show. This was said to be reflected in his decision to pick designs that emphasized not his classic creations but recent works that were still for sale. According to the reasoning proposed, he did so because the latter allowed him to benefit financially and in this way served his personal vested interests rather than the interests of good design, history, or art.

Issues of vested image have been highlighted in discussions of Google that have criticized its power in the digital world. In a 2010 blog on Google (www.angrylemming. info/2010/04/21/t-800-android-follow-up-google), we read that Google, "which fuels and controls the vast majority of search engine traffic, has a vested interest in turning us to their products and obscuring the products of their competition."

The claim is not that Google does this (the blogger does not definitely claim that it does) but that we can't trust Google because (a) there is no way to know this isn't the case and (b) the financial interests of Google are so significant that it can't be trusted not to do so. The same issue was raised in the lead story in a 2004 issue of *Time* magazine, which asked whether it was possible to "trust Google with our secrets" given its growth and its interest in creating and branding products with the Google name.

Others have raised similar issues. In 2011, Scott Cleland and Ira Brodsky published a book called *Search & Destroy: Why You Can't Trust Google, Inc.* (St Louis, MI: Telescope Books), in which they argue that Google cannot be trusted, that it violates its users' privacy, and that it should be regulated by the government. They suggest that Google is not the benevolent lamb it has been thought to be, and is better identified with its mascot, the Tyrannosaurus Rex ("a terrifying predator"). In keeping with this theme, their cover, Illustration 2.1, depicts Google as a T-Rex in sheep's clothing. A veiled criticism of Google along similar lines appeared in the London underground, in a "guerilla" advertising campaign that asked whether it was proper for one company to have so much control over the information on the web. One of the subway advertisements is reproduced in Illustration 2.2.

Behind these issues is the principle that we should be wary of sources that have a significant financial interest in a particular point of view. Of course, this is a principle that must be applied to Google's critics as well as Google itself. In the case of Scott Cleland, some have argued that his attack on Google should not be taken seriously because he has worked for Microsoft and other Google competitors. In the case of the guerilla campaign in London, the advertisements that criticized Google referred viewers to an "Information Revolution" website which was later discovered to be run by one of Google's competitors, Ask. com. These observations don't show that the arguments against Google must necessarily be mistaken, but

Source: Telescope Books. Used with permission.

Illustration 2.1   "Search and Destroy"

Illustration 2.2   "Information-Revolution.org"

they do show that vested interests surround us in cases like this, and that we need to be wary of the role they play in attempts to convince us of this or that point of view.

In cases that involve advantages other than financial benefits, vested interests may be less obvious. In such contexts, it is helpful to remember that an arguer may benefit from a particular perspective in all kinds of ways that are not directly tied to monetary gains. The acceptance of particular conclusions may serve one's pride or one's view of right and wrong rather than one's wallet. An arguer may be attracted to a particular conclusion because the argument increases the prestige of the institution from which the arguer graduated, because it vindicates a stand the arguer has publicly defended, because it fosters a particular image of his or her congregation, ethnic group, or political party, or because it promotes policies or beliefs that are in some ways in keeping with the arguer's loyalties and commitments.

The existence of a vested interest need not in itself show that an argument is mistaken. When an arguer has a vested interest, you should treat his or her arguments with caution. You should be circumspect and careful to ask whether the arguments are characterized by illegitimate biases and have fairly presented the issues that are to be discussed. But an arguer may have a vested interest in an issue and still offer strong premises for a conclusion. Anyone defending himself or herself against a charge that he or she has done wrong has a considerable vested interest in the discussion of his or her case. It would be a mistake to think the individual's arguments can be dismissed offhandedly on this account. It is important to detect an arguer's vested interests and to be aware of his or her biases. But the question of whether an argument is to be accepted or rejected should lie with the quality of the premises and their relationship to the conclusion.

Conflict of Interest

In some cases, vested interests are so significant that they give rise to a **conflict of interest**. This occurs when someone, usually in a professional situation, is in a position to make a decision that might unfairly provide them with important benefits. Though the legal and ethical issues that arise in such contexts are too complex to be discussed in detail here, it can generally be said that someone who has a conflict of interest has a duty to declare it and to refrain from the decision it might interfere with.

The following are three examples of conflict of interest:

Example 1

The case
You are a shareholder in a corporation that has been accused of polluting the river that runs through the city in which you live. The government has decided to investigate. They appoint you to the expert panel that has been established to investigate the matter.

The conflict of interest
You have something to lose from a decision that the corporation acted wrongly. It could affect share prices and decrease the value of the shares you hold.

Example 2

The case
You are a judge in criminal court. Your sister has been charged with theft, and break and enter. You are assigned the case.

The conflict of interest
You have something to gain by deciding that she is innocent, both because it will save someone you love from unpleasant consequences and because it will save you the embarrassment that you might feel if you had a sister who was a convicted thief.

Example 3

The case
You are a member of the hiring committee of the Archaeology Department at your university or college. Your committee plays a major role in deciding who is hired for new appointments that are open. The department has advertised an opening for an expert in Near Eastern archaeology. Your partner, who is qualified, has decided to apply.

The conflict of interest
You have a great deal to gain by favouring your partner in the selection process, because hiring that person will substantially increase your combined revenue and award a very significant benefit to someone you are close to. It may provide you with other advantages as well by increasing your power and influence in the department.

In cases of conflict of interest, the issue is someone's ability to act as an impartial decision maker in some circumstance in which he or she has a vested interest in the outcome of the decision. In such contexts, the very possibility that one might be swayed by personal interest is enough to undermine one's role as a decision maker, for this is a possibility that could cast doubt on the validity of the process by which the decision is made.

EXERCISE 2A

1.* Suppose the federal government has established an initiative program that provides grants to businesses in order to stimulate the economy in depressed areas of the country. It is discovered that a good friend of the president or prime minister has received a large grant to support the building of a golf and country club. Is this a case of conflict of interest? Why or why not? What would you need to know to be certain?

2. Go to the "Full Comment" page of the *National Post* and review the comments by John Moore in "A Reality Check for Conrad Black" (5 July 2011) and Black's response "A note to my critic" (9 July 2011). Identify the main conclusion of each piece and then consider the biases that are reflected or discussed there. Are they legitimate? Explain why.

3. Many of those who have argued that global warming is not the result of human activity have been closely associated with the oil industry, an industry that would be seriously affected by any significant attempt to reduce emissions of greenhouse gases. Is this a case of vested interest that produces an illegitimate bias? Why or why not? Find arguments against (or for) the claim that global warming is the result of human activity, and discuss whether they are illegitimately biased.

2   Detecting Illegitimate Biases

Some cases of bias can be judged illegitimate through what is said and what is not said. Consider part of a story in the *New York Times*, 18 May 2011, p. A19, entitled "Church abuse report authors defend findings as critics weigh in." It reports on the findings of a study of the sex abuse crisis in the Catholic Church by a group of criminologists from the John Jay College of Criminal Justice at the City University of New York who were hired by the Roman Catholic bishops. The report's principal investigator was Karen Terry.

> Among the most controversial findings in the report is the mountain-shaped graph that shows the number of abuse victims climbing through the 1960s, peaking in the 1970s and sharply declining from 1985 onward.
>
> The report theorizes that priests coming of age in the 1940s and 1950s, growing up in families where sexuality was a taboo topic, and trained in seminaries that did not prepare them for lives of celibacy, went on to violate children during the social chaos of the sexual revolution.

Ms Terry said in an interview that she could not say for sure that the abuse did not predate the 1960s. The researchers were contracted to study only the 1950s and onward.

There are several things we might say about this report and the study it is reporting. But with respect to the question of bias, particular things come to the fore. The study shows a peak in the abuse by priests in the 1970s (this is questioned elsewhere in the story) and then correlates this with another social phenomenon—the sexual revolution. Whether or not this is intended to defend the behaviour, it is noteworthy that the study only concentrated on the period that would in a sense confirm the theory (the period of the sexual revolution) and did not look at what occurred prior to the 1950s. This is because this was the period the researchers were specifically contracted by the Church to study. So the Church has a stake both in the nature of the study and its release. If a comparable level of abuse occurred before the 1950s, then this would challenge the implication that the sexual revolution was somehow causally involved. Moreover, it could be that the reason for the graph's findings peaking in the 1970s could be explained by the wide-spread *reporting* of abuse during that period. We might charge bias here, then, not on the part of the researchers—they have no more vested interest than any researchers who are contracted to do work—but on the part of those who contracted the study with its specific limits and then released the results.

Though this is a controversial example, it displays a feature common in cases of illegitimate bias. It has a tendency to arise when arguers are dealing with matters that are of great importance to them—matters that pertain directly to themselves, their loved ones, their livelihood, or their cherished beliefs and convictions. Illegitimate biases are common in these contexts because they are contexts in which it is difficult to weigh the evidence dispassionately.

Slanting by Omission and Distortion

Illegitimate biases tend to manifest themselves in techniques that are used to distort reports and arguments. Learning these techniques of slanting can help you detect arguments that have been distorted by biases of one sort or another. Even more importantly, it can help you avoid such techniques in the construction of your own arguments.

The first technique is called *slanting by omission*. Anyone who describes a situation must select particular facts and issues to emphasize. Given that time and space are limited, it is unavoidable that other facts or issues must be summarized or ignored entirely. In the process of deciding what will and will not be reported and emphasized, it is relatively easy for an arguer to report those facts and details that favour the impression the arguer wishes to create. In the process, the arguer can downplay or leave out altogether those facts that suggest an alternative conclusion. The arguer does present "nothing but the truth" but fails to give "the whole truth" by avoiding aspects of the situation that may raise doubts about his or her perspective.

The following is the opening of a newspaper article that appeared in the *Chronicle Herald*:

No Viable Energy Alternative to Nuclear Power, Churchmen Told

Sackville (Special)—Two professors from the University of New Brunswick in Saint John told United Churchmen here Saturday that there is no viable alternative to nuclear energy if Canadians wish to maintain their present lifestyle.

The rest of the article expands on this opening remark, outlining the views of the two professors. The article was accurate in this regard, but it neglected to point out that there were *three* professors who spoke to United Churchmen. The third offered a critique of nuclear energy and of the positions of the other two professors. By omitting this central fact, the article slanted its story in favour of the arguments that were offered for the pro-nuclear position. The conclusion that there is no viable alternative to nuclear power may be the correct one, but trying to establish it this way creates an illegitimate bias. Proper reasoning on a controversial issue of this sort must demonstrate balanced conclusions that consider opposing arguments, especially when they have been an explicit part of the discussion.

We take our next example from two news reports of an American law authorizing military trials for terrorism. The US Supreme Court had earlier ruled that trying detainees in military tribunals violated American and international law, so the administration of President George W. Bush introduced changes to American law, which would allow such trials, ones that did not require detainees to have legal counsel and prohibited them from filing habeas corpus. The first report is from *The Windsor Star* of 17 October 2006; the second is from the *Detroit Free Press* of the same date. *Both* papers are using a common source for their information—an Associated Press writer. *The Windsor Star* report notes that President Bush had signed the legislation, calling it a vital tool against terrorism. It gives the history of court decisions that had led to the new law and lists the names of some of the individuals who would now face justice. It quotes Bush saying that with this bill he would save lives, linking it to the 11 September 2001 attacks. Secretary of Defense Donald Rumsfeld is singled out for praise, and some details of the law, including the restrictions we have noted, are provided. It notes that "Bush said the process is 'fair, lawful and necessary'." Thus, we have a clear report of events that took place and the reasons for them, with some suggestion of the consequences likely to follow.

What might strike a critical reader of *The Windsor Star* report is that such a law, coming as it did late in the second term of a president with declining popularity, would seem extremely controversial. It takes away rights that were previously granted to a class of individuals and does so, given the earlier Supreme Court ruling, in violation of international law. It is surprising that there were no dissenting voices to the legislation and that the report itself avoids any critical comment. That Bush saw fit to stress the fairness of the law suggests there was some criticism of it, but the implication of this is all that remains.

In fact, the *Detroit Free Press* report corrects this picture by reporting not only the facts in *The Windsor Star*'s report (in the same language, since they have a common source) but also the considerable opposition to the bill from several corners, including within Bush's own party. The lengthier *Detroit Free Press* report stresses that the bill also authorizes "harsh interrogations of terror suspects" and comes after months of "highly publicized dispute with key Republicans." It identifies and quotes civil libertarians and leading Democrats who "decried the law as a violation of American values" and notes the protest of a coalition of religious groups. It also provides further details of the nature of the bill, including special powers of interpretation of international prisoner standards that it grants to the president. Finally, the *Detroit Free Press* reported the White House's refusal to disclose any of the techniques of interrogation that would be used.

From the perspective of both reports, with the fuller picture provided by the second, it seems clear that *The Windsor Star* report is guilty of omission. Of course, the space available to report a story can vary from one newspaper to another, and so some omissions are understandable. But *The Windsor Star*'s omissions are noticeable in that what is explicitly omitted is one side of the story—the dissenting side. As a result, the story is slanted in favour of the Bush Administration and its statements on the new law. Readers without access to other sources for the same events will be left with a false impression of what went on. We charge *The Windsor Star* with slanting by omission.

As in the American terrorism bill case, slanting by omission is common in news reporting that promotes short accounts of a news story rather than in-depth analysis. Most notably, slanting by omission is a problem in television news, which relies on short, memorable copy with accompanying visuals. Two minutes is a long television news report, and it is difficult to fit all the relevant aspects of a complex issue into such a short span of time. Some critics conclude that TV news is inevitably misleading, for it always omits crucial aspects of the issues and events that it reports on. In place of the important—albeit boring—details that an informed report requires, it frequently substitutes sensational pieces of information and captivating visuals that grab our attention. An understanding of slanting by omission can help you combat these tendencies, not only when you watch television but in any context in which you are gathering the kind of information that may play a role in argumentative discussion.

A second slanting technique is called *slanting by distortion*. It occurs when one describes or exaggerates or colours the facts that one is reporting in a manner that enhances an impression one wishes to create. Newspaper reporters or editors can, for example, twist the facts that they report by using terms with suggestive overtones in place of words that are neutral and descriptive; by inserting insinuating phrases; or by using headlines, the position on a page, or accompanying illustrations to foster the perspective that they favour.

Slanting by distortion can be very subtle because it can be hard to find words that are entirely neutral and easy to use descriptions that lean one way or another. The adage that "a half-empty glass is half-full" well captures the point that the same fact can be cast in a positive or negative light. A good historical example of slanting by distortion is provided in the following Paris newspaper headlines, announcing the journey of Napoleon across France on his return from Elba (9–22 March 1815; this example is given by Eleanor MacLean in *Between the Lines: Detecting Bias and Propaganda*, Montreal, QC: Black Rose Books). Each headline reports that Napoleon is in such-and-such a place but colours the report in a way that sends more extreme messages that change according to the bias of the newspaper in which the headline appears. The slanted messages are not themselves arguments, but it is easy to imagine how they might provide the background for argumentative debate.

9 March

THE ANTHROPOPHAGUS [the monster who eats people] **HAS QUITTED HIS DEN**

10 March

THE CORSICAN OGRE HAS LANDED AT CAPE JUAN

11 March

THE TIGER HAS ARRIVED AT CAP

12 March

THE MONSTER SLEPT AT GRENOBLE

13 March

THE TYRANT HAS PASSED THROUGH LYONS

14 March

THE USURPER IS DIRECTING HIS STEPS TOWARDS DIJON

18 March

BONAPARTE IS ONLY SIXTY LEAGUES FROM THE CAPITAL
He has been fortunate to escape his pursuers

19 March

BONAPARTE IS ADVANCING WITH RAPID STEPS, BUT HE WILL NEVER ENTER PARIS

20 March

NAPOLEON WILL, TOMORROW, BE UNDER OUR RAMPARTS

21 March

THE EMPEROR IS AT FONTAINBLEAU

22 March

HIS IMPERIAL AND ROYAL MAJESTY
arrived yesterday evening at the Tuileries amid the joyful acclamations of his devoted and faithful subjects

None of these headlines explicitly says that Napoleon is good, bad, loved, feared, hated, admired, or despised, but the choice of words very clearly implies a variety of claims in this regard. The slanting by distortion that results reflects the vested interests of the newspapers that carried these headlines, for they are, of course, more likely to be furthered by positive headlines as Napoleon comes closer and closer to Paris.

Slanting by distortion or omission is a likely possibility whenever an individual or group has a perspective, a product, or a cause they are dedicated to promoting. Slanting is found not only in newspaper and television news but in strategic analyses, feasibility studies, union and management reports, political platforms, scholarly defences of particular points of view, and attempts to promote "special interests" of one sort or another (milk producers, the dot-com industries, a particular religious perspective, a sports franchise, etc.). The crux of slanting is the use of omission and distortion to create an illegitimate bias that insinuates a particular interpretation of the facts or issues that are reported and debated. A good reasoner watches for the possibility that someone arguing has imposed a particular "slant" on the issues.

Slanting is particularly evident in propaganda, which the *Oxford English Dictionary* defines as "information, especially of a biased or misleading nature, used to promote a political cause or point of view." Propagandists are willing to exaggerate in extreme ways that employ self-serving analogies, shifts of meaning in the use of key terms in the course of an argument, controversial hidden premises, and an aura of certainty that is often promoted by name-dropping and pseudo-technical jargon. Ironically, the extreme slanting that characterizes propaganda often makes their lack of objectivity transparent, rendering their arguments unconvincing rather than convincing. Films like *Reefer Madness*, which shows high school kids smoking pot and quickly doing insane things, and *The Atomic Café*, which parodies the extreme propaganda that promoted things like the atomic bomb, have become popular comedies because we can, in hindsight, see how crude and heavy-handed earlier attempts at propaganda were.

Looking for Balance

Slanting is an indication of illegitimate biases that can help us determine how we should respond to arguers and arguments. But an argument may be influenced by such bias even if it is not obvious that it is slanted. Someone reading the article from the *Halifax Chronicle Herald*, noted earlier, will not know that it has left out important details unless they were at the colloquium on nuclear power it discusses or have learned, in some other way, about the events of the evening. In many circumstances, an article or argument may not appear slanted to someone who does not have a comprehensive understanding of the issues or the circumstances it discusses.

This underscores the point that deciding whether an argument is illegitimately biased may, in some cases, depend on an examination of arguments forwarded by those who have opposing points of view. Especially when assessing an arguer's attempt to provide a comprehensive overview of some issue or concern, it is important to see what those with opposing views maintain, for this is the only way we can be sure that the comprehensive overview is fair to them and their arguments. In order to judge whether the arguments supporting Conrad Black are illegitimately biased, we may have to spend time looking at the arguments of those who are critical of Black. Thus, an attempt to consider bias and perspective must often evolve into an attempt to understand the broader context in which debates, arguments, and controversies occur.

In trying to determine whether arguments are affected by illegitimate biases, you may follow a three-step method, outlined as follows:

1. Note vested interests.
2. Look for slanting.
3. Survey opposing views.

In dealing with many arguments, there is no need to survey opposing views, which can be a long and laborious task. If an arguer has no vested interests, if his or her claims are relatively straightforward, or if there is little reason to believe that he or she is misrepresenting his or her own or his or her opponents' points of view, then the argument he or she presents can be considered on its own terms, without a survey of the broader argumentative context in which it occurs. However, if there is good reason to think that bias may be a problem, surveying opposing views is the best way to determine whether, and to what extent, an argument is illegitimately biased.

EXERCISE   2B

Develop a case study as an individual, group, or class project. Carefully watch a current documentary film that is garnering popular attention. *The Undefeated* (2011), *Sicko* (2007), *An Inconvenient Truth* (2006), *Super Size Me* (2004), *Food, Inc.* (2008), *Crude: the Real Price of Oil* (2009) or *The Greatest Movie Ever Sold* (2011) are examples of films that would be suitable. As you watch, make note of any apparent vested interests on the part of people whose views are solicited or considered (these may appear on both sides of the issue). Then explain your judgement of whether these interests have resulted in illegitimate biases. Look for instances of slanting by omission and distortion, defending your identifications in all cases. Finally, summarize the film in terms of how well it handles questions of bias. Remember, we expect people who feel strongly about an issue to be biased in regard to it. Our aim here is to judge the difference between legitimate biases and those that are not.

3   Difficult Cases

In some circumstances, issues of bias make it very difficult for you to know how you should regard particular arguments. In cases of this sort, don't be shy about identifying the problems and recognizing the limits of your analysis.

Consider a sensational case of alleged child abuse that surfaced in 1992, when a Manitoba woman robbed a bank at gun point and took the money to the Manitoba minister of justice, declaring, "Here's some money to help my abusive husband get into a treatment program." In the hearings that followed, one of the central issues that arose was whether or not the woman's husband, Ambrose, was guilty of child abuse. Below is a list of some of the charges and counter-charges that were made during the course of the case:

> *Charge:* Ambrose, in his affidavit, stated that Mary Ann admitted to his lawyer that she fabricated the abuse charge. Mary Ann admitted this in her second affidavit.
>
> *Counter-charge:* Mary Ann claimed she was under a great deal of pressure to say whatever Ambrose wanted.
>
> *Charge:* An independent witness swore in an affidavit that Mary Ann told him the accusation was false.
>
> *Counter-charge:* Mary Ann accused the witness of lying.
>
> *Charge:* Mary Ann and her supporters made much of the point that Ambrose pleaded guilty to a charge of abuse.
>
> *Counter-charge:* Ambrose said that Mary Ann promised to reconcile with him if he pleaded guilty, and Mary Ann admitted in court that she had threatened to keep the child away if he didn't plead guilty.

This is only a small selection of the charges and counter-charges that characterized this case. Even if we ignore the others, these ones usefully demonstrate how clashes of vested interest and the possibility of illegitimate bias may make it almost impossible to decide what should be believed.

If two individuals are implicated in a murder and the only account of the situation we have is their two reports, how can we reconcile their accounts when each points a finger at the other? Each has a substantial vested interest (to be free from blame and punishment), and there are good reasons to suspect that each of them may be providing an account of the situation that is illegitimately biased in his or her favour. In some circumstances (in which one of them has divulged "what really happened," to a friend, perhaps), there may be a way to get to the bottom of the situation, but there are cases in which we have no way to choose between them.

In our attempt to be critical thinkers who assess the evidence and arguments we come across carefully it is important to always keep in mind the limits of this evidence and the possibility that it might be biased. We can illustrate this point with the following two photos taken from coverage of one night of the "Occupy Oakland" protests of 2011 (see Illustration 2.3 and Illustration 2.4). They were part of a worldwide wave of protests that began with a September "Occupy Wall Street" protest against social and economic inequality (the bottom "99 per cent" versus the top "1 per cent"), high unemployment, greed, corruption, and the influence of large financial corporations on government policy.

Taken by themselves, the two photos suggest a very different view of the protest that took place on 3 November. The first suggests violence and anarchy—two masked protesters (looking like terrorists); an out-of-control fire from a car that has been set on fire; a knocked over garbage bin covered with graffiti; and frenzied activity in the background. If one is presented with just this photo as a representation of what happened, one is likely to conclude that the protest was a night of mayhem and out-of-control protestors causing violence and property damage. In sharp contrast, the second photo suggests a very different view of the protest, presenting a quiet, unassuming

Illustration 2.3   Occupy Wall Street, 3 November, 2011

Illustration 2.4   Oakland Protests, 3 November, 2011

protestor beside an intimidating row of aggressive-looking police officers with helmets and batons at the ready. In place of a weapon, the young woman, who appears to be a student, has been carrying a brief case, which she has laid on the ground at her feet. Her hands are clasped together in a prayerful pose.

While the first photo is likely to evoke sympathy for the police (who must find a way to contain the damage caused by out-of-control protestors), the second is more likely to evoke sympathy for the protestors (who are portrayed as peacefully in pursuit of a better society, unarmed, and no match for a professional paramilitary force). Which photo best represents what happened at the protest? Without knowing a great deal more about the protest, it is impossible to say, though the two together suggest that neither photo can be said to represent a long, complex event made up of many actions and moments. In a discussion of bias, the important point is that it would be easy to use either photo (or a collection of similarly themed photos) as the basis for a biased account of the demonstration which favours the conclusion that the protestors behaved improperly (and the police were forced to do what they could to control them) or that the police behaved improperly (and provoked peaceful protestors). In situations of this sort (situations which characterize much of the media coverage we consume each day) it is difficult to judge bias without further research. In such cases, you should try to eliminate or understand bias by considering and comparing the different perspectives and accounts of an issue offered by arguers and their opponents. In some cases it may be impossible (or not practically feasible) to do so. In such situations, you will do best to recognize the potential biases and admit that you have no clear way to establish how biased the coverage in question is.

Balancing Your Arguments

In the course of constructing arguments, be mindful of the dangers of illegitimate biases, and strive to avoid them. If your perspective is informed by vested interests and previous commitments that are pertinent to the case at hand, be open about them. Be explicit about your views, and do your best to ensure that any opinions or feelings you express are justified by an unbiased understanding of opposing views of the issue or situation you discuss.

In the process of putting your arguments together, be cautious about emotionally charged modes of expression. It is appropriate to feel strongly about some things, but strong claims need to be backed by convincing arguments, and you must be cautious of overstatement and terms that colour your claims in a way that is slanted in favour of your own view. In the end, the strength of your own perspective will depend on your willingness to be fair to the views of your opponents. The most convincing argument is one that recognizes and fairly states opposing points of view and then deals adequately with the issues that they raise.

In constructing arguments, you need to judge those of other people. In many cases, the manoeuvres used in slanting can alert you to the possibility of its presence. Obvious symptoms of slanting—and possible symptoms of propaganda—include the use of inflammatory terms where neutral ones suffice, sensational words that promote moralistic judgements, unnecessary phrases filled with innuendo, and suggestions that are implied but never explicitly stated. As you read an argument, you should be able to identify some of the facts an argument depends on. Once you do, you can ask whether the account proposed is slanted. As you read or watch or listen, ask yourself: Does this commentary push its audience unreasonably toward a particular perspective? By assessing the facts and issues in a loaded way or by letting the facts "speak for themselves"? Has the arguer made appropriate judgements in deciding which details should be emphasized and which should be treated as inconsequential or as secondary matters? Could one "juggle the facts" in a way that creates a very different impression?

In many cases, you may be aware of slanting only when someone who has been offended raises their voice to correct some omission or some distorted commentary. But there are ways to take a more active role in diagnosing and exposing illegitimate biases. If you detect significant vested interests (and especially vested interests that have not been declared) or if the terms used in an argument jump out at you, try to compare the argument before you with a report or argument written by someone with a competing point of view. Studying two reports of the same event—especially reports from sources with opposing commitments and loyalties—is one of the best ways to establish a more accurate understanding of the issues you discuss.

DETECTING BIAS

1. Note vested interests.
2. Look for slanting.
3. Survey opposing views.
4. Admit the problems with difficult cases.

EXERCISE 2C

1. Read the lead article from your daily newspaper (in print or on the web). Is the article illegitimately biased? Slanted? Why or why not?

   a) Rewrite the article in a slanted way that unfairly promotes a different view of the situation than that suggested in the article.

   b) Write a mock letter to the editor criticizing your own article on the grounds that it is illegitimately biased.

   c) Rewrite the original article in another way that reflects a different set of illegitimate biases (your first rewrite might be from a liberal point of view, the second from a conservative point of view, etc.).

2. Review major news stories reported in at least two newspapers or on-line news sources. The online editions of newspapers (to which your institution likely subscribes) make these readily accessible. You want to find at least two reports of the same story, perhaps from the same journalistic source. Compare the stories for suggestions of slanting by omission or distortion, defending your judgements in each case.

4   Summary

Chapter 2 has focused on the role that bias plays in arguments. All arguers are biased in favour of the positions they defend, but some are open about the commitments and allegiances they have and don't hide such matters. Illegitimate biases occur when arguers assume things that should be argued for. We have considered how to distinguish legitimate and illegitimate biases. In the course of this, we have explored some central ideas associated with bias: vested interest and conflict of interest. In both cases, an arguer has a stake in what is being argued such that the case they make may lack the objectivity good arguments require. We have also looked at ways in which arguments and even news stories can be slanted in favour of a particular perspective. This can occur by omitting important details or by distorting the details that are provided.

MAJOR EXERCISE 2M

1. Consider the following arguments or reports and identify any concerns about vested interest and possible bias:

a)* [Ms Pat Curran, Canadian Automobile Association, quoted in *TransMission*, 1995] We at the CAA believe that reducing the speed to 30 kilometres per hour on city streets would be unreasonable and unenforceable. Motorists will only obey the speed limits that they perceive as reasonable. Further, we feel that such a low speed limit . . . could have the detrimental effect of increasing fuel consumption and exhaust pollution.

b) [From an advertisement in *Wired* magazine, January 2003]
    **WE COULD TELL YOU HOW WE GOT THESE NUMBERS
    BUT THEN WE'D HAVE TO KILL YOU.**
    OUR MISSION: BECOME THE LEADER IN MANAGED HOSTING

    MISSION STATISTICS:

    0
    Seconds to talk to a real person

    97%
    Of our customers would recommend us

    100%
    Network uptime for the last 18 months

    6,000+
    Servers managed at Rackspace

    550,000+
    Domains hosted
    rackspace MANAGED HOSTING

c)* [Adapted from a public advertisement from Canada Post in favour of "advertising mail," which is popularly referred to as "junk mail"] The people who send you ads-in-the-mail do a lot of nice things for you, and for us. Advertising

Mail allows you to shop from the comfort of your home. Advertising Mail adds $50,000,000 revenue to the Post Office and that keeps postal rates down. Advertising Mail creates employment for tens of thousands of men and women. . . . Probably someone you know.

d) [From *The Windsor Star*, "Docs Want New Vaccine for Kids," 4 October 2010] "We think (the vaccine) is safe, it's effective, it's going to prevent severe infections and it will, we believe, save the provinces money," says Dr. Robert Bortolussi, chair of the Canadian Paediatric Society's infectious disease and immunization committee and a professor of pediatrics at Dalhousie University in Halifax.

e) [From the introduction to an article in *O: The Oprah Magazine*, January 2003]

IS SHE THE MOST

SHOCKING

WOMAN

ON TELEVISION?

She looks like a plainspoken, modest, homey grandmother. In fact, cable TV sex therapist Sue Johanson is an authority on (among other things) vibrators, clitoral sensitivity, and how to get semen out of silk. Lise Funderburg sits down with Canada's favorite lay person.

f) [From an article in *Wired* magazine, January 2003]

Google Sells Its Soul

It's inevitable that a company of Google's size and influence will have to compromise on purity. There's a chance that, in five years, Google will end up looking like a slightly cleaner version of what Yahoo! has become. There's also a chance that the site will be able to make a convincing case to investors that long-term user satisfaction trumps short-term profit. The leadership of the Internet is . . . [Google's] to lose. For now, at least, in Google we trust.

g) [From "Marx after Communism," in *The Economist*, 21 December 2002] When Soviet communism fell apart towards the end of the 20th century, nobody could say that it failed on a technicality. A more comprehensive or ignominious collapse—moral, material, and intellectual—would be difficult to imagine. Communism had tyrannized and impoverished its subjects, and slaughtered them in the tens of millions. For decades past, in the Soviet Union and its satellite countries, any allusion to the avowed aims of communist doctrine—equality, freedom from exploitation, true justice—had provoked only bitter laughter.

2. Each of the following passages is a comment on the kinds of issues discussed in this chapter. Explain what the author is saying in terms of vested interest, illegitimate bias, conflict of interest, slanting, and any other concepts introduced in the chapter. If the passage contains an argument, identify its premises and conclusion. Do you think this is a case of illegitimate bias? Why or why not? If you would need more evidence to decide the issue, where would you go to get it? Make sure you explain what the author is saying *before* you judge their claims.

a)* [A Letter to the Editor, *The Economist*, May 1997] Sir: Your assertion that public smoking should not be banned, on the grounds that "other people's freedoms . . . sometimes get in your eyes," is biased. Our societies ban or restrict any number of activities that are minor irritants: begging, loud music, nudity, skateboarding. Although each of these restrictions on individual liberty is the result of intolerance, *The Economist* seldom champions their causes; yet your newspaper seems unable to mention tobacco without commenting on dangers to the rights of smokers.

b)   [From *The Windsor Star*, Opinion, "Star rejects conflict allegations," p. A7; 13 October 2010, p. A7]
Last Monday at a press conference it was suggested that *The Windsor Star* has a conflict of interest with the Mayor's office and this is reflected in the opinions that we publish.

As Publisher I can assure you that *The Windsor Star* does not have a conflict of interest with respect to the mayor, or the mayor's office or the municipal election. Since we don't have a conflict of interest, the allegations made last week were not supported with evidence.

c)   Some have suggested that we make Pulp Press Publishers a publicly owned company. We could make a great deal of money by doing so. But we think we would pay in a different way. As a private company, Pulp Press Publishers answers to one master: the readers it has cultivated for a unique brand of pulp fiction. As a public company, Pulp Press would have shareholders to worry about. And shareholders are primarily concerned with profits.

Pulp Press has demonstrated its loyalty to its readers by continuing to publish unique titles with a small but devoted readership. If Pulp Press goes public, will it cave to pressure from its shareholders and streamline its publishing list if stock prices begin to cave?

d)   [From a Letter to the Editor, the *Toronto Sun* (1 April 1996) concerning police violence in a controversial strike] It was okay for the union goons to harass citizens crossing the picket lines to the point of tears or even scuffle or skirmish, but as soon as the shoe was on the other foot they wimped out and cried police brutality.

e)* [A "disclaimer" pasted into high school biology textbooks in Clayton County, Georgia] This textbook may discuss evolution, a controversial theory some scientists present as a scientific explanation for the origin of living things, such as plants, animals and humans. . . . No human was present when life first appeared on earth. Therefore, any statement about life's origins should be considered a theory, not fact.

f)   [From an advertisement for a vitamin pill called "Within," in *Ms.* magazine, August 1987]
Most multivitamins don't know you from Adam.
WITHIN
With the extra calcium and extra iron women need
. . . The most complete multivitamin created for women.

g)   [From a response to a decision in Dover, Kansas, by the court judge (Jones) that intelligent design is religion and cannot be taught as science in state schools. The respondent is a member of the Intelligent Design Network, which is the source of the extract: www.intelligentDesignnetwork.org (visited 12 October 2006)]

The twisted decision of the court in Dover today [20 December 2005] effectively establishes a state sponsored ideology that is fundamental to non-theistic religions and religious beliefs. By outlawing the inference of design that arises from observation and analysis, the court has caused the state to endorse materialism and the various religions it supports. Thus the court actually inserted a religious bias into science while purporting to remove one.

The incorrect assumption implicit in the decision is that there is only one kind of "religion"—the kind that subscribes to God. In fact religion includes other kinds, those that reject any God that might intervene in the natural world—Atheism, Agnosticism, Secular Humanism, etc. The Court's second error was to ignore the obvious: any explanation of origins will unavoidably favor one kind of religion over another.

For Judge Jones "religion" seems to be a term that describes only one particularly kind of religion—Christianity. Although the Judge was quick to note theistic friendly implications of an intelligent cause for life, his opinion omits any discussion of the religious implications of evolution and the acknowledged naturalistic/materialistic philosophy which has protected it from scientific criticism.

h) [From www.vix.com/men/media/manucon.html (accessed 2 January 2003)] Statistics show that men and women suffer roughly equal rates of violence. Media coverage of male victimization, however, is virtually non-existent. . . . [In a study I did on newspaper headlines,] I found that the few headlines on men were quantitative, providing data on the amount of violence they experienced without placing it in any societal context. Headlines on women were rarely quantitative: those that were used words like "epidemic" or provided statistics only on women. . . . In the end, I argued that while the media appeared willing to address violence against women, and rightly so, the media did not appear willing to address a second type of violence, that against men, although statistics show that rates of violence against men are at least as high as those for women.

i) [David L. Katz, in "How to Spot a Diet Scam," *O: The Oprah Magazine*, January 2003] Ads for fad diets generally offer convincing quotes from highly satisfied customers. These are as easy to obtain as they are meaningless. The quotes may come from the brief period of peak satisfaction. How do these folks feel six months later, when the weight is likely to have come back? The ads don't say.

j) [Under the headline "The Times's slip is showing," in "The Goldberg File," from *The National Review* www.nationalreview.com/goldberg/goldberg 052499.html, 3 January 2003] Speaking of hegemonic liberal orthodoxy (was that what I was speaking about? I can't remember), today's *New York Times* is a great example. The *Times* has a huge article on the US Court of Appeals for the Fourth Circuit. It wrings its hands about the fact that this cell of conservatives is trying to do conservative things and it's succeeding. Is it possible to think that the *Times* would ever run a hand-wringing piece about a liberal circuit succeeding at doing liberal things?

k) [A map of the world, claiming to represent the world as seen by Americans]

Illustration 2.5   "The world according to Americans"

l) [From Robert Fisk, in "When journalists forget that murder is murder," *Z-magazine*, www.bulatlat.com/archive1/034us-fisk2.html, 18 August 2001] What on earth has happened to our reporting of the Middle East? George Orwell would have loved a Reuters dispatch from the West Bank city of Hebron last Wednesday. "Undercover Israeli soldiers," the world's most famous news agency reported, "shot dead a member of Yasser Arafat's Fatah faction yesterday in what Palestinians called an assassination." The key phrase, of course, was "what Palestinians called an assassination." Any sane reader would conclude immediately that Imad Abu Sneiheh, who was shot in the head, chest, stomach and legs by 10 bullets fired by Israeli "agents" had been murdered, let alone assassinated. But no. Reuters, like all the big agencies and television companies reporting the tragedy of the Palestinian-Israeli conflict, no longer calls murder by its real name.

m) [From a report in www.newsmax.com on 3 January 2003] Clonaid founder "Rael," whose disciple Dr Brigitte Boisselier conned almost the entire media over the weekend into covering her claim that Clonaid scientists had successfully cloned a human being, announced Saturday that he would clone Nazi Führer Adolf Hitler if he had the chance.

    While the press has taken note of Mr Rael . . . reporters were apparently too embarrassed over their own gullibility to cover the Clonaid founder's comments to Fox News Channel's Page Hopkins on Saturday. But we think Hopkins and Fox performed a genuine public service by exposing the media's ill-considered rush to report Clonaid's claims, with her probing questions of the group's white suited, shoulder-padded, ponytailed cult leader.

n) [From the cover of a "prize envelope"]

> **YOU ARE NOW IN POSSESSION OF A COLOUR-CODED PRIZE SEAL THAT COULD MAKE YOU RICH FOR LIFE WITH OUR BIGGEST CASH AWARD EVER.**
>
> *If you reply in time and win, we'll say . . .*
>
> **LEO GROARKE, YOU'VE MADE THE FINAL CUT—YOU'RE ONE OF TEN LUCKY PRIZE WINNERS GUARANTEED UP TO $11,000,000!**

 For more online exercises, review questions, and quizzes related to the material in this chapter, please go to www.oupcanada.com/GoodReasoning5e

3

ARGUMENTS, WEAK AND STRONG

We evaluate arguments to distinguish those that are weak and those that are strong. In this chapter, we introduce the basic concepts of argument evaluation. You should emerge with an understanding of the following key concepts:

▶ burden of proof
▶ strong and weak arguments
▶ acceptability
▶ valid and invalid arguments
▶ argument schemes and counter-schemes
▶ contextual relevance
▶ fallacies
▶ red herring
▶ straw man.

We evaluate (or "assess") arguments to determine whether they are strong or weak or somewhere in between. We use the terms "strong" and "weak" to emphasize the point that the strength of an argument is not a black-or-white affair. A strong argument should convince a reasonable audience that its conclusion is plausible, but it will rarely be so strong that it cannot be strengthened or responded to. A weak argument may be so weak that it cannot be rehabilitated, but many weak arguments are better described as weak but capable of strengthening (by, for example, adding more premises). Argument evaluation encompasses a continuum from very weak to very strong that contains abundant, perhaps infinite, shades of grey. In this chapter, we explore the essential features of strong arguments.

1   Burden of Proof

Not every claim or situation calls for argument. In assessing arguments—or someone's failure to defend their claims with argument—this means that we must begin by understanding when we ought to argue. The answer to this question is tied to a notion called **burden of proof**. A "burden" is something that is carried. It might be an object—a backpack or a sack of coal—but it can also be something abstract, like the responsibility to take care of a difficult person or home. In circumstances where there is disagreement, the person who carries the *burden of proof* is the person who has an obligation, or *onus*, to defend (and in this way "prove") their views with argument.

In addressing a criminal court, the burden of proof rests with the prosecution, which accuses the defendant of a crime. In England, Canada, and the United States, this means that a defendant and his or her lawyer are not required to prove that the accused is innocent. Innocence is assumed, and the prosecution must proceed by trying to prove the defendant's guilt. The French legal system sometimes assigns burden of proof on some issues to the defendant, but generally also presumes the innocence of a person accused of crime. Internationally, the Universal Declaration of Human Rights places the burden of proof on the prosecution, stating that everyone has the right to be presumed innocent before the law.

Questions about burden of proof and an arguer's obligation to defend premises lie behind every argument, because every argument offers premises in support of its conclusion. In deciding such questions we must distinguish those cases in which the burden of proof rests with the arguer and those in which it rests with those who might challenge them. In the first case, the arguer will have to build sub-arguments that back their premises; in the second, the premises can be assumed without further argument.

We explore burden of proof in greater detail in Chapter 8. For now you should decide questions about burden of proof by asking whether it is reasonable to accept a premise, or whether it needs to be supported. In making such judgements, a key consideration will be the specific audience to whom the argument is directed, for different audiences will accept different premises without support. In a Spanish newspaper, one can assert without argument that bull fighting is a laudable cultural endeavour. In North America, where bull fighting is seen as cruelty to animals, the burden of proof reverses, requiring that those individuals who view it as a worthy endeavour defend their premises.

Over time, the burden of proof in a particular area changes as our view of the world changes. Economics is an established and revered discipline but the recent collapse of financial markets has raised questions about its credibility. James Galbraith, himself an economist, expresses this change in attitude in the following testimony, which he presented to the United States Congress on 18 May 2010:

> I write to you from a disgraced profession. Economic theory, as widely taught since the 1980s, failed miserably to understand the forces behind the financial crisis. Concepts including "rational expectations," "market discipline," and the "efficient markets hypothesis" led economists to argue that speculation would stabilize prices, that sellers would act to protect their reputations, that caveat emptor could be relied on, and that widespread fraud therefore could not occur. Not all economists believed this—but most did.

Such testimony challenges the assumptions that characterize standard economic theory, which assumes a model of behaviour which was unable to predict or properly account for the fall of the American housing market and the global financial crisis it precipitated. In the wake of these events, Galbraith is no longer willing to assign burden of proof in a manner that accepts without argument the standard premises that underlie traditional economic theory.

As this example shows, questions about burden of proof may themselves be the subject of argument. Some have argued that the practice of employment drug tests, instituted by some employers, is unfair (*conclusion*) because it places an unfair burden of proof on employees who must prove they are innocent of using illegal drugs (*premise*). In a much debated incident in 2006, Duke University expelled three players from its lacrosse team and cancelled the team's season when they were accused of sexual assault. When DNA evidence proved that they were innocent, the university and the prosecuting attorney were rebuked on the grounds that they had assumed the students were guilty, instead of assuming them innocent and placing the onus on those who alleged otherwise.

EXERCISE   3A

For each of the following arguments, discuss whether the burden of proof would lie with the arguer who puts forward the premises or with a challenger who might dispute them:

a)* [Lindsey Murtagh and David Ludwig, the authors of a commentary in *The Journal of the American Medical Association* entitled "State intervention in life-threatening childhood obesity," (2011, Vol. 306, No. 2, pp. 206–7), argued that in extreme cases the government should be allowed to intervene and remove children from their parents' custody. Their argument included the following premises] Ubiquitous junk food marketing, lack of opportunities for physically active recreation, and other aspects of modern society promote unhealthy lifestyles in children. Inadequate or unskilled parental supervision can leave children vulnerable to these obesigenic environmental influences.

b) [Bioethicist Art Caplan challenged some of the conclusions drawn in the above study, in comments reported in the *Toronto Star* (13 July 2011)] The debate risks putting too much blame on parents. Obese children are victims of advertising, marketing, peer pressure and bullying—things a parent can't control.

c) [The Omega watch company withdrew its advertising from *Vogue* magazine in protest over what it called distasteful pictures of an emaciated model in the June 1996 issue. The brand director of Omega argued as follows (source: the *New York Times*, 31 May 1996)] Since *Vogue* presumably targets an audience that includes young and impressionable females, its creators must surely be aware that they will inevitably be influenced by what laughably passes for fashion in these pages. It was irresponsible for a leading magazine that should be setting an example to select models of anorexic proportions.

d) [From the same news story. The publisher of *Vogue* responded] [The brand director's] comments appear to be motivated by sour grapes, because he had objected to the way Omega watches had been photographed for a feature on watches.

e)   [Excerpted from a Letter to the Editor, *The Washington Times*, 6 June 2011, by the executive director of the International Climate Science Coalition based in Ottawa]

Referring to those of us who do not support the climate scare as "climate-change deniers" is both a mistake and a logical fallacy. It is a mistake because no reputable scientist on either side of the debate denies that climate changes. The only constant about climate is change—it changes all the time no matter what we do.

The term "deniers" is often used by supporters of the hypothesis that our greenhouse gas emissions are causing a climate crisis. They use it in order to equate their opponents to Holocaust deniers and so elicit negative emotions. This is the logical fallacy referred to as "ad hominem" in that it is against the man, not the idea. It is a common but offensive public relations trick and should be shunned by all honest citizens.

Use of the phrase "fossil-fuel industry-funded" to discredit our point of view is also a logical fallacy, by saying that we are funded by vested interests, appear to have a motive to lie, and, therefore, what we say is wrong is clearly illogical. It also implies that our scientific opinions can be bought and thus we are dishonest, which would again be an ad hominem logical fallacy. Besides, many skeptical scientists have nothing to do with the energy industry, fossil fuel or otherwise.

2   Strong Arguments

Burden of proof tells us when we are obligated to provide an argument. In doing so, our goal is a *strong* argument: an argument that provides evidence that will convince a reasonable audience that they should accept our conclusion. In the paradigm circumstance in which an argument is required—when we must address an audience that does not accept our conclusion—we might compare a successful argument to a journey which takes our audience from their current beliefs to the argument's conclusion. In doing so, a strong argument must satisfy two conditions.

(i) Premise Acceptability

One essential feature of good arguments is acceptable premises—i.e. premises the intended audience will (or should) accept. If they believe that the premises are false or misconceived or in some other way unacceptable, then the argument does not provide them with reasons for believing the conclusion. In a strong argument, the premises of an argument function like a vehicle that takes the audience to its conclusion. In an argument with unacceptable premises, the members of the audience might be compared to passengers who refuse to get on a bus which cannot, in view of this, take them to its destination.

When we say that an argument's premises should be "acceptable" we mean that they should be accepted as true by the audience it is addressed to. We leave for an advanced course in philosophy the complex questions raised by debates about the meaning of "true." In evaluating arguments, we hold that premises should be 'acceptable' rather than 'true' because there are many circumstances in which it is reasonable to rely on premises that are plausible or probable, or judged correct in some other provisional way. This is an inevitable aspect of many—perhaps most—arguments because they occur in circumstances characterized by uncertainty. Suffice it to say that the premises of a strong argument may be acceptable even though a reasonable audience might hesitate to go so far as to call them "true."

The kinds of issues raised by premise acceptability can be illustrated with a simple example we have taken from a debate in *Runner's World* magazine (December 2010). It features two experts who take opposite stances in response to the question whether one should listen to music while running. In the course of arguing the pro side of the debate, the expert who supports running with music argues as follows.

> **Premise:** Studies find that music reduces your perception of how hard you are running by about 10 per cent.
> **Conclusion:** Music can sometimes make running feel easier.

In gauging the strength of this argument, we must consider whether its premise is acceptable. What are we to make of its claim that scientific studies show that music reduces our perception of the effort we are making when we are running?

In the course of reading this debate, one might accept this claim on the grounds that it is offered by someone who is described as a "Ph.D., a sports psychologist, who has studied music's positive influence on athletes." In doing so, one grounds the premise on an appeal to authority of the sort we discuss in Chapter 12. This is a reasonable stance, but someone skeptical of the argument might adopt an opposing point of view. They might emphasize the point that the argument is offered in a context in which another expert—described as a "Ph.D., a sports sociologist and coach"—takes issue with the suggestion that it is a good idea to run with music. In such a situation, the skeptic may not be willing to accept a general claim about unspecified scientific studies, even if it is made by an expert. Without a more detailed account of the studies that are alluded to—one that allows them to check the credibility of the studies and their conclusions—they may find the premise unacceptable and maintain that the argument fails to provide compelling evidence for the conclusion that music can sometimes make running feel easier.

We will not attempt to resolve this debate. Our aim is to illustrate the kinds of issues raised by premise's acceptability, and the role it plays in evaluating arguments. Ideally, all the premises of a strong argument are acceptable, though there may be times when an argument is convincing even though it has some unacceptable premises.

(ii) Logical Consequence

Acceptable premises are the first component of good arguments. The second is a conclusion that is a logical consequence of its premises—i.e. a conclusion that "follows" from these premises. Put another way, the conclusion of a good argument is a conclusion we have good reason to accept if we accept its premises. If we think of an argument as a journey, the conclusion is the destination the argument is supposed to take us to. When the conclusion offered is not a logical consequence of the premises, the premises lead in the wrong direction. Even if they are acceptable, this means that they cannot lead us to the conclusion. In this case, the argument is like a bus which picks up its passengers but fails to take them to its intended destination.

We can illustrate the notion of logical consequence in terms of the example we have already outlined. Let's assume that we accept the conclusion that "Music can sometimes make running feel easier." In the context of the broader debate in *Runner's World*, this claim functions as a premise in support of running with music. We can summarize this argument as follows.

> **Premise:** Music can sometimes make running feel easier.
> **Conclusion:** Running with music is a good way to run.

When we evaluate this argument we need to ask whether its conclusion follows from (is a logical consequence of) its premise.

This is a more complex question than it might at first appear. Intuitively, one might think that conclusion of our new argument follows from its premise because it suggests that running with music will require less effort, and this seems to be a good idea. But one might argue for a very different point of view. In *Runner's World*, the expert who opposes running with music opposes it because listening to music distracts us from the signals our bodies send us when we are running—signals we should pay attention to if we want to avoid injury, over exertion, or an accident. As he puts it, "One big problem is that listening to music can remove you from the other sounds that running produces, such as breathing and foot strike, which are essential cues. They give you feedback on your effort." Looked at from this perspective, the premise "Music can sometimes make running feel easier" is a reason for thinking, not that you should run with music, but that one shouldn't do so—for it confirms the claim that listening to music interferes with our perception of our bodily state when we are running.

This makes the argument we are discussing an argument in which the second component of strong arguments—a conclusion that follows from the premises—is not present. Even when we assume that its premise is acceptable, it follows that the argument is weak without further backing. The latter might be provided by further premises or other arguments that qualify or elaborate the premise in a way that helps it establish the conclusion—by showing that listening to music makes running feel easier without interfering with our perception of the key signals we need to be attuned to if we are to run safely.

If we think of a strong argument as an argument that provides evidence that should convince its audience to accept the conclusion, and a "weak" argument as one that fails to, then the notions of premise acceptability and logical consequence allow us to more precisely elaborate the features of strong arguments in that:

A strong argument is an argument with (1) acceptable premises and (2) a conclusion that follows from them.

A *weak* argument is, in contrast, an argument without acceptable premises or with a conclusion that does not follow from them, and possibly both.

Argument Criticism

By definition a weak argument is an argument that fails to satisfy one or both of the criteria for strong arguments: i.e. an argument that has unacceptable premises or a conclusion that does not follow from its premises. Good argument criticism exposes one or both of these flaws.

We illustrate good argument *criticism* with an example from a talk radio show on CFRB Toronto. In it, host John Oakley responded to a Canada-wide speaking tour conducted by the well-known environmentalist, David Suzuki. Suzuki had emerged from his tour arguing that the Canadian government should institute a carbon tax on the carbon content of fuels. In support of this conclusion he said that he had consulted with Canadians across Canada and found them "overwhelmingly" in support of such a tax. One might summarize this argument as: "The people I have talked to overwhelmingly want a carbon tax (*premise*), which shows that Canadians overwhelmingly support such a tax (*conclusion*)."

Oakley was not convinced and took Suzuki to task for his claim that Canadians overwhelmingly want a carbon tax. Summarized, his position is that Suzuki's conclusion about Canadians does not follow from his premise. As we shall see when we look at polling in detail in Chapter 9, Suzuki's argument provides a paradigm example of a poor generalization. It is not surprising that the people he met and spoke to on his tour were overwhelmingly in favour of a carbon tax, for he is a famous environmentalist and it is people who support his strong environmentalism who are attracted to his talks. His experience talking to them does support the claim that these sorts of people are overwhelmingly in favour of a carbon tax, but it would be a mistake to conclude from this that the "average citizen" shares such views. On his own radio show, Oakley demonstrated the point by surveying his own listeners, finding that only 8 per cent of his respondents supported such a tax. Oakley's survey is no better proof of what Canadians believe (because there is no reason to think that those who like to listen to his views represent the views of most Canadians), but it does illustrate the problem of bias such generalizations involve, and this raises questions about Suzuki's claims.

Our criticism highlights problems with Suzuki's conclusion that Canadians overwhelmingly support a carbon task. This weakens the further argument in which this is used as a premise, which we can summarize as follows:

The Canadian government should institute a carbon tax (*conclusion*) because Canadians overwhelming want a carbon tax (*premise*).

The issues we have already raised show that this argument fails to satisfy the first criterion of strong arguments—premise acceptability. There are, in contrast, no obvious problems with the link between the premise and the conclusion, for it is reasonable to assume that a government should do what the majority of its citizens want (there are, of course, all kinds of situations in which this does not happen, and for good reasons, but there is no obvious way in which they apply). In view of this, it is easy to see how the conclusion follows from the premise. It is the unacceptability of the premise, not its relation to the conclusion, which weakens this particular argument. Our two examples illustrate how good argument criticism assesses the two components of good arguments, premise acceptability and logical consequence. In responding to such criticism we can strengthen an argument by addressing the problems it highlights. In our second case, this would require the replacement of the weak premise we identified.

Our criticisms of Suzuki's arguments do not by themselves settle the question of whether Canada should institute a carbon tax. The arguments we have considered fail to show that this is so, but there may be other arguments that are more convincing (Suzuki himself enunciates many other arguments). A proper poll or vote would provide evidence establishing whether the majority of Canadians do support a carbon tax. Even if it doesn't one might argue that this is a situation in which the environmental consequences of a carbon tax are so important (for future generations as well as our own) that one should be instituted anyway.

In the course of evaluating arguments it is important to distinguish the criticism of a particular argument from an evaluation of the conclusion it presents. One may accept the conclusion of an argument without accepting the argument. The argument "Every intelligent person will read this book. You are intelligent, so you are reading this book," has a true conclusion but its first premise is (regretfully) implausible and makes this argument weak (our confidence in the second premise cannot remedy this flaw). A decision about the plausibility of any conclusion would require a comprehensive review of the evidence that might be marshalled for or against it.

EXERCISE   3B

1. The following examples of argument are derived (and in some cases adapted) from the debate on running with music we have already discussed. In each case, identify the premise(s) and conclusion of the argument and evaluate it as strong or weak, addressing the questions of premise acceptability and logical consequence.

    a) Running while listening to music also removes you from the environment you're in, which can be unsafe. You may not hear a car or person behind you. You may not hear thunder in the distance. And in races, it makes you oblivious of other runners and you can't hear the directions being given by officials.

    b) The ability to be at peace and be calm is something we've lost in our culture in favour of multi-tasking. We can recover this peace with running but I would argue that listening to music—or podcasts or audio books—while running is a form of multi-tasking. So find yourself by running without music.

    c) In the "flow state," which is complete immersion in the task at hand, time almost seems to stand still. You're enjoying what you are doing, you feel at one with yourself. But there's good research showing that music can help enhance flow state during running. So it can actually be part of this holistic experience, not necessarily detached from it or a detriment to it.

2. In each of the following examples, identify the premise(s) and conclusion of the argument and evaluate it as strong or weak, addressing the questions of premise acceptability and logical consequence.

    a)* [From Pliny the Elder, *Natural History* Book 7, Line 50] People may be born the same moment but have entirely different fates. So astrology is not reliable.

    b)* Cigarettes are the most flagrant example of drug pushing, since most tobacco is pushed on teenagers, who are led by advertising into thinking it's cool to smoke.

    c) University education should be free in the United States. It is free in Australia and many European countries that do not have the resources America has.

    d) It was once rare to find a professional with an MBA. Now they are a dime a dozen. Because value reflects scarcity, an MBA isn't worth what it once was.

3. Assess the following example of argument criticism, adapted from the "Citizen Tom" blog. Identify the premises and conclusion in both the argument in favour of compact fluorescent light bulbs (CFLs) and the argument against them.

    It is true that CFLs use two-thirds less energy than standard incandescent bulbs to provide the same amount of light, and last up to 10 times longer. Environmentalists conclude that we should convert.

    But the pros and cons of CFLs are not so simple. Why? Because there are, in addition to advantages, disadvantages to CFLs as well: i.e. because they contain mercury; because they are almost all made in China, which has poor environmental standards for production; and because light bulbs are used at night, which means that replacing all our household light bulbs will do little to reduce peak demand and mitigate the need for . . . power.

3   Logical Consequence: Deductive and Inductive Validity

The second criterion for strong arguments is logical consequence, which we have defined as "a conclusion that follows from the premises." Put in another way, a strong argument must have premises that *lead* to its conclusion. Those who study argument have debated the nature of this link between premises and conclusion. Some emphasize one kind of link that they attribute to all arguments, others differentiate between two kinds of links, and still others distinguish more than two. We will not pursue a theoretical account of these differences here, but we will refine our account of logical consequence by introducing the two most commonly distinguished ways in which a conclusion may follow from a set of premises.

In "deductive" arguments the link between premises and conclusions is so strong that the conclusion *necessarily* follows from the premises. In arguments of this sort, it is impossible for us to accept that the premises are true and still reject the conclusion. We call arguments of this sort **deductively valid**. Consider the following example:

(**Premise 1:**) The fetus, even in the case of a pregnancy resulting from rape or incest, is an innocent human being. (**Premise 2:**) The killing of innocent human beings is never permissible. (**Premise 3:**) Abortion kills the fetus. (**Conclusion:**) Abortion is never permissible.

In a case like this, someone who accepts premises 1, 2, and 3 must accept the conclusion, for as soon as you accept that the fetus is, in all cases of abortion, an innocent human being, that abortion kills the fetus, and that the killing of innocent human beings is never permissible, it is impossible to reject the conclusion that abortion is never permissible.

In deductively valid arguments, the link between the premises and the conclusion is as strong as it can be. Anyone who understands the argument must accept the conclusion if they accept the premises. If they do not, they have misunderstood the meaning of the statements that make up the argument or they are fundamentally irrational. The strength of the link between the premises and conclusion in a deductively valid argument means that it always satisfies the requirement that the conclusion of a strong argument must be a logical consequence of its premises. It does not follow that all deductively valid arguments are strong arguments, for they may not have acceptable premises.

In the example we have given, Premise 1 assumes that the fetus is a "human being"—a claim that has been widely debated. Premise 2 is also controversial, for it does seem to be permissible to kill innocent people in certain circumstances (in self defence and in times of war, for instance). Premise 3 is acceptable in our current circumstances but there might come a time in the future when it might be mistaken: if, for example, technological innovation allowed a doctor to remove a fetus from a pregnant mother without killing it (say, by placing it in an artificial womb). At the very least, such considerations show that the burden of proof in this case requires the arguer who forwards the argument to justify its first two premises (the third premise is acceptable in our current circumstances). Because they are not acceptable without further support, the argument is weak even though it is deductively valid.

Deductively *invalid* arguments contain a conclusion that does not necessarily follow from the premises. In these cases, one can reject an argument's conclusion even while accepting that its premises are true. This means that the link between an argument's premises and conclusion is not as strong as the link in deductively valid reasoning, but it does not mean that all deductively invalid arguments should be rejected. In the case of inductively valid arguments we can imagine that the premises of an argument are true and the conclusion false, but the premises still make the conclusion likely, and in this way provide reasonable support for it.

Consider an example from Vancouver, where the BC Court of Appeal ordered the city to amend their bylaws after it forced Falun Gong protestors in 2009 to take down a hut used in demonstrations outside the Chinese consulate. According to the court, this action violated the right to protest that is a key element of the freedom of expression that is essential in a democratic society. In response to the Court's decision, Vancouver's City Council discussed a new by law entitled "Structures for Public Expression on City Streets" in 2011. It was supposed to make room for protest structures, but the initial version of the law was widely criticized on the grounds that it was too restrictive: it would charge protestors $1200 to set up a structure; would prohibit structures in residential areas; would limit the size of the displays; and would require a traffic management plan for every structure. On the basis of these restrictions, some concluded that the law would inevitably lead to further court challenges that the city would lose.

We might summarize the latter argument as follows.

Premise: The proposed "Structures for Public Expression on City Streets" is restrictive in a great many ways (by charging protestors $1200, prohibiting structures in residential areas; limiting the size of the displays; and requiring a traffic management plan).

Conclusion: The law would lead to further court challenges the city would lose.

This is an argument which is not deductively valid, for we cannot say that the conclusion *necessarily* follows from the premise. The possibility that the city would lose future court challenges depends on many things: on the city's interpretation of the law; on the extent to which protest groups would be willing to invest the time and fiscal resources to challenge the law; on legal technicalities; and so forth. It is certainly possible that one or more of these factors would prevent future court challenges the city would lose.

This does not mean that the argument can be dismissed out of hand. The finding of the Appeal Court shows that it takes the issue of freedom of expression very seriously; the proposed law places many impediments that interfere with protesters' right to protest in public; and a number of incidents in the city's past suggest that protesters will zealously defend their right to protest. In such circumstances it is reasonable to suppose that a decision to pass the proposed law makes it plausible or likely that the city would lose further court challenges.

This is a good example of an inductively valid argument. Such arguments are characterized by a more tentative link between their premises and their conclusions. They function as an essential part of ordinary reasoning. We rely on them in many situations characterized by uncertainty in which they serve as an alternative to deductive arguments. In contrast, inductively *invalid* arguments are always weak, for their conclusions are not a logical consequence of their premises.

Relevance and Sufficiency

When judging validity, it may help to consider the premises of an argument from two points of view. First, we can ask whether the premises in an argument are *relevant* to the conclusion. We count a premise or group of premises as relevant when it provides some—that is, any—evidence that makes the conclusion more or less likely. Premises are *positively* relevant when they make a conclusion more likely and *negatively* relevant when they make it less likely. The following statements are all positively relevant to the claim that "University education is a way to build a better economic future":

- University graduates have, on average, much higher salaries than people who don't go to university.
- University graduates are more likely to occupy professional and managerial positions.
- University graduates are more likely to be promoted.

A strong argument proposes premises that are positively relevant to its conclusion. If it failed to do so, it would provide no support for this conclusion. But positively relevant premises do not guarantee a strong argument. In addition to positively relevant premises, a strong argument requires premises that are *sufficient* to establish that a conclusion is more likely than not. This implies something more than positively relevant premises, which may provide some support for a conclusion without providing *enough* support to convince a reasonable audience. We can, therefore, develop the notion of logical consequence by saying that an argument's conclusion follows from its premises if they are (1) relevant to the conclusion, and (2) sufficient to establish it as probable.

In a deductively valid argument, the premises are always relevant and sufficient to the conclusion, for it is impossible to accept the premises and reject the conclusion. One cannot have premises that are more relevant and sufficient than this. In an inductively valid argument the link between the premises and conclusion is weaker, but the argument may still be strong, and may provide sufficient evidence to convince us of its conclusion. In an inductively invalid argument, the link between premises and conclusion is too weak to do so.

Deciding when we have relevant and sufficient evidence for a conclusion can be a complex task. Consider a popular blog entitled "100 Reasons NOT to Go to Graduate School" (http://100rsns.blogspot.com). The author describes the blog as "an attempt to offer those considering graduate school some good reasons to do something else." The reasons given include the claims that:

- Graduate school is expensive and there are few jobs waiting for graduates.
- Graduate school forces you to put other important aspects of your life (e.g., marriage and a family) on hold.
- Universities use graduate students primarily as a source of cheap labour.

A full analysis of the overall argument would be a very complex endeavour requiring an assessment of the relevance and sufficiency of the 100 reasons given (and the relevance and sufficiency of the sub arguments provided in defence of each of the 100 reasons). To illustrate the notions of relevance and sufficiency, we consider just part of the evidence the blog provides for the claim that "The Smart People Are Somewhere Elsewhere"—the first reason it gives for not going to grad school.

> According to FinAid.org: "The median additional debt [the debt that graduate students pile onto the debt that they acquired as undergraduates] is $25,000 for a Master's degree, $52,000 for a doctoral degree and $79,836 for a professional degree. A quarter of graduate and professional students borrow more than $42,898 for a Master's degree, more than $75,712 for a doctoral degree and more than $118,500 for a professional degree." This is not intelligent behavior. The smart people are somewhere else.

Here the large debt that students accumulate in graduate school is used as a premise for the conclusion that going to grad school is not intelligent behaviour (and "The smart people are somewhere else").

Is this an argument that gives relevant and sufficient reasons for its conclusions? In addressing this question we would note that the premise tells us that a particular website,

FinAid.org, provides the figures it gives for graduate student debt. Certainly the statement on that website is relevant to the claim that graduate students acquire unreasonable debt, but is it sufficient to establish that this is so? One issue this raises is whether this website is a credible authority which is providing a reliable account of student debt—if the website is not credible, then there is no reason to accept its data as evidence for the claim that graduate student debt is unreasonable. To determine whether it is credible, we would have to learn more about FinAid.org and its claims. In the final analysis, this probably requires an assessment of the authorities *it* depends on when it makes its claims.

Assuming that the figures given can be established as reliable, the premise of our argument is relevant to the conclusion that it is not wise for most people to go to graduate school—for it isn't wise to accumulate large debts. But it does not provide sufficient evidence to establish the conclusion that going to graduate school is not an intelligent decision, for the wisdom of this debt depends, from a financial point of view, on the financial consequences of the decision to go to graduate school. If the result is likely to be a lucrative job with a high paying salary, then this may compensate for the expense that one occurs in graduate school. It may, to take one example, be expensive to become a medical doctor, but the ultimate financial rewards may outweigh the expense of doing so.

Of course, the argument for and against graduate school could continue. In answer to our analysis of one of its arguments, one might point out that the *100 Reasons* blog provides evidence for thinking that it is a mistake to imagine that most or even many of the graduates of graduate school will find lucrative jobs. We take no position on the question whether you should go to graduate school, but we would say that it behooves you to consider the arguments pro and con if you are thinking of doing so, and that they provide ample illustrations of the complexities that arise when we try to determine whether the premises of an argument are relevant and sufficient to establish its conclusion. This underscores the point that much more could be said about validity, and relevance and sufficiency, something we do in Chapter 8. Until we get there, our outline of validity and the criteria for establishing it will provide helpful background as we turn to the more complex aspects of argument analysis and evaluation.

EXERCISE   3C

In each of the following cases, identify the premise(s) and conclusion in the argument. Are the premises relevant and sufficient to establish the conclusion? Are the arguments deductively or inductively valid? Why or why not? Be sure to explain your judgements in each case. (Note that this exercise does not ask you judge whether the premises of the argument are acceptable. In this case you are asked only to consider whether the argument is valid or not.)

a)* Since large carnivores like grizzly bears and wolves are majestic creatures in their own right and are also critical to maintaining the health of the ecosystem, it is wrong to indiscriminately destroy them.

b) Medieval portrayals of Plato and Aristotle with haloes cannot be taken to mean that these two were seen as "saints." "Sainthood," and the attainment of it, is directly related to the following of Christ himself.

c)* We should not extend the status of the family to same-sex couples. There are two reasons for this. First, some discrimination is always necessary in complex societies. Secondly, a family by definition must have both a mother and father.

d) [From a Letter to the Editor, *The Globe and Mail*, 8 February 1997] An independent Associated Press poll (December 1995) showed that 59 per cent of the American public thought that it was "always wrong to kill an animal for its fur." A 1997 fur industry poll, specifically targeting fur coat wearers, found that a mere 17 per cent said that a fur coat represented fashion and 14 per cent said social status. From this information it follows that the public views those who wear coats as callous, showing arrogant disregard for the suffering of fur-bearing animals.

e) [From the *Wall Street Journal*, 4 June 2003, p. A3]

TAKE A CHANCE ON LOVE.

NOT ON YOUR PRIVATE JET.

You have to throw caution to the wind when it comes to affairs of the heart. Purchasing a private jet, however, demands a rational approach. When you choose fractional jet ownership with NetJets, you'll have access to the world's largest fleet of business jets, which means you're guaranteed a plane in as little as four hours. The best-trained pilots in the industry assure your safety and it's all backed by the financial strength of Berkshire Hathaway. Maybe that's why people who can fly any way they want choose NetJets.

NETJETS. LEAVE NOTHING TO CHANCE.

f) [From the *Wall Street Journal*, 4 June 2003, p. A8]

Considering NetJets? If You Think Performance Matters, Call Flexjet.

BOMBARDIER FLEXJET'S HIGH PERFORMANCE FLEET STRETCHES YOUR HOURS.

Bombardier is a world-leading expert in the design and manufacturing of sleek, aerodynamically efficient aircraft. The superior speed advantage of Flexjet aircraft significantly shortens your trip time and delivers a lower cost per mile than NetJets. With Flexjet you'll fly faster, higher and more efficiently. So, you can use the hours you save towards more trips.

Flexjet Gives You the Equivalent of 12% More Hours Per Year.

Flexjet: Equivalent of 112 Hours

Netjets: 100 Hours

Bombardier Flexjet

4 Contextual Relevance

The relevance of premises to the conclusion is not the only type of relevance that interests us when evaluating argumentation. We are also concerned to ensure that our own arguments and those we are considering are relevant to the contexts in which they arise. If a context assumes one understanding of an issue and then an arguer ignores or misrepresents that meaning, then the argument will be contextually irrelevant. Strong arguments will avoid this error and remain relevant to the appropriate context.

An argument that is contextually situated properly addresses whatever issue is at hand, responds appropriately to any prior argument it answers or builds upon, and anticipates reasonable objections from opponents. When arguments fail in this respect, they can exhibit the kind of weaknesses that have been traditionally identified as "fallacies." A fallacy is *a common mistake in argument.* The focus of this text is on *good* reasoning, so although we will have occasion to discuss several fallacies in the chapters ahead, we do so in terms of how arguments fail to meet the various criteria of strength that are our primary concern. In this chapter, however, we will illustrate specific kinds of weakness by introducing two fallacies of contextual *irrelevance.* They highlight problems that tend to characterize arguments that are not properly situated in their context.

Red Herring

A red herring is an attempt to shift debate away from the issue that is the topic of an argument. Instead of addressing the strength or weakness of the argument, it deflects attention to a new topic that is not relevant to the one at hand. The term "red herring" is commonly said to originate in the use of a real red herring (i.e. the fish) in fox hunting. Hunters who wanted to save an exceptional fox for another chase would drag a red herring across its scent, diverting the chasing hounds after the stronger scent of the red herring. Whether this is true or not, there is no doubt that the argumentative counterpart of this strategy is a common tactic in debate.

We take our first example from an Internet debate about Lance Armstrong, the seven time winner of the Tour de France. His status as a cancer survivor who has raised millions for cancer treatment has made him a hero to some, but others regard him as a fraud whose success was due to the use of illicit drugs. On the occasion of his retirement from cycling, *Velonews: The Journal of Competitive Cycling* posted an article on its website entitled "Armstrong's 25-year Journey is Over" (17 February 2011). It sparked an Internet exchange between readers who roundly criticized Armstrong, and others who rejected suggestions that he was guilty of doping. Here is a portion of that exchange:

road_bikerider

Can't anyone just be happy for Lance and enjoy all of the drama and excitement that he has given us over the years? He is a great athlete and has accomplished much in his lifetime, both before and after his cancer.

birillothedog

He's not a great athlete, he's a fraud, a cheat, and a liar. That's why not everybody is "happy for Lance."

lboogie6029

Jealousy is a bummer.

We can understand the first comment in this exchange as an argument. It suggests that we *should* "just be happy for Lance and enjoy all of the drama and excitement that he has given us over the years" (*conclusion*) because "He is a great athlete and has accomplished much in his lifetime, both before and after his cancer" (*premise*). The next commentator, birillothedog, answers with a different argument, maintaining that there is a good reason that "not everybody is happy for Lance" (*conclusion*) because "He's not a great athlete, he's a fraud, a cheat and a liar" (*premise*). Putting aside the question whether we should accept these arguments, we want to note the next contribution to the exchange, which abruptly dismisses birillothedog's argument, accusing him of jealousy.

In the next chapter, we will discuss how to detect the implicit argument behind assertions like this. Here, we will assume that lboogie6029 believes that the previous contributor is not a fan of Armstrong *because* he is jealous. This is a good example of red herring. For the topic at issue is the question whether Armstrong should, at the end of his career, be celebrated. The first commentator presents an argument for thinking so. Birillothedog provides an argument for the opposite conclusion. This second argument may be weak. If lboogie6029 wishes to reject it, then he or she should provide his or her own argument that shows that this is so. He or she could, for example, attempt to show that the premise is false, that the conclusion doesn't follow, or that there is other compelling evidence that shows that Armstrong should be celebrated. Instead of doing this, lboogie6029 changes the topic. The new topic is the question whether birillothedog is jealous.

This new question deflects attention away from the issue at hand: the question of whether Lance Armstrong should be celebrated. The new question is, moreover, a question that makes little sense as a topic for argument in the debate in which it is embedded. It is very difficult to see how lboogie6029 or anyone else could know that birillothedog is jealous by reading two sentences that might instead be taken as an instance of conviction, indignation, or anger. More importantly, it doesn't really matter whether birillothedog is jealous. In a debate about Lance Armstrong, the important question is whether his arguments criticizing Armstrong are strong or weak. This issue does not turn on the question whether he is jealous—even if he is, that cannot show that the argument he proposes must be mistaken. People who are jealous may still forward good arguments, so something more is needed if one wants to reject the argument he provides.

Straw Man

One kind of diversion that warrants special mention is called straw man. Historically, a "straw man" was a figure made of straw used to represent a man. Straw men were used in military drills that aimed to teach recruits how to fight with an opponent. In other circumstances, they were burnt as effigies to protest against leaders they were said to represent. In the world of argument, a *straw man* is a false account of an opponent's point of view. Presenting such an account violates our obligation to represent opposing positions fairly and accurately.

RED HERRING

The fallacy red herring is an attempt to shift attention away from the topic of an argument, in another direction that is not contextually relevant.

Usually, straw man arguments employ a weakened version of an opponent's position that is, like the straw men traditionally used in military training, more easily disposed of than their real counterpart. Within the scope of the argument in question, this makes it easier for an arguer to refute their opponents, but it is a false victory, for one has not defeated the real opponent, but a weaker replica that lacks the strength of the original.

In our discussion of proponents and opponents in Chapter 1, we noted the historical debate between al-Ghazali and Ibn Sina (Avicenna). In the context of straw man it is worth noting that al-Ghazali's critique of Avicenna's arguments was preceded by another book, titled *The Aims of the Philosophers* (*Maqasid al-falasifah*), which was a summary of Avicenna's philosophy. In the West, al-Ghazali was originally known for this work, because it was a superb guide to the tenets of Islamic Aristoteleanism—so good that al-Ghazali himself was at one point incorrectly thought to be an adherent. But as al-Ghazali himself said, one must be well versed in the ideas of others before setting out to refute them. This is the attitude we should all have when criticizing the views of our opponents. We should understand their views thoroughly (ideally, as well as they do), to ensure that our criticisms are not just fair and reasonable, but also telling, for this is the only way to ensure that our criticisms will themselves stand up to scrutiny.

Straw man arguments represent the other side of this spectrum, occurring when an arguer misrepresents the views of those he or she criticizes. To illustrate this, we return to the Internet debate about Lance Armstrong. The following is another contribution to the discussion posted by Samaway:

> Moral judgments of whether he doped, and whether his accomplishments are then somehow valid, are simply reflections of cultural constructs. . . . I can't condone doping, but nor do I get angry at riders who do. I think doping signals something much more troubling about our culture.

In answer to these remarks, "S" provides the following retort:

> So the end justifies the means? Whoever is the best at cheating wins and should receive our adulations? Who the hell cares about the guy who raced "clean" but came in 6th right?. . . It's about whether you won, placed or showed . . . anything less is for saps.

It should be evident that this seriously misconstrues Samaway's position. Samaway neither condones nor condemns (gets angry about) doping, which implies that they *don't* think "it's about whether you, won, placed or showed" and that "anything less is for saps." What Samaway suggests is something different: that the "troubling" issue that should be discussed and debated is what it is in our culture gives rise to doping. As they themselves write in response to this: "It seems that focusing on whether a cyclist is a cheater is a little short sighted, given the mix of political economy and cultural values that the sport embodies."

If S wishes to take issue with Samaway's views evidence should be provided that he or she is mistaken. This might be done by arguing that cheating is wrong no matter what cultural influences give rise to it, or by arguing that Samaway might as well argue that it is permissible to cheat on one's taxes or text while you are driving because our culture makes this a prevalent practice. Whether or not these are good arguments, they are arguments that respond to Samaway's real position, and that some such argument is what is needed if one wants to show that Samaway is mistaken. Instead, S constructs a straw man, dismissing Samaway's claims in a way that seriously misrepresents them.

We finish our discussion of red herring and straw man with an example from a Manitoba controversy that arose when a judge sentenced a convicted rapist to a conditional sentence—a sentence that meant the man would not spend time in jail. In explaining his decision, the judge described the case as a situation in which the defendant never threatened the woman and genuinely misperceived what the victim wanted. "This is a different case than one where there is no perceived invitation," he said. "This is a case of misunderstood signals and inconsiderate behaviour." ("Rape victim 'Inviting,' so no jail," *Winnipeg Free Press*, 2 February 2011, p. A3)

One might summarize the judge's main argument as the claim that the defendant should get a conditional sentence (*conclusion*) because (a) this was a case where he genuinely misunderstood what the woman wanted (*premise 1*) and (b) he never threatened the victim (*premise 2*). In a further account of the factors that were alleged to contribute to the miscommunication, the judge included the woman's attire—tube tops with no bra, high heels, and makeup; her suggestive comments; her willingness to accompany the man into the woods; and her flirtatious conduct, which included consensual kissing.

When the decision was reported, it produced a wave of comments and debate, which included many calls for the judge's dismissal. In less than a day, there were three hundred responses to the initial report on the website of the *Winnipeg Free Press*. Many of these responses focussed on the judge's comments about the woman's attire. A commentator called CDNinJPN wrote that:

> according to the judge "wearing tube tops with no bra, high heels and plenty of make up" means "let's have sex" no matter what the woman actually says. Seriously, I thought that kind of thinking went out the door with 8-tracks, rotary phones, and Betamax.

On the day following the report, the *Winnipeg Free Press* featured the following comment, by Denial Awareness, as the "Comment of the Day":

> The premises of this whole "she was wearing a tube top . . ." argument is that women control men's actions. If a woman is wearing a tube top, no bra, and make up, a man has absolutely NO control over himself and no responsibility for his actions. The woman MADE him rape her. He had no choice. He was forced by his uncontrollable

chemical reaction to seeing her in a tube top. This judge talks about "signals being misunderstood" as though "signals" are some sort of accurate way to communicate. I was once told by a guy that I had been "giving signals" that I wanted to have sex with him and he went on to describe how I lifted my arm and turned my head a certain way. It was ridiculous! I'm shocked that a judge even uses the term "signals" as a justification for vindicating a rapist!

In considering these comments, it is important to say that there are many ways that one might argue against the judge's decision—by arguing that it sets an unacceptable precedent, does not take the issue of sexual assault seriously enough, and so on. That said, the remarks that we have quoted are problematic because they seriously misrepresent the judge's explanation of his reasons for assigning the sentence he did. The following five problems with their characterization of the judge's argument may serve as premises in an argument for the conclusion that they are instances of the fallacy straw man.

- **Problem 1.** The judge did not argue that a man "has absolutely NO control over himself and no responsibility for his actions" when he sees a woman in a tube top. Nor does he hold that these are circumstances in which "The woman MADE him rape her. He had no choice. He was forced by his uncontrollable chemical reaction to seeing her in a tube top." Nothing in the judge's comments suggest that this is (as "Denial Awareness" suggests) a basic premise in his argument. His remarks imply the opposite: that the man *was* in a position to make a conscious decision to have—or not have—sex with the woman. The defendant was not given a mitigated sentence on the grounds that he could not help himself, but on the grounds that he misunderstood the woman and made a mistaken decision, not one that he could not have made otherwise.

- **Problem 2.** "Denial Awareness" incorrectly claims that the judge talks "about 'signals being misunderstood' as though 'signals' are some sort of accurate way to communicate." The judge very clearly thinks that that "signals" are *not* an accurate way to communicate, for this is implied by his suggestion that it is possible to misunderstand them and what they mean.

- **Problem 3.** It is unclear how the example that Denial Awareness gives from her own experience (when a "ridiculous" man told her that she was giving signals to have sex because she lifted her arm and turned her head) is relevant to the judge's assessment of this case. There is no reason to believe he would accept the claim of the man described, for the scenario in question shares little with the case before the judge.

- **Problem 4.** The claim that the judge uses the term "signals" as a justification for "vindicating a rapist!" greatly exaggerates the judge's views and actions. To "vindicate" means "to free from allegation or blame" but the judge found the defendant guilty, gave him a criminal record, and assigned a penalty that involved work in the community. It goes without saying that this may be too light a sentence (because the penalty does not include jail time) but one cannot equate it with vindicating the man in question.

- **Problem 5.** The judge did not say what CDNinJPN says he did, i.e. that "wearing tube tops with no bra, high heels and plenty of make-up means let's have sex." He listed these as factors that *contributed* to a miscommunication, and said that this *plus* other aspects of the situation (the kissing, the suggestive remarks, etc.) resulted in the alleged misunderstanding. One might compare the meaning of other claims qualified in a similar way: if an astrobiologist says that the presence of carbon is one of the factors that contributes to the possibility of life, then we would seriously misrepresent his or her position if we described it as the claim that "the presence of carbon means the presence of life." In the case at hand, the judge maintained that it was a series of factors *and still other* aspects of the situation (notably, the lack of threatening behaviour) that warranted the conditional sentence.

When we describe the comments we have quoted as instances of straw man, that does not mean that the judge's own argument is a good one. That remains to be established. The important point is that straw man criticisms of the judge are weak criticisms because they fail to address his real views. If we want to forward strong (even devastating) criticisms of the judge—or any other opponent, then we must do so in a way that carefully and accurately presents their views. When we fail to do so, our arguments become contextually irrelevant.

The examples of red herring and straw man we have given are not extraordinary. In the give and take of ordinary argument, it is common for arguers to deflect attention from the issues at hand. Often this is done by misrepresenting their opponents, typically by ignoring the nuances of their position and creating a simplified version of it that is easily derided. Especially when arguments are heated and the stakes are high, it is easy for our reactions to push us in this direction. Resisting this inclination is one way to establish yourself as an accomplished arguer and ensure you produce strong arguments.

STRAW MAN

The fallacy straw man is a type of diversion that attempts to shift attention from the proper topic of an argument against an opponent's point of view by misrepresenting the views that are the subject of criticism.

EXERCISE 3D

Assess each of the following examples in terms of how well the arguers comply with the requirements of contextual relevance. Identify the arguments, and in the case of fallacies of irrelevance explain what has gone wrong and why.

a) The government's healthcare bill is designed to pass the costs onto the public and this is a bad idea. The post office is a similar example of government mismanagement. It is extremely inefficient compared to private couriers, losing taxpayers billions of dollars a year, and there is no incentive to improve matters because of the government monopoly.

b)* The government's healthcare bill promises much but will likely deliver very little. It's impossible to believe it will make Americans healthy overnight. It should therefore be defeated.

c) A: Why are you not willing to support the gun-control legislation? Don't you have any feelings at all for the thousands of lives that each year are blotted out by the indiscriminate use of handguns?

B: I just don't understand why you people who get so worked up about lives being blotted out by handguns don't have the same feelings about the unborn children whose lives are being indiscriminately blotted out. Is not the sanctity of human life important in all cases? Why have you failed to support our efforts concerning abortion legislation?

d) [From "Europes elites are destroying the grand project" (*Der Spiegel* Online International, 9 June 2009, http://www.spiegel.de/international, which attempts to account for the poor turnout in European Parliamentary elections. The center-left political party *Süddeutsche Zeitung* is being quoted]

All opinion polls show that the majority of European's value the EU, that they would not like to do without it, that they appreciate the advantages of the community and that they would like to see more Europe when it comes to dealing with the big questions of the present and future such as climate change, energy supplies or foreign and security policy.

Why then does this majority not turn out to vote? Because no one has convinced them that it is important. Almost every party in every country in the EU has failed in the task of encouraging the voters to take part in the decision-making process.

e) [From a Letter to the Editor, *The Peterborough Examiner*, 20 May 1992, p. A3]

I am concerned by the recent letters to the editor that portray the Women's Health Care Centre as an abortion clinic I would like to point out that the Women's Health Care Centre provides many valuable services . . . pregnancy non-stress testing; colposcopy clinic; lactation consultant (breastfeeding support); counselling and information on a wide range of health issues of concern to women and their families; workshops covering PMS, menopause, body image, living alone, and many others.

I feel that the services provided by the Women's Health Care Centre work in conjunction with physicians and provide comprehensive information and support for the women of Peterborough and the surrounding areas.

5   Schemes and Counter-Schemes

In judging arguments, we can distinguish questions of acceptability from questions of validity. In many cases, we judge the validity of an argument by relying on our intuition—on our intuitive appreciation of what does and does not follow from a set of premises. This is what Sherlock Holmes tends to do when he reflects on his investigations and announces the unexpected verdict that "So-and-so committed the crime." In response to Watson's quizzical response, he claims that his reasoning is "Elementary, my dear Watson." By this, Holmes means that the conclusion is easy to see once his argument is properly understood. Typically, Holmes goes on to explain his argument in a way that clearly demonstrates that its conclusion follows from the evidence at hand.

We have all listened to and proposed many arguments. This gives us an intuitive appreciation of what makes sense and what does not which we can use to determine whether a straightforward and uncomplicated argument is valid or invalid. This is in some ways an easier task than judging whether premises are acceptable, for we can judge the relationship between premises and conclusion without having to marshal evidence for and against the premises. We rely on this intuitive skill when we follow Holmes's step-by-step explanation of his conclusions. Like Holmes, we use this skill when we try to demonstrate that our own inferences are valid.

Consider a simple example. In working through the exercises in this text, you wonder whether the answer to a particular question is included in the answers collected on the website that supports this text. In the process, you might employ the following reasoning:

> **Premise 1:** All the starred exercise questions are answered on the text website.
> **Premise 2:** Exercise question number 5 is starred.
> **Conclusion:** Exercise question number 5 must be answered on the text website.

This argument is deductively valid. If you are unsure why, try to imagine that you accept the premises but reject the conclusion. This would mean that exercise question number 5 is, contrary to the conclusion, not answered on the text website. But it would also mean that premise 1 is true—i.e. that all answered questions are starred. It would necessarily follow that question 5 is not starred, but this contradicts premise 2. This "mental experiment" shows that it is impossible for the conclusion to be false when the premises are true—i.e. that the argument's conclusion deductively follows from the premises.

Consider another example. Let's suppose you have an interest in nuclear science. You have heard that the person who discovered radioactivity won two Nobel prizes. You discover that this person is Marie Sklodowska Curie. You argue with a friend over the date when she discovered radioactivity. To settle the matter, you ask a professor and go back to your friend and say, "Marie Curie discovered radioactivity in 1898. Professor Szabo, who studied this in graduate school, told me so." Your argument is inductively rather than deductively valid, but it is a strong argument. Professor Szabo could have slipped up and confused this date with another one, but he is an expert in the matter, has studied the issue you have asked about, and betrayed no doubts when you asked him. In all likelihood, you and your friend will intuitively see that your conclusion should be accepted.

Relying on intuition is one way to judge whether an argument is valid or not. It will work in many cases, but it is difficult to intuit whether a long extended argument is valid, especially as intuitions may prove to be mistaken. Clearly, the principle "Trust your intuition" is not a sure guide to the strength of arguments, for people do present weak arguments and this is a situation in which the argument seems intuitively valid to at least one arguer—i.e. the arguer who proposed it. In these and many other cases, argument evaluation must provide us with a way to choose *between* competing intuitions.

In developing a more systematic approach to argument, and one that can tell us how to construct valid arguments, we can rely on the observation that individual arguments come in a variety of repeating patterns that can be identified in terms of the kinds of premises and conclusions they involve. We call these patterns argument schemes. By isolating particular schemes that apply to different kinds of argument, we can distinguish strong and weak patterns of reasoning, and judge arguments accordingly.

The last two examples we have given can illustrate this approach. The inductively valid argument that established the conclusion that Marie Curie discovered radioactivity in 1898 is an instance of a scheme called "appeal to authority." Arguments employing this scheme provide the word of an authority or expert as evidence for a conclusion (we discuss this scheme in detail in Chapter 12). The previous example, about exercise question 5, was an instance of a scheme that deduces a particular affirmative from a universal affirmative. We discuss this and similar schemes when we examine syllogisms in Appendix 1.

When we define schemes, we do so in a way that lets us separate the scheme from the particular instance of it conveyed in a specific argument. In the case of our argument about starred exercises, we can do this by letting "X" stand for "starred exercise questions," by letting "Y" stand for "questions answered on the text website," and by letting "z" stand for "question number 5." On this basis, we can represent the scheme of our example as follows.

SCHEME 1 (UNIVERSAL INSTANTIATION)
> **Premise 1:**   All X are Y.
> **Premise 2:**   z is X.
> **Conclusion:** z must be Y.

This scheme is sometimes called "universal instantiation."

Once we identify this scheme we can see that the example we have given shares its structure with many other arguments that can be represented in the same way. For any groups X and Y, and any individual z, an argument that has the same form of Scheme 1 will be deductively valid. Scheme 1 is, for example, implicit in the following argument about BMW automobiles:

> All luxury cars are expensive vehicles. Your BMW is a luxury car, so it must be an expensive vehicle.

If we let X = luxury cars, Y = expensive vehicles, and z = your BMW, you will see that this new argument is an instance of scheme 1. Our ability to represent both arguments in terms of this same scheme shows that they share a common structure even though their contents are different.

It is easy to build other arguments that are examples of universal instantiation. To do so, we only need to let X, Y, and z represent different groups and individuals. If we let X = logic professors, Y = people who read a lot, and z = Jan, then this produces the following argument of this form:

> All logic professors are people who read a lot. Jan is a logic professor. So Jan must read a lot.

Here again the result is a valid argument, for it is impossible for the conclusion to be false (i.e. for Jan *not* to read a lot) if its premises are true.

In developing our account of argument evaluation we have often compared an argument to a journey that takes one from accepted premises to a destination that is the conclusion. In understanding schemes and how they work, we might compare the distinction between an argument's scheme and its content to the distinction between directions and a particular location. If we say you need to go south 10 kilometres, then go east seven kilometres, this will take you to a different location depending on where you start. The same directions may, in view of this, take us to drastically different places: to a location in Saskatoon or Alaska or Singapore. Some directions will almost always make sense ("The location is 10° west and 10° south of you") and others not ("Turn left and right at the next traffic light"). The directions function in the same way in each case, but take us to very different destinations. In a similar way, a scheme of argument is a pattern or structure that can take us to a variety of conclusions.

When we embark on an analysis of complex arguments, it is helpful to identify any scheme of argument they incorporate, for different schemes have different criteria that can be used to assess the strength or weakness of instances of the scheme. These standards tell us what kinds of "critical questions" we should ask when evaluating an argument that is an instance of the scheme. In judging an appeal to authority, for example, we will need to ask questions about the authority's credentials, trustworthiness, and any bias they might have that might interfere with their judgement in this instance. These kinds of questions help us distinguish valid and invalid instances of the scheme.

"Counter-schemes" are schemes that are used to criticize arguments of a particular type, by showing that the premises in question are unacceptable or that the argument is not valid. The counter-scheme "argument against authority" is used to criticize appeals to authority. Some of the arguments we have to deal with in our reasoning will not correspond to any scheme or counter-scheme. In other cases, arguments are so complex that identifying an argument scheme requires a substantial amount of interpretation. That said, an understanding of schemes and how they work will significantly improve your ability to assess and create all types of arguments. The most common schemes are discussed in Chapters 9, 10, 11, and 12.

Discuss each of the following argument schemes. Do you think they are schemes that define deductively or inductively valid arguments? In each case, construct three arguments that are instances of the scheme.

    a)* All X are Y, all Y are Z, therefore all X are Z.
    b) After a thorough search, we have not been able to find any evidence of hypothesis X, so it is probably false.
    c) If X, then Y. If Y, then Z. So if X, then Z.

6   Summary

In Chapter 1 we introduced the notion of argument. In this chapter we looked at the difference between strong and weak arguments and how to evaluate them. In particular, we have explored how strong arguments must have conclusions that follow from premises, and learned that those premises must be acceptable. These two criteria will be developed in important ways in later chapters. We have also considered that strong arguments must be relevant to the contexts in which they arise. In this respect, we have looked at two failures of this requirement characterized by certain weak arguments, these are the Red Herring and Straw Man arguments. Finally, we have introduced a key tool that will be the focus of our accounts of argument: argument schemes and counter-schemes. These are regularized patterns of reasoning that can be evaluated according to specific ways in which the criteria for strong arguments arise for each scheme.

    1. For each of the following topics, construct short arguments that adequately satisfy the two basic criteria for strong arguments. Be sure to consider and meet your obligations with respect to the burden of proof. Once you have done this, exchange your arguments with another member of your class and constructively evaluate each other's efforts. Discuss the results.

        a)* Appropriate email etiquette.
        b) The right to smoke in enclosed public spaces.
        c) Publicly funded health care.
        d) The best student restaurant in town.
        e) The danger of a world wide flu pandemic.
        f) Our obligations to help with the AIDS epidemic in Africa.

    2. [The following arguments explore both sides of the controversial practice of factory farming. They are adapted from International Debate Education Association, www.idebate.org, accessed 20 June 2011. For each example, identify the argument, consider whether it is contextually relevant, and then assess it using the two basic criteria for strong arguments]

a)* Factory farming sees animals as "products," "commodities" for production and sale just like bricks or bread. But animals are conscious and aware and know pleasure and pain.

b)* Unless the state is going to impose vegetarianism (and that's not being proposed here) the business of food will continue, and that business should be efficient and productive like any other—that's in the interest of the producer, who makes a profit, and the consumer, who gets a low price.

c) Health risks to humans are also greatly magnified by factory farming, with epidemics swiftly spread between overcrowded animals and antibiotic resistance encouraged by medicated feed.

d) This intensive type of farming brings meat down to a price affordable to the poorest in our community on a regular basis. Without factory farming the poor will have an even worse diet.

e) Factory farming is very cruel. Confinement to the point at which suffocation is commonplace is the norm. Many animals never touch the ground or see direct sunlight. Chickens are bred selectively and genetically modified until the birds cannot stand up and their bones cannot support their weight. Battery hens are crammed into tiny cages and to stop them doing damage when they attack each other (as they inevitably do in such unnatural conditions) their beaks and toes are cut off. Pigs, highly social animals, are kept singly in cages they can't turn around in—and a number of diseases are very common because of the cramped conditions.

f) There is very little cruelty or suffering in factory farming—certainly no more than in traditional forms of farming. Foie gras has been produced since time immemorial by the force feeding of geese. Animals have always been herded together, confined, branded, killed and eaten. This is not the fault of the modern intensive (or "factory") industry, it's just the way things are when people eat meat.

3. For each of the following arguments from *The Sporting News* (24 July 1995), identify the argument and assess it as a strong or weak argument. Explain your decisions.

a)* [Dave Kindred, arguing against major league baseball's decision to institute new rules designed to speed up the game] There is pleasure knowing that events and not an expiring clock will decide when the evening's entertainment is done.

b) [Mike Schmidt, talking about the content of his speech on his induction into baseball's Hall of Fame] Children and their dreams must have positive reinforcement from parents, coaches, and friends. I truly believe that this reinforcement is not only important, but imperative. . . . Without parental encouragement to reach their goals, it is more difficult for children to develop self-esteem and become successful.

c) [Letter to "Voice of the Fan"] So Rockets' general manager John Thomas . . . doesn't think changing the logo after back-to-back titles won't hurt their luck? Well, I subscribe to Crash Davis's theory, as stated in the movie *Bull Durham*— "Never (mess) with a winning streak." . . . Ask the Penguins if they're sorry they changed logos. They did after their second consecutive Stanley Cup title but haven't made it past the second round since.

4. For each of the following arguments, say whether the argument is deductively or inductively valid. Explain your decision.

    a)* The conclusion of the argument can be false when the premises are true, so the argument is invalid.

    b) Most people find that their logical abilities improve with practice. So you should do fine if you work regularly on the exercises in this book.

    c)* In order to avoid the intricacies of theories of truth, we will rely on our earlier remark that the objective of an argument is to convince an audience. If this is so, then it is sufficient for our purposes that the premises of a good argument be accepted as true by both us and our audience. So this is what we will aim for.

    d)* [Greg Gutfeld, in "Be a jerk," *Men's Health*, 1995]
        A long time ago, I had this health problem. . . . Almost immediately, my doctor laid my worries to rest. He told me to relax. He sat with me and we talked for a long while. . . .We bonded. We became pals. . . . Over the course of a few months, I began to look forward to my visits. . . . But there was a small problem. I was still sick.

        Finally, I gave up and went to see another doctor. He was not a pleasant guy, more like a scowl in a white jacket. He took one look at me and spat out a diagnosis. . . .

        A week later I was cured.

        I learned something valuable here: When it comes to your health and other important matters, you can usually count on a jerk . . . .

    e) [From the same article] Nice bosses can ruin your career by not challenging you to do better. They won't tell you when your ideas stink, your work has been slacking or your fly is down. . . . A nice-guy boss will happily nod as you explain how elevator shoes for dachshunds is the wave of the future.

5. Provide argument criticism for each of the following passages. Begin by deciding whether the passage contains an argument. If it contains an argument, identify the conclusion and premise(s), and indicate the audience and opponents. For any arguments that you find, discuss where the burden of proof lies and whether contextual irrelevance has been avoided. Then assess whether they are strong arguments by applying the two basic criteria.

    a)* Certain non-human primates have been known to exhibit grief at the loss of a family member. But if they do that, then they are capable of abstract thought, and creatures with those capabilities must have a self. So, certain non-human primates must have a sense of self.

    b)* Certain non-human primates have been known to exhibit grief and be capable of abstract thought. And if they have those kinds of capabilities, then they are demonstrating some of the key indicators of personhood. Therefore, certain non-human primates are moral agents, since if they exhibit indicators of personhood then they are moral agents.

    c) [From a Letter to the Editor, *Wired* magazine, January 2003]
        Current chipmaking processes may require dangerous substances, but those cited in "Cleaning up clean rooms" are hardly carcinogenic franken-chemicals.

Hydrogen peroxide is what our mommies had us rinse our mouths with (albeit in diluted form) and pour into our ears (full strength) to help remove wax. Isopropyl alcohol we swab on cuts and abrasions.

Sometimes just the word chemical frightens people, so we need to be cautious. After all, dihydrogen oxide keeps us alive, but a few years ago a survey revealed that people were terrified of it and would want the FDA to ban it from foods.

d) [The following is a response to a news item (April 2008) that researchers in the United Kingdom had produced hybrid embryos, part-human and part-animal. The embryos did not survive beyond three days. The response is from Dr David King of Human Genetics Alert, http://news.bbc.co.uk, accessed 3 May 2010] For anyone who understands basic biology, it is no surprise that these embryos died at such an early stage. Cloning is inefficient precisely because it is so unnatural, and by mixing species it becomes even more unnatural and unlikely to succeed. The public has been grossly misled by the hype that this is vital medical research. Even if stem cells were ever to be produced, like cloned animals, they would have so many errors of their metabolism that they would produce completely misleading data.

e) [Robert F. Hartley, in *Business Ethics: Violations of the Public Trust*, 1993, Hoboken, New Jersey: J. Wiley] Lest we conclude that all takeovers involving heavy borrowing are ill-advised, reckless, and imprudent, let us look at a positive example. A&W root beer is part of America's motorized culture. . . .In 1986, Lowenkron engineered a leveraged buyout for $74 million, with $35 million in junk bonds. . . . By 1989, the company's sales surpassed $110 million, more than triple what they were before the buyout; profits reached $10 million, compared to a small loss in 1986.

f) [Al Bugner, on his heavyweight fight with Frank Bruno, in *Facing Ali: The Opposition Weighs In*, by Stephen Brunt, 2002, Alfred A. Knopf, Toronto, p. 160] The fight was the most disgraceful affair ever in a boxing ring. . . . I was rabbit-punched eight or ten times in the back of the head. Even in the eighth round when I was on the ropes he was doing it. There's no doubt in my mind that the whole affair was rigged. It was a set-up.

g)* [From *Life Extension* magazine, December 2002, p. 75] Carnosine may play a role in improving and increasing exercise performance. A study examined 11 healthy men during high-intensity exercise for concentration of carnosine in their skeletal muscle. . . . Carnosine was able to significantly buffer the acid-base balance in the skeletal muscles, which becomes unbalanced by the overproduction of hydrogen ions occurring in association with the build-up of lactic acid during high-intensity exercise.

h) [From "No chicken in this game," *Star Weekly*, 3 October 1959] Cock-fighting is one of the oldest and bloodiest sports in the world. The natural spur of the cock is replaced by one of steel, two inches long, which is tied on with leather throngs. The spurs are needle sharp and can do terrible damage. Matches are sometimes over in a few seconds or they may last for over an hour. The fight is always to the finish.

i) [The following is from a Letter to the Editor, *The Windsor Star*, 1 February 2007, by the chief electoral officer of Leamington, Ontario] Mail-in balloting is not a threat to democracy. . . . This form of balloting makes voting more accessible to many voters and promotes participation in our democratic process. And it is a system that is greatly appreciated by the many voters who have to manage mobility and accessibility issues.

j)   [From an article on automated chicken catching machines, "Poultry in motion," in *The Wall Street Journal*, 4 June 2003] Human catchers are expected to snag as many as 1,000 birds an hour. As the men tire during eight-hour shifts, they accidentally slam birds against the cages, breaking wings and legs. Up to 25 per cent of broilers on some farms are hurt in the process. By contrast, a recent study in the British scientific journal *Animal Welfare* found that a mechanical catcher in use in Germany reduces some injuries by as much as 50 per cent. That's good news for the birds, and also for the industry.

k)*   [From a personal email on "why to stop drinking Coke"] In many states the highway patrol carries two gallons of Coke in the trunk to remove blood from the highway after a car accident. You can put a T-bone steak in a bowl of coke and it will be gone in two days. The active ingredient in Coke is phosphoric acid. Its pH is 2.8. It will dissolve a nail in about four days.

l)   [Excerpted from "At Risk: Vaccines: How a legal case could cripple one of modern medicine's greatest achievements," by Paul A. Offit, the *Boston Globe*, 3 June 2007] No single medical advance has had a greater impact on human health than vaccines. Before vaccines, Americans could expect that every year measles would infect four million children and kill 3,000; diphtheria would kill 15,000 people, mostly teenagers; rubella (German measles) would cause 20,000 babies to be born blind, deaf, or mentally retarded; pertussis would kill 8,000 children, most of whom were less than one year old; and polio would paralyze 15,000 children and kill 1,000. Because of vaccines all of these diseases have been completely or virtually eliminated from the United States. Smallpox—a disease estimated to have killed 500 million people—was eradicated from the face of the earth by vaccines. And we're not finished; vaccines stand as our only chance to prevent pandemic influenza, AIDS, and bioterror, and our best chance of preventing certain cancers.

m)   [From an editorial on how to deal with the proliferation of nuclear weapons, in *The Wall Street Journal*, 4 June 2003, p. A16] For our part, we don't have much faith in UN inspections, which tend to see only those things the host nation wants to be seen. North Korea hid its clandestine uranium program for years, even as IAEA inspectors "safeguarded" its plutonium program. Then Pyongyang simply shut off even those TV cameras and booted the inspectors out of the country.

n)   [From a 2007 advertisement for Broil King barbecues] Unlike folded steel, cast aluminum ovens retain heat for superior cooking performance and have no seams for heat and drippings to escape. Most importantly, the thick aluminum will NEVER rust, and even features a Lifetime Warranty.

6.   Go to your local newspaper or your favourite magazines and find five examples of simple arguments and assess them as strong or weak.

For more online exercises, review questions, and quizzes related to the material in this chapter, please go to www.oupcanada.com/GoodReasoning5e

4

DRESSING ARGUMENTS

We have already introduced the key components of arguments and the concepts that we apply when evaluating them as weak and strong. Our account has focused on **simple arguments** because the fundamental elements of arguments are more easily distinguished in such cases. In this chapter we turn to more complex arguments and questions of interpretation they raise. In doing so, we discuss:

▶ simple and extended arguments
▶ explanations
▶ inference indicators
▶ argument narratives.

In a discussion of argument and argument analysis, John Woods has distinguished between arguments "dressed" and "on the hoof." These are terms normally used to refer to meat as it appears in a grocery store or butcher's shop, and on a live animal before it is butchered. Arguments on the hoof are arguments as they actually appear in the exchange that characterizes the use of arguments in science, social commentary, political and philosophical discussion, and so on. "Dressed" arguments are arguments as they appear after we clarify and delineate their structure, recognize their premises and conclusions, and label and identify them and their component parts. Woods's terminology underscores the point that it takes some significant work to dress an argument on the hoof, and that the result often looks different than the argument did before this work began.

Learning to dress arguments is a key part of learning to understand, construct, and evaluate them. Doing it well allows one to present an argument in a way that clarifies its structure, and prepares the way for a detailed evaluation. But dressing can itself be a difficult task and requires an understanding of a number of the complications that arise when we present and express arguments in the contexts in which they naturally occur.

1 Simple and Extended Arguments

So far, we have restricted our discussion of arguments to simple arguments. A **simple argument** has one conclusion supported by one or more premises. We contrast a simple argument with an **extended argument**—an argument which has a main conclusion supported by premise(s) and some premise(s) that are supported by other arguments. In an extended argument, sub-arguments support the premises that support the argument's principal conclusion.

Philip Yancey is a Christian author who wrote a book expounding the Christian notion of grace (P. Yancey, *What's So Amazing about Grace?*, Zondervan, 2002, p. 247). In it, he writes that the church has "for all its flaws" dispensed grace and justice to the world. "It was Christianity, and only Christianity, that brought an end to slavery, and Christianity that inspired the first hospitals and hospices to treat the sick. The same energy drove the early labour movement, women's suffrage, prohibition, human rights campaigns, and civil rights." This passage is naturally interpreted as a simple argument. It presents a claim—that the Christian church has, despite its flaws, dispensed grace and justice to the world—and backs it with reasons for thinking that this is so: that it was only Christianity that brought an end to slavery, inspired the first hospitals and hospices, and so forth.

Yancey's argument appears in a book written for Christian readers. His argument may convince—or rather reinforce—his audience's conviction that there is something valuable and worthwhile in the Christian church. But it is easy to imagine how his simple argument would have to evolve into an extended argument when it is presented to a broader audience; for those skeptical of his point of view (atheists, agnostics, adherents of non-Christian religions) are unlikely to accept his premises without debate. They are, for example, likely to need some evidence before they are willing to accept the claim that it was only Christianity that brought an end to slavery or that Christianity made women's suffrage possible.

In turning Yancey's simple argument into an extended argument, someone who advocates his views might back the claim that Christianity brought an end to slavery by providing evidence that shows that the abolitionists who succeeded in eliminating slavery were motivated by their commitment to Christian religious beliefs. It is in this way that a simple argument naturally evolves into an extended argument.

In analyzing such an argument (in dressing it for evaluation) we need to recognize (a) a principal argument that establishes the arguer's main conclusion, and (b) the various sub-arguments that are used to back the premises of the principal argument. In each case, we will need to identify the premises and conclusion of the arguments involved. In many cases, we will have to go even further, for the sub-arguments backing the premises of the principal argument are themselves extended arguments which have premises backed by further arguments.

> A **simple argument** is an argument that has one conclusion supported by one or more premises. An **extended argument** is an argument that has a main conclusion supported by premises, some of which are conclusions of subsidiary arguments.

EXERCISE 4A

1. Dentists, medical researchers, and health activists have debated the risks of "silver" amalgam fillings. The principal ingredient in these fillings is mercury, which is toxic to human beings. Those opposed to amalgam fillings argue that the mercury in the fillings does not remain inert and enters the body, where it can cause serious illness and multiple side effects. Those committed to amalgam fillings (including professional dentistry associations) have argued that there is no convincing evidence to back these claims. Identify and analyze the argument put forward in the following excerpt from the website of the American Dental Association, www.ada.org/news/881.aspx, (accessed 29 July 2009). How would one go about turning it into an extended argument?

   Are dental amalgams safe?
   Yes. Dental amalgam has been used in tooth restorations worldwide for more than 100 years. Studies have failed to find any link between amalgam restorations and any medical disorder. Amalgam continues to be a safe restorative material for dental patients.

2. Take any potential topic for argument and construct first a simple argument and then an extended argument that results when you back some premises of your simple argument with sub-arguments.

3. In each of the following cases, identify the argument as a simple or extended argument. In the latter case, identify the premises and conclusion in the principal argument and the sub-arguments that support its premises.

   a) The death penalty process is inherently flawed and broken, and can thus never be administered fairly, quickly, and with good faith that all the fail-safes are effectively employed. Given this, it should be abandoned in all societies that profess to be established on humane principles.

   b) The quality of political campaigns has been seriously degraded by the increase in attack advertisements because they detract voters from the real issues and focus attention on issues of personality.

   c) We should be grateful when people choose to care for ailing relatives. Not only does that choice allow the sick person to remain in more comfortable surroundings, it also alleviates the burden on hospitals, nursing homes, and an inadequate home care system.

   d) [From *The Vancouver Sun*, Opinion, "No reason to delay warnings, help line on cigarettes," 7 October 2010, www.vancouversun.com] Of all the risks we can do something about, smoking is the most clearly defined. There is no argument about the health effects of tobacco. There are no offsetting benefits, and we can easily see the needless suffering and loss of vitality caused by tobacco-related illness.

   e) [Adapted from a Letter to the Editor, *The Los Angeles Times*, November 5, 2010, www.latimes.com, accessed 5 November 2010] McDonald's spends tens of millions of dollars a year on advertising that uses toys to get kids to prefer junk food and demand it from their harried parents. What parent wants to constantly compete against that?

Most Happy Meals contain fatty meat, fatty fries, sugary drinks and white flour. That's pretty much the opposite of what kids should be eating. As the kids grow older, they almost certainly will graduate to the restaurants' bigger burgers and drinks, while graduating into overweight adolescence and obese adulthood.

2   Inference Indicators: Distinguishing Arguments and Non-Arguments

We have defined an argument as a conclusion and a set of statements ("premises") offered in support of it. The first step in learning how to deal with arguments "on the hoof" is learning how to recognize arguments and their components in the contexts in which they naturally occur. In doing so, it is important to remember that the claim that something is an argument must not be confused with the claim that it is a good argument. Arguments on the hoof may be strong or weak, plausible or implausible, convincing or unconvincing. We leave a further discussion of these distinctions for later chapters. In this and the next chapter, our only concern is recognizing, identifying, and dressing arguments and their components. In passing we will note that you are likely to be a more adept arguer if you learn to separate the attempt to dress an argument from the attempt to evaluate its strength.

Some people are poor reasoners because they fail to recognize arguments and their components. But some enthusiastic (or pugnacious) arguers go too far in the opposite direction, interpreting almost anything as an argument. This is a mistake. In looking for arguments and creating them, remember that many claims and remarks are not properly understood as attempts to provide evidence for some conclusion. We use communication for many purposes—to convey our feelings, to report facts, to ask questions, to propose hypotheses, to express our opinions, and so on. Arguing is only one of the ways in which we communicate. It is a pervasive practice, but the first step in learning how to analyze and assess arguments on the hoof is, learning how to distinguish arguments and non-arguments.

In deciding whether or not a set of sentences is an argument, it is important to remember that arguments, even when they are explicit, may be expressed in a variety of ways. Sometimes the conclusion comes first and is followed by premises. Sometimes the premises come first and are followed by the conclusion. At other times, some of the evidence is given first, followed by the conclusion, followed by further evidence. In many cases, the premises and conclusion are interspersed with opinions, questions, and judgements that are background or comment on the argument itself. Our first task in dressing arguments will be recognizing them and extracting their premises and conclusions in a way that makes the argument clear.

Inference indicators are words and phrases that tell us that particular statements are premises or conclusions. The words "consequently," "thus," "so," "hence," "it follows that," "therefore," and "we conclude that" are conclusion indicators. When you come across these and other words and phrases that function in a similar way, it usually means that the statement that follows them is the conclusion of an argument. Consider the following examples:

> All the senior managers here are members of the owner's family. *So* I'll have to move if I want to get promoted.
> A human being is constituted of both a mind and a body, and the body does not survive death; *therefore*, we cannot properly talk about personal immortality.

In cases as simple as these, we can easily identify the premises of an argument, for they are the statements that remain after we identify the conclusion.

In other cases arguments are designated by **premise indicators**. Common premise indicators include the expressions "since," "because," "for," and "the reason is." The argument in our last example can be expressed with a premise indicator rather than a conclusion indicator as follows:

> *Since* a human being is constituted of both a mind and a body, and the body does not survive death, we cannot properly talk about personal immortality.

The following simple arguments also employ premise indicators:

> Nothing can be the cause of itself, *for* in that case it would have to exist prior to itself, which is impossible.
> Sheila must be a member of the cycling club, *because* she was at last week's meeting and only members were admitted.

In these and cases like them, premise indicators identify the reasons offered for some conclusion. The conclusion is the statement they support. In the last case, the conclusion is "Sheila must be a member of the cycling club."

Arguments may contain both premise and conclusion indicators, but this is unusual. An argument with a premise indicator *or* a conclusion indicator is usually a clear argument. In constructing arguments, you should always use inference indicators so that other people can clearly recognize both that you are forwarding an argument and the evidence you are offering for what conclusion.

COMMON INFERENCE INDICATORS

Premise Indicators

Since	Because	For
As can be deduced from	Given that	The reasons are

Conclusion Indicators

Consequently	Thus	Therefore
So it follows that	Hence	We conclude that

EXERCISE 4B

For all of the following examples, either (a) identify all premise and conclusion indicators and the structure of the argument they inform (i.e. what premises lead to what conclusions) or (b) insert premise or conclusion indicators, and revise the sentences in any other way that clarifies the argument, the premises, and the conclusion.

1.* We have defined an argument as a unit of discourse that contains a conclusion and supporting statements or premises. Since many groups of sentences do not satisfy this definition and cannot be classified as arguments, we must begin learning about arguments in this sense by learning to differentiate between arguments and non-arguments.

2. In other cases, indicator words are used, but not to indicate premises and a conclusion. When you come across indicator words that have more than one use, you must therefore be sure that the word or phrase is functioning as a logical indicator.

3. [Clara explaining why she isn't ready to go to school] "Because there's a blizzard outside and they close Detroit schools whenever there's a blizzard."

4. Sun Tzu's famous book *The Art of War* tells us that a successful military force must act swiftly and cannot sustain a military operation for a protracted period of time. But Hitler's decision to attack Russia inevitably committed him to a long war. Because of this, he was bound to fail once he decided to attack Russia.

5. It is important that you be alert to variations from the usual indicator words, for the richness of our language makes many variations possible.

6. We have already seen that an argument is a unit of discourse consisting of a group of statements. However, genuine questions are not statements but requests for information. As such, a genuine question cannot serve as a premise or conclusion.

7. Misinterpreting someone else's thinking is a serious mistake. It's important to proceed with caution when we are trying to decide whether a particular discourse is or is not an argument.

8.* [From a travel brochure] You'll like the sun. You'll like the beach. You'll like the people. You'll like Jamaica.

9. [Adapted from "The world needs our military, but we need to shed some burdens'," Commentary, *The Globe and Mail*, www.theglobeandmail.com, accessed 30 October 2010]

   The belligerents today are often warlords, terrorists or militia groups that rarely play by anyone else's rules. Canada has a moral duty to help where help from the international community is desperately needed. Canada can no longer be a nation of traditional peacekeepers, because the world needs something else.

10. [From a Letter to the Editor, *The Globe and Mail*, 19 August 2004] A.B. implies that hunting is unethical because it is akin to killing. If this were true and killing were wrong, then we would all be walking contradictions. Finding, killing, and consuming life of all kinds is a requirement of life, human and non-human alike. Therefore, there is not much hope for those who believe unconditionally that killing is wrong.

11. [Adapted from a Letter to the Editor, *The Walrus*, April 2007] Great architecture involves sophisticated engineering and material experimentation. It must negotiate the social relationships of the day. It must perform well in its urban infrastructure. Great architecture is more than nifty aesthetics.

12. [Aristotle, *Metaphysics*, 1084a] Number must be either infinite or finite. But it cannot be infinite. An infinite number is neither odd nor even, but numbers are always odd or even.

13. [A variant of the second proof of God's existence in St Thomas Aquinas's *Summa Theologica*: sometimes called the "argument from first cause"] The second proof of God's existence is from the nature of cause and effect. In the world we find that there is an order of causes and effects. There is nothing which is the cause of itself; for then it would have to be prior to itself, which is impossible. Therefore things must be caused by prior causes. So there must be a first cause, for if there be no first cause among the prior causes, there will be no ultimate, nor any intermediate cause, for to take away the cause is to take away the effect. If there were an infinite series of causes, there would be no first cause, and neither would there be an ultimate effect, nor any intermediate causes; all of which is plainly false. Therefore it is necessary to admit a first cause, to which everyone gives the name of God.

14. [From the *New York Times*, Opinion, "In vitro fertilization," by Robin Marentz-Henig, 6 October 2010, www.nytimes.com/2010, accessed 6 October 2010] Science fiction is filled with dystopian stories in which the public blindly accepts destructive technologies. But in vitro fertilization offers a more optimistic model. As we continue to develop new ways of improving upon nature, the slope may be slippery, but that's no reason to avoid taking the first step.

3 Arguments without Indicator Words

Inference indicators are signposts that help us identify arguments. But many arguers do not use inference indicators in their arguments. They simply assume that their meaning is clear, even when this is not the case. In some specific contexts, the argumentative purpose of claims is understood in a way that makes inference indicators less important. Many editorials, political cartoons, and advertisements contain no inference indicators, though they are clear attempts to convince us that we should accept one conclusion or another.

In dealing with cases such as these, we need to be able to determine when arguments occur without premise or conclusion indicators. When you come across a group of sentences without an indicator, you can start by considering whether it appears in a context in which something is in dispute or controversial. Ask yourself whether this is a circumstance in which we would expect someone to justify their claim(s) by offering reasons in support of it. Consider the following excerpts from negative reviews of the film *What Women Want*, taken from www.rottentomatoes.com:

Shallow characters the audience cares little about, an unbelievable situation rather than a potent plot, and, for those who don't find men-in-pantyhose or poodle-poop jokes hilarious, not many funny lines.

Susannah Breslin, *TNT ROUGH CUT*

Women are from Venus; men are from the gutter. That's more or less the view of things at work in *What Women Want*, a sporadically funny, rigidly formulaic romantic comedy about a chauvinistic man's man named Nick Marshall (Mel Gibson) who suffers a standard-issue comedy-fantasy freak accident that gives him telepathic access to the thoughts of women. Nick may be a male chauvinist, but the film verges into misandrism. . . . In *What Women Want*, no male character ever does anything noble or generous or compassionate . . . (except of course for the ultimately-redeemed Nick of the last act), and no female character ever does anything self-serving or insensitive or underhanded.

Steven D. Greydanus, *Decent Films Guide*

Both of these comments forward arguments. In part we know this because they are excerpts from film reviews. Film reviews are inherently argumentative, for they function as assessments of films in which the writer provides reasons for their judgment that the film is outstanding, not worth seeing, a must see, disappointing, and so on. In the present case, we do not need to be told that both reviews conclude that the film *What Women Want* is a "rotten tomato": that is indicated on the website visually, via the splattered tomato that appears beside the review 🍅 (some other reviewers make this judgement in another visual way, with a "thumbs up" or a "thumbs down"). In the first case, three reasons are given for thinking that this is so: (a) shallow characters the audience cares little about; (b) an unbelievable situation rather than a potent plot; and (c) not many funny lines (for those who don't find men-in-pantyhose or poodle-poop jokes hilarious). In the second case, the reviewer criticizes the film makers of a simple-minded sexism against men (misandrism). In both cases we have clear arguments even though these passages do not contain premise or conclusion indicators—no "therefore," "since," or "because."

It is important to recognize argumentative contexts, for we should approach them with a critical attitude to the arguments they present. It is especially important to be critical when the arguments are not explicit, for this might easily lull us into an uncritical acceptance of the reasons and conclusions they suggest. When we consider whether we will download Mary Gordon's *Joan of Arc* to an e-reader, we need to recognize that the praise for her other books noted on a publisher's announcement is an attempt to persuade us to purchase it. In such a context, the critical reader will ask how strongly quotes from a handful of selected newspaper reviews (a handful of reviews out of possibly thousands, in a context in which reviewers often disagree radically) support the conclusion that we should buy this book.

Context is one factor that can help us decide whether a set of sentences with no inference indicators should be classified as an argument. In making this decision, other clues may be found in the wording of the sentences themselves. Consider the following paragraph from a letter on the history of South America:

The artistic motifs that characterize the ruins of ancient Aztec pyramids are very similar to those found in Egypt. And the animals and vegetation found on the eastern coasts of South America bear a striking resemblance to those of West Africa. From all appearances, there was once a large land mass connecting these continents.

These sentences do not contain indicator words. Yet the first two report observational data that appears to justify a speculative third statement—a statement that is the sort of statement that needs to be supported. This reading seems confirmed by the expression "from all appearances," which suggests that the first two sentences appear to lead to the third. In this way, the internal clues in this passage convince us that this is a case in which the author offers the first two statements as premises for the last.

Borderline Cases

The ability to detect arguments on the basis of context and internal clues is a skill that everyone has to some degree, but it is a skill that improves with practice. Your skill will improve as you spend more time looking for, detecting, and analyzing arguments. But no amount of skill will resolve all of the issues raised by borderline cases, where it is difficult to know whether something should be interpreted as an argument. In a typical case, we must decide whether a set of statements is an argument or simply an expression of opinion. This is a key decision for expressions of opinion and arguments call for different responses. In the first case we may agree or disagree with the opinion (and may construct an argument for or against it). In the second case, we need to go further and dress the argument embedded in the statements. This requires us to identify its premises and conclusions in a way that prepares the way for an evaluation that assesses the argument as strong or weak.

The following example is adapted from a letter to the *Hamilton Spectator*, written on the occasion of a strike by steel workers in the city:

> Haven't we had enough letters to the editorial page of the *Spectator* every day from cry-baby steel workers talking about how the Stelco strike is killing them? I am sure there are hundreds of pro-union letters going into the *Spectator* office, but only the anti-union ones are printed. I would not be a bit surprised if Stelco and the *Spectator* were working together to lower the morale of the steel workers who chose to strike for higher wages.

It is not easy to say whether this passage contains an argument. Certainly an opinion is expressed. But does the author offer reasons to support it?

If we want to distil an argument from the letter, we might dress it as follows:

Premise 1: We have had enough letters to the editorial page from cry-baby steel workers talking about how the Stelco strike is killing them.

Premise 2: I am sure there are hundreds of pro-union letters going into the *Spectator* office, but only the anti-union ones are printed.

Conclusion: There is reason to believe that Stelco and the *Spectator* are working together to lower the morale of steel workers.

This interpretation of the letter contains some linguistic adjustments. The final sentence in the published letter reads like a privately held suspicion. We have reworded it so that it carries the impact of a conclusion (but have tried to preserve the tentative tone of the author's comments). Given that the writer has decided to express such a controversial claim publicly, it is plausible to suppose that she wants to persuade readers that it is true on the basis of her claims about letters to the editor. For this reason, we have interpreted "I would not be a bit surprised if . . ." as the claim, "There is reason to believe that . . ."

In creating our first premise, we have put into statement form what appeared in the letter as a question, changing "Haven't we had enough letters . . . ?" to "We have had enough letters . . ." This is not an arbitrary change. It highlights a common stylistic feature shared by many ordinary language arguments. Genuine questions are not statements but requests for information. They cannot function as a premise or conclusion in an argument. But not all questions are requests. Some are implicit statements or assertions that are expressed as questions for "rhetorical" effect. They ask the person who hears or reads them to answer the question in a suggested way. We call such questions rhetorical questions. In the case at hand, the writer is not genuinely asking whether there have or have not been enough letters to the editorial page. Rather, her question is a way of asserting that there *have* been enough letters. Our revised wording clarifies this meaning.

We could have constructed a more complex representation of the chain of reasoning that seems to be contained in this letter about steel workers. In this and many other cases, one may interpret a set of sentences in more than one way. The question remains: Does the writer argue? Does she assert a claim and provide evidence for it? Do our proposed premises and conclusion capture reasoning in the letter? Is this a situation in which the author has given reasons for some conclusion? There are no definitive answers to these questions. There is no way to exactly discern the author's intentions, for she does not make them clear. On the one hand, this is a context in which an argument would be appropriate—the letter is, after all, published in the context of a debate about the steel workers' strike—but one might also hold that this is a context in which she might reasonably express an opinion instead of arguing for one. If an argument is intended, she would have done better to make this clear by using explicit or even oblique indicator words

In dealing with borderline cases, it is best to recognize the uncertainty of one's interpretation. In the present cases, we can do so by recognizing that there is no certain way to establish whether the author of the letter intended it as an argument. We might, for example, respond to the *Hamilton Spectator* letter by remarking that:

> The author of this letter suggests that the *Spectator* is acting in collusion with Stelco. She appears to believe that this is so on the grounds that . . . If this is her reasoning, then . . .

Here the expressions "She appears to believe" and "If this is her reasoning" clearly recognize our uncertainty in a way that nonetheless allows us to deal with the argumentative issues raised by the letter. Dealing with these issues in this manner is the proper way to further the discussion and debate.

In cases where we wish to analyze a possible argument but are unsure of our interpretation, we can note the uncertainty of the arguer's intention by introducing our discussion with a statement like the following:

> It is not clear whether the author intends to argue for the claim that . . . He appears to think that this claim can be justified on the grounds that . . . If this is what he intends, then it must be said that . . .

We can go on to outline the tentative argument we wish to discuss and analyze it as we would analyze other arguments. The simple fact that someone might interpret the claims in question as an argument warrants this discussion.

Whenever we attempt to identify and assess arguments, it is important to be conscious at the risk of misinterpreting someone's claims. When you construct your own arguments, aim to construct them in a way that prevents misinterpretation. In dealing with other people's claims, avoid interpretations that turn their claims into bad arguments they may not have intended. In the midst of controversy and debate, remember that the attempt to avoid misinterpretation is no reason to avoid issues raised by someone's remarks. If it is unclear what some potential arguer intends, say so, but go on and discuss whatever issues are raised by their remarks.

EXERCISE   4C

Are the following passages arguments? Borderline cases? For any possible argumentative passages, how would you identify the premises and conclusion if you were responding to it?

1.* [Excerpted from a Letter to the Editor, from The Royal Canadian Legion, Ottawa, to *The Petrolia Topic*, June 2011, www.petroliatopic.com/ArticleDisplay.aspx?e=3175744&archive=true]

Sir: As the combat mission in Afghanistan transitions into other military activities, The Royal Canadian Legion would like to extend a heartfelt thanks to those service men and women, and their families, who have served with distinction and sacrificed on behalf of Canadians during these past several years.

Their contribution to the well-being and care of another country's populace is a tremendous reflection of Canada's efforts toward maintaining global peace and we are proud of the way you have represented us.

2. [Stephen Brunt's book *Facing Ali: The Opposition Weighs In* (Alfred Knopf, New York, 2002) consists of interviews with the opponents who boxed against Muhammad Ali. On the back of the jacket cover, one finds three quotes under the heading *Praise for Facing Ali*. The following is attributed to Bert Sugar, identified as the "co-author of *Sting Like a Bee* and former editor and publisher of *Ring Magazine*."]

Just when you think that everything about Muhammad Ali and his career has been written, re-written and over written, along comes Stephen Brunt to give us a valuable new perspective to the Ali story in this extraordinary look at the parties of the second part: his opponents. *Facing Ali* has "winner" written all over it. And through it.

3.* [From a letter to *National Geographic*, November 1998] The laboratory where I am a consultant obtained a hair sample of an alleged 1,200-year-old Peruvian mummy. Our analysis revealed levels of lead, cadmium, and aluminum 5 to 13 times higher than would be acceptable in the typical patient of today. . . . consensus was that he received the contaminants from improperly glazed clay pottery.

4. [Martha Beck, in "Looking for Dr Listen-Good," *O: The Oprah Magazine*, January 2003, p. 42] You can steer clear of all these nightmare councillors by remembering Goethe's phrase "Just trust yourself, then you will know how to live." Rely on this truth at every stage of the therapeutic process. Trust yourself when your aching heart tells you it needs a compassionate witness. Trust yourself when your instincts warn you that the therapist your mother or a minister recommended isn't giving you the right advice. Trust yourself when, sitting in a relative stranger's office, you suddenly feel a frightening, exhilarating urge to tell truths you've never known until that very moment.

5.* [From *PC Gamer*, December 2002]. In Battlefield 1942, airpower is a strong weapon, . . . but it comes with high dangers. Ground-based anti-aircraft guns can chop you to pieces with flak, and enemy fighters are a constant dogfighting threat. But when you land your payloads, it's a devastating blow to the enemy.

6. [From the same article] American, British, Russian, German, and Japanese forces are all modelled. Each map pits two forces against one another in a re-creation of a historic battle.

7. [From an interview, "Ayaan Hirsi Ali on Islam, Catholicism and democracy," *El País* (Spain), 13 February 2008, www.eurotopics.net, accessed 25 September 2008. The former Dutch deputy Ayaan Hirsi Ali is analyzing the links between democracy and religion in an interview with Jose Maria Marti] As a group of principles, Islam is very consistent, very coherent, very simple and not at all compatible with liberal democracy. The principles of liberal democracy consider human life an end in itself, whereas Islam says that a satisfactory life can only be obtained by submitting oneself to the will of God . . . Catholicism isn't compatible with democracy either, but Christian societies have established a separation between Church and State. As a result, this religion does not have the power to punish those who fail to respect its principles.

8. [From a letter to the *National Post*, 10 December 2007] No amount of studies will change the fact that parallel private health care systems are splendidly efficient. One need look no further than the systems in place in Sweden, Switzerland, and Japan. All these countries deliver timely health care, with comparable or better outcomes than we have in Canada, and at a lower cost.

4   Arguments and Explanations

Attempting to distinguish arguments from non-arguments can sometimes be confusing when the words that can be used to indicate premises and conclusions are used in other ways. The "since" in the sentence "Since you arrived on the scene, my life has been nothing but trouble" is not a premise indicator but rather used to indicate the passage of time. The "for" in the sentence "I work for IBM" is not a premise indicator, and "thus" does not signal a conclusion in "You insert the CD in the CD-ROM drive thus."

In such cases, it is obvious that we do not have an argument. In other cases, this is less clear, especially where indicators like "so," "since," "therefore," and "because" are used in *explanations*: attempts to provide the reasons why something is the way it is. To understand how indicator words function within explanations—and to appreciate the difference between arguments and explanations—we need to separate two different meanings that can characterize our talk of "reasons." When we talk of "reasons" in the context of arguments, we mean "reasons for believing." It is in this sense that premises are reasons for believing some conclusion. In contrast, the word "reasons" means "causes" when we are discussing explanations. In this context, the *reason* something happened is the *cause* that brought it about.

Hugh Rawson begins a book on folk etymology (*Devious Derivations*, Castle Books, 2002, p. 1) with the remark that: "One of the most basic of all human traits is the urge to find reasons for why things are as they are. Ancient peoples heard thunder and created gods of thunder. They witnessed the change of seasons, and devised stories to explain the coming of winter and the miraculous rebirth of spring. The tendency is universal, appearing in every aspect of human thought and endeavor." Here the reasons alluded to are those things that bring about—i.e. cause—thunder, the seasons, and everything else that humans aspire to explain.

The kinds of contemporary issues we typically want to explain might include catastrophic weather patterns; the fall of the Greek, Irish, and Portuguese economies; the reasons that some people manage to live so long; mad cow disease; and how bird flu moved from birds to humans. In explaining such phenomena, we often use indicator words in their causal sense. We say that global warming is intensifying *since* we burn too much fossil fuel; that Aunt Sally lived so long *because* she didn't drink or smoke or engage in arguments; that the virus that causes bird flu is destroyed by cooking, *so* we cook chicken and eggs thoroughly.

In deciding whether indicator words are being used to indicate an explanation rather than an argument, you must consider the status of the claim that is backed by the "reasons" given. If "X, therefore Y" is an argument, then it is Y (the conclusion) that is in dispute. If it is an explanation, then the issue in dispute is whether X caused Y. In an explanation, we know what happened. What we are trying to establish are the reasons (causes) for it. In an argument, we know the reasons (premises). What we are trying to establish is a conclusion that is in doubt.

In the statement that "The house burnt down because they were smoking in bed," the indicator word "because" is used to indicate an explanation, not an argument. It would be an obvious mistake to interpret it as the argument:

Premise: They were smoking in bed.
Conclusion: Their house burnt down.

Something similar can be said of the following remarks in which an expert witness explains to a court what happened in an accident:

> The minivan was carrying a load in excess of the maximum recommended and was hauling a trailer that had been improperly attached to the vehicle. Consequently, when the driver veered suddenly to the left—trying to avoid a stalled truck—he lost control of the vehicle and crashed into the oncoming vehicle.

These remarks give the reasons why (according to the expert) the accident occurred. No one doubts that the crash occurred, so it is not a matter of dispute.

It goes without saying that the expert's explanation in this case might be debated. It probably will be if it is testimony in a trial that accuses the minivan driver of breaking the law. In such a context, an explanation may generate an argument. But this does not change the fact that it is not an argument. It would be a mistake to interpret it as one because it contains a word ("consequently") that is frequently used as a conclusion indicator.

In most cases, you can distinguish arguments and explanations by putting them into the general scheme "X, therefore Y" (or "Y because X") and asking whether they are an attempt to explain the cause of Y or an attempt to argue for Y. If Y (the conclusion) is in dispute, the sentences are an argument. If the question whether X (the set of reasons) caused Y is in dispute, they form an explanation. In the case of an explanation, Y must be a present or past fact or event. If it is a prediction, an evaluation, a recommendation or a classification, then the passage is an argument.

Arguments within Explanations

Explanations complicate our attempts to identify and dress arguments, because they use indicator words in a different way than arguments. Still more complex cases arise in situations in which explanations contain arguments because they outline a chain of reasoning, or because arguments themselves may act as causes (causing people to believe and do the things they do). This means that there will be times when an explanation incorporates an argument that we will, in the process of recognizing and dressing arguments, need to recognize and analyze.

Consider the following comment from a business article in the *New York Times* entitled "Shares fall on lower oil and commodities prices" (12 April 2011). It appeared in the wake of a major tsunami that severely damaged the Japanese nuclear reactor in Fukushima.

> Analysts cited several reasons for Tuesday's decline in the oil and commodities markets, including expectations of lower demand in Japan as that economy slows in the aftermath of the earthquake, the tsunami and the nuclear crisis.

In this case, the word "reasons" in the first sentence indicates an explanation. But this is a situation in which the explanation suggests that a particular argument—one implicitly attributed to investors—has led to the decline in the oil and commodity markets. We might summarize this extended argument as follows.

> **Premise:** The Japanese economy will slow in the aftermath of the recent earthquake, tsunami, and the nuclear crisis.
>
> **Conclusion 1:** This will mean less demand for oil and commodities.
>
> **Conclusion 2:** This is not a time to invest in these markets.

The passage we have quoted alludes to other arguments that have influenced investors, but this is the only one that it makes explicit. In doing so, the commentator provides an explanation which incorporates an argument that can be isolated, identified, and discussed.

Another example can illustrate the difference between arguments that do and do not contain arguments. In a history lesson, someone might forward the hypothesis that "Germany lost World War II because Hitler turned his attention to Russia when he had England at his mercy." Some would criticize this as a simplistic explanation of Germany's turn of fortune. The important point is that this is a paradigm instance of an explanation which is not an argument. The statement that Germany lost the war is not a matter of dispute. The speaker offers a controversial explanation why it happened but he has not attempted to provide evidence to back it. This makes this a case where "because" indicates an explanation *rather* than an argument.

We may, however, easily imagine someone challenging the proposed explanation of Germany's defeat. Let us suppose that the initial speaker answers such a challenge as follows:

> Sun Tzu's famous book *The Art of War* says that a successful military campaign must move swiftly. No army can sustain a war for a protracted period of time. Hitler ignored this. His decision to attack Russia committed him to a long and protracted war. Because of this, he failed.

In this remark, our interlocutor offers a more detailed *explanation* of the reasons that led to Hitler's fall. But this is now a case in which his explanation incorporates an argument. For it indicates a chain of reasoning that should, if it is correct, cause one to believe that Hitler was bound to lose the war when he decided to turn his attention to Russia. We can dress this chain of reasoning as follows:

> **Premise 1:** Sun Tzu's famous book *The Art of War* tells us that a successful military campaign must move swiftly—no army can sustain a military operation for a protracted period of time.
>
> **Premise 2:** Hitler's decision to attack Russia ignored this wisdom, committing him to a protracted war.
>
> **Conclusion:** Once Hitler decided to attack Russia, he was bound to fail.

Once we recognize and dress the argument incorporated in the explanation we have cited, it should prompt a variety of questions. Does Sun Tzu say what our speaker claims? Is the proposed principle of military success debatable? Are there counterexamples? Did the decision to attack Russia inevitably mean a long war? Were there other factors that extended it? It is in this way that recognizing and dressing the argument is a first step toward a rational scrutiny of the issues that it raises.

An argument is a set of reasons forwarded as premises for a conclusion. Most explanations present reasons in a different sense—i.e. reasons that are the purported cause of some event or circumstances. That said, there are times when an explanation of the cause of something incorporates an argument. Typically it will do so by providing a chain of reasoning within the explanation, or by suggesting an argument as the reason for some belief or behaviour. In identifying and dressing arguments, and in distinguishing between arguments and non-arguments, this means that we need to carefully distinguish between explanations that do and do not incorporate an argument.

EXERCISE   4D

Identify any argument (or explanation) indicators in the following passages. Put the reasoning in each case into "X, therefore Y" (or "Y because X") form and discuss whether it is an explanation and/or an argument. In the case of arguments, identify the premises and conclusion.

  a)   The company lost a lot of money last year, so we are not getting a wage increase this year.

  b)* Drugs should be legal because the attempt to ban them creates more problems than it solves.

  c)   The debt crisis in Greece is no mystery. Various studies, including one by the Federation of Greek Industries, have estimated that the government loses as much as $30 billion a year to tax evasion.

  d)   Everybody inside and outside Afghanistan is aware of the high illiteracy rate, particularly within the Afghan police. Moreover, this fact about a high illiteracy rate has been known for years. In particular it is known for years among the Afghan ministers in charge! How can this not be seen as an internal Afghan problem which it should be a top priority to address?

  e)   [Adapted from a Letter to the Editor, *Times Literary Supplement*, 17 January 2003] Galileo was faced with the choice of whether to recant the Copernican theory or face almost certain death by torture at the hands of the Inquisition. He chose the disgrace of recanting, rather than an honourable death as a martyr to science, because his work was not complete. He was subsequently able to develop, among other things, a physics involving concepts of constant velocity and acceleration that were crucial to Newton's development of the laws of motion.

  f)   [From a Letter to the Editor, *Skeptic* magazine, Vol. 4, 2006, p. 13] Many accident reports include claims like "I looked right there and never saw them". . . . Motorcyclists and bicyclists are often the victims in such cases. One explanation is that car drivers expect other cars but not bikes, so even if they look right at the bike, they sometimes might not see it.

  g)   [From About.com, http://autism.about.com, accessed 12 January 2011] Do vaccines cause autism? Two theories link autism and vaccines. The first theory suggests that the MMR (Mumps-Measles-Rubella) vaccine may cause intestinal problems leading to the development of autism. The second theory suggests that a mercury-based preservative called thimerosal, used in some vaccines, could be connected to autism. The medical community has soundly refuted these theories, but a very passionate group of parents and researchers continues to disagree, based on anecdotal evidence.

h)* [From Peter King's web site http://users.ox.ac.uk/~worc0337/note.html, accessed 19 December 2002] The smug and offensive (and ignorant) tone of this [comment from another web site] gets up my nose, and is a sure-fire way of ensuring that I don't include a link to the site in question.

i) [From *Life Extension* magazine, December 2002, p. 32] the fact is that millions of women all over the world don't need Premarin because they don't get the [menopause] symptoms Western women get. By now most people have heard that the Japanese have no word for "hot flash." But did you know that the Mayan and Navajo indigenous peoples don't either? The women in these cultures don't get "hot flashes." In fact, they get virtually no menopausal symptoms at all. And it's not because they have strange rituals or odd lifestyles. They simply eat differently. Sounds boring, but these women incorporate things in their diet that keep menopausal symptoms away.

5   Argument Narratives

The most obvious examples of arguments are directly conveyed to us by the words of the arguer. Most of the examples in this book are arguments of this sort. But we will end our chapter on the complications that arise in arguments on the hoof by noting that there are cases in which arguments are conveyed in a way that does not use the words and expressions of the actual arguer.

Consider the novel *Redwork*, in which Michael Bedard describes a liaison between one of his main characters, Alison, and a philosophy Ph.D. student she nicknames "Hegel." When her liaison with Hegel leads to pregnancy, "His solution to the problem was as clear, clean and clinical as a logical equation—get rid of it. Instead, she had got rid of him. She hadn't had much use for philosophy since" (p. 24). In this passage, the narrator provides a second-hand account of reasoning—what we will call an "argument narrative." We do not have the reasoning attributed to Alison expressed in her own words, but it is clear that it was her negative experience with her boyfriend that convinced her that she had no use for philosophy. We might summarize the argument as "Hegel is a philosopher who deals with human situations in the way of a philosopher (as clean and clinical as a logical equation), so philosophy is of no use to me."

Like borderline cases, the arguments implicit in argument narratives have to be treated with care, for they represent cases in which we do not have the original arguer's actual words, and it is always possible that the person who narrates the argument may not present it accurately. This is a significant disadvantage when one wants to accurately capture the details of an argument, but it is still useful to consider the arguments conveyed in narratives for they may be important topics to discuss. Consider, for example, the following CBC report of the reaction of Elizabeth May, the leader of the Green Party of Canada, after a federal leader's debate from which she was excluded (14 April 2011).

Green Party Leader Elizabeth May, excluded from Tuesday's leaders debate by the broadcast consortium, blasted the event as a "sad spectacle of a partial leaders' debate" . . . May said the list of issues left out of the debate is long, including First Nations issues, Canada's position in Libya, food policy, homelessness, energy policy, arts funding and the environment.

This is an argument narrative. It does not exactly present May's words, but it still out-lines an argument for the conclusion that the debate was a "sad spectacle." It includes this conclusion and the premise that the list of issues left out of the debate is long, including First Nations issues, Canada's position in Libya, food policy, homelessness, energy policy, arts funding and the environment. We cannot be sure what words May used to convey this argument and it is always possible that the reporter has missed some nuance in her comments, but this is still a worthy argument for analysis—one which usefully highlights some of the key issues raised by the debate.

In dealing with argument narratives, it is important to recognize that we are work-ing with someone else's summary of an argument, and that this has limitations, which we acknowledge. In particular, we need to guard against the possibility that a criticism of an argument as it is described in an argument narrative may be a straw man argu-ment because the person reporting the argument has not done so accurately. Provided we recognize this possibility, we should be able to avoid it. We can still usefully analyze the arguments we find in argument narratives, and should bear in mind that doing so may shed light on some of the significant issues we need to explore and understand.

EXERCISE 4E

Identify the arguments reported in the following argument narratives:

a) [From "Prayful science," *Skeptic* magazine, 2006, Vol. 12, No. 4, p. 11] The issue of intercessory prayer was recently in the news again when a study reported no significant health benefits among those who received prayer . . . In 1999, the medical journal *Lancet* published a critical report that analyzed studies from around the world on the efficacy of prayer and the role of religion in medicine. The researchers found that nearly all studies lacked proper scientific controls, or their conclusions were too broad and inconsistent to be useful.

b) [From *The Expositor* newspaper,12 April 2007, p. A7] Ontario's Liberal government asked Transport Canada Wednesday to release the latest studies on seatbelts in school buses following an accident in Brampton, Ont., that left several children injured. But an official with the federal agency said there is no need to do so, as all studies show that children are much safer in buses that are designed to protect them in the event of an accident than they would be with seatbelts holding them rigidly in place.

c)* [From *Xinhua*, 13 April 2007, http://news.xinhuanet.com/english/2007-04/13/ content_5971431.htm] In the 1993 Oscar-award-winning movie *Jurassic Park* and again in the 2001 *Jurassic Park III* flick Sam Neill, portraying the character of dinosaur expert Dr Alan Grant, expounds the theory dinosaurs really never went extinct, they just evolved into birds. . . .

Once again, science fiction becomes science fact.

Now a team of scientists from North Carolina State University have extracted collagen tissue from a 68-million-year-old T. rex thigh bone and found protein that is structurally similar to chicken protein, offering further evidence of the evolutionary link between dinosaurs and birds.

d) [The following is taken from a news report titled "Opinion polls undermine trust, says Dutch minister" in *NRC Handlesblad* newspaper, 26 September 2008. Dutch home affairs minister Piet Hein Donner (Christian Democrat) was speaking at a conference on "the economics of trust"] Donner said opinion polls undermine trust in the government, parliament and official authorities. He was referring only to regular surveys that indicate confidence in politicians and the government, and mentioned a recent poll by RTL News which concluded that 70 percent of Dutch people do not have faith in the current Christian-Labour cabinet. He referred to academic studies which show that the results of voter surveys can be disputed. Answers to questions concerning people's confidence in the government depend on a variety of factors, he said. They are based on a combination of personal preferences and general sentiment at the time.

6 Summary

Chapter 4 has dealt with more complex questions surrounding the identification and treatments of arguments. In particular, we have moved beyond the simple arguments of earlier chapters to look at extended arguments. A further complexity has been the similarity between argument and explanation, and here we have discussed the differences between these two types of discourse. We have also explored further tools for identifying arguments, like the presence of indicators words, and discussed how to proceed when such aids are absent. Finally, we have looked at argument narratives.

MAJOR EXERCISE 4M

1. Provide two examples of each of the following:
   a)* extended argument
   b) inference indicator
   c) premise indicator
   d)* rhetorical question
   e) conclusion indicator
   h) argument narrative

2. Identify the argument forwarded by each of the following editorial cartoons.

a) [An Anthony Jenkins cartoon from *The Globe and Mail*, November 2011, in preparation for the Christmas shopping season]

Illustration 4.1   "Turbulence"

b) [A comment on the BC Reform Party's opposition to photo radar]

Illustration 4.2   "All opposed to photo-radar . . . ?"

3. Explain why you are reading this book. Since this explanation will have to explain your reasoning, it will contain an implicit argument. Identify the premises and conclusion in the argument.

4. For each of the following, decide whether an argument and/or explanation is present, and explain the reasons for your decision. (Some examples may contain non-arguments that are not explanations.) Be sure to qualify your remarks appropriately when dealing with borderline cases. In the case of arguments, dress them (i.e. identify their premises and conclusions).

    a)* Religion is nothing but superstition. Historians of religion agree that it had its beginnings in magic and witchcraft. Today's religious belief is just an extension of this.

    b)* [A comment by an observer who visited the seal hunt on the east coast of Newfoundland] The first time I went out onto the ice and saw the seal hunt, it sickened me. I could not believe that a Canadian industry could involve such cruelty to animals and callous brutalization of men for profit.

    c)* The island of Antigua, located in the Caribbean, boasts secluded caves and dazzling beaches. The harbour at St John's is filled with the memories of the great British navy that once called there.

    d) [Overheard at a train station] These trains are never on time. The last time I took one, it was two hours late.

    e) [From an advertisement for Ceasefire, the Children's Defense Fund and Friends, 1995] Each year, hundreds of children accidentally shoot themselves or someone else. So if you get a gun to protect your child, what's going to protect your child from the gun?

    f) [From a Letter to the Editor, *The Globe and Mail*, 14 July 2011] One reason waitlists for orthopedic surgeons are so long is the number of inappropriate referrals from general practitioners who don't have enough specific training in orthopedic injuries.

    g)* [Donald Wildmon, an American United Methodist minister, quoted in *Time* magazine, 2 June 2003] Could somebody have a husband and a woman partner at the same time and be a Christian? . . . I doubt that seriously.

    h) [From Robert Wilson, *The Hidden Assassins*, (Harper (Re-issue) edition), 2009, pp. 86–7]
        "Why are you certain that this could not have been a gas explosion?"
        "Apart from the fact that there's been no reported leak, and we've only had to deal with two small fires, the mosque in the basement is in daily use. Gas is heavier than air and would accumulate at the lowest point. A large enough quantity of gas couldn't have accumulated with anybody noticing," he said. "Added to that, the gas would have had to collect in a big enough space before exploding. Its power would be dissipated. Our main problem would have been incendiary, rather than destruction. There would have been a massive fireball, which would have scorched the whole area. There would have been burn victims. A bomb explodes from a small, confined source. It therefore has far more concentrated destructive power. Only a very large bomb, or several smaller

bombs, could have taken out those reinforced concrete supporting pillars. Most of the dead and injured we've seen so far have been hit by flying debris and glass. All the windows in the area have been blown out. It's all consistent with a bomb blast."

i)* [Richard Stengel, *You're Too Kind: A Brief History of Flattery*, New York: Simon & Schuster, p. 14] In many ways, flattery works like a heat seeking missile, only what the missile homes in on is our vanity. And vanity, as the sages tell us, is the most universal human trait. . . . Flattery almost always hits its target because the target—you, me, everybody—rises up to meet it. We have no natural defense system against it.

j)* [From *Time* magazine, 2 June 2003, p. 4] As a single father who, when married, held down a demanding job and fully participated in child rearing and household chores, I was offended by Pearson's fatuous attempt to mine the worn-out vein of humour about useless males. She defines a husband as "a well-meaning individual often found reading a newspaper." None of the fathers and husbands I know come anywhere close to this stereotype. I was dismayed that *Time* would publish such tired pap and think it's funny or relevant.

k) [From an advertisement in *University Affairs*, March 2003, p. 51] UBC hires on the basis of merit and is committed to employment equity. We encourage all qualified people to apply. There is no restriction with regard to nationality or residence, and the position is open to all candidates. Offers will be made in keeping with immigration requirements associated with the Canada Research Chairs program.

l) [From a Letter to the Editor, *The Globe and Mail*, 14 July 2011] A history with a powerful US neighbour in many ways pushed Canada to work at alternative ways of addressing conflict. This, along with the deep roots and influence of aboriginal culture—and its ethos of acceptance and enlarging the circle—had far more of a profound impact on what Canada is today than military action. For these reasons, Canadians always have been uncomfortable with the use of military force.

m) [Hugh Rawson, in *Devious Derivations*, Castle Books: Victoria, BC, 2002, p. 2] False conclusions about the origins of words also arise . . . as a result of the conversion of Anglo-Saxon and other older English terms into modern parlance. Thus a crayfish is not a fish but a crustacean (from the Middle English crevis, crab). A helpmate may be both a help and a mate, but the word is a corruption of help meet, meaning suitable helper. . . . Hopscotch has nothing to do intrinsically with kids in kilts; scotch here is a moderately antique word for a cut, incision, or scratch, perhaps deriving from the Anglo-French escocher, to notch or nick.

By the same token, people who eat humble pie may have been humbled, but only figuratively. The name of the dish comes from umbles, meaning the liver, heart, and other edible animal innards.

n) [From a local, Brantford, Ontario, church pamphlet, 2006] None of us on the Leadership Team, here at Brant Community Church would claim to have received an infallible picture of the future, but we do believe that forecasting and planning is part of the job that God has called us to do.

o) [A quote from "Midwifery on trial," *Quarterly Journal of Speech*, February 2003, p. 70] The difficulty I find with the judge's decision [to dismiss a charge against a midwife] . . . is that these people are completely unlicensed. They are just a group of people, some with no qualifications, whose only experience in some cases is having watched five or six people give birth. They have no comprehension of the complications that can arise in childbirth . . . we are about to embrace totally unqualified people . . . I think the judge is out of his mind.

p) [The *Expositor* newspaper, Brantford, 12 April 2007] As I drove to a school for my volunteer work this morning, I once more noticed some truly dedicated people. These men and women occupy busy street corners three times per day in all sorts of weather, while most of us look out the windows from warm rooms. Their role is to protect our children from dangers—traffic and otherwise . . . . So, a big thanks to the crossing guards. Be sure to wave as you go by (with all five digits) and when you have an opportunity, say thank you!

q) [From the Disability Discrimination Act of the United Kingdom, available online at www.parliament.the-stationery-office.co.uk/pa/ld200102/ ldbills/040/ 2002040.htm, accessed 8 January 2003] Where (a) any arrangements made by or on behalf of an employer, or (b) any physical feature of premises occupied by the employer, place the disabled person concerned at a substantial disadvantage in comparison with persons who are not disabled, it is the duty of the employer to take such steps as it is reasonable, in all the circumstances of the case, for him to have to take in order to prevent the arrangements or feature having that effect.

r)* [From a Letter to the Editor, in *National Geographic*, May 1998, which is a comment on an article on the aviator Amelia Earhart, who disappeared on a flight over the Pacific in July 1937] I was sorry to see Elinor Smith quoted, impugning Amelia's flying skills, in the otherwise excellent piece by Virginia Morell. Smith has been slinging mud at Earhart and her husband, George Putnam, for years, and I lay it down to jealousy. Amelia got her pilot's license in 1923 (not 1929 as Smith once wrote) and in 1929 was the third American woman to win a commercial license.

s) [John Beifuss, in "Timing's right for Kissinger portrait," a review of the film *Trials*, at gomemphisgo.com, "Movie reviews," www.gomemphis.com/mca/ movie_reviews/ article/ 0,1426,MCA_ 569_ 1592636,00.html, accessed 24 December 2002] At the very least, Trials serves as an overdue corrective to the still active cult of Kissinger. Even viewers who aren't convinced that the former national security adviser, Secretary of State and Nobel Peace Prize winner fits the definition of "war criminal" likely will emerge shocked that presidents still call for advice from the man who may have been responsible for such clandestine and illegal foreign policy initiatives as the 1969 US carpet bombing of Cambodia, the 1970 overthrow and murder of democratically elected Chilean president Salvador Allende and the 1972 "Christmas Bombing" of North Vietnam, which Hitchens, in an onscreen interview, describes as "a public relations mass murder from the sky." As journalist Seymour Hersh comments: "The dark side of Henry Kissinger is very, very dark."

t)   [An exchange attributed to a reporter interviewing a former Miss Alabama] Question: If you could live forever, would you and why? Answer: I would not live forever because we should not live forever because if we were supposed to live forever then we would live forever but we cannot live forever which is why I would not live forever.

u)   [A controversy connected with the Internet resource Wikipedia has been the practice of Alphascript Publishing to collect related articles from the site and publish them as stand-alone books. This has resulted in a lot of criticism. The following is an extract from an interview between a journalist of the *Guardian* newspaper and a representative of Alphascript. It can be found on Alphascript's site: www.alphascript-publishing.com, accessed 1 June 2011]

   Q: . . . do all of Alphascript's books take their content from Wikipedia?
   Alphascript: Yes, since we believe that the quality of the Wikipedia articles is so good that it is worthwhile creating books with them. Wikipedia themselves give an impulse for this. The articles published on their sites are free in every respect and without any limitations as to further use. All authors participating in texts of Wikipedia know this or should at least know it.

   The vice-versa procedure by now seems to have become "normal." For years Google has been scanning books and published them in internet.
   Of course there are also protests, but then the rights for the material concerned are still with the author or the publishing house.

v)* [From a Letter to the Editor, *New Woman* magazine, July 1995, in support of a commitment to cover New Age issues] When I was going through a recent bout with depression, I discovered the "goddess spirituality" movement. I chose Artemis as the goddess I would seek comfort in . . . I built an altar to her in my room, burned incense, and meditated, and I found comfort in these ritualistic practices. I think this type of paganism can be an important tool for women to discover their inner strengths.

w)   [From a *New York Times* editorial, "A virus among honeybees," www.nytimes.com, visited 11 September 2007 Two other factors may also have played a role in this die-off [of honeybee populations]. One is drought, which in some areas has affected the plants that bees draw nectar and pollen from. The other—still unproved—may be the commercial trucking of bees from crop to crop for pollination, a potential source of stress. These may have made bees more vulnerable to the effects of this virus.

   In some ways, this newly reported research seems all the more important given all the speculation about what has been killing off the honeybees. These hive losses have inspired a kind of myth-making or magical thinking about their possible environmental origins. The suspected culprits include genetically modified crops and cellphones, to name only two.

x)   [From a Letter to the Editor, *National Post*, 27 November 2007] I wanted to share a recent experience that shows how draconian the Ontario Provincial Police's new approach to speeding really is. I received a ticket for driving 20 kilometres over the limit, on a straight stretch of highway outside of built-up areas in light traffic. I was not driving aggressively and I had been following other traffic at a safe distance for several kilometres. When I questioned the officer, he seemed to accept that my speed wouldn't normally be a problem, but he said he had to write the ticket because "we have a new commissioner now and he has changed the rules and he wants us to crack down on this type of speeding craziness."

Is driving 20 kilometres an hour over the limit with the flow of traffic in safe conditions really the type of "speeding craziness" we need to crack down on?

y) [What is the argument propounded in the following advertisement?]

Illustration 4.3   "It's a small world"

4. An earlier example was excerpted from the current debate over the safety of traditional dental amalgams (so called "silver fillings"). Go to the Internet and explore this debate, finding sites that discuss the safety of amalgam fillings. Extract three arguments on the issue, identifying their premises and conclusions.

For more online exercises, review questions, and quizzes related to the material in this chapter, please go to www.oupcanada.com/GoodReasoning5e

ARGUMENT DIAGRAMS

One of the most effective ways to represent arguments is by "diagramming"—by constructing diagrams that identify their premises and conclusions, and illustrate the relations between them. The present chapter introduces diagramming and how it works. The key concepts are:

▶ argument diagrams
▶ linked and convergent premises
▶ supplemented diagrams
▶ diagramming in argument construction.

We have already introduced the distinction between arguments dressed and "on the hoof." In dressing arguments, we identify their premises and conclusions and, in the case of extended arguments, the sub-arguments that support the premises that lead to their main conclusion. Up to this point we have been dressing the arguments we discuss by labelling their premises and conclusions. This is one way to dress arguments, but it is a clumsy way to present the structure of complicated arguments and does not represent different premises in a way that makes it clear when they may provide different strands of evidence for a conclusion. To provide a more precise and effective way of dressing arguments, this chapter introduces a method of diagramming that does not have these shortcomings. As you continue to practise argument analysis, you will find it a convenient way to map the structure of an argument and in doing so prepare the way for evaluation.

1   Argument Diagrams: Simple Arguments

Once we recognize something as an argument, we need to dress it in a way that delineates its structure. This is the first step in deciding how we should assess it. As we have already seen, the task of dressing arguments is not always easy, for arguments on the hoof are frequently confusing. A conclusion may be stated first or last, or sandwiched in between the premises. Premise and conclusion indicators may not always be used, and the same ideas can be repeated in a number of different ways. Extraneous comments, digressions, and diversions (insinuations, jokes, insults, compliments, and so on) may be interspersed with the content that really matters to the arguer's attempt to provide evidence for a conclusion.

In analyzing arguments, we call the remarks and comments that accompany but are not integral to an argument *noise*. Your first step in dressing an argument is eliminating noise. Sometimes noise exists in the form of introductory information that sets the stage or background for an argument that follows. Sometimes it consists of statements that are intended only as asides—statements that have no direct bearing on the argument but may add a flourish or a dash of humour. In discarding noise, you must be careful to ensure that you do not, at the same time, discard something that is integral to the argument.

We can discard the noise that accompanies an argument by drawing an argument "diagram" that maps and clarifies the argument's structure. Diagramming is an especially important tool when you are first learning how to understand an argument (your own or someone else's), for it shows you how to isolate the essential components and plot their relationship to each other. Even when you have developed your logical skills, diagramming will be an invaluable aid when dealing with complex arguments or with arguments presented in confusing ways, something that is common in ordinary discourse.

Having extracted noise, we proceed to diagram an argument by extracting its components. It is easiest to start with the conclusion, because it is the point of the whole argument. After we determine the conclusion, we can identify the premises by asking what evidence is given to support the conclusion. When we are constructing a diagram, we create a "legend" that designates the argument's premises as P1, P2, etc., and the conclusion as C. In an extended argument, we list the intermediary secondary conclusions as C1, C2, etc., and designate the main conclusion as MC. Once we have constructed a legend for a diagram, we use the legend symbols (P1, P2, MC, C1, etc.) to represent the argument's premises and conclusion and connect them with arrows that indicate what follows from what.

We will illustrate the fundamental principles of argument diagramming with some examples of simple arguments. The argument "Thinking clearly and logically is an important skill, so all students should study the rudiments of logic," we construct a legend as follows:

P1 =   Thinking clearly and logically is an important skill.
C =   All students should study the rudiments of logic.

Once we have this legend, we can diagram the argument as:

This diagram portrays the essential structure of our argument. It shows it to consist of one premise that leads to one conclusion. Together with our legend, the diagram shows the argument's components and their relationship. The only thing that might seem missing is the conclusion indicator "so," but this is represented by the arrow in the argument, which tells us the direction of the inference.

Many arguments can be represented by the same diagram. If we let:

P1 =   We have over 150 hotels in nearly 30 countries, and even more are on the way.

C =   Wherever you go, we're already there with a great stay in big cities, on the beach, by the airport and in the suburbs.

then our diagram represents the following argument, found in a flyer in a hotel room in the Four Points by Sheraton (hotel): "We have over 150 hotels in nearly 30 countries, and even more are on the way, so wherever you go, we're already there with a great stay in big cities, on the beach, by the airport and in the suburbs." Once we dress the hotel's argument with this diagram, we may proceed to argument evaluation and consider whether its premise is acceptable and its conclusion follows.

Consider another example. The following argument is taken from an article about one of the CEOs at RIM (Research In Motion, the makers of BlackBerry) published in *PC Magazine*, 13 April 2011:

Today the co-CEO of RIM, Mike Lazaridis, got upset and cut short a BBC interview after the reporter asked him a (fair) question about the company's issues with security in India. This comes shortly after he played Rodney Dangerfield to the New York Times, complaining about how his company doesn't get any respect . . . What's got Lazaridis so rattled?

In this case the question at the end of the passage is a rhetorical question which functions as a way of introducing a conclusion and inviting us to reflect on it. The conclusion is that Lazaridis is rattled, which is used as an opening for a discussion of the reasons this is so: reasons that have to do with RIM's position in the market and the success of their competitors. Keeping this in mind, we can diagram the argument in the passage as follows:

P1 =   Today the co-CEO of RIM, Mike Lazaridis, got upset and cut short a BBC interview after the reporter asked him a (fair) question about the company's issues with security in India.

P2 =   This comes shortly after he played Rodney Dangerfield to the New York Times, complaining about how his company doesn't get any respect.

C =   Lazaridis is rattled.

In this case our diagram shows that our commentator offers two premises for the conclusion they offer, i.e. two pieces of evidence that support the claim that Lazaridis is rattled.

EXERCISE 5A

Diagram each of the following arguments:

1.* [An argument from Aristotle's *Nichomachean Ethics*] Politics appears to be the Master Science because it determines which of the sciences should be studied in a state. . . .

2. It seems that jurors are more willing to convict for murder when the death penalty is abolished, so maintaining the death penalty makes it more likely that more murderers will roam the streets.

3. The beach is the best place to go to really relax. The sound of the surf is one of the most soothing sounds I know.

4. [From *Adbusters* magazine, March/April 2007] Al Jazeera [Television] is a breath of fresh air. . . . There are half the number of commercials, no pro-war or anti-war bias, and a fearlessness no longer seen at the other networks. And it does it all in style.

5. [Excerpted from *The Windsor Star*, "A one-term president?" by Toby Harnden, 17 September 2010, p. A8] Obama is the first black American president, an established author, multimillionaire and acclaimed figure beyond American shores. It seems unlikely that he will decide not to run in 2012.

2   Diagramming Extended Arguments

These first examples of argument diagrams dress simple arguments, but it should be readily apparent how the same diagramming can be extrapolated to apply to extended arguments. Consider a case where someone uses our first argument—"Thinking clearly and logically is an important skill, so all students should study the rudiments of argument"—as support for the further conclusion that "Courses on critical thinking should be mandatory." In this case, the corresponding diagram would be a "serial" diagram, where:

P1 = Thinking clearly and logically is an important skill.
C1 = All students should study the rudiments of logic.
MC ["Main Conclusion"] = Courses on critical thinking should be mandatory.

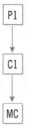

Our third argument—the argument for the conclusion that "Lazaridis is rattled"—might also be made the basis of an extended argument. We will relabel this conclusion C1. If we imagine a situation in which the value of RIM stock has declined rapidly in the last week, we can further imagine someone combining this observation with C1 to establish the new conclusion that "I should sell my RIM stocks." Using the legend that we have previously established, and allowing MC to represent our new main conclusion, this new argument can be diagrammed as:

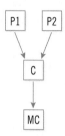

As this illustrates, the diagram of an extended argument will incorporate the diagrams of the simple arguments it contains.

A Complex Example

When diagramming arguments, especially extended ones, you will often need to make minor (and sometimes major) linguistic adjustments to clarify the argument. We have already seen that we delete inference indicators, since the arrows and symbols in our diagram perform the task of indicating premises and conclusions and the ways in which they are connected. A more difficult task is eliminating sentences that repeat ideas, as well as remarks, words, and phrases that are, for some other reason, properly classified as noise. In many cases, changes in the wording (but not the meaning) of an argument's premises and conclusion will make the structure of the argument clearer. Sometimes, we may need to change verb tenses and reformulate exclamations, rhetorical questions, and sentence fragments so that they are easily recognizable as statements that function as a premise or conclusion.

The following excerpt illustrates the kinds of linguistic changes that may be necessary in order to diagram the kinds of arguments that we may find "on the hoof." It is taken from an article entitled "$40,000-plus for eggs of clever, pretty women," by Kate Cox, posted on the *Sydney Morning Herald* web site www.smh.com.au, 15 December 2002). Consider, in particular, the argument it attributes to Shelley Smith:

> Karen Synesiou, a director of Egg Donation, Inc., said women [in Australia who are willing to donate their eggs to American couples] could earn up to $US25,000 ($44,000), although the average payment was between $US5,000 and $US10,000. American fertility specialist and former model Shelley Smith, who runs the Egg Donor Program in the US, said it was unethical for US agents to tout for business overseas. "I vehemently oppose what they do," she said. "We work frequently

with Australian couples, more and more over the years because they just can't find donors there. But we don't import Australian donors.

It's just terrible that they purposely take a woman from there and bring them here when there are dozens of couples desperately needing donors in their own country. It's a roundabout way . . . and it really exploits everybody, the girls and the couples. Everybody gets hurt."

Ms Smith said recipient couples would most likely receive less information about their donor, and Australian egg donors would be offered less than US citizens get paid for their eggs, not have adequate access to counselling services, and possibly regret it later.

The controversial nature of the egg donor issue and Smith's explicit opposition to the practice of employing Australian donors suggest that the criticisms she makes of this practice function as premises in an argument. Once we recognize that this is so, we can proceed to diagram the argument in question.

In this and other cases, we recommend that you begin your analysis by trying to identify the principal point the arguer is trying to establish. This will help you cut through the noise the argument contains. In the case of an argument the main point will be the argument's main conclusion. In this passage, Smith's main conclusion is indicated early in the excerpt, when she is attributed the claim that it is unethical for American agents to use Australian egg donors. We take the following statements:

"I vehemently oppose what they do."
"[I]t really exploits everybody, the girls and the couples. Everybody gets hurt."
"[W]e don't import Australian donors."

as another way to make this same point. As the discussion is focused on the use of Australian women donors, we will identify the main conclusion as:

MC =   It is unethical for American companies to solicit human egg donations
        from Australia.

Having established this main conclusion, we need to ask what evidence Smith gives in support of it. We detect a number of premises.

P1 =   It's just terrible that they purposely take a woman from Australia and
        bring her here when there are dozens of Australian couples desperately
        needing donors.

P2 =   American couples involved in such transactions will most likely receive
        less information about their donor.

P3 =   Australian egg donors will likely be offered less money than US citizens
        get paid for their eggs.

P4 =   Australian egg donors will not have adequate access to counselling services.

The last of these premises is included in Smith's suggestion that "Australian egg donors would not have adequate access to counselling services and possibly regret it later." We think that this is plausibly interpreted as a sub-argument, for it suggests that Australian women may regret their decision later *because* they will not have adequate access to counselling services. In order to capture this aspect of the reasoning we will include a sub-conclusion in our legend, which we will identify as:

C1 =   Australian egg donors who donate to American couples may regret their decision later.

This completes our legend, allowing us to diagram the argument attributed to Smith:

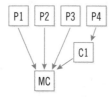

This example is more complex than our other examples, and better illustrates the complexities that arise when we "translate" ordinary language arguments into diagrams. It is especially important to observe the way we constructed a clear diagram by eliminating background information, digressions, and significant repetition of the original. In this case, the first sentence in the excerpt is noise that provides background information rather than the content of an argument: it explains the context of Smith's argument, but it is not a part of it. Hence it contains nothing that needs to be included in our diagram. The finished diagram presents a well dressed argument that provides the key information we need to evaluate the reasoning: it shows us how many lines of support there are for the main conclusion and how many of those lines are also supported.

Since diagramming is a skill that improves with practice, it is by completing exercises with examples such as this one that you will learn how to make the linguistic adjustments that will allow you to clearly represent an argument in a diagram.

DIAGRAMMING: A SHORTCUT METHOD

In most cases in this book, we will present a diagram by defining our legend in the way we have already outlined. But in dealing with arguments on a more casual basis, we can use a quicker method. Instead of writing out each premise and conclusion, we circle the relevant statements in a passage and number them consecutively. We can then sketch a diagram that shows the relationships between the numbered statements. Those sentences or words that can be considered "noise" can be crossed out or left unnumbered. The following is a simple example:

I have spent some time thinking about university education. What should a student should study when they go to university? (Thinking clearly and logically is an important skill) so (all students should study the rudiments of logic.)

In diagramming with this shortcut method, our first example might be diagrammed as follows:

This shortcut method of diagramming can help you complete practice exercises much more quickly than the long method, which requires you to write out an argument's premises and conclusion in full. Use the shortcut when it is convenient, as we will on occasion, but be aware that there are cases in which this method is unsuitable. In these cases, the premises and/or conclusion of the argument need to be identified by making revisions to the actual statements that the arguer uses (in order to eliminate "noise," to clarify the arguer's meaning, to recognize the argument's implicit components, or for some other reason).

EXERCISE   5B

1.   Diagram each of the following extended arguments (use the long method or the shortcut method as you prefer):

a)* The conservative government did the right thing when it abolished the Canadian Firearms registry in 2012, because it wasn't an efficient instrument for fighting crime, since criminals are the people least likely to register their firearms.

b)   [From a *National Geographic*, July 2011, article on species extinction "Food ark" found at: http://ngm.nationalgeographic.com/2011/07/food-ark/siebert-text] Food varieties extinction is happening all over the world—and it's happening fast. In the United States an estimated 90 percent of our historic fruit and vegetable varieties have vanished. Of the 7,000 apple varieties that were grown in the 1800s, fewer than a hundred remain. In the Philippines thousands of varieties of rice once thrived; now only up to a hundred are grown there. In China 90 per cent of the wheat varieties cultivated just a century ago have disappeared. Experts estimate that we have lost more than half of the world's food varieties over the past century. As for the 8,000 known livestock breeds, 1,600 are endangered or already extinct.

   Why is this a problem? Because if disease or future climate change decimates one of the handful of plants and animals we've come to depend on to feed our growing planet, we might desperately need one of the varieties we've let go extinct.

c) Wikipedia is no substitute for serious research in a library. The articles on Wikipedia have no guarantee of reliability because what is written may only just have been entered without anyone else checking what is said. Moreover, Wikipedia articles rarely have the depth of information available in good libraries.

d) [From *The Windsor Star*, Editorial, "All-year school: At least, let's discuss it," 8 October 2010, p. A6] Do children benefit from attending school all year long? Studies show they do, for one obvious reason: Lots of valuable facts can be lost during that two-month gap called summer vacation.

e)* [Adapted from an editorial in *The Globe and Mail* (14 July 2011) responding to the proposal of Shawn A-in-chut Atleo, the National Chief of the Assembly of First Nations, that the Indian Act be repealed and the Department of Aboriginal Affairs abolished] An entity smaller than a department might not be an improvement because the needs of First Nation communities are so great, and so urgent. The provinces have more political power in relation to Ottawa and vastly more revenues of their own than first nations communities. Thus, the breakup of the Department of Aboriginal Affairs could result in a dangerous neglect of aboriginal policy.

3 Linked and Convergent Premises

In order to make diagrams a more effective way to represent the structure of an argument, we draw them in order to distinguish between premises that are "linked" and those that are "convergent." **Linked premises** work as a unit—they support a conclusion only when they are conjoined. **Convergent premises** are separate and distinct and offer independent evidence for a conclusion.

Some simple examples can illustrate the difference between linked and convergent premises and the ways in which they can be represented in a diagram. Consider, as a first example, the Sherlock Holmes argument we discussed in Chapter 1. It can be diagrammed as follows:

P1 = Although the living room window is open, there are no footprints outside despite the softness of the ground after yesterday's rain.

P2 = The clasp on the box was not broken but opened with a key that had been hidden behind the clock.

P3 = The dog did not bark.

C = The crime was committed by someone in the house.

The premises in this argument are convergent: each premise has a separate arrow leading to the conclusion, indicating that it provides an independent reason for that conclusion. You can see this by imagining that the only premise in the argument is either

P1 or P2 or P3. In each case, our reasoning would be weaker, but the single premise would still provide some evidence for C. The premises do not require each other to provide support for the conclusion.

The situation would be very different if Sherlock Holmes used the following reasoning to conclude that the crime could not have been committed by the butler, George:

> It is clear that the crime was committed by someone who is very strong. But George is singularly weak. So he cannot be the culprit.

In this new argument, the premises are linked: they provide support for the conclusion *only* if they are considered as a unit. The first premise—the claim that the crime was committed by someone very strong—provides *no* support for the conclusion that George "cannot be the culprit" unless we combine it with the second premise—that George is singularly weak. Similarly, the second premise provides no support for the conclusion unless it is combined with the first.

In an argument diagram, we recognize the linked nature of these two premises by placing a plus sign (+) between them, drawing an underline beneath them, and using a single arrow to join the two of them to the conclusion. Our finished diagram looks like this:

P1 =   The crime was committed by someone very strong.
P2 =   George is singularly weak.
 C =   George cannot be the culprit.

We can easily imagine Sherlock Holmes combining this argument with further reasoning. If he has already decided that "Either George or Janice is guilty of the crime," he may now conclude that Janice is the culprit, for the argument above has eliminated the only other possibility. In this case, Holmes's entire chain of reasoning may be diagrammed by extending our initial diagram:

P1 =   The crime was committed by someone very strong.
P2 =   George is singularly weak.
C1 =   George cannot be the culprit.
P3 =   Either George or Janice is guilty of the crime.
MC =   Janice is guilty of the crime.

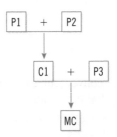

In this new diagram, C1 and P3 are linked premises for the main conclusion, for they support it only when they are combined.

In drawing diagrams, it is important to make sure that you distinguish between linked and convergent premises, for this distinction will determine how you assess particular premises. If you have difficulty deciding whether some premise P is linked to other premises, ask yourself whether P provides any support for the conclusion when it is considered independently of the other premise(s). Some premises need to be considered together, others not, and when you diagram your argument you need to group them accordingly. To some extent, this is a judgement call. You must be prepared to defend your decision to link premises by showing that one of those premises could not serve as support for the conclusion unless it is combined with at least one other premise.

Some Examples

To better acquaint you with argument diagrams, we have designed the following examples to illustrate the application of our diagramming method to particular arguments.

EXAMPLE 1

Argument

The ruins of ancient Aztec pyramids are very similar to those found in Egypt. Also, animals and vegetation found on the eastern coasts of South America bear a striking resemblance to those of West Africa. From all appearances, there was once a large land mass connecting these continents. This implies that the true ancestors of the indigenous peoples of South America are African.

Diagram

P1 =   The ruins of ancient Aztec pyramids are very similar to those found in Egypt.

P2 =   Animals and vegetation found on the eastern coasts of South America bear a striking resemblance to those of West Africa.

C1 =   There was once a large land mass connecting these continents.

MC =   The true ancestors of the indigenous peoples of South America are African.

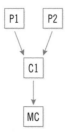

EXAMPLE 2

Argument

[In a famous incident in Homer's *Odyssey*, Odysseus and his men land on an island inhabited by one-eyed giants called "Cyclops." When Odysseus speaks to a Cyclops inside a cave, he reminds him that Zeus requires the Cyclops to treat guests well. The Cyclops responds with the following argument] "Stranger, you must be a fool, or must have come from very far afield. For you warn me to take care of my responsibilities to Zeus and we Cyclopes care nothing about Zeus and the rest of the gods. . . ."

Diagram

P1 = You warn me to take care of my responsibilities to Zeus.
P2 = We Cyclops care nothing about Zeus and the rest of the gods.
 C = You must be a fool or have come from very far afield.

EXAMPLE 3

Argument

[Adapted from a Letter to the Editor, *The Globe and Mail*, 9 October 1998] Re. Lord Elgin's Greek Marbles: Robert Fulford advocates that the sculptures should be kept at the British Museum. He's wrong. I can think of three reasons why the marbles should be returned to Greece. They are part of the cultural heritage of Greece, not Britain. They were taken from Greece with the consent of the Ottoman empire, which had no cultural claim on the antiquities. And there is no evidence that the marbles were in danger of "destruction or dispersal," as he puts it, when Lord Elgin shipped them off to Britain.

   Mr Fulford should think again.

Diagram

P1 = The Elgin Marbles are part of the cultural heritage of Greece, not Britain.
P2 = The Elgin Marbles were taken from Greece with the consent of the Ottoman empire, which had no cultural claim on the antiquities.
P3 = There is no evidence that the marbles were in danger of "destruction or dispersal" (as Fulford puts it) when Lord Elgin shipped them off to Britain.
C1 = The marbles should be returned to Greece.
MC = Robert Fulford is wrong when he advocates that Lord Elgin's Greek marbles should be kept at the British Museum.

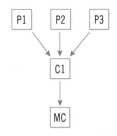

DIAGRAMMING AN ARGUMENT

1. Determine the main conclusion of the argument: the major point the arguer is trying to establish.
2. Mark the text into blocks that have a unified logical purpose, such as stating a premise or drawing a conclusion.
3. Cross out digressions and noise.
4. Express the content of each block in statement form. In doing so, try to capture the author's intended meaning.
5. Create a legend listing the premises as P1, P2, etc., the subsidiary conclusions as C1, C2, C3, etc., and the main conclusion as MC.
6. Join each independent premise to the conclusion it supports with an arrow.
7. Conjoin linked premises with a plus sign (+) and an underline, and connect them to the appropriate conclusion with an arrow.

EXERCISE   5C

Diagram the following arguments, using the bracketed words to define premises and conclusions:

a) [Thinking requires the capacity for abstraction], so [computers cannot think].

b)* [White Jaguar automobiles are unusual in this area]. [The defendant owns a white Jaguar]. And [the car from which the shots were fired has been identified by several witnesses as a white Jaguar]. Therefore, [there is reason to believe that the defendant is guilty of the drive-by shooting].

c) Because [the hospital has been in debt for over a decade] and [all debt-ridden public institutions should be closed], [this hospital should be closed]. Besides, [the technology in the operating rooms is outdated].

d)* [The sun is bigger than the Earth]. It follows that [the Earth revolves around the sun], due to the fact that [smaller objects revolve around bigger objects and not vice versa].

e) [Explanations depend on the laws of nature, either explicitly or implicitly], and [they seek to tell a story of how something came to be the way it is]. In distinction, [arguments don't depend on the laws of nature in any way], and [they don't tell a story of how something came to be]. We must conclude that [arguments are not explanations].

f)* [It is fair that anyone who intentionally takes another's life should forfeit their own]. Hence, [capital punishment is not wrong]. In addition, [it is cheaper to execute someone than to keep them in prison for 50 years], and [society has a right to save money whenever it can]. Also, [executing murderers serves as a deterrent to others who might be contemplating similar crimes]. Thus, [society should execute murderers].

g) [University graduates tend to occupy a higher place in society than those who do not graduate from a university]. Hence, [if university were a privilege, it would become a means of perpetuating an elitist society]. Therefore, [university should be a right and not a privilege], since [all means of perpetuating an elitist society should be avoided] because [elitist societies are unjust societies]. Moreover, [elitist societies are economically inefficient].

4   Supplemented Diagrams

A diagram is an efficient way to summarize the content of an argument. Its legend presents the premises and conclusion(s). The diagram provides a visual representation of the relationships that exist between them. When we want to assess an argument, constructing a diagram is a good way to begin our assessment of the reasoning it contains.

It is important to remember that, as useful as they may be, diagrams do not, in themselves, provide all the information we need to assess any argument. We have already noted that there is more to an argument than premises and conclusions. Arguments are situated in a context of communication that includes arguers, audiences, and opponents. A careful analysis of an argument must frequently discuss these parties. In order to prepare the way for this discussion, we may, in drawing the diagram for an argument, decide to identify one or more of them. In discussing the strength of the argument, this information may provide the basis for a discussion of the arguers (which may address their credibility or our past experience in dealing with their arguments, etc.), the audiences for whom the argument is constructed (which may explain aspects of the argument that might otherwise make little sense), or the opponents (for we may need to assess the extent to which the arguers have adequately dealt with objections to their views).

A *supplemented* diagram is a diagram of an argument to which has been added information about the arguer, the audience to which the argument is directed, or those who oppose this point of view. A *fully supplemented* argument contains information on all three. The following advertisement for Scotiabank illustrates the construction of a fully supplemented diagram. It appeared in a variety of university newspapers in an effort to promote the bank among students:

Being a student has its advantages. With Scotia's student bank account—*Student Banking Advantage*® Plan for post-secondary students, there is no monthly fee and no transaction limits.

PLUS other free benefits include:

- 2,000 SCENE®* rewards points[1] (2 free movies) and an additional 1 point for every $5 you spend on debit purchases. You may never have to pay for movies again!
- *Bank the Rest* ®—turn debit purchases into savings automatically by rounding up[2] each purchase to the next multiple of $1 or $5.
- Access to your accounts 24/7 via Scotia Online, smart phone, telephone, Interac Online, or one of Scotiabank's 3,000 ABMs.

Speak to your local branch for details.

® Registered trademarks of the Bank of Nova Scotia.
®* Registered trademark of SCENE IP LP, used under license.

[1] 1,000 SCENE points will be added to your SCENE membership account when you obtain a SCENE® *ScotiaCard*® debit card on a new Student Banking Advantage® Plan. This bonus points offer will be awarded once per customer per SCENE membership. For joint accounts, if at the time of awarding either offer, each customer has registered an eligible individual SCENE membership, points will be split equally. This offer does not apply to existing SCENE-eligible Scotiabank account holders. Additional 1,000 points will be added to your SCENE membership when you transfer your payroll or two pre-authorized debits/credits.

[2] *Bank the Rest* savings program can only be set-up on Personal *ScotiaCard* bank cards. Conditions apply.

To construct a fully supplemented diagram for this argument, we proceed by preparing a standard diagram, combining it with an account of the arguer, the audience, and the opponents. When we do so, the resulting account of the argument might look like this:

> The *arguer* is Scotiabank.
>
> The *audience* is students, for this particular advertisement speaks only to students, not to other potential customers.
>
> The *opponents* include competing banks, who are likely to argue that their banks are as student-friendly as Scotiabank, as well as those who might oppose banking in a more fundamental way. The latter may believe that there are moral reasons that show that we should not use banks and should support credit unions in their place.

> P1 = With Scotia's student bank account—Student Banking Advantage Plan for post-secondary students, there is no monthly fee and no transaction limits.
>
> P2 = Other benefits include 2,000 SCENE®* rewards points[1] (2 free movies) and an additional 1 point for every $5 you spend on debit purchases.
>
> C1 = You may never have to pay for movies again.

P3 = If you have a Scotia student bank account, *Bank the Rest* will allow you to turn debit purchases into savings automatically by rounding up[2] each purchase to the next multiple of $1 or $5.

P4 = You can access your Scotia accounts 24/7 via Scotia Online, smart phone, telephone, Interac Online, or one of Scotiabank's 3,000 ABMs.

MC = You should speak to a Scotiabank branch about Scotiabank's student account.

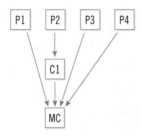

This fully supplemented diagram provides a very complete background for argument analysis. On the one hand, it clearly delineates the premises and conclusion of the argument and the pattern of support within the reasoning. At the same time, it provides us with the information on the arguer, the audience, and the opponents that may play an important role in our attempt to determine whether this is a good argument. For example, the recognition that the arguer is Scotiabank is not inconsequential, for this is a case where the arguer has an obvious vested interest, where there are financial benefits that accrue to Scotiabank if the intended audience accepts its conclusion. This is something we may need to consider in deciding whether the argument is biased in a way that reflects this vested interest.

In dealing with most arguments, we will not provide fully supplemented diagrams. Why? Because this is a time-consuming task, especially if we are analyzing a whole series of arguments. Instead of providing fully supplemented diagrams, we will normally provide diagrams that are supplemented only with whatever information about the arguer, the audience, or the opponents we believe is relevant to a critical assessment of the argument. We suggest you do the same, while keeping in mind that someone who fully understands an argument should be able to provide a fully supplemented diagram that discusses the features of argument we have outlined in this and the previous chapter. Even when you don't provide a fully supplemented argument, you should, in principle, be able to do so.

EXERCISE 5D

1. Illustrate each of the following concepts with two examples of your own:

   a)* diagram legend

   b) linked premises

c)   convergent premises

d)   supplemented diagrams

2.   Decide whether each of the following passages is an argument. If it is an argument, provide a supplemented diagram that illustrates its structure.

a)   Since everyone has a right to free access to the best health care and few could afford the high costs of private health care, it would be wrong to move to a predominantly private system, and hence the government has an obligation to fund all health care programs.

b)   Not only does having an on-line presence give academics exposure to new audiences, it is also fundamental to their role as educators. How can academics be relevant to students if they are not engaged with the most powerful research medium ever? Students use social media, and if teachers want to understand their students, they must understand social media. And the only way to do that is to use it.

c)   [Richard Stengel, in *You're Too Kind: A Brief History of Flattery*, Simon & Schuster, 2000, p. 234] Compliments, favours, and self-enhancement aren't good bets when ingratiating upward, because they seem manipulative and even impertinent.

d)   [Hillary Clinton, quoted by David Heinzmann in the *Chicago Tribune*, 28 October 1999] "[I]n many ways, the story of Chicago blues is the story of the African-American experience," she said. "The blues found its beat with the polyrhythms of Africa; gained words and form and pain and emotion on the plantations of the South; travelled up the Mississippi; collaborated with white musicians and discovered electricity, volume and fame right here in the Windy City."

e)*   [Adapted from www.openair.org, (accessed 4 June 2003)]
      Urge Hillary Clinton to Save Maxwell Street, An American Treasure
      Hillary Clinton has an appreciation for and understanding of the blues and played an instrumental role in ensuring that the Chess Studios have been saved and rehabbed. If preserving the Chess Studios is essential to the legacy of the blues, certainly Maxwell Street must be preserved also. Blues is, at root, a folk idiom. Its creation comes from the folk at the grassroots street level. The music got recorded at Chess, VJ, and other labels but it got created on Maxwell Street.

f)   [From a university debate over the proposed North American "missile shield," which would protect North America from incoming missiles] The proposed missile defence system would be the first step toward weapons in space. So far, space has been preserved as a military-free zone. It is important—for the safety of us all—that we keep it that way. So we should reject the proposed missile shield.

g)   [Robert Sullivan, "Adventure: An attempt at a definition" in *LIFE: The Greatest Adventures of All Time*, Life Books, Time Inc., 2000, pp. 8–9] We will not deny that when the Norwegian Viking Leif Eriksson sailed to Vinland in the year 1000, . . . he had quite an adventure. We will not deny that when Marco Polo traveled the Silk Road at the end of the 13th century, he had many adventures. We will not deny the adventurousness of Christopher Columbus. . . . But adventurers first? We would argue not. Most were explorers, principally, while others were variously conquistadors, missionaries and mercenaries. Among their reasons for venturing, adventure was low on the list. . . . Yes, on paper an explorer may look quite the same as an adventurer. They share several traits—boldness, stoicism, strength. But the reason for the enterprise is fundamentally different, and an adventurer is, therefore, a very different beast.

h)* [From *Time* magazine, 2 June 2003, p. 23] Swing voters have always been elusive creatures, changing shape from election to election. . . . This axiom is proving true again with that most-talked-about slice of American political demography: the Soccer Mom. Since 9/11, polls suggest she has morphed into Security Mom. . . . The sea change in these women has already reshaped voting patterns. Their new attitude helps explain why the gender gap that had worked to the Democrats' advantage since Ronald Reagan was in office narrowed sharply in last year's congressional elections.

i) There are several key reasons to not use social media for marketing. First of all, it's all hype. If you explore the issue, you'll find that very few companies have successfully followed this route. Also, it doesn't generate profit. If it did, then everyone would be on the bandwagon. But the biggest reason is that social media is just too distractive. Because of this, it is easy to waste time, and wasted time means low productivity.

j) [Excerpted from a Letter to the Editor, *The Globe and Mail*, 19 August 2004] Vancouver—A.B. implies that hunting is unethical because it is akin to killing. If this were true and killing were wrong, then we would all be walking contradictions. Finding, killing, and consuming life of all kinds is a requirement of life, human and non-human alike.

Therefore, there is not much hope for those who believe unconditionally that killing is wrong and who subscribe to Kantian ethics.

5 Diagramming Your Own Arguments

Our examples have already demonstrated that diagramming is a useful tool when we need to plot the structure of someone else's argument. We will end our discussion by noting that diagramming can also be used to analyze and construct arguments of our own. How extensively you use diagrams will depend on your own inclinations. Some people find a diagrammatic representation of an argument an invaluable tool in argument construction. Others who are not inclined to visual representations may not make extensive use of them. Though you will need to decide what works for you, there are two ways in which a supplemented diagram can help you construct an argument, especially if you feel some trepidation as you approach the task before you.

First, a diagram will provide you with a precisely defined set of premises and conclusions and illustrate the way in which the premises support particular conclusions. Because the structure in a diagram is clear, using one will encourage you to plot straightforward patterns of argument with clear lines of reasoning. Second, diagramming will help you see for yourself whether the premises you provide work independently to support a conclusion or rely upon each other to provide support.

Once you sketch a diagram, turning it into a written or a spoken argument is a simple task. It requires only that you substitute premise or conclusion indicators for the arrows in the argument and make any minor adjustments that the sense of the argument requires. If there are sub-arguments, you will want to include them as separate paragraphs (or separate sections) in a written argument. The argument that results will have a clear structure because it has been built upon a structure that was clearly delineated in your diagram.

A supplemented diagram is an especially useful tool when preparing an argument, because it requires you to think about the audience for and opponents of your argument and their own beliefs and attitudes. This can help you develop an argument that takes them into account. A long extended argument should appeal to the beliefs, convictions, and concerns of the audience and should address counter-arguments that opponents to your position are likely to raise. The ability to prepare supplemented diagrams will be important to your development as a reasoner.

To illustrate this use, consider one of the most controversial contemporary debates—that of embryonic stem cell research—and consider how you might use diagramming in constructing a position in this debate. This will be an issue that recurs in examples throughout the text and will form the context for an extended argument in the final chapter. Imagine that you want to defend the position that human embryonic stem cells should *not* be used in research. You have the main conclusion, so you need to decide what central lines of support to provide for it: these will form the sub-arguments in your diagram. You also need to consider the audience and the opponents. The *audience*, we will assume, is the public, since this issue is a broadly discussed issue which is discussed in the public media. Your *opponents* would be those who do favour using embryos in research. Identifying this group helps us to focus on what their principal argument might be for that position (addressing this argument should form part of the argument you construct).

Let's take as reasons for your conclusion the following:

Premise 1:   All humans are subject to respect and dignity
                     And (+)

Premise 2:   The embryos in question are human by nature.
                     Furthermore,

Premise 3:   there are other means to achieve the outcomes for which embryonic stem cells are to be used.

The corresponding diagram has two linked premises and a third premise converging on the conclusion. But now you need to consider where the burden of proof lies with respect to these three premises. Premise 1 seems relatively uncontroversial in Canadian society (your target audience), so you can leave this without further support. The burden of proof lies with someone who would challenge it. But premise 2 could be deemed controversial and needs some support if only by way of clarification. Perhaps you could offer the following: P4: "Anything composed of human material is human by nature." This makes P2 a conclusion (C1) and expands your argument so that it is now extended rather than simple. Likewise, P3 needs to be supported, because this is the premise that most directly addresses the position of your opponents. They believe that the use of embryonic stem cells is essential for developing remedies of major diseases like, for example, Parkinson's disease. P3 says there are other means to achieve some positive ends. What are they? A review of the issue would indicate that a lot of people put their trust in research using *adult* stem cells. So P5: "Research in adult stem cells promises important results" would be support for P3, making that in turn C2. Now you have a more complex argument and diagramming it shows where your lines of support lie.

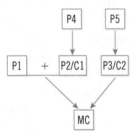

Of course, this argument could be developed further and it still has several points that would be vulnerable to counter-argument. But the point of the exercise has been to show how diagramming can serve as an aid to argument construction.

The arguments you present should be ones that can easily be diagrammed; it should not be difficult for someone who wishes to diagram it to identify your premises and conclusions in a legend. Premise and conclusion indicators will make clear which premises are tied to which conclusions, allowing an observer to easily determine how arrows connect the different components of the argument and whether premises should be linked in the diagram or left to converge on the conclusion.

EXERCISE   5E

1. Go back to exercise 1M. Pick four arguments in the exercise. In each case, dispute the argument's conclusion by providing a supplemented diagram (specifying an audience and an opponent) for a simple argument for the opposite conclusion. Present the argument in a paragraph.

2. Construct and diagram simple arguments supporting or disputing five of the following 10 claims. In each case, let the audience be the general public, and define some group of likely opponents. Present the argument you have diagrammed in a paragraph.

   a)* A college education is a privilege rather than a right.
   b)* Genetic experiments should be banned.
   c)* Capital punishment is wrong.
   d) The threat of terrorism justifies greater security measures in airports.

e) Climate change is the number one challenge facing our generation.
f) Water is a resource that should be protected from commercial exploitation.
g) Newspapers should not exploit their position by supporting causes.
h) Research using embryonic stem cells should be permitted.
i) The right to bear arms does not extend to assault weapons designed for killing humans.
j) University education should be free for all who qualify.

A Cautionary Note

Having extolled the virtues of diagramming, we offer you a few words of caution and some practical suggestions. In diagramming—and in constructing arguments—aim for simplicity. Plot the structure of your argument so that it is relatively simple and stands out as clearly as possible. Do not defeat your purpose by creating a small-scale version of a confusing city map, with myriad roads and intersections. Do not push the possibilities for diagramming to extremes. All you need is a diagram that shows clearly the role that each premise plays in the total scheme of your argumentation. Too much elaboration tends to be confusing.

Leo Groarke

Illustration 5.1 "Not a successful diagram"

PREPARING ARGUMENTS

1. Decide on your conclusion.
2. Pick your premises and diagram your argument.
3. Diagram an argument against likely objections.
4. Keep your diagrams as simple as possible.
5. Base your finished argument on your diagrams.

6   Summary

This chapter has introduced a diagramming method as a tool for constructing and evaluating simple and extended arguments. We have looked at how such diagrams can depict the relationships between components of an argument. We have introduced serial diagrams, as well as linked and convergent diagrams. All extended diagrams are composed of these basic structures. We have finally discussed supplemented diagrams, which involve adding information about the arguer, audience, and opponents.

MAJOR EXERCISE   5M

Decide whether each of the following contains an argument, and explain the reasons for your decision. Diagram any arguments you find. In at least four cases, provide a fully supplemented diagram of the argument.

a)* The room was sealed from the inside. Hence, no one could have left it. Therefore, the murderer was never in the room.

b) Few monographs are successful in introducing readers to the manifold benefits of a new theory or idea while at the same time making clear its weaknesses and limitations. The author is to be commended for what she has accomplished here.

c)* Literacy skills are essential for the development of productive citizens. This program has been teaching people basic literacy skills for over two decades. Providing continued funding for the program is clearly justified.

d) Active euthanasia, or assisting someone to die, is a practice that will come to be accepted in the future. For when people become old or debilitated by illness, they may lack the strength to end their own lives. Such individuals may try many times, unsuccessfully, to end their own lives, causing themselves and others great suffering. Therefore, the need to have assistance in ending terminal pain is becoming more evident.

e) [From an editorial in *The Globe and Mail*, 10 July 2010, commenting on the announced $925-million cost of the 2010 Winter Olympics in Vancouver.] Canada brought home a record number of gold medals . . . [held] a large international competition with few hitches, and . . . [enjoyed] a resurgence of national pride. How do you place a price on that?

f) Pakistan is at a crossroads in its history. It needs the support of Western countries now more than ever, because without them it cannot battle the Islamic extremists trying to destabilize the country from within. Abandoning a nuclear-armed Muslim nation would only bring catastrophic consequences.

g)* [From the web site of the US Food and Drug Administration Center for Devices and Radiological Health, www.fda.gov, (accessed 5 January 2003)] FDA and other organizations of the US Public Health Service (USPHS) continue to investigate the safety of amalgams used in dental restorations (fillings). However, no valid scientific evidence has ever shown that amalgams cause harm to patients with dental restorations, except in the rare case of allergy.

The safety of dental amalgams has been reviewed extensively over the past ten years, both nationally and internationally. In 1994, an international conference of health officials concluded there is no scientific evidence that dental amalgam presents a significant health hazard to the general population, although a small number of patients had mild, temporary allergic reactions. The World Health Organization (WHO), in March 1997, reached a similar conclusion. They wrote: "Dental amalgam restorations are considered safe, but components of amalgam and other dental restorative materials may, in rare instances, cause local side effects or allergic reactions. The small amount of mercury released from amalgam restorations, especially during placement and removal, has not been shown to cause any other adverse health effects." Similar conclusions were reached by the USPHS, the European Commission, the National Board of Health and Welfare in Sweden, the New Zealand Ministry of Health, Health Canada, and the province of Quebec.

h) [From St Augustine's *Confessions*, Book vii, paragraph 10] I turned my attention to the case of twins, who are generally born within a short time of each other. Whatever significance in the natural order the astrologers may attribute to this interval of time, it is too short to be appreciated by human observation and no allowance can be made for it in the charts which an astrologer has to consult in order to cast a true horoscope. His predictions, then, will not be true because he would have consulted the same charts for both Esau and Jacob and would have made the same predictions for each of them, whereas it is a fact that the same things did not happen to them both. Therefore, either he would have been wrong in his predictions or, if his forecast was correct, he would not have predicted the same future for each. And yet he would have consulted the same chart in each case. This proves that if he had foretold the truth, it would have been by luck, not by skill.

i) [The Guerrilla Girls are an American group of women who aim to fight discrimination with facts and humour. One of their campaigns is in support of women film directors, who are judged to be under-represented when it comes to recognition through awards. The following announcement accompanied a billboard depicting a female Kong dressed in a designer gown. The poster and text can be found on the web site www.guerrillagirls.com/posters/unchained. shtml, (accessed 26 February 2007)]

> The 500-pound gorilla in Hollywood isn't King Kong—it's discrimination against women directors!
>
> THE GUERRILLA GIRLS AND MOVIES BY WOMEN UNVEIL A NEW BILLBOARD AT SUNSET AND CAHUENGA IN HOLLYWOOD, FEB. 1– MARCH 5, 2006
>
> We took Kong, gave him a sex change and a designer gown, and set her up in Hollywood, just a few blocks from where the Oscars will be awarded March 5, 2006.
>
> Why? To reveal the sordid but True Hollywood Story about the lack of women and people of color behind the scenes in the film industry: Only 7% of 2005's 200 top-grossing films were directed by women.

Only 3 women have ever been nominated for an Oscar for Direction (Lina Wertmuller (1976), Jane Campion (1982), and Sofia Coppola (2003). None has won.

More embarrassing Hollywood statistics:

Of 2004's top-grossing films: 5% had female directors 2% had female writers 3% had female cinematographers

16% had female editors. Only 8 people of color have ever been nominated for an Oscar for Direction. None has won.

Hollywood guilds are 80 to 90% white.

Only 3% of the Oscars for acting have been won by people of color.

In the 21st century, low, low, low numbers like this HAVE to be the result of discrimination, unconscious, conscious or both. Hollywood likes to think of itself as cool, edgy and ahead of its time, but it actually lags way behind the rest of society in employing women and people of color in top positions.

There may be women heading studios these days, but what are they doing for women and people of color? Why do they keep the white male film director stereotype alive? Here's an easy way to change things: open up that boys' club and hire more women and people of color. It worked in medicine, business and law. It worked in the art world. Now it's Hollywood's turn. Rattle that cage, break those chains!

LET WOMEN DIRECT!

 For more online exercises, review questions, and quizzes related to the material in this chapter, please go to www.oupcanada.com/GoodReasoning5e

6

HIDDEN ARGUMENT COMPONENTS

Communication frequently depends on an ability to understand what isn't said or what is said obliquely. To help understand and diagram arguments that employ communication of this sort, this chapter discusses:

► principles of communication
► abbreviated arguments
► hidden premises and conclusions
► verbal, non-verbal, and visual arguments.

The examples of argument we have examined so far are relatively straightforward combinations of premises and conclusions. Arguments are more difficult to analyze in cases that require more interpretation. This is especially the case with arguments that depend on claims or assumptions that are left unstated or obliquely indicated. In the latter case, a claim may be made by means of a picture or by pointing or by saying something that has hidden implications. Everyone is familiar with the classic example of a "loaded" question: "Have you stopped battering your wife?" One cannot answer "Yes" or "No" (as one is asked to do) without implicating oneself. We say the question is "loaded" with an implicit assumption: that you have battered your wife. The right way to answer the question is by exposing this assumption (by "unloading" it) and disposing of it.

In some ancient texts on argument, authors recommend that an arguer hide controversial components of his or her arguments so that they will not be readily apparent to an audience. In some cases, an important component of an argument is not stated because the arguer is clumsy and does not express his or her reasoning clearly. In other cases, a point may be more precisely made in other ways (by showing a photograph or video). We call the unstated components of arguments "hidden," not because they are purposely hidden in every case, but because they are not immediately apparent and you need to search for them when you are confronted with an argument. In this chapter, we introduce you to the principles and concepts that can make this search proceed more efficiently and effectively.

Speech Acts and the Principles of Communication

Attempts to communicate are called **speech acts**. The most obvious kind of speech act is the uttering of a statement, but such acts encompass any attempt to communicate, including attempts to do so that are not confined to spoken language. A remark in a conversation is a speech act, and so is a paragraph in a term paper, a "thumbs-up" gesture, a film, or a map that someone draws to show you where they live.

In trying to understand and interpret speech acts, it is helpful to note three principles of communication, which can guide us as we try to understand the meaning of a speech act:

Principle 1 (Intelligibility):	Assume a speech act is intelligible.
Principle 2 (Context):	Interpret a speech act in a way that fits the context in which it occurs.
Principle 3 (Components):	Interpret a speech act in a way that is, as much as possible, in keeping with the meaning of its various elements (the words, gestures, music, etc., it explicitly contains).

Principle 1—the Principle of Intelligibility—directs us to approach speech acts with the assumption they are meaningful. This raises the question how a particular speech act should be interpreted. Principle 2—the principle of Context—directs us to interpret a speech act by considering the context in which it occurs. This context includes the other speech acts it is connected to and the broader social context in which it occurs. If a speech act is an answer to a question, then it must be understood in terms of this question. If someone approaches you in the middle of an election campaign with a button that says VOTE WRIGHT and begins telling you why Wright is remarkably well qualified to represent you in Ottawa or Washington, then it is reasonable to understand their comments as an argument for the conclusion that one should vote for Wright.

The third principle of communication—the principle of Components—tells us that we should, in interpreting a speech act, do so in a way that makes sense of its elements (the words, music, pictures and other carriers of meaning) and their relationship to each other. In the anti-smoking advertisement shown in Illustration 6.1, created by the California Department of Health Services, we can distinguish two key elements: (a) a beautiful image of a sunset—the kind of image we associate with advertisements for Marlboro cigarettes, and (b) a comment ("I miss my lung,") that alludes to the negative effects of smoking. When we interpret the image we need to resolve the tension between dissonant messages—that conveyed by Marlboro cowboy images, which promote smoking as an attractive, even beautiful, pastime; and that conveyed by the allusion to the negative effects of smoking (which may result in lung cancer). We can readily resolve this juxtaposition by understanding the advertisement as a rejection of the view of smoking inherent in Marlboro's advertising images. The message can be roughly summarized as the following argument: The attractive view of smoking presented in Marlboro advertisements should be rejected (*conclusion*), because smoking can have extremely serious health effects—such as lung cancer (*premise*).

California Department of Public Health

Illustration 6.1   "I miss my lung, Bob."

Any attempt to interpret a speech act implicitly depends on our three principles of communication. When we try to understand arguments as they actually occur in our lives, the principles can be an aid as we interpret, diagram, and assess argumentative exchanges. We have already seen the role that the components of speech acts (e.g. inference indicators) and context play in determining what is an argument. The role that intelligibility plays can be illustrated by a Cox & Forkum commentary on one of the editorial cartoons featured on their website (www.coxandforkum.com, accessed 07 July 2012). In the case we are considering, the commentary explained a cartoon about Iran:

> **Iran says its nuclear drive is solely aimed at generating energy and that it does not aspire to nuclear weapons.**
> Yeah right. Here are some recent examples of Iran's "peacefulness.". . .
>
>> Iraqi insurgents are being trained in Iran to assemble weapons and Iranian-made weapons are still turning up in Iraq, the US military said Wednesday.
>> The statement comes two months after the United States said it had asked Tehran to stop the flow of weapons into Iraq.
>> Coalition forces found a cache of Iranian rockets and grenade launchers in Baghdad on Tuesday, spokesman US Maj. Gen. William Caldwell said Wednesday. . . .
>> He accused the Quds Force of supplying Iraqi insurgents with armor-piercing roadside bombs. . . .
>> He said Shiite extremists are being trained inside Iran. . . .
>
> Here is a list of articles indicating that Iran is not waging "peace" against the US in Iraq:
>
>> US troops attacked by Iranian military last year (*The Jerusalem Post*, 25 March 2007)
>> Iran's influence grows in Iraq, region (*Chicago Tribune*, 7 March 2007)
>> Iraqi extremists trained in Iran: US intelligence (AFP, 28 February 2007)
>> Military: more evidence of Iran-made explosives (*Seattle Times*, 27 February 2007)

Rumsfeld: Iraq bombs "clearly from Iran" (CNN, 10 August 2005)

And finally MEMRI reminds us of the kind of government confronting us: "Thief's hand amputated in public in Iran; Official cleric calls for reinstating Islamic punishments."

This passage is obviously an argument—it forwards a series of reasons in defence of the conclusion that Iran is *not* a peaceful nation and aspires to nuclear weapons.

How do we know that this is the conclusion of the argument? The passage contains no logical indicators, and it begins not with the conclusion we suggest, but with a statement describing Iran's claims followed by the expression "Yeah right." How do we know to interpret these as a conclusion that Iran is not peaceful and does aspire to nuclear weapons? Because this is the only way to render the passage intelligible. It simply makes no sense to suppose that Cox & Forkum agree that Iran is only interested in the peaceful use of nuclear power in a passage where they go on to list a number of reasons for believing otherwise. In keeping with this, we interpret "Yeah right" as a sarcastic way of disagreeing with the statement that precedes it. It is this that gives us the conclusion we have noted.

THE PRINCIPLES OF COMMUNICATION

Principle 1 (Intelligibility): Assume that a speech act is intelligible.

Principle 2 (Context): Interpret a speech act in a way that fits the context in which it occurs.

Principle 3 (Components): Interpret a speech act in a way that is in keeping with the meaning of its explicit components.

EXERCISE 6A

1. Take two of the arguments you analyzed in Exercise 3M. Explain how the principles of communication were implicitly applied in your analysis of the argument.

2. Suppose you are writing a term paper on the ancient sophist Protagoras and on his claim that "Humans are the measure of all things." According to the principles of communication, how should you go about trying to understand his claim?

3. In the 2011 Canadian federal election campaign, many people were confused by the daily reporting of opinion polls that seemed to provide conflicting and often contradictory results. Writing in *The Globe and Mail*, a columnist argued in favour of the practice of polling. Part of his argument is given in the following. Analyze this and explain how your interpretation depends on intelligibility, context, and explicit elements.

    [P]olling is regularly criticized for turning the election into nothing more than a horse race—and a confusing one at that. But survey the role of public-opinion research more closely and a greater good may emerge from the backstretch dust: Thanks to the largely unmediated power of statistics, a small sampling of the population gives the entire body politic a collective voice, in both campaigns and in government.

In the messiness of democracy, electoral polling offers a semblance of order, a numerical corrective that lets the thoughts of the people rise above the cries and whispers of party politics. "Good public-opinion research plays a grounding function in a campaign," says pollster Nik Nanos of Nanos Research. "It reveals how Canadians feel about public-policy issues and that prevents the parties from making claims that aren't founded in reality."

4. In 2007, the *National Post* reported on the gender gap in Canadian universities, suggesting that a larger proportion of females to males was not a problem. The report elicited several letters in response. The following is part of one of them (*National Post*, 5 December 2007). Analyze this argument and explain how your interpretation depends on intelligibility, context, and explicit elements.

I have always been opposed to preferential treatment. . . . I would be the first in line to applaud the university administrators who balk at implementing affirmative action for men, except for two things. . . .

So far, no one has promised to dismantle the existing institutions of preferential treatment for women that are rampant at Canadian universities, including female-only scholarships, women's centres (with no analogous men's centres), preferential hiring for female faculty and set-asides for research grants for women.

Second, if universities are not inclined to make any special efforts to attract men, the least they could do is end the things that repel them. The typical Canadian university is a hostile environment for men, who are constantly exposed to the most venomous and ill-informed nonsense emanating from women's studies departments, and who are disproportionately targeted by ever more draconian speech and behaviour codes by "equity commissars" run amok.

2 Hidden Conclusions

"Abbreviated" arguments are arguments that depend on hidden premises and/or conclusions that are not explicitly stated. In the process of analyzing arguments and constructing diagrams, we need to identify these hidden components so that their role in the argument can be recognized and assessed.

The principles of communication suggest that we identify an argument's hidden premises and conclusions by considering the context in which the argument occurs and by looking for clues in its explicit components. In doing so, you will want to identify all the hidden components relevant to the argument: you need to recognize the whole argument. But you must at the same time make sure that you do not add too many components and in this way misrepresent the argument. In identifying hidden components, you should work like an archaeologist rather than an architect: you do not want to build up an argument but to discover what is already there, even though it is there implicitly.

An argument is said to have a hidden conclusion when its premises propose a conclusion that is left unstated. Often, the argument contains some indication that the arguer is offering reasons for accepting the conclusion. Consider the following comment on seatbelts:

I think there is enough evidence to justify a reasonable conclusion. In the vast majority of cases that have been examined, wearing seatbelts has prevented injuries that would have resulted from automobile accidents. And these cases appear to vastly outnumber the relatively few cases in which people have avoided injury because they were not wearing seatbelts and were thrown clear of a vehicle.

The first sentence in these remarks suggests that a conclusion follows from the evidence that is given. No conclusion is explicitly stated, but the rest of the passage makes it clear that the hidden conclusion is the claim that wearing seatbelts is a good way to avoid injuries in automobile accidents. We can recognize the hidden conclusion in this abbreviated argument by diagramming the argument as follows:

P1 = In the vast majority of cases that have been examined, wearing seatbelts has prevented injuries that would have resulted from automobile accidents.

P2 = Cases where seatbelts have prevented injuries appear to vastly outnumber the relatively few cases in which people have avoided injury because they have been thrown clear of a vehicle.

HC = It is reasonable to believe that wearing a seatbelt is a good way to avoid injuries in automobile accidents.

Within legends and diagrams, we indicate hidden components by prefixing "H" to the symbols that we use to represent them. In this case, our conclusion is represented as "HC."

In supplying the hidden conclusion in this example, we have tried to capture the tone and content of the author's explicit statements. It is significant that she emphasizes that some of the accidents investigated do not confirm her point, qualifies one of her statements with the word "appear," and says that the conclusion is "reasonable to believe" rather than certain. In the midst of such qualifications, we would overstate her intentions if we expressed the conclusion as "Wearing seat belts always prevents injury." The conclusion "The wearing of seat belts should be required by law" would be equally out of place, for it introduces a new issue the writer has not touched upon, namely that of legislation. For all we know, she may not believe in legislation (she may be a libertarian opposed to government regulation) and may only advocate the voluntary use of seat belts.

Consider a different kind of example. The *National Post* reported, in April 2010, on a case in which a dispute over table manners was being reviewed by a human rights tribunal. A comment in response to this ["Now table manners are a human right?" *National Post*, 26 April 2010] provided the following argument:

Human rights tribunals offer an incentive to pursue frivolous cases which should never be in the legal system in the first place. If matters are really serious enough to warrant litigation, let plaintiffs go through the regular court system, where they will have to pay their own lawyers, court fees, and the like. Perhaps that will encourage more people to settle minor matters privately, instead of making them into a public circus at taxpayers' expense.

The logic of the passage indicates that the argument can be summarized as follows:

P1 =   Human rights tribunals offer an incentive to pursue frivolous cases which should never be in the legal system in the first place.

P2 =   If matters are really serious enough to warrant litigation, let plaintiffs go through the regular court system, where they will have to pay their own lawyers, court fees, and the like.

P3 =   Perhaps that will encourage more people to settle minor matters privately, instead of making them into a public circus at taxpayers' expense.

HC1 = This is not an issue that should be heard by a human rights tribunal.

We identify this as a hidden conclusion, because the writer is clearly offering reasons against the proposed hearing. But this is a case in which our analysis can go further, for there is another implicit conclusion that is implied by the premises. The author does not explicitly say so, but the author's comments suggest that this example supports the case for not having separate human rights tribunals (and that human rights cases should be heard in the regular courts). In a diagram we can represent the full argument as follows:

HMC = This kind of case shows that human rights tribunals should be disbanded in favour of using the regular court system.

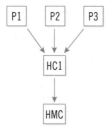

FINDING HIDDEN CONCLUSIONS

Ask yourself whether the remarks in question defend or invite some unstated conclusion. If the answer is "Yes," represent this claim as a hidden conclusion, "HC."

EXERCISE   6B

1. Each of the following comments is from a variety of sources debating the question whether Canada should increase immigration numbers. Each comment can be understood as an argument with a hidden conclusion. Diagram each argument.

a) A former Director of Federal–Provincial Relations at Immigration Canada has pointed to the fact that Canada's native labour force is declining and birth rates in most provinces are not expected to increase in the near future.

b) A recent study from the Fraser Institute suggests that immigration costs Canada up to $23.6 billion a year, since each immigrant received an average of $6051 more in benefits than they paid in taxes (according to data from the 2006 census).

2.* [From the back of a package of Novitra, a cream for treating cold sores] Clinically Proven. In a randomized double-blind, placebo-controlled study, NOVITRA is proven to shorten duration of cold sores, and goes to work immediately to reduce severity of symptoms.

3. [From an opinion piece criticizing a movement to ban incandescent light bulbs for environmental reasons (Andrew Potter, "Not the brightest bulbs in the pack," *Maclean's* magazine, 9 April 2007)] If a government believes it is entitled to micro-manage the preferences of its citizens with respect to electricity consumption, there is no reason to stop at light bulbs. Why not ban sales of 72-inch plasma screen tele-visions, or outlaw central air conditioning? Why not legislate limits on the number of hours a day I can spend surfing the Internet, or playing video games?

3   Hidden Premises

Hidden premises are unstated claims an argument depends on. Without assuming them, there is no way to move from the argument's explicit premises to the conclusion. Consider the following argument adapted from a letter to *Time* magazine, which responded to an article on reproductive technologies (surrogate motherhood, in vitro fertilization, cloning, etc.) used to help infertile couples have children of their own.

> We should stop aborting innocents, as that would eliminate the need for unnatural methods of making babies.

This is an interesting example because the argument is so condensed. Looking at the explicit claims the arguer makes, we can see that she is opposed to abortion, for she describes it as "aborting innocents," and, apparently, to technological methods of dealing with infertility, which she describes as "unnatural." We might diagram her argument as follows:

P1 =   By stopping the abortion of innocent fetuses, we could eliminate the need for unnatural methods of making babies.

C =   We should stop aborting fetuses.

You may sense that there is something right and something wrong with this diagram. This is the general structure of the reasoning, but there is something missing. There is a gap that must be bridged. Someone could accept P1 and not draw the proposed conclusion—because they might hold that unnatural ways of making babies are a legitimate way to satisfy some people's desire to have a baby. This tells us that our arguer must hold that unnatural methods of making babies are wrong and should, if possible, be avoided. It is this claim *together* with P1 that takes us to the conclusion.

Once we recognize the hidden premise in the argument, our diagram becomes:

P1 =   By stopping the abortion of innocent fetuses, we could eliminate the need for bizarre and unnatural methods of making babies.

HP2 =   Unnatural methods of making babies are wrong and should, if possible, be avoided.

C =   We should stop aborting fetuses.

It is important to identify hidden premises when they are controversial claims. In the present case, we need to recognize HP2 because many people would argue that unnatural methods of making babies are not wrong. They might back their position by arguing that we all depend on unnatural methods of doing things (driving, flying, emailing, etc.) that are based on technological innovation. The last argument of the previous section (on human rights tribunals) also depended on a controversial claim that was assumed by the arguer. A full diagram of that argument would need to also include this assumption as a hidden premise:

HP =   A dispute over table manners is a frivolous case.

This assumption is controversial (and thus elevated to the status of hidden premise) because whether such a case is frivolous is one of the things the human rights tribunal should be deciding. At the very least, the arguer has the burden of proof to support this assumption. Including it as a hidden premise in the diagram ensures we focus on this problem when we come to analyze the argument.

In diagramming, then, our aim is to make explicit all aspects of the argument we will want to discuss when we assess the argument. This sometimes means that we identify as hidden premises assumptions that the arguer has taken for granted. We cannot treat every assumption as a hidden premise, for every argument presupposes an endless number of assumptions that are too numerous to be catalogued (in the abortion argument above, they include assumptions like "Science has made unnatural ways of making babies possible," "Making babies naturally is not wrong," and "The words used in this argument are meaningful English words").

Every argument makes many assumptions. There is no reason to enumerate them when they are not controversial assumptions, for they do not need to be discussed. They can be taken for granted because they reflect widespread agreement about the world, about language, and about what is right and wrong. In contrast, those assumptions that are speculative or debatable need to be represented as hidden premises in the diagramming of an argument, so that such assumptions can be recognized and discussed.

In some cases, the process of identifying hidden premises forces you to choose between different possibilities. In such cases, we encourage you to be cautious. Be charitable when you identify the hidden premises in an argument. Make sure any unstated claim you attribute to the arguer is both necessary to the argument and something the arguer would accept.

Consider the following response to a Canadian Senate committee's recommendation in the fall of 2002 that marijuana use be decriminalized. One supporter of the report wrote the following to *The Globe and Mail* (6 September 2002):

> Adults should have the right to decide whether or not to use it because no scientific study has ever shown marijuana to be even as harmful as alcohol.

The premise indicator "because" shows us that the second statement is intended as support for the first, and hence we have an argument. Initially, we might diagram it as:

P1 =   No scientific study has ever shown marijuana to be even as harmful as alcohol.

C =   Adults should have the right to decide whether or not to use marijuana.

It should be clear that there is something missing from this diagram. Indeed, the reasoning is somewhat peculiar, for why should the absence of a scientific study showing marijuana to be as harmful as alcohol count as a reason for adults having the right to use it? One possibility, which focuses on the references to a scientific study and harm, is that the arguer believes that adults have a right to decide for themselves in cases where a significant harm has not been scientifically proven. Adopting this interpretation, the hidden premise in the argument is:

HP2 =   Adults have a right to decide for themselves in cases where a significant harm has not been scientifically proven.

The diagram becomes:

This interpretation is plausible, but it commits the arguer to a very general claim that may have applications beyond her or his intention. Because we are committed to as charitable an interpretation of the argument as possible, we prefer a different diagram that uncovers an assumption that commits the author to no more than he or she is likely to believe. Thus, we identify the hidden premise in the argument as:

> HP2 =   Adults have the right to decide whether or not to use alcohol or other substances that are less harmful.

This is a weaker claim than our first HP2. The new HP2 reports something that is debatable (one might argue that there are prescription drugs that are less harmful than alcohol, but that this does not mean that we have the right to decide whether to use them) but it is not as controversial. This HP also allows us to see how the expressed components of the argument are connected. In choosing this as our hidden premise, we are not saying that the argument is, in the final analysis, a good one—only that this hidden premise is sufficient to explain the inference it incorporates.

Our next example comes from the same dispute over the Canadian Senate report on the decriminalization of marijuana:

> The criminalization of marijuana use cannot be justified. In spite of the eagerness of the police to devote many hours to the enforcement of pot legislation, the logical course of action would leave the police free to investigate crimes that actually hurt people.

If we wanted to diagram the expressed reasoning we might begin by establishing the following legend:

> P1 =   In spite of the eagerness of the police to devote many hours to the enforcement of pot legislation, the logical course of action would leave the police free to investigate crimes that actually hurt people.
>
> C =   The criminalization of marijuana use cannot be justified.

But this is a case in which the move from P1 to C depends on at least two assumptions that may be identified as hidden premises. The first is the assumption that the enforcement of pot legislation requiring many hours of police work is not logical. The second is the assumption that marijuana use does not hurt people. It is only by accepting these two (controversial) assumptions that one can move from P1 to the conclusion, so we need to include them as two hidden premises on which the reasoning depends.

FINDING HIDDEN PREMISES

Ask yourself whether the stated premises lead directly to the conclusion or depend on some unstated assumption. If the latter, and if this assumption needs to be assessed, present the unstated assumption as a hidden premise.

EXERCISE   6C

1. Each of the following passages can be read as a simple argument but with hidden components that should be made explicit. Diagram each argument:

   a)* God is all good. So God is benevolent.
   b) You can't rely on what that witness said. Two other witnesses contradict her.
   c) Politicians of today are no longer leaders. Democracy forces them to do whatever will get them elected.
   d) Let's go see *Harry Potter and the Deathly Hallows: Part 2*. The first Part was a fine example of filmmaking.
   e)* Sports are good for kids because they teach discipline.
   f) Father-only families are single-parent families. So we should make special efforts to help them.
   g) Strengthening the Endangered Species Act should be a legislative priority, because doing so will preserve genetic diversity on the planet.
   h) The Endangered Species Act needs to be watered down. In its current form, it severely damages the economy.
   i) Cheerleading should be a recognized sport because cheerleaders belong to squads (or teams), try out, train, compete, and hone specialized skills.
   j)* It's morally wrong to treat human beings as mere objects. So it is wrong to genetically engineer human beings.
   k) It is morally acceptable for humans to eat animal flesh. Humans have teeth designed for eating animal flesh.
   l) We have a duty to provide food for future generations. So we have a duty to develop genetically engineered crops.
   m) The environment is under enormous stress as a result of human activity, and we have the means to do something about this.

2. The following excerpts are from different Internet discussions of the question whether humans are naturally meat eaters or vegetarian. Each passage can be interpreted as an argument with hidden components. Diagram the argument in each case.

   a)* Our early ancestors from at least four million years ago were almost exclusively vegetarian.
   b) The animals most similar to us, the other primates, eat an almost exclusively vegan diet. Their main non-plant food often isn't meat, it's termites.
   c) Our closest relatives among the apes are the chimpanzees (i.e. anatomically, behaviorally, genetically, and evolutionarily), who frequently kill and eat other mammals (including other primates).
   d) Some who claim we are meat eaters point to our so-called "canine teeth," but they are "canine" in name only. Other plant-eaters (like gorillas, horses, and hippopotami) have "canines," and chimps, who are almost exclusively vegan, have massive canines compared to ours.
   e) As far back as it can be traced, clearly the archeological record indicates an omnivorous diet for humans that included meat. Our ancestry is among the hunters and gatherers from the beginning. As soon as we began domesticating food sources, they included both animals and plants.

3. Diagram the reasoning attributed to the Chinese in the following argument narra-
    tive on Chinese-American relations in the wake of "the bloody suppression of the
    Tiananmen Square democracy movement" [adapted from *Time* magazine, July 1995]:

    Since the Tiananmen incidents, a series of disputes have arisen with the United States.
    The only logical conclusion the Chinese have been able to draw is that Washington
    is making a concerted and coordinated attack on the Chinese government.

4   Non-Verbal Elements in Argument: Flags and Demonstrations

In interpersonal argument, we frequently use gestures, facial expressions, and other
non-verbal means of communication. Especially as information technology has made
it easier to convey images and sounds, public arguments are often conveyed in ways
that do not rely on words alone. Many of the arguments you encounter every day
exploit images, music, and other non-verbal carriers of meaning. **Visual arguments**
convey premises and conclusion with non-verbal visual images one finds in drawings,
photographs, film, videos, sculpture, natural objects, and so on. In most cases, they
combine visual and verbal cues in a manner that can be understood as argument.

In trying to understand and diagram some of these arguments, you must identify and interpret their non-verbal aspects. This is less difficult than it might at first
appear, for these non-verbal speech acts can, like the verbal aspects of argument, be
understood by applying the principles of communication we outlined at the beginning of this chapter. The intelligibility principle suggests that there is a "logic" to
non-verbal attempts to communicate argumentative ideas, i.e. that these speech acts
are in principle intelligible. Context and essential elements suggest that we must try to
make sense of them by considering the contexts in which they occur and the explicit
components (visual, musical, etc.) they employ.

In many cases, the non-verbal aspects of a speech act that constitutes an argument do not play a significant role in the reasoning it contains. The visual backdrop
to an argument—the room or other surroundings in which it is presented—may not
have any argumentative significance. In such cases, it is not a key component of the
argument and need not be considered in argument analysis. In other cases, the background to an argument is more significant and needs to be discussed, for it has been
consciously chosen specifically to facilitate the argument in one way or another.

In the simplest cases, an image or some other non-verbal aspect of a situation functions as an **argument flag** that draws attention to an argument. Flags play a significant
role in ordinary argument because an argument cannot convince someone of its conclusion unless they take the time to consider it. Flags attract the attention that allows arguments to do their work. An arguer may, for example, announce their argument with a
drum roll or piece of music, present it before a stunning natural landscape or while sitting
in the high-backed chair of a judge, or convey it through an announcer with eye-catching
good looks. Insofar as these non-verbal means are intended as attempts to attract our
attention (and not as content in the actual argument), they are examples of argument flags.

We have already seen an example of an argument flag in the anti-Marlboro advertisement from the California Department of Health Services. It—and other advertisements like it (including Marlboro advertisements) typically use images (or on television or video, images and music) to grab our attention. In a world in which we are accosted by millions of advertisements every month—a situation that teaches us to ignore most advertisements—this is one of the things that makes artistic creativity so important to successful advertising. Once the advertiser captures our attention, they usually attempt to convince us of something, often in a manner that can be understood as argument.

A historical example of a visual flag is the 1920s illustration of a cricket we have reproduced below (Illustration 6.2). It was featured in an early advertising campaign for home insurance. This image is properly classified as a visual argument flag because it was used to attract the reader's attention to the argument that accompanied it. In doing so, it exploited the way a picture on a page may "jump out" at you. In this case, the image's ability to catch the viewer's eye was enhanced by the quality of the artwork and by the vivid colour in the original, which was published at a time when colour printing was rare and remarkable. In a case like this, the non-verbal cue that catches our eye is only a flag and not itself an element of argument, for the flag is not used to convey the argument and only functions as a means of directing us to the text that conveys the actual argument. Within that text, we are told that the painting is of a field cricket building a home, a theme that introduces the argument that we should purchase insurance, for we, like the cricket in the illustration, care about our homes.

Source: Traveler's Insurance. Used with permission.

Illustration 6.2   1920s ad campaign for home insurance

Visual and musical flags are a common element in argument, especially at a time when technology makes it easier and easier to present arguments with images, sound and multi-media. Arguers use these tools to attract our attention, especially in contexts in which there are many other arguments that vie for our attention. They take advantage of the fact that we are naturally drawn to a stunning photograph or piece of music. Some flags serve only to attract attention and are not themselves arguments or argument components. In interpreting arguments in which they function in this way, we should learn to recognize flags for what they are, but we treat them as noise rather than as an argument component. They might be compared with many headlines and striking verbal claims that are used to draw attention to an argument but cannot themselves be classified as a premise or conclusion.

Non-Verbal Demonstrations

The most basic way in which non-verbal elements function as argument components occurs when music, sounds, images, or even aromas provide evidence for some conclusion. This is one of the most primitive forms of argument, which we use when we try to prove something by literally presenting it (in a case of murder it might be a murder weapon, the body of the person who has been murdered, or visual evidence that allegedly records the murder). Demonstrations of this sort appeal to evidence in favour of a conclusion, not with words (or not only with words), but by using images, sounds and other non-verbal elements. In a situation in which one wishes to prove something about Victorian homes in San Francisco; the anatomical structure of a fly; van Gogh paintings; ancient fertility gods; the symptoms of a particular disease; urban blight in Calgary; or the rituals of a particular indigenous people, etc., images and sounds may be the most important element of your argument.

In some cases it is visual evidence which is the heart of an argument, as in the most discussed controversy in North American ornithology, which debates the question whether the Ivory-billed Woodpecker (the species which was the inspiration for that animated classic *Woody Woodpecker*) is extinct or not—a debate that revolves around a controversial video alleged to document a sighting in Louisiana. Our first example of visual evidence is the photograph of an eight-legged starfish found by a fisherman in the North Sea, reproduced in Illustration 6.3. Beside it is a normal starfish, which is smaller and has five legs. In this case, the image—and for those who have seen it, the actual specimen (now named "Stan") functions as a premise which shows that our ordinary assumptions about starfish—that they

Photo by Rex Features

Illustration 6.3   "Stan"

have five legs—are in some cases mistaken. The question how this should be accounted for—by seeing Stan as a genetic mutation or a different species—remains a matter of argument and debate.

Our second example of a visual demonstration arises in the context of the 1999 renovation of the Brantford Carnegie Library. It was an important heritage building and one of the issues raised by the renovation was whether it would be renovated in a manner that successfully preserved the look of the original. Of course, one could provide many different kinds of evidence to this effect (for example, the Heritage award that the renovation received from Brantford's heritage committee), but the most effective way to do so is by comparing photographs of the library in the early 1900s and after the renovation, as we have done with Illustration 6.4 and Illustration 6.5. To keep things simple, we have included only two photos (of the exterior, which is typically considered the most significant part of a building from a heritage point of view) but such a presentation could, of course include tens or hundreds of photographs or video evidence (as in a documentary that was done on this and other heritage buildings in Brantford). In a case such as this, we might diagram our own simple argument as follows:

P1 = In 1999, the library looked as it does in our first photograph.
P2 = In 1910, the library looked as it does in our second photograph.
 C = The 1999 renovation of the Brantford Carnegie Library successfully preserved the look of the original.

When we analyze a visual argument like this, we build a reference to the image into the premises or conclusion. In this way, the sentences in our legend do not replace the images the argument includes, but direct us to them and the evidence they provide.

Like any other argument, visual and other non-verbal demonstrations need to be evaluated by considering the acceptability of the premises and the question whether the conclusion follows. In many ways, such evidence can be misleading—images and sounds can be "doctored" (more easily all the time), can be misinterpreted, and may provide a very limited view of a circumstance or situation. One of the reasons to recognize a visual argument as an argument is precisely because that paves the way to an assessment of the reasoning proposed. In many cases, non-verbal evidence can convey shapes and features that would be difficult to describe in words. In many cases effective arguments combine non-verbal elements with words that discuss them. A sophisticated attempt to make our argument about the Carnegie library the basis of an extended argument for the conclusion that its renovation was an important project in heritage renewal would, for example, probably combine the visual demonstration available through photographs with a detailed account of the building's Beaux Arts style, the heritage significance of Andrew Carnegie libraries, and so on.

Illustration 6.4   The Carnegie Library as the Brantford Public Library (circa 1910)

Brant Museum and Archives

Illustration 6.5   The Brantford Carnegie Library renovations (2000)

Leo Groarke

Non-verbal demonstrations are common in science. The identification and classification of a species, for example, often depends on a visual identification which is accomplished through photographs or video or a comparison with an actual item taken from a specimen collection. In other cases, microscopic or diagnostic imaging may provide images that are the heart of a conclusion. One sometimes finds more questionable uses of non-verbal demonstrations in advertising, where before-and-after photographs are used to promote a particular weight loss program, a trailer is used to advertise a new movie, and the scent sprayed from a sample bottle is used to promote a perfume. In such cases, non-verbal demonstrations are a means of supporting some conclusion the arguer hopes to convey to you—that you can lose *this* kind of weight, that this movie is *this* compelling, or that this perfume smells *this* good.

In the case of a movie, the aim is to convince you that you should see a particular film on the basis of the compelling nature of the sample presented in the trailer. We might diagram the general form of such arguments as follows:

P1 =   The trailer is compelling (funny, motion packed, poignant, etc.).
HC =   The movie is compelling (funny, motion packed, poignant, etc.).
HMC =   This is a movie you should go to see.

So construed, we can see that the main conclusion of the argument is founded on a prior inference that the trailer is an accurate sample of the movie. This is a generalization and needs, in view of this, to be evaluated according to the criteria for good generalizations we introduce in Chapter 9.

Traditionally, non-verbal demonstrations were highly regarded forms of argument, for they present evidence more directly than an argument expressed in mere words. A witness who tells you that she saw a person wearing a ring that was stolen from you may be lying, but not if she points to a person and you can identify the ring on his right hand. A photograph or video is one step removed from this kind of presentation, but it captures evidence in a relatively direct way. At a time when technology makes it relatively easy to record sounds and visual images, non-verbal demonstrations of this sort are increasingly prevalent and important. They are accompanied by challenges as well as benefits, for the technological advances that have made it easier to provide visual evidence also make it easier to manipulate it. It would be naïve to assume that they necessarily convey "things as they are."

These caveats being noted, non-verbal demonstrations are an especially compelling form of argument in many circumstances. The image in the advertisement for the province of Newfoundland and Labrador that we have reproduced in Illustration 6.6 is a case in point. Especially when you consider it together with the many other photographs posted on the website of the provincial tourism office www.newfound-landlabrador.com), the image is a reasonable way to demonstrate some of the sights and experiences available on a trip to Newfoundland and Labrador. We might diagram the intended argument as:

P1 =   If you visit Newfoundland and Labrador, you will be able to experience sights like this.

HP2 =   Experiencing this is something you should pursue.

C =   You should visit Newfoundland and Labrador.

Illustration 6.6   The glacier-carved freshwater fjord at Western Brooke Pond, Newfoundland and Labrador

EXERCISE 6D

1. Analyze the visual demonstration in the following popular poster.

Illustration 6.7   Fast Food

2.   Go to your university or college website. Go to the section for "Prospective Students." Analyze the images and statements (and music and sounds). Identify flags and demonstrations. What messages do they communicate? How do the non verbal aspects of the pages contribute to the overall attempt to attract students to your school?

3.   The following photograph is a Robert Croft image of figures in a fresco on St Mary's Cathedral in Lincoln, Lincolnshire, England (available on Wikimedia). Like many medieval paintings and statues it functions as a visual argument that reinforces a key message of the church? What is the message? How might you diagram the argument the fresco proposes?

Illustration 6.8   Lincoln cathedral: sculptured relief of the sufferings of the damned on the western front

5   Symbols and Metaphors

Argument flags and non-verbal demonstrations are the most direct ways in which arguments may employ non-verbal elements. In such circumstances, these elements are understood in a straightforward, literal way. In other cases, such elements may be used in a more figurative way to convey a message that turns on the proper interpretation of the non-verbal elements.

A political cartoon that depicts a politician as a devil with horns employs non verbal elements, but it is not a demonstration. The artist is not claiming that this is how the politician actually looks. He is, rather, using his drawing as a way of saying that the politician is engaged in wrongdoing, which is the business of a devil. In this and similar cases, the non-verbal elements of arguments function as symbols that can replace words, represent some idea, or refer to someone or something. You use and interpret non-verbal symbols every day. You know that a crucifix represents Christ, that a skull represents death, that "The Star Spangled Banner" symbolizes the United

States of America, that a peace sign stands for peace, that a thumbs-up means "Okay!," and that a "swoosh" represents Nike sports equipment. Even if you don't follow the NHL, you probably recognize the blue maple leaf that stands for the Toronto Maple Leafs and the CH symbol for the Montreal Canadians.

In contexts of argument, visual symbols are often used either to state a position or to make a case for one. Consider the image below, posted on a website which asked visitors to give their "reasons why abortion rights must be protected." By now you should recognize this as a request for arguments that provide premises (reasons) for this conclusion. In response, one visitor posted the image below. The context in which this image appears makes it plausible to interpret the image as a visual argument, but what is the argument that the image forwards?

In answering this question, we can begin by recognizing that the context (in which the image functions as the answer to a question) makes the (hidden) conclusion in the argument relatively straightforward: it is the claim that we should protect a woman's right to an abortion. To understand the premises that have been conveyed in support of this conclusion, we need to interpret two elements of the image that function as visual symbols: the (red) circle with a diagonal line and the coat hanger. The first of these symbols is readily understood as a visual symbol of negation that is typically used as an injunction in signs that tell us: no smoking, no guns, no rights, no swimming, and so on. In this case, the no sign clearly qualifies the coat hanger, which has

become a symbol for "coat hanger abortions"—illegal abortions carried out by back street abortionists, often with coat hangers, when abortion was illegal. Such abortions were notorious because of their frequently disastrous consequences for the desperate women who sought them. Understanding this background, we can plausibly interpret the visual image as the following argument:

HP1 =   Coat hanger abortions have disastrous consequences for the desperate women who are forced to seek them.

C1 =   We must not allow coat hanger abortions.

HP3 =   If we do not protect a woman's right to an abortion, there will be coat hanger abortions.

HMC =   We should protect a woman's right to an abortion.

In diagramming the argument we have designated C1 as the only explicit argument component because it is what the image explicitly asserts. We have designated the other premises and the conclusion as hidden components because they are not asserted, visually or verbally. It is important to recognize HP2 as a hidden premise in the argument because it provides the unexpressed crucial link that that ties the explicit claim to the main conclusion.

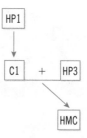

Metaphors

A fourth kind of non-verbal meaning is conveyed when arguments use **non-verbal metaphors**. A metaphor describes one thing as though it were another. "Jill is a block of ice" and "The world's a stage" are verbal metaphors. They make no sense if we try to understand them literally, for people are not made of ice and the world is not a theatre. We therefore understand them, in a figurative way, as claims that Jill is unfriendly and that our lives are like roles in a stage play.

Non-verbal metaphors operate in a similar way. Political cartoons are a form of political commentary that frequently uses visual metaphors to comment on matters of political significance. The Henry Payne cartoon in Illustration 6.9 (from www. henrypayne.com) is a comment on Mitt Romney in the midst of his 2011 campaign to become the Republican Presidential candidate for the 2012 American election. At the root of the message is a drawing of President Obama's health care plan ("Obama Care") as Frankenstein. This depiction, which Payne uses in a number of cartoons that address the plan, is a metaphorical way of saying that Obama Care, which has been severely criticized by Republicans, is monstrous and horrific (as was Frankenstein). In the cartoon, this visual metaphor is employed in a criticism of Romney, who played a key role instituting a similar health care program in Massachusetts while he was governor. This plan, which Payne dubs "Romney Care," is presented as a twin of Obama Care, and is depicted as another Frankenstein. The application of the same visual metaphor in both cases (and the look of surprise and uncertainty on the face of "Romney Care") suggests that Romney is denying the obvious when he claims that there is no relation between the two. We might summarize the argument the cartoon forwards as the claim that (*premise:*) Romney Care is, despite Romney's denials, similar to Obama Care; therefore (*conclusion:*) Romney is not a credible Presidential candidate for the Republican party.

Our second example of a visual metaphor is a cartoon commenting on the Canadian seal hunt by the Victoria artist, Adrian Raeside (Illustration 6.10). It shows a woman in a fur coat, which casts a shadow in which we see a crazed Atlantic fisherman

Illustration 6.9   "No. No relation"

with a wild grin who holds a bloody seal pup that he has clubbed to death. The cartoonist is not, of course, suggesting that this is the shadow that is really cast by a woman in a seal fur coat. Rather, he metaphorically suggests that the brutal killing of the seal pups used to create such a coat "casts a shadow" on the wearing of it. We can understand the cartoon as a simple argument which criticizes such fashion and those who wear such coats, who are represented by the unflattering image of the woman in the cartoon. We might summarize this argument as:

Illustration 6.10   "Seal Hunter's Shadow"

P =   Behind each seal coats lies the brutal killing of seal pups.
C =   Those who wear such coats are acting without conscience.

Our final example of a non-verbal metaphor employs sounds rather than images. It is taken from a series of radio advertisements that helped Durex Condoms become the largest condom manufacturer in the world (available on the Durex website, www. durex.com). One of the advertisements (which the company calls "Guitar") can be summarized as follows:

1. [An enticing female voice:] "This is what sex is like with an ordinary condom."
2. [One hears the sound of:] A pedestrian, slow march.
3. [The female voice returns:] "This is what sex is like with a Durex Sheik condom."
4. [One hears the sound of:] A rock and roll tune with a driving beat.
5. [The female voice returns:] "Feel what you've been missing. Set yourself free with the condom designed for excitement. Durex Sheik condoms. For super sensitivity. So you can enjoy all of love's pleasures. Now safer sex doesn't have to feel like safe sex. Set yourself free with Durex Sheik condoms."

The crux of this advertisement is the difference between the two pieces of music it contains, the first representing ordinary condoms, the second representing Durex. In a context in which Durex is obviously promoting its condoms, we have no problem recognizing that the energy and the driving beat in the second clip, when contrasted with the boredom and lack of vigour conveyed in the first piece of music, suggests that sex with an ordinary condom is ho-hum in comparison to sex with a Durex condom and that Durex condoms can "set you free" so that you can "enjoy all of love's pleasures."

If we eliminate the repetition in the argument and isolate the reasons it provides for its conclusion, we can diagram it as follows:

P1 =   Durex Sheik condoms will provide a more exciting sex life than ordinary con-
       doms (one that includes all of love's pleasures; one that doesn't feel like safe sex)
P2 =   Durex Sheik condoms are designed for super sensitivity.
C =   You should use Durex Sheik condoms.

When you recognize and diagram this as an argument, it you should see that it is weak. Durex is attempting to convince us that we should buy Durex Sheik condoms on the grounds that they will make our sex life more exciting. But there is no proof that they will do so. Indeed, this claim is inherently peculiar. For why should we think that a particular condom can turn a pedestrian sex life into one that we would associate with rock and roll? There are ways in which one might plausibly argue for Durex Sheik condoms (by comparing their properties to those of competing brands, by appealing to testimony, etc.), but the radio advertisement for Durex is a clear instance of a company deciding to try to sell their product by charming us with music and humour, not by engaging in a reasonable attempt at argument.

A Complex Example

Non-verbal means of communication have a strong emotional appeal. Images and music captivate us. They make us laugh and smile and can play upon our fears and frustrations, our likes and dislikes. At times, the emotional pull of non-verbal messages can be used legitimately in argument. For instance, in an attempt to convince you that you should help the homeless, photographs (or an actual tour) of a shelter may be the best way to convey to you the needs of homeless people.

But there are many circumstances in which arguments are couched in non-verbal terms because this encourages us to be emotional *rather* than critical when we relate to them. It is important to recognize the communicative role that non-verbal elements play in many arguments, because this will encourage us to properly recognize them as something that needs to be subjected to criticism and inquiry. The Durex radio advertisements are clever and witty, but we need to see them as something more than this, especially if we are considering buying condoms—i.e. if we are part of the audience to which the advertisements are directed. In that case, we should be concerned that this attempt to persuade us to buy Durex condoms rather than some other brand has little argumentative force because it fails to provide reasons.

Of course, many of the arguments we encounter are complex combinations of verbal and non-verbal elements. In cases such as this, we need to interpret the argument as a whole. Consider Mazda's popular "zoom, zoom" advertisements for the Mazda Tribute, its popular sport utility vehicle. These advertisements have been carefully crafted to include stirring music with an African beat, stunning visuals, and a verbal commentary that all lead to the inevitable conclusion that one should drive a Tribute. In diagramming and analyzing the argument, we need to recognize that these are all parts of a package and need to be interpreted together. We might begin by summarizing the advertisement for the Tribute, which unfolds as follows:

1. Music
2. [Male voice:] "What would happen if an SUV was raised by a family of sports cars?"
3. Pause with visuals (wheat blowing in the wind)
4. [A boy in a suit whispers:] "Zoom, zoom."
5. [Male voice:] "Introducing the 200-horsepower Mazda Tribute, the SUV with the soul of a sports car."
6. [One hears a driving African beat, scat singing with the sounds:] "zoom, zoom, zoom . . . heh . . . zoom, zoom, zoom . . . yah . . . zoom, zoom, zoom . . . ."

7. The music is accompanied by scenes on the open road, where a Mazda Tribute weaves its way through a pack of sports cars racing along a highway.
8. After the Tribute emerges at the front of the pack, it refuses to take a turn in the highway and races off the road into open country.

What is the message conveyed in this advertisement? Clearly, it is an attempt to sell the Mazda Tribute. But what are the reasons it offers for the conclusion that this is a car one would want to own? To understand these reasons, we need to understand both the verbal and the non-verbal elements of the advertisement. The non-verbal elements include instances of all the forms of non-verbal communication we have already noted. They might be summarized as follows:

- **Argument flags.** The vivid music and the visuals function as argument flags that capture our attention.
- **Non-verbal demonstrations.** The visuals demonstrate the principal message of the advertisement—that the Mazda Tribute combines the qualities of a sports car (the speed, the handling, etc.) with the SUV's ability to drive off-road. The qualities of the sports car are demonstrated as the Tribute weaves its way through a pack of sports cars. The off-road capability is demonstrated when it refuses to take a turn and drives off the highway into the outback.
- **Metaphor.** The "zoom, zoom" theme is Mazda's (highly successful) attempt to adopt a slogan that captures what it has called "the joy of motion." This is a theme enunciated in the words that accompany the advertisement and in the music, which is strong, fun, lively, energizing. The Tribute itself is alleged to embody all these traits.
- **Symbols.** The boy in the suit may initially seem perplexing. Why a boy? Boys don't drive automobiles. And why a boy in a suit? Boys don't wear suits. To understand this aspect of the advertisement, we need to consider the implicit symbolism. Men are the traditional market for automobile advertisements. And the professional men who can afford a Mazda Tribute wear suits. The boy in the advertisement is the boy who still exists inside the businessman—the boy who still enjoys the simple thrill of motion. It is this "inner child" who whispers the crucial "zoom, zoom" in the advertisement. He whispers because his comment is a thought inside the head of the man that he is speaking to— the man thinking about the Mazda Tribute.

When we combine these non-verbal elements with the statements made in the advertisement, we can see an argument that we can begin to diagram as follows:

P1 =   The Mazda Tribute combines the driving qualities of a sports car (the speed, the handling, etc.) with the SUV's ability to handle off-road driving.
C1 =   The 200-horsepower Mazda Tribute is an SUV with the soul of a sports car.
P2 =   Driving the Mazda Tribute (like driving other Mazdas) is boyishly fun, thrilling, and energizing.
MC =   You should purchase a Mazda Tribute.

We can develop this further by recognizing that the sub-argument from P2 to MC depends on two unstated premises that can be expressed as follows:

HP3 =   One should purchase an automobile that is fun, thrilling, and energizing.
HP4 =   The tribute is *more* fun, thrilling, and energizing than the competition.

HP3 is needed because the fun of driving a Tribute provides significant support for the conclusion that one should purchase the Tribute only if this is what really matters in an automobile (and not safety, economy, etc.). We can see why we must add HP4 to our diagram if we imagine that the Tribute is *not* more fun than its competitors, for in these circumstances, the assumption that one should buy a car that is fun and appeals to one's youthful sense of play (HP3) may lead to the conclusion not that one should purchase a Tribute but that one should purchase a competing vehicle. Our full diagram is:

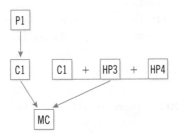

Once we have this diagram, a number of debatable aspects become apparent. Despite its emotional appeal (especially to the "boy inside the man" that Mazda is targeting), HP3 could easily be debated. HP4 is also open to debate, as is the staged visual presentation that is supposed to demonstrate the qualities claimed in P1.

But these and other concerns lie beyond the scope of our present discussion, where we want only to demonstrate that complex arguments employing non-verbal elements can be identified and diagrammed by recognizing the different forms of non-verbal meaning we have noted. Once we have identified and diagrammed the elements of such arguments, we can assess them the same ways we will assess other arguments, by asking whether their premises are plausible and their conclusions follow.

FOUR KINDS OF NON-VERBAL MEANING

There are four kinds of non-verbal elements that may function in an argument:

1. **Argument flags** draw our attention to an argument.
2. **Non-verbal demonstrations** provide some direct evidence for a conclusion.
3. **Symbolic references** make a non-verbal reference to some idea, person, or thing.
4. **Metaphors** figuratively ascribe some characteristic to the subject of the metaphor.

In some complex arguments, all four kinds of non-verbal meaning may be used. Sometimes the same non-verbal elements (e.g. a particular piece of music) may convey more than one kind of non-verbal meaning.

EXERCISE   6E

1. Visit the web site Ads of the World at http://adsoftheworld.com. Pick an advertisement that can be understood as an argument. Dress and analyze the arguments, and then explain how the principles of communication were applied in your treatments of the arguments. What kinds of non-verbal meaning were evident?

2. The following is an advertisement for the French newspaper, *Aufait*. What is the role of the visual image in the advertisement. Analyze its meaning in terms of the kinds of non-verbal meaning we have introduced.

Source: Au Fait

Illustration 6.11   "The Facts" from *Aufait* newspaper

3. What is the visual argument forwarded by the following illustration, labelled "The downward spiral of debt."

Leo Groarke

Illustration 6.12   The State and Investors

4. The lithograph reprinted in Illustration 6.13 was created by Adolfo Mexiac and turned into a political poster during the 1968 Mexico Olympics, when over 300 student protestors were killed in the Plaza de las Tres Culturas, in an incident known as the Tlatelolco Massacre. Explain the message in terms of our account of non-verbal meaning.

Illustration 6.13   "Libertad de Expresion: Mexico 68" by Adolfo Mexiac

Image © Victoria and Albert Museum, London.

6   A Note on Argument Construction

In many circumstances, we communicate in ways that are not entirely explicit. This is not a bad thing. If we could communicate only in ways that were explicit and used only words, communication would be cumbersome, difficult, and mundane. But there are circumstances where explicitness is a goal we should aim for. The attempt to identify and diagram an argument is one such case, for it is an attempt to reveal *all* the important parts of the argument. Identifying these parts prepares us for the inspection of them that will allow us to decide whether the argument is strong or weak.

In the process of dressing arguments, we can "fill in the blanks" and recognize their implicit aspects by applying the three basic principles of communication outlined at the beginning of this chapter. They suggest that the interpretation of any speech act should aim for a coherent meaning that is in keeping with its context and its explicit elements. In earlier chapters, we implicitly relied on the process of interpretation this suggests in deciding what is and is not an argument and in deciding how the components of ordinary arguments should be identified and diagrammed. In this chapter, we have explained how this process can be used in identifying hidden premises and conclusions and in understanding the non-verbal elements of many arguments.

In constructing arguments of your own, your goal should be arguments that do not depend on implicit elements in a way that makes them difficult to interpret or easy to misconstrue. The first step toward this goal is a commitment to use premise and conclusion indicators whenever you construct an argument. This is the only way to ensure that your arguments will be recognized as arguments.

In the body of your arguments, you can avoid confusion by using words and, if you decide to use them, non-verbal elements that clearly and precisely express what you want to say. Though no one can expect to avoid hidden premises in every circumstance (because our audiences will, in some cases, want to take issue with assumptions that seem to us obvious and unproblematic), you should try to explicitly express any important premise your argument depends on. In Chapter 1, we introduced the device of imagining an opponent for your argument to help you see what objections might be raised. You can use the same device to anticipate what statements will be controversial. If you can reasonably expect a premise to be controversial to such an opponent, then you should not hide it. Instead, you should create an extended argument that includes a sub-argument to support the premise in question.

In constructing arguments, especially in public contexts that are conducive to images, music, and other elements, it is not unreasonable to use non-verbal elements, so long as they are not exploited in order to promote poor reasoning or substitute purely emotional appeals for combinations of premises and conclusions that will stand up to scrutiny. It is a positive thing to be clever, witty, and creative, but not in a way that undermines the force of the arguments you construct.

EXERCISE   6F

Construct an extended argument for or against the death penalty (no more than three paragraphs long). Use non-verbal elements if you choose. After you have constructed the argument, discuss it from the point of view of clarity: How have you presented your argument and structured it so that it is clear what you are saying? What potential confusions did you need to avoid? How have you avoided them? What mistakes might occur in a poorly constructed version of your argument?

7   Summary

The focus of this chapter has been the implicit nature of much argumentative material. We have discussed ways in which both conclusions and premises may be hidden and left unstated. These need to be drawn out and made explicit. We have also explored the non verbal nature of some argumentative components, when images and sounds are used as evidence. We have also explored the more figurative ways to convey messages, through symbolic references and metaphors.

MAJOR EXERCISE   6M

1. For each of the following passages, say whether it contains an argument. If it contains an argument, dress it with a diagram, adding hidden premises and conclusions as necessary. (Don't assume that all passages are arguments or that all contain hidden components. Qualify your discussion of borderline cases.)

    a) Section 598b of the California Penal Code makes it illegal to eat domesticated animals like cats and dogs. But the only community in California that eats such animals is the Vietnamese community. So section 598b of the California Penal Code discriminates against the Vietnamese community.

    b)* [From an advertisement for "Arthur's Pom Plus Smoothie"] A healthy diet containing foods high in potassium and low in sodium may reduce the risk of high blood pressure, a risk factor for stroke and heart disease. Arthur's Pom Plus Smoothie is high in potassium and low in sodium.

    c) [The same advertisement continues]: A healthy diet rich in a variety of vegetables and fruit may help reduce the risk of some types of cancer. Arthur's Pom Plus contains 2½ servings of fruit per serving as per the Canada Food Guide.

    d) [Adapted from a column in the *Detroit Free Press*] Airlines are funny. They make sure you aren't carrying a weapon of destruction and then sell you all the booze you can drink.

    e) [An old-fashioned advertisement:] ARE YOU GULLIBLE? Then our product is for you. For years people believed there was no simple cure for this ailment. People who succumbed to its ravages were considered beyond help. They studied critical thinking, they worked hard to develop a critical attitude. All with little chance of success. Why work so hard? Now there's TINDALE'S CREDULITY FORMULA. $25 for the completely gullible. Smaller bottles, priced at only $10, are available for the slightly gullible.

f)   [The following is part of a response to the long-gun registry debate in Canada. It was published as a letter to the editors of *National Post*, 22 September 2010] The most frustrating part of the whole gun registry debate is hearing the phrase "if it saves even one life it's worth it." This is the argument of those who have no concrete evidence to support their position. We keep statistics on many things in Canada and we can identify pretty well those things which actually save lives.

g)* [From a discussion of Bill Moyers's PBS television series on poetry in *Time* magazine, 7 March 1995] Moyers makes virtually no attempt to place the poet in a larger social context—to view poetry as a profession (or, perhaps more to the point, to analyze what it means that ours is a culture where it's all but impossible to be a professional poet). Ezra Pound once pointed out that history without economics is bunk. To which one might add that poetry without economics—without some sense of the ebb and flow of the megamercantile society surrounding the poet—is bunk too.

h)* [From a discussion in a philosophy class] Abortion is not murder. The soul does not enter the body until the first breath is taken. Up to this point, the fetus is a biological entity only.

i)* [From a comment on an article that appeared in the *National Geographic*, November 1999, which declared the Archaeraptor Fossil to be "a true missing link in the complex chain that connects dinosaurs to birds"] How did the *National Geographic* come to publish the fraud with such fanfare? This was due to the fossil's origins being cloaked in mystery since it was discovered in China, and to there being insufficient time to have the article peer-reviewed [reviewed by experts in the field].

j)   [Odysseus in the *Odyssey*, Book 7, 215] For nothing in the world is so shamelessly demanding as a man's confounded stomach. However afflicted he may be and sick at heart, it calls for attention so loudly that he is bound to obey it.

k)   [Pierre Théberge, the organizer of an exhibit of automobiles at the Montreal Museum of Fine Arts in 1995] In design circles the automobile is still something of an "orphan" because it has been looked upon as essentially an outgrowth of technological development.

l)   [Gene Laczniak and Patrick Murphy, in *Ethical Marketing Decisions*, Boston: Allyn & Bacon, 1993, p. 263] A final argument that can be made for televised political advertising is that it motivates voters. TV advertising is thought to reach and vitalize individuals who otherwise might not participate in the election.

m) [From *The Calgary Herald*, Opinion, "Lessons on obese kids,"2 November 2010, www.calgaryherald.com, p. A12] Parents, schools, teachers and society all have a role to play in getting kids off the couch and stopping children from becoming overweight. Overweight otherwise leads to obesity, which can soon turn into a lifelong sentence.

n)   Cigarettes are the greatest public health problem we have, and the most flagrant example of drug pushing, since most tobacco is pushed on teenagers, who are led by advertising into thinking it's cool to smoke.

o)* [A sign on a public bench] You just proved Bench Advertising Works.

p)   [From a radio advertisement for a Subaru four-wheel drive] Have you ever seen an agile dog on two legs? For better agility and handling, see your Subaru dealer today.

2.   We have already seen that arguments tend to reflect the values of the times in which they are constructed. We have included two advertisements below. The first is an advertisement for "Motor Bus Lines of America" that appeared during the Second World War. The second is a contemporary advertisement promoting the use of Amorim natural cork stopper in wine bottles. Analyze and dress the arguments proposed in each case. How does each reflect the consciousness of the time in which it appeared?

© American Bus Association

Illustration 6.14   "To keep the flames of America burning . . ."

Illustration 6.15 "Save Miguel"

3. The following is a controversial advertisement featuring Pamela Anderson, created by PETA (People for the Ethical Treatment of Animals). It created much controversy and was banned in Montreal, where the official in charge of issuing permits with the city's television and film office defended this decision, writing that "We, as public officials representing a municipal government, cannot endorse this image of Ms. Anderson. It is not so much controversial as it goes against all principles public organizations are fighting for in the everlasting battle of equality between men and women." In light of this controversy:

a) Dress, diagram, and analyze the visual argument the advertisement presents (explain the elements of visual meaning).

b) Dress, analyze and diagram the city's argument against it.

c) Construct your own argument supporting one side of the debate or the other.

d) Dress, analyze and diagram your own argument.

Illustration 6.16 "All animals have the same parts"

4. Pick a topic (on women's or men's health, government debt, the environment, human rights, poverty, etc. and construct an argument using visual images you create of find on the web, in a newspaper, on YouTube, etc.).

 For more online exercises, review questions, and quizzes related to the material in this chapter, please go to www.oupcanada.com/GoodReasoning5e

DEFINITIONS:
SAYING WHAT YOU MEAN

In Chapter 1, we discussed the principles of communication that arguments depend on. In this chapter, we take our study of language further, discussing it in the context of the issues that arise when we construct or analyze an argument. To this end, we look at:

► vagueness and ambiguity
► equivocation and verbal disputes
► extensional and intensional definitions
► ways to ensure that you express what you mean.

We have all been interrupted in the course of an argument by someone who asks us to clarify something we said. The point or term that is obscure may have seemed perfectly clear to us. We may be surprised to find that our meaning has not been communicated in the way that we expected.

When this occurs in conversation, we can explain ourselves. The problem is more acute if the confusion arises in an argument we are trying to communicate in writing. In an ongoing exchange, we may have the opportunity to clarify our meaning, but there will be many circumstances in which we have only one opportunity to convey what we mean. This chapter is designed to teach you how to communicate clearly and precisely in argumentative contexts. It explains some of the common ways in which meanings are lost or misconstrued and how to avoid such problems. You need to keep these concerns in mind when you are constructing arguments (especially written arguments) and be able to discuss them when you analyze and critique other people's reasoning.

The principal way to make meanings clearer is through definitions that explain important terms we use. The ability to construct definitions, as well as to evaluate them, is a crucial skill in the good reasoner's repertoire. This is especially important because many disputes are founded on arguments about the meaning of some term or concept or the way it should be defined. We recognize the significance of definitions in good reasoning by making definitions and the arguments that hinge on them a central topic in this chapter.

1   Using Words Precisely

Human cloning is an important contemporary issue. Suppose you are involved in a discussion of the rights and wrongs of cloning. Imagine that someone sitting across the table from you declares that "human cloning contravenes the most fundamental requirements of reverence in dealing with human life." You want to evaluate this statement. As you will appreciate from our earlier discussion of the criteria for judging strong arguments, your evaluation will turn on the question of whether this premise—that "human cloning contravenes the most fundamental requirements of reverence dealing with human life"—is a good reason for the conclusion that "human cloning is wrong."

But we cannot decide whether a premise is acceptable unless we are clear about what it means. To this end, we must isolate the different terms and phrases used and be sure we understand them. In the case in question, we need to ask what is meant by "the fundamental requirements of reverence" and, more specifically, what is meant by "reverence." The answers to these questions may lie elsewhere in an arguer's discussion, so we must pay careful attention to all that has been said. We cannot evaluate whether a particular statement is a reasonable premise—or conclusion—in an argument if we cannot establish what that statement or one of its component terms means.

In approaching the words used in arguments, and in using them ourselves, we need to remember that languages change over time. Dictionaries are constantly updated because language is fluid and the meanings of words shift. New words are coined, and old words acquire additional meanings or different meanings. Consider, to take one example, how the evolution of computer technology has affected our language, introducing terms like "software" and "Internet" as well as new meanings for old terms like "crash" or "mouse" or "web." It is important to remember the fluid nature of language when you are reviewing the arguments of arguers from previous generations: it would be wrong to artificially impose on their arguments the meanings that words have for us today.

In contexts in which our own use of language may be misunderstood, we need to take steps to avoid this possibility. If we are using a term in an idiosyncratic way that does not correspond to a standard meaning of the term, we need to say so. If there are different uses of a term that need to be distinguished, we should make clear which use we are employing. If our use differs from that of an author we are quoting, we must note the distinction. What we require of ourselves and other arguers is precision in the use of terms.

Euphemisms and Emotional Language

Euphemisms substitute mild and indirect ways of speaking for ways that might seem blunt and harsh. They may neutralize remarks that would otherwise be filled with emotion. Many euphemistic words and phrases play an integral role in our ordinary vocabulary. In the interests of social grace or politeness, they function as inoffensive substitutes for coarse, harsh, or inelegant expressions. We say that someone "passed away" instead of saying that the person "died." We do not say that a veterinarian "kills" a family pet but that she "puts it to sleep." Euphemisms of this sort are in many circumstances acceptable. Insofar as they soften a harsh reality, they may be advantageous, as long as they do not muddle someone's intended meaning.

In contrast, there are times when meanings and claims are distorted by the use of euphemisms. Political activists often accuse politicians and the military of using intentionally misleading euphemisms to soften the images of weapons and their effects. Think of what is not being said when a term like "collateral damage" is employed to describe the consequences of a military engagement. Or consider how the impact of bombs on civilian marketplaces in Iraq is lessened by referring to such incidents as "sectarian differences." The term "smart bomb" may attempt to promote a positive attitude to this kind of device (for we admire things that are smart) and suggest that it is much less likely to cause unwarranted destruction than other explosives. The American philosopher and peace activist John Somerville argued that the term "nuclear war" is fundamentally misleading and proposed that we replace it with the term "omnicide," formed by analogy with terms like "infanticide," "fratricide," and "genocide" to capture nuclear war's capacity to kill all things. According to Somerville, nuclear war is as different from other kinds of war as murder and suicide are from disease, and we invite confusing conclusions if we treat it as something that is comparable (John Somerville, "Nuclear 'war' is omnicide" *The Churchman*, Vol. 196, January, 1982, pp. 10–12).

Other euphemisms that may be disturbing include terms used to refer to business notions like "casual labour" and "downsizing" (sometimes called "rightsizing"). Such terms are, critics argue, specifically designed to allow us to talk about important moral and social issues without properly addressing the dire consequences they can have. Novelist George Orwell famously expressed these sentiments in "Politics and the English language," where he wrote that "political language has to consist largely of euphemisms, question-begging and sheer cloudy vagueness. . . . Such phraseology is needed if one wants to name things without calling up [disquieting] mental pictures of them."

In contrast to euphemism, which softens or neutralizes emotional content, *emotional language* consists of words or phrases infused with an emotional charge. This kind of language is often used by arguers who are strongly attached to the issues they address. In many cases, a hasty emotional response to an issue is unintentionally substituted for a careful argument. When the Supreme Court of Canada ruled that homosexual people must be included under Alberta's human rights legislation, a group calling itself Canada's Civilized Majority attacked the court's decision in a full-page advertisement in a national newspaper. The advertisement railed against "the barbaric agenda of militant homosexuals" and accused the Supreme Court of imposing a "bathhouse morality."

Many readers who thought the advertisement crossed the line of tolerance and good taste wrote letters to the editor attacking the newspaper involved for agreeing to run it. But many of these letters used language that was just as incendiary as the original advertisement, saying that the advertisement was guilty of a "horrifying viciousness and bigotry"; a "hysterical and sensationalistic tone" that indicated "outright fear-mongering and exploitation"; and a "misinformed and hateful rhetoric." In each of these instances, emotionally charged phrases were used instead of reasoned argument.

Perhaps the authors of these letters believed, as writers overcome with rage or dismay often do, that the viciousness, hysteria, or exploitation was obvious. You will see that this sort of appeal to obviousness cannot resolve the issue if you consider the fact that the sentiments of outrage expressed by those who placed the original advertisement were equally strong. The lesson to learn from such examples is that emotional language is no substitute for argument. Indeed, it invites problems and confusion, for it tends to violate the principle that we should use language with precision. For instance, in the example we have just noted, there is no precise meaning to such expressions as: "a barbaric agenda," "bathhouse morality," "horrifying viciousness and bigotry," "outright fear-mongering and exploitation," and so on. It might be possible to explain some of these terms, but no serious effort was made to do so, and they are, therefore, a weakness rather than a strength of the remarks expressed. In this way, emotion-laden language is, like the use of unacceptable euphemisms, another obstacle to the clear communication of arguments.

EXERCISE   7A

1. The following are two responses to the Massachusetts Supreme Court ruling of February 2004 that found restricting gay couples to civil unions and not full marriage rights would violate the state's constitution. Identify all the terms or phrases that have emotional import. Is the use of emotion legitimate?

    a)* "This decision is on an order of magnitude that is beyond the capacity of words. The court has tampered with society's DNA, and the consequent mutation will reap unimaginable consequences for Massachusetts and our nation.—senior trial attorney, American Family Association Center for Law and Policy."

    b) "It is reprehensible for left-wing judges, such as these four radical Massachusetts judges, to disregard the will of the overwhelming majority of the American people who believe that marriage is only the union of one man and one woman. Traditional marriage is one of the last obstacles to the complete normalization of homosexuality in America.—president, Christian Coalition of America."

2. The following is from an advertisement in *Mother Jones* magazine (June/July 1987). Provide a fully supplemented diagram of the argument it contains. Circle all the terms within it that might need to be discussed or defined. How might someone argue that this is a case of overly emotional language? How might someone argue that it is, in fact, exposing an illegitimate use of language?

In America Violence Starts Young!

Of all western countries only in the United States are helpless infant boys routinely strapped to a board, spread-eagled and without anesthesia their foreskins are clamped, slit, torn, crushed and sliced off while they scream and struggle from the diabolical torture, usually vomiting and excreting before losing consciousness. The bloody stumps that result from this mutilation are open to constant irritation from hot, urine-soaked diapers and faeces. Infection is an obvious problem in addition to the needless accidents where too much foreskin is removed or a tiny penis is totally destroyed. For lists of medical pamphlets and groups working to stop this savage custom, send a stamped, self-addressed envelope to CIRCUMCISION IS CHILD ABUSE.

2   Vagueness and Ambiguity

The use of words or phrases that are vague or ambiguous is one common way in which arguers fail to be clear and precise. In assessing other arguers' arguments, we need to be able to recognize vagueness and ambiguity. In creating our own arguments, we need to make sure that we construct arguments that are not undermined by either.

A word or phrase is *vague* if it has no clearly specifiable meaning for an audience. Words like "the American dream," "existential situation," "conservative," and "liberal," when used without qualification, are vague terms. When we use such terms, we allow our audience to read into them whatever meanings they prefer, and we run the risk of miscommunication.

Vagueness can affect whole sentences as well as single words and phrases. A professor who was asked to provide support for a student requesting more funding for research that had been prematurely terminated explained that "the student had legitimate problems related to the maintenance and survival of his experimental organisms." What this meant would not have been clear to the review committee if the student had not provided his own straightforward explanation: "My fish died." Similarly, advertisers may purposely use vagueness in their copy. A claim that a laundry detergent "gets clothes up to 50 per cent cleaner" appears to promise a great deal until we realize how difficult it is to understand precisely what the company has promised: for what does "50 per cent cleaner" mean? Cleaner than what? And how is the 50 per cent to be measured?

It is important to try to resolve instances of vagueness when preparing an argument diagram, which should present premises and conclusions in clear language that remains true to the intended meaning of the arguer. Sometimes an "initial vagueness" can be resolved by reading the context in which the argument arises, including any previous argumentation on the issue. If so, the argument has been expressed in a weak way, but our analysis of it will not be seriously hindered. In contrast, cases in which the claims of an arguer and the context cannot help us determine a clear meaning of a term or phrase involve serious weaknesses in the argument. In the most difficult cases, we will not be able to evaluate the argument. The problem is less serious when the vagueness is restricted to a sub-argument in the reasoning. Then we may be able to proceed with our evaluation.

Like vagueness, ambiguity may undermine our ability to fully evaluate an argument. Words or phrases are *ambiguous* when they can have more than one specifiable meaning in the context in which they arise. An "amphibole" (also called a syntactic ambiguity) is an ambiguity that results from a confusing grammatical construction. A person who says "Last night I shot a burglar in my pyjamas" has said something ambiguous because the structure of the sentence makes it unclear whether the shooter or the burglar was wearing the pyjamas. Other cases of ambiguity (called semantic ambiguity) result when words with multiple meanings are not used carefully. In puns, such ambiguity is intentional. The joke "I don't see how it's possible to have a civil war. I've never seen enemies being civil to each other" elicits a smile because "civil" in this context can be interpreted to mean something that takes place between citizens of the same country or the act of being polite.

Equivocation and Verbal Disputes

Although ambiguity is indispensable in entertainment and creative writing, it is usually a problem in argumentative discourse. When an arguer conflates two or more meanings of a term or phrase, we charge them with the fallacy equivocation. Consider the following argument:

> Since, as scientists tell us, energy neither comes into being nor goes out of being, there should not be an energy crisis.

The problem with this reasoning lies in the meaning of the term "energy." In its first occurrence, it refers to the total amount of energy in the universe. In its second, it refers to our diminishing supplies of gas and oil and electricity. The premise—that scientists tell us that energy neither comes into being nor goes out of being—does not support the conclusion that there shouldn't be an energy crisis, because the two statements refer to different things. The ambiguity of the word "energy" makes the confusion possible.

Consider a second example:

> Science has discovered many laws of nature. This surely constitutes proof that there is a God, for wherever there are laws, there must be a lawgiver. Consequently, God must exist as the Great Lawgiver of the universe.

We can diagram this argument as follows:

P1 =   Science has discovered many laws of nature.
P2 =   Wherever there are laws, there must be a lawgiver.
 C =   [Science shows us that] God, the Great Lawgiver of the universe, must exist.

This argument might seem convincing until you think carefully about the meaning of

the word "laws," which is used in two different senses. The laws laid down by a legislative body or lawgiver are "prescriptive" laws. In contrast, "descriptive" laws identify regularities or patterns in the world. Once we make this distinction, we can see that P1 holds only if the word "laws" is interpreted to mean "descriptive laws." But P2 holds only if "laws" is interpreted to mean "prescriptive laws." The conclusion seems to follow only because the arguer equivocates on these two different meanings of the word "laws."

When a group of arguers is involved in discussion or debate, an equivocation may take the form of a verbal dispute, which can be contrasted with a *real dispute*. In a real dispute, the parties to the dispute must utter opposing statements. In a verbal dispute, the disputants appear to disagree, but this is an illusion that reflects different meanings they assign to some key term or phrase. What appears to be a real difference is only verbal.

We have already noted an instance of a verbal dispute at the beginning of this book. You will remember that we began with an account of Monty Python's "argument room" skit. At one point in the exchange, the paying client and the professional arguer enter into a long debate about whether they have had an argument. The professional arguer maintains they have; the client maintains they have not. It is unclear from the discussion that they really disagree because they are, as we have already noted, using the word "argument" in two different ways. According to one meaning (used by the professional arguer), an argument is any disagreement. According to the other (used by the client), an argument is a connected series of propositions, which includes premises and a conclusion. In such a context, there is, despite the emotion that accompanies the disagreement, no genuine dispute. The arguers agree about what is going on in the argument room—it appears otherwise only because they have decided to use the word "argument" in two contrasting ways.

Of course, verbal disputes often take place in more serious contexts. Imagine two people arguing whether euthanasia (popularly known as "mercy killing") should be legalized. One maintains that euthanasia is morally justifiable because it allows terminally ill patients the opportunity to die with dignity rather than prolonging their lives with life-support machines. The other argues that you cannot disguise the reality with euphemisms, and that euthanasia is morally wrong because it is, in the final analysis, nothing less than murder. In this context, the opposing conclusions—"Euthanasia is morally justifiable" and "Euthanasia is not morally justifiable"—appear to signify a real dispute. This is possible, but not necessarily so. The first person may be talking about "passive" euthanasia, which occurs when one withholds extraordinary systems of life support (thereby allowing the individual to die), while the second may be talking about "active" euthanasia, which involves a direct intervention like the injection of a lethal drug. In such a context, there is no real dispute—not because we cannot debate the morality of either type of euthanasia but because the two disputants are focusing on different aspects of the issue.

Like disputes, agreements may be merely verbal. A real agreement must be built upon a mutual understanding of crucial terms and phrases. Two individuals who think they share a belief in "capitalism" may in fact disagree because one of them believes in a completely unrestrained capitalism that leaves no room for government intervention in the economy, while the other believes in a capitalism that allows government regulation in order to establish minimum wages and protect the environment.

Even in a debate, disputants may mistakenly think that they agree on the meaning of key terms they use. Creationists and evolutionists seem to be speaking the same language when they debate whether there is any "proof" of the theory of evolution. An evolutionist who puts forward proofs may be perplexed by a creationist who denies that what has been put forward constitutes proof. In such a case, the assumption that the two disputants use the term "proof" in the same way may be mistaken. Some Christian groups use the word "proof" to mean a "proof with holy text." According to this idea, any scientific notion, if it is to be considered credible, must be backed by Scripture. When a creationist of this ilk says that there is "no proof" of evolution, they may mean that there are no Scriptures that support it. The evolutionist who claims that there is proof may, on the other hand, mean that evolution is supported by the biological and geological evidence available. The point here is not to comment on the merits of the positions in the dispute but to recognize how confusion over a central term like "proof" can impede understanding in the debate itself.

Avoiding vagueness and ambiguity in our own disputes is not easily accomplished. Like other aspects of good reasoning, it demands an ability to view one's own work from a different perspective. Often, we are so close to our own arguments that we are unable to appreciate the confusions they may foster. We do not see the vagueness and the ambiguity in what we have said or written.

You can combat such problems by preparing drafts of arguments, setting them aside, and coming back to them. A few days later, you may have achieved a little distance and can probably read your work with a more critical eye. In doing so, ask yourself whether your intended meaning is clear and unambiguous. Clarify your meaning where necessary. Do not worry about implausible meanings that might be artificially attributed to your remarks. Good reasoners will be judicious and charitable and will not assign outlandish interpretations to what you say.

For your own part, you should not spend your time attributing implausible meanings to someone else's arguments. Focus on plausible meanings, and in cases where more than one might be applied, try to resolve the ambiguity by looking at the context and considering your knowledge of the author and the background. In cases in which you cannot resolve the ambiguity, you will want to charge the arguer with a problematic argument or claim, depending on the impact the ambiguity has on their argument and your ability to evaluate it. It may be possible to continue by offering alternative evaluations of an argument that depend on the different ways existing ambiguities might be resolved. In such cases, you will still want to say that there is a major problem with the argument.

EXERCISE   7B

1. Are the following claims vague or ambiguous or both? If vague, explain why. If ambiguous, state whether it is a case of amphibole (syntactic ambiguity) or semantic ambiguity, and provide at least two alternative interpretations.

    a) [First sentence in a report in the *Toronto Star*, 20 August 1998, p. A2] Bank tellers are harder on low-income Canadians than bank presidents.

    b)* Jennifer is a wealthy woman.

c) [Headline from the *Portola Reporter*, quoted in *The New Yorker* magazine, 15 November 15 2010, p. 93] Marijuana eradication calls for joint help.

d) "The best investigator is one who will stop at nothing," Holmes asserted confidently.

e)* Vitamin E is good for aging people.

f) [From Cleveland Amory, *The Cat Who Came for Christmas*, 1988, Madison, WI: Demco Media] I, for example, am a terrible dream rememberer.

g) Democracy is government by the people.

h) A recent survey shows that teenagers are smoking and drinking less than they were four years ago.

i) [Sign in a shop window] Watch repairs here.

j) Harper pledges to shrink government.

k)* [From Shakespeare's *Henry VI*, Act 1, Scene 4] The duke yet lives that Henry shall depose.

l) [A politician responds to the demand that he apologize for calling a colleague a liar.] I called him a liar. It is true, and I am sorry for it.

m) [From an essay on donor conception by Margaret Somerville in *The Globe and Mail*, 10 July 2010, discussing the need to ensure safety in such procedures] And that safety goes beyond . . . only physical harm to the future child and includes existential harm to him or her, and risk and harm to our societal values and ethics.

2. The following "medical bloopers" circulated on a list claiming that "this varicose vein of anguished English has in no way been doctored." In each case, diagnose the problem (vagueness, ambiguity, or something else) and, if possible, rewrite the medical comment to make it clear and precise.

a)* The patient has been depressed ever since she began seeing me in 1983.

b) Patient has chest pain if she lies on her left side for over a year.

c) Discharge status: Alive but without permission.

d) By the time he was admitted, his rapid heart had stopped, and he was feeling better.

e)* The patient refused an autopsy.

f) The patient's past medical history has been remarkably insignificant with only a 40-pound weight gain in the past three days.

g) The patient left the hospital feeling much better except for her original complaints.

h) The bugs that grew out of her urine were cultured in the ER and are not available.

3. Each of the following claims has two plausible senses that might easily give rise to equivocation or a verbal dispute. To practice avoiding such problems, distinguish the senses and express each interpretation in a way that makes it clearer than the original.

a)* Convicted criminals must be made to pay for their crimes.

b) The good life is a life of pleasure.

c)* Life continues after death.

d) The universe is a giant thought.

e)* Enabling legislation should be introduced to make euthanasia possible.

f) Genetic experimentation must be restricted.

g)   Rape trials are unfair to victims.

h)   I am free to act as I choose.

i)   Machines can think.

j)   The end of the world is in sight.

4.   The following arguments involve instances of ambiguity, vagueness, or equivocation. Diagram the arguments, and discuss the seriousness of the problem with language. Are we able to use context to resolve the vagueness or ambiguity?

a)* Every society is, of course, repressive to some extent. As Sigmund Freud pointed out, repression is the price we pay for civilization.

b)   [This argument refers to the debate over the use of human embryos in research to find cures for serious illnesses that affect many people. Concerns are raised when embryos used in this kind of research are destroyed.] As a moral being, I cannot understand the debate. We all agree that it is the potential of the embryo that is important. It should have the potential to help other people through its role in research. It can liberate millions of lives that might be helped by the results of the research.

c)   [Excerpted from "Keeping up the patriotism," *The Gazette: Western's Daily Student Newspaper*, 10 March 2005] Canadian sovereignty is the most important thing we must fight for so that we can maintain our diverse values and cultures. . . .
I actually prefer Quebec culture to Ontario. Montreal is the soul of Canada. Its rich history is a key part of what it means to be Canadian. Let us not forget the loyal Canadians from Montreal Island who saved our country in the 1995 Referendum.
     Doing more for ourselves or going our own way does not imply unilateral action. Patriotism is not always doing what is practical. It is not about bowing to those stronger than us for economic gain or protection. Patriotism is an ideal we must defend to preserve our freedoms and what is uniquely special to Canada.
     Although diverse, we do have shared values. We are a peacekeeping society rather than a warlike society. Those that sacrifice the Canadian ideal for the easy, practical route of self-gain are collaborators. Those of the collaborator mentality will never understand the patriotic ideal.

d)   [From the copy on the packaging of Snyder's of Hanover pretzels] Nearly a century of pride goes into every batch of Snyder's of Hanover bakery pretzels. You can taste it in our natural ingredients. You can feel it in each carefully crafted shape. And you can see it in our continued dedication to baking the world's best tasting, most innovative new pretzel varieties.

e)   [This is adapted from Rex Murphy, "Selling something, Dr Suzuki?," *The Globe and Mail*, 28 September 2002. Mr Murphy is responding to remarks made by David Suzuki at a press conference hosted by Canadian doctors advocating the ratification of the Kyoto Protocol. Among the claims advanced was that 16,000 Canadian deaths are caused each year by global warming] Dr Suzuki makes claims that sound scientific, but this is something we shouldn't buy. 16,000 deaths a year is an "advocacy number." A number like this doesn't have much to do with science. It is better compared to a phrase like "more dentists recommend this toothpaste." When someone uses advocacy numbers they are out to sell a cause rather than reveal a scientific finding. Advocacy numbers are part of an advertising culture that doesn't do investigations; they are argumentative quickies that make the sale without going into the details and complications and labour that a real investigation would require.

f)   [From Shinichiro Morinaga, "The current debate on human embryo research and human dignity," *Journal of Philosophy and Ethics in Health Care and Medicine*, No. 3, pp. 3–23, July 2008, p. 20] A "crime against mankind" is a crime against the human status, or human nature itself. In other words, an attack on mankind's diversity, which is such an important characteristic of the "human status" that, if mankind did not have it, terms such as mankind and human nature would become meaningless, that is, it is a threat to human existence.

3   Formulating Definitions

Two recent reports in the media illustrate the importance of definitions to how we live and understand the world as well as their potential controversial nature. The Australian journal *InvestorDaily* (21 April 2011) announced the opposition of the National Institute of Accountants to an attempt by the financial services sector to establish a legal definition of "financial planner." In the eyes of the accountants, this was an attempt to exclude other professionals (like accountants) from providing financial advice. In response, a spokesperson for the Financial Planners Association argued that the lack of legislation containing a restrictive definition of "financial planner" had allowed many non-professionals to offer advice, leading to a lack of consumer confidence in the industry when that advice proved bad.

Or consider the following image:

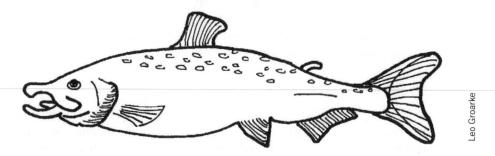

Leo Groarke

Illustration 7.1   Fish?

Is this a fish? The answer may seem obvious, but a recent controversy errupted when the United States Food and Drug Administration (FDA) chose to place new genetically modified salmon under the label (and hence definition) of a drug rather than treating it as food. In deciding to regulate the salmon—designed in a laboratory on Prince Edward

Island—using the rules for veterinary drugs, the FDA thus subjected it to a different set of evaluations than those which govern new food products. Consumer groups opposing this worry that such regulations do not allow for the scientific study of food-safety issues surrounding the human consumption of fish. So, is it a drug or a fish?

Or consider the following: In an interview about his book *Animal Rights and Wrongs* (*Philosophy Now*, June 2000, p. 36), the British philosopher Roger Scruton criticizes those who refer to "animal rights":

> [W]hen people refer to animal rights, either they are making a mistake about the nature of animals, or they are using the word "rights" in a very loose way to refer to our duties towards animals. If animals really have rights in the way we do, then they have to be fully part of the moral realm, the realm of negotiation. Therefore, they must be accorded not only the benefits of morality, but also the burdens, which are huge. Cats would have to be treated as serial killers, for a start. And we don't want to inflict the penalties on them that that would imply.

Scruton's remarks can be interpreted as an instance of the argument scheme called an **argument by analogy**, which we discuss in Chapter 11. For the present, we are interested in the way his argument depends on a particular understanding of the key term "rights." He assumes an account that ties rights to responsibilities that are tied to negotiation. On the basis of this definition, he argues that animals cannot have rights.

Such examples illustrate the central role that definitions play in many arguments. This is one reason why a good reasoner must understand the different kinds of definition and the ways in which they can be used. Another reason is the need to use definitions to resolve problems of vagueness and ambiguity that we saw earlier in the chapter.

The purpose of a definition is to enable your reader or audience to understand quickly and precisely how you are using a particular term, and to point out how a term is generally used. When you are writing and when you are attempting to make explicit the meaning of a term used by another author, you should recognize that there are several kinds of definition. We will look at some principal kinds and then discuss how they can be employed in constructing arguments.

Two Different Kinds of Definition

In the example from Roger Scruton's argument he makes implicit reference to the way in which we naturally classify things. One of the principal ways in which we use language is to create or refer to categories and assign things to them. In this way, we decide what things mean. Some of the meanings we confront are conventional. That is, they are widely used and understood by speakers and writers in a broad community. Groups can have their conventions, but so too does society at large. Dictionaries tend to capture the conventional uses of words and modify their definitions as those conventions change. Other meanings might be described as non-conventional. Here a word or phrase is given a specific meaning for a purpose. When someone stipulates how a word is being used in a particular context, they implicitly acknowledge that their meaning may not be conventional. Scruton is assuming a conventional meaning for "rights," but he is insisting that the subcategories of "animal rights" and "human rights" do not necessarily coincide, so we cannot transfer the meaning of one to the other.

When we use definitions in everyday contexts (rather than as lexicographers), we are indicating something about what a word or phrase means. We can do this in two principal ways: by giving an extensional definition or an intensional one.

Extensional definitions clarify a term by identifying members of the class of things it names. The following are examples of extensional definitions:

"That," as one points to people engaged in a particular activity, "is a game."
"Humanistic studies" means "studies in language, literature, philosophy, fine arts, religion, and music."

Extensional definitions may be constructed by pointing to or naming instances of the things to which the term applies, as in our first example, or, as in the second case, by noting how the larger class of things comprises a series of representative subclasses.

Intensional definitions clarify the meaning of a term by identifying the essential qualities that make something a member of the class of things it names—that is, by reference to its meaning, or "intension." The following are examples of intensional definitions:

"Rubella" is a measles-like disease that is sometimes called "German measles."
"Scapula" is a bone in the shoulder.
"Nom de plume" is a pseudonym used by a writer.

These are all instances of the simplest form of **intensional definition**, which substitutes a familiar term for an unfamiliar one. By invoking the familiar term, the definition explains to an audience the essential characteristics of the thing in question.

In formal situations, where we take pains to ensure that something is defined as precisely as possible, we may employ an intensional definition by *genus* and *differentia*. It designates the class to which a thing belongs (its *genus*) and the characteristics that distinguish it from other members of the class (its *differentia*). The following are definitions by genus and differentia:

A "chair" is "a piece of furniture (genus) designed for the purpose of seating one person and providing a support for the back (differentia)."

"Happiness" is "a state of mind (genus) characterized by the satisfaction that one has achieved what one deems to be worthwhile and by the absence of mental anguish (differentia)."

In each of these examples, the definition identifies the larger class to which something belongs and then specifies the way in which it is distinguished from other members of this class. Though they can be difficult to construct, the details that definitions by genus and differentia require can make them the best way to clarify a contentious term or phrase.

We can easily see how conventional meanings will be captured in both extensional and intensional definitions, since the extension conveys the boundaries of the intension. But this can also work for non-conventional meanings that we use in particular contexts. We may, for example, want to define a "hero" as "someone who performs a routine everyday task on which we all depend" (intension) and then point to a garbage collector or police officer as examples (extension). The difficulty with these cases is that it can be difficult to judge where the extension begins and ends. But if the intentional definition is clearly given, that should help us in such a judgement.

In most circumstances, conventional understandings suffice. But there will be times when conventional meanings do not fit your precise purpose, and you will need to indicate that you are using a term or phrase in a very specific way. In a sociology paper, you may want to restrict the meaning of "the unemployed" to "those people who are actively seeking employment" and define "actively seeking employment" as "making at least two inquiries a week." In such circumstances, we stipulate the meaning of a term or phrase.

Such definitions can help you avoid vagueness, ambiguity, and verbal disputes. Even if your audience—an instructor, perhaps—does not agree with your definition, he or she will be able to better understand what you mean because you have explicitly stated how you intend a key term or phrase to be understood. "Democracy" normally means "government by the people either directly or through elected representatives." But you may want to use the term in a more restricted sense. You may use an extensional definition: "By the term 'democracy' I mean the kind of rule by the people found in Canada and the US, not in Korea and Singapore." Or you could use an intensional definition: "By the term 'democracy' I mean rule by the people through the representatives chosen by popular votes in free multi-party elections." The most important thing is that you inform your audience that the definition you are providing has a non-conventional meaning, so that they understand how you are using it.

Many arguments and remarks are difficult to understand because authors use familiar words as key terms in specific ways without stipulating their meaning—often because they take their meaning to be self-evident. Consider the claim "The law of the church forbids the marriage of priests." Suppose that the context does not make it clear whether the marriage of priests is forbidden by the church's understanding of the will of God or by the church's administration for strictly practical purposes. The former circumstance would make the non-marriage of priests a "divine law," the latter an "ecclesiastical law." The claim, then, is subject to two interpretations: (1) divine law forbids the marriage of priests, and (2) ecclesiastical law forbids the marriage of priests. Because the alternative meanings pivot on the single term "law," this is the kind of situation that could easily give rise to an equivocation or a verbal dispute.

The different kinds of strength that characterize these definitions dictate the kinds of contexts in which they might best be used. Extensional definitions link our words and our arguments to the world of experience. If terms did not have extensions, the definitions in our dictionaries would be circular, for they would, in every case, define terms by means of other terms that had no foothold in reality. In view of such considerations, we can use an extensional definition to anchor the meaning of an important word in the world beyond our language. On the other hand, an extensional definition is rarely able to indicate every application of the term defined. For practical reasons, it can, in most cases, do no more than indicate a sample of the things included in a term's extension. A large and representative list would be unwieldy. And even if we provided such a list, this definition would not identify the common features that establish that the items it lists are included in the extension.

Because it focuses on the essential features shared by those things in a term's extension, an intensional definition that defines a term in a single, relatively simple, well-constructed sentence is, in many cases, the clearest and most convenient way to proceed. If you are unsure as to how you should construct such a definition, you might try a definition by genus and differentia. Begin by specifying the kind of thing you are defining, and proceed to an account of the differences between it and other things of the same sort.

In constructing your own arguments, be prepared to define key terms, especially unfamiliar and technical terms, as well as terms that are vague or ambiguous or ones that are used in a way that deviates from conventional usage. This task may sound more formidable than it is. Normally, the number of terms that require definition is not large. The vast majority of the words you use will be common ones that have a meaning that your audience will appreciate. Even in cases where you use words with several meanings, the context will usually make the intended meaning clear.

Definition through Argument

Moreover, on some occasions, you may construct arguments that have the intent of arguing about a definition, whether it be a modified sense of a term, assigning a certain object or event under a specific definition, or introducing a new term altogether. The astronomers of the International Astronomical Union (IAU), which has been the official naming body for astronomy since 1919, created controversy simply by modifying the definition of "planet" during their general assembly in 2006. The revised definition had the result of changing the extension of the term by removing Pluto and designating it under the category of "dwarf planet."

Arguments involving or advancing definitions are among some of the more controversial that we will encounter or possibly construct. In dealing with them, and in dealing with arguments that modify, debate, or introduce definitions, it is important to be clear about the adequacy of the definitions involved. To that end, our discussion of some of the central types of definition should assist you in making your judgements.

EXERCISE   7C

Each of the following involves the use of argument to present or modify definitions or debate how something should be defined. For each example, provide a supplemented diagram, and then identify the key term being defined and the type of definition employed. Is the definition adequate?

a)* [From Robert Aunger, "What's the matter with memes?" in *Richard Dawkins: How a Scientist Changed the Way We Think*, A. Graffen and M. Ridley (eds.), Oxford University Press, p. 177] A meme, of course, is defined as the fundamental unit of a cultural transmission. From an evolutionary perspective, it plays the role in cultural change equivalent to that of the gene in biological change: as the basic unit of inheritance allowing the accumulation of adaptations. The idea is that, like a gene, a meme is a replicator. . . . Genes replicate through the duplication of DNA strands; cultural replication, or the duplication of memes, takes place through the social transmission of information.

b) [From a Letter to the Editor, *The Globe and Mail*, 2 March 2007] C.J. (Every one or no one—letter, 1 March 2007) says we are in a war against terror and must be willing to sacrifice some of our human rights until it is won. This is not a war, it will never be truly won: Therefore, a moment will never arrive when all the human rights can be reinstated. A war entails mass mobilization, battle lines and, in the end, a surrender. Resistance to terrorism has none of these. The word "war" should be used sparingly and with clear definition. We must deal with poverty, global warming, HIV and, yes, terrorism. But these are not wars. They are problems to be confronted.

c) [Commentators are constantly debating what constitutes a "just war," and reach conflict, like that begun in Afghanistan in the fall of 2001, tends to be measured against an understanding of that concept. The following is a further contribution to that discussion.] Richard Falk ("Defining a just war," *The Nation* magazine, 29 October 2001) has argued that it was the only just war since World War II because it was aimed at "neutralizing" the perpetrators of the 11 September attack on New York, political negotiation was not an option, the military force was proportionate to the provoking cause and what was needed for a military result, and force was directed only against military targets.

d) [In Jose Cibelli et al., "The first cloned human embryo" (*Scientific American*, Vol. 286, 24 November 2001, pp. 44–51), scientists from Advanced Cell Technology described the processes they used to clone early-stage human embryos—processes that put therapeutic cloning (cloning to further medical treatments) within reach. The authors of the report were acutely aware of ethical concerns that their work could provoke. They countered these concerns in part in a sidebar to the report ("The Ethical Considerations") prepared by their ethics advisory board]
[U]nlike an embryo, a cloned organism is not the result of fertilization of an egg by a sperm. It is a new type of biological entity never before seen in nature. Although it possesses some potential for developing into a full human being, this capacity is very limited. At the blastocyst stage, when the organism is typically disaggregated

to create an embryonic stem cell line, it is a ball of cells no bigger than the period at the end of this sentence. . . . It has no organs, it cannot possibly think or feel, and it has none of the attributes thought of as human. Although board members understood that some people would liken this organism to an embryo, we preferred the term "activated egg," and we concluded that its characteristics did not preclude its use in work that might save the lives of children and adults.

e) [From Owen Gingerich, "Planet politics: How I tried and failed to save Pluto," the *Boston Globe*, 2 September 2006, p. D2, http://pqasb.pqarchiver.com/boston/access/1124647021.html?FMT=ABS&date=Sep+3%2C+2006, (visited 1 February 2007) Dr Gingerich was chair of the IAU committee to investigate Pluto's planetary status] There are two distinct scientific ways to approach the problem of defining planethood. One is extrinsic, to define a planet in terms of its neighbors and its interactions with its environment. This route would select the dominant bodies in the solar system, the ones whose gravity perturbs one another.

It was the flash of insight that not only the sun holds the planets in orbit, but that each planet attracts each other one, that led Isaac Newton to the concept of *universal* gravitation. Neptune attracts Pluto, locking it into a resonant orbit so that in the time Neptune takes to round the sun three times, Pluto revolves exactly twice. But Pluto is too lightweight to have an observable effect on giant Neptune. The eight dominant heavyweights, from Mercury to Neptune, are big enough to rule their zones and swallow up most of the smaller bodies or kick them out of the way.

Choosing such dominance is a comfortable way to go when defining what constitutes a planet: While it would dismiss Pluto, it would forever place the other eight planets in an exclusive club.

An alternative way to define a planet, however, is intrinsic—that is, by the properties of the body itself, more or less independent of its environment. This is the way planetary geologists look at the problem, and pretty much the way astronomers looking at the hundred-plus planets circling other stars do. The idea of using the basic physics of the object appealed to our committee as the forward-looking way to define planets, for it could apply not only to the far stretches of the solar system, but to the objects being found around distant stars as well.

Rather than arbitrarily drawing a line in the sand that would either include or exclude Pluto, we opted to let nature pick a dividing line between planets and the hundreds of thousands of lumpy asteroids now known—nearly 140,000 numbered objects and an equal number awaiting their catalog numbers. If a body is massive enough, with enough self-gravity to pull itself into a ball, let it be planet. If it's just a lump, let it be an asteroid or a comet. . . .

In August our committee took this recommendation to Prague, to the triennial IAU [International Astronomical Union] congress. . . . The IAU thereafter defined a planet in our solar system as an object large enough to clear the smaller bodies from its orbit, a definition just murky enough to give teachers a considerable challenge to explain precisely what this means. Taking the exclusive club approach for the heavyweights, the IAU went on to create a class of "dwarf planets," including

Pluto, that by definition are not planets. To me this is a linguistic absurdity, a contradiction that could have been avoided if they had chosen to define only the eight classical planets as the basic type of planets, allowing dwarf planets to be considered planets too, albeit of a different kind.

f)   From Steve Fuller, *Dissent Over Descent: Intelligent Design's Challenge to Darwinism* (Cambridge, UK: Icon Books, 2008, pp. 44–45).

Here we must be clear what we mean by "science," which is a theoretical whole much greater than the sum of techniques needed to get by on a day-to-day basis, the *modus operandi* of every other species. All animals have sophisticated cognitive capacities for dealing intelligently with the physical world, not least by reconstructing their habitats in ways that enhance their chances of survival . . . . To be sure, scientific progress is sometimes portrayed as the distinctly human extension of this general evolutionary proclivity. But this is to miss entirely the point of science, which is to do with a *unified* understanding of *all* reality, not just the specific bits that permit specific groups reproductive advantage. Science does not make sense unless reality possesses a *depth* that eludes our normal sensory encounters with the world but can nevertheless be accessed with sufficient application under the right conditions. Thus, science presupposes the *intelligibility* of reality; that its organization, whatever its ultimate cause, is tractable to the human mind.

DEFINITIONS

- **Extensional definitions** define a term by referring to its *extension*, the group of things to which it refers.
- **Intensional definitions** define a term by referring to its *intension*, the set of characteristics that determines what it refers to.

4   Rules for Good Definitions

To help you construct definitions, we offer the following four rules that good definitions must follow.

Rule 1: The Rule of Equivalence

The defining phrase should include neither more nor less than the term being defined.

If "A" stands for the term defined and "B" for the defining phrase, then A and B must be equivalent. Those things designated by A must be the same as those things designated by B. The definition of "violin" as "a stringed musical instrument" is too broad because there are many stringed musical instruments that are not violins. The definition of "portrait" as "a large oil painting of a person's head and shoulders" is too narrow because portraits are not necessarily large and are not always done in oils. The rule of equivalence is respected in the extensional definition "*That* [pointing to a cow] is a cow" because it is understood that the extension includes all animals of this sort.

Rule 2: The Rule of Essential Characteristics

In an intensional definition, the defining phrase must specify the essential features of the thing defined, i.e. the traits that are indispensable to its being what it is, rather than accidental features.

The definition of "the moon" as "the large object in the sky that is sometimes said to be made of green cheese" satisfies the rule of equivalence (for there is only one astronomical object with this reputation), but it does not pick out the moon in a useful way because it has fastened on an aspect of it that is not particularly informative. In most contexts, we will do better to define the moon as "the earth's natural satellite, which shines at night by the sun's reflected light."

In specifying essential characteristics, keep in mind that different characteristics may be counted as essential in different contexts. In introducing a book on the history of comic strips, one might begin by defining human beings as "the only animals that read comic strips." In such a context, this may be what matters, though a similar definition of human beings would probably be unhelpful in a lecture on moral responsibility.

Rule 3: The Rule of Clarity

The defining phrase must clarify the meaning of the term defined by using words that make it readily understood by the intended audience.

Since we use definitions precisely when we want to clarify meaning, we undermine our definitions when they do not successfully explain our meaning to our intended audience. Plato's definition of "time" as "the moving image of eternity" presupposes familiarity with his theory of reality. In another context and, some would argue, even against the background of his theory, this definition of "time" violates the principle of clarity. An attempt to define "architecture" in terms of "frozen music" might suit an informal talk on the aesthetics of architecture but only if it is backed by an explanation that makes it clear how this comparison is to be understood.

The rule of clarity is often violated by arguments that make use of *circular definitions*. A circular definition defines a word in terms of the word itself or, in some cases, by using terms or phrases so similar that the meaning of the original term is not made any clearer. If someone says, "By 'human rights' I mean the rights of human beings," they can be charged with a circular definition. We need, instead, a definition like "Human rights are rights (such as freedom from unlawful imprisonment, torture, and execution) that are believed to belong to all human beings." In cases like this, the repetition of some part of the term defined is permissible, provided it will not confuse the audience. When we define a term like "isosceles triangle" or "watchdog," we will probably want to repeat the modified term ("triangle," "dog") within our definition. If the use of the term "rights" in our definition of human rights is likely to confuse our audience, then it must itself be defined, perhaps, as "something to which one has a just claim."

In some cases, circular definitions use defining phrases that include obvious synonyms and correlative phrases without properly explaining the idea that the term or its synonyms refer to. The definition "a homosexual is a gay person" uses a synonym and does not explain what a homosexual, or a gay person, is. The definition "a cause is something that produces an effect" illustrates the use of correlative terms. There may be rare contexts in which these definitions are useful (as when someone who does not speak English well understands the synonym or the correlative term but not the term defined). However, in most circumstances, these definitions will count as circular definitions.

Like synonyms, antonyms may also violate the rule of clarity. An "evil person" can be defined as "a person who is not good" and "night" as "not day," but such definitions rarely explain these notions to an unsure audience.

Rule 4: The Rule of Neutrality

The defining phrase must avoid terms heavily charged with emotion.

Earlier in this chapter, we noted the problems that arise when arguers use euphemisms and emotional language. These problems are compounded when arguers offer or assume persuasive definitions that betray ulterior motives. One violates the rule of neutrality if one defines "socialism" as "that form of government that steals wealth from energetic people and divides it among the lazy poor" or "capitalism" as "a system built on greed that ensures that the poor suffer and the rich get richer."

Constructing Good Definitions

The rules for good definition are easier to understand than to apply. In dealing with real definitions, you will find that many of them violate more than one of the rules or that the same problem might be described in terms of different rules. It can also be difficult to identify the unique, essential, and defining differentia that distinguish one group of things from the other members of a larger class.

In some cases, defining properties are not at all obvious. What are the unique defining characteristics of a "human being"? Rationality? A capacity to create symbols and communicate by means of them? A sense of moral responsibility? The ability to create and use sophisticated tools? If you see the last three of these characteristics as expressions of human rationality, where do you propose to draw the line between "higher animals," such as chimpanzees, and human beings with a very low IQ? Especially in moral contexts, where our judgements of individuals may depend on a definition, controversies surrounding the meaning of a term are common. In July 2005, Canada became the fourth country in the world to legalize same-sex marriages. The change in the status of marriage provoked much debate in the country both before and after Parliament passed the law. The previous definition of marriage, based on the British common law definition, was "the lawful union of one man and one woman to the exclusion of all others." On these terms, only two people of different sexes could legally marry. Bill C-38, also known as the Civil Marriage Act, introduced a new definition of marriage: "Marriage, for civil purposes, is the lawful union of two persons to the exclusion of all others." This expanded definition resulted in a major shift in the way a significant number of Canadians were treated.

The problems that arise when trying to define something like "human being" or "marriage" can be seen as expressions of the difficulties that arise when we try to decide the extension of important terms. Does the human embryo belong within or outside the class of "human beings"? If outside, then at what point does it become a human being? If within, is it entitled to "rights and freedoms," including the right to life, liberty, and security of the person? The bearing of these considerations on the debate surrounding human cloning is apparent.

In constructing your own definitions, and in judging those of others, remember that good definitions must recognize the audiences to which they are directed and be suitable to their intended purpose. The definition of "water" as "a liquid compound of 11.188 per cent hydrogen and 88.812 per cent oxygen by weight, which freezes at 0 and boils at 100 degrees Celsius" may be useful in an introductory science lecture, but it would be quite unserviceable in an article about sailing or about what measures to take when our bodies retain too much water.

A good arguer constructs an argument in a way that makes it clear and convincing to the intended audience. In formulating definitions, a good arguer constructs them with the same concerns in mind.

EXERCISE 7D

1. What kind of definition is each of the following?
   a) By "western Canadian provinces" I mean Saskatchewan, Alberta, and British Columbia.
   b)* A kitten is an immature cat.
   c) A textbook is the sort of thing you are now reading.
   d) A financial planner is a professional licensed to give advice on investments.
   e) "Macabre" means "gruesome."
   f) "Terrorism" is a form of violence to achieve political goals.
   g)* By "social sciences" is meant economics, history, anthropology, sociology, and psychology.
   h) The UN Security Council is a body of the United Nations charged with maintaining peace and security around the globe.
   i) By "primary caregiver" I mean that parent who bears greater responsibility for the raising of a child.
   j) An argument consists of at least two statements, one of which is a conclusion and the other a premise.
   k) An "activated egg" is a biological entity that is not the result of fertilization of an egg by a sperm.

2. What rule(s) of definition, if any, does each of the following definitions violate? In each case, explain your answer in one sentence.

    a)* Child abuse is the physical and/or psychological violence inflicted on a child as an expression of parental anger and frustration.

    b)* [The definition of "obscenity" in the Canadian Criminal Code] For the purposes of this Act, any publication a dominant characteristic of which is the undue exploitation of sex . . . .

    c)* Noon means 12 o'clock.

    d)* Nonsense is what one is speaking or writing when what one speaks or writes is devoid of all sense.

    e)* Prayer is a form of religious mumbo-jumbo.

    g)   Sonar is a system using transmitted and reflected acoustic waves.

    f)   "Terrorism" is the tactic or policy of engaging in terrorist acts.

    g)* Canada is a country that lies north of the 49th parallel.

    h)   Taxation is a form of theft in which the government acts as a criminal, victimizing citizens by taking a big bite of their income without their willing cooperation.

    i)   A circle is a geometric plane figure.

    k)   A laser printer is the pen of the contemporary scribe.

    l)* Distance is the space between two points measured by the yard.

    m)* "Terrorism" is a method of war that consists in intentionally attacking those who ought not to be attacked.

    n)   Global warming is the heating of the globe.

3. The following passages involve terms or phrases that have controversial meanings. Identify the terms or phrases in question and their importance to the arguments concerned. What kinds of definitions are given? Are the definitions given adequate? Do they respect the rules of good definitions?

    a)   [Michael Ignatieff, in "The value of toleration," *The Rushdie File*, L. Appignanesi and S. Maitland, (eds.), Fourth Estate, 1989, p. 251] In the heated competition to appear full of conviction, some liberals have taken to saying that they hold freedom sacred. This, I think, is a misuse of "sacred." If the word means anything it means something that is inviolate to criticism or rational scrutiny. Freedom is not a holy belief, nor even a supreme value. It is a contestable concept.

    b)   [From a Letter to the Editor, *The Globe and Mail*, 1 September 2007] "I am a carnivore," Jonathan Zimmerman twice proclaims in Why Is It A More Serious Crime To Kill A Dog Than Hit A Woman? (Aug. 29). If he thinks he's using the word effectively in its core sense, he's setting himself apart from the species, Homo Sapiens, to which I and most Globe readers belong.

    Mammals of the order Carnivora (cats, dogs, bears, seals, etc.) are the ones that have "powerful jaws and teeth adapted for stabbing, tearing, and eating flesh" (*Canadian Oxford Dictionary*). They have these features because they cannot survive without the specific kinds of nourishment available only from animal flesh. Humans, by contrast, can—and many do—survive on a meatless diet. True carnivores inflict cruelty and death on other creatures only out of necessity, unlike human beings.

c)* The distinguishing characteristic of a "person" is rationality: being able to reflect on one's own existence, remember one's past, and project oneself into the future. It follows from this that a person is a creature of culture, capable of sophisticated, higher-order brain activity. A person is able to enjoy art, literature, and culture. No matter what respectful status we accord to non-human primates, they will never be persons.

d) [From the law of blasphemy in England, as formulated in article 214 of *Stephen's Digest of the Criminal Law*, 9th edition, 1950] Every publication is said to be blasphemous that contains any contemptuous, reviling, scurrilous or ludicrous matter relating to God, Jesus Christ or the Bible, or the formularies of the Church of England as by law established. It is not blasphemous to speak or publish opinions hostile to the Christian religion, or to deny the existence of God, if the publication in couched in decent and temperate language. The test to be applied is as to the manner in which the doctrines are advocated and not to the substance of the doctrines themselves.

e)* [From a statement by Andrea Dworkin and Catharine MacKinnon] Pornography does not include erotica (defined as sexually explicit materials premised on equality) and it does not include *bona fide* sex education materials, or medical or forensic literature. In short, we define pornography as depicting a combination of the sexual objectification and subordination of women, often including violation and violence.

f) [Barbara Dority, in "Feminist Moralism, 'Pornography,' and Censorship," *The Humanist*, 1989, November/December, Volume 49, No. 6, pp. 8–9, p. 46] "Pornography" is the depiction of erotic behavior (as in pictures or writing) intended to cause sexual excitement.

g) [From the Vegetarian Society of the United Kingdom Limited information sheet, www.vegsoc.org/ info/definitions.html] A vegetarian is someone living on a diet of grains, pulses, nuts, seeds, vegetables and fruits with or without the use of dairy products and eggs (preferably free-range). A vegetarian does not eat any meat, poultry, game, fish, shellfish or crustacea, or slaughter by-products such as gelatine or animal fats.

h) [From "To stop terrorists we must know the roots of terrorism," *The Independent*, 19 December 2008]
In Afghanistan, women have played a key role de-escalating the violence, as they have in other conflict zones like the Balkans, Somalia and Northern Ireland. However, despite being a signatory to United Nations agreement to include women in preventing and resolving violence, Britain is reluctant to engage with what this means in practice—be it training significant numbers of police women or supporting their role in development and education.

This aversion means losing out on opportunities to deliver a powerful kind of "human security," based on addressing human needs and grievances that, if frustrated and ignored, may fuel violence.

Paul Rogers, Professor of Peace Studies at Bradford University, uses the term "liddism" to describe the current mindset. He defines this approach as "keeping the lid on things rather than acknowledging the underlying problems."

Britain's commitment to nuclear weapons, for example, stems from a belief that one day we may need to contain all kinds of unimaginable horrors and will require the ultimate in force to do so. Yet for most people the greatest threats they face are socio-economic and environmental.

4. You must define a key term for the audience you are addressing. Formulate a definition that would be appropriate for each of the following circumstances:

a) You are telling your grandparents what is meant by "social media."

b) You are explaining to your parents, who are not college or university graduates, the nature of the discipline (anthropology, sociology, etc.) in which you are majoring.

c)* You are a candidate in a forthcoming election addressing a public meeting on the merits of "liberalism."

d) You are a financial adviser speaking to a group of middle- and upper-class homemakers about "preferred shares."

e) You are explaining AIDS to a high school class.

f)* You are the keynote speaker at a convention of newspaper journalists talking about "objectivity" in reporting.

g) You are a participant at a political rally speaking to whoever will listen about "climate change."

h) You are writing a letter to the editor of your local newspaper arguing for more "international aid."

i) You are addressing an assembly of college and university students on sexual "ethics."

j) You are urging the local board of education to adopt a sabbatical policy as a measure to prevent teacher "burnout."

5   Expressing Your Intended Meaning

For a variety of reasons, you will often find yourself at a loss to grasp clearly the claim an arguer is making. The problem may be psychosocial. We noted earlier in the text how as individuals, we have different backgrounds, environmental influences, peer groups, political commitments, problems, loves, and loyalties, all of which contribute to a network of beliefs that we bring to bear on arguments we encounter. This network colours our interpretation of all arguments.

Alternatively, the problem may arise in the context of the issues discussed in this chapter. A claim will be unclear whenever the person to whom it is directed does not understand a term or phrase. Often this is because the term is vague or ambiguous. It is an author's responsibility to ensure that any key terms are clear and used consistently throughout the text. An author who shifts between two different meanings of a term is guilty of equivocation. If an author fails to stipulate a special meaning for a crucial but familiar term, you must identify alternative senses that are possible within that context. If an arguer uses an unfamiliar term without providing a definition, you will have to identify the meaning or meanings justified by the arguer's use of it, perhaps with the help of a dictionary. In your own arguments, you will want to spare your audience such frustrations by carefully considering your choice of words, by using the different kinds of definitions as appropriate, and by employing your terms consistently.

Even after you have addressed the problems of meaning that stem from an author's use of specific words and phrases, you may find that a claim is open to alternative senses or interpretations. Once you have established plausible meanings of an author's claims, you will need to determine which interpretation the author intended. This is something you can do by a process of elimination that is guided by a sense of fidelity to the text, common sense, and the principle of charity. Use whatever hints you can locate in the rest of the author's writing. If one of the plausible senses stands in blatant contradiction to what is clearly the main claim of the text, then common sense (and the principles of communication we introduced in the previous chapter) dictates that you reject it. If other interpretations appear irrelevant or trivial or uninteresting or obviously false, you should eliminate them unless you have good reason for not doing so. Eventually, you should be left with a plausible interpretation of the author's intended meaning or, perhaps, two different interpretations that could each qualify as the intended meaning.

This entire procedure should not be necessary and would not be necessary if the author had communicated clearly and precisely. The lesson for you, as you go about constructing extended units of informative and argumentative discourse, should be clear. Be willing to endure some labour pains in the process of giving birth to your claims and arguments. After you formulate a claim, think about it; ask yourself whether it says precisely what you mean or whether it can be interpreted in different ways. Be prepared to amend it—several times, if necessary. Don't be satisfied until you have a way of expressing your views that communicates exactly what you mean.

6 Summary

The focus of this chapter has been the words and phrases of which arguments are composed. Many arguments are affected by problems with language, like vagueness, ambiguity, and emotional terms. We have explored what is involved in each of these and how to recognize them. Then we have turned to treating problems with language by providing good definitions. To this end we have given an account of the basic kinds of definition and how to construct them.

MAJOR EXERCISE 7M

1. Diagram the reasoning in each of the following arguments and then, in a few paragraphs, assess the strengths and weaknesses of the language employed. Look in particular for problematic instances of vagueness, ambiguity, and emotional language. Determine whether any key terms are left undefined, and in the case of definitions provided and argued for, assess them according to the ideas in this chapter.

   a)* You can consult all the experts you like, write reports, make studies, etc., but the fact that pornography corrupts lies within the common sense of everybody. If people are affected by their environments, by the circumstances of their lives, then they certainly are affected by pornography. The mere nature of pornography makes it impossible that it should ever affect good. Therefore, it must necessarily affect evil. Even a fool has the sense to see that someone who wallows in filth is going to get dirty. This is intuitive knowledge. People who spend millions of dollars to try and prove otherwise are malicious or misguided, or both.

b)* [Victor P. Maiorana, in *Critical Thinking across the Curriculum: Building the Analytical Classroom*, 1992 Bloomington, IN: EDINFO Press] The purpose of critical thinking is, therefore, to achieve understanding, evaluate view points, and solve problems. Since all three areas involve the asking of questions, we can say that critical thinking is the questioning or inquiry we engage in when we seek to understand, evaluate, or resolve.

c) [Daniel J. Kurland, in *I Know What It Says . . . What Does It Mean?*, 1995 Bloomington, CA: Wadsworth] Broadly speaking, critical thinking is concerned with reason, intellectual honesty, and open-mindedness, as opposed to emotionalism, intellectual laziness, and closed-mindedness. Thus, critical thinking involves: following evidence where it leads; considering all possibilities; relying on reason rather than emotion; being precise; considering a variety of possible viewpoints and explanations; weighing the effects of motives and biases; being concerned more with finding the truth than with being right; not rejecting unpopular views out of hand; being aware of one's own prejudices and biases, and not allowing them to sway one's judgment.

d) [From a response to a decision in Dover, Kansas, by the court judge (Jones) that intelligent design is religion and cannot be taught as science in state schools. The respondent is a member of the Intelligent Design Network, which is the source of the extract www.intelligentdesignnetwork.org]
The twisted decision of the court in Dover today [20 December 2005] effectively establishes a state sponsored ideology that is fundamental to non-theistic religions and religious beliefs. By outlawing the inference of design that arises from observation and analysis, the court has caused the state to endorse materialism and the various religions it supports. Thus the court actually inserted a religious bias into science while purporting to remove one.

The incorrect assumption implicit in the decision is that there is only one kind of "religion"—the kind that subscribes to God. In fact religion includes other kinds, those that reject any God that might intervene in the natural world—Atheism, Agnosticism, Secular Humanism, etc. The Court's second error was to ignore the obvious: any explanation of origins will **unavoidably** favor one kind of religion over another.

For Judge Jones "religion"" seems to be a term that describes only one particularly kind of religion—Christianity. Although the Judge was quick to note theistic friendly implications of an intelligent cause for life, his opinion omits any discussion of the religious implications of evolution and the acknowledged naturalistic/materialistic philosophy which has protected it from scientific criticism.

e) [A response to the same court judgement by the science writer, Richard Dawkins. From "The Kitzmiller Decision" at www.philosophyexperiments.com (accessed 15 October 2007)]

It would have been a scandal if any judge had not found against the ID [intelligent design] charlatans, but I had expected that he would do so with equivocation: some sort of "on-the-one-hand-on-the-other-hand" consolation prize for the cavemen of creationism. Not a bit of it. Judge Jones rumbled them, correctly described them as liars and sent them packing, with the words "breathtaking inanity" burning in their ears. The fact that this splendid man is a republican has got to be a good sign for the future. I think the great republic has turned a corner this week and is now beginning the slow, painful haul back to its enlightened, secular foundations.

f)   [From a news report, Associated Press, 16 March 2007] Santa Fe, NM, — Astronomers may have stopped calling Pluto a full-fledged planet, but it's on its way to regaining that status whenever it's visible over New Mexico.

A nonbinding memorial approved this week by the state House of Representatives declares that Pluto be designated a planet whenever it "passes overhead through New Mexico's excellent night skies."

The International Astronomical Union reclassified Pluto as a dwarf planet last August because its orbit overlaps with Neptune's. That caused hard feelings in New Mexico, home of Clyde Tombaugh, the astronomer who located Pluto in 1930.

g)*   [From Stuart Umpleby, www.asc-cyberneticcs.org/foundations/defs.htm, 1982; rev. 2000] Cybernetics takes as its domain the design or discovery and application of principles of regulation and communication. Cybernetics treats not things but ways of behaving. It does not ask "what is this thing?" but "what does it do?"" and "what can it do?" Because numerous systems in the living, social and technological world may be understood in this way, cybernetics cuts across many traditional disciplinary boundaries. The concepts that cyberneticians develop thus form a metadisciplinary language through which we may better understand and modify our world.

h)   The following is excerpted from an internet discussion of the Obama Administration's Health Care Reform Bill ("No Government Health Care—Stop Socialized Medicine!" www.facebook.com/group.php?gid=103797767015, visited 24 October 2011):

Obama's socialized medicine would result in a decrease in the number of doctors, and decrease in the quality of physicians due to the reduced incentives among young people to pursue careers in a field where they are not compensated for their work, and where they cannot make their own decisions regarding treatment of patients. . . .

Obama's socialized medicine would result in the reduction of overall quality of treatment for everyone, based on reduced number of physicians, overworked and underpaid physicians and staff, reduced time to treat patients, reduced materials and medicines available for treatment, reduced autonomy of physicians to practice medicine, rationing of care based on Eugenics-based judgments by politicians, reduced number of hospitals, and reduced number of adequately trained health care practitioners.

Obama's socialized medicine would ration care away from older individuals regardless of their willingness or ability to pay, based on "social justice" theories of treatment that are connected to the principles of Eugenics which have historically been supported and advanced by the political Left.

i)*   [From a Letter to the Editor, *The Globe and Mail*, 25 March 1996] The analysis of many of those who oppose the principle of prohibiting discrimination on the basis of sexual orientation is fundamentally flawed. . . . They say that because sexual orientation is "a personal choice" (which of course is highly debatable, given recent studies indicating that sexual orientation is likely genetically determined), it does not deserve human-rights protection. Well, religion is also "a personal choice," but we rightly prohibit discrimination on the basis of a person's creed.

The principle is this: If there is evidence that people are being discriminated against because they possess a particular personal characteristic, that characteristic is a suitable candidate for human-rights protection. "Sexual orientation" clearly meets the test. Put simply: There is no evidence that being gay (or being Protestant) affects job performance. Is it fair then to allow employers to deny someone a job because that person is gay (or Protestant)? Unless we put sexual orientation in the federal Human Rights Code (as we have done with religious creed), we are in effect saying "Yes."

j)   The central question is whether the state has a right to prevent an adult citizen from consuming materials that, though not dangerous, are considered by other citizens to be disgusting. Is it proper to make criminals out of people who wish to produce, show, or transmit these socially benign materials? Does the state have the right to impose the values of moralistic meddlers upon the rest of us? The state has no such right in a free and democratic society.

k)   [Ian Wilmut, Keith Campbell, and Colin Tudge, in *The Second Creation: Dolly and the Age of Biological Control*, Farrar, Straus and Giroux, 2000, p. 9] Beyond technology, and in harness with it, is science. People conflate the two: Most of what is reported on television by "science" correspondents is in fact technology. Technology is about changing things, providing machines and medicine, altering our surroundings to make our lives more comfortable and to create wealth. Science is about understanding how the universe works and all the creatures in it. The two pursuits are different, and not necessarily linked. Technology is as old as humankind: Stone tools are technology. People may produce fine instruments and weapons, cathedrals, windmills, and aqueducts, without having any formal knowledge of the underlying science—metallurgy, mechanics, aerodynamics, and hydrodynamics. In contrast, science at its purest is nothing more nor less than "natural philosophy," as it was originally known, and needs produce no technologies at all.

l)*   [From an example discussed by George Orwell in his essay "Politics and the English language," 1946] If a new spirit is to be infused into this old country, there is one thorny and contentious reform that must be tackled, and that is the humanization and galvanization of the BBC. Timidity here will bespeak canker and atrophy of the soul. The heart of Britain may be sound and of strong beat, for instance, but the British lion's roar at present is like that of Bottom in Shakespeare's *A Midsummer Night's Dream*—as gentle as any sucking dove.

A virile new Britain cannot continue indefinitely to be traduced in the eyes, or rather ears, of the world by the effete languors of Langham Place, brazenly masquerading as "standard English." When the Voice of Britain is heard at nine o'clock, better far and infinitely less ludicrous to hear aitches honestly dropped than the present priggish, inflated, inhibited, school-ma'amish arch braying of blameless bashful mewing maidens!

m) [From a Letter to the Editor, *The Independent* newspaper, 1 January 2009]

To watch a fox hunt is to enter a stark, dark and frightening world, a world filled with fear and threat, a chaotic event in which hounds can run all over a busy road, a village can be invaded by a pack in full cry as they pursue an animal frantic to escape. This activity fills the human participants with an unholy excitement and a feeling of power. As well as the mounted field, there are quad bikes carrying terriermen, their terriers contained in tiny boxes mounted on the quads, the bike also loaded with spades and drain rods. Believe me, unless your taste runs to animal abuse, this is no jolly, frolicking bit of British eccentricity: it is a very dark world, dressed up like a sinister pantomime.

n) [The following is a further contribution to the debate over the nature of "just war" and which wars should qualify. From Howard Zinn, "A just cause, not a just war," *The Progressive*, December 2001]

And yet, voices across the political spectrum, including many on the left, have described this as a "just war." One longtime advocate of peace, Richard Falk, wrote in *The Nation* that this is "the first truly just war since World War II." . . . I have puzzled over this. How can a war be truly just when it involves the daily killing of civilians, when it causes hundreds of thousands of men, women, and children to leave their homes to escape the bombs, when it may not find those who planned the September 11 attacks, and when it will multiply the ranks of people who are angry enough at this country to become terrorists themselves?

This war amounts to a gross violation of human rights, and it will produce the exact opposite of what is wanted: it will not end terrorism; it will proliferate terrorism.

I believe that the progressive supporters of the war have confused a "just cause" with a "just war." There are unjust causes, such as the attempt of the United States to establish its power in Vietnam, or to dominate Panama or Grenada, or to subvert the government of Nicaragua. And a cause may be just— getting North Korea to withdraw from South Korea, getting Saddam Hussein to withdraw from Kuwait, or ending terrorism—but it does not follow that going to war on behalf of that cause, with the inevitable mayhem that follows, is just.

For more online exercises, review questions, and quizzes related to the material in this chapter, please go to www.oupcanada.com/GoodReasoning5e

8

WEIGHING EVIDENCE

In Chapter 3, we outlined the key components of strong arguments. In this chapter, we focus on evaluation and return to that discussion with a more in depth account of premise acceptability and (deductive and inductive) validity. You should emerge with a better understanding of three key concepts:

▶ acceptability
▶ relevance
▶ sufficiency.

In Chapter 3 we saw that a strong argument is an argument that has acceptable premises and a valid conclusion, i.e. a conclusion that follows from its premises. In the case of both inductively and deductively valid arguments, this makes it difficult (and in the case of deductive validity, impossible) to accept an argument's premises and reject its conclusion. In our discussion of validity we saw that a valid argument has premises that provide evidence that is (a) relevant and (b) sufficient to establish its conclusion.

In view of this, acceptability, relevance and sufficiency provide a basis for our attempts to weigh the evidence an argument gives for its conclusion. In applying these notions to a broad range of arguments on the hoof, we want to emphasize the complexity inherent to such arguments. This is rooted in the fact that argumentative discussion revolves around multiple perspectives endorsed by arguers who have different (and frequently opposed) political, moral, and even religious inclinations, and many different opinions about the "facts" on almost any subject. In Chapter 1 we saw that the "public" is not a homogeneous group of people, but a conglomerate of many different groups who have diverse and conflicting perspectives and vested interests. This makes the systems of belief that characterize individuals and the audiences they make up an important consideration when assessing and constructing arguments.

In part because of the plethora of perspectives that characterizes argument, much of our reasoning is infused with uncertainty, disagreement, and dispute. Other factors that contribute to the complexities this produces are the partial and incomplete nature of our knowledge of the world and the limited view we may have of issues that still matter to us. It is not easy to know what the population of the world will be fifty years from now, and whether it will precipitate an environmental crisis; what should or is likely to happen in Middle East politics; whether we can reclaim the Alberta tar sands after extracting the oil that they contain; or whether cell phones increase the likelihood that we will have certain kinds of brain cancer and what we should do to regulate them; and so on.

Although our experience of the world does not yield certainty, the important point is that it can be used to establish claims that are reasonable and acceptable—claims that can be used as premises in arguments that establish reasonable conclusions. In the context of many arguments on the hoof, much the same can be said of the uncertainties and differences of opinion that characterize moral, political, and religious opinions. Here, too, it would be too much to expect the conclusion of an argument to be certain. Instead of undermining reasoning, this lack of certainty serves to emphasize the need to reason carefully, to consider opposing points of view, and to weigh all the relevant evidence in determining what should and should not be believed.

1 Acceptable, Unacceptable, or Questionable?

In judging the acceptability of the premises in an argument propounded by others or ourselves, we must ask (1) whether they are claims that the audience the argument is addressed to would accept without further support, and whether (2) they are reasonable claims. When arguments address a broad range of people who have many different perspectives—in arguments in public debates, in news commentaries, or on the editorial or letters to the editor section of a newspaper, for example—satisfying criterion (1) is equivalent to satisfying criterion (2), for in this case a premise must be acceptable to anyone who is reasonable. Put in another way, this is a case where premises must be acceptable to the audience which is commonly called the "universal" audience.

In Chapter 3 we saw that questions about burden of proof are tied to questions of acceptability. In judging burden of proof in a particular case, we must ask whether a claim or position is acceptable as it stands. If it is, then the onus, or burden of proof, in the argument rests with anyone who thinks the premise should not be accepted. If we recognize that a premise we want to use is not acceptable without support, then the burden of proof shifts to us. Any supporting premises we provide in such a circumstance must also be subjected to this same test. Ultimately, we should be able to ground our arguments in premises that are basic enough that their claims should be accepted by reasonable people.

For each premise provided in support of a conclusion, ask yourself whether there is any evidence that conflicts with the statement and undermines its claim to be acceptable or whether you lack the evidence needed to decide either way. If you answer "Yes" to the first question, then the premise is unacceptable. It may conflict with empirical evidence, or it may be rejected by definition, or it may be inconsistent with another premise in the same argument. If you must answer "Yes" to the second question, then the premise is **questionable**. It cannot be accepted as given, but we do not currently have grounds to judge that it is unacceptable.

When evaluating arguments, remember that you must support a judgement that a premise is questionable. When doing so you should ask yourself what evidence would be required to make it acceptable. What are you looking for that has not been provided? In some cases, you may find that when you scrutinize a premise in this way, what you had thought to be questionable is in fact unacceptable, since the evidence that would be required to make it acceptable could not, in principle, exist.

Consider the debate that ensued in Canada during 2011 over whether legislation was needed to provide sex-trade workers with safe environments. One contribution to this debate, published as a letter to the *Cape Breton Post* (4 July 2011) argued that sex workers should not be protected in this way because prostitution [as the writer explained, "I refuse to dignify the buying and selling of human beings with euphemisms such as "sex work" or "sex workers"] is not just another business. The writer's point was not against legislation to provide a safe environment, but against the trade itself. Prostitution should not be encouraged by any legislation. There is an element of contextual irrelevance in the overall argument since the topic has been shifted, but our interest is in premises associated with this debate.

One of this writer's premises in support of the central claim that prostitution is not just another business was the following:

> **Premise:** It is an affront to the innate dignity of the human person to regard her (or his) body as just a commodity to be bought or sold.

This premise appears to be questionable, primarily because of the vagueness of "innate dignity." No support is provided that would explain its meaning, but we also have no initial reason to reject the premise out of hand.

The situation changes when we ask what sort of evidence we *would* need to accept this statement. Then we begin to recognize the difficulties involved. What is meant by "dignity" in this context? This is a notoriously vague concept in many moral debates. And how is such dignity determined to be innate? A charitable audience might allow that it is consistent with Canadian values to view human beings as having a certain kind of importance that sets them apart from other things in nature, and this importance could be termed "dignity." But it should be clear that the associated concept of innateness increases the premise's controversial nature for many people. Still, we can imagine how someone might support this premise in a way that is acceptable to part of the audience.

A later contribution to the debate from another individual was even more problematic. Here the premise read:

> **Premise:** No woman would choose prostitution if she were warm and fed.

No matter how charitable we are, this assumption seems unsupportable in principle. It is difficult to conceive of any legitimate evidence that would corroborate the statement.

Perhaps a portion of the audience would accept that no woman *should* do this (again, assuming certain common values), but that is not what is asserted. The claim is about all women, and we can see that it would be impossible to acquire confirming data about *all* women and what they would choose (including those of the past and the future). In this case, the difficulty is so great that we deem a claim that might at first have seemed questionable to be, on reflection, unacceptable.

Keep in mind that it is not enough to dismiss a premise as unacceptable or questionable out of hand. In analyzing arguments you are obligated to support such judgements by stating the grounds of unacceptability or possible unacceptability. In many cases, this means that you should state what missing evidence or information is needed to determine the acceptability or unacceptability of a premise.

DETERMINING ACCEPTABILITY

There are three decisions we can make with respect to a claim's acceptability:

1. **It is acceptable without further support.** The statement itself is of such a nature, or is supported by other statements to such a degree, that a reasonable audience will accept it.
2. **It is unacceptable.** The statement conflicts with what is known to be the case such that a reasonable audience (and evaluator) has reason to reject it.
3. **It is questionable.** The statement is neither clearly acceptable nor clearly unacceptable because insufficient information is presented to decide either way.

EXERCISE 8A

Each of the following claims is from an article entitled "Living milk maids," in *Time* magazine, 30 April 2007. It discusses a trend that sees more American mothers hiring other mothers to breastfeed their children (or "cross-nursing," in which different mothers share breastfeeding for infants who are not their own). Decide whether each claim is acceptable without further support, unacceptable, or questionable. Explain your answer in each case.

1.* They say breast milk is the perfect food for baby's mind and body.
2. Studies show that children who nurse may be healthier and happier and, if they breastfeed for longer than seven months, have a higher IQ.
3.* Many believe that breastfeeding develops an intense bond between mother and child.
4. Cross-nursing "takes female friendship to another level. You're trusting another person to nurture your child."
5. Cross-nursing is "also a way of building that village or community that a lot of us crave."
6. Robert Feinstock, who owns A+ Certified Household Staffing, an agency that supplies wet nurses across the United States, says "demand has steadily risen in the past four years."

2   Conditions of Acceptability

Keeping in mind the account of audiences and belief systems we introduced in Chapter 1, we can elaborate our account of premise acceptability as follows.

Premise acceptability

A premise is judged acceptable if:

(1)   it would be accepted *without further support* by the audience for which it is intended, given the background knowledge of its members and the beliefs and values they hold; *and*

(2)   it is a premise that would be accepted by reasonable people.

The second part of this account raises a natural question: what do we mean when we say that a premise is a claim that "would be accepted by reasonable people"? It is not easy to categorize claims as those that would and would not be accepted by reasonable people, what you need to consider is whether a premise:

a)   conforms to (does not violate), alone or in combination with other premises, the principles of good reasoning; and

b)   could in principle be defended in front of the universal audience.

What can and cannot be defended in front of a universal audience is a matter open to argument, so this does not settle issues of acceptability in any simple way, but it does tell us how to argue in discussing and defending claims about acceptability. To make it even clearer how this must be judged, we can compile a list of conditions for acceptability that will help you judge when a premise is acceptable.

Acceptable by Definition, *or* Self-evidently Acceptable

Some claims can be established as acceptable by appealing to definitions. We know from the meanings of its component terms that the statement "All squares are four-sided figures" must be acceptable. Other claims are self-evident for different reasons. "Your phone bill will be more, less, or the same as last month's bill" is obviously the case because it exhausts all the possibilities. Sometimes we take moral principles to be self-evident. "One should not cause unnecessary pain" is an example of a moral principle many people consider to be self-evident.

A claim that is acceptable by virtue of the meaning of its component terms is acceptable in view of the way in which we use language and so relies to some extent on what is commonly known by a community of language users (as will be discussed below). This is the strongest type of self-evident claim, because the attempt to deny it results in an absurdity.

Acceptable as a Factual Statement Reporting an Observation or as a Statement of Eye-witness Testimony

Observation is another way of establishing the acceptability of some claims. It is on the basis of this that we would determine whether it is or is not the case that "There has been virtually no snowfall during the last two hours." If someone presents us with such a statement, we really have no grounds to reject it unless it contradicts other observations available to us.

This leads to the more difficult cases of claims that are based on a person's own eye-witness testimony but not verifiable by shared observations. In general, we have no reason to dispute what someone claims to have experienced or perceived. In normal conversation there is a presumption in favour of a speaker's truthfulness, and this principle transfers to the realm of argumentation. In ordinary circumstances we would have little reason to reject the claim that "I have driven my Toyota every day for two years without any mechanical problem" as acceptable based on the testimony of the speaker. If we did not accept such statements, we would be constantly skeptical of what we are told. While a degree of critical doubt is important in our social relations, total scepticism would disrupt them unnecessarily.

There are obvious limits to this. If someone has proved repeatedly that he or she is untrustworthy, then that is a reason not to accept what he or she says. If the statement lacks plausibility, as when someone claims they were removed from their car in broad daylight and taken up into an alien spacecraft, then we are justified in doubting it. We expect personal testimony to conform to the general structure of experience. In other cases, testimony is difficult to rely on because different individuals provide inconsistent testimony. In cases such as this we must carefully compare the credibility of those providing testimony.

Acceptable by Common Knowledge or Assent

Common knowledge is so often invoked as a reason for the acceptability of a statement that we need to treat it cautiously. Many treat virtually any claim as though it were a part of some community's shared experience. Others fail to distinguish between factual claims and value judgements, confusing value judgements that are not common knowledge with factual claims that are. "The government has proposed a separate justice system for minority groups" is a factual claim. "The government's proposed separate justice system for minority groups is an outrage" is a value judgement. Value judgements may convey the same information as a corresponding factual claim but add the claim that it is right or wrong.

Under "common knowledge or assent" we include factual claims of a descriptive nature that we can *expect* to be *commonly* known, and value judgements that are not open to reasonable dispute. "Misleading the public is wrong in an election campaign" is a generally accepted value judgement that may be, for example, the basis of a debate over the question whether a political party should be criticized for doing so. In the case of factual claims, we could dismiss many of the premises aimed at specific audiences because they report or depend on information not generally known by a larger (universal) audience. But that would be uncharitable. Unless the argument is specifically aimed at a universal audience, we allow statements based on the common knowledge of the community being addressed.

At the other extreme, people sometimes reject statements because they are not commonly known by *all* members of an audience. This again is uncharitable. For the most part, we do not know what is actually known by all individuals making up audiences and communities. We cannot see into other minds and certainly not the minds of large groups of people. But we do know what we *expect* people to know, and that is what information they have access to in their daily lives. We live in environments where certain ideas ("Slavery is wrong, "The Mona Lisa is a remarkable painting," "We have a right to express our ideas freely.") are almost universally accepted and where certain kinds of information ("Paper books are less prevalent than they once were" "Victoria is susceptible to earth quakes," "Barack Obama is the President of the United States") are readily available. They can help us make sense of the common knowledge or assent condition. In considering it, we are not speaking about what people actually know in common but what we can reasonably expect them to know given the environments in which they live and work.

In considering the common knowledge or assent condition, this means that we should consider the universality of the argument and the audience being addressed. We should generally allow statements like "Cruel and unusual punishment is wrong," "The Roman Catholic Church does not allow women to be priests," or "The Rolling Stones are a popular rock band." They are common bits of information or an indelible part of our moral and political points of view. Statements with more restricted exposure in the media may only be judged common to more restricted audiences.

Acceptable Because it is Defended in a Reasonable Sub-argument

An arguer is obligated to support those premises that would not be otherwise acceptable to the audience being addressed. They must accept this burden of proof where required to do so. When an arguer fulfills this obligation, and the support provided is reasonable, then we have grounds for finding the supported premise to be acceptable. Once supported in this way, the premise in question becomes a conclusion of a strong sub-argument.

Consider the following:

We have good reason to believe that juries are more likely to convict those accused of murder when capital punishment is not an option. For 1960–74, when the death penalty was in place, the conviction rate for crimes punishable by death was about 10 per cent. Capital punishment was abolished in 1976 and the conviction rate rose to 20 per cent by 1982. If you think about it, this suggests that if we bring back the death penalty, as the Conservatives have suggested, this is likely to mean that murderers will have a smaller, not a greater, chance of being convicted for their crimes.

[Adapted from an article in *The Globe and Mail*, 9 January 1987; commenting on a report from the research and statistics group of the Department of the Solicitor General of Canada]

Using the short cut method we introduced in Chapter 5, we can diagram this argument as follows.

We have good reason to believe that juries are more likely to convict those accused of murder when capital punishment is not an option. For 1960–74, when the death penalty was in place, the conviction rate for crimes punishable by death was about 10 per cent. Capital punishment was abolished in 1976 and the conviction rate rose to 20 per cent by 1982. If you think about it, this suggests that if we bring back the death penalty, as the Conservatives have suggested, this is likely to mean that murderers will have a smaller, not a greater, chance of being convicted for their crimes.

When evaluating the acceptability of the premises in this argument, we begin with statement 1, which is a premise in support of the main conclusion. Taken by itself, the claim that (Canadian) jurors are more willing to convict for murder since the abolition of the death penalty is controversial, and could not be accepted it as it stands. Recognizing this, the authors have provided statistical data needed to support 1 in statements 2 and 3. Each describes the conviction rate for murder in Canada, statement 2 prior to the abolition of capital punishment, statement 3 after the abolition. Thus, 2 and 3 represent the kind of premises needed to support the sub-conclusion 1. Of course, once we see that this is so, our look at acceptability would then shift to the acceptability of the premises in 2 and 3. The acceptability of these two factual statements relies largely on the authority of their source, which is in this case a research and statistics group of the Solicitor General. As this is a (highly) reputable source, we judge these premises acceptable, on the basis of our next ground for acceptability.

Acceptable on the Authority of the Arguer or an Expert

Sometimes premises are accepted simply because the arguer or an expert says they are acceptable. If you have no reason to doubt the reliability of an arguer, then you should accept, at least provisionally, claims they make. If they tell you that the United Nations' Fourth World Conference on Women was held in Beijing, for example, it is reasonable to accept their claim until you have reason to doubt it. In this way, arguers can reasonably rely on uncontroversial knowledge that they have.

A more explicit appeal to an expert or authority occurs when a premise is considered acceptable because it carries the support of, or appeals to, an expert or authority. The appeal to authority is an argument scheme that will be treated in detail in Chapter 12. Here, we wish only to introduce the notion of expertise and indicate its role in assessing the acceptability of a premise.

Experts are people, institutions, or sources who, by virtue of their authority, knowledge, or experience, can be used to support the claims made in premises. Consider an example:

> As the Surgeon General says, second-hand smoke is bad for your health. So you are hurting your children when you smoke at home.

The simple argument here is: "Second-hand smoke is bad for your health, so you are hurting your children when you smoke at home." Is the premise in this argument acceptable? The arguer attempts to establish its acceptability by appealing to the authority of the Surgeon General. If such an authority is appropriate here—that is, the right kind of authority, speaking on the right issue, with the right motive—then the premise is acceptable.

Note that the premise may not be *enough* to carry the conclusion. But in cases where we do not have access to the information we would need to judge a premise, or where we simply lack the expertise to make such an assessment ourselves, it is legitimate to rely on an authority. Authorities act as proxy support for a premise. The information they have is available somewhere, so their support provides a presumption in favour of the premise.

Experts and authoritative sources come in many forms, like the Department of the Solicitor General of Canada in the earlier argument, which, as an objective body, gives legitimate support to the premise given there. Other authoritative sources may include professionals who are renowned in their fields, objective consumer advocacy groups, documentaries, dictionaries, and textbooks.

CONDITIONS OF ACCEPTABILITY

1. Acceptable by definition, or self-evidently acceptable.
2. Acceptable as a factual statement reporting an observation or as a statement of eye-witness testimony.
3. Acceptable by common knowledge or assent.
4. Acceptable because it is defended in a reasonable sub-argument.
5. Acceptable on the authority of the arguer or an expert.

1. Each of the following claims can be taken as an acceptable premise in an argument. In each case, explain the acceptability in terms of the conditions of acceptability we have introduced.

    a)* The presence of a cause is demonstrated by the existence of its effects.

    b) The former Soviet Union included Uzbekistan.

    c) [Stated by the chief of police] The intersection of these two major roads is the worst location for accidents in the city.

    d) Human beings cannot always be trusted to tell the truth.

    e) [Stated by a tourist guide] Hamburg has more bridges than Amsterdam and Venice combined.

    f) Computer technology will either improve daily life, or it will not.

    g) [Explain why the first sentence can be used as an acceptable premise] Russell and Enns have defied the preconceptions of wildlife officials and the general public. For they have lived unthreatened—and respected—among the grizzlies of Kamchatka. In the process they demonstrate that it is possible to forge a mutually respectful relationship with these majestic giants, and provide compelling reasons for altering our culture.

3   Conditions of Unacceptability

In many instances, a premise will be judged unacceptable because it fails to satisfy—i.e. it specifically violates—one or more of the conditions of acceptability. In other cases, the failure to satisfy a condition of acceptability may render the premise questionable but not explicitly unacceptable. However, beyond these considerations, there are some additional conditions of unacceptability that should be recognized.

Unacceptable Because of an Inconsistency

Inconsistency is a weakness in argumentation that is brought to light by carefully reading an argument's components and considering their meaning. It is possible for two (or more) premises in an argument to be perfectly acceptable when considered individually. But when they are appraised together we encounter a situation where they cannot both be acceptable as support for the same conclusion. Consider the inconsistency between the following premises:

P1 =   Only claims that can be verified can be trusted.

P2 =   Enough people have reported encounters with ghosts to make their existence likely.

These two statements could issue from the belief system of someone who has not carefully evaluated their own beliefs and considered how they sit with each other. At first glance, P2 might seem to be consistent with P1, since a person's experience is a type of verification. But the kind of verification intended by P1 is objective, third-person verification. If claims are to be trusted, there must be some way of subjecting them to testing. As they stand, P1 and P2 appeal to quite different criteria. If both were to be used in a single piece of argumentation, the inconsistency between them would render them unacceptable.

Sometimes premises are problematic because they are **inconsistent** with other claims or related behaviour. In *Reverse Aging* (Miami, FL: JSP Publishing, 2000), Sang Whang claims to reveal the secrets of longevity that his father discovered. But he himself notes that his father died in strange circumstances at 78. In the middle of an interview on his secrets of longevity, he suffered a stroke and passed away. Here the acute reader should see a potential inconsistency. If, as Sang Whang and his father claimed, they had discovered the secrets of longevity, how is it that his father passed away at the unexceptional age of 78? Shouldn't someone who knows the secrets of longevity live longer than that?

Unacceptable as a Result of Begging the Question

Sometimes "begs the question" is used to mean "raises the question." But this is a relatively recent use of the phrase. The original use of the expression belongs to logic, where "begging the question" is a specific violation of the principles of good reasoning. It occurs when arguments are "circular"—when the premises assume the very things that should be established by the conclusions. The following argument illustrates the problem:

> How do we know that the Bible is the right criterion of truth? All through the Scriptures are found . . . expressions such as "Thus says the Lord," "The Lord said," and "God spoke." Statements like "Thus says the Lord" occur no less than 1,904 times in the 39 books of the Old Testament.

> [Adapted from *Decision Magazine*, January 1971]

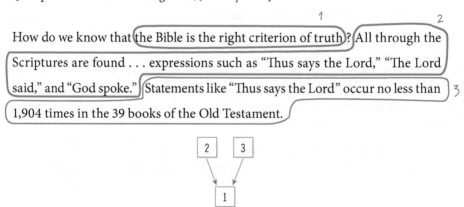

Here the argument in support of 1 (the main claim) might be judged sufficient and accepted by an uncritical audience already sympathetic to it. But the argument is not convincing because statements 2 and 3 assume precisely what they are supposed to prove. No reasonable person who has doubts about the truth of the Bible will accept its own testimony that this is so, for doing so assumes that what the Bible says is true. In this way the argument assumes the very principle it is supposed to prove. It therefore begs the question.

In order to avoid begging the question, you also need to resist the temptation to use premises that merely restate the claim you are trying to establish. The premise "People living below the poverty line ought to receive a basic income" is not a separate and distinct reason for the claim "The poor should be given financial subsidies up to a pre-established minimum." It simply recasts the same idea in different language. To use one of these statements as a premise to support the other as a conclusion is to beg the question.

Unacceptable Because of Problems with Language

After reading the discussion of language in the last chapter, you should be able to recognize a number of language problems that would be grounds for finding a premise unacceptable. There may be cases in which an audience cannot be expected to understand an arguer's meaning. And there are also clear-cut cases in which no audience could be certain of a premise's meaning—where the statement is irresolvably vague or a definition, although not internally contradictory, is too broad or narrow to be persuasive.

Even premises that report personal testimony can be rejected because they fail to communicate clearly. A statement like "I have driven my 2004 Ford every day for three years without any major problem" flounders on the vagueness of "major problem," for a constant series of "minor" problems might itself be considered a major problem.

FURTHER CONDITIONS OF UNACCEPTABILITY

1. Unacceptable because of an inconsistency.
2. Unacceptable as a result of begging the question.
3. Unacceptable because of problems with language.

EXERCISE 8C

1. Explain the grounds you would use in judging the acceptability, questionability, or unacceptability of each of the following statements:

   a) Of all the people in the South American countries I have visited, I have found Chileans to be the most hospitable.

   b) Several extinct species can be found in the rain forest.

   c)* Prisoners in federal penitentiaries should be allowed to vote because they still retain their citizenship, and elected officials oversee the regulations that govern the running of penitentiaries.

   d) Most people prefer the company of those from their own culture.

   e) Many problems in language use are hard to identify because of their indeterminate nature.

2. From the perspective of a general, reasonable audience, assess the acceptability of the premises in each of the following arguments. Be sure to explain fully the grounds for your decisions.

a) Nobody likes a quitter. So I won't give up smoking.

b)* To every man unbounded freedom of speech must always be, on the whole, advantageous to the state; for it is highly conducive to the interests of the community that each individual should enjoy a liberty perfectly unlimited of expressing his sentiments.

c) [Mary Gordon, in *Joan of Arc: a Life*, New York: Peguin, 2000, pp. 2–3] Joan's family does not seem to have been of much consequence to her. When she decided to obey her voices and go off to crown the king of France, she left home with a cousin, who was her godfather, employing an ordinary, adolescent lie. She told her parents she was going to help out with the cousin's wife's labor, and then with the new child. She never spoke to her parents again, and when she was asked during her trial if she felt guilty about what could only be construed as a sin of disobedience, she said, "Since God commanded it, had I had a hundred fathers and a hundred mothers, had I been born a king's daughter, I should have departed." So we would do well not to linger over Joan's family for explanations of anything.

d) Since animals can experience pain and are also capable of nurturing relationships, it is wrong to use them indiscriminately in experiments, and hence there should be strict guidelines governing such use.

e) [Marcus Aurelius, in *Meditations*, Book XII] The gods must not be blamed, for they do no wrong, willingly or unwillingly; nor human beings, for they do no wrong except unwillingly. Therefore, no one is to be blamed.

f) Some diseases have been known to fool even the experienced medical professional. According to the *New England Journal of Medicine*, human error can affect both physicians' diagnoses and laboratory test results. In cases of serious illness, a second opinion is often desirable.

4   Internal Relevance

We have already introduced the concept of relevance in two discussions in Chapter 3. A strong argument, we have seen, must have, in addition to acceptable premises, a conclusion that *follows* from these premises. A conclusion follows from a set of premises when they are (a) (internally) relevant to the conclusion and (b) sufficient to establish it as plausible. In deductively valid arguments, the premises are both relevant and sufficient, for they guarantee the conclusion. Once we accept the premises, we must accept the conclusion. Especially when we consider arguments that are inductively valid, we need to distinguish between relevance and sufficiency. An argument must also be relevant to the context in which it arises. We called this contextual relevance.

Internal relevance is distinct from this in being a measure of the relationship between an argument's premises and conclusions. But a conclusion's premises may be relevant to it even though they raise questions about that conclusion. Consider the premise:

Premise: UN members from Africa will support the US proposal.

In a circumstance in which we are trying to establish the conclusion "The UN will support the US proposal," this would be a relevant premise. It shows that a significant block of countries will support the US proposal in question. It increases the likelihood of the conclusion. And yet the premise does not, by itself, guarantee the conclusion: for even if all the members from Africa support the proposal, this may not mean that a majority do (that may require the African members plus other blocs of votes as well). We can accept the premise without having to accept the conclusion. We see, then, that internal relevance is something apart from deductive validity.

Consider another possible premise in this context:

Premise 2: The US proposal will soon be debated in the UN General Assembly.

Like the first premise, premise 2 may be acceptable. But unlike the first premise, it makes no obvious contribution to the argument—it is not a reason for believing the conclusion that "The UN will support the US proposal." Premise 2, then, is not relevant to the conclusion.

Relevant premises increase (or decrease) the probability that the conclusion should be accepted. It is not enough that they simply "talk about the same subject." When we argue, our goal is to make our conclusion more plausible and more likely to be accepted. We do this by providing premises that are internally relevant to our conclusion. That said, there are times when arguments introduce evidence that actually undermines or goes against a conclusion. We discover relevance in this negative way when we engage in counter-argumentation and look for premises that decrease the probability of a conclusion.

In our earlier example, the first premise, "UN members from Africa will support the US proposal," actively increases the probability of the conclusion. It is the kind of positive evidence we would look for to establish the claim. What we require further is information about the other member nations. As more indicate their support of the proposal, the likelihood of the conclusion increases. If we then learn that a number of members oppose the proposal, that counts as negatively relevant evidence that starts to decrease the likelihood of the conclusion.

In contrast to premise 1, premise 2, "The US proposal will soon be debated in the General Assembly," has a neutral relation to the conclusion, neither increasing nor decreasing its likelihood. This demonstrates the point that premises we have judged acceptable are not necessarily relevant. Acceptable premises can be irrelevant to the conclusion they are intended to support.

In extended arguments, some premises will not be relevant to the main claim because they are intended only as support for subsidiary claims. This is another place where the use of diagrams is valuable. The following example serves as a fuller application of our rule:

The right to a lawyer is crucial to our justice system .... An accused is vulnerable to intimidation, conscious or not, by the authorities who arrest him.

Since our society considers him innocent unless proved guilty, and believes he should not be compelled to testify against himself, justice requires that he be counselled by someone who knows the law and can advise him on which questions he must legally answer.

We diagram this argument as follows.

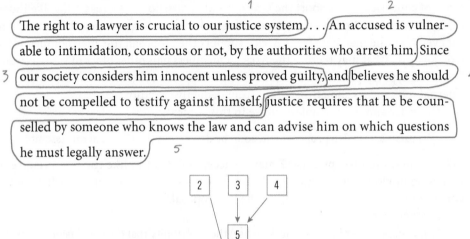

The diagram reveals a subsidiary argument within the main argument. Accordingly, in assessing relevance, we must look at the bearing each of statement 2 and statement 5 has on statement 1, the MC, and the bearing each of statement 3 and statement 4 has on statement 5. Although we may legitimately wonder whether a paralegal could take the place of a lawyer in providing the required service, we have no difficulty seeing that statement 2 and statement 5 are the right kind of evidence needed to increase one's acceptance of statement 1. Likewise, statements 3 and 4 actively increase the likelihood of statement 5 being accepted. Applying our requirement of internal relevance requires judgement on our part. But there seems to be nothing in this argument with which we can legitimately disagree.

INTERNAL RELEVANCE

If a premise increases the likelihood of the conclusion it is intended to support, or if it decreases the likelihood of that conclusion, then the premise is relevant to the conclusion. If neither of these conditions holds, then the premise is not relevant.

RELEVANCE AND HIDDEN PREMISES

You are by now familiar with the notion of "hidden premises," which we introduced in Chapter 6. If you are still having trouble identifying hidden premises, you should find the requirement of internal relevance useful. Before you dismiss a premise as irrelevant to a conclusion, consider whether it is plausible to suppose that there is a hidden premise that will, when it is identified, combine with the explicit premise and make it relevant to the conclusion. You may not find this helpful in every case, but you will find it helpful in many. Consider the following argument:

> It is morally permissible to experiment on human embryos at a developmental stage prior to the formation of the brain, since there is no possibility of causing pain or distress to the organism.

If we let "1" be the statement "It is morally permissible to experiment on human embryos at a developmental stage prior to the formation of the brain" and let "2" be the statement "There is no possibility of causing pain or distress to the organism" then it is clear that statement 2 is given as a reason for statement 1. But we might at first glance judge it irrelevant to this conclusion. How do we get from causing pain to having a brain? What would make the premise relevant to the conclusion (that is, what would provide active support for it)? Would it be an explicit connection between permissible experiments and experiments that do not cause pain or distress? which the author has not provided. Drawing out the following hidden premise is, then, a reasonable assumption to attribute to the author. Once drawn out, it combines with the explicit premise to provide relevant support for the conclusion.

HP =   It is morally permissible to experiment on organisms if the experiment cannot cause them pain or distress.

1.   Assess the relevance of the reasons offered for the following claims. For the purposes of this exercise, assume that each reason is acceptable.

 a)* **Claim:** It is wrong to inflict suffering on animals.
      Reasons:
      i)   It is wrong to inflict suffering on any creature that can experience pain.
      ii)   All animals can experience pain.
      iii) Circuses exploit animals for human profit.

    iv)   Some medical advances for humans can only be achieved at the price of inflicting pain on rats and rabbits.

    v)   In keeping with Christian doctrine, we are to be the stewards of Nature.

b)   **Claim:** There should be stricter gun-control laws.

    Reasons:

    i)   Children already witness too much violence on television.

    ii)   Few people would be killed by handguns if those guns were more rigidly controlled.

    iii) The right to bear arms is written into the Constitution.

    iv) Police associations across North America support stricter gun laws.

    v)   Stricter gun-control laws would assist police in keeping law and order.

c)   **Claim:** Government-sponsored daycare is needed to promote equality of the sexes.

    Reasons:

    i)   Welfare costs will be reduced if single parents are free to take remunerative employment.

    ii)   Sexual equality requires that women be free to pursue the same employment opportunities as men.

    iii) The lack of government-sponsored daycare is an impediment to equality of the sexes.

    iv) Daycares provide young children with an environment in which they can learn to interact and acquire essential social skills.

    v)   Economic pressures often force women to choose between motherhood and a career.

d)   **Claim:** Drunk drivers who are convicted of causing accidents in which others are injured should be compelled to compensate the victims or their families.

    Reasons:

    i)   This would force repeat offenders to take responsibility for their actions.

    ii)   The costs arise as a result of the drunk driver's actions.

    iii) Courts often treat drunk drivers too leniently.

    iv) Costs incurred in accidents are the responsibility of the insurance companies.

    v)   It's unfair to expect the victims to bear the costs of someone's negligence.

e)   **Claim:** Vikings of 1000 BCE visited North America centuries before Columbus did in 1492.

    Reasons:

    i)   The Vikings were exceptional sailors, and their ships were built to withstand the travails of long voyages.

    ii)   What is believed to be a Norwegian silver penny dating to the reign of Olaf Kyrre, minted between 1065 and 1080 BCE, was found at the Goddard site, a large Indian site in Penobscot Bay, Maine.

    iii) Native North American legends speak of contact with white men long before Columbus.

    iv) Vikings were known to be fearless warriors.

    v)   No replica of a Viking ship has been able to traverse the Atlantic Ocean in modern times.

f) **Claim:** Fox hunting is a cruel sport that should be banned in Britain.
Reasons:
i) Fox hunting involves setting a pack of trained dogs against a single small animal that cannot defend itself.
ii) Fox hunting is destructive to the environment.
iii) Repeated public opinion polls have shown that seven out of 10 people in Britain believe that fox hunting is cruel.
iv) Each year, fox hunting is responsible for the deaths of between 15000 and 20000 animals.
v) The fox is killed by the lead hound, trained to be first on the scene and snap the neck in less than a second.

g) **Claim:** Fox hunting in Britain provides important services and should be continued.
Reasons:
i) Fox hunting is a sport with a 250-year tradition, enjoyed by kings and queens.
ii) Fox hunting has important economic value to rural Britain.
iii) In the absence of any other natural predators, environmental checks and balances cannot limit the number of foxes preying on British farm animals.
iv) Foxes are capable of vicious and wanton destruction of livestock.
v) The campaign against fox hunting is merely one of political correctness.

h) **Claim:** Restrictions should be placed on the press to protect individuals' privacy.
Reasons:
i) Invasion of privacy can be a serious harm in our society.
ii) A series of scandals has shown that members of the press to go to any lengths to get a story.
iii) Freedom of speech is an important value in our society.
iv) The public's right to know supersedes any claims to privacy.
v) The press has too much power.

2. Each of the following examples gives a response to the cost-cutting measures proposed in 2011 by Toronto mayor Rob Ford, who campaigned partly on a promise to stop the "gravy train" at City Hall. The comments are from thestar.com, July 2011, (www.thestar.com/news). Set out the argument in each case, and provide an analysis of relevance.

a) The mayor has no financial background and he throws a "bogeyman" $700 millon number for our deficit, when in fact he has not factored in the surplus handed to him by the previous administration. He is also throwing away the important revenue side—even though we have one of the most cost-efficiently run cities in North America. Proof is the attempt to cut essential service bits which are not gravy (with the exception of the $350,000 report Ford commissioned).

b)* A Mayor who was a true leader, a consensus builder, would understand that he needs to involve the other members of council in the decision-making process, by being open and transparent. He would want to share his plans, discuss the pros and cons, and would build consensus by giving in now and again. But, sadly, that's not the guy Toronto elected as its Mayor.

c) "So far, the biggest savings identified would come from closing city-run daycares and long-term-care homes"—to cut these essential services in an urban centre like Toronto would be cruel for the financially strapped and elderly. I cannot believe these would even be considered in these economic times.

d) Cut the fluoridation of drinking water. It's a useless and ridiculous program anyway. Always has been. Do you people really think it reduces tooth decay? People get enough fluoride from toothpaste. No point in paying to have it dumped in our water.

5   Sufficiency

In judging whether arguments are inductively—as opposed to deductively—valid, we need to consider questions of sufficiency as well as relevance. Consider our earlier premise: "UN members from Africa will support the US proposal." In a context where we are attempting to establish the conclusion "Most members of the UN support the US proposal," we judge the premise to be acceptable and relevant to the claim, but *insufficient* to establish the conclusion.

A strong argument must create a presumption in favour of its conclusion. It must make an audience more likely to adopt it than reject it and shift the burden of proof to those who do not to provide a counter-argument. But how much is enough evidence? Experience tells us that this will vary from argument to argument. There are no precise rules for determining when enough evidence has been put forward. Nor can we think in terms of the number of premises, since a single premise in one argument can carry as much evidence for its claim as three or four premises in another argument. But some important considerations can assist you in making judgements of sufficiency.

1. When assessing the sufficiency of evidence in an argument, consider how strongly the conclusion has been expressed. Suppose a resident of an average-size city argues on the basis of her experience that the postal service is inadequate, by which she means that delivery is slow and unreliable. There is no denying the details of her personal testimony. We may sympathize with her, given our own frustrations with the postal service, yet we can see that the evidence of her experience alone is not sufficient to convince a reasonable audience of a general claim about the postal service. In fact, it is difficult to see what non-trivial conclusion can be drawn from her experience.

But suppose the same person undertakes to canvass her neighbourhood and other neighbourhoods throughout the city and finds numerous households with similar complaints. If she can argue on the basis of a broader range of experience, her argument becomes stronger. But it is still not strong enough to support the claim that the postal service, in general, is inadequate. What she may have is sufficient evidence, if it is representative of all neighbourhoods, to show that the postal service *in her city* is inadequate. Not until she has managed to cull supporting evidence from regions and cities right across the country would she have sufficient evidence to support her claim about the postal service in general. But this, we recognize, would be very difficult for an individual to accomplish.

The point of this example is that what constitutes sufficiency of evidence must be decided relative to the claim the evidence is intended to support. The more general the claim, the more evidence is needed. For this reason, you are advised to keep your claims as specific as possible. Without the support of something like a national poll behind you, you are likely to experience difficulty in marshalling sufficient evidence for general claims like this one.

Claims that are expressed with high degrees of certainty are particularly difficult to support without sufficient evidence. Consider the following example:

> Thor Heyerdahl crossed the Atlantic in a raft designed after carvings on an ancient Egyptian tomb. Heyerdahl landed at the island of Barbados. This proves that Barbados was the first landing place for humans in the Western world.

The two premises do not come close to *proving* the conclusion that "Barbados was the first landing place for humans in the Western world." But they do provide the right sort of relevant evidence to support a weaker claim such as "This raises the possibility that . . ."

2. Do not draw a conclusion too hastily. We sometimes find ourselves "jumping to conclusions" that we afterwards need to modify or withdraw once the excitement abates. Traditionally, arguments of this sort have been termed "hasty conclusions" or "hasty generalizations." They involve conclusions drawn before enough evidence is in. This does not mean that we can't make tentative claims that we test in order to see if we can gather the evidence for them. Scientific progress often proceeds this way, with hypotheses being put forward and then subjected to rigorous testing. We would be alarmed to learn that the latest drug on the market had been tested on only a few subjects before its manufacturers concluded that it "worked." In fact, government agencies are supposed to make sure that this does not happen. A similar check needs to be made on our own hypotheses. But still, some judgement is required. How many tomatoes in the basket do we have to check before we decide they are a good value? We're generally required to check some before we can draw a reasonable conclusion. But beyond that, circumstances will determine how many we'll have to check before we'll be willing to conclude we have a good buy.

On the other hand, less evidence may be enough to draw some kinds of conclusions. No matter how many times a hypothesis is verified, if there is one instance in which it fails, and the prediction had not allowed for any failures, then that one instance can be enough to reject the hypothesis. One negative experience touching a hot stove is enough to convince a child not to do so again. In theory, the hot stove might not burn next time, but the negativity of the experience is enough to discourage further testing. We would be reluctant to charge the child with drawing a hasty conclusion.

3. Ensure that the arguer has provided a balanced case and discharged all of his or her obligations. Better arguments—that is, arguments that are more likely to receive serious attention from others and to impress them with the arguer's reasonableness—are arguments that try to give a balanced picture of an issue. If you present only the evidence supporting your position and ignore evidence that detracts from it, your audience is likely to be suspicious about what you have left out. It does not help the postal critic's argument if she presents a lot of supporting evidence only to have her opponents present evidence indicating that most people are satisfied with the service.

Selectively presenting only one side of an issue is to engage in what is called "special pleading." Consider the following argument:

> The government should not be returned for another term in office. It has hurt the country by paying too much attention to foreign policy and neglecting domestic affairs.

Beyond the vagueness of the charges, the argument makes no attempt to recognize anything positive the government may have done. It is possible that the arguer believes that nothing positive has been done. But a more complete evaluation of the government's performance will have a wider appeal to a broader audience. By explicitly outlining and then addressing the views of those who believe that the government was right to emphasize foreign policy, someone who forwards this particular argument will substantially increase the likelihood that their audiences will find their argument convincing.

We should strive wherever possible to dress our arguments with a sense of objectivity and balance. If there is evidence that goes against your position, honesty demands that you introduce it and respond to it. If you cannot counter it, you probably should not be advancing that argument in the first place. In assessing the arguments of others, however, do not judge them too harshly for not anticipating all the objections to their claim. Rarely are all conditions for sufficiency satisfied, but a well-constructed argument should make a reasonable attempt to respond to key objections.

On the other hand, we do expect arguers to discharge their obligations, particularly those that arise from charges and promises made in the argument. If the arguer claims a position is inconsistent, then the onus is on him or her to substantiate the charge. The failure to do so is a violation of the sufficiency condition. Likewise, if the arguer promises to show that a position has no reasonable objections to it, then the subsequent argument should be judged on whether that promise is fulfilled.

A final obligation is to define key terms in an argument. If a definition required to establish a claim is omitted, then the evidence for that claim is insufficient.

EXERCISE   8E

Assess the sufficiency of different combinations of the premises offered for each of the following claims:

a)* **Claim:** Boxing should not be outlawed.
   Reasons:
   i)   Boxing gives many young men the opportunity to escape lives of poverty.
   ii) Boxing is no less dangerous than other contact sports.

iii) The art of boxing reflects an age-old human love of physical challenge and excellence.

iv) While there are some serious injuries, these are relatively rare and proportionately fewer than in other popular sports.

v) No one is coerced into boxing or watching the sport.

b) **Claim:** Critical thinking courses are certainly the most important courses in the curriculum.
Reasons:
i) Critical thinking teaches the fundamentals of good reasoning.
ii) It helps people learn how to detect bad reasoning in the arguments they hear and read.
iii) Critical thinking principles underlie all the academic disciplines.
iv) Critical thinking teaches skills that are useful in the everyday world.
v) A critical thinking course is part of a well-rounded education.

c) **Claim:** The service in the local department store is always excellent.
Reasons:
i) I was there yesterday, and three assistants asked if they could help me.
ii) There's a sign over the main entrance that says "We Aim to Please."
iii) The store is usually busy when I'm there, unlike its competitor.
iv) I've always been treated courteously by the sales staff.
v) My father has had the same good experience with the store.

d) **Claim:** Lee Harvey Oswald probably did not act alone in assassinating President John F. Kennedy.
Reasons:
i) He was alleged to have shot Kennedy from the sixth floor of the Texas School Book Depository where he worked, but shots were also fired from a grassy knoll to the side of the president's car.
ii) Several witnesses reported seeing armed men running away from the vicinity of the shooting.
iii) Studies of the direction of the bullets that hit the president indicate they came from more than one direction.
iv) Investigations found that Oswald, who was known to have Cuban sympathies, was involved in the assassination.
v) The 1976 US Senate inquiry concluded that more than one gunman had been involved.

e) **Claim:** A critical thinking course is useful for most post-secondary students.
Reasons:
i) These courses discuss the basic elements used in producing strong, convincing arguments.
ii) Students who have taken a critical thinking course generally perform well in other courses.

iii) Such courses force students to defend the decisions they make and the claims they advance.

iv) Such courses aid students in recognizing themselves as thinking creatures with specific beliefs.

v) Critical thinking fosters an environment in which students are required to consider the beliefs and perspectives of others.

6   Applying the Criteria

In completing this chapter, we want to illustrate the way that our accounts of acceptability, relevance, and sufficiency apply when we attempt a comprehensive assessment of an extended argument. The argument concerns a debate over whether it is good to expose children to some traditional children's stories.

> Many people dismiss out of hand the suggestion that certain children's stories should be banned because of things like violence and stereotyping. But there is at least one reason to consider censoring some children's stories. In several common children's stories the stepmother is an evil person who mistreats her stepchildren and wishes them ill.
>
> For example: Her stepmother wishes Snow White dead and later tries to poison her. Cinderella's stepmother treats her as a servant and mocks her in front of her stepsisters. And the stepmother of Hansel and Gretel has them abandoned in a deep forest. Since children hear these stories at an impressionable age, such stories may be instrumental in creating for young children a negative image of stepmothers.

We can diagram this argument as follows:

> Many people dismiss out of hand the suggestion that certain children's stories should be banned because of things like violence and stereotyping. But there ⟩ 1
> is at least one reason to consider censoring some children's stories. In several ⟩ 2
> common children's stories the stepmother is an evil person who mistreats her
> stepchildren and wishes them ill. For example: Her stepmother wishes Snow ⟩ 3
> White dead and later tries to poison her. Cinderella's stepmother treats her as a ⟩ 4
> servant and mocks her in front of her stepsisters. And the stepmother of Hansel ⟩ 5
> and Gretel has them abandoned in a deep forest. Since children hear these sto- ⟩ 6
> ries at an impressionable age, such stories may be instrumental in creating for
> young children a negative image of stepmothers. ⟩ 7

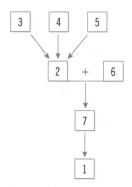

The first statement in this discourse is taken as background. It announces the context in which the argument arises, indicating its controversial nature and stating the position with which the author disagrees. In weighing the evidence the argument gives for its main conclusion, we will consider acceptability, relevance, and then sufficiency.

We have three arguments here: the support proposed for statement 2 by statements 3, 4, and 5; the support proposed for statement 7 by statements 2 and 6; and the support proposed for statement 1, the main conclusion, by statement 7. In judging acceptability, we work backwards through the diagram, starting with statement 7.

The claim that certain children's stories may be instrumental in creating a negative image of stepmothers for young children (7) is weakened in a positive sense by the qualifying phrase "may be." The writer does not have to establish that the stories *do* have this effect, only that they *may*. While the claim is still not acceptable as it stands (if it were common knowledge, there would be little need to argue for it), it is supported, and we can look to see if that support is reasonable.

The claim that children hear these stories at an impressionable age is unsupported, so it must be evaluated on its own merits. While it may suffer from the vagueness of what constitutes an "impressionable age," we are prepared to allow the premise on the grounds that people commonly understand young children to be impressionable and these stories are intended for quite young children. A reasonable audience should accept it. To assess statement 2, we need to again consider the evidence offered for it. Each of statements 3, 4, and 5 reports a central and commonly known element in a very popular children's story. Each is acceptable, given the common currency of these stories. And they are enough to establish statement 2 with its reference to "several common" stories. Together, then, 2 and 6 are acceptable as support for 7 (and, we will soon see, relevant to it). So this argument fares very well on the acceptability condition.

To consider internal relevance, we look at the arrows in the diagram. They indicate five decisions to be made about internal relevance. The structure of the diagram is important here. The irrelevance of statement 7 to the main conclusion (1) would be far more detrimental to the argument than the irrelevance of one of the premises given in support of statement 2. As it happens, statement 7 is relevant to the MC. We are told that there is at least one reason to consider censoring some children's stories.

We expect statement 7 to provide such a reason, and it does. The creation of a negative image for young children is a reason to consider censorship.

Statements 2 and 6 are linked in support of 7. Why should we believe the stories may be instrumental in creating a negative image for young children? The premises give us the kind of information relevant to answering this question: each story portrays the stepmother as an evil character, and children hear this at an impressionable age. So here, also, the premises are internally relevant to the conclusion they are given to support.

Finally, three arrows lead to statement 2. Statement 2 claims the image of the evil stepmother exists in "several common" stories. The kind of evidence that would be relevant to establishing this claim would involve examples of such stories. That is exactly what each of statements 3, 4, and 5 provides. So all of them are internally relevant to 2. The argument passes the relevance condition for strong arguments.

To complete our assessment, we must decide whether the evidence is sufficient to establish the main claim and its sub-conclusions. It is important to note that both the main conclusion and the sub-conclusion in statement 7 are expressed in a qualified way with no suggestion of certainty. The main conclusion maintains that "there is *at least one* reason to *consider* censoring some children's stories." It falls short of actually advocating censorship (for which this argument would not be sufficient), nor does it concern all children's stories. Hence, evidence concerning one reason to raise the possibility of censorship would be enough, and this the argument provides.

In considering the sub-conclusion in statement 7, it is important to recognize its claim that the stories *may be* instrumental in creating a negative image of stepmothers in young children. Again, it does not suggest a definitive causal relationship between children's stories and negative attitudes toward stepmothers. Such a claim would be harder to defend. Thus, we judge that statements 2 and 6, together, are enough support for 7. To decide otherwise would require us to say what more would be needed, and there is little more that we could expect (beyond, perhaps, the testimony of children or stepmothers who have felt this influence). Whether the three instances cited in statements 3, 4, and 5 are sufficient support for statement 2 is a matter of judgement. But statement 2 refers only to "several" stories, and the supporting premises provide three.

The argument passes all three conditions for good arguments and is, hence, a strong one. Note that the sufficiency of the evidence in the argument has been judged according to the expectations raised by the argument's own claims. This is a point to take to heart when performing your own assessments. Applying the general criteria to the "stepmother" argument reveals it to be strong all round. We could charge that it lacks balance because it provides no instances of stories containing good stepmothers, but its merits outweigh this minor defect.

Revising Arguments

Our three criteria for strong arguments tell us, not only whether an argument is strong or weak, but what needs to be done to make it stronger. In short, that requires moves that make its premises more acceptable, relevant and sufficient. When you find arguments that are weak or have flaws, this means that you should not, in a comprehensive analysis, reject them out of hand, but should consider how their flaws might be remedied. If some of its premises are irrelevant, for example, this is a serious flaw. But it does not follow that you can definitively conclude that the argument has no merits. If there are sufficient other relevant premises, or if there is a way to make the irrelevant premises relevant (typically by adding another premise), then there may be a way to adequately support the conclusion.

We can illustrate the way in which our criteria for strong arguments can be applied to arguments which are not fully convincing with an example. Consider the following argument, which we have extracted from an article ("The trouble with dams") which appeared in the American magazine, *Atlantic Monthly* (August 1995, p. 74). According to the author, American water policy should be changed to enforce conservation measures, because "we squander so much [water] that following through on just the easiest conservation measures would save vast amounts of water." We can diagram the intended argument as follows:

P1 =   Following through on just the easiest water conservation measures would save vast amounts of water.

C =   We should follow through on conservation measures.

If we want to ensure that the diagram captures all of the author's reasoning, we may include, as a hidden premise, HP2, the implied assumption that it is wrong to waste water that could easily be saved. The diagram then appears as follows:

A detailed analysis of P1 and HP2 is beyond the present discussion. At first look, the premises seem acceptable and the conclusion appears to follow from them, making this an example of a strong argument. But if you think about it you should be able to see that there are ways in which one might try to criticize this reasoning. One might, of course, take issue with premise 1. And even if one deemed it acceptable, one might argue that it is not sufficient to establish the conclusion because the United States has an abundance of water and has, therefore, no need to save water, even in easy ways. Alternatively one could deny the sufficiency of the premises by arguing that there are disadvantages to even the easiest conservation measures: because they would mean, for example, the cancellation of the dam projects that the author is criticizing, and they create significant employment in a time when jobs are scarce and the economy needs to be stimulated.

We will not discuss these objections in detail here, except to say that they do not only show potential problems with the argument: they show how its potential weaknesses can be remedied. If the issue is the acceptability of P1, then what is needed is a convincing sub-argument that features P1 as its conclusion. If the problem is the sufficiency of the premises then one can address the argument's weaknesses by adding premises to show that there is, for example, a shortage of water in the United States, or that there aren't major disadvantages to the easiest conservation measures (the latter claim seems to be implied by the very suggestion that these measures are "easy").

As this example illustrates, the three criteria for strong arguments—acceptability, relevance, and sufficiency—provide both a basis for criticizing weak arguments and, at the same time, a positive basis for addressing their weaknesses and remedying the faults that make them so.

7   Summary

This chapter has explored in more detail how we should evaluated arguments. To that end, we have discussed the three key criteria of acceptability, relevance, and sufficiency, illustrating each. We have then applied these to an extended argument in order to see how they can be used to weigh the strengths and weaknesses of argumentation and come to a reasonable judgement.

MAJOR EXERCISE 8M

Assess each of the following passages in terms of the basic criteria of acceptability, relevance, and sufficiency. Be sure to defend your assessments and comment on the overall strength of the argument in each case.

a)   [From "The Rebirth of News," *The Economist*, 14 May 2009, www.economist. com/opinion, p. 15] Up to now, most [newspapers] have been offering their content free online, but that is unsustainable, because there isn't enough advertising revenue online to pay for it. So either the amount of news produced must shrink, or readers must pay more. Some publications, such as the *Financial Times* and *The Wall Street Journal*, which has more than 1m online subscribers and has just promised to develop a new system of micropayments for articles, already charge for content. Others will follow: Rupert Murdoch, the *Journal*'s owner, has said he expects his other titles to start charging too. With news available free on Google and Yahoo!, readers may, of course, not be prepared to pay even for deeper or more specialised stuff; but since they do in the paper world, where free-sheets and paid-for publications coexist, there seems no reason why they wouldn't online.

b)*   Elementary school teachers should be better paid than university professors. The reasons for this are as follows. The complex material dealt with at university requires that students be well grounded in basic skills of reading and writing. And according to many educators, elementary school teachers teach students in their most formative years when basic skills are best taught. Therefore, the job of elementary school teachers is more important than that of university professors. Furthermore, people should be paid according to the importance of their jobs to society. And lastly, university professors are already overpaid.

c)*   [Phillip Flower, in *Understanding the Universe*, West Publishing Co., 1990] Astronomy, however, is accessible to everyone. For only a modest investment, anyone can purchase or build a telescope and begin viewing the sky. . . . Magazines such as *Sky & Telescope and Astronomy* are written for amateurs and help them keep up with the latest research results. In addition, many books for the nonscientist have been written on a variety of astronomical subjects, from the origin of the solar system to the future of the universe.

d) [From "Nudity on film: Sauce for the Goose. . .", the *New York Times*, 15 November 1992, p. B14] Audiences don't want to see male nudity because it's too private, less attractive than female nudity, and somewhat threatening, so directors avoid it (male nudity) at almost any cost.

e) [From a subscription renewal letter from the *London Review of Books*] The *London Review of Books* is becoming a "must-read" among scholars, journalists and opinion leaders—not only in Britain but in North America, too. And until recently, you were among this select group, participating in the international exchange of ideas.

You were in an enviable position. Many people who would enjoy the *London Review of Books* do not yet know about it. You did. You took advantage of that.

I can't imagine that you would want to forego the pleasure of subscribing, especially since we have made the renewal rates so attractive. Surely, you're not renewing must be an oversight. This is your last chance to correct it.

f) [Daniel D. Polsby, in "The false promise of gun control," *Atlantic Monthly*, March 1994] Everyone knows that possessing a handgun makes it easier to intimidate, wound or kill someone. But the implication of this point for social policy has not been so well understood. It is easy to count the bodies of those who have been killed or wounded by guns, but not easy to count the people who have avoided harm because they had access to weapons. Think about uniformed police officers, who carry handguns in plain view not in order to kill people but simply to daunt potential attackers. And it works. Criminals generally do not single out police officers for opportunistic attack. Though officers are expected to draw their guns from time to time, few even in big-city departments will actually fire a shot (except in target practice) in the course of a year. This observation points to an important truth: people who are armed make comparatively unattractive victims. A criminal might not know if one civilian is armed, but if it becomes known that a large number of civilians do carry weapons, criminals will become warier.

g) [From a Letter to the Editor, *National Post*, 6 December 2007] I belong to the demographic of the single young female (SYF), part of the so-called New Girl Order. However, I don't relate to the type of woman portrayed on Sex and the City. The few times I watched the show I saw boring, self-involved, neurotic women, who have no awareness of their dignity.

It's a myth that these women are happy. Perhaps they are self-satisfied, but not happy. The overwhelming #1 goal of any SYF is to find a good man and have a family. That some women do aspire to live the Sex and the City lifestyle makes me think that their family and society have failed them.

h) [From *The Windsor Star*, Opinion, "Keep phones out of class," 24 September 2010, p. A7] The school board thinks it would be good for students and allow them to take notes on their phones. I think this is outrageous. I am a student at the university and have seen first-hand that many students just sit there and text all class. . . . The world is far too complicated these days and the only way we are going to move in the right direction is by simplifying things. In my opinion, all you need to do well in school is paper, a pen and, most importantly, your mind.

i)* [From a Letter to the Editor, the *Windsor Star*, 17 December 2007]
Lately, I have noticed men, sometimes well-dressed men, will open two or three buttons on their shirts. It does not look neat. It is obviously giving notice that they are fed up with being choked. If they have been to a formal affair or party, where they feel necessary to have their shirts buttoned up to the Adam's apple and a tie to make them look snazzy, the first thing they do when they get to their car is to loosen the tie and the top button.

Obviously, most hate wearing uncomfortable clothing. So why not have fashion designers design men's clothing that is dressy and comfortable?

j) [Adapted from I.F. Stone, *The Trial of Socrates*, Little, Brown and Company, 1988, p. 62] It seems paradoxical for Socrates to say that he was not a teacher. One can imagine three possible reasons for such a claim. They are political, philosophical, and personal. The political reason is tied to Socrates' rejection of democracy. He held that "one who knows" should rule, but such rule would be undermined if knowledge and virtue were things that one could teach. The philosophical reason is the impossibility of attaining the absolute certainties that Socrates wanted to attain. The personal reason may be Critias and Alcibiades, two of Socrates' students who turned out badly and did Athens a great deal of harm.

k)* [From Norman Kretzmann's introduction to *William of Sherwood's Introduction to Logic*, University of Minnesota Press, 1968, pp. 3–4] Whether or not [William of Sherwood] was a student at the University of Paris, we have several reasons for believing that he was a master there. In the first place, he lived at a time when "scholars were, indeed, to a degree which is hardly intelligible in modern times, citizens of the world" and when "almost all the great schoolmen . . . taught at Paris at one period or other of their lives." Secondly, in each of his two main works Sherwood uses an example with a Parisian setting: in one case the Seine, and in another the university. Finally, all the philosophers who show signs of having been influenced directly by Sherwood or his writings were in Paris at some time during a span of years when he certainly could have been lecturing there.

l) [From the *Washington Post*, Opinion, "Same-sex marriage isn't the threat to African-American families," 4 March 2011, http://voices.washingtonpost.com/]
It's still beyond me how gay marriage affects the already married or heterosexuals who want to get married.

I understand even less, if that's possible, the concentration of conservative black pastors on gay marriage when the real and present danger is the decline of marriage among African Americans—an ominous trend that has nothing to do with the desire of two people of the same sex to marry.

At least there are gays and lesbians who want to get married. Would that the same could be said of African Americans. . . . Gay, lesbian and transgender people and their desire to get married have nothing to do with the decline of marriage and family in the African American community. What ails us comes from within and from societal conditions unrelated to same sex marriage. If anyone should know that, it's the black preacher.

m) [Environment Canada, Ottawa, *State of the Environment Reporting Newsletter*, No. 7, December 1991] Canada is truly a forest nation. The forest sector provides important social, environmental and economic benefits to every Canadian. Forests not only supply wood and fibre, they also provide a habitat for many plants and animals and a retreat from the pressures of daily life. Canada's forests are a backdrop for a multi-million-dollar tourism and recreation industry. They also play an important environmental role by recycling carbon, nitrogen and oxygen, influencing temperature and rainfall, protecting soils and supplying energy.

n) [From a generally distributed flyer titled "Voting rights for children": (www.coursehero.com/tutors-problems/Other-Homework/7080389-For-the-following-passage-write-a-short-essay-500-words-or-less-in/)] There is a gaping inconsistency in the logic of our democracy in denying children this fundamental democratic right. Many argue that children haven't the intelligence and experience to vote in a meaningful way. This argument was used years ago as a reason for denying non-male, nonwhite people the right to participate in elections. Nobody's intelligence or experience is of more value that someone else's. We all bring our own attributes to the ballot box when we select a candidate.

Others might say that children don't work and thus don't really contribute to society and therefore shouldn't vote. Well, school is work. And with a double digit unemployment rate and many people on social assistance, this rational is also absurd. Would we deny the unemployed the right to vote?

Some argue that parents or guardians will manipulate or force their children to vote for candidates they themselves endorse. We as adults are constantly bombarded with messages and attempted manipulations by all sorts of media and institutions. Just as we learn to sort out our own beliefs from those of others, so will our children. The issue of pressuring children to vote a particular way would be discussed and become a topic of public discourse. Thus children would come to know their rights and practise these rights in the privacy of the polling booth.

It is time we broaden and enrich our lives by realizing that children's views merit substantial validation.

o) [Samuel V. LaSelva, in "Pluralism and hate: Freedom, censorship, and the Canadian identity," *Interpreting Censorship in Canada*, K. Petersen and A.C. Hutchinson, (eds.), University of Toronto Press1999, p. 51] [Pluralism] is connected to harm in at least two ways. First, a society that is pluralistic will have a different conception of harm than one that is not. Thus, a society that endorses multiculturalism brings into existence categories of harm and offensiveness that are not universally recognized. Second, a pluralist society not only recognizes distinctive kinds of harm but is itself a source of them. "One of the difficulties in making multiculturalism politically acceptable," writes Joseph Raz, "stems from the enmity between members of different cultural groups." Such enmity is not simply due to ignorance but is endemic to multiculturalism and other forms of value pluralism. By insisting that there is no single scale of value and that different forms of life are worthwhile, multiculturalism requires people to choose between rival values and commitments, and thereby to value what they choose and disapprove of those who choose differently.

For more online exercises, review questions, and quizzes related to the material in this chapter, please go to www.oupcanada.com/GoodReasoning5e

9

LOOKING FOR THE FACTS

In Chapter 3, we introduced the notion of argument schemes as tools in the construction and evaluation of arguments. In this and subsequent chapters, we explore some of the more popular schemes employed in different types of argumentation. Here, we introduce "empirical" schemes of argument that are used when arguers debate factual issues. In each case, we outline the basic structure and conditions of the scheme and sketch the conditions for a good "counter-argument" that can be used to combat reasoning of this sort. Our discussion focuses on three key ways of arguing that we employ when we "look for the facts" in such circumstances:

▶ generalizations
▶ polling
▶ causal reasoning.

In Chapter 8 we discussed the general criteria for strong arguments. Every strong argument must have premises that are relevant, acceptable, and sufficient to establish its conclusion. When we evaluate a particular argument, we always do so by applying these criteria to the case at hand.

In our preliminary review of argument schemes in Chapter 3, we described them as patterns of argument that commonly occur in arguments on the hoof. By identifying them, and by learning to recognize them in the arguments we analyze (our own as well as others' arguments), we can enhance our ability to assess reasoning. In identifying individual schemes we specify the conditions that must be satisfied to ensure that an instance of a scheme meets the standards of acceptability, relevance, and sufficiency required for a strong argument. In each case, these conditions allow us to identify a "counter-scheme" that may be used to contest conclusions based on the scheme in question. Counter-schemes reject a particular instance of a scheme by arguing that it fails to meet the conditions necessary for good instances of that scheme.

The schemes we introduce in this chapter apply to "empirical" or "factual" issues. We use them when we are looking to establish "facts" about the world: what causes certain things to happen, or how individuals or groups think or behave. In the next chapter we will take our discussion further by looking at other schemes and methods used to establish what the facts are. Because an exhaustive list of schemes used in empirical arguments is beyond the scope of this book (and arguably impossible to construct), there will be times when you must deal with arguments about the facts that do not fit any of the patterns that we will introduce. This is something to keep in mind as you work your way through empirical arguments on the hoof. But you should not think of it as a problem, for you are already equipped to deal with arguments of this sort. In such cases where you cannot rely on the definition of a specific scheme you can revert to the general criteria for strong arguments we discussed in Chapter 8 (i.e. our general account of acceptability, relevance, and sufficiency).

1 Generalizations

Generalization is the process of moving from specific observations about some individuals within a group to general claims about the members of the group. Occasionally, we make generalizations on the basis of a single incident. One painful experience may convince children not to place their tongues on a frozen lamp post, and one good experience may convince us that the Magic Carpet Cleaning Co. does a good job cleaning carpets. More frequently, generalizations are based on a series of observations or experiences. By recording a series of experiences or observations, researchers who conduct polls, surveys, and studies try to determine whether the majority of the population favours capital punishment, whether mandatory seatbelt legislation really reduces injuries in traffic accidents by 40 per cent, and so on.

Generalizations are, by definition, based on an incomplete survey of the evidence. In most cases, this is because a complete survey is, for practical reasons, impossible. Consider the following example: Suppose you operate a small business that assembles cell phones, and you have ordered a thousand microchips for them from a firm in Japan. The firm has agreed to produce them to your exact specifications. Upon their arrival, you open one of the 10 boxes at random, pull out five of the 100 chips it contains, and examine each one carefully to ensure that it meets your requirements. You find that all five do. At random, you open another box from the 10 and test five more chips, finding once again that they have been properly manufactured. You do the same with a third and a fourth box, with the same results. By this time you have carefully examined 20 of the 1000 chips and are fully satisfied. Twenty out of 1000 is a small ratio, but you conclude that "The computer chips meet our specifications."

As we shall see, this is a good inference, even though the premises, consisting of limited observations, do not guarantee the truth of your conclusion about the entire order. You could guarantee the truth of the conclusion if you examined all 1000 of the chips sent and found each and every one to meet your specifications. For practical reasons, we are rarely able to undertake such a complete review. Nor is it necessary, given that we have the basis for a reasonable generalization, even though it remains *possible* that a significant portion—indeed, most or even all the remaining chips—are not what you had ordered. You may, by accident, have happened to pick out the only good chips in the entire order. We must accept that this is possible, but the chance of it is very small, so we accept the reasoning and let the generalization stand.

Sometimes, the end result of such a generalization is a *universal* claim. A universal claim has the form "All Xs are Y." Appendix 1 discusses syllogistic arguments that involve such claims. For the present example, the universal conclusion would read, "All the microchips are good." In other cases, generalizations support *general* claims. A general claim has the form "Xs are, in general, Y," or "Xs are Y," or "Each X is probably Y." In the case at hand, you could express a general claim by concluding that "The microchips meet our specifications."

General claims are not as strong as their universal counterparts. The statement "The microchips meet our specifications" is not as strong a claim as "All the microchips meet our specifications." The general claim implies that the microchips are, on the whole, satisfactory. It leaves open the possibility that some chips may be defective. In contrast, the universal claim allows no exceptions. It is proved mistaken if we find one microchip that is defective. This is why such claims are deemed to be defeasible, that is, they are always open to revision. Defeasible reasoning comes in many forms. It is good reasoning in situations characterized by uncertainty, but it is reasoning that carries the proviso that its conclusions may always be revised if further relevant evidence comes to light.

General claims do not assert as much as universal claims, so they are easier to defend. When we say that "Salmon is good to eat," we may mean that it is usually palatable, and our claim is not refuted if we are served a piece of salmon of poor quality. It is wise to draw general rather than universal conclusions unless you are confident that there are no exceptions to your generalization. In the microchip case, this suggests that you should favour a general conclusion over a universal conclusion.

In some cases, generalizations lead to neither universal nor general claims but to *proportional* claims. Suppose that you had found a defective microchip among the first five you examined. In that case, you would probably have pulled out a few more—say, four more chips—from the same box and inspected them. Suppose you found them to be satisfactory. From one of the 10 boxes you have found one out of nine chips to be defective. Having found one defective chip, you may be more wary than you were. Suppose you open all 10 boxes and at random select a dozen chips from each. You examine them all and conclude that the proportion of defective chips is probably three out of every 120, or that 2.5 per cent of the chips fail to meet your specifications. More generally, you conclude that the vast majority of the chips meet your specifications but that some proportion of them is defective. In both cases, you are making a "proportional" claim.

We have seen that generalizations can lead to universal, general, or proportional claims. In all three cases, the key to a good generalization is a sample of the members of the group that is free from any errors in its selection. If such errors are avoided the sample will represent the group such that we can reasonably draw inferences from the one to the other such that what is true of the sample is true of the group.

Other considerations have to do with what is being sampled. In the case of microchips, which are manufactured using sophisticated technology capable of producing identical items on a production line, we can assume a high level of consistency and predictability. The situation changes if your business is selling fresh fruit rather than computers and the product you received is not microchips but perishable goods like strawberries or bananas. In this case, it is more difficult to assume the consistency of the product, for bananas are not "produced" identically in the way that microchips are, nor do they retain their quality over an extended period of time. Given that fruit will be affected by many factors that can cause imperfections, there is a greater chance that its quality will vary and good generalizations will require a more careful sampling.

In everyday life, we are inclined to make generalizations without a good sample. Often this is because our generalizations rely on "anecdotal evidence," which consists of informal reports of incidents that have not been subjected to careful scrutiny. Though anecdotes of this sort are rarely collected in a systematic way and are sometimes biased and unreliable, they are often used as a basis of generalizations about the unemployed, welfare recipients, professors, women drivers, the very rich, "deadbeat dads," particular ethnic groups, and so on. You should be wary of such generalizations, which are often based on a few instances that may have been embellished and slanted according to the prejudices of those who proffer them.

The "hasty generalizations" that frequently characterize ordinary reasoning have convinced some people that it is wrong to generalize. But bad generalizations do not rule out the possibility of good generalizations, and we can, if we are careful, use our critical faculties and our common sense to decide whether a generalization is based on a good sample. Two kinds of considerations must play a key role in this assessment.

Sample Size

The first thing you must consider in determining the suitability of a sample is its size. Samples that are too small are unreliable and more likely to be affected by pure chance. In the cell phone example, you examined 20 of 1000 microchips and concluded that they met your specifications. Assuming that you have confidence in the firm that manufactured the chips and the process by which they were produced, you have good reason to accept your conclusion, despite the small sample you examined. In contrast, a sample size of one or two or three chips chosen from one box is too susceptible to the luck of the draw. As more and more chips are examined, the chances that your results are mere coincidence diminish.

In the case of the proportional generalization, the discovery of a defective chip led you to enlarge your sample. Problems can occur on a production line. So to get a more accurate picture of the condition of the microchips, you examined more of them. If you had settled for your first five chips, you would have concluded that 20 per cent of the order was defective. As it turns out, a larger sample suggests that there are only problems with 2.5 per cent.

Sample Bias

A sample must be sufficiently large to give us confidence that its characteristics are not due to chance. A good sample must also avoid bias. Anecdotal evidence is problematic because it tends to be biased. Thus, individuals tend to accept and repeat anecdotes that conform to their own perspective in the process of eliminating counter cases.

In a sample used for generalizations, a bias is some way in which the individuals in the sample differ from other individuals in the larger group specified in the generalization. If the microchips in your order had been made in two distinct ways, "A" and "B," and your sample comprised only chips made by process A, then your sample would be biased. This is a serious bias, for each process is likely to have its own potential problems and you cannot expect to detect problems caused by process B if no process-B chips are included in your sample. In this case, a representative sample must include chips from process A and process B (ideally in equal portions, if the same number of chips were made in each way).

A common source of bias is a natural tendency to generalize from the situations with which we are familiar without asking whether these situations are representative. When social workers generalize on the basis of their experiences with single-parent families, they must keep in mind that they are working in a specific geographic area with particular social, ethnic, economic, and political characteristics. They must therefore ask themselves whether single mothers and fathers elsewhere share a similar situation. Otherwise, their generalizations cannot be extended beyond their sphere of experience.

Bias is particularly problematic when generalizations are made about groups of people. Problems easily arise because humans are not a homogeneous group and people are characterized by differences in religious commitment, political affiliation, ethnic background, income, gender, age, and so on. In Chapter 1, we saw how these factors may contribute to someone's belief system, which affects his or her opinions and attitudes about virtually anything we may wish to investigate. Consequently, any attempt to generalize about people and their behaviour must carefully avoid a sample that is imbalanced in any way, by taking account of relevant differences and variations in perspective.

Criteria for Good Generalizations

We can summarize our discussion of generalizations by defining good generalizations as strong arguments (i.e. with acceptable, relevant, and sufficient premises) that conform (implicitly or explicitly) to the following scheme:

> **Premise 1:** S is a sample of Xs.
> **Premise 2:** Proportion 1 of Xs in S are Y.
> **Conclusion:** Proportion 2 of Xs are Y.

In this scheme,

- **Xs** can be anything whatsoever—dogs, cats, worlds, dreams, cities, etc.
- **Y** is the property that Xs are said to have.
- **Sample (S)** is the group of Xs that has been considered—the particular microchips selected for examination, the bananas inspected in a shipment, the people questioned in a poll, etc.

- **Proportion 1** and **Proportion 2** refer to some proportion of the Xs—*all* Xs, *some* Xs, *most* Xs, Xs *in general*, etc., or some specified percentage, e.g. 2.5 per cent, 10 per cent, 70 per cent, and so on. Proportion 1 must be equal to or greater than Proportion 2.

An explicit instance of this scheme would be the following:

P1 = The group of microchips examined (Sample S) is a sample of the chips sent (Xs).

P2 = All (Proportion 1) of the microchips examined (i.e. in Sample S) are made to specification (Y).

C = All (Proportion 2) of the microchips sent (Xs) are made to specification (Y).

In this case, Proportion 1 and Proportion 2 are the same proportion "All," which is normally the case, though it is possible that they will be different. In this example, we could have let Proportion 2 = "Most" and made our conclusion the general (rather than the universal) claim that "Most of the microchips sent are made to specifications."

Our scheme for generalizations raises the question of how we can establish its first premise. This will be explored further in the section on polling. For now we will simply say that we expect a sample that is (a) large enough not to be overly influenced by chance and (b) free of bias. In considering whether a generalization is a strong generalization or not, we will, therefore, need to spend much of our time considering arguments like the following:

The researchers considered a reasonable number of Xs.
The group of Xs considered is not biased.
Therefore, the sample considered is a good sample.

In ordinary reasoning, you need to consider the kinds of things that are being sampled in order to decide whether a particular sample of them is reasonable and unbiased.

As you do exercises and consider other examples of ordinary reasoning, you will see that generalizations are often presented in implicit ways in ordinary argument. An arguer may not explicitly address the question of whether a sample is biased or reasonably sized. Sometimes they will not even recognize that they have based their general, universal, or proportional claim on a process of generalization that needs to be evaluated. In such contexts, it is up to you to recognize the issues that the implicit generalization raises. In this way, you can subject the argument to proper critical assessment.

Counter-arguments against Generalizations

A strong argument against a generalization must show that strong reasoning does not support the conclusion allegedly established by the generalization. This can be done in one of two ways: (1) by showing that the sample of Xs in question is not characterized by the property alleged (Y); or (2) by showing that the sample of Xs does not accurately reflect the group. In the latter case, we need to argue that the sample is too small or that it is biased in one way or another. In the process, we must, of course, clearly explain why we believe the sample to be inadequate.

GENERALIZATIONS

Generalization is the process of moving from specific observations about some individuals within a group to general claims about members of the group. Generalizations can be the basis for universal, general, or proportional claims. A strong generalization shows:

1. That the individuals in the sample have some property Y, and
2. That the sample is good—i.e. that it is (a) of reasonable size and (b) free of bias.

A good counter-argument to generalization shows that one or more of these criteria is not met.

EXERCISE 9A

1. For each of the following topics, state whether you are in a position to make a reasonable generalization, and why. In each case, discuss the issues this raises and the problems you may encounter in forming a generalization. Giving examples of possible generalizations, discuss how you could improve the sample in order to yield a more reliable generalization and/or modify your generalization to fit your sample more accurately.

   a) Students' work habits at your institution.
   b) The policies of a particular political party.
   c)* Bus service where you live.
   d) The exams of one of your instructors.
   e) Psychology courses.
   f)* The attitudes of Americans.
   g) The spending habits of tourists to California.
   h) The colour of squirrels.
   i) The price of automobiles.
   j) The reliability of your make of car.

2. Identify the generalizations contained in the following examples and assess their strength:

   a) [From "Women like practicality in cars, men go for the looks—study" DETROIT—Reuters, 11 April 2011] Men prefer their cars beefy or fast, while women go for lower price tags and better fuel economy, according to a new survey. TrueCar.com, which studied data from 8 million purchases in the United States last year, found BMW AG's Mini had the highest percentage of female buyers at 48 per cent, while 93 per cent of buyers for Fiat SpA's Ferrari were men.

   "The study shows that women car buyers are more cost-conscious and purchased fuel-efficient vehicles while male buyers were completely the opposite, purchasing vehicles that were either big and brawny, like a large truck, or chose a high-priced, high-performance vehicle," TrueCar analyst Jesse Toprak said in a statement.

Following Mini with the women were Kia Motors Corp (47 per cent) and Honda Motors Co Ltd (46 per cent) branded vehicles, according to the study. Last year, General Motors Co's Saturn and Kia tied at 45.2 per cent, followed by Mini at 45 per cent.

There were 15 brands with more than 40 per cent female buyers, TrueCar said.

Maserati (84 per cent), Porsche (80 per cent) and General Motors' GMC (74 per cent) followed Ferrari for the highest percentage of male buyers, according to the study.

The top-selling model for women, with a minimum of 1,000 retail sales, was Volkswagen AG's New Beetle at 61 per cent, while for men it was the Porsche 911 at 88 per cent, TrueCar said.

b)* "I've owned two Toyota's with no problems. My wife bought a Toyota that she is still driving seven years later with only minor repairs in the course of tune-ups. I'll never drive another vehicle."

c) [From *Redbook* magazine, 3 March 2011, p. 72] If your little one is anti broccoli, spinach, and veggies in general, it is okay to surrender and stop stressing, says New Jersey-based dietician Erin Palinski, R.C. A recent study at the University of Bristol in the United Kingdom followed more than 13,000 children from infancy to age 7 and found that picky eaters met the same calorie and nutrient quotas as veggie-loving kids. And there were no major differences in weight and height between the two groups.

d) [From the manifesto of the "Unabomber," widely available on the Internet] It is said that we live in a free society because we have a certain number of constitutionally guaranteed rights. But these are not as important as they seem. The degree of personal freedom that exists in a society is determined more by the economic and technological structure of the society than by its laws or its form of government. Most of the Indian nations of New England were monarchies, and many of the cities of the Italian Renaissance were controlled by dictators. But in reading about these societies one gets the impression that they allowed far more personal freedom than our society does.

2   Polling

One context in which generalizations play an important role is polling. Media outlets regularly release the results of professionally conducted polls under headlines that make claims like "Most Americans believe the economy will improve in the next year," or "Over 90 per cent of people support increased health care spending," or even "Few people trust the results of polls." Beneath these headlines we read an array of details that supposedly justify them. They may tell us who was polled (how many), what was asked, how it was asked, who conducted the poll, and how reliable the results are deemed to be (the "margin of error"). Given the prevalence of conclusions inferred from polls, it is important to learn how to judge them—in order to distinguish strong conclusions from weak ones, to know what information to expect to be present, and to appreciate when a problem lies in the poll itself or in the way it is being reported.

In deciding whether a poll is a reasonable generalization, we need to begin by identifying three aspects of it:

1. *The sample:* the group of people polled—who they are and how many of them there are.
2. *The population sampled:* the larger group to which the sample belongs and is deemed to be representative of.
3. *The property in question:* the opinion or characteristic studied in the poll about which a conclusion has been drawn.

These three concepts can be illustrated with the following example.

Under the headline "41% of US doctors would aid executions" (Andre Picard, *The Globe and Mail*, 20 November 2001, p. A9—available in the paper's archives under the headline), we read that 1000 practising physicians were asked whether they would carry out one or more of 10 acts related to lethal injection. In this example, the *sample* is 1000 practising American physicians, the *population* is all practising American physicians, and the *property* is "willingness to aid in executions." As the headline indicates, the researchers conducting the poll concluded that 41 per cent of practising American physicians have the property "would aid in executions." They based this conclusion on the fact that 41 per cent of their sample said they would, at least according to the news story.

Implicitly or explicitly, polling arguments are instances of the general scheme for generalizations. Good arguments from polling are strong arguments that have the form:

> **Premise 1:** S is a sample of Xs.
> **Premise 2:** Proportion 1 of Xs in S are Y.
> **Conclusion:** Proportion 2 of Xs are Y.

where:

- **Xs** are the population—the group of people about whom the conclusion is drawn.
- **Y** is the property the people in the population are said to have.
- **Sample S** is the sample of people studied.
- **Proportion 1** and **Proportion 2** are the proportion of people in the sample and the population who are said to have property Y.

In most arguments from polling, Proportion 1 and Proportion 2 are identical, as with the 41 per cent assigned to both sample and population in the above example. In many arguments, premise 1 (the claim that the sample is of the population) is a hidden premise.

Because polls may study more than one property in a sample, many arguments from polling will specify not only the proportion of the sample and the population that has the principal property investigated but also the proportion that has other properties. In trying to determine the percentage of physicians who would act in executions, for example, a poll is likely to reach conclusions about the percentage opposed to such actions, the percentage who have no opinion, and so on. For this reason, the second premise in a polling argument often has the form "Proportion 1 of Xs in S are Y; Proportion 2 of Xs in S are Z; Proportion 3 of Xs in S are W. . . ." In such cases, the conclusion of the polling argument will be "Proportion 1 of Xs are Y; Proportion 2 of Xs are Z; Proportion 3 of Xs are W. . . ." This can be illustrated with respect to the above poll, by going to the newspaper's own source, the *Annals of Internal Medicine*. The information contained there varies from *The Globe and Mail*'s report in significant ways, and we will comment on this below. But using the newspaper's interpretation and information from the study we can produce the following argument:

P1 =   The 1000 practising American physicians polled constitute a representative sample of practising American physicians.

P2 =   Forty-one per cent of the physicians polled indicated that they would perform at least one action related to lethal injection disallowed by the American Medical Association; 25 per cent said they would perform five or more disallowed actions; only 3 per cent knew of any guidelines on the issue.

C =   Forty-one per cent of practising American physicians would perform at least one action related to lethal injection disallowed by the American Medical Association; 25 per cent would perform five or more disallowed actions; only 3 per cent know of any guidelines on the issue.

In this case, the sample is the physicians polled, the population is practising American physicians, and the properties investigated are the three properties mentioned in premise 2.

Sampling Errors

In determining whether a polling argument is a strong argument, we need to assess the acceptability of the premises. There are two kinds of issues that can arise in this regard, which correspond to each of our two premises.

The first issue that polls raise is tied to premise 1. It concerns the sample used. In deciding whether it is representative, we need to ask questions like: *Is the sample reliable? Is its size sufficient? How was it selected? Does it include all relevant subgroups? Is the margin of error it allows within reasonable bounds?* If these kinds of questions cannot be answered satisfactorily, we say that the poll contains a *sampling error* and that the polling argument is a weak one. It can be compared to other kinds of generalizations with samples that are biased or too small.

In many cases, the reports we read of polling results will not give us the answers to all our questions. In considering what has been omitted, remember that sample size is important. As we have seen in our discussion of generalizations, too small a sample will not permit reliable conclusions. How much is enough? For most studies pollsters aim for samples of around 1000. That may seem small to you, given that the population in question involves a national membership. But as populations grow, the sample sizes required for reliable results increase by only small amounts. A number of 1000 is adequate for the kinds of national polls you are likely to find reported in the media. Where populations are smaller, such as the number of people in your year at your institution, much smaller samples can be used.

Even when a sample is large enough, there may be problems with the group chosen as a sample. When you judge a sample to determine whether there is a sampling error, consider how it was selected. Did people self-select, say, by voluntarily answering a mail survey or by logging on to a website? If so, you need to judge what kind of people are likely to do so and whether conclusions based on such results actually reflect the populations identified. A certain portion of the public does not use the Internet. Another portion will not answer surveys. These portions of the public will not be represented in a self-selected Internet poll. In such a case, we need to ask whether this creates a bias—whether it means that the sample does not accurately represent the population it is drawn from.

One of the most famous unrepresentative samples in the history of polling was used by *The Literary Digest* to predict the results of the 1936 US presidential election. It sent surveys to 10 million individuals, with 2.4 million responses. This should have given them statistically significant information. *The Literary Digest* predicted that the election would result in 370 electoral college votes for Landon and 161 for Roosevelt. History showed the pollsters to be drastically mistaken as Roosevelt won hands down. How could this be? How could such a large sample fail to be representative? The problem lay with polling techniques flawed in ways that biased the results. They surveyed their own readers—a group with incomes above the national average. And they used lists of automobile owners and telephone users. Again, in the Depression years of the 1930s, both of these groups had higher incomes than the national average. The sample represented an economic class that was overwhelmingly predisposed to Landon's Republican party. The error cost the magazine its life.

The preferred means of sample selection is one that is random. A sample is "random" if every member of the population has an equal chance of being selected. In the survey of American physicians, we are told that the participants were randomly selected. In this and other cases of random sampling, we need to determine whether relevant subgroups of the population have been included. Relevant subgroups can include men, women, and people of a particular age, education, geographical location, etc. As you can imagine, there are many possibilities. In any particular case, the possibilities that matter are those that are likely to affect the property in question. In the poll of American physicians, we would want to know how many of the 1000 doctors who participated in the survey practise in states that carry out executions and how many are from states that do not, because it is plausible to suppose that the possibility that one really will be asked to assist with an execution may influence a participant's response.

Because truly random samples are difficult to obtain, polls and surveys conducted by professional pollsters tend to use a method called "stratified random sampling." In stratified random sampling, a group of people polled is divided into categories relevant to the property in question, ensuring that a suitable number of individuals from each group is included in the sample. If 25 per cent of Americans have an income under $20,000, then a poll aiming to discover what percentage of Americans support their present government should attempt to have 25 per cent of its surveys answered by Americans with an income under $20,000. The sample should be selected in a way that ensures that all other significant subgroups are considered.

Most reports on polls include a margin of error that gives the confidence interval this size of sample allows. While this is a complex matter, it is sufficient for our purposes to understand how to read margins of error. As scientific as polling has become, the results are still approximations that tell us what is *probably* the case. To underscore this point, statisticians report results that fall within a margin of error that is expressed as a percentage ("plus or minus 3 per cent," or "± 3%") that indicates the likelihood that the data they have collected are dependable. The lower the margin of error, the more accurately the views of those surveyed match those of the entire population. Every margin of error has a "confidence level," which is usually 95 per cent. This means that if you asked a question from a particular poll 100 times, your results would be the same (within the margin of error) 95 times.

Margin of error is particularly important when it leaves room for very different possibilities, for this raises questions about the significance of the results. For example, if a poll tells us that in the next election 50 per cent of people will vote for party "A" while 45 per cent will vote for party "B" (the rest undecided or refusing to tell) and that there is a margin of error of ± 3 per cent, then we need to proceed with caution. For although it looks as if party A is ahead, the margin of error tells us that party A's support could be as low as 47 per cent (–3) or as high as 53 per cent (+3); party B's support lies between a low of 42 per cent and a high of 48 per cent. Who is ahead in the polls? In this situation, the overlap makes it too close to call.

Measurement Errors

Assuming that a poll does not contain a sampling error, we still need to ask whether it has attained its results in a manner that is biased or in some other way problematic. Otherwise, the results reported in premise 2 in our polling scheme may be unreliable. Here we need to ask: *How reliable is the information collected about the measured property? What kinds of questions were asked? How were the results of the immediate questions interpreted? Were the questions or answers affected by biases (of wording, timing, sponsors, etc.)?* If these kinds of questions cannot be answered satisfactorily, we say that the poll contains a *measurement error.* Here the problem may be that the results of the poll are biased because of the way in which the sample was studied. A current suspicion of polling during political election campaigns, fuelled in part by the very different results announced by different polling companies, reflects the possibility that measurement errors are at work in at least some of the published polls. In the 2011 Canadian federal election disparities between voter preferences reported by pollsters were as high as 15 percentage points (from John Allemang, "In the messiness of democracy, polling offers semblance of order," *The Globe and Mail*, 8 April 2011, p. A7). As Allemang notes, some of this is due to the obsolescence of traditional techniques. A generation ago, telephone samplings achieved 70 per cent response rates; now call-display features have lowered this to 20 per cent. All of which should encourage you to look carefully for possible measurement errors in published polls.

We know from Chapter 6 that statements can be vague or ambiguous. If survey respondents have been asked questions that lend themselves to different interpretations or are vague ("How do you feel about X?"), then we may question the reliability of the results. If a sample of university students is asked whether they "use condoms regularly," it matters whether the respondents are left to decide what should count as "regularly" or are given an indication of what the pollster means by the term.

It can also be important to ask how pollsters arrive at percentages from the types of questions asked. To learn that 70 per cent of health club members in a certain city are males seems unproblematic because we can imagine what kind of straightforward question was asked. People tend to know whether they are male or female, and it would be no problem for the pollsters to take the numbers of each and convert them into percentages. But when we are told that 70 per cent of adults are "largely dissatisfied" with the government's response to crime, then the matter seems not so straightforward. What questions have the pollsters asked to arrive at this percentage? People may not know their views in quite the same way as they know their sex, and so the clarity of the questions and any directions accompanying them become crucial.

There are other ways in which the questions, or the way they have been posed, may result in a measurement error. Psychologists tell us that people are more likely to answer truthfully when participating in face-to-face interviews. Interviews conducted over the phone are less reliable, as are the results of group interviews, where participants feel pressure to answer in certain ways. In judging polls, we need, therefore, to ask whether some factors may have influenced people to answer in ways that did not reflect their real behaviour or opinions.

In other cases, a poll may contain a measurement error in view of the time when it was conducted, who conducted it, or who commissioned it. We are usually told when a poll was conducted. At this point, we should ask ourselves whether there were things occurring at that time that may have influenced the responses. A poll assessing people's views on their country's involvement in a war just after a number of casualties have been incurred may elicit a different set of responses from those elicited by the same poll conducted at another time. In view of this, the poll may not reflect how people *generally* feel about the issue. Likewise, we may ask whether the group or agency that commissioned the poll released the results in a timely fashion or held on to them until a time that suited them. If they have waited, the results may no longer be reliable because intervening events could have altered the views given.

Finally, when dealing with polls reported in the media, be charitable. To properly assess a poll, you need a significant amount of information on the way it was conducted. When this information is omitted, ask yourself whether the problem lies with the poll itself or with the media outlet reporting it. Sometimes the report does not give the information we require to properly assess the poll. Our analysis of the reasoning should mention this, and we should refrain from making conclusions that the information we have does not justify. Also, be alert to the way that both editors and reporters (and those quoted in reports) themselves have interpreted the results of polls, as reflected in the headlines they choose and the statements they make. Sometimes such headlines and statements are not justified by the information provided, as an analysis of that material (according to the procedures we have explained) will tell you. Our opening headline—"41% of US doctors would aid executions"—is an eye-catching claim. But it also exploits the vagueness of the word "aid." The details provided in the report tell us that only 19 per cent of the doctors included in the survey said they would actually give the injection. So the reporter's lead statement that "More than 40 per cent of US physicians are willing to work as executioners" is misleading. More problematic, the actual study in the *Annals of Internal Medicine* indicates that the 1000 number important to the report was the number of surveys distributed. Only 413 responded—a serious omission in the newspaper report—and the sample of 41 per cent who were willing to do one or more of the actions involved in capital punishment is the percentage of *this* lower number. The authors of the study rightly worry that the number of nonresponses produced a biased result. So the report on the poll is quite misleading. As always with second-hand reports, we are vulnerable to the kinds of selection and distortion we discussed in Chapter 2. The lesson is that before we act on such information, we should investigate further.

Counter-arguments to Polls

Once we understand polls and the ways in which they can support good generalizations, we can also understand how to construct counter-arguments to contest the conclusions based on them. This requires that we show that the features of good arguments from polls are missing in the case at hand. In such cases, the poll (or media source) misreports the results of the polling or suffers from a sampling or a measurement error. In this way, the criteria for good arguments from polls can help us construct and assess arguments against a poll result.

POLLING

A poll is a kind of generalization that surveys a sample of a larger population in order to establish what proportion of this population has one or more properties. A strong generalization based on a poll shows:

1. That the individuals polled have the properties in question to the extent claimed; and
2. That the sample is (a) free of sampling errors and (b) free of measurement errors.

A good counter-argument to a generalization based on a poll shows that one or more of these criteria is not met.

EXERCISE 9B

For each of the polls reported here, identify the sample, population, and property, and set out the argument scheme. Then assess the reliability of the conclusion by means of the questions raised for dealing with polls. Where you identify problems, determine whether they lie with the poll itself or the way it has been reported.

a) [From Brian Lilley "Canadians still want to marry: Poll," *Toronto Sun*, 23 July 2011] With or without the statistics, most single Canadians say they want to marry, and the overwhelming majority of adults consider a successful marriage an important life goal, according to a new survey.

When asked—in a poll conducted for Sun News Network by Abacus Data—how important it was to have a successful marriage, 82% of those surveyed said it was either "the most important" or "very important but not the most." A successful marriage came second only to being a good parent on the list of life goals, which also included owning a home, being successful in a high-paying career and living a very religious life.

When single Canadians, representing 237 of those surveyed were asked whether they wanted to get married, 64% said yes while 36% said no. The online poll of 1,005 adult Canadians was conducted June 23 and 24 (2011)

b)* [From a report in the journal *Nature*, December 1997] Cheating remains widespread among students at US universities, according to a recent survey of 4,000 students at 31 institutions. The survey found that incidents of serious malpractice have increased significantly over the past three decades and, although highest among students on vocational courses such as business studies and engineering, they are also significant in the natural sciences.

The survey report by Donald McCabe, professor of management at Rutgers University in New Jersey, appears in the current issue of the journal *Science and Engineering Ethics* (Vol. 4, No. 433–45, 1997). Based on the experience of the university departments, McCabe concludes that strict penalties are a more effective deterrent than exhortations to behave morally. Cheating is more common at universities without an "honour code"—a binding code of conduct for students, with penalties for violation. More than half of science students at universities with no honour code admitted falsifying data in laboratory experiments.

More than two-thirds of all students polled said they had cheated in some way. Seventy-three per cent of science students from universities without an

honour code admitted "serious cheating." The figure for those from universities with a code was 49 per cent. "Serious cheating" includes copying from someone during an examination and using crib notes.

c) [From an Angus Reid survey of British Columbia residents after the riots that followed the last game of the Stanley Cup. We have focused on one question asked: the actions of the Vancouver police force. *Angus Reid Public Opinion*, 20 June 2011, www.angus-reid.com/polls/43930/british-columbians-want-vancouver-rioters-and-looters-to-face-justice]

British Columbians Want Vancouver Rioters and Looters to Face Justice

Residents of British Columbia and Metro Vancouver are dismayed at the events that unfolded after the conclusion of the Stanley Cup Final, and call for those responsible for the rioting and looting that took place in Downtown Vancouver to be prosecuted to the full extent of the law, a new Angus Reid Public Opinion poll has found.

The online survey of a representative provincial sample of 906 adult British Columbians also shows support for new measures to deal with crowds, and opposition to the idea of banning street parties.

Two-thirds of British Columbians (66%) and Metro Vancouver residents (64%) are satisfied with the way the Vancouver Police Department (VPD) handled the events that took place after the conclusion of the Stanley Cup Final. In addition, practically all respondents (96% in BC, 95% in Metro Vancouver) want the people who took part in riots to be prosecuted to the full extent of the law. For the most part, British Columbians agree with some of the prevailing arguments that have emerged in the aftermath of the riots . . . that police officers handled the situation properly, and that those who broke the law must be brought to justice.

The level of satisfaction with the way the VPD handled the events is high. *Methodology: From June 16 to June 17, 2011, Angus Reid Public Opinion conducted an online survey among 906 randomly selected British Columbia adults, including 515 Metro Vancouver adults, who are Angus Reid Forum panelists. The margin of error—which measures sampling variability—is +/- 3.3% for the British Columbia sample and +/- 4.3% for the Metro Vancouver sample. The results have been statistically weighted according to the most current education, age, gender and region Census data to ensure a sample representative of the entire adult population of British Columbia. Discrepancies in or between totals are due to rounding.*

3 General Causal Reasoning

Often, generalizations are used to establish cause-and-effect relationships. When dieticians tell us that people with low-fat diets tend to be healthier overall, it suggests that it is the diet that causes the health effects. When a university tells you (or potential students) that graduates earn such-and-such an impressive average income, it is suggesting that a high income is, at least in part, a causal consequence of the stature of their institution and the quality of education it provides.

General causal arguments attempt to establish general or universal causal claims. We make general causal claims when we say that students from a particular school are better prepared for university, or that wearing seatbelts saves lives. Scientists use general causal reasoning to show that a chemical behaves in a specific way under certain conditions, that smoking causes lung cancer, or that car emissions and the burning of other fossil fuels are causing global warming.

Two kinds of causal conditions play a role in general causal reasoning. A constant condition is a causal factor that must be present if an event is to occur. For example, the presence of oxygen is a constant condition for combustion: without oxygen, there cannot be combustion. This gives oxygen an important causal role in combustion, but we would not, under normal circumstances, say that oxygen causes combustion. The event or condition we designate as the cause is the *variable condition*, i.e. the condition that brings about the effect. Since dry foliage is a constant condition for a forest fire and oxygen is a constant condition for combustion, we would normally designate the carelessly tossed match—the variable condition—as the cause of a particular fire.

We call the set of constant and/or variable conditions that produce some event its *composite cause*. A comprehensive account of the composite cause of some event is difficult to produce, for most events are the result of a complex web of causal relationships and a number of constant and/or variable conditions. Often, our interest in a composite cause is determined by our interest in actively affecting the outcomes in some situation. If we can establish that the (variable) condition in the cause of forest fires is the embers from campfires, we may be able to reduce this risk by educating campers. If we are concerned about spring flooding, we must accept that we cannot control the variable conditions that produce such floods (e.g. spring rains and runoff), but we may build dams and reservoirs that allow us to control the constant conditions that make these floods possible (e.g. the height of a river).

Our interest is in constructing and evaluating causal arguments in everyday reasoning, so we will keep our discussion as simple as possible. We will begin with arguments for general causal claims, i.e. claims of the form "X causes Y," where X is either a variable condition or a composite cause. In the next chapter, we will look at particular causal arguments.

A good general causal argument is a strong argument that establishes (implicitly or explicitly) three points in support of a general causal conclusion. We can summarize these points in the following scheme for general causal reasoning:

> **Premise 1:** X is correlated with Y.
> **Premise 2:** The correlation between X and Y is not due to chance.
> **Premise 3:** The correlation between X and Y is not due to some mutual cause Z.
> **Premise 4:** Y is not the cause of X.
> **Conclusion:** X causes Y.

One key to a good argument for the general claim "X causes Y" is a demonstration that X and Y are regularly connected. This is captured in the first premise of our scheme, for in a case of such regularity we say that there is a **correlation** between X and Y. The claim that gum disease is caused by the build-up of plaque is ultimately based on the work of scientists who have established a correlation between the build-up of plaque and gum disease. That is, they have observed a regular connection between the two phenomena.

Every causal relationship implies the existence of a correlation between two events, X and Y, but the existence of a correlation does not in itself guarantee a causal relationship. The assumption that this is the case is the most common error made in causal reasoning. The problem is that an observed correlation may be attributable to other factors. Most notably, it may be the result of simple chance or of some third event, Z, which really causes Y or causes both X and Y and is referred to as a "second" cause. Our scheme guards against these two possibilities in its second and third premises.

Moreover, given an established correlation between X and Y, we must also have some reason to rule out a causal relationship whereby Y is actually the cause of X. Our fourth premise addresses this. In many instances, the context alone will suffice to support this premise: we can be confident, for example, that house fires do not cause careless smoking. In other cases, the relationship may not be so clear and can lead to the problem of confusing cause and effect. Does stress during exams cause errors, or do errors cause stress? The fourth premise requires us to consider carefully whether the causal relationship may be the reverse of what is being concluded.

In many cases, a good argument for the claim that X causes Y will be built on sub-arguments that establish the four premises in our scheme. In arguing that there is a correlation between X and Y, the results of a study or even casual observations may be cited. In arguing that this correlation is not due to chance, a sub-argument may explain why it is plausible to see X and Y as causally connected. In arguing that there is no mutual second cause, a sub-argument may try to eliminate the likely possibilities. And in arguing that Y does not cause X, a sub-argument will aim to show that this is implausible or unlikely.

Consider a case of causal investigation reported on the CBC radio program Dispatches (www.cbc.ca/dispatches/episode/2011/06/02/june-2-5-from---lima-peru---amsterdam---syria---rondonia-brazil---lomardi-italy), under the headline "Why Are Italian Soccer Stars Coming Down with Lou Gehrig's Disease?" This disease, also known as ALS, is a fatal muscle-wasting disease with no known cause. Apparently, over the last 30 years there has been a high incidence of ALS in Italian soccer players, nearly 50 out of 40,000. This means that Italian soccer players are 20 times more likely to contract the disease than the rest of the population. Why?

One hypothesis is that the cause is doping. Unfortunately, because of the timeline involved, it has been very difficult for investigators to test for toxicity in former players. But they did look at another sport—cycling, which is notorious for its doping scandals. And there are no incidences of ALS among professional cyclists. A second hypothesis is trauma. But when investigators looked at professional basketball, with a high incidence of trauma injuries, they again found no incidence of ALS among present or former players.

The issue is compounded by the fact that all the cases of ALS involve only four teams: AC Milan, Como, Fiorentina, and Torino. Investigators then turned their attention to the fields involved. While the Italian Soccer Federation has not cooperated in the studies, they have found heavy metal under the pitch at Como. But as an official of the Como ground points out, many players have played on that pitch without contracting the disease. So if it turns out something in the fields like heavy metal is the constant condition, investigators will still need to uncover a variable condition that brings about the effect in some players but not others. At the time we write this, no such condition has been uncovered.

It is possible to understand the scheme for good general causal reasoning as a variant of the scheme for good generalizations. This is because the correlation that is the heart of an argument for a general causal claim is a sample of the instances of the cause. If we claim that "Taking a vacation in February is one way to cure the winter blahs," on the basis of our own experience and the experience of our friends, then we have made a general claim on the basis of a sample of vacations in February (i.e. those taken by ourselves and our friends). In our reasoning, we have used the correlation between these vacations and the curing of the winter blahs as a basis for a causal generalization. In any general causal argument, the correlation between the cause and the observed effect in the sample studied is used to justify the broader claim that the cause always, or in general, leads to the effect. "X causes Y" is a general claim in which the property "causes Y" is assigned to X. As in any generalization, we must be sure that the sample offered is representative, that it is not biased in any way, and that its connection to the alleged effect is not due to coincidence. The second premise in our scheme discounts the first possibility; the third rules out bias as an explanation for the existence of Y in the correlation.

Given our account of general causal reasoning, good arguments *against* a general causal claim can be constructed by showing that the reasoning the claim depends on violates the conditions for good causal reasoning. In such cases, we will need to show:

1. That the claimed correlation does not exist;
2. That the correlation is due to chance;
3. That there is a second cause that accounts for the correlation between the alleged cause and effect; or
4. That it is more likely that the causal relation is the other way around.

Most problematic causal arguments are undermined by the third possibility.

Key features of general causal reasoning are evident in a study published in the journal *Pediatrics* (Lee et al., "Weight status in young girls and the onset of puberty," 5 March 2007) and widely discussed in the media. Researchers studied 354 girls from the National Institute of Child Health and from the Human Development Study of Early Child Care and Youth Development. The girls were measured and weighed at 36 and 54 months and grades 1, 4, 5, and 6 and with assessment of pubertal stage by physical examination and maternal report in grades 4 through 6. The researchers discovered a correlation between body mass index and early puberty such that the higher a girl's body mass index (or fat mass) by age three, the more likely she was to reach puberty by her ninth birthday. "Puberty" was determined by breast development and first menstruation.

Some media outlets saw this as "Obesity may cause early puberty" (CanWest News Service, 5 March 2007), a clear causal claim drawn from the correlation. But the researchers themselves were less definite in their conclusions. Lead author Dr Joyce Lee, an assistant professor in the division of pediatric endocrinology at the University of Michigan, stated, "By no means have we proven weight gain causes early onset of puberty." But the study's finding adds further evidence to the hypothesis that excess body fat is a potential cause of early sexual maturation in girls. Other studies have found that girls are entering puberty at younger ages compared with 30 years ago, and rates of childhood obesity have increased dramatically over the same period, supporting the hypothesis of a link between the two. The mechanism by which obesity might trigger puberty in girls is unclear. One theory is that the higher the body mass index, the more fat cells, and that those fat cells secrete hormones that kick-start puberty. But Lee pointed out that that is "all speculation." She also stated in an interview that it was unclear "if puberty is causing the weight gain, or the weight gain is causing puberty." But the study now favours the latter.

The study, then, has serious causal import. In terms of the questions we have raised, the tracking of the girls from 36 months through grade 6 found that increased body mass (or fat) and early puberty were "consistently and positively associated," thus presenting a strong correlation between the two variables. Nor, given the number of girls and time frames involved, does chance seem to be a factor in the correlation. That the causal relationship may be the other way around (with early puberty causing obesity), a possibility before this study, is also addressed by the systematic measurements taken at 36 and 54 months and grades 1, 4, 5, and 6. What had not been explicitly ruled out is the possibility of a third factor accounting for both the variables. But the study decreases this likelihood. In terms of the possible consequences, given the increases in obesity among North American children and the social and psychological problems associated with early puberty (higher rates of depression and anxiety, increased likelihood of drinking alcohol and having sex at an earlier age, increased risks of teenage pregnancy as well as obesity and breast cancer as adults), then prudence favours accepting the causal claim.

GENERAL CAUSAL REASONING

General causal reasoning attempts to establish general causal principles that govern causes and effects. A good general causal argument is an argument that establishes that X causes Y (where X is a variable condition or a composite cause) by showing:
1. That there is a correlation between X and Y;
2. That this correlation is not the result of mere coincidence;
3. That there is no second cause, Z, that is the cause of Y or of both X and Y; and
4. That Y is not the cause of X.

EXERCISE   9C

Discuss the following arguments from the point of view of the account of causal arguments we have provided. Diagram the arguments. Are the arguments made for or against causal claims plausible or implausible, weak or strong? What would be needed to strength the claim?

a) [An advertisement in *Redbook*, 3 March 2011, p. 36. The line "brings fever down faster" is in red type in the advertisement]

> FACT:
> Children's Advil
> **brings fever down faster**
> than Children's Tylenol.
>
> Children's Advil also keeps your
> child's fever down longer.
>
> Nothing is proven better on fever.
> Not even Children's Motrin.
>
> Look for Children's Advil in
> the cough/cold aisle today.

b) [Bjørn Lomborg, in *The Skeptical Environmentalist: Measuring the Real State of the World*, Cambridge University Press, 2001, p. 10] Recent research suggests that pesticides cause very little cancer. Moreover, scrapping pesticides would actually result in *more* cases of cancer because fruits and vegetables help to prevent cancer, and without pesticides fruits and vegetables would get more expensive, so that people would eat less of them.

c)* Every time there's a test on a Friday morning after Thursday pub night, the class tends to do terribly. So if we move the test to Wednesday, results should improve.

d) [From Mark Kingwell, 'Number-crunching satisfaction and desire,' *The Globe and Mail*, 23 June 2007, p. F6. Regarding a study from the US National Bureau of Economic Research] The paper argues that there is a significant correlation of low blood pressure and happiness. Countries with higher reported rates of happiness showed lower national levels of hypertension. "[I]n constructing new kinds of economic and social policies in the future, where well-being rather than real income is likely to be a prime concern," the authors say, "there are grounds for economists to study people's blood pressure."

But which came first, the calmness of the happiness—and why? Social policy is indeed important, but how exactly do we get there from blood pressure?

e)* [From Michael Kesterton, "Social Studies: a daily miscellany of information," *The Globe and Mail*, 13 May 1997 p. A20] The murder rate in Britain would be at least triple what it is now if it weren't for improvements in medicine and the growing skills of surgeons and paramedics, experts believe. "The murder rate is artificially low now," says Professor Bernard Knight, a leading pathologist.

"People say there were far more murders in the old days, but the woundings that happen now would have been murders then," he told the *Independent* on Sunday. "If you look at the rise in [the] murder rate, it is very small, but look at the wounding figures and the graph goes up 45 degrees. If that number of woundings had occurred years ago the murder rate would have been massive."

4   Summary

In this chapter we have begun looking in detail at the most popular argument schemes. The ones here are schemes that tend to be employed in empirical reasoning, where people are trying to establish facts. To this end, we have looked at the schemes for generalization, and an extension of this in the reasoning used for polling. Then we have begun to explore causal reasoning by looking at the scheme for general causal arguments.

MAJOR EXERCISE   9M

1. This assignment is intended to test your understanding of argument schemes by using some of them in conjunction with specific issues.

    a) How might one construct arguments employing the following schemes (one for each argument) in support of the claim "Public ownership of assault rifles should be prohibited":
        i)   generalization
        ii) causal reasoning
        iii) polling.

    b) How might one employ the same schemes in support of the opposite claim, "Public ownership of assault rifles should be allowed."

    c) Using any of the argument schemes of this chapter, construct a short argument on one of the following issues:
        i)   industrial safety
        ii) nuclear testing
        iii) pollution.

2. Decide whether each of the following passages contains an argument. If it does, assess the reasoning. For any specific argument schemes dealt with in this chapter, explain whether the argument fulfills the conditions for good arguments of that scheme.

    a)* Walking in the bird sanctuary I again saw my neighbour with his dog, and as on previous occasions, the dog had a bird feather in his collar. My neighbour now tells me that when his dog wears a feather, he thinks he's a bird and thus doesn't chase other birds. I assume he's relying on the hidden premise that "birds don't chase birds." But that's not the case: birds do chase other birds.

    b)* [From "The Corrosion of the Death Penalty," www.globeandmail.com, 21 May 2002, p. A18] This month, the Governor of Maryland temporarily banned the death penalty in his state, over concerns that gross racial disparities exist in the way it is used. Illinois has had a moratorium on the death penalty for two years, after its governor said the risk of executing the innocent was unconscionably high. These states are opening their eyes to the obvious. Race matters in who is put to death. Between 1977 and 1995, 88 black men were executed for killing whites; just two white men were executed for killing blacks. Two years ago, a federal Justice Department study found that white defendants were almost twice as likely as black ones to be given a plea agreement by federal prosecutors that let them avoid the death penalty. Of the 13 on death row in Maryland, nine are black. Only one of the 13 was convicted of killing a non-white.

c)   [From Steven Pinker, "A History of Violence," *The New Republic*, 19 March 2007, www.edge.org/3rd_culture/pinker07/pinker07_index.html] In the decade of Darfur and Iraq, and shortly after the century of Stalin, Hitler, and Mao, the claim that violence has been diminishing may seem somewhere between hallucinatory and obscene. Yet recent studies that seek to quantify the historical ebb and flow of violence point to exactly that conclusion.

Some of the evidence has been under our nose all along. Conventional history has long shown that, in many ways, we have been getting kinder and gentler. Cruelty as entertainment, human sacrifice to indulge superstition, slavery as a labor-saving device, conquest as the mission statement of government, genocide as a means of acquiring real estate, torture and mutilation as routine punishment, the death penalty for misdemeanors and differences of opinion, assassination as the mechanism of political succession, rape as the spoils of war, pogroms as outlets for frustration, homicide as the major form of conflict resolution—all were unexceptionable features of life for most of human history. But, today, they are rare to nonexistent in the West, far less common elsewhere than they used to be, concealed when they do occur, and widely condemned when they are brought to light. . . . Social histories of the West provide evidence of numerous barbaric practices that became obsolete in the last five centuries, such as slavery, amputation, blinding, branding, flaying, disembowelment, burning at the stake, breaking on the wheel, and so on. Meanwhile, for another kind of violence—homicide—the data are abundant and striking. The criminologist Manuel Eisner has assembled hundreds of homicide estimates from Western European localities that kept records at some point between 1200 and the mid-1990s. In every country he analyzed, murder rates declined steeply— for example, from 24 homicides per 100,000 Englishmen in the fourteenth century to 0.6 per 100,000 by the early 1960s.

d)* [From *The Globe and Mail*, 9 March 1987, from London (Reuters), p. A16] Farmer John Coombs claims his cow Primrose is curing his baldness—by licking his head. Mr Coombs, 56, who farms near Salisbury, in southwestern England, says he made the discovery after Primrose licked some cattle food dust off his pate as he was bending down.

A few weeks later hair was growing in an area that had been bald for years.

The farmer has the whole herd working on the problem now, The Daily Telegraph reported yesterday.

Mr Coombs encourages his cows to lick his head every day and believes he will soon have a full head of hair.

e) [From a Letter to the Editor, *Omni* magazine, September 1983] I am surprised that a magazine of the scientific stature of *Omni* continues to perpetuate a myth. Bulls do not charge at a red cape because it is red. Bulls, like all bovines, are colour-blind. They see only in shades of black, white, and gray. The reason a bull charges at a red cape is because of the movement of the cape. By the time a matador faces a bull, the animal has been teased into a state of rage by the picadors. They run at it, shout, wave their arms, and prick it with sword points. Any old Kansas farm girl, like me, can attest to the fact that when a bull is enraged it will charge at anything that moves.

f) [From "Gas prices up, auto deaths down," Associated Press, 11 July 2008] WASHINGTON—Today's high gas prices could cut auto deaths by nearly one-third as driving decreases, with the effect particularly dramatic among price-sensitive teenage drivers, the authors of a new study say.

Professors Michael Morrisey of the University of Alabama and David Grabowski of Harvard Medical School found that for every 10-per-cent increase in gas prices, there was a 2.3-per-cent decline in auto deaths. For drivers ages 15 to 17, the decline was 6 per cent and for ages 18 to 21 it was 3.2 per cent. The study looked at fatalities from 1985 to 2006, when gas prices reached about $2.50 a gallon (about 66 cents Canadian a litre). With gas now averaging over $4 a gallon ($1.07), Prof. Morrisey said he expects to see a drop of about 1,000 deaths a month.

With annual auto deaths typically ranging from about 38,000 to 40,000 a year, a drop of 12,000 deaths would cut the total by nearly one-third, Prof. Morrisey said.

"I think there is some silver lining here in higher gas taxes in that we will see a public-health gain," Prof. Grabowski said. He warned, however, that their estimate of a decline of 1,000 deaths a month could be offset somewhat by the shift under way to smaller, lighter, more fuel-efficient cars and the increase in motorcycle and scooter driving. Prof. Morrisey said the study also found the "same kind of symmetry" between gas prices and auto deaths when prices go down. "When that happens we drive more, we drive bigger cars, we drive faster and fatalities are higher," he said.

g) [The following is from the report *Study Links Obesity to Protein in Infant Formula*, Nutra ingredients-USA.com, 20 April 2007, www.nutraingredients-usa.com/, accessed 4 May 2009] The results of the EU Childhood Obesity Programme indicate that low-protein content in infant formula may have metabolic, endocrinal and developmental benefits for babies—which may also have an impact on obesity at a later age. Subject to further follow-up, the findings add weight to the idea that a tendency towards obesity is set in earliest childhood. They come shortly after another study indicated that tendency towards obesity could be genetic. Professor Berthold Koletzko, project co-ordinator from the University of Munich, Germany, said the results "*emphasise the importance of promotion of and support for breastfeeding, together with the development of the right composition of infant formula, and support for the choice of appropriate complementary food."*

The study involved 990 infants and ran from October 2002 to July 2006, when the youngest participants reached the age of two. The researchers hypothesised the primary hypothesis that one possible causal factor for the difference in long-term obesity risk between breast and formula-fed infants is the much lower protein content of breast milk compared to infant formula. The infants were randomised to receive either a low-protein formula (1.8g/100kcal, then 2.25g/100kg in follow on formulas) or a high protein formula (3g/100kcal, then 4.5g/100kcal). The intervention lasted for 12 months from birth, and the infants were followed until they reached the age of two. A group of breast-fed children was also followed. In addition to a body growth rate similar to that of breast-fed babies, those in the low protein group were seen to have metabolic and endocrinal benefits too.

h) [Barbara Dority, "Feminist Moralism, 'Pornography,' and Censorship," in *The Humanist*, November/December 1989, p. 46] In many repressive countries—whether in Central America, Asia, Africa, eastern Europe, or the Middle East—there is practically no "pornography." But there is a great deal of sexism and violence against women. In the Netherlands and Scandinavia, where there are almost no restrictions on sexually explicit materials, the rate of sex-related crimes is much lower than in the United States. "Pornography" is virtually irrelevant to the existence of sexism and violence.

i) [From Xenophon, *On Hunting*, Book 12] Nobler, I say, are those who choose to toil.

And this has been proved conclusively by a notable example. If we look back to the men of old who sat at the feet of Cheiron—whose names I mentioned—we see that it was by dedicating the years of their youth to the chase that they learnt all their noble lore; and therefrom they attained to great renown, and are admired even to this day for their virtue—virtue who numbers all men as her lovers, as is very plain. Only because of the pains it costs to win her the greater number fall away; for the achievement of her is hid in obscurity; while the pains that cleave to her are manifest.

j) [The following is part of a response to claims members of the media were exaggerating the danger of a flu pandemic: "Flu pandemic not nonsense," *NRC Handelsblad*, 12 May 2009, http://vorige.nrc.nl/international/opinion/article2239709.ece] According to a report by the World Health Organisation, the mortality rate of the current H5N1 birds-to-humans infection is still 60 percent, again despite antibiotics and other modern treatments (Cumulative Number of Confirmed Human Cases of Avian Influenza A/(H5N1), 2009). This high mortality rate, it seems, is not the result of a bacterial superinfection (pneumonia) but rather of a "cytokine storm" (or hypercytokinemia), a strong reaction of the immune system to the new virus, which affects the entire body. The patients die because all their internal organs—lungs, heart, kidneys, liver, the blood-forming organs and the brain—fail simultaneously (multiorgan failure), and antibiotics are no help.

Eyewitness accounts of the 1918 Spanish influenza indicate a similar multio-rgan failure reaction. (See: John M. Barry: *The Great Influenza: The Epic Story of the Deadliest Plague in History*, New York: Penguin) Ekkelenkamp's claim that the high death toll in 1918 was so high because the world population was exhausted and underfed because of World War I has long been discredited. The mortality rate in the United States, where there was no food shortage, did not vary substantially from the one in Europe.

Of course, there is no certainty that a new subtype of human-to-human influenza with serious virulence will ever see the light of day. But influenza experts from all over the world think the risk is substantial. It is also uncertain whether the H5N1 bird-to-human infection will be as lethal if it should mutate to a human-to-human infection; influenza viruses often lose virulence when they mutate.

But history teaches us that the consequences of even a mildly virulent pandemic should not be taken lightly. Ten serious influenza pandemics have been documented in the past three centuries. The mortality of the Spanish influenza—which caused 50 to 100 million deaths—was comparable to that of the 1830–1832 pandemic, except that the world population was much smaller then.

If a virus with the same pathogenicity as the Spanish influenza should return today, it will probably kill 100 million people worldwide—despite all the anti-viral and anti-bacterial medication, the vaccines and the prevention system available to modern medicine. Given a world population of 6.7 billion, even a moderately virulent pandemic could kill millions of people (see: Jeffrey Taubenberger and David Morens "1918 influenza: the mother of all pandemics," Vol. 12, No. 1, 2006, Emerging Infectious Diseases, pp. 15–22) On top of that will come the economic effects of a disrupting pandemic with 1.6 billion sick people worldwide.

For more online exercises, review questions, and quizzes related to the material in this chapter, please go to www.oupcanada.com/GoodReasoning5e

10

MORE EMPIRICAL SCHEMES AND THE REASONS OF SCIENCE

The last chapter introduced several empirical schemes that use patterns of reasoning to arrive at conclusions about facts. Some of these schemes are clearly involved in scientific discovery and communication, as we saw with the discussions of generalization and general causes. In this chapter, we continue to explore schemes of this nature, and end our investigation of empirical schemes with a discussion of the principles behind scientific reasoning—principles that are traditionally said to provide a **"scientific method."** To that end, this chapter investigates:

▶ particular causal reasoning
▶ arguments from ignorance
▶ scientific reasoning.

1   Particular Causal Reasoning

We begin with what amounts to our continuation of causal reasoning introduced in the previous chapter. As we will see, particular claims about causes often assume general causal principles on which they implicitly depend. In Chapter 3, we distinguished between arguments and explanations. We saw that many of the indicator words we use in constructing arguments are also used in explanations. One kind of explanation that plays a particularly important role in lives gives the cause of some event or situation.

Consider the following statements:

- The fire was the result of smoking in bed.
- He died of a massive coronary.
- You brewed the coffee too long. That's why it's so bitter.
- The reason the car wouldn't start is that the battery was dead.
- Motivated by greed, the banker embezzled the money.

Though none of the above statements uses the word "cause," they all express causal relationships. And they all refer to some particular case that requires a causal explanation.

Note also that these statements are not arguments. They are explanations; they seek to explain an event by pointing to the cause.

The causal arguments we discussed in Chapter 8 are arguments for general claims that express general causal principles. When we make particular causal claims, we usually invoke these general principles, scientific claims, or some generally established theory as a basis for the particular claims. In the most straightforward cases, such reasoning takes the form

X causes Y.
Therefore, this y was caused by this x.

where "x" and "y" are instances of the general categories of X and Y. If "X causes Y" means "Carelessly tended campfires (can) cause forest fires," then "This y was caused by this x" means "This particular forest fire was caused by this (particular) carelessly tended campfire." In more complex cases, we may not have a unique general causal principle that we can apply to a particular causal claim. If someone says that "Sarah was depressed because she did not get an A on her exam," they are not, thereby, committed to the simple principle that "Failing to get an A on an exam causes depression." In such a case, we need to investigate a more complex set of causes and interaction (perhaps involving Sarah's attitude and upbringing, her rivalries with siblings, and so on) that precipitated the event or circumstance in question. In simple and complex cases, an argument for an explanation of a particular causal claim is dependent on general causal principles.

In view of this, the following scheme captures the essence of a good argument for a particular causal explanation:

Premise 1:   X causes Y.
Premise 2:   This is the best explanation of the y in question.
Conclusion: This x caused this y.

A strong particular causal argument establishes (implicitly or explicitly) these two premises and, in view of this, the conclusion.

In keeping with this scheme, a good argument *against* a particular causal explanation must show that it is inconsistent with general causal claims (that the general claim X causes Y is not defensible) or that there is a better causal explanation of the event or circumstance in question. In showing that the general causal claim that a particular causal explanation depends on is problematic, we must typically appeal to the conditions for good general causal reasoning and show that there is no strong argument for establishing the general claim in question.

A dubious example of particular causal reasoning arises in the following excerpt from an opinion piece in the *Detroit Free Press* (8 November 2010):

When we fill up at the pump, we are pouring millions of dollars a day into the treasuries of hostile nations. Much of that money funnels into the coffers of those same terrorist groups our soldiers, sailors, airmen and Marines face every day. Enemy bullets and IEDs are bought with our dirty oil money and fired back upon our own men and women—often imported or funded by countries like Iran. This cycle is unacceptable, dangerous, and must be stopped. Congress failed to pass energy and climate legislation this summer, but there is still much that can be done to solve this threat to national security.

By raising our fuel efficiency standards we can dramatically lower the amount of oil we require as a nation to go about our daily lives, thereby stemming the flow of money to enemy nations and diminishing the disastrous consequences of climate change.

Several issues seem to occupy this writer, including a concern with climate change. But what interests us are the causal claims around the security of troops. Asserted here is a causal relationship between the everyday act of filling up with gas, and the threats faced by troops in other parts of the world. Many advocates for social justice in other parts of the world will point to the impact that our everyday behaviour has on others elsewhere. Buying regular coffee, for example, is said to contribute to the exploitation of coffee workers in the world. The reasoning here is similar. Because there is no attempt to identify any general causal principles, the first premise of our scheme would be implicit. We will present the key argument according to our scheme for particular causal reasoning:

Premise 1:   X causes Y.
Premise 2:   This is the best explanation of the y in question.
Conclusion: This x caused this y.

Perhaps we could understand X = economic activity in the United States, and Y = providing money for hostile nations. Then, in this case, x would = filling up at the gas pump, and y = threats to military personnel. Setting it out in this way allows us to see the problematic intermediate step that the argument requires, since it is Y that causes y by virtue of the hostile nations using oil money to fund those attacking American military personnel. This is the crucial causal claim that needs support. Read a different way, we could track back from the effect, which is the threat to military personnel, to the series of causes that arrives at the everyday practice of buying gasoline.

Clearly, the argument depends on the speculative leap from Y to y. The burden of proof lies with the writer to support this link and give reasons to believe the causal chain involved. As we have noted, our everyday practices often do have consequences for people elsewhere in the world. The point here is to *show* that *this* practice has *this* consequence. As it stands, the reader has been given no reason to believe this. The reasoning fails to conform to the standards governing good particular causal reasoning. Without fulfilling this obligation, the author cannot expect the further argument (to address the alleged situation) to follow, and change practices so as to raise fuel efficiency standards. This is not to say there would not be good reasons to raise such standards, but only that the argument given does not provide such reasons.

PARTICULAR CAUSAL REASONING

Particular causal reasoning attempts to establish the cause of some specific state of affairs. A good instance of particular causal reasoning shows that a certain event or state of affairs, *y*, is caused by *x*, by showing:

1. That this is consistent with good causal principles; and
2. that this provides the most plausible explanation of the state of affairs in question.

EXERCISE 10A

For each of the following, identify the causal claim, then evaluate and discuss the reasoning:

a)* After his criminal record was disclosed, the local politician's standing dropped in the polls, and he lost the election to his opponent.

b) My client had the right of way when she obeyed the left-turn signal and turned. The other driver should not have been entering the intersection at that point and is thus entirely at fault for what transpired.

c) [From Tim Flannery, *The Weather Makers*, HarperCollins, 2005, p. 19] Greenhouse gases are a class of gases which can trap heat near Earth's surface. As they increase in the atmosphere, the extra heat they trap leads to global warming. This warming in turn places pressure on Earth's climate system and can lead to climate change.

d)* Whenever Bob plays poker, he wears his suspenders, because he has never lost at poker while wearing his suspenders.

e) [From a Letter to the Editor, *The Windsor Star*, 8 November 2007] Out of a job yet? You can thank the Liberals. How many have forgotten the trade missions to China by Mr. Chrétien and Mr. Martin?

   Tainted dog food, lead paint on toys, and now humidifiers that can cause fires. How many Canadians who made goods of all types have been affected by this flood of one-way trade from China? Thank you Liberals.

f) [From "Sixteen Scandals" http://drdawgsblawg.ca/2011/03/sixteen-scandals.shtml, accessed 1 July 2011] It only got a small mention in Finance Minister Jim Flaherty's Budget Speech of February 27, 2008—a proposal to re-establish passenger rail service between Peterborough and Toronto on an existing rail line—but it caught federal bureaucrats off guard and caught the attention of national media. . . . Commentators immediately noticed that the rail line happened to pass through Flaherty's Whitby-Oshawa federal riding, the same provincial riding for which Flaherty's wife, Christine Elliott, is the Ontario MPP. The rail line would also pass through Peterborough, a city of about 80,000 held by federal Conservative Dean Del Mastro.

2   Arguments from Ignorance

The last empirical argument scheme we will consider applies to cases in which we have no specific evidence—scientific or otherwise—to use in supporting or rejecting a particular claim. These arguments "from ignorance" (often referred to by their Latin name as arguments *ad ignorantiam*) take our inability to establish a proposition as evidence for its improbability or, conversely, our inability to disprove it as evidence in favour of it. We construct an argument from ignorance when we argue that ghosts do not exist because no evidence has been given that proves that they do. Traditionally, such arguments have been regarded as fallacious, but there are instances where they constitute good reasoning.

Arguments from ignorance are prominent in legal proceedings, where an accused person is presumed innocent until proven guilty, and in scientific reasoning, where hypotheses may be rejected if no confirming evidence is found. The failure to find evidence of living dodos or of certain kinds of subatomic particles does contribute to the evidence against their (present) existence. Everyday examples of arguments from ignorance are found in remarks like: "I've looked for my car keys everywhere and can't find them, so someone must have taken them." Here, a failure to find evidence confirming that the keys are where we might have put them is used as evidence for the conclusion that they are no longer there.

The criteria for good arguments from ignorance are implicit in these examples. In essence, a good instance of the scheme demonstrates a responsible attempt to garner evidence that confirms or disconfirms the claim in question. Accordingly, we define the scheme for good arguments from ignorance as follows:

> **Premise 1:** We have found no evidence to disprove (or prove) Proposition P.
> **Premise 2:** There has been a responsible attempt to garner evidence.
> **Conclusion:** Proposition P is improbable (or probable).

It is important to recognize that we can construct a strong argument from ignorance *only* after a careful search for evidence to disprove or prove the proposition that appears in our conclusion. It would not be convincing to argue that our car keys have been taken on the basis of our failure to see them unless we have made some effort to locate them. It is the responsible attempt to establish a claim that makes an appeal to ignorance plausible.

The first premise in an argument from ignorance is usually indisputable: if someone tells you they have found no evidence for a particular event or circumstance, this should probably be accepted. This means that when we are arguing against an argument from ignorance, we will normally need to show that the argument we are criticizing is not founded on a thorough enough investigation of the issue in question.

Consider the following extract from a letter to *The Globe and Mail* (15 July 2011), responding to an earlier correspondent who had claimed that South Africa's apartheid policy had been based on Canada's Indian Act.

This is a discomforting idea, one commonly deployed by Canadian academics and activists alike to highlight not only the injustices of Canada's policies toward its aboriginal peoples, but also the moral shortcomings of Canada's relationship with South Africa in the era of white settler domination.

Unfortunately, the idea is arguably no more than a bold assertion, lacking historical evidence from South Africa, and based on only the most doubtful evidence from Canada. Numerous historians (including myself) have searched diligently for hard evidence to support the idea, but none has been uncovered.

Quite independently of Canada, the settler colonies that became South Africa developed "native reserves" and elaborate segregation laws of their own in the 19th century, making it largely unnecessary to look elsewhere for models in the 20th.

We can show this to be a good argument from ignorance as follows:

Premise 1:   We have found no evidence that South Africa's apartheid policy was based on Canada's Indian Act.

Premise 2:   Numerous historians (including myself) have searched diligently for hard evidence to support the idea, but none has been uncovered.

Conclusion: It is improbable that South Africa's apartheid policy was based on Canada's Indian Act.

This is an argument from ignorance because the author uses the *lack* of supporting evidence of the Canadian association with apartheid South Africa as evidence against that association. And we can judge his argument a strong example because it indicates a serious attempt to investigate the matter on the part of historians (the relevant kind of investigators in such a case). Moreover, the last paragraph suggests an alternative reason that can account for the phenomenon in question (apartheid South Africa).

As this example indicates, strong arguments from ignorance can teach us the importance of supporting our rejection of a claim with some indication of a responsible attempt to find evidence for it. Here of course, our evaluation is dependent on someone's testimony that they carried out the right kind of investigation. But the writer is a historian from the University of Western Ontario, and thus the right kind of authority for judging historical questions. We look at the argument scheme associated with authority claims in Chapter 12. A good critical thinker is willing to admit that they are not in a position to know much about certain issues. Above all, they will recognize that they should not yield to an all-too-human tendency to hold tenaciously to prejudices and assumptions.

ARGUMENTS FROM IGNORANCE

Arguments from ignorance attempt to prove or disprove some claim *x* by appealing to the *lack* of evidence for or against it. A good appeal to ignorance claims that *x* is probable (or improbable) after the failure of a *responsible* attempt to find evidence for its improbability (or probability).

EXERCISE 10B

1. Describe specific circumstances in which you would or would not be in a position to construct a good argument from ignorance about each of the following topics:

   a)* ghosts
   b) the alleged racism of a provincial or state ombudsman
   c) the hypothesis that there is a tenth planet
   d) the question of whether someone is guilty of murder
   e) ESP
   f) the irradiation of food.

2. Dress each of the following in the scheme for appeals to ignorance and then decide whether they are strong instances of the scheme.

   a) [The following excerpt criticizes comments on "snuff films" made by the American lawyer Catherine MacKinnon in a speech on pornography, *The Globe and Mail*, 24 March 1987] I wonder if Ms MacKinnon has ever seen a snuff film, especially since no one else seems to have. In the absence of a genuine example, I continue to believe that snuff films are a fabrication of censorship crusaders, the purpose of which is obfuscation.

   b)* [Periodically, newspapers publish obscure photographs alleged to show Bigfoot. Such occurred in *The Globe and Mail*, 21 April 2005 eliciting the following response] The Loch Ness monster, UFOs and other such "mysteries" have one thing in common—the shadowy, grainy photo. Considering how many hunters are combing North America every year, it seems highly unlikely that one of them wouldn't have shot a Bigfoot by now.

   c) [From "The Myth of Voter Fraud," an Opinion in the *New York Times*, 13 May 2008] There is no evidence that voting by noncitizens is a significant problem. Illegal immigrants do their best to remain in the shadows, to avoid attracting government attention and risking deportation. It is hard to imagine that many would walk into a polling place, in the presence of challengers and police, and try to cast a ballot. There is, however, ample evidence that a requirement of proof of citizenship will keep many eligible voters from voting. Many people do not have birth certificates or other acceptable proof of citizenship, and for some people, that proof is not available.

3   Scientific Reasoning

Though one of the aims of "science" is precision, our use of the word is vague. Today, we might describe science as a set of disciplines (math, physics, biochemistry, geomorphology, etc. and disciplines like psychology and economics if we include the "social sciences") that study and attempt to understand different aspects of the world. The word "science" comes from the Latin word *scientia*, which means "knowledge." Though we often talk as though all science is based on one approach to understanding, it encompasses many different methods and approaches. Computer modelling, epidemiological studies (studies of patterns of health and illness in a population), and archaeological debates about the way of life that characterized early peoples assume, for example, distinct criteria for judging what should and should not be counted as scientific fact.

What we can say is that science is a rigorous attempt to generate evidence that allows us to draw conclusions about the subjects of scientific study. In this way, science is a key component of many of the arguments which play a key role in our debates, not only about the nature of the world, but also about public policy, the nature of knowledge, religious and metaphysical beliefs, and moral and political issues, which are predicated on assumptions about the way the world works. In considering such arguments, it would be naive to think that science and scientific conclusions are immune from controversy. The question whether science itself resists the development of new and better ways of understanding the world is itself a matter of dispute. Certainly it can be said that many of the views science now takes for granted—the Copernican view of the Earth's relationship to the sun, plate tectonics, the rejection of phlogiston theory, etc.—were once rejected out of hand.

However one views science, there can be no doubt that it is a major force in our attempt to understand that world. In some ways it is the engine that has driven the social and economic developments that characterize the modern (and postmodern) world. In view of this, an account of it must play a key role in our attempt to understand, analyze and assess many of the arguments we contend with. It is with this in mind that this chapter ends with a look at the method of inquiry which is the backbone of scientific inquiry.

4   The Scientific Method

Considering science from a general point of view, we might distinguish two types of scientific reasoning. On the one hand, there is the reasoning that scientists engage in as they go about their tasks of discovery and explanation. On the other, there is the reasoning that scientists use to communicate their conclusions to others, be they other scientists, members of the general public, or a funding agency. We expect scientists to communicate their ideas to other scientists in a different way than they do to the general public, but a scientist (or someone reporting on scientific findings) must in both cases communicate in a way that reflects the basic principles of scientific research. In elaborating these principles, we will outline a sequence of steps which much scientific reasoning uses to generate the evidence for its conclusions—a sequence of steps commonly referred to as "the scientific method."

At the core of the scientific method one finds hypotheses. They are tentative—and sometimes imaginative and ingenious—solutions to a problem or explanations for some strange and unexpected phenomenon. They are designed to be verified or falsified by some subsequent observation or experiment. It is the testing of hypotheses that is the crux of the arguments founded on the scientific method. In the course of confirming and rejecting hypotheses, many different kinds of evidence may be employed. The three schemes of argument we discussed in the previous chapter—generalizations, polling, and causal reasoning—and the particular causal arguments and appeals to ignorance of this chapter, are, for example, all common modes of reasoning in this context.

We can describe the general process that constitutes the scientific method as follows.

i) Understanding the Issue

The use of the scientific method begins with a problem or issue that arises from the examination of some data or phenomena. The issue may be generated by industry or by government, or it may arise in the speculative atmosphere of the laboratory, but we want to emphasize that the scientific method is a very general method that can be used to answer questions and solve problems. To this end, we will illustrate the method with three simple situations that pose issues that can be (or have been) tackled using the scientific method.

Example 1: Phlogiston Theory

Our first example is from the early history of chemistry. In the 1600s, chemists and alchemists saw combustion (fire, burning) as the most important chemical reaction, recognizing that it included phenomena like corrosion in metals and respiration in living things. A German physician, Johann Joachim (J.J.) Becher, suggested a hypothetical substance, which he called "inflammable earth," which every flammable substance contains. Georg Stahl called this mysterious substance "phlogiston" (pronounced "flow-giss-ton"), understanding combustion as the process that occurred when the phlogiston in a substance was given off into the air. The issue in this case was a basic one for chemistry: *what is combustion?*

Example 2: The Stradivarius Violin

Everyone knows the name Stradivarius. A "Stradivarius" is a violin made by the Stradavari family, the most notable luthier in the family being Antoni Stradavari (1644–1737). Violins made by the latter are highly prized musical instruments that may sell for more than a million dollars (in comparison with a well constructed contemporary violin, which might sell for $10,000). Owning and playing a Stradivarius is a mark of great distinction in the world of classical music. The issue we might pose in this case is: *What makes a Stradivarius so special? What makes it more valuable than other violins?*

Example 3: "Earthing"

A recent trend in "health and spirituality" promotes the notion that direct contact with the earth encourages better sleep and health. Walking in bare feet, sleeping on the ground, and other practices that accomplish this have, on these grounds (so to speak), been recommended by those who promote such "Earthing." The traditional teachings of Native American elders are said to support such practices. Here we may put the issue as the question: *should we believe that earthing promotes better sleep and health?*

ii) Formulating a Hypothesis

Once we understand the problem or issue we want to investigate, the next step in the scientific method is the formulation of a hypothesis. There may be a number of competing hypotheses, each offering a solution to or explanation of the problem. Observation is important, along with imagination and creativity. We might, for example, compare the problem we are considering to past phenomena in the hope of detecting common traits, which would suggest an appropriate hypothesis. In other cases, we might strive to think of possible solutions or explanations that are novel and challenge our way of looking at the world. In view of the other steps in the scientific method, we want a testable hypothesis: a hypothesis that it will be practical to test in one way or another. We can approach the three examples we have identified in the following way.

Example 1: Phlogiston Theory

In the case of phlogiston, the initial hypothesis is simply the hypothesis that combustion is a process of giving off phlogiston. This is a theory that derives from an earlier theory that sulfur was the ingredient that caused combustion. Evidence for this included the observations that it burned completely and was given off when wood burned. But it was clear that combustion did not yield ordinary sulfur in other cases. Such considerations were the basis of Becher's hypothetical substance, and the corresponding hypothesis that *combustion is a process that occurs when phlogiston leaves a substance and flows into the air.* This is the explanation of the problem that we began with (what is combustion?) that is the core of phlogiston theory.

Example 2: The Stradivarius Violin

In the case of the Stradivarius violin, its fame has precipitated scientific speculation on the reasons why it is a superior instrument. To this end, investigators have hypothesized that the wood used to build a Stradivarius had different properties than contemporary wood, that the use of pozzolana volcanic ash (Roman hydraulic cement) as a treatment for the wood imbued it with special properties, and that there is something special about the varnishes used by the Stradivari family and other Cremonese violin makers. But all of these hypotheses (and the scientific studies based on them) assume a more basic hypothesis that we will focus on: i.e. the hypothesis that *Stradivarius violins have a superior sound quality that makes them better to listen to* (typically put as the claim that they have better "sonority"—resonance—than other violins). Obviously, this hypothesis is one way to explain the extraordinary high value of Stradivarius violins.

Example 3: "Earthing"

The notion of Earthing as it is popularized today is founded on the thinking and personal experience of Clint Ober, whose views were the result of his experience with insomnia and his curiosity when he measured and thought about the electromagnetic fields in the house in which he lived. Having recorded different voltages in different parts of his house, and an extremely very high voltage in his bedroom, he grounded his bed to eliminate the correspondent electromagnetic fields and immediately slept better. This led him to the hypothesis that *grounding—an electrical connection to the earth—is a key ingredient of good sleep and health.* This gives rise to Earthing theory, which might be described as an attempt to explain the (alleged) health benefits of a direct connection to the earth that can be maintained by walking with bare feet, sitting on the ground, and so forth.

iii) Identifying the Implications of the Hypothesis

Having established a hypothesis, the next step in the scientific method is determining what observable consequences must follow if the hypothesis is correct. Such inferences use argument schemes founded on the premise that:

> "If h is the case, then x would have to occur,"
> where h is the hypothesis and x is the observable consequence.

These schemes are discussed in the appendices to this book. In our present context, we will simply note that this kind of statement is called a *conditional*. It is made up of two constituent claims, one that occurs after the "if" and before the "then," and one which occurs after the "then." The first ("h is the case") is called the **antecedent** of the conditional, the second ("x would have to occur") is called its **consequent**. In identifying the consequences of a hypothesis we need to identify the consequent in the above conditional. In our three examples, we can do so as follows.

Example 1: Phlogiston Theory

The testing of phlogiston theory is an important event in the birth of chemistry because those scientists who put the theory to the test did so by carefully weighing the effects of combustion (and in this way illustrated the importance of the careful measurement of physical properties in chemistry). They reasoned that *if it is true that combustion is a process that occurs when phlogiston leaves a substance and flows into the air, then the weight of what remains after combustion should be less than the weight before.*

Example 2: The Stradivarius Violin

We invite you to stop for a moment and think about the way that you would identify testable implications of the Stradivarius hypothesis we have already noted. It is not improbable that you will come up with the same conditional as those who have put this hypothesis to the test: i.e. *if Stradivarius violins have a superior sound quality that makes them better to listen to, then this should be evident in tests where listeners compare works performed on a Stradivarius and on other violins.*

Example 3: "Earthing"

In the case of Earthing we will follow the reasoning of Clint Ober, who identified consequences of his hypothesis by reasoning that: *if grounding is a key ingredient of good sleep and health, then grounding should help those who suffer from insomnia and sleep problems.*

iv) Testing the Hypothesis

Once we have identified the implications of our proposed hypothesis, the next step in the scientific method is an attempt to devise and conduct tests to determine whether the consequences do follow. Ideally, the tests will be designed to confirm or refute the hypothesis with observable consequences. If a hypothesis is not testable in practice, it should at least be testable in principle. Scientists have, for example, identified the implications of a nuclear winter that would follow a large-scale nuclear war. There is no experimental way to test these implications (fortunately so), but something approximating a test can be carried out using computer models. In our three examples, the hypotheses and implications we have identified have been tested as follows.

Example 1: Phlogiston Theory

A Russian chemist, Mikhail Lomonsov tested the phlogiston hypothesis by weighing a sealed bottle containing magnesium before and after it was burnt. Since phlogiston (like heat) was supposed to pass through glass, the theory implied that the sealed bottle should have weighed less after burning. Lomonsov discovered that the bottle weighed the same, contradicting phlogiston theory,

Example 2: The Stradivarius Violin

The hypothesis that a Stradivarius violin is a superior violin from a listening point of view has been tested many times. In the early 1900s, a series of rigorous tests were carried out under very careful conditions. They had listeners listen to a Stradivarius and other violins in blind and double blind tests where the listeners (and in the latter case the players) did not know which violins were being played. The tests showed that even accomplished listeners and players could not distinguish between violins and could not uniquely identify the Stradivarius. Other tests since that time have produced similar results. In a test in 2009, reported in *Science Daily* (14 September 2009), the British violinist Matthew Trusler played his 1711 Stradivarius and four modern violins made by the Swiss violin-maker Michael Rhonheimer to an audience of experts. One of Rhonheimer's violins, made with wood that a researcher had treated with fungi, received 90 of 180 votes for the best tone. The Stradivarius came second with just 39 votes, and the majority (113) of the listeners misidentified the winning violin as the Stradivarius.

Example 3: "Earthing"

Clint Ober, the founder of the Earthing movement, tested his hypothesis with the help of students at a university sleep clinic. He assembled 60 volunteers from spas (38 women and 22 men) who complained of sleep problems and joint and muscle pain. He split them into two groups. Thirty slept on beds that were grounded, thirty slept on beds that were not. There was no way for the volunteers to know whether the platform they slept on was one of the ones that was grounded. The subjects who slept on grounded beds reported very significantly improved sleep and relief from the symptoms they had suffered. One hundred per cent of those sleeping on grounded beds reported less muscles stiffness and pain, for example, while one hundred per cent of those who slept on beds that were not grounded reported that there was no change in their health from this point of view. Ober published the results in the *ESD Journal* (the journal of the Electrostatic Discharge Association: the paper is available at www. esdjournal.com/articles/cober/ground.htm). In this case, the results of the test provide confirming evidence for the hypothesis.

Re-evaluating the Hypothesis

In a case like the latter one, it is important to note that the confirmation of the implications of a hypothesis does not guarantee that it is correct. In Appendix 2, we shall see that the argument:

> If h, then x.
> x.
> Therefore, h.

is an instance of the argument scheme **affirming the consequent**, which is not a valid argument. The Austrian philosopher Karl Popper, therefore, argued that scientific theories are inevitably conjectural and more decisively disproved than confirmed (for the argument "If h, then x; not-x; therefore not-h" is always valid). In the present context it is enough to say that the implications of a hypothesis h may not show that it is true, because there may be other ways to explain them. If there are, then these implications will confirm these alternative hypotheses as much as they confirm h. For our purposes, it suffices to say that the confirmation of the implications of a theory does provide strong evidence for it if there are no clear counter-hypotheses.

Considering counter-hypotheses is one aspect of the final step of the scientific method, which is the re-evaluation of the proposed hypothesis in light of the evidence produced in testing. One might, in light of these results, reject the hypothesis, revise it in some way that the evidence suggests is appropriate, or consider it confirmed and adopt it as the best current solution to the problem or explanation of the phenomenon. The latter is an important rider, for our knowledge and understanding of the situation in question is inevitably incomplete and it is likely that new evidence and arguments may make us want to refine or revise a confirmed hypothesis in the future. To this extent, there is no "final" step in the scientific method, but rather a perpetual consideration and re-evaluation of new hypotheses on the basis of previous and new evidence. This "forward progress" is one of the hallmarks of science that has made it such a powerful tool in our attempts to understand the world. The consequences of the re-evaluation of the three hypotheses we have noted show how things tend to progress in practice.

Example 1: Phlogiston Theory

The discussion and testing of phlogiston theory led, not only to the conclusion that the theory was mistaken, but eventually to a new theory of combustion developed by Antoine Lavoisier. It held that combustion is not a process which gives off phlogiston, but one that occurs when it combines with another element (oxygen). The discussion and testing of this new theory set the stage for another, caloric, theory of combustion. The phlogiston debate became a significant one in the history of chemistry because it demonstrated the importance of the quantitative measuring of the physical properties, something that has been a central aspect of chemistry ever since.

Example 2: The Stradivarius Violin

The extensive evidence against the hypothesis that a Stradivarius is a superior violin from a listening point of view makes it difficult to uphold this hypothesis. In a context in which this has not inhibited the fame of Stradivari violins or their market value, this raises the question as to why? We cannot pursue a detailed exploration of this question here, but will refer you to an article by R.L. Barclay in *Skeptic* magazine in 2011 ("Stradivarius pseudoscience: The myth of the miraculous musical instrument"), which suggests that it is bad science that has maintained its prestige.

Example 3: "Earthing"

In the wake of the experiment we have described, Clint Ober and others have pursued systematic testing and theorizing about Earthing and its effects. This has included the investigation of a number of hypotheses beyond the one we have mentioned. They include the hypothesis that grounding reduces electromagnetic fields on the body; that grounding effects circadian rhythms; and, more specifically, that they affect the circadian secretion of cortisol (a steroid hormone which is related to stress). At this point, mainstream science and medicine has paid little attention, and it will take many studies to establish whether Earthing will be accepted as a theory.

Beyond the Scientific Method

In looking at scientific reasoning and arguments about science, it is important to note that they are not limited to what is incorporated in the scientific method. Scientists will, for example, use models or analogies to draw conclusions about something unknown based on some similar phenomena that is better known or understood. Early attempts to describe the structure of atoms included an analogy with the solar system, since it was reasoned that an atom resembled a very small solar system. Like the solar system with its sun, an atom has its positive charge at the centre, and just as the planets move in orbits around the sun, so electrons carry a negative charge around the atom's centre. Such analogies highlight the role that reasoning from analogy may play in our attempt to understand the physical world. Scientists examining the meteorite ALH84001, collected in Antarctica and recognized as originating from Mars, argued for the existence of past life on Mars based on its similarities to life in rock formations on Earth. While our next chapter does not focus on scientific reasoning, the discussion will include argument by analogy as a scheme of argument that is used in empirical as well as moral reasoning.

The scientific method as we have discussed it emphasizes observable experimental results. In contrast, some scientific arguments depend on mathematical models rather than empirical observation and some branches of science cannot provide immediate observations or experiments that support their conclusions. Stephen Jay Gould gave an example of this kind of scientific reasoning in a discussion of science in *Discover* magazine in 1987:

> Since we can't see the past directly or manipulate its events, we must use the different tactic of meeting history's richness head on. . . . Thus plate tectonics can explain magnetic strips on the sea floor, the rise and later erosion of the Appalachians, the earthquakes of Lisbon and San Francisco . . . the presence of large flightless birds only on continents once united as Gondwanaland, and the discovery of fossil coal in Antarctica.

No matter how scientific reasoning varies in its procedures, you might note that some hypothesis-forming is always present, whether it be the hypothesis that the solar system is a suitable model for explaining the structure of the atom or that plate tectonics can account for the diverse phenomena identified by Gould. Looked at from this point of view, hypothesizing lies at the heart of scientific reasoning.

THE SCIENTIFIC METHOD

As a general procedure, the scientific method involves five steps for proposing and testing a hypothesis:
1. *Understanding the problem* that requires a solution or explanation.
2. *Formulating a hypothesis* to address the problem.
3. *Deducing consequences* to follow if the hypothesis is correct.
4. *Testing the hypothesis* for those consequences.
5. *Re-evaluating the hypothesis* after testing.

EXERCISE   10C

1. Consider the following account of "How Gertie the chicken mysteriously switched genders," adapted from an April 2011 report by Alasair Wilkins at io9 (available at http://IO9.COM). How might you investigate what is happening using the five steps of the scientific method (note that the key question is what hypotheses you might investigate)? On the completion of your investigation, what further investigations might be warranted as your theory of sex change develops?

Gertie is one of two hens kept by Jim and Jeanette Howard in Cambridgeshire in England. Both their hens produced fewer eggs last winter, when Gertie then stopped laying eggs completely, and began losing her feathers. She emerged from the molting with more feathers and a stronger physique. She then developed the neck wattle of a rooster, and her comb grew. She began behaving like a rooster, and began to crow. "I'm not really sure whether Gertie has actually changed sex, but to all intents and purposes she's now a cockerel," said Jim. A veterinarian has suggested that something in her feed had acted as a synthetic hormone, causing her to suddenly develop male characteristics. But recent research shows that a chicken's cells are either inherently male or female, regardless of their hormones. So how did Gertie's "inherently female" cells allow her to look and act like a male? "We're not sure."

2. Find an account of scientific research in a recent magazine (read a scientific magazine or journal if you need to) or on a science website on the Internet. Explain the research in terms of the account of the scientific method introduced in this chapter.

3. Analyze the following account of the scientific process of discovery in terms of the five steps of the scientific method:

[Alfred Wallace, in *My Life: A Record of Events and Opinions*, Vol. 1, New York, 1905, pp. 360–2] It was while waiting at Ternate in order to get ready for my next journey, and to decide where I should go, that the idea already referred to occurred to me. It has been shown how, for the preceding eight or nine years, the great problem of the origin of the species had been continually pondered over. . . .

But the exact process of the change [of one species into another] and the cause that led to it were absolutely unknown and appeared almost inconceivable. The great difficulty was to understand how, if one species was gradually changed into another, there continued to be so many quite distinct species, so many that differed from their nearest allies by slight yet perfectly definite and constant characters. . . . The problem then was, not only how and why do species change, but how and why do they change into new and well-defined species, distinguished from each other in so many ways. . . .

One day something brought to my attention Malthus's "Principles of Population," which I had read twelve years before. I thought of his clear exposition of "the positive checks to increase"—disease, accidents, war, and famine—which keep down the population of . . . people. It then occurred to me that these causes or their equivalents are continually acting in the case of animals also; and as animals usually breed much more rapidly than does mankind, the destruction every year from these causes must be enormous in order to keep down the number of each species. . . .

Why do some die and some live? And the answer was clearly, that on the whole the best fitted lived. From the effects of disease the most healthy escaped; from enemies, the strongest, the swiftest, or the most cunning; from famine, the best hunters or those with the best digestion; and so on. Then it suddenly flashed upon me that this self-acting process would necessarily *improve the race*, because in every generation the inferior would inevitably be killed off and the superior would remain—that is, *the fittest would survive*.

5   Summary

In this chapter we have continued our examination of empirical schemes by examining first Particular Causal arguments and then Arguments from Ignorance. In each case we have approached the topic by understanding the schemes involved. Then we have turned to the primary place in which empirical schemes might be expected to be found—scientific reasoning. Traditionally, the reasoning in scientific discovery has been understood in terms of a five-stage method. We have detailed and illustrated that method, while also noting other aspects that can go into scientific reasoning.

MAJOR EXERCISE 10M

1. This assignment is intended to test your understanding of argument schemes by using some of them in conjunction with specific normative issues.

    a) Construct short arguments employing the following schemes (one for each argument) in support of the claim "technology has improved the lives of average citizens":
       i)* particular causal argument
       ii) appeal to ignorance.

    b) Employ the same schemes in support of the opposite claim, "Technology has not improved the lives of average citizens."

    c) Using any of the argument schemes of this chapter, construct a short argument on one of the following issues:
       i) global warming
       ii)* the use of placebos in studies
       iii) built-in obsolescence of common household appliances.

2. Decide whether each of the following passages contains an argument. If it does, assess the reasoning. For any specific argument schemes dealt with in this chapter, explain whether the argument fulfills the conditions for good arguments of that scheme. Note that examples may involve more than one argument scheme and may also include applications of the scientific method.

    a)* It would be basically illogical to state that miracles cannot occur. This is because in order to state this, a person would have to have logical proof that miracles cannot occur. And no such proof is available.

    b) [From a Letter to the Editor, *The Globe and Mail*, 15 March 1997] So the Liberals have not come close to making the point that restrictions on tobacco advertising will lead to a reduction in the incidence of smoking among young people (Speaking Freely about Smoking—editorial, March 5). The following Statscan figures are provided with your March 8 front-page article: one in five deaths in Canada are attributed to smoking; in Quebec, the number is one in four. The average age of becoming a "regular smoker" in Canada is 15; in Quebec, it is 14. Fifty per cent of all sponsorship dollars provided by tobacco companies are spent in Quebec. Coincidence?

    c)* [From a report in *The Canadian Press*, 27 September 2007, titled "Teens with part-time jobs more likely to smoke: study"] High school students who take part-time jobs for pocket money may be more likely to start smoking than teens who don't join the after-school and weekend work force, a study suggests.

The study of Grade 10 and 11 students in Baltimore shows that those who took jobs, often in retail outlets and fast-food or other restaurants, had a greater propensity to begin lighting up—and that trend was strongest among teens who worked the most hours per week. "Of those who didn't smoke at Grade 10, kids who (began working) were at least three times more likely to start smoking than kids who didn't start working," lead author Rajeev Ramchand, a psychiatric epidemiologist, said Thursday from Arlington, Va. "What we found was the kids who worked more than 10 hours a week on average had an earlier age of initiation. So they started to smoke ahead of their peers," said Mr. Ramchand, who conducted the study with colleagues while a graduate student at the Johns Hopkins School of Medicine in Baltimore, Md. He now works for the Rand Corp.

The researchers posit a number of reasons for the change in smoking status: For one, teens may be exposed on the job to older youth or to adults who are more likely to smoke and where smoking is more common and acceptable, said Mr. Ramchand.

"Second is that they can now buy cigarettes, as before they may have not had the means, the money, to buy cigarettes," he said. Taking a part-time job also changes a teen's relationship with family members, and that can strongly affect behaviour. "When kids start working, we know from previous research, their bonds with their parents tend to weaken. So whereas in the past some have proposed that your bonds to your parents actually prevent you from drug-using behaviours like tobacco smoking, when you work, a parent kind of releases those bonds and . . . that freedom may increase the likelihood to smoke."

Stress may also be another factor, Mr. Ramchand offered. "Kids don't report that their jobs themselves are very stressful, but what they will report is that managing their time and their responsibilities—getting all their homework done, sports if that's part of their lives, as well as their work responsibilities—the combination of those things creates stress."

"And they may turn to cigarettes as a kind of self-medication to relieve that stress."

The research, published Friday in the *American Journal of Public Health*, is part of a larger, ongoing study of almost 800 Baltimore children, who were enrolled in Grade 1.

d)* [From *The Windsor Star*, 24 October 1995] Seven out of 10 women wear the wrong size bra, according to surveys by Playtex, a bra manufacturer . . . this statistic was based on women who came to Playtex bra-fitting clinics.

e) David M. Unwin concludes in *Nature* (May 1987) that the winged reptiles, pterosaurs, spent most of their lives hanging upside down from cliffs and trees because, while they may have been agile in the air, they could do no more than waddle clumsily on the ground.

This conclusion was drawn in part from recent discoveries in Germany and Australia of two relatively uncrushed pterosaur pelvises. In these pelvises, the acetabulum, a socket into which the tip of the femur bone fits, is oriented outward and upward, and this suggests that the pterosaurs' legs were splayed out, giving them a clumsy gait. Had the acetabulum pointed out and down instead, the pelvises would have supported another theory, held since the 1970s, that pterosaurs stood erect with their hind limbs beneath their bodies and were agile on the ground.

f)   [The following comes from a report on the Air France disaster in May 2009, "The riddle of flight AF447," *The Independent* newspaper, 10 June 2009] Airline disasters are meat and drink to conspiracy theorists. Several alternative explanations still exist for the Concorde disaster in Paris in 2000 and the terrorist bombing of a Pan Am jumbo over Lockerbie in 1988. The confusion and misinformation surrounding Flight AF447 will inevitably lead to similarly fevered speculation.

g)* [The following comes from a BBC News report on a study on obesity, published in full in the *International Journal of Obesity*, "Obesity 'link to same-sex parent'" 12 July 2009, http://news.bbc.co.uk] There is a strong link in obesity between mothers and daughters and fathers and sons, but not across the gender divide, research suggests. A study of 226 families by Plymouth's Peninsula Medical School found obese mothers were 10 times more likely to have obese daughters. For fathers and sons, there was a six-fold rise. But in both cases children of the opposite sex were not affected. The researchers believe the link is behavioural rather than genetic. They say the findings mean policy on obesity should be re-thought.

Researchers said it was "highly unlikely" that genetics was playing a role in the findings as it would be unusual for them to influence children along gender lines. Instead, they said it was probably because of some form of "behavioural sympathy" where daughters copied the lifestyles of their mothers and sons their fathers. It is because of this conclusion that experts believe government policy on tackling obesity should be re-thought. . . .

Study leader Professor Terry Wilkin said: "It is the reverse of what we have thought and this has fundamental implications for policy. We should be targeting the parents and that is not something we have really done to date." His team took weight and height measurements for children and parents over a three-year period. They found that 41 per cent of the eight-year-old daughters of obese mothers were obese, compared to 4 per cent of girls with normal-weight mothers. There was no difference in the proportion for boys. For boys, 18 per cent of the group with obese fathers were also obese, compared to just 3 per cent for those with normal-weight fathers. Again, there was no difference in the proportion for girls.

h)   [From a cosmetics advertisement] Research among dermatologists reveals a lot of skepticism regarding anti-aging claims. Research also shows that 95% of the doctors surveyed recommended Overnight Success's active ingredient for the relief of dry to clinically dry skin.

The Overnight Success night strength formula dramatically helps diminish fine, dry lines and their aging appearance. . . . And after just 3 nights' use, 98% of women tested showed measurable improvements.

Discover Overnight Success tonight. Wake up to softer, smoother, younger looking skin tomorrow.

i) [From a Letter to the Editor, *Saturday Night* magazine, 15 July 2000] According to an article published in the *New England Journal of Medicine*, marking territory with urine may prevent incontinence in old age. The *Journal* looked at two patients' reports of using their urine to keep cats and dogs out of their garden. The male, clad in sandals and kilt, walked around the garden's edge, urinating a small amount every few steps. This constant use of the pubococcygeal muscles keeps the bladder and rectal sphincter strong, and is what scientists believed prevented incontinence among our ancestors.

j) [From a Letter to the Editor, *Kitchener-Waterloo Record*, 1 December 1984] I would like to respond to the news stories that have warned of possible increases in the taxes of cigarettes and liquor in the next government budget. As a smoker I am very upset. Does the government not realize that if people cannot afford to buy tobacco and stop smoking, many people will be out of work? By raising the price of tobacco, people will have to stop smoking because they cannot afford to buy cigarettes. So the cigarette companies and tobacco farmers will have to lay people off. The government exists to create jobs not to lose them, and if the government raises cigarette prices any more, the unemployment and welfare lines are going to get a lot longer.

k)* [The following is from *The Darwinian Paradigm: Essays on its History, Philosophy and Religious Implication*, Michael Ruse, Routledge, 1989, p. 38. Ruse is discussing Darwin's *Origin of the Species* (1859)]

Coming to selection itself, we find the same emphasis on the individual. For instance, to illustrate how natural selection might work Darwin gave the imaginary example of a group of wolves, hard-pressed for food (1859, p. 90). He suggested that the swiftest and slimmest would be selected, because it will be they alone who will catch the prey. Hence, there will be evolution towards and maintenance of fast, lean wolves. Obviously, the crux of this explanation is that some wolves survive and reproduce whereas others do not. There is no question here of selection working for a group; rather it is all a matter of individual against individual.

l) [Tim Radford, "Genes say boys will be boys and girls will be sensitive," in the *Guardian*, 22 June 1997, p. 14] The sensitive sex was born that way. And boys are oafish because they can't help it. Blame nature, not nurture. The gene machine switches on feminine intuition long before birth, British scientists reported last week. The same mechanism switches off in boy babies after conception, leaving them to grow up awkward, gauche and insensitive. The irony is that a girl's talent for tact, social deftness and womanly intuition comes from father, not mother.

"What we might call feminine intuition—the ability to suss out a social situation by observing nuances of expression in voice and so on—is a set of skills of genetic origin that has nothing at all to do with hormones, as far as we know," said David Skuse of the Institute of Child Health in London. Prof. Skuse and colleagues from the Wessex Regional Genetics Laboratory in Salisbury were actually studying Turner's syndrome, a rare condition that affects one female in 2,500.

"A high proportion of girls had serious social adjustment problems, which started around the time they entered school and continued right through to adolescence," he said. Intelligence was normal, but the girls were often short, and in adult life infertile. As children they were less aware of people's feelings, interrupted conversations, made demands of other people's time, and could not "read" body language.

Girls have two X chromosomes, boys an X and a Y. But girls with Turner's syndrome have only one. Some inherited their one X from the mother, some from the father. The ones with the mother's X had the more severe problems. So, the researchers reason, there would be a gene or set of genes switched on or off in the egg, according to the parent from whom they are inherited. Girls normally get the switched on version from fathers, and boys inherit a single X chromosome from their mothers, with the genes switched off. "Others might feel that men are somehow doomed. Well, we can learn social skills," Prof. Skuse said. "Women will pick them up intuitively."

This raised an evolutionary puzzle. "Why would it be advantageous for males to be socially insensitive? If you wanted to recruit boys into an army, a hunting party or a football team, it is an advantage to have those boys socially unskilled so the dominant male in that group can impose a set of social mores," he said.

m) [The following is excerpted from "Cinema fiction vs. physics reality: Ghosts, vampires, and zombies," by Costas J. Efthimiou and Sohang Gandhi, *Skeptical Inquirer*, Vol. 31.4, July/August 2007] Anyone who has seen John Carpenter's *Vampires*, or the movies *Dracula* or *Blade*, or any other vampire film is already quite familiar with the vampire legend. The vampire needs to feed on human blood. After one has stuck his fangs into your neck and sucked you dry, you turn into a vampire yourself and carry on the blood-sucking legacy. The fact of the matter is, if vampires truly feed with even a tiny fraction of the frequency that they are depicted as doing in the movies and folklore, then humanity would have been wiped out quite quickly after the first vampire appeared.

Let us assume that a vampire need feed only once a month. This is certainly a highly conservative assumption, given any Hollywood vampire film. Now, two things happen when a vampire feeds. The human population decreases by one and the vampire population increases by one. Let us suppose that the first vampire appeared in 1600 CE. It doesn't really matter what date we choose for the first vampire to appear; it has little bearing on our argument. We list a government website in the references (US Census) that provides an estimate of the world population for any given date. For 1 January 1600, we will accept that the global population was 536,870,911. In our argument, we had at the same time one vampire.

We will ignore the human mortality and birth rate for the time being and only concentrate on the effects of vampire feeding. On 1 February 1600, one human will have died and a new vampire will have been born. This gives two vampires and 536,870,911–1 humans. The next month, there are two vampires feeding, thus two humans die and two new vampires are born. This gives four vampires and 536,870,911–3 humans. Now on 1 April 1600, there are four vampires feeding and thus we have four human deaths and four new vampires being born. This gives us eight vampires and 536,870,911 – 7 humans.

By now, the reader has probably caught on to the progression. Each month, the number of vampires doubles, so that, after n months have passed, there are

$$\underbrace{2 \times 2 \times \ldots \times 2}_{n \text{ times}} = 2^n$$

vampires. This sort of progression is known in mathematics as a geometric progression—more specifically, it is a geometric progression with ratio two, since we multiply by two at each step. A geometric progression increases at a tremendous rate, a fact that will become clear shortly. Now, all but one of these vampires were once human, so that the human population is its original population minus the number of vampires excluding the original one. So after n months have passed, there are 536,870,911 – $2n$ + 1 humans. The vampire population increases geometrically and the human population decreases geometrically. We conclude that if the first vampire appeared on 1 January 1600, humanity would have been wiped out by June of 1602, two and a half years later.

We conclude that vampires cannot exist, since their existence would contradict the existence of human beings.

n) [Chandra Wickramasinghe, Milton Wainwright, and Jayant Narlikar, in "SARS—A clue to its origin?," Letter to the Editor, *The Lancet*, Vol. 361, No. 9371, 24 May 2003] Sir—We detected large quantities of viable microorganisms in samples of stratospheric air at an altitude of 41 km.[1,2] We collected the samples in specially designed sterile cryosamplers carried aboard a balloon launched from the Indian Space Research Organisation/Tata Institute Balloon Facility in Hyderabad, India, on Jan. 21, 2001. Although the recovered biomaterial contained many microorganisms, as assessed with standard microbiological tests, we were able to culture only two types; both similar to known terrestrial species.[2] Our findings lend support to the view that microbial material falling from space is, in a Darwinian sense, highly evolved, with an evolutionary history closely related to life that exists on Earth.

We estimate that a tonne of bacterial material falls to Earth from space daily, which translates into some 10^{19} bacteria, or 20,000 bacteria per square metre of the Earth's surface. Most of this material simply adds to the unculturable or uncultured microbial flora present on Earth.

[1] Harris M.J., Wickramasinghe N.C., Lloyd D., et al. The detection of living cells in stratospheric samples. *Proc. SPIE Conference* 2002; 4495: 192–198. [PubMed].

[2] Wainwright M, Wickramasinghe N.C., Narlikar J.V., Rajaratnam P. Microorganisms cultured from stratospheric air samples obtained at 41 km. *FEMS Microbiol Lett* 2003; 218: 161–165. [CrossRef] [PubMed].

The injection from space of evolved microorganisms that have well-attested terrestrial affinities raises the possibility that pathogenic bacteria and viruses might also be introduced. The annals of medical history detail many examples of plagues and pestilences that can be attributed to space-incident microbes in this way. New epidemic diseases have a record of abrupt entrances from time to time, and equally abrupt retreats. The patterns of spread of these diseases, as charted by historians, are often difficult to explain simply on the basis of endemic infective agents. Historical epidemics such as the plague of Athens and the plague of Justinian come to mind.

In more recent times the influenza pandemic of 1917–19 bears all the hallmarks of a space-incident component: "The influenza pandemic of 1918 occurred in three waves. The first appeared in the winter and spring of 1917–1918. . . . The lethal second wave . . . involved almost the entire world over a very short time. . . . Its epidemiologic behaviour was most unusual. Although person-to-person spread occurred in local areas, the disease appeared on the same day in widely separated parts of the world on the one hand, but, on the other, took days to weeks to spread relatively short distances."[3]

Also well documented is that, in the winter of 1918, the disease appeared suddenly in the frozen wastes of Alaska, in villages that had been isolated for several months. Mathematical modelling of epidemics such as the one described invariably involves the ad hoc introduction of many unproven hypotheses—for example, that of the superspreader. In situations where proven infectivity is limited only to close contacts, a superspreader is someone who can, on occasion, simultaneously infect a large number of susceptible individuals, thus causing the sporadic emergence of new clusters of disease. The recognition of a possible vertical input of external origin is conspicuously missing in such explanations.[4,5]

With respect to the SARS outbreak, a prima facie case for a possible space incidence can already be made. First, the virus is unexpectedly novel, and appeared without warning in mainland China. A small amount of the culprit virus introduced into the stratosphere could make a first tentative fallout east of the great mountain range of the Himalayas, where the stratosphere is thinnest, followed by sporadic deposits in neighbouring areas. If the virus is only minimally infective, as it seems to be, the subsequent course of its global progress will depend on stratospheric transport and mixing, leading to a fallout continuing seasonally over a few years. Although all reasonable attempts to contain the infective spread of SARS should be continued, we should remain vigilant for the appearance of new foci (unconnected with infective contacts or with China) almost anywhere on the planet. New cases might continue to appear until the stratospheric supply of the causative agent becomes exhausted.

[3] Weinstein L. Influenza: 1918, a revisit? *N Engl J Med* 1976; 6: 1058–1060. [PubMed].

[4] Hoyle F, Wickramasinghe N.C. *Diseases from Space*. London: JM Dent, 1979.

[5] Wickramasinghe N.C. *Cosmic Dragons: Life and Death on Our Planet*. London: Souvenir Press, 2001.

o) [From C.D.B. Bryan, *Close Encounters of the Fourth Kind: Alien Abduction, UFOs, and the conference at M.I.T.*, Knopf, 1995, p. 230] During the days immediately following the conference, I am struck by how my perception of the abduction phenomenon has changed: I no longer think it is a joke. This is not to say I now believe UFOs and alien abduction are *real*—"real" in the sense of a reality subject to the physical laws of the universe as we know them—but rather that I feel something very mysterious is going on. And based as much on what has been presented at the conference as on the intelligence, dedication, and sanity of the majority of the presenters, I cannot reject out-of-hand the *possibility* that what is taking place isn't exactly what the abductees are saying is happening to them. And if that is so, the fact that no one has been able to pick up a tailpipe from a UFO does not mean UFOs do not exist. It means only that UFOs might not have tailpipes. As Boston astronomer Michael Papagiannis insisted, "The absence of evidence is not evidence of absence."

p)* [Carl Sagan, in *The Dragons of Eden: Speculations on the Evolution of Human Intelligence*, Random House, 1977, pp. 92–3] So far as I know, childbirth is generally painful in only one of the millions of species on Earth: human beings. This must be a consequence of the recent and continuing increase in cranial volume. Modern men and women have braincases twice the volume of Homo habilis's. Childbirth is painful because the evolution of the human skull has been spectacularly fast and recent. The American anatomist C. Judson Herrick described the development of the neocortex in the following terms: "Its explosive growth late in phylogeny is one of the most dramatic cases of evolutionary transformation known to comparative anatomy." The incomplete closure of the skull at birth, the fontanelle, is very likely an imperfect accommodation to this recent brain evolution.

For more online exercises, review questions, and quizzes related to the material in this chapter, please go to www.oupcanada.com/GoodReasoning5e

SCHEMES OF VALUE

> In this chapter, we introduce schemes "of value" that play an important role in or-
> dinary reasoning. Because these schemes play a particularly important role in mor-
> al and political reasoning, we focus on examples from these areas. The schemes
> that we discuss are:
>
> ▶ slippery-slope arguments
> ▶ arguments from analogy
> ▶ appeals to precedent
> ▶ two-wrongs reasoning
> ▶ two-wrongs by analogy.

In the last two chapters, we have discussed schemes of argument that address factual issues. In this chapter, we discuss a set of schemes that are used in reasoning
about "values" or "morals." By this we mean that such arguments can be used when we
debate what is right and wrong, what should be done in particular circumstances, and
what policies or laws should be adopted. As it is often said, factual claims and arguments are claims and arguments about what is the case; moral (or "value") claims and
arguments are claims and arguments about what ought to be the case.

Of course, moral and factual reasoning are not entirely distinct. In ordinary discussion, they are usually intertwined. When we debate political uprisings in the Arab
world, we are likely to debate both factual issues (the conditions under which people
live, what actually happened in controversial incidents, who controls and acts for
whom, etc.) and issues of morality and value (what rights individuals have, how one
can legitimately deal with violent threats, under what circumstances a group of people
has the right to rise up and protest, etc.). In introducing a series of argument schemes
that can be applied to moral and political reasoning, we shall see that there are times
when these schemes are used to establish factual rather than moral conclusions and
that they often blend empirical and moral reasoning.

As we have noted before, the schemes that we are introducing are not exhaustive
or definitive. They are the basis of a broad range of important moral and political

arguments, but in your dealings with ordinary arguments, you may find instances of moral and political reasoning that do not fit any of the schemes that we introduce. In such cases, you can again assess such arguments by relying on the general criteria for good arguments that we have already identified (i.e. acceptability, relevance, and sufficiency). In fact, each of the schemes in this chapter involves specific applications of the general criteria for a good argument.

1 Slippery-Slope Arguments

The first scheme that we will consider in our account of reasoning about values illustrates the ways in which moral and empirical reasoning are often combined in the discussion of moral and political issues. Because "slippery-slope arguments" are used in debates about actions and their consequences, they combine causal reasoning about the consequences of particular actions and moral considerations about the consequences that should or should not be prevented.

Using uppercase letters to refer to actions, we can represent the scheme for slippery-slope arguments as follows:

Premise 1: A causes B, B causes C, and so on to X.
Premise 2: X is undesirable (or X is desirable).
Conclusion: A is wrong (or right).

Arguments that abide by this scheme are called "slippery-slope" arguments, because the negative version of this argument maintains that a given action, "A," initiates our "sliding down a slippery slope of causal sequences to some inevitable consequence" that we should avoid.

One might compare slippery-slope arguments to some of the schemes in the Appendices that explore propositional logic. The causal chain in a slippery-slope argument is like a conditional series, i.e. *if X then Y, if Y then Z, etc., therefore, if X then Z,* where the conditionals are causal statements that declare that if X occurs, then this causes Y to occur, and so on. Because a slippery-slope argument can be based on a long chain of cause-and-effect relationships, premise 1 in our scheme will often appear as a series of premises of the form:

A causes B
B causes C
C causes D
D causes X

A strong slippery-slope argument is (explicitly or implicitly) a strong instance of the scheme for such reasoning. Here, we need to consider two questions that correspond to each of our two premises. An answer to the first—"Does the causal chain really hold?"—requires empirical reasoning. The second—"Is the final consequence properly judged to be desirable (or undesirable)?"—requires moral reasoning. A good argument against slippery-slope reasoning must argue that the claimed causal chain will not develop as proposed or that the value of its ultimate consequence has been misjudged. The causal chain can be challenged by questioning one of the causal links, either by pointing out that it lacks support or that it is supported by poor causal reasoning.

An example of slippery-slope reasoning in the political arena is found in the following illustration, fashioned after a World War II cartoon by David Low. It is a criticism of the indifference of the English public when Germany moved against Czechoslovakia. Low criticizes this indifference by suggesting that it will precipitate a series of causal effects that will lead to disaster. He does so by drawing (quite literally) a slippery slope that represents the chain of consequences that will transpire if Germany is allowed to take Czechoslovakia.

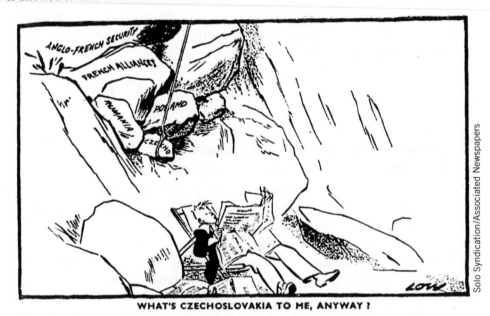

WHAT'S CZECHOSLOVAKIA TO ME, ANYWAY ?

Illustration 11.1   "What's Czechoslovakia to me, anyway?"

We can diagram Low's argument as follows:

P1 =   If Germany takes Czechoslovakia, then Romania and Poland will fall.

P2 =   If Poland and Romania fall, then the French alliances will fall.

P3 =   If the French alliances fall, then Anglo-French security will be unstable.

P4 =   We do not want Anglo-French security to be unstable.

MC =   We should not continue to ignore Germany's incursions on Czechoslovakia.

In assessing this argument, we need to ask whether the causal chain that it proposes is plausible. In retrospect, history tells us that it was. But at the time, an assessor would have had to judge the likelihood of each step in the causal chain. Given the military might of Germany at that time, combined with the relative weakness of countries like Czechoslovakia and Romania, and given the geographical facts of the situation, a reasoner could indeed have judged each link in the proposed causal chain as plausible. Also, the final consequence of this causal chain—the fall of Anglo-French security—is something that is clearly undesirable to Low's audience (the British public) as well as to a broader universal audience (which would not, for moral reasons, support the rise of Nazi Germany). We, therefore, judge Low's argument to be a good instance of slippery-slope reasoning.

We take as our second example of slippery-slope reasoning an article by William Saletan in the online magazine *Slate* (www.slate.com, posted 19 May 2006). He argues that "We've just taken another step down the slippery slope toward eugenics" by allowing PGD—"preimplantation genetic diagnosis," a process in which clinics take sperm and eggs, make embryos in laboratory dishes, and screen them for genetic flaws. The process was first approved to "weed out genes that were nearly certain to cause a grave childhood disease or were certain to cause a grave adult disease," but the new rules expanded the use of the procedure to allow the elimination of embryos for diseases that are more treatable and less likely to affect the person an embryo would become.

Saletan argues that there are some good reasons for allowing PGD: that it will "spare many families a lot of suffering. But so will the next step down the slope, and the step after that. And there's no sign of a foothold ahead that will brake our slide." In the remainder of his article, Saletan develops detailed arguments for the claim that the decision about PGD promotes a slide toward eugenics and the manipulation of genes: by creating weaker standards for "penetrance," "treatability," and "age of onset." We will not consider these concepts in detail here but simply note that they are used in a paradigm instance of slippery-slope reasoning. It argues that we should not do something (change the rules on PGD) because it will ultimately lead to something we want to avoid (eugenics: the improper manipulation of genes). The key to the assessment of this particular argument will, then, be the assessment of Saletan's causal claims that ultimately link PGD to eugenics.

SLIPPERY-SLOPE ARGUMENTS

A slippery-slope argument is one that shows either (1) that an action should not be performed or allowed because it will begin a causal chain leading to an undesirable consequence or (2) that an action should be performed or allowed because it will begin a chain of causes leading to a desirable end. A good slippery-slope argument must be founded on a plausible causal chain and an acceptable claim about what is or is not desirable.

EXERCISE 11A

Assess the slippery-slope arguments in the following passages:

a)* The UN Security Council's resolution authorizing states to take "all necessary measures" to protect Libyan civilians goes beyond a simple no-fly zone. Banning flights of Libyan military forces will lead to targeted air strikes on military installations, and when that fails to shift the war in favour of the rebel forces, as it will, we will inevitably see "boots on the ground" in spite of the wording of the resolution. Such an invasion will confirm the suspicions of all sceptics in the region that the real goal is to control Libyan oil, with dire consequences for future UN missions. We can avoid this only by withdrawing now.

b)   [Adapted from J. Gay-Williams, "The wrongfulness of euthanasia," In *Intervention and Reflection: Basic Issues in Medical Ethics,* Ronald Munson, Ed., Wadsworth, 1979] Euthanasia as a policy is a slippery slope. A person apparently hopelessly ill may be allowed to take his own life. Should he no longer be able to act, he may be permitted to deputize others to do it for him; then the judgment of others becomes the ruling factor. At this point it becomes a matter of others acting "on behalf of" the patient as they see fit, and this may incline them to act on behalf of other patients who have not authorized them to act on their behalf. It is only a short step, then, from voluntary euthanasia (self-inflicted or authorized), to directed euthanasia administered to a patient who has given no authorization, to involuntary euthanasia conducted as part of a social policy. As social policy, it would give society or its representatives the authority to eliminate all those who might be considered too "ill" to function normally any longer.

c)   [John Hofsess, in *Maclean's* magazine, October 1973] If you don't get into the habit of exercising regularly when you're young, you are less likely to keep exercising during your later 20s and 30s when career, home, and family take up more and more time and interest. You'll then tend to become sedentary and physically unfit. That will set you up for various heart and lung diseases during middle age. No one wants to have a heart attack at 45 or 50, so to lessen that danger, you ought to get into the habit of exercising when you're young.

d)   [Arthur Schafer, in "There can be another me, but should there be another ewe?," *The Globe and Mail*, 28 February 1998] Ethicist Arthur Schafer challenges those who claim our acceptance of biomedical technologies puts us on a slippery slope, as we gradually come to accept things we at first rejected.
Yes, but is this always a bad thing? . . . Does public acceptance of assisted reproduction prove that our moral sensibility has been coarsened? Or have we, rather, discarded an unthinking prejudice?

2   Arguments from Analogy

Analogies add richness to our language. An analogy makes a comparison between two different things by identifying similar features they both possess. A neurosurgeon delivering a lecture on the structure of the human brain might introduce her lecture by saying, "The brain is like a highly efficient and compact computer," and then organize her remarks around specific similarities.

As long as no conclusion is drawn from the comparison between the brain and a computer, we do not have an argument. It is an analogy, but one used simply for elucidation. It is only when the comparison is used as a basis for drawing a conclusion that we have an argument by analogy. Typically, the reasoning is that two things are analogous in a certain respect because they are analogous in one or more other ways. If, based on similarities between the human brain and the computer, the neurosurgeon concluded that "Humans are (like computers) just complicated machines" or "Human beings have the same moral status as a very complex machine," we would have an argument by analogy.

We call the two things compared in an analogy "**analogues**." In presenting a scheme for analogical arguments, we will label the analogues X and Y. Those respects in which X and Y are said to be alike can be represented as p, q, r, and so on. Each of these letters represents a statement or characteristic that is true of both X and Y. Since Y is like X in possessing the qualities p, q, r, etc., we conclude that Y possesses some additional property z, a property we call "the target property." It is a property that X possesses. Schematically, the argument can be depicted as follows:

> **Premise 1:** X is p, q, r, . . . , z.
> **Premise 2:** Y is p, q, r, ...
> **Conclusion:** Y is z.

The analogues do not have to be single entities. One or the other or both may be groups of things, in which case the form of the argument may look like this:

> **Premise 1:** X, W, R, S are p, q, r, . . . , z.
> **Premise 2:** Y is p, q, r, ...
> **Conclusion:** Y is z.

You must analyze analogical reasoning in terms of the similarities between the analogues. In the strongest cases, the analogues, X and Y, will be identical, i.e. the same in all essential characteristics. In that event, we say that the claimed similarities are "tightly" tied to the target property. The conclusion necessarily follows, for any property of X will be shared by Y. If X and Y are identical ("monozygotic") twins, then finding out something about X's genetic make-up allows us to conclude the same of Y. If X and Y are two actions that are in all morally relevant ways similar, then we can be certain that the conclusion we draw about the rightness or wrongness of one can be applied in the other instance. But the cases we usually consider are cases where X and Y are not identical and where the conclusion that X has target property z is only probable. In these cases we say that the target property is more loosely tied to the similarities that the analogues are claimed to share. In a good argument by analogy, the strength of the tie between the similarities in the analogues and the target property must be tight enough to make the conclusion probable.

Arguments by analogy can be used to establish empirical or moral conclusions. In scientific contexts, medical researchers often use discoveries about the effect that particular substances have on rats or other mammals as a basis for conclusions about the effects they will have on humans. In such cases, medical researchers use a species with a physiological system analogous to that of humans and conclude that humans would probably be similarly affected.

Arguments by analogy also play a central role in moral and legal discourse. The basis of law is the principle that "justice is blind," which means that the law is obliged to treat similar actions in similar ways. Morality similarly obliges us to judge analogous actions as good or bad or permissible or not permissible. When we are forced to deal with new kinds of moral situations—those that result from new technological innovations, for example—we often proceed by looking for analogous situations with which we are familiar and by applying relevant moral principles in a similar way to the new circumstance. For instance, if we want to decide whether a new method of dealing with male sterility should be subsidized by the government, we may begin by considering whether this method can be compared to other medical interventions that are (or are not) supported by the government (say, other methods that are supported, or methods used to treat female sterility).

A convincing argument by analogy must enumerate real, and not just apparent, similarities between the analogues. Because different kinds of similarities and differences matter in different contexts, the argument must enumerate the similarities that matter to the case at hand. In sentencing someone convicted of a crime, a judge may decide to look at cases that are similar or different in terms of the seriousness of the offence, premeditation, callousness, the pain caused to innocent victims, etc. Many other similarities and differences will not matter, though the distinction between those that matter and those that don't is not always clear. When Keith Richards of the *Rolling Stones* was given a suspended sentence for possessing a large quantity of heroin and cocaine, critics argued that the principle that like cases be treated similarly had been violated, because his unexpectedly light sentence was, they claimed, a consequence of the fact that he was a rock star rather than an ordinary addict. Their claim can be expressed as the claim that this kind of difference in personal status is irrelevant when in a courtroom, where judges are obliged to treat analogous cases in the same way.

In view of these kinds of considerations, a good argument by analogy typically depends on an assumption that we can represent by adding a hidden premise to our standard scheme:

> **Premise 1:** X, W, R, S are $p, q, r, \ldots, z$.
> **Premise 2:** Y is $p, q, r, \ldots$.
> **Hidden Premise:** p, q, r are the properties relevant to z.
> **Conclusion:** Y is z.

This implies that a strong argument of this sort will (implicitly or explicitly) establish z as a property of some Y by pointing out (1) that z applies to X; (2) that Y is similar to X in sufficient relevant respects; and (3) that X and Y are not relevantly dissimilar. A strong argument by analogy has premises establishing that property z is a property of the first analogue and that the analogues are similar in ways that are relevant to the conclusion and does not overlook any relevant dissimilarities. Because the premises in an analogical argument must be combined to warrant the conclusion, they will always be linked in a diagram that represents the argument.

One of the most famous historical examples of an argument by analogy is the "argument from design." It states that the universe exhibits a particular order, predictability, and design and maintains that it is reasonable to infer from this the existence of a designer. This designer is, of course, God, and the argument from design is one of the traditional proofs of the existence of God. The eighteenth-century Scottish philosopher David Hume discusses this argument in his *Dialogues Concerning Natural Religion*. His own argument takes place in the context of a dialogue involving several participants, which allows Hume both to present the argument by analogy and then to criticize it. When he presents the argument, he suggests that scientific study shows us that the world is like a machine, with different parts that are made up of other parts that work together in a precise way:

> Look round the world … you will find it to be nothing but one great machine, subdivided into an infinite number of lesser machines, which again admit of subdivisions to a degree beyond what human sense and faculties can trace and explain. All these various machines, and even their most minute parts, are adjusted to each other with an accuracy which ravishes into admiration all men who have ever contemplated them. The curious adapting of means to ends, throughout all nature, resembles exactly, though it much exceeds, the productions of human contrivance—of human design, thought, wisdom, and intelligence. Since therefore the effects resemble each other, we are led to infer, by all the rules of analogy, that the causes also resemble, and that the Author of nature is somewhat similar to the mind of man, though possessed of much larger faculties, proportioned to the grandeur of the work which he has executed.

The manner in which everything in nature appears to work together, to happen for a reason, to fulfill a particular purpose, suggests the product of a specific design, akin to human design but far superior. This resemblance in the origins or causes suggests that the "Author" of nature is analogous to the human mind, though on a much greater scale, appropriate to the larger scale of creation as a whole. Hume's principal concern is the nature of God: we infer the nature and mind of God by analogy with our nature and mind, extended to divine proportions.

In the next part of Hume's dialogue, another participant, Philo, proclaims that the argument from design is a very weak analogy. Suggesting that analogies weaken the moment we shift our terms of reference, Philo states that we conclude that a house had an architect or builder because this is the kind of effect we have observed to result from that kind of cause. However:

> Surely you will not affirm that the universe bears such a resemblance to a house that we can with the same certainty infer a similar cause, or that the analogy is here entire and perfect. The dissimilitude is so striking that the utmost you can here pretend to is a guess, a conjecture, a presumption concerning a similar cause.

Philo's point is that the dissimilarities between the universe and a house are so great that they threaten to undermine the necessary similarities, and the analogy breaks down; therefore, the attempt to infer, on the basis of one thing, a similar cause in the other—or any cause at all in the case of a proof of God's existence—is fruitless. What we have is a guess, not a fully convincing argument. Hume's discussion goes on to elaborate the ways in which the universe and a house differ, much of it rooted in the basic tenet of his philosophy, that only things we can know from experience can be proven or accepted. It follows that we can know where houses come from but cannot say the same about the universe.

One might write a whole book on the argument from design. In the present context, our purpose is to illustrate a basic, and renowned, philosophical example of an argument by analogy. Philo's response to the argument is an example of a counter-argument to analogy, which we will discuss next.

Counter-arguments to Analogy

Given our understanding of good arguments by analogy, a strong counter-argument against an argument by analogy must demonstrate that the criteria for a good argument by analogy are not (or cannot be) met in a specific case. This can be done in two ways.

In some cases, we may criticize an argument by analogy by accepting the proposed analogues but denying that the property emphasized in the conclusion applies to either. Suppose we discipline students for some misbehaviour—say, cheating on an exam— by failing them in our course. Suppose they complain that they have been unfairly treated because other students in the same situation received a zero on the exam but were allowed to complete the course. This is an argument by analogy. It maintains that two groups of students are in analogous situations and should, as a consequence, be treated in an analogous way. As people in these kinds of situation often rely on unreliable anecdotal information, it is easy to imagine that we might respond to the situation by investigating the matter and reporting that "This is not in fact the case; the students in question were given a failing grade in their course." In this situation, we have constructed a strong counter-argument to an argument by analogy by showing that the analogue that is the basis of the argument does not have the property assigned to it.

More commonly, a counter-argument against analogy will be an *argument by* **disanalogy**, which attempts to show that two purported analogues are not analogous. This is done by showing that they do not share necessary similarities or that there are relevant differences that distinguish them. In the case above, we would construct an argument by disanalogy if we told the students who complained that those students they had compared themselves to were not in an analogous situation (say, because their cheating was on a relatively minor test rather than on an exam).

Another example of argument by disanalogy is found in a letter to *Euro Know* (www.euro-know.org/letters017.html, accessed July 2002). The letter begins with the comment that "The ideal of the European Union is the integration of, so far, fifteen different political and economic structures not one federal state like the USA controlled by Brussels." In the rest of his letter, the arguer proposes evidence that attempts to show that this analogy does not make sense (that the histories are different, that attitudes are different, and so on). On the basis of this disanalogy, he maintains that it makes no sense for the European Union, as opposed to the United States, to have one currency. The conclusion that it makes no sense to model the European Union on the United States is based on the argument that the two are not analogous.

We construct an implicit counter-argument to analogy whenever we criticize an argument by analogy. Consider the following letter to the *Toronto Star* (27 April 1983), which focuses on a definition argued from analogy:

> Whether or not a fetus is a human being is a matter of personal opinion, but nobody can deny that forcing a woman to carry and give birth to a child against her will is an act of enslavement. Consider: someone approaches you and demands to be hooked up to your life support system for nine months, on the grounds that this is necessary for survival. It would be an unselfish gesture to comply, but you have every right to refuse. After all, it's your body—isn't it?

We can diagram this argument as follows:

P1 =   In forcing a woman to carry and give birth to a child and in forcing you to allow someone to be hooked up to your life support system, it is one's own body that is being used.

P2 =   In both cases, the use of one's body is necessary to ensure survival, of the person or the fetus.

C1 =   Forcing a woman to carry and give birth to a child against the woman's will is like forcing you to allow someone to be hooked up to your life support system for nine months.

P3 =   In the second case, you would have the right to refuse to comply (it would be an act of enslavement to force you to comply).

MC =   A woman has every right to refuse to carry a child (it would be an act of enslavement to force her to carry it).

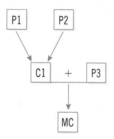

This is a version of a famous analogy used in moral reasoning, and at first glance, the argument may seem strong. One of the analogues appears somewhat fanciful, but there are grounds for comparing these two situations because (allowing that the fetus is a person) they both involve the dependence of one person on another. There are, however, two major dissimilarities that have been omitted. Once they are identified, the main conclusion is clearly problematic, and the argument can be recognized as weak.

If someone did approach you and demand to be hooked to your life support system, it would be quite reasonable to first point out that you are in no way responsible for that individual's predicament and to then require an explanation why that demand should be made specifically of you. A mother carrying a child is in a different situation, for she may bear some responsibility for her situation, in which case the justification for the demand implicitly made by the fetus is quite unlike that in the other analogue. Second, a person approaching you comes from "the outside" and already has some autonomous existence. But in the case of a pregnancy, the fetus has developed from within and has had no antecedent existence. If the two situations really were analogous, they could not be characterized by such significant dissimilarities. The main conclusion will not, therefore, be acceptable to any reasonable audience. Within the scope of an argument, we could eradicate these differences (imagine, for the moment, that you are responsible for the predicament of the person who needs to be hooked up to your life support system), but in that case it is no longer obvious that it would be wrong to force us to support the sufferer in question.

ARGUMENTS BY ANALOGY

Arguments by analogy are founded on claims that people or situations are analogous. A good argument by analogy attributes a target property to Y on the basis of a premise that show (1) that the target property belongs to X; (2) that Y is similar to X in sufficient relevant respects; and (3) that X and Y are not relevantly dissimilar. In a good argument by analogy the tie between the claimed similarities and the target property are tight enough to make the conclusion probable. A good counter-argument to analogy shows that one or more of the criteria for a strong argument by analogy cannot be satisfied.

EXERCISE 11B

1. Imagine that you are going to buy a new car. You choose to use an argument by analogy to decide what car you should purchase. You decide you want a car that is analogous to one a friend owns. What would be the structure of your argument? What is the target property? What would be the relevant similarities? What differences would not matter?

2. In each case, comment on the appropriateness of arguing the stated claim by means of the analogies suggested:

    a) **Claim:** Marijuana should be legalized.
       Analogies:
       i)   Legalizing marijuana is like legalizing cocaine.
       ii) Banning marijuana is like banning alcohol.
       iii) Making marijuana illegal is like banning novels in that it entices more users.
       iv) Smoking marijuana is like giving people an easy fix rather than the opportunity to accomplish things by hard work.

b) **Claim:** Rich nations should provide aid to poor ones.
   Analogies:
   i) Aid is like a handout people don't deserve.
   ii) Teaching a person to fish is like feeding the person for the rest of his or her life.
   iii) Aiding poor nations is like putting too many people on an already over-crowded lifeboat.
   iv) Refusing aid is being like Ebenezer Scrooge; providing aid is being like Jesus Christ.

3. Analyze the analogical reasoning in the following arguments. In each case identify the target property in the proposed argument by analogy (or in the argument being criticized). Is the argument in question a strong example of arguments from analogy or disanalogy? Provide your reasons.

   a)* The human brain is like a cell phone. We know the people we hear on the phone are not actually *in* the phone; the phone is just a receiver of voices of people who exist elsewhere. Likewise, the mind exists elsewhere, and the brain is just for the mind's thoughts.

   b) [From Pliny the Elder's *Natural History*, 7.56] We do not breathe differently from the other animals, and there are some that live longer than us, so why do we not assume they, too, are immortal? . . . These [beliefs about the soul] are fictions of childish absurdities.

   c)* [Deana Pollard, in "Regulating violent pornography," *Vanderbilt Law Review*, Vol. 43, No. 1, pp. 125–159, 1990] Speeding is known to increase the likelihood of car collisions, and drivers are punished for this dangerous behaviour whether or not their particular sprees cause collisions. Violent pornography, like speeding, is intrinsically dangerous, and legislatures may regulate it on the basis of its known propensity for harm without a showing of particular harm.

   d) [From a Letter to the Editor, *The Globe and Mail*, 11 March 2003] Crawford Kilian equates the specificity of recruiting a black person as head of the Johnston Chair for Black Canadian Studies at Dalhousie University to establishing segregated public toilets for blacks. The analogy is spurious.

   There is nothing black-related about a toilet; there is a great deal black-related about a Department of Black Canadian Studies.

   Does Mr Kilian, however painstaking and detailed his study of Canadian blacks, really believe that he, as a non-black, could successfully defend his credibility as head of such a department? Could he accurately communicate the total experience of being black? Indeed, would anyone listen?

   In a perfect world, of course, it wouldn't matter that he was white. In a perfect world there would be no such chair for black Canadian studies. It wouldn't be relevant.

   Today, alas, it is extremely relevant. And it absolutely requires a black leader.

   e) [Adapted from a letter to the *Toronto Star*, 5 November 1983] A man who drives his car into the rear of another is not guilty of careless driving if his brakes failed. Similarly, a man should not be found guilty of murder if his mind failed to perceive reality due to mental illness.

f)   [Excerpted from *The Wall Street Journal*, "His Dark Material: The unsubtle atheism of Philip Pullman's books," 14 December 2007]
So is the ferment about "His Dark Materials" just Harry Potter vs. Fundamentalists redux, a clash that generates heat but no light? Probably not.

First of all, "His Dark Materials," unlike the Harry Potter series, is real literature and, as such, deserves serious attention. Mr. Pullman, a graduate of Oxford University with a degree in English, knows his stuff. The books are loaded with allusions to Greek mythology and philosophy, Milton, Blake and the Bible, with images ranging from the obvious (the Garden of Eden) to the obscure (the bene elim, or angelic Watchers mentioned in Genesis 6:1–4). These allusions, unlike the throwaway Latinisms of Hogwarts' spells, drive the plot, characters and themes of Mr. Pullman's series. Indeed, a child who investigates them would begin to gain the rudiments of a classical education.

Moreover, again in contrast to J.K. Rowling's books (which were criticized by some Christians for their use of magic and witchcraft), Mr. Pullman's series is bluntly anti-Christian. In the third book, "The Amber Spyglass," a former nun tells the two child protagonists, Lyra and Will, that "the Christian religion is a very powerful and convincing mistake, that's all." The church and its members do nothing but evil.

3   Appeals to Precedent

Morality and law require consistency. In both cases, we are obliged to treat similar cases in a similar way. In view of this, we may appeal to precedents (i.e. to previously established decisions) to establish that a particular situation should be treated in a particular way. If an analogous case was treated in a certain way in the past, or if we want to treat future cases as analogous to those that are current, then our reasoning will be based on precedents. If two householders, for example, are granted a permit to add an addition to their house, this sets a precedent for other people in the neighbourhood to do likewise.

When we make an appeal to precedent, we are arguing by analogy. In view of this, arguments by precedent are a variant of the scheme we have given for arguments by analogy, that is:

Premise 1: X is $p, q, r, \ldots, z$.
Premise 2: Y is $p, q, r, \ldots$.
Hidden Premise: p, q, r are the properties relevant to the moral or legal assessment of X and Y.
Conclusion: Y is z.

In the case of appeal to precedent, X is the event or circumstance that is used to establish a precedent. It may be a previous or a future event (if the latter, the argument is used to establish a precedent to ensure that future cases of this sort are treated in a particular way). *Y* is the analogous event or circumstance that we are faced with. The hidden premise recognizes the assumption that *X* and *Y* are relevantly similar.

In dealing with new precedents, one may argue positively for a precedent or negatively against one. In the latter case, we argue that some action or decision will set an undesirable precedent, paving the way for actions or situations that are unacceptable. A professor may argue that it would be unfair to accept a late paper from one student because he or she must then accept late papers from other students in similar situations. In other cases, we use appeals to precedent to argue that a given case should be treated in a particular way because it will establish a good precedent for the future. In such a case, we might argue that we should prosecute a particular industrial polluter and not forgive a first offence, since consistency would then demand that we forgive other first offenders.

An example that illustrates how precedents may be used is the "Powell Doctrine," named after the former American secretary of state Colin Powell. In this case, the precedent appealed to is the Vietnam War and the perceived mistakes committed by the United States both in how the decision to go to war was made and in how the campaign was carried out. These perceived mistakes, which include entering the conflict with little popular support at home and no clearly defined military objective, are said to have had undesirable consequences. According to Powell, the United States was, as a result of these mistakes, trapped in an extended police action, suffering heavy casualties and low morale. On the basis of this understanding of Vietnam, Powell and others have concluded that it sets a negative precedent, i.e. a precedent that establishes how *not* to conduct military action. Thus, the Powell Doctrine holds that the United States should in the future not become involved in military action without a clear and pre-established military objective, a high level of support from the public, and a clearly winnable position. (For more on this, see *The New Republic*, 16 October 1995.)

Another example of arguing against a precedent is found in a response to the decision of an Ontario court that ordered that a man's extensive collection of old newspapers, magazines, and papers be seized and destroyed (reported in *The Globe and Mail*, 25 October 1995). The basis of this decision was the argument that the collection, comprising numerous stacks of paper material that he had collected and stored in his basement for years, represented a fire hazard. In response to the decision, other collectors of old books and materials immediately protested, arguing that this decision set an undesirable precedent, one that could be extended potentially to all collectors of any old or antiquarian materials. Booksellers argued that such a decision could prove a threat for antiquarian collectors, setting a precedent for the suppression of private book collections.

This example highlights the way in which arguments for or against a new precedent share similarities with slippery-slope reasoning insofar as they maintain that some action, used as a precedent, will lead to an undesirable (or desirable) consequence. It is important, though, to distinguish arguments that rely on causal reasoning from those based on analogical reasoning. This identification will help us decide whether what we have is principally a slippery-slope argument or an appeal to precedent. While we would not want to rule out the possibility of both types of reasoning arising in a particular argument, we should strive to avoid confusing the two. When constructing your own arguments of these sorts, decide whether the strategy you have in mind is one that uses causal reasoning of a future chain or analogical reasoning of comparing cases, and adopt the appropriate scheme.

As with other cases of analogy, a strong appeal to precedent establishes that the analogues compared—in this case, the precedent and the other situation said to be similar—are, in fact, analogous and that a particular moral or legal judgement applies in the situation that is associated with the precedent. Sub-arguments may be used to establish both these claims as acceptable. In constructing a *counter-argument to an appeal to precedent*, one must argue against one or both of these claims. In practice, you will find that the strength of most appeals to precedent turns on the question of whether the particular case that is said to be a precedent is analogous to the other cases with which we compare it. In particular, you must determine whether there are any relevant dissimilarities that separate the case at hand from the past or future situation(s) to which it is compared.

APPEALS TO PRECEDENT

Appeals to precedent argue for or against a situation or course of action by appealing to previous or future cases that are analogous.

A strong appeal to precedent shows that some action X should be allowed (or disallowed) because some analogous case has been allowed (or disallowed) or because future analogous cases should be allowed (or disallowed).

A strong counter-argument to an appeal to precedent shows that one of these claims is unacceptable because the cases being compared are not relevantly analogous.

EXERCISE   11C

1. Taking the following topics, sketch (a) an appeal to past precedent; (b) an argument against precedent; and (c) an argument for a new precedent. In each case, which argument is strongest?

    a) censorship of child pornography on the Internet
    b) using social media sites to identifying alleged criminals
    c) human cloning

2. Evaluate the strengths and weaknesses of the following argument by precedent:

    > Several publishers that had been planning books about prominent people or companies have been threatened with lawsuits by their potential subjects. Once threatened, these publishers felt they had no choice but to cancel the plans to publish the controversial books. The situation, known as "libel chill," will discourage writers, publishers, and commentators in the future from pursuing certain subjects. This situation represents undemocratic media control, censorship, and loss of freedom of expression.

4　Two-Wrongs Reasoning

In her biography of Ayn Rand, the well-known political thinker, Anne Conover Heller notes some of the moral complexities in Rand's own life and thought:

> "One must never attempt to fake reality in any manner," she would write in her famous description of the ethical man. That she could sometimes invent, exaggerate, or hide events in her own life in order to advance her hopes or bolster her public image may be partly due to her experience in Russia, especially as a Jew; for generations, small deceptions were a matter of safety or survival for Russian Jews. She made this point explicit when, in middle age, she told friends that an obligation to be truthful ends where the immoral behavior of others makes truth telling damaging to one's own interests. (*Ayn Rand and The World She Made*, New York, Doubleday, 2009, p. 34)

Here Heller contrasts the universal prescription that one must *never* falsify reality (a prescription Rand once ascribed to the ethical man) with Rand's later view: that there may be circumstances when this is permissible because it is the only way to protect one's interests from the immoral behaviour of others. Rand's experience as a Jew in Russia is suggested as a case in point, for it was necessary for Jews to hide their identity to protect themselves against discrimination and possibly even violence. Heller's comments highlight the complexities of moral and political reasoning, which often require that we weigh the reasons for and against some policy or course of action. In cases such as these, we use an argument scheme called "two-wrongs reasoning" when we justify a questionable action or policy on the grounds that it is a necessary way of correcting or avoiding some injustice.

There are two kinds of two-wrongs arguments. In the first, an action or policy that might be questioned is justified as a response to another wrong it attempts to cancel or alleviate. In the second, called "two-wrongs by analogy," an action is justified by pointing to similarly questionable actions that have been allowed. In this case, the argument maintains that consistency justifies the current action. Two-wrongs by analogy is discussed in greater detail below. For the moment, it will help to remember those arguments are a subset of the more basic two-wrongs argument and that our comments about it apply to both kinds of two-wrongs reasoning.

If correctly argued, the conclusions of two-wrongs arguments are plausible. Justifications of self-defence or civil disobedience typically take this form. We don't have to look far in the world for examples of people being denied the right to assemble (in India at the time of Gandhi or in the former Soviet Union on in China's Tiananmen Square). As we saw in what has been dubbed the "Arab Spring" of 2011, in response to perceived wrongs in countries like Tunisia and Egypt, people defied government edicts and congregated to protest, leading to the overthrow of dictatorial regimes. In these cases, they justified breaking the law by pointing to the wrongness of the policy that restricted them. In another context, a government may justify subsidies that are seen as "propping up" an industry by arguing that the same practice goes on in other countries and that, regrettably, they must also do so to make the domestic industry competitive on the international market.

These arguments are examples of two-wrongs reasoning. In our first example, the case of the Arab uprisings people apparently believed they had no better alternative than to defy what they considered unjust laws. In our second example, a principle of fairness is at stake, and analogical reasoning plays an important role in the argument. In both examples, the two-wrongs argument does not deny that the action or policy defended is less than morally ideal. It admits this but still tries to justify the action, maintaining that it is the lesser of two-wrongs and in this way arguing for its acceptability to an impartial universal audience.

In order to be legitimate, two-wrongs arguments must meet three conditions. These conditions are represented by the three premises in the scheme for two-wrongs reasoning, which has the following form:

Premise 1: X is a response to another wrong, Y, the unjust consequences of which it is designed to cancel or alleviate.

Premise 2: X is less wrong than Y.

Premise 3: There is no morally preferable way to respond to Y.

Conclusion: X is justified.

A good argument against two-wrongs reasoning must demonstrate that one of the conditions for good two-wrongs reasoning imbedded in the three premises has not been satisfied (i.e. that one of these premises is unacceptable in the case at hand). In this way, it is possible to show that the particular wrong being proposed cannot be justified by another wrong.

We can see how these conditions for two wrong reasoning apply by reconsidering the cases that Heller alludes to in her account of Ayn Rand. In the case of Jews in Russia, the conditions for good two-wrongs reasoning seem met, for here the deceptions in question appear to be the only way to avoid the much more serious injustice implied by discrimination and violence against those who identify themselves as Jews. The other cases that Heller alludes to—situations in which Rand would allegedly "invent, exaggerate, or hide events in her own life in order to advance her hopes or bolster her public image"—are more problematic, for these are not cases where the fabrications in question are clear attempts to correct or compensate for other wrongs that are more serious. At the very least these cases will require more discussion.

In constructing your own versions of two-wrongs reasoning, you will be called on to decide what is "less" wrong in a specific situation and whether there is (with respect to the third condition) a morally preferable response. The complexities of two-wrongs reasoning illustrate the extent to which the domain of moral argumentation is one in which you cannot always expect to easily grasp a right or wrong answer with which everyone will agree.

Argument schemes like two-wrongs reasoning shed light on the issue, tell us the kind of questions we should be asking, and facilitate our own reasoning on the issues as we strive to come to reasonable positions on them.

The following two-wrongs argument appeared in an editorial from *The Wall Street Journal* (January 1984) addressing the actions of Bernard Goetz in a famous incident in which he shot four black youths who he believed were going to rob him on a New York subway train:

> If the "state of nature" has returned to some big cities, can people fairly be blamed for modern vigilantism? Is it more "civilized" to suffer threats to individual liberty from criminals, or is it an overdose of sophistication to say individuals can never resort to self-protection?

Since this reasoning is phrased in rhetorical questions intended as assertions and the conclusion is hidden, it is important to diagram this argument:

P1 =   If the "state of nature" has returned to some big cities, people cannot be blamed for modern vigilantism.
HP2 =   The "state of nature" has returned to some big cities.
P3 =   It is not "civilized" to have to suffer threats to individual liberty from criminals.
P4 =   It is an overdose of sophistication to say individuals can never resort to self-protection.
HC =   Self-protection in the form of modern vigilantism is justified.

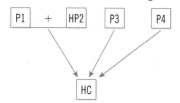

Despite an awkward presentation, the thrust of this reasoning is quite evident. To justify the kind of self-protection in which Goetz engaged, the argument claims that big cities are characterized by a "state of nature," understood as an everyone-for-his-or-herself struggle to survive. It is important to acknowledge this aspect of the argument because, as a general statement about inner-city life—especially in the big cities of the United States—this claim may appeal to some people.

But Goetz's actions are difficult to justify on the basis of two-wrongs reasoning, for the existence of a first wrong is questionable. When we apply the first condition for a strong two-wrongs argument, we find that it is not clear that Goetz was responding to an actual wrong, since the youths didn't actually rob him but only asked him for five dollars. There are also doubts as to whether the second condition is satisfied. Was Goetz's act less wrong than the one he anticipated? The writer of the editorial clearly believes it was. But the writer also begs the question in an important sense, for P3 already assumes the truth of the conclusion (that the act was justified) when it refers to "criminals." There are no clear criminals in this case. To accept Goetz's labelling of people as criminals in a society where the law requires people to be assumed innocent until proven guilty is to grant Goetz status as both judge and executioner. The third condition for strong two-wrongs arguments is also not satisfied. Given that the claim that there is a first wrong is so weak, there are undoubtedly morally preferable ways in which Goetz could have responded (by ignoring the youths, by calling for help, or even by leaving the situation).

We have found a more plausible instance of a two-wrongs argument associated with Maori protests against the British Royal Family in Australia and New Zealand. The following is a long excerpt from a discussion of these protests by Dr Augie Fleras in an article entitled " 'Crude' form of protest a Maori tradition," (*Kitchener-Waterloo Record*, 2 April 1986, p. A7):

> The Royal Family has once again experienced several embarrassing incidents while on tour of the South Pacific. Efforts by activists to disrupt the visit of Queen Elizabeth and Prince Philip to New Zealand and Australia have focused worldwide attention on the antipodes.
>
> . . . of the various gestures of defiance exhibited to date, none has attracted the same degree of press coverage as the attempt by a Maori activist to expose his buttocks to the Queen. . . . Those of us outside of New Zealand might wonder at the folly of such a seemingly juvenile gesture, more likely to be associated with drunken "moons" outside of moving vehicles. Even native New Zealanders appear perplexed by the audacity of such outrageous behaviour.
>
> But as is commonly known among the indigenous population of that country, this behaviour is commensurate with Maori cultural tradition. Exposing one's buttocks is nothing less than a legitimate and traditional symbol of "ritualized derision" ("whakapohane"). . . .
>
> It is one thing to establish the cultural rationale for "whakapohane," it is another to explain why the Royal Family has been singled out for this insulting treatment.
>
> An understanding of New Zealand history is useful here. In 1840, representatives of the British Crown and a group of Maori leaders signed the Treaty of Waitangi.
>
> Under the terms of the treaty the Crown acquired the right of sovereignty over what was known then of New Zealand. The Maori in turn were bestowed the benefits of imperial protection. . . .
>
> They also received the right of access to those resources—land, fish, forests—necessary to procure their survival. But for the most part successive governments have reneged on their end of the agreement.
>
> Maori land has not been protected from encroachment by land-hungry settlers with the result that only three million acres (of the original 66 million) remain in Maori possession. . . .
>
> In an effort to vent their frustration and draw royal attention to the plight of the indigenous people, Maori activists have taken advantage of opportunities to embarrass the Royal Family and the New Zealand government.
>
> Protest is conducted in a manner consistent with Maori cultural traditions, and guaranteed to garner maximum exposure.

In this case, the author of the passage is not presenting an argument of his own but explaining the reasoning behind Maori protests. It should be clear that this reasoning is an instance of two-wrongs reasoning, for the Maori protesters believe that what would otherwise be outrageous acts of rudeness are justified because they are a response to other wrongs—i.e. the wrongs of the Royal Family and the New Zealand government, who have not kept their side of an agreement they signed with the Maoris.

To see if this is a good instance of two-wrongs reasoning, we need to consider whether it is a strong instance of the two-wrongs scheme, i.e. an instance that legitimates the conclusion that rude acts of protest against the Royal Family are justified. Certainly the first premise required for such an argument is acceptable. The rude protests are an attempt to respond to a previous wrong, i.e. the Royal Family's and the New Zealand government's failure to respect commitments made to the Maori people. By drawing media attention to their plight, they hope to provoke public and international pressure that will alleviate the unjust circumstances. It is also clear that the second premise necessary for good two-wrongs reasoning is acceptable, for, as rude as it is to expose one's buttocks to the Queen, this is not as wrong as a concerted attempt to deprive a whole people of millions of acres of land and other resources they were promised.

The question whether this argument is a strong two-wrongs argument thus hinges on whether there is a morally preferable way for the Maori protesters to respond to the injustice they are trying to alleviate. We are not in a position to judge this question well (for we do not know what alternative ways of pursuing redress are feasible); however, we can say that it may be plausible to argue that the only way to rectify the injustice is to bring a great deal of political pressure to bear on the situation, and it is conceivable that protests like the one in question are the only feasible way to do so. (The whakapohane protests are, it might be argued, particularly appropriate because they are commensurate with Maori tradition.) In such circumstances, it would be possible to present a strong two-wrongs argument in the following way:

P1 = Rude acts of protest against the British Royal Family are a response to another wrong—the violation of the Treaty of Waitangi and the taking of Maori land and resources—and are an attempt to alleviate this wrong.
P2 = Rude acts of protest are less wrong than the unjust taking of (millions of acres of) Maori land and Maori resources.
P3 = There is no morally preferable way to bring about an attempt to alleviate this injustice.
C = Rude acts of protest against the British Royal Family are justified.

Though our discussion is not in this case definitive, it should help you see what kinds of considerations must play a part in an attempt to construct a good two-wrongs argument.

TWO-WRONGS REASONING

Two-wrongs reasoning attempts to justify an action normally considered wrong by pointing out that it cancels or alleviates some worse wrong. A good two-wrongs argument establishes that (1) the wrong that is said to be permissible is a response to another wrong; the unjust consequences of which it tries to cancel or alleviate; (2) the wrong that is said to be permissible is less wrong than any injustice it attempts to cancel or alleviate; and (3) there is no morally preferable way to respond to the injustice in question.

Two-wrongs by Analogy

"Two-wrongs by analogy" is a more specific kind of this argument that merits separate treatment because it plays an important role in ordinary reasoning. We introduced a two-wrongs-by-analogy argument earlier when we said that one argues by two-wrongs reasoning if one claims that subsidies for one country's industries are legitimate if similar subsidies are offered by other countries to their industries. In this and other circumstances, two-wrongs-by-analogy arguments apply because fairness demands that analogous situations be treated in a similar way. We noted the importance of this principle in our discussion of appeals to precedent. Two-wrongs by analogy differs from an appeal to precedent in its acknowledgement that the action it justifies is less than morally ideal.

Often, two-wrongs-by-analogy arguments can be diagrammed as follows:

Premise 1: An action or policy *X* is similar to action or policy *Y*.
Premise 2: *Y* has been accepted/allowed.
Conclusion: *X* should be accepted/allowed.

In many instances of two-wrongs by analogy, there are sub-arguments that justify P1 and P2.

We can judge two-wrongs-by-analogy reasoning by appealing directly to the criteria for strong two-wrongs reasoning. In this kind of case, the wrong that is said to be alleviated is the inconsistent treatment of similar situations, and a convincing argument must show that the remedy (allowing some new wrong) is not worse than the inconsistency (the wrong) that is said to have been allowed and that there is no preferable way to deal with the inconsistency in question. In view of this, a fully explicit two-wrongs by analogy argument will conform to the following scheme:

Premise 1: A wrong, X, is analogous to other wrongs ($Y, Z, W, \ldots$) that have been permitted.

Premise 2: Fairness in the form of consistency is more important than preventing X.

Premise 3: There is no morally preferable way to respond to the situation.

Conclusion: X should be accepted/allowed.

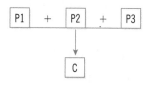

Both bad and good examples of two-wrongs-by-analogy arguments come readily to mind. If it is common practice not to ticket cars parked illegally on a city lot, it would be unfair to pick one car—a car owned, let us say, by a vocal critic of the municipal administration—and ticket it. In such circumstances, the individual who has been ticketed can reasonably propound the following two-wrongs-by-analogy argument:

> where P1 = Other people who park their cars in the lot are not ticketed, P2 = I am entitled to the same treatment as other people, especially for such a petty wrong, P3 = There is no other way of treating me fairly, and C = I should not have been ticketed.

To refute this argument, one would have to show that one or more of the premises is unacceptable. (If they are acceptable, then the argument's adherence to the scheme for good two-wrongs-by-analogy reasoning ensures that they are relevant and sufficient to the conclusion.) One might, for example, argue that the offence is not in fact a petty one (say, because illegal parking is interfering with city workers) and that ticketing a few individuals on a random basis is the morally best way to respond to the situation, given that the city is short of parking officers. This counter-argument is in fact another instance of two-wrongs reasoning, for it grants that it would be best if all of the individuals who parked in the lot were treated consistently (i.e. if all were given tickets) but justifies a deviation from this policy on the grounds that random ticketing is the morally preferable way to deal with the problem. This counter-argument can, therefore, be assessed by considering the criteria for good two-wrongs arguments.

An example of poor two-wrongs-by-analogy reasoning is the argument that a crackdown on drunk driving is wrong because police and the courts have been lax in prosecuting past offenders. A consistent treatment of future offenders would require that they go free, but such consistency is not as desirable a goal as preventing the potential damage, injury, and loss of life that may be caused by drunk drivers. It follows that the proposed new wrong—turning a blind eye to new offenders—is not preferable to a crackdown. The principle of consistency suggests that it is wrong to treat differently individuals who commit the same offence. If one offender is not charged, then one can argue on these grounds that none of them should be. But in circumstances in which we are dealing with serious offences, a preferable way to deal with the situation would be to charge all offenders. In terms of the criteria for strong two-wrongs-by-analogy reasoning, the argument that consistency demands that none be prosecuted fails to satisfy the third condition for good reasoning of this kind.

TWO-WRONGS REASONING BY ANALOGY

Two-wrongs reasoning by analogy is a specific form of two-wrongs reasoning that justifies an action normally considered wrong by pointing out that it is analogous to other actions that have been permitted. A good two-wrongs-by-analogy argument establishes that (1) the wrong that is said to be permissible is analogous to other wrongs that have been permitted; (2) fairness in the form of consistency is more important than preventing the wrong in question; and (3) there is no morally preferable way to respond in the situation.

Counter-Arguments to Two-Wrongs Reasoning

Like arguments that conform to the other argument schemes we have considered, two-wrongs arguments have counterparts that attempt to show that some instance of two-wrongs reasoning is a weak argument. In this case, a good counter-argument will show that some (actual or potential) case of two-wrongs reasoning does not meet the criteria for good two-wrongs arguments embedded in our detailed argument schemes. In practice, this means that such an argument will show that some potential wrong is not a response to another wrong that attempts to alleviate its unjust consequences, that it is not less wrong than the wrong it tries to alleviate, or that there is or was some morally preferable way to handle the wrong in question.

A detailed discussion of counter-arguments to two-wrongs reasoning is beyond the present book, but we will note two ways in which many two-wrongs arguments fail to meet the conditions required for strong instances of this scheme.

1. Two-wrongs reasoning justifies only "wrongs" that are an attempt to alleviate other wrongs. Imagine that a student is found guilty of plagiarism on an essay. Suppose the student argues, "I know seven other people who were guilty of plagiarism." This is an implicit appeal to the two-wrongs scheme. It maintains that this particular indiscretion is acceptable because others are guilty of the same indiscretion. But there is a fundamental problem with the reasoning, for the wrong that is said to be justified in these circumstances is *not* a response to other wrongs that it tries to minimize or rectify. This is clear, for if the situation really is as the student has suggested, he or she could easily rectify the problem by notifying the course instructor of the indiscretions of the other students. The failure to do so suggests that the student's interest is not in alleviating other wrongs but in excusing a wrong of their own. This motivation is fundamentally at odds with the motivation that must lie behind a convincing two-wrongs argument.

One might reply that the student in question can claim that it is wrong that they, but not others, have been punished for plagiarism and that this is the wrong that they are trying to eliminate. But how would the other students' markers know this was the case? The markers did not knowingly excuse other students who were clearly guilty of plagiarism, so they cannot, on grounds of consistency, be reasonably asked to do so in this case.

2. Strong two-wrongs reasoning requires "proportionality." The second and third conditions required for good two-wrongs reasoning imply a principle of proportionality that plays an important role in moral, political, and legal reasoning. It dictates that the response to a wrong that someone commits must not be out of proportion with the wrong in question. The principle implies that we must not overreact to a wrong that has been committed. If someone commits a crime, society has the right to respond to this, but not in any way whatsoever. It does not, for example, give us the right to torture people or to give them extreme sentences (say, 30 years in jail for smoking in a non-smoking area). The wrongs that two-wrongs reasoning justifies must always be proportional to the original wrongs. You may legitimately respond to insults by telling someone to leave your office—but not by pulling a revolver from your desk and shooting them. In the latter case, you have violated the principle of proportionality.

COUNTER-ARGUMENTS TO TWO-WRONGS REASONING

A strong counter-argument to two-wrongs reasoning shows that the conditions for good two-wrongs reasoning are not met, or cannot be met, in some instance of (actual or potential) two-wrongs reasoning.

EXERCISE 11D

1. In each of the following scenarios, explain whether the two-wrongs reasoning is legitimate or not. Give reasons for your decisions.

   a)* In response to a law that restricts the immigration of South Americans, forcing many to be sent home to face possible torture and death, citizens hide in their homes people whom they believe to be genuine refugees. They argue that the law is morally wrong.

   b) An elderly man kills his wife of 58 years. She is terminally ill and dying slowly in great pain. He defends himself by arguing that his was an act of euthanasia and that his wife's suffering was a greater wrong that his action terminated.

   c) *In vitro* fertilization involves the surgical removal of an egg from a woman's ovary, fertilizing it by mixing it with semen in a dish, and then transferring this back to the uterus once it has started to divide. By means of drugs, "superovulation" can produce several eggs in the same cycle. These can be collected in one surgical operation and then fertilized. Then, one or more of the embryos can be introduced into the uterus while the rest are frozen, either to be introduced into a uterus at a later date or to be used in research. Usually, embryos used in research would then be destroyed. The question arises about the morality of this last activity: producing human embryos for research with no intention of allowing them to develop. But if such research produces a cure for, say, cystic fibrosis—through the discovery of the defective gene, which can then be treated or replaced—then the initial moral wrong of using embryos in research would be justified.

2. Imagine that you wish to be exempted from a final exam in some course you are taking. You know that in the past, students have sometimes been exempted because of serious medical conditions. Explain why a two-wrongs by analogy argument could or could not be used to defend the claim that you should be exempted for the following reasons:

a)* Your father is very ill.
b) You have just gone through an acrimonious divorce.
c) You panic in test situations.
d) You have to attend a funeral.
e) You have been recovering from an accident for the last year.

5 Summary

This chapter turns from schemes used in the search for facts to schemes likely to be used in value-based arguments. Thus, much of what has been discussed here involves moral reasoning. We have employed the details and use of the following schemes: Slippery Slope Arguments; Arguments from Analogy; Appeals to Precedent; and Two-Wrong Reasoning. In each case we have discussed how to construct such schemes, as well as constructing counter-schemes.

MAJOR EXERCISE 11M

1. In support of the claim "Public ownership of assault rifles should be prohibited," construct a short argument using each of the following schemes:

a)* slippery slope
b) argument by analogy
c) appeal to precedent

2. Use the same argument schemes in support of the opposite claim, "Public ownership of assault rifles should be allowed."

3. Construct arguments on the issue of euthanasia using an argument by analogy.

4.* A current topic of discussion is the extent to which Western banks and nations should help developing countries by forgiving the huge debt these countries have accumulated. Take each form of reasoning we have discussed, and outline how you could use it in your deliberation on the issue. Write a "letter to the Editor" using the argument scheme you regard as best suited to justify your position.

5. Construct an argument scrapbook by collecting from magazines and newspapers five examples of the argument schemes we have introduced. In each case, explain whether it is a good or bad argument. If it is a bad argument, explain how it could be strengthened or corrected.

6. Decide whether each of the following passages or illustrations contains an argument. If it does, assess the reasoning. Using any of the argument forms dealt with in this chapter, explain whether the argument fulfills the conditions for good arguments of that form. Note that examples may involve more than one argument form and that you may need to use the concepts we introduced in earlier chapters to explain the examples.

a)* If we allow embryonic stem cell research, which sacrifices early-stage embryos, the next thing will be that infanticide and euthanasia of the terminally ill will be permitted so that we can use their body parts for research or cures. If you don't hold all life to be sacred, then none will be sacred.

b) [Arthur Shafer, in "Top judges got it wrong in this case," the *Toronto Star*, 19 January 2001. Schafer is commenting on the Robert Latimer case, in which a Saskatchewan man was convicted of murder for killing his 12-year-old daughter to end her suffering from a severe form of cerebral palsy] Interestingly, however, in the half-dozen or so mercy killing cases in recent Canadian history, some involving doctors who hastened the death of their painfully dying patients with a fatal dose of potassium chloride, not one person served even a single day in prison. Charges have been dropped, or a guilty plea accepted to a lesser charge.

c) [From a Letter to the Editor, *Los Angeles Times*, 5 November 2010] The death penalty process is inherently flawed and broken, and can thus never be administered fairly, quickly and with good faith that all the fail-safes are effectively employed. Given its crippling cost to taxpayers, we have a proposition just begging to be put on the ballot to crush this barbarous and slow process once and for all. Letting our convicted killers die with a whimper in a cell is no less retributive in my opinion, but it makes a lot more sense.

d) [A Letter to the Editor, the *Telegraph* newspaper, 2 November 2007] Sir: The poor of India and the Indian tiger ("The face of a doomed species," 31 October) have much in common in their lack of habitat and conditions to make life tolerable, and a sometimes monumental indifference to the efforts drawing attention to their plight.

The poor have recently been able to mobilise and march on Delhi in numbers and make the government sit up and take notice. The tiger can neither speak nor march anywhere, except on the path to extinction—and there are no votes attached to it.

Often the tiger and poor have to compete for habitat, giving the tiger a bad name when domestic livestock replace the tiger's natural food. The recent Recognition of Forest Rights Act, which grants some of India's most impoverished communities the right to own and live in the forests, further marginalises tiger populations. "If you are not going to set aside habitats where there are no humans then you cannot have tigers," according to Mr Valmik Thapar, a tiger expert.

And to make the plight of the tiger grimmer, poaching to meet the illegal demand for tiger pelts and body parts, seen as valuable not only outside the Indian sub-continent but also by an expanding indigenous middle class, ensure that the tiger has a bigger price on its head dead than alive.

The lack of will of governments to deal with both the plight of the poor and the tiger is disgraceful, but while their actions are unlikely to see the extinction but rather expand the numbers of the poor, they will certainly lead to the demise of a magnificent species which is mocked as a national emblem symbolising India's strength and natural beauty. God protect the tiger from the human race.

e) [After Ontario teacher Paul Fromm was censored for racist actions outside of the classroom, the following letter appeared in the *National Post,* 12 November 2007] I have never met Paul Fromm and although I have only a cursory knowledge of his white supremacist views, I find them repugnant. However, the Ontario College of Teachers has started us on a dangerous and slippery slope; Mr. Fromm's competence and behaviour in class are apparently not at issue.

Why are teachers singled out for special treatment for their views and behaviour outside the workplace? Who decides what views are "contrary to the values of the profession and the educational system, and which have a negative impact on the education system"?

The Ontario College of Teachers claims that "this case is not about the member's right to hold political views that are unpopular or to participate in legal political activities," but it sounds very much like it is.

f) [The cartoonist Gary Larson has taken legal action to prevent the unauthorized use of his cartoons on the Internet. In a letter explaining why, he has described his cartoon as his "children of sorts" and said that he is, like a parent "concerned about where they go at night without telling me." The cartoon below parodies his comparison and suggestion to "Please send my 'kids' home."

Illustration 11.2 "Famous cartoonist charged for selling kids"

g) [Kathleen Gow, in *Yes Virginia, There Is Right and Wrong*, John Wiley and Sons, 1980, p. 92. In an article discussing various pedagogical techniques, Kathleen Gow questions the use of exercises that put students in imaginary situations where they have to make difficult moral decisions] Children may become so confused by all the qualifications and situational dilemma exercises—many of which are extreme and very far removed from everyday life—that they will decide that the world is totally without moral or social order. As one grade seven student asked, "Isn't there anything you can count on?"

When we are caring for babies, we do not give them a whole apple to eat. We know that their digestive systems are not sufficiently sophisticated to process the skin, the flesh, and the core. The risk that they will choke is very high. So instead of the whole apple, we give them applesauce—the essence of the apple. This does not mean that we are cheating them of their independence.

h) [Janet George, in "Saboteurs—The real animals," the *Guardian* 28 February 1993, p. 24] People who believe that killing animals for sport is wrong might assume that banning field sports would solve the problem. They are wrong. Hunting is merely the first in a long list of targets. . . .

Already, butchers' shop windows are frequent targets for damage, and incendiary devices have been used against department stores selling furs and leather goods. If another private member's bill is introduced successfully, and hunting is banned, animal rights extremists will see it as a vindication of their methods.

i)* [John Searle, in *Minds, Brains and Science*, Harvard University Press, 1985, pp. 37–8] Why would anybody ever have thought that computers could think or have feelings and emotions and all the rest of it? After all, we can do computer simulations of any process whatever that can be given a formal description. So, we can do a computer simulation of . . . the pattern of power distribution in the Labour party. We can do computer simulation of rain storms . . . or warehouse fires . . . . Now, in each of these cases, nobody supposes that the computer simulation is actually the real thing; no one supposes that a computer simulation of a storm will leave us all wet . . . . Why on earth would anyone in his right mind suppose a computer simulation of mental processes actually had mental processes?

j)* [Adapted from a Letter to the Editor, the *Toronto Star*] If pro-choice doctors are allowed to go ahead and open abortion clinics under the banner of women's right to abortion on demand, then members of organized crime should be allowed to open gaming casinos because people have the right to gamble, and producers of pornographic movies to open theatres because people have the right to view what they wish. If pro-abortion groups can do it, so can other groups.

k)   [An image posted on the website *Pundit Kitchen* http://news.icanhascheezburger.
      com/]

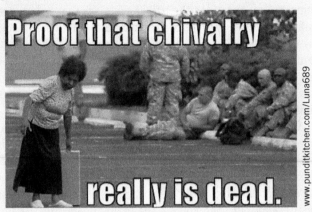

www.punditkitchen.com/Luna689

Illustration 11.3   "Proof that chivalry really is dead"

l)   [St. John of Chrysostom, in the *Post-Nicene Fathers*, Vol. 9, p. 442] To
      laugh, to speak jocosely, does not seem an acknowledged sin, but it leads to
      acknowledged sin. Thus laughter often gives birth to foul discourse, and foul
      discourse to actions still more foul. Often from words and laughter proceed
      railing and insult; and from railing and insult, blows and wounds; and from
      blows and wounds, slaughter and murder. If, then, thou wouldst take good
      counsel for thyself, avoid not merely foul words, and foul deeds, or blows, and
      wounds, and murders, but unseasonable laughter itself.

m)*   [From a letter to the *Independent*, 27 October 2007] Sir: While agreeing with
      Joan Smith that "men have responsibility for abortions, too" (Comment, 26
      October) and hoping that male responsibility might go so far as to say no to
      abortion, I find the rest of what she has to say repellent in its lack of concern
      for human life. Implicit in her article is her belief in a woman's "right to chose
      [*sic*]." This is a choice between the life or death of a human being. That the
      human being is developing and dependent is neither here nor there. No other
      group in society claims such a right of life or death over another human being.

      And those who oppose abortion do not so on "ideological grounds": they
      oppose abortion on moral grounds. In a truly compassionate society, we would
      not allow unfortunate women to take life, but would help them through their
      difficulties with understanding and practical help.

n)   Smokers are the most persecuted group on Earth. First all the non-smokers
      decided that we should be segregated to separate parts of restaurants. Then they
      passed by-laws preventing us from smoking in most public places. Next they'll
      be storming our houses to arrest us for smoking in the privacy of our home, since
      even there "we don't own the air." This is a bad model for how to set social
      policy. Once a state begins over-regulating its citizens, the door is opened to any
      number of infringements on personal liberty and freedom of expression.

o)   [Francis Bacon, from *Francis Bacon: A Selection of His Works*, Odyssey Press,
      1965, p. 17] There are seven windows given to animals in the domicile of

the head, through which the air is admitted to the tabernacle of the body, to enlighten, to warm and to nourish it. What are these parts of the microcosmos: Two nostrils, two eyes, two ears and a mouth. So in the heavens, as in a macrocosmos, there are two favourable stars, two unpropitious, two luminaries, and Mercury undecided and indifferent. From this and from many other similarities in nature, such as the seven metals, etc., which it were tedious to enumerate, we gather that the number of planets is necessarily seven.

p) [From a letter sent out by IIFAR—Incurably Ill For Animal Research, March, 1988]
[W]hat it all boils down to, after you eliminate all the hype, is that medical research is being conducted to alleviate human suffering, and testing on animals prior to testing on humans is essential. As long as society believes it is okay to kill cows for food, exterminate mice and rats that infect our homes, and kill more than 10 million cats and dogs each year in public pounds because they are nuisances, it surely must be okay to use animals to find cures for unfortunate human beings who suffer from incurable illnesses.

q) [Gary E. Jones, in "On the permissibility of torture," *Journal of Medical Ethics*, 1980, Vol. 6, p. 12] Consider, for example, solar energy. It presently suffers from the same poor cost-benefit ratio as the use of torture allegedly does. However, the promise of future benefits from the use of solar energy, along with the assumption that the cost-benefit ratio will improve, are sufficient grounds for many to conclude that its use should be promoted. Analogously, it could be argued that technical improvements in the methods used to extract information in as humane a way as possible will improve the cost-benefit ratio of the use of torture.

r) [From *World Press Review*, February, Vol. 50, No. 2, 2003, p. 18] But there are dangers to China's explosive growth. If the government neglects the growing gap between rich and poor, or the displacement of its massive rural population . . . serious social unrest will ensue. And if China's 1.2 billion people get a taste for SUVs, air conditioning, and other trappings of its affluent neighbors in the West, the environmental costs alone will be staggering.
Slow, steady, patient, controlled: The Chinese government must keep a leash on its economy to avoid self-implosion. If done well, the new century will belong to the dragon. Too much, too fast, too open, and we're all in trouble.

s)* [In May 1987, Klaus Barbie, the so-called "Butcher of Lyon," was put on trial in France for crimes against humanity during the Second World War. With respect to the defence of Barbie, the following quote from Jacques Verges, Barbie's lawyer, was reported in *The Globe and Mail*, 2 May 1987] We will see during the course of this business that what Mr Barbie did as a loyal officer of his country was no different than what hundreds of loyal officers of this country did during the Algerian war. We will see that Mr Barbie operated under a legally accepted premise at the time and that he was assisted by citizens and officials of France. We will see that even French Jews and members of the Resistance assisted Mr Barbie in his work.

t) [The following is excerpted from an article titled "Life's essence, bought and sold," *The Globe and Mail*, 9 July 2010. Full article available at www.catholiceducation.org/articles/medical_ethics/me0155.htm) by Canadian ethicist Margaret Somerville. She is concerned about future children who are the products of reproductive technologies]

Donor conception may be a completely avoidable human tragedy in the making, one for which we might be holding a truth and reconciliation commission at some future date, when offspring ask, as some are already doing, "How could you have done this to us? How could you have allowed this to happen?"

Is donor conception the 21st-century version of the wrongs we now recognize we did to some children in the 20th century? Are we repeating in a new context and in new ways the terrible errors and grave injustices that occurred with Australia's "stolen generation" of aboriginal children, the United Kingdom's "home children" sent to Canada and other British Commonwealth countries, and the "scoop" of native children from reserves into Canadian residential schools and white adoptive homes, all of which deliberately separated children from their biological families.

In all these instances, our intentions, as is true in donor conception, were to "do good." In donor conception, however, we primarily intend to "do good" to the adults who want a child, rather than to the child, as was the motive—although a grossly mistaken belief—in the other historical wrongs I have mentioned.

u)* [Both of the following excerpts are from letters responding to aspects of the Somerville article. *The Globe and Mail*, 12 July 2010. Full article available at www.catholiceducation.org/articles/medical_ethics/me0155.htm] Margaret Somerville's essay on egg and sperm donation (Life's Essence, Bought And Sold—July 10) argues that conceiving children with donated eggs and/or sperm is a "completely avoidable human tragedy," which she compares in moral terms to Canada's residential school atrocity.

The comparison is fallacious. The aboriginal children who were placed in residential schools were old enough to feel searing psychological trauma at losing loving attachments to their families. In contrast, eggs and sperm form no loving attachments. Indeed, when someone donates eggs or sperm to another person in order to create a child, that donation produces feelings of generosity, rather than trauma.

v) [Somerville] asks, "Is there something gravely ethically wrong with the commercialization of the miracle of the passing on of human life?" and refers to the Assisted Human Reproduction Act, which makes it illegal to undertake certain commercial (and non-commercial) activities in relation to assisted reproduction. This raises issues similar to those in the debate over the legal prohibition of abortion.

When you ban these activities, you drive them underground or push them offshore, making them more dangerous. The better approach in both cases is regulation, not prohibition.

For more online exercises, review questions, and quizzes related to the material in this chapter, please go to www.oupcanada.com/GoodReasoning5e

ETHOTIC SCHEMES

The last three chapters discussed empirical and moral schemes of arguments. In this chapter, we discuss "ethotic" schemes that, in one way or another, base conclusions on premises about the people who stand behind arguments: those who argue, provide support for premises through their character or expertise, or adjudicate reasoning. The schemes discussed include:

- ► *pro homine*
- ► *ad populum* arguments
- ► *ad hominem* reasoning
- ► appeal to authority
- ► appeal to eyewitness testimony
- ► guilt by association.

In Aristotle's *Rhetoric*, one of the most famous books written in the history of argumentation theory, the perceived character of an arguer—his or her *ethos*—is said to play an important role in influencing an audience. As Aristotle puts it, we are more likely to accept arguments and conclusions offered by people of whom we think highly.

Sometimes the influence of *ethos* is subtle and implicit. Aristotle's credibility may make us more ready to accept what he says, while disdain for someone we know may make it difficult for us to take their claims seriously. In these circumstances, *ethotic* arguments explicitly address the character of an arguer. In many cases they use judgements about their *ethos* as a basis for the conclusion that we should treat their claims and arguments in a particular way (that we should accept them, be cautious of them, pay attention to them, reject them outright, and so on). The present chapter provides an introduction to different kinds of ethotic argument.

Ethotic considerations often arise in circumstances in which we do not have the time, the means, or the ability to investigate a question in sufficient detail to decide the proper answer to it. We may accept or reject particular views in part by considering whether they are offered and defended by individuals or groups we trust or do not trust, or by arguers we do or do not deem competent to address the issue at hand. Such arguments are called **pro homine** ("for the person") and "**ad hominem**" ("against the person") because they defend or attack a claim or point of view by defending or attacking its proponent. There are different kinds of *pro homine* and *ad hominem* reasoning that can usefully be distinguished when we deal with ordinary argument.

 ### Pro Homine

In 1987, congressional hearings investigated allegations that the American government's administration acted improperly and illegally by selling arms to Iran and diverting the money from the sales to rebels trying to overthrow the Sandinista government in Nicaragua. One of the witnesses who testified at the hearings, Lieutenant Colonel Oliver North, became a special focus of media attention. His appearance in marine uniform, his distinguished military record, and his patriotic fervour captured the imagination of many Americans.

One *New York Times* columnist described North's appeal as the attraction of an "underdog, true believer, one man against the crowd: there was a lot of Gary Cooper in him, the lonesome cowboy, a lot of Jimmy Stewart, too, the honest man facing down the politicians, and quite a bit of Huck Finn" (6 July 1987). Given that North admitted that he lied to Congress and the public, such a description is ironic and underscores the extent to which a person's "image" in the media can influence our perceptions of an individual.

Much of the public accepted what North said as true because they were impressed by him as a man. In the process, they relied on *pro homine* reasoning. We engage in such reasoning whenever we defend or accept a conclusion because it is propounded by someone whom we trust to have the correct opinion. Often, *pro homine* arguments have the form "*X* believes *y*, so I accept it too," but a strong *pro homine* must (implicitly or explicitly) be an instance of the following scheme:

> **Premise 1:**   *X* says *y*.
> **Premise 2:**   *X* is knowledgeable, trustworthy, and free of bias.
> **Conclusion:**   *y* should be accepted.

In proposing *pro homine* reasoning, we take our past experience of certain individuals as intelligent and honest as good grounds for accepting their opinions now and in the future. We rely on *pro homine* reasoning in many informal circumstances, such as trusting an individual's recommendation of restaurants, listening to the commentaries of the sports we watch, or receiving an edifying account of political developments in a particular country.

In deciding whether an argument is a strong or weak *pro homine*, we need to consider whether the person whose opinion is appealed to is knowledgeable, trustworthy, and free of bias. This judgement will depend on the circumstances involved, though one consideration that can usually be brought to bear is the quality of a person's reasoning. If the arguer is someone who has previously demonstrated that they do or do not have a grasp of the difference between weak and strong arguments (say, the difference between reliable and unreliable *pro homine* arguments), then this is evidence to consider when they provide further *pro homine* reasoning.

What, then, can we make of the *pro homine* appeal to Lieutenant Colonel North? Although we concede that he was a knowledgeable person, there are some problems with a *pro homine* appeal to his testimony, for one might dispute the claim that he is trustworthy or free of bias. Indeed, it is arguable that patriotism (or any other over-riding motive) and obedience to authority—the factors that make North attractive to some—may have blinded him to propriety and made him an untrustworthy judge of what was right and wrong in the relevant circumstances. More problematic is the question of his bias, for he was himself accused of wrongdoing, a situation that makes it difficult for him to be objective and more difficult for us to know whether his claims are motivated by vested interest or a sincere desire to tell the truth.

Above and beyond the specific problems with a *pro homine* in North's case, there are more general concerns that suggest that we should be cautious in accepting or making any *pro homine* argument. While it is sometimes reasonable to accept the opinions of individuals we respect in one way or another, it would be a mistake to slip into an uncritical acceptance of their views. Ultimately, an in-depth investigation of a position cannot be replaced by an appeal to the person who defends it. That said, an appropriate appeal to a person does count as evidence for a position.

PRO HOMINE REASONING

Pro homine reasoning argues for a claim by showing that it is held by some person X. A good *pro homine* argument maintains that it should be accepted because X is:

1. knowledgeable
2. trustworthy
3. free of bias.

EXERCISE 12A

1.* The following is the opening passage of Martin Luther King's famous "Letter from a Birmingham Jail," a response to eight fellow clergymen who had publicly criticized King for going to Birmingham in April 1963 and defying the law. Explain how King uses this opening of his letter to establish his own *ethos*, demonstrating how he would be the subject of a fitting *pro homine* appeal.

> I think I should indicate why I am here in Birmingham, since you have been influenced by the view which argues against "outsiders coming in." I have the honor of serving as president of the Southern Christian Leadership Conference, an organization operating in every southern state, with headquarters in Atlanta, Georgia. We have some eighty-five affiliated organizations across the South, and one of them is the Alabama Christian Movement for Human Rights. Frequently we share staff, educational and financial resources with our affiliates. Several months ago the affiliate here in Birmingham asked us to be on call to engage

in a nonviolent direct-action program if such were deemed necessary. We readily consented, and when the hour came we lived up to our promise. So I, along with several members of my staff, am here because I was invited here. I am here because I have organizational ties here.

2. Describe a context in which you could make a strong *pro homine* argument for a conclusion about each of the following:
   a) eating in a particular restaurant
   b)* subscribing to a particular magazine
   c) believing what an acquaintance says
   d) reading a particular book
   e) going on a particular holiday.

2 *Ad Populum* Arguments

Ad populum arguments, also called "appeals to popularity," attempt to establish a conclusion on the basis of its popular appeal. They are an instance of *pro homine* because they justify conclusions by noting that particular people—i.e. most people (or most people in a group)—subscribe to them.

Many appeals to popularity are poor arguments, even though they are effective when they exploit a strong desire to belong to a group. The following are examples of *ad populum* arguments:

- *25 million people own a Maytag washer. Maybe they know something you don't.*
- *Ruffles: America's best-selling chip.*
- *Everyone who's anyone will be there.*
- *Tonight, a special episode of Comedy TV that everyone will be talking about.*

In each case, the claim that something is popular among some group is used as a basis for a hidden conclusion (that one should own a Maytag, eat Ruffles, "be there," or watch the special episode).

Appeals to popularity can be problematic because popularity is not a good gauge of what is acceptable or unacceptable, true or false, or right or wrong. Indeed, popular opinion is frequently influenced by prejudice, superstition, outdated theories, and ill-considered judgements. In Columbus's time, the popular view of the world (at least in Europe) was that it was flat. Columbus, like other significant figures in the history of thought, was able to advance our knowledge of the world by refusing to be tied to popular opinions and independently developing his own view.

In a world where we had the time and ability to investigate every issue we had to resolve, we would not need to rely on *ad populum* arguments. Certainly, appeals to popularity have no significant role to play in scientific investigation or in other attempts to carefully investigate what is true and false. But there are two contexts in which appeal to popular opinion can be reasonable. We have already discussed the first context, for it occurs when we are preparing arguments for a popular audience and need to use its beliefs as premises in our argument. In keeping with our general account of *pro homine*, the second context occurs when we can reasonably proceed on the assumption that popular opinion is knowledgeable, trustworthy, and free of bias.

In such contexts, an *ad populum* argument is an instance of *pro homine* that can be schematized as follows:

Premise 1: It is popularly held that *y*.
Premise 2: This is a context in which popular opinion is knowledgeable, trustworthy, and free of bias.
Conclusion: *y* should be accepted.

There are many contexts in which this kind of argument will be weak because premise 2 is not acceptable. But there are also contexts in which this scheme justifies a provisional conclusion. Suppose, for example, that we are in a hardware store buying a handsaw. Without significant experience with different handsaws and little time to investigate and study the different saws available, we might reasonably purchase a particular saw because we trust the dealer and she tells us that "This is the most popular saw we sell." In doing so, we accept this claim as a premise for the conclusion that "This is the saw I will buy." In the process we accept an *ad populum* argument.

In reasoning this way, we are accepting, as a hidden premise, the claim that popular opinion about handsaws is knowledgeable, trustworthy, and free of bias. Thus, we assume that the saw in question is the best-selling handsaw because buyers have found it to be a good saw. The group of buyers who have purchased it are in this sense judged knowledgeable, trustworthy, and free of bias. A critical thinker will recognize that this is not a certain claim. It is always possible that the saw is popular for another reason, say, because the company that produces it has such compelling advertisements or because it is among the less expensive handsaws. If we were determined to decide which was the best handsaw—because we were comparing handsaws for a consumer magazine, for example—we would eliminate this possibility by testing the saws and not relying on an appeal to popularity. But in a context in which we have limited time at our disposal and want to resolve an issue quickly, it is reasonable to rely on an *ad populum* as a useful heuristic. In a similar way, the fact that Shakespeare's plays are so popular provides some evidence for their value and may be a strong reason for someone to decide to read them.

Because *ad populum* arguments are relatively weak arguments, it is important that you think carefully about particular instances of them. Ask yourself whether this really is a circumstance in which popular opinion is knowledgeable, trustworthy, and free of bias, or at least a circumstance in which there are good practical reasons to rely on this assumption (perhaps because this is the best judge of something that is available in the circumstances).

EXERCISE 12B

1. For each of the contexts given in exercise 12A, question 2, discuss circumstances in which it would and would not be acceptable to use *ad populum* arguments.

2. Set out and then evaluate the *ad populum* arguments in each of the following:

    a) [From the website www.rdglobaladvertising.com, where *Reader's Digest* issues several statements designed to attract global advertisers to place their advertisements with the magazine] *Reader's Digest* is the best read magazine in the world.

    b) [From a website promoting a private primary school in Manchester, England—www.whgs-academy.org/] The Manchester Evening News revealed William Hulme's as the most popular Primary School in Greater Manchester! Last year the school received five times more applications than reception-year places.

    c)* [From " 'Godless'? Hardly," *National Post*, 20 January 2007] Agnostic media commentators point with delight to the alleged decline of the Church in Latin America, but this too, is largely a canard. . . . A widely publicized Latino-Barometro poll of 2005 revealed that 18% of Latin Americans trusted any of the political parties in their countries, 28% their national congresses, 38% private business, 42% trusted the military, and 43% trusted their national presidents. The Roman Catholic Church was trusted by 71%, including leftist-governed countries such as Venezuela (74%), and even Cuba, and including a representative sampling of non-Catholic opinion.

3   Arguments from Authority

Though simple *pro homine* and *ad populum* arguments can be adequate support for a conclusion, they are relatively weak argument schemes. Some of the issues that they raise may be alleviated through an argument scheme called "argument from authority," or "appeal to expert opinion." This is a form of *pro homine* argument that recommends a claim on the grounds that it is held by someone who is an authority. This makes the claim believable because they are knowledgeable about the issues the argument addresses.

In straightforward cases, we are given grounds to believe something because of the expertise or credentials of someone who also believes it. This can be someone as familiar as the park ranger who warns us of potential fires in the park due to conditions, to the scientist who reports on her or his research into unfamiliar areas. In many of the more controversial cases, the question is not so much what to believe as who to believe, as the following case indicates.

In March of 2011, the *Journal of Cosmology* (Vol. 13) published a paper "Fossils of cyanobacteria in CI1 carbonaceous meteorites." The central claim of the paper is that a rare meteorite holds the fossilized evidence of alien life. Naturally, this is a sensational claim and had attracted the kind of attention that we would expect of such a claim. It matters, then, who has said this and what credentials that person has. The author of the paper is Dr Richard B. Hoover, an astrobiologist with NASA's Marshall Space

Flight Center. Given his background, he is the right kind of authority to be making this claim. Dr Hoover is convinced that he has found fossils within an extremely rare class of meteorites, called CI1 carbonaceous chondrites. As he writes:

> I interpret it as indicating that life is more broadly distributed than restricted strictly to the planet Earth. This field of study has just barely been touched—because quite frankly, a great many scientists would say that this is impossible.

Indeed, as will see, other scientists have seriously questioned the claim. To this end, the journal itself has solicited the opinions of 100 scientists, and has taken pains to defend itself. After all, as you should appreciate, it is not just people who serve as authorities for evidence in arguments, sources also have this status. We trust such diverse sources as a dictionary, Statistics Canada, and the bus timetable, expecting in each case to receive reliable information. It is reliability that is a key to the right kind of authority, along with knowledge. Since the journal has been defending and appealing to the authority of Dr Hoover, we will take the journal as the source of the argument, and set it out as follows:

Premise 1: Dr Hoover is an authority in astrobiology.
Premise 2: Dr Hoover has found fossils within a rare class of meteorites and believes these are evidence of alien life.
Conclusion: The fossils found in the meteorites are evidence of alien life.

As an example of an argument from authority this is an instance of the basic scheme:

Premise: *X* is an authority (expert) who believes and states *y*.
Conclusion: *y* should be accepted.

In our presentation of the argument, we included a premise stating that Dr Hoover is an authority, but in almost all such arguments this will be unstated. We recognize the type of argument scheme involved from the context and kind of appeal on which the reasoning depends. As we proceed with our discussion of this scheme we will have more to say about the strengths of this particular argument. As we have indicated, not all appeals to authorities are straightforward, and this is a case in point.

In dealing with arguments from authority, it is important to distinguish "argument from authority" from arguments *given by* a person in a position of authority. The latter may not be appeals to authority but other kinds of arguments that back the authority's point of view. In contrast to this, an argument from authority is an appeal to an authority's claim that uses their expertise as a basis for the conclusion that their views should be accepted.

It is arguable that we adopt the majority of our beliefs because we accept the views of authorities who recommend them. We see this in practical affairs, where we depend on doctors, plumbers, electricians, and appliance and automobile mechanics as authorities with special competencies. To a very significant extent, education depends on students accepting the authority of their instructors. Corporations hire consultants. In such cases, we depend on others' views, and it is difficult to see how we could get by without them.

Nonetheless, we must balance our reliance on arguments from authority and general *pro homine* arguments by consistently questioning such appeals. We should keep in mind that the very best appeal to an authority is a secondary way of establishing a conclusion. The suggestion that we accept someone's claim is predicated on the assumption that the person has good reasons for it, and these reasons, rather than the person's authority, ultimately determine the plausibility of their claims. A *pro homine* appeal is simply a promissory note assuring us that the experts—or, in the simple case, "people with good sense"—have good reasons for their views.

Another problem inherent in some appeals to authorities arises when we are presented with expert opinions that conflict and we must ask whose judgement we can trust. We all know that there are good and bad doctors, lawyers, plumbers, electricians, and professors, but it can be difficult to sort out the competent from the incompetent. If we know virtually nothing about an issue, we may have little basis for judging who is genuinely knowledgeable and who is not. We can circumvent this problem by appealing to well-established experts and paying particular attention to their views, but even these appeals can be problematic. We tend to think of science as the place where authority is most easily established, but science is characterized by great differences of opinion.

Recent philosophers (among them, Thomas Kuhn and Paul Feyerabend) have argued that science suppresses views that go against accepted paradigms, even when they are logically persuasive. And the Hoover case could appear to be a good example of this. Other scientists have been quick to challenge his findings and particularly his interpretations of them, and these challenges have included attacks on the authoritative status of the *Journal of Cosmology* itself.

The problem of disagreement among authorities is magnified when we move outside the field of science. The ancient skeptics argued that discrepancies between different people and different authorities show that truth cannot be found. We still face that problem. The views of Kuhn and Feyerabend conflict with those of other scientific authorities who have a more positive view of science and the scientific method. Numerous issues of immense significance to us, such as the existence of global warming and the nature of climate change, are characterized by disagreement and debate among respected scientists.

We do not raise such problems to dissuade you from using arguments from authority but to alert you to their potential weaknesses. These problems underscore the importance of constructing and assessing arguments from authority in a way that recognizes their provisional nature and ensures that they are free from common errors. Remember that the basis of any argument from authority is the claim that we should accept someone's views because he or she has special expertise that makes his or her claims persuasive. The individual's expertise is proven by his or her "credentials," which are usually educational or professional qualifications.

There are five conditions that must be satisfied, implicitly or explicitly, by a good argument from authority. They can be summarized as follows:

1. A strong argument from authority must identify the authority appealed to and state that authority's credentials. Anonymous experts lend little weight to a claim, and an audience has no reason to accept the views of the authority if you fail to state the credentials that make them an authority whose opinion should be well regarded.

Often, what is required is relatively straightforward. If you want to establish some basic fact about chemical properties, then it makes sense to use someone with a degree in chemistry as your authority. Perhaps it will be necessary to appeal to someone who specializes in a particular branch of chemistry. On other occasions, specifying credentials may be more complicated. If you are appealing to a panel that has been appointed to investigate a public scandal, you will not be able to say that they have degrees in "public scandal investigation." You would have to appeal to the general intelligence, character, and specific knowledge of the members of the panel.

The Hoover case meets this first condition: Both Hoover and his credentials are clearly stated. If we needed to, we could conduct further research into his background, the kind of expert he is, and the institution for which he works.

2. A strong argument from authority relies on an authority with credentials that are relevant to the issue discussed. Strong appeals to authority require relevant specialized knowledge on the part of the authority cited. In 2008, Gillette began running advertisements on British television featuring three sports stars, Thierry Henry, Tiger Woods, and Roger Federer (replacing a previous series of advertisements with David Beckham) and featuring text that read "champion," and "player of the year." Like most advertisements that display celebrities endorsing products, this is a bad argument from authority, for though these experts have established their expertise in some field—tennis, soccer, and golf—they are usually ill-qualified to judge whether a certain product is more dependable than another. If we really want to know whether a razor gives the best shave possible, we should turn to someone who understands the science of such matters.

Again, the Hoover case gives us the right kind of authority. If we are unsure whether there are authorities on meteorites and non-terrestrial life, the title of "astrobiologist" suggests itself as a probable candidate, and the organization for which he works—NASA—supports this inference.

3. A strong argument from authority appeals to authorities who are not biased. As we saw in Chapter 2, an obvious kind of bias arises when individuals have a vested interest, when they stand to gain from expressing some view or making a claim. This is, of course, a further problem with the kinds of endorsements found in advertisements. It is also evident in appeals to the authority of individuals who are in some substantial way committed to one side of a debate and in this way have a vested interest in it. A good argument could not, for example, cite the authority of scientists employed by the nuclear industry in a debate over the question of whether, say, a nuclear power plant or food irradiation is safe. Such individuals may reasonably argue for a particular view of such an issue, and their arguments may be convincing, but we must use their arguments rather than their authority to defend their conclusions. An appeal to an authority with a vested interest to protect or promote does not carry the same weight as the views of independent authorities and researchers.

This is where we need to look closer at the Hoover case. On the face of it, he is a scientist conducting objective studies that we expect from scientists. But like all of us, scientists can become deeply invested in their work. This is the kind of good bias we expect from dedicated people. But it can also lead to hasty conclusions and statements when a longed for outcome seems suddenly to be confirmed. The media report of the Hoover case (FoxNews.com, 7 March 2011), mentions earlier work in this field, including similar claims of life in meteorites made in 2004 and 2007 by Dr Hoover. So it is possible he has a strong interest in seeing his work finally acknowledged.

4. A strong argument from authority is possible only when there is wide agreement among the relevant experts. The failure of members of an investigative panel to come to an agreement lessens the extent to which we can appeal to them to decide an issue. A selective appeal to an authority who takes a stand with which other authorities disagree is usually inappropriate. We may say, "My claim is supported by X, but I must confess that no one else in the field agrees with her on this"; however, such a claim will provide minimal evidence for our view. It would have to be combined with other considerations if it were to be the basis of a convincing argument. This does not mean that lack of agreement is a clear sign that a claim is false. Revolutionary thinkers like Galileo and Darwin, whose claims eventually gained widespread acceptance, stood alone against other contemporary experts. But in such a case, it must be an argument scheme other than argument from authority that is used to establish that a claim should be accepted.

This is the weakest part of the Hoover case. Publication of the article has resulted in a serious debate on both sides, and there is clearly no consensus. This is not an instance where other scientists looked at the evidence and immediately acknowledged the correctness of the claim. In fact, even Hoover's own institution has challenged him. NASA's Chief Scientist Paul Hertz has stated "While we value the free exchange of ideas, data, and information as part of scientific and technical inquiry, NASA cannot stand behind or support a scientific claim unless it has been peer-reviewed or thoroughly examined by other qualified experts." Clearly, in Hertz's (and NASA's) judgement, this review has not taken place, and this seriously weakens the argument.

5. A strong argument from authority must appeal to an authority who belongs to an area of knowledge where a consensus among authorities is in principle possible because there are universally accepted criteria for making judgements in that field. In judging and constructing arguments from authority, remember that some topics do not lend themselves to appeals to authority because they refer to fields in which authority is not possible or yet available. Many new areas of inquiry are characterized this way, and some people would hold that this is also the case with disputed fields, like those in parapsychology. Are there, for example, authorities on ghosts? Other people insist that matters of taste are subjective and that it is not, therefore, possible for authorities to reach a consensus on what constitutes good or bad music, or art, or cuisine. Generally, in appealing to authorities, you must be prepared to argue that the issue at hand is one in which broad agreement is possible because it relates to an appropriate field in which it makes sense to speak of "authorities."

On this fifth point, the Hoover case seems to qualify. The fact that a debate has emerged among a defined set of scientists who have a background in the relevant issues indicates that this is a field in which authorities exist and where agreements in principle are possible.

Given these conditions, a fully developed strong appeal to authority will be an instance of the following scheme:

Premise 1: *X* is an authority with credentials *c*, who believes and states *y*.
Premise 2: Credentials *c* are relevant to *y*.
Premise 3: *X* is not biased.
Premise 4: There is wide agreement among the relevant experts over *y*.
Premise 5: *y* is an appropriate field in which consensus is possible.
Conclusion: *y* should be accepted.

The kinds of concerns that must be taken into account when we judge authorities have a significant role to play in our interactions with the World Wide Web. It has been a boon to arguers insofar as it has made a remarkable amount of information readily available. At the same time, it is a means of communication that does not clearly separate authoritative and non-authoritative views. Web sites may be characterized by a lack of attention to detail, a failure to properly consider opposing points of view, and ill-considered argument. The sources available in a university library have probably been acquired because someone who is an authority (a librarian or a faculty member) has decided that they were significant enough to be included. They have likely been influenced by other experts who write reviews and make recommendations. In contrast, no critical evaluation need inform a site on the Web, which may be constructed in a way that inadvertently or intentionally propagates misinformation.

In dealing with web sites, apply the criteria we have developed in our account of arguments from authority. Any web site, whether or not it has been developed by a recognized authority, may have arguments worth considering. But one cannot quote and depend on such sites in the way that we quote and depend on authorities unless these sites promote the conditions for good appeals to authority. This means that to use a web site's endorsement of some claim as evidence for a conclusion, the endorsement must be presented in a way that allows you to identify the author and his or her credentials and to eliminate the possibility of bias and vested interest (which may be evident when you investigate who sponsors a website). The relevance of the author's credentials, the agreement of other experts, and the appropriateness of the field must also be clear if one is to construct a strong argument from authority in such a case. One way to test some of these conditions is by checking other sites on the same topic.

ARGUMENTS FROM AUTHORITY

Arguments from authority provide evidence for a claim by establishing that it is endorsed by authorities. A good argument from authority supports a claim on the basis that the person or group that endorses it is deemed to have (1) certain stated credentials, which are (2) relevant to the claim in question, and (3) no biases that are likely to interfere with their assessment of the claim, provided that (4) the claim in question concerns an area in which there is wide agreement among the relevant experts, and that (5) the claim concerns an area of knowledge in which consensus is possible.

EXERCISE   12C

1. Find three instances of argument from authority in a magazine. Diagram them. Are they strong or weak arguments from authority?

2. Find one web site that can be used in a strong argument from authority and one that cannot. Explain why in each case.

4   Ad Hominem

Ad hominem arguments are counter-arguments to *pro homine* reasoning. An *ad hominem* argument gives us reasons for not taking someone's position seriously or for dismissing it altogether. A good *ad hominem* bases this claim on premises that show that someone is in some way unreliable. The version of *ad hominem* we call an "argument *against* authority" argues that a person is not a reliable authority and should not, therefore, be taken seriously.

The general scheme for a good *ad hominem* argument is the reverse of the scheme for a good *pro homine* and can be represented as follows:

> **Premise 1:** *X* says *y*.
> **Premise 2:** *X* is unreliable (i.e. not knowledgeable, trustworthy, and/or free of bias).
> **Conclusion:** *Y* should not be accepted (on the grounds that *X* says *y*).

The essence of an *ad hominem* is an attack against the credibility of a particular individual. We use *ad hominem* for the same reason we employ *pro homine*: it is impossible to investigate every claim we come across. If we hear, for example, that a professor whose work we are familiar with has just published another book on social psychology and decide not to read it because we have read her other six hefty tomes and found reading them a waste of time, we are using a reasonable *ad hominem*, for we have evidence that she is not knowledgeable.

We have evidence of such an attack in the Hoover case. NASA science chief points out that Hoover did not advise the agency he had submitted the paper to a journal, indicating there were internal protocols involved that had not been followed. More seriously,

Hertz stated that the article had failed to get published "in a more established peer-reviewed journal," thus casting doubt on the authority of the *Journal for Cosmology*. In this vein, David Morrison, senior scientist at the NASA Astrobiology Institute, NASA Ames Research Center, said he felt the choice of scientific journal was enough to call the report into question. "Extraordinary claims require extraordinary evidence. At a bare minimum this would require publication in a prestigious peer-refereed scientific journal—which this is not." All of this constitutes an *ad hominem* attack on Dr. Hoover's reliability, suggesting that he had specific reasons for not publishing the paper in a peer-reviewed journal according to the accepted standards of his profession.

Good *ad hominem* arguments usually appear in contexts where an appeal to a *pro homine* has occurred or might occur. Consider an advertisement that the Rolling Stones placed in British music publications when the record label Decca released an album called *Stone Age* without the Stones' permission. (The album contained eight songs recorded on other albums and four new releases—see Tony Sanchez, *Up and down with the Rolling Stones*, Da Capo Press, 1996, p. 214.) The advertisement, paid for by Mick Jagger and signed by all members of the band, read as follows:

> Beware! Message from the Rolling Stones Re: Stone Age. We didn't know this record was going to be released. It is, in our opinion, below the standard we try to keep up, both in choice of content and cover design.

This is an interesting argument, for in it the members of the Rolling Stones make a *pro homine* appeal to themselves, suggesting that the reader should accept their own judgement that the record in question is of substandard quality.

We can assess this *pro homine* in the way that we assess any other *pro homine*. In this case, it is clear that the Rolling Stones made the claim in question, so we must ask whether they are knowledgeable, trustworthy, and free of bias and in this way individuals whose opinions should be accepted. Though we must accept that they know their own music, and this might seem to make the argument a strong one, this is a case in which one might reasonably question the Rolling Stones's status as reliable commentators. Their claim that the music in question is below their normal standard raises, to begin with, the question of whether their judgement can be trusted, for the majority of the songs on the record were released on those records that are claimed to be superior. Putting aside the questions that this raises, the most serious problem is one of bias, for the advertisement in question was produced at a time when the Rolling Stones had left Decca and established their own competing record company. To that extent, they were angered at the release of their songs by a competing record label. This suggests that they were motivated by their own vested interests, making this a case where a *pro homine* appeal is unreliable.

In producing this criticism of the Rolling Stones's advertisement, we have been constructing an *ad hominem* argument that illustrates the logic of such reasoning. That is, we have dismissed the conclusion advanced because we judge the arguer unreliable in the ways we have indicated. There may be other good reasons that could support the Rolling Stones's conclusion, but our point is that their say-so is not a good reason to accept it.

It is important to distinguish *ad hominem* attacks that discredit a person's position because of their character from attacks on the person alone. The latter is often called an *abusive ad hominem* because it does little more than hurl abuse. An example of this occurs in a letter the late actor Richard Harris wrote to the British *Sunday Times* newspaper (8 June 1995) in response to a feature interview they had conducted with actor Michael Caine. The article discussed Caine's acting career as well as his successes as a businessman and art collector, and it applauded his return to England from a self-imposed exile in Hollywood. In several direct quotations, Caine numbered himself among the premier English actors of his generation (including Harris) and implied that he had out-achieved these men in several respects—as an actor, a television star, and a businessman. In responding, Harris wrote the following:

> Any suggestion that he [Caine] has eclipsed the names of Finney, O'Toole, Burton, Bates, Smith and Courtenay is tantamount to prophesying that Rin-Tin-Tin will be solemnised beyond the memory of Brando....
>
> In truth, he is an over-fat, flatulent 62-year-old windbag, a master of inconsequence now masquerading as a guru, passing off his vast limitations as pious virtues.

These particular remarks are a study in abusive *ad hominem*. While heavy with insult, they don't successfully meet the challenge required by the criteria for a good *ad hominem*—i.e. the challenge to demonstrate that Caine is unknowledgeable, untrustworthy, or biased. Because insult has been substituted for substance, this *ad hominem* is very weak.

Buried in other aspects of Harris's remarks are some indications of more proper *ad hominem* reasoning. Elsewhere in the letter he argues, for example, that readers should dismiss what Caine is reported to have said about fellow actors because he has tried to achieve greatness by associating with great actors; that Caine is not in a position to criticize the low standard of British television because his own contributions to that medium are part of the problem; and that Caine should not pose as an expert on "oenology and art" because he admits to buying things for their resale value and so recognizes only their price, not their worth. Each of these cases constitutes a sub-argument that needs to be evaluated. Though the strength of each might be debated, and though Harris's letter is not an example of a better *ad hominem* argument, these aspects of his argument are not abusive in the transparent way that is evident in the remarks provided above.

In your own dealings with *ad hominem* reasoning, be sure to distinguish what is abusive from what is substantial. As always, your goal should be to uncover a clear argument.

AD HOMINEM REASONING

Ad hominem reasoning can be considered the reverse of *pro homine* reasoning. A good *ad hominem* argument establishes that a person's views should not be given credence or should be rejected outright because the person is deemed to be:
1. not knowledgeable
2. untrustworthy
3. biased.

EXERCISE (**12D**)

1. For each of the topics listed in exercise 12A, question 2, describe a context in which one could construct a good *ad hominem* argument. Give reasons for your answer.

2. Discuss and evaluate the following pieces for *ad hominem* reasoning:

   a)* [As world media were eulogizing Pope John Paul II in April 2005, cultural critic Terry Eagleton took a less appreciative stance; the following is an excerpt from "The Pope Has Blood on His Hands," the *Guardian* newspaper, 4 April 2005] John Paul, however, acknowledged equality with nobody. From his early years as a priest, he was notable for his exorbitant belief in his own spiritual and intellectual powers. Graham Greene once dreamed of a newspaper headline reading "John Paul canonises Jesus Christ." Bishops were summoned to Rome to be given their orders, not for fraternal consultation. Loopy far-right mystics and Francoists were honoured, and Latin American political liberationists bawled out . . . .The result of centring all power in Rome has been an infantilisation of the local churches. Clergy found themselves incapable of taking initiatives without nervous glances over their shoulders at the Holy Office. It was at just this point, when the local churches were least capable of handling a crisis maturely, that the child sex abuse scandal broke. John Paul's response was to reward an American cardinal who had assiduously covered up the outrage with a plush posting in Rome. The greatest crime of his papacy, however, was neither his part in this cover-up nor his neanderthal attitude to women. It was the grotesque irony by which the Vatican condemned—as a "culture of death"—condoms, which might have saved countless Catholics in the developing world from an agonising AIDS death. The Pope goes to his eternal reward with those deaths on his hands. He was one of the greatest disasters for the Christian church since Charles Darwin.

   b) [From the "tipping debate" at Starbucks Gossip, http://starbucksgossip.type pad.com/_/2004/09/tipping_debate_.html] Starbucks employees don't DESERVE a tip. Jeez, get a grip people—you aren't performing a personalized service of any sort, you're pouring coffee (wildly overpriced coffee no less). I polled co-workers who frequent Starbucks (I don't) and couldn't find a single person who had ever seen a Starbucks employee do anything that went the least bit beyond their job description. Of course, nobody could even think of anything that would qualify in the first place!

   Someone else here also pointed out that customers have to wait in line as well. Even in a hash house, the waitress has to lug your food from the kitchen.

   Bottom line—you don't deserve a tip of any sort. Consider it the highest form of kindness that you ever get one since you do absolutely nothing that warrants it.

   c) [From a Letter to the Editor, *National Post*, 12 November 2007] Re: Spain's King Tells Venezuela's Chavez To "Shut Up," Nov. 10. I'm glad to see that someone has finally put Venezuela's loudmouth president, Hugo Chavez, in his place. Chavez has a habit of making provocative remarks about other politicians in a style inappropriate for any communication outside of a professional wrestling ring. Before his accusations of "fascism" regarding a Spanish prime minister, he referred to US President George W. Bush as the Devil.

Such international grandstanding is indicative of the quality of his socialist government. Instead of focusing on how command economics and authoritarian rule have driven Venezuela further and further into poverty and resulted in high crime rates and political violence, Chavez is trying to make international headlines and create an "us vs. them" mentality. His acts mimic George Orwell's "Two Minute Hate" of 1984.

5   Arguments against Authority

Just as an appeal to authority is a more specific form of the *pro homine*, so an argument against an authority is the more specific form of the *ad hominem*. Its general form is:

Premise 1:   *X* is not an authority on *y*.
Conclusion: *X*'s advocating some claim about *y* does not provide support for it.

Arguments against authority are counter-arguments that cast doubt on the reliability of a proposed authority's views by showing that an appeal to his or her opinion fails to meet the criteria we have introduced for good arguments from authority. In view of this, a good argument *against* authority is one that rejects an alleged authority by establishing one of the following:

1.   that the authority's credentials are questionable;
2.   that the credentials cited are irrelevant to the issue in question;
3.   that the alleged authority is biased;
4.   that the topic under scrutiny is one where there is significant disagreement among the relevant experts; or
5.   that the topic is one where expertise cannot be claimed.

These requirements can be understood in light of the considerations we introduced in connection with appeals to authority. Because a failure to satisfy even one of the conditions for a good argument from authority makes such an argument weak, any such failure can be the basis of an argument against authority.

Our earlier criticism of commercial endorsements by celebrities as representing vested interests was an argument against authority. The following example involves an *ad hominem* and an appeal to authority. It arises in the context of a disagreement among contemporary commentators over the authorship of an ancient text called the *Magna Moralia*. The following, which refers to a passage from the *Magna Moralia*, is from a footnote in a work by one commentator, A.W. Price:

John Cooper attaches great weight to this passage. . . . It is consistent that he ascribes the *Magna Moralia* to Aristotle himself. . . . Others will find the author's treatment of "goodwill" here . . . typical of his [the author of the *Magna Moralia*'s] "constant botching," as Anthony Kenny has termed it. [A.W. Price, 1989, *Love and Friendship in Plato and Aristotle*, Oxford: Clarendon Press, pp. 122–3]

Both Cooper and Kenny can be considered "experts" in the field by virtue of their published work and its reception. Price thinks that the *Magna Moralia* was not written by Aristotle and backs this claim by invoking Kenny's claim that the author of the *Magna Moralia* is a "constant botcher" (thereby implying that it is not Aristotle's work). Here, then, one has an implicit argument from authority that can be diagrammed as follows:

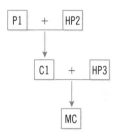

where:

P1 =   Kenny claims that the author of the *Magna Moralia* is a constant botcher.
HP2 =   Kenny is a noted expert.
C1 =   The author of the *Magna Moralia* is a constant botcher.
HP3 =   Aristotle is not a constant botcher.
MC =   Aristotle is not the author of the *Magna Moralia*.

The passage in question contains an implicit argument *against* authority as well as an argument from authority, however, for the appeal to one authority (Kenny) is used to dismiss the views of another (Cooper). The argument against authority can be summarized as the claim that "The author of the *Magna Moralia* is a constant botcher (C1), so Cooper is not a good judge of the passage in question, and he is not a credible authority." In essence, this implicit argument calls into question Cooper's credentials by pointing to his alleged poor judgement.

Because, however, this is a case characterized by disagreements between the authorities, the appeal is of little value. Academia is renowned for its contentious debates, and where disagreements arise it is always important to have both sides of the story. In this case, we have neither the grounds for Cooper's high opinion of the author of the *Magna Moralia* nor the grounds for Kenny's low opinion of the same author. In the face of their disagreement, the fourth condition of good appeals to authority cannot be met. Since the *ad hominem* critique of Cooper's credentials depends on the appeal to authority, it is also problematic. In this instance, Price can better make his point by showing how Cooper's interpretation of the passage could be considered a case of "botching." To his credit, it is this that he proceeds to attempt next.

ARGUMENTS AGAINST AUTHORITY

Arguments against authority can be considered the reverse of arguments from authority. A good argument against authority rejects an alleged authority by establishing that:

1. the authority's credentials are questionable; or
2. the credentials cited are irrelevant to the issue in question; or
3. the alleged authority is biased; or
4. the topic under scrutiny is one where there is significant disagreement among the relevant experts; or
5. the topic is one where expertise cannot be claimed.

EXERCISE   12E

Find three poor examples of arguments from authority in magazines or on web sites. Construct a strong argument against authority in response to them. Present your argument in the form of a letter to the editor.

6   Appeal to Eyewitness Testimony

In Chapter 8, we discussed the testimony of witnesses as a way to determine the acceptability of premises. Clearly, such appeals are ethotic in nature, and so we return to them here for a fuller consideration. Eyewitness accounts are important, of course, in institutions like the law. But it is also the case that much of the information we acquire about the natural and social world derives from the testimony of other people and so our dependence on this source for evidence in argumentation is likely to be equally important. However, as our experience with law courts also indicates, eyewitness testimony is not perfectly reliable and can be influenced by a host of factors like a person's vision, attentiveness, memory, and the anticipation of what they expected to see. According to a CBS News report of 8 March 2009, 235 people in the United States who had been convicted of serious crimes have been exonerated by DNA evidence. And in more than three quarters of those cases, the conviction was based on eyewitness testimony.

To evaluate good eyewitness testimony, we need conditions that will factor out as many of these influences as possible. Accordingly, we introduce the following scheme for eyewitness testimony:

Premise 1: O was in a good position to observe X.
Premise 2:   There are no obvious factors that would bias the account given.
Premise 3: O has documented the observation.
Conclusion: *O's account of X is reliable.*

where: O = the observer and X is the object or event observed.

The first premise addresses the central issue of what gives this person their authority as an eyewitness. They must have been present at the time of the event in question or in close proximity to the object. How close is close enough will depend on the context and the event or object in question. Being in the midst of a crowd during a riot gives someone a direct experience of what is going on around them. But their viewpoint is restricted to the position they are in. Overseeing a riot from a balcony or bridge would give another person a much better view of the event and the relationships between components of that event. Essentially, we are asking here about the conditions involved and whether they were optimal for the observations being made and reported.

In asking whether someone was in a good position to observe we are also interested in his or her intellectual and emotional condition. Did he or she have the skills necessary for making an accurate report of the event? Could he or she understand the language of those around him or her, for example? Was he or she in an environment with which he or she were familiar? And was he or she unaffected by factors like fatigue or emotional excitability? Some of these questions may be difficult to answer because the source for such answers will be the very same as the source of the report—the eyewitness.

It is important to distinguish between observations and interpretations, because the latter introduces a further layer of uncertainty. Quite often when two eyewitnesses disagree that disagreement lies in how they have understood or interpreted what they saw. An evaluation of premise 2 must cover that distinction. It must also consider factors like the timeline involved. If a person is relating something that happened to them or that they saw decades ago, then it is reasonable to expect that the intervening years may have altered the memory in some way, thus influencing the reliability of the account.

It is also important, of course, to consider under premise 2 whether a person has a conflict of interest in saying what they do. On this point, our related discussion of this in Chapter 2 is relevant. To this end we are interested in learning about the person's allegiances and commitments. Does she or he have an association now or in the past that may incline him or her to say what he or she does or to encourage him or her to see things in a specific way? Here, we are searching for objectivity in the account. The best eyewitnesses will be those who have no involvement in the issues being reported.

Finally, under premise 3 we look for documentation of the observation. It is the case that most eyewitness appeals will not contain this component, since many people do not, as a matter of course, document what they see (by keeping a journal, for example). But this is a condition that, where met, can make the difference between stronger and weaker eyewitness appeals. In the case of such documentation, we are interested in how soon after the observation in question it was made. Obviously, the sooner the better. We are also interested in whether it is contradicted by other documented accounts of the same event. Finally, in the age of cell phones with cameras,

APPEAL TO EYEWITNESS TESTIMONY

Appeal to eyewitness testimony argues for a claim by showing that it is supported by the report of a reliable observer. A good appeal to eyewitness testimony argument maintains that it should be accepted because O:
1. is in a good position to make the observation,
2. is free from biases, and
3. has documented the observation in some way.

many unusual events or objects that a person witnesses will be recorded. Such visual records will both supplement and confirm an eyewitness account and so count as a valuable contribution to the evidence of the report.

EXERCISE   12F

> Use the Internet to find an example of a report based on an eyewitness (news sites would be a good source for these). Decide whether the eyewitness testimony is reliable according to the conditions of our scheme.

7   Guilt (and Honour) by Association

An argument scheme closely related to *ad hominem* is what is known as **guilt by association**. As the name implies, this argument attributes "guilt" to a person or group on the basis of some association that is known or thought to exist between that person or group and some other person or group of dubious beliefs or behaviour. A variant of this scheme of argument that we call "honour by association" uses a positive association as a basis for the conclusion that they are in some way creditable.

Guilt-by-association arguments are variants of the following scheme:

Premise 1: A person or group X is associated with another person or group Y.
Premise 2: Y has questionable beliefs or behaves in a questionable way.
Conclusion: X's character and/or claims are questionable.

An honour-by-association argument has the form:

Premise 1: A person or group X is associated with another person or group Y.
Premise 2: Y has creditable beliefs or behaves in a creditable way.
Conclusion: X's character and/or claims are creditable.

What does "associated" mean in this context? In cases in which the association claimed in premise 1 of either of these arguments exists, guilt or credit can sometimes be legitimately transferred or inferred in the way proposed. But it is important to be wary of such arguments, for they often serve as a vehicle for generalizations based on stereotyping, which should be avoided because they inhibit careful moral assessments.

A guilt-by-association argument is strong when, and only when:

1. there is good reason to believe that the alleged association between X and Y really does exist;
2. there is good reason to question the beliefs or the behaviour of Y; and
3. there is no good reason to differentiate X from Y.

In keeping with these conditions, the conditions for a good honour-by-association argument are the same, except that condition (2) becomes:

2.   there is good reason to *credit* the beliefs or the behaviour of *Y.*

Because many guilt-by-association arguments are problematic, it is a good idea to develop an argument of this sort fully if you decide to use one. When you do so, the main premises in your argument will be variants of the three conditions already noted. These principal premises may have to be backed by sub-arguments that support them.

Association arguments cannot serve as definitive substitutes for thorough critical examinations of the views of a person or group. But there are cases in which association arguments are reasonable. For instance, if someone spent 20 years as an active member of the Salvation Army, this does lend credence to their observations about social issues. On the negative side, if someone who offers social criticisms has close connections with extremists, say, because he has acted as a spokesman for an extremist organization, then we have grounds for being skeptical about his analysis of social problems and even his character. Especially when we have limited time at our disposal, positive and negative arguments by association can be a further heuristic in deciding what arguments we should and should not take the time to consider and discuss.

Association arguments can also combine with others to weaken (or strengthen) a case. We have an example of this in the Hoover case, involving his choice to publish in the *Journal of Cosmology*. There is no doubt that this association exists, and if the journal does not conduct peer-reviews of articles before it publishes—as is standard in professional and academic fields, then this is a relevant reason for transferring the journal's apparent lack of a key standard onto one of its authors. The journal's editor insisted that the attacks that complained Dr Hoover's article should have been published in another journal were "just sour grapes and should not be taken seriously." But this is not a good response to a very serious challenge.

Difficult cases involve situations in which we might question the relevance of a particular association. Consider the following, taken from Janet George's article on the British anti-hunting campaign, entitled "Saboteurs—The Real Animals" (the *Guardian*, 28 February 1993, p. 24):

[O]ne can condemn . . . the dishonesty of the campaign against hunting. If the anti-hunt literature said "We are against killing animals for any purpose: killing animals for food is morally as unacceptable as killing animals for sport but impossible to ban," financial and political support for the campaign would be so greatly reduced as to make it unsustainable. Such an extreme view would be held by less than 2 per cent of the population, so a little misrepresentation is necessary to keep funds flowing.

Whatever claims are made by spokesmen of the anti-hunting campaigns, the truth is that more and more hunt saboteurs express their disapproval of legal activities with illegal acts. Anti-hunt organizations pay lip-service to peaceful protest, but by producing emotive and misleading propaganda . . . they must accept some responsibility for the actions of their supporters.

These remarks shift some of the guilt of the "hunt saboteurs," who have been guilty of increasing violence, onto the anti-hunt organizations who advocate peaceful protest (though there may be some confusion over the identities of the associated parties).

Set out as guilt-by-association reasoning, this argument is as follows:

P1 =   The anti-hunt organizations are associated with the hunt saboteurs.
P2 =   The hunt saboteurs behave in a questionable (violent) way.
C =   The motives of the anti-hunt organizations are questionable.

The first condition for appropriate guilt-by-association arguments requires that the alleged association really does exist. Consider how many conspiracy theories rely upon alleged associations that are implausible from the outset. In the current case, we will grant the association for the moment. It seems charitable to allow that the anti-hunt organizations and the anti-hunt "saboteurs" (accepting that this may be a loaded term and open to challenge) will share ideological views at least to the extent that they are working for the same end.

The second condition asks whether there is good reason to question the behaviour of the one group. There is less doubt here. Although we may shy from the term "saboteurs," it is established (in the media) that the groups discussed engage in violent acts against property and persons, including law enforcement officers. Such acts are clearly questionable.

The third condition focuses on the relevance of the association in this instance. Is there good reason to disassociate the two groups on this issue? Here we look to the evidence provided by the first paragraph. The link that establishes guilt in George's eyes is the dishonest literature. Although the anti-hunt organizations pay lip-service to peaceful protest, they must accept some responsibility for the violence because they produce misleading and emotive propaganda. Given that she grants that the groups pay lip-service to peaceful protest, we must believe that the propaganda does not explicitly incite violence. So it is difficult to see just how the "propaganda" establishes a significant enough connection.

The misleading nature of the literature, according to George's first paragraph, lies in its failure to tell the full extent of the group's position. Honesty here would, allegedly, lead to a loss of political and financial support. The people who would disassociate themselves from anti-hunt organizations if the literature was honest are a different group altogether. No connection is established between the failure of the literature to be honest and the violence of the "saboteurs." In fact, the literature seems irrelevant to this group, since their actions do not appear to be a result of being misled by any *softer* goal expressed in the literature. At the very least, George has not established the association she requires if she wants to criticize anti-hunt organizations on the basis of their association with violent offenders.

GUILT AND HONOUR BY ASSOCIATION

An argument form that attributes guilt (or credit) to a person or group, X, on the basis of some association that is known or thought to exist between that person or group and some other person or group, Y. In a good guilt-by-association argument:

1. there is good reason to believe that the alleged association between X and Y really does exist;
2. there is good reason to question the beliefs or the behaviour of Y; and
3. there is no good reason to differentiate X from Y.

In a good honour-by-association argument, conditions 1 and 3 remain, and the second condition becomes (2) there is good reason to credit the beliefs or the behaviour of Y.

EXERCISE 12G

1. The well-known German philosopher Martin Heidegger is known to have been a member of the German Nazi party. This has sparked a controversy over whether this association in any way discredits his work as a philosopher. Do you think one could build a strong guilt-by-association argument on this basis? Why or why not?

2. Assess the different associations and the implicit guilt- and honour-by-association reasoning in the following passage, from www.friesian.com/rockmore (accessed 4 February 2003):

> The controversy about Martin Heidegger's membership in the German Nazi Party ultimately reveals one very important thing: The very principles that attracted Heidegger to Hitler and the Nazis are also the principles that attract Heidegger's defenders to him. That most of Heidegger's defenders are leftists and "progressives" (like Richard Rorty) simply reveals a characteristic of the history of the 20th century: that the Left. . . has far more in common with the far Right . . . than anyone on the Left has ever wanted to admit—except perhaps for Susan Sontag's classic, politically incorrect statement that "Communism is fascism with a human face'"—though one must then explain Alexander Dubcek's claim that the revolution in Czechoslovakia in 1968 was to produce "Communism with a human face"; presumably he didn't think that it already had one. Since Dubcek had to live under communism and Sontag didn't, we can count on him to have gotten it more right. Sontag, however, who also said that Americans could learn more about the Soviet Union reading *Reader's Digest* than *The Nation*, got it far more right than most of her intellectual peers. (Rockmore, "Sartre holds that Marxism is unsurpassable as the philosophy of our time," p. 147).

8   Other Cases

Our account of guilt-by-association arguments ends our discussion of different argument schemes. In closing, we reiterate the point that some arguments do not fit neatly into the categories we have introduced. Sometimes no specific argument scheme is used, and sometimes the premises contain a mixture of specific schemes. Where there is no specific scheme at all, we must depend on the general criteria of relevance and sufficiency and acceptability in assessing an argument. If an argument is a mixture of a variety of specific schemes, we must appeal to a variety of specific criteria.

To illustrate such complexities, imagine that a homicide investigator argues that White is the murderer the police are looking for on the basis of the following reasoning:

P1 = Green says White is the murderer.
P2 = White is a vicious person at the best of times.
P3 = No one has been able to provide any evidence to the contrary.
C = White is the murderer.

Note that P1, P2, and P3 appeal to very different sorts of evidence. P1, implicitly appealing to Green as someone who should know who the murderer is, is a *pro homine* argument. P3 is an argument from ignorance. P2 does not conform to any of our specific argument schemes. (Note that it is an attack on White, not an attack on White's views and, hence, not an *ad hominem* argument.)

The diagram for this argument would be a simple one, with three convergent premises. In assessing the argument, we must consider the weight each specific subargument lends to the conclusion. Then the overall strength of the argument must be evaluated by asking whether the conclusion is probable, given the cumulative force of the different kinds of evidence introduced to justify it. Individually, each aspect of the total argument may be questionable and, therefore, only marginally convincing. But in conjunction with the others, it can contribute to a strong argument, especially if there are no fundamental objections to the reasoning. The strength of the final conclusion is a result of the three separate kinds of considerations providing supporting evidence for it. Thus, although Green may not be the most trustworthy character, his claims must be taken seriously when they are corroborated by other evidence.

Other complications arise when different parts of the conclusion are established by different premises. We can add complexity to the example we have been considering by adding a fourth premise and rewriting the conclusion as a conjunction:

P1 = Green says White is the murderer.
P2 = White is a vicious person at the best of times.
P3 = Nobody has been able to provide any evidence to the contrary.
P4 = All those who have met him agree that Brown could not commit such a heinous crime.
C = White is the murderer, and Brown is innocent.

We can now represent the argument as consisting of four premises leading to conclusion C. Premises P1, P2, and P3 clearly go together to establish that White is the murderer, while P4 establishes that Brown is innocent. For purposes of assessing the argument, we can represent Brown's innocence as a hidden conclusion (HC2) following from P4 and the conclusion of our earlier argument, that White is the murderer, as HC1, following from P1, P2, and P3. The final conclusion thus follows from HC1 and HC2, and we can diagram the argument as follows:

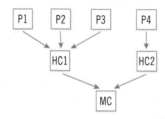

where:

HC1 =   White is the murderer.
HC2 =   Brown is innocent.
MC =   White is the murderer, and Brown is innocent.

Using this diagram, we can assess the argument in the normal way.

It is because of the need for different kinds of assessment that we must separate premises that provide different types of support for a conclusion: by appealing to analogies, to causal reasoning, to *pro homine* considerations, and so on. If you keep in mind your goal, which is an honest and logically useful representation, then you should be able to deal effectively with whatever specific argument schemes you come across.

EXERCISE 12H

Construct an argument for the conclusion that "White is the murderer, and Brown is innocent" that has the same form and diagram as the example just given, except that the premises P1–P4 are linked (and not convergent) and in this way establish the plausibility of the conclusion.

9   Summary

The schemes introduced in this chapter are all based in some aspect of the character or person who is advancing the argument, or who is appealed to in the argument. The schemes involved are Pro Homine, the *Ad Populum* Argument, Argument from Authority, the *Ad Hominem*, Argument Against Authority; Appeal to Eyewitness Testimony, and Guilt by Association. We explore the nature of these schemes and the conditions involved in evaluating them.

MAJOR EXERCISE 12M

1. This assignment is intended to help you test your understanding of the schemes of argument introduced in this chapter by asking you to use some of them in conjunction with specific normative issues.

    a) Construct short arguments employing the following forms (one for each argument) in support of the claim "Capital punishment should not be reinstated where it is currently disallowed":
        i)   *pro homine*
        ii) appeal to authority
        iii) guilt- or honour-by-association

    b) Employ the same argument forms in support of the opposite claim: "Capital punishment should be reinstated where it is currently disallowed."

    c) Using any of the argument forms of this chapter, construct a short argument on one of the following issues:
        i)   global warming
        ii) the rights of indigenous peoples
        iii) insider trading

    d) The Canadian Supreme Court decided the "Ottawa/Quebec Secession-Rights Case" on 28 February 1997. The court was asked to rule on whether the province of Quebec had the legal right to declare itself separate from Canada. The federal government's argument that it did not have this right was supported by the opinions of two specialists in international law: James Crawford of the University of Cambridge and Luzius Wildhaber of the University of Basel in Switzerland (a judge of the European Court of Human Rights). In appealing to these authorities, was the Canadian government making a strong argument from authority?

2. Decide whether each of the following passages contains an argument. If it does, assess the reasoning. Identify any instances of argument schemes dealt with in this chapter, explaining whether they fulfill the conditions for good arguments of that form. Note that examples may involve more than one argument form. Diagram all arguments.

    a)* [From a flyer advertising "Astro-Guard Security Systems"] You don't have to be a statistic! The experts admit "it's not *if* you will be the victim of a break-in . . . but **WHEN**." Astro-Guard security systems stops burglars before they get inside. ONE OUT OF FOUR! Those are the statistical chances of you and your family being the victims of a break-in **within the next 12 months**. . . . Psychiatrists, Psychologists, Criminologists, Security Experts and Police Officials all agree: "The earlier the intruder is discovered, the more effective the security system."

    b) [From an advertisement in *The Saturday Evening Post* magazine, February 2003] **Our most popular cookbook** FREE **when you subscribe**. What could be more appropriate? A better-health cookbook of delicious high-fiber diet recipes to accompany the legendary all-American magazine that has said no to booze and tobacco advertising and replaced those pages with an emphasis on a long, happy, healthy lifestyle! More than 1,000,000 copies of this 8¼" × 10¾" publication attest to the popularity of *The Saturday Evening Post Family Cookbook*, the joint effort of Cory SerVaas, M.D., and Charlotte Turgeon.

c) [From: "Climate change: Questionable coverage?" by Daniel Kitts, Thursday, 15 April 2010, TVO's Inside Agenda Blog, http://theagenda.tvo.org/blog/agenda-blog/climate-change-questionable-coverage]

Yesterday I came across an article on climate change in the Financial Times, a British newspaper. Being from the venerable FT, as the paper is sometimes known, it was a typically well-written article. But what struck me most about the piece was not that it was well written, but that it's the kind of article on climate change that drives environmentalists such as blogger and one-time Agenda guest Joseph Romm nuts.

Here's the headline and the lead sentence:

Global warming graph attacked by study

A key piece of evidence in climate change science was slammed as "exaggerated" on Wednesday by the UK's leading statistician, in a vindication of claims that global warming sceptics have been making for years.

My, my. Those climate skeptics have been right all along, haven't they? Well, not exactly. Because when you read the whole article you find out that the UK's leading statistician, Professor David Hand, said that while the graph in question did indeed exaggerate the warming trend, the underlying data used indeed points to evidence of a warming planet. Furthermore: Prof Hand said his criticisms should not be seen as invalidating climate science .

. . . He accused sceptics of "identifying a few particular issues and blowing them up" to distort the true picture. The handful of errors found so far . . . were "isolated incidents," he said. "If you look at any area of science, you would be able to find odd examples like this. It doesn't detract from the vast bulk of the conclusions," he said.

I should also mention that this article was based on a report on the infamous "Climategate" email scandal that largely exonerated the scientists involved, stating they had behaved "honestly and fairly" and showed "no evidence of any deliberate scientific malpractice."

d) [From "The Skeptic's Skeptic," *Scientific American*, 3 November 2010]

Although he has no formal training in science, I would pit Hitchens against any of the purveyors of pseudoscientific claptrap because of his unique and enviable skill at peeling back the layers of an argument and cutting to its core. We would all do well to observe and emulate his power to detect and dissect baloney through pure thought. To wit, after watching a quack medicine man fleecing India's poor one Sunday afternoon, the belletrist scowled in a 2003 *Slate* column, "What can be asserted without evidence can also be dismissed without evidence." The observation is worthy of elevation to a dictum.

Of course, as scientists we prefer to tether evidence, when it is available, to logical analysis in support of a claim or to proffer counterevidence that disputes a claim. A radiant example of Hitchens's insightful thinking, coupled to the effective employment of counterevidence, is his reaction to an episode of the television series *Planet Earth*. As he watched, he had a revelation of creationism's profound flaws. The episode was on life underground, during which Hitchens noticed that the blind salamander had "eyes" that "were denoted only by little concavities or indentations," as he recounted in a 2008 *Slate* commentary. "Even as I was grasping the implications of this, the fine voice of Sir David Attenborough was telling me how many millions of years it had taken for these denizens of the underworld to lose the eyes they had once possessed."

Creationists make a big deal about the eye, insisting that the gradual stepwise process of natural selection could not have sculpted such a complex instrument because of "irreducible complexity," meaning that the removal of any part would render it useless. Even Charles Darwin fretted about the eye in *On the Origin of Species*: "To suppose that the eye, with all its inimitable contrivances for adjusting the focus to different distances, for admitting different amounts of light, and for the correction of spherical and chromatic aberration, could have been formed by natural selection, seems, I freely confess, absurd in the highest possible degree."

If God created the eye, then how do creationists explain the blind salamander? "The most they can do is to intone that 'the Lord giveth and the Lord taketh away,'" Hitchens mused. "Whereas the likelihood that the postocular blindness of underground salamanders is another aspect of evolution by natural selection seems, when you think about it at all, so overwhelmingly probable as to constitute a near certainty."

e) [From a Letter to the Editor, the *Peterborough Examiner*, 12 November 1994] What people must understand is that if you support one aspect of the animal rights agenda you are supporting it all. You may not be against fur, but your support is helping animal rights groups in their anti-fur campaigns, and you may be against cosmetic testing, but that support also supports their stand against vital medical research that each and every one of us benefits from every day of our lives.

f) [From *The Telegraph*, "What has Al Gore done for world peace?," 12 October 2007. This piece refers to the former American vice-president and his documentary, *An Inconvenient Truth*] So Al Gore is the joint winner of the Nobel Peace Prize. Admittedly, he has to share it with the United Nations' climate change panel—but, even so, I think we need to declare an international smugness alert.

The former US Vice-President has already taken over from Michael Moore as the most sanctimonious lardbutt Yank on the planet. Can you imagine what he'll be like now that the Norwegian Nobel committee has given him the prize?

More to the point, can you imagine how enormous his already massive carbon footprint will become once he starts jetting around the world bragging about his new title?

Just after Gore won an Oscar for his global warming documentary, *An Inconvenient Truth*—in which he asked American households to cut their use of electricity—the Tennessee Centre for Policy Research took a look at Al's energy bills.

It reckoned that his 20-room, eight-bathroom mansion in Nashville sometimes uses twice the energy in one month that the average American household gets through in a year. The combined energy and gas bills for his estate came to nearly $30,000 in 2006. Ah, say his defenders, but he uses rainwater to flush his lavatories. Is there enough rainwater in the world, I wonder?

g)* [The following, from a Letter to the Editor, the *Toronto Star* (September 1982), concerns a suggestion that noted Canadian doctor Norman Bethune should be honoured for his service to humanity. Bethune died in 1939 while assisting Communist Chinese forces in their struggle against Japanese invaders] Is it possible to honour Dr Norman Bethune as a humanitarian, despite the fact that he was a self-confessed Communist? Only a negative rejoinder is possible, for the morality of a person's acts must be judged by their consequences. Thus when Dr Bethune placed his medical skills and humanism at the service of international Communism, he unquestionably contributed to an evil ideology that has produced many mountains of corpses. When Canadians naively eulogize such a person as Dr Bethune, such praise unwittingly constitutes an endorsement of Communist ideology.

h)* [Adapted from a report on the effects of smoking on the economy, "Smoking benefits amazing," in the *Peterborough Examiner*, 10 September 1994] According to economist Jean-Pierre Vidal in a study commissioned by Imperial Tobacco, while smoking kills, those deaths have economic benefits for society. A person who dies of lung cancer at age 70 will not be hospitalized later with another disease, and the costs of hospitalization tend to increase substantially for people after the age of 70. Furthermore, wages forfeited by deceased former smokers cost neither the government nor the taxpayer, since they will not be paid for work they will not do.

i) [In spite of the accolades his documentary received, Vice-President Gore also suffered the ignominy of having a British High Court Judge find that *An Inconvenient Truth* had made "exaggerated" claims. After a BBC report on the story, the Spinwatch newsletter (www.spinwatch.org.uk) published a response (11 October 2007), an extract of which follows] As the trailers finished the BBC's Anchorman Huw Edwards said: "A controversial film on climate change being shown in British schools is heavily criticized by a high court judge for making alarmist and exaggerated claims."

The overriding theme of the piece, by the BBC's environmental analyst Roger Harrabin, was that Gore's film was flawed with nine significant errors. The judge had pointed out it was "a political film."

However what the BBC spectacularly failed to do in its programme last night was give any background to the "political" nature of the attack against the film. The BBC reported the fact the High Court case against the film was brought by Stewart Dimmock, a "school governor in Kent" who called the film a "political shockumentary."

What the BBC did not mention was Dimmock's own political connections. Dimmock is a member of the political group, the New Party. The founder and chair of the New Party is Robert Durward, whose political party is so right-wing it has been labeled "fascist" by the Scottish Tories.

More importantly, there is a cross-fertilisation between the New Party and Durward's other pet project—he is the founder of the anti-environmental

Scientific Alliance. Both the New Party and Scientific Alliance work closely with the PR company Foresight Communications.

j)   [Daniel D. Polsby, in "The false promise of gun control," *The Atlantic Monthly*, March 1994] If firearms increased violence and crime, then rates of spousal homicide would have skyrocketed, because the stock of privately owned handguns has increased rapidly since the mid-1960s. But according to an authoritative study of spousal homicide in the *American Journal of Public Health*, by James Mercey and Linda Saltzman, rates of spousal homicide in the years 1976 to 1985 fell. If firearms increase violence and crime, the crime rate should have increased throughout the 1980s, while the national stock of privately owned handguns increased by more than a million units every year of the decade. It did not.

j)   [From an advertisement in the *Saturday Evening Post*, February 2003] Discover why thousands of people with low vision have purchased the VidoEye power magnification system to continue reading and doing everyday tasks.

k)   [From Sharon Kirkey, "Docs want new vaccine for kids," *The Windsor Star*, 4 October 2010] "We think (the vaccine) is safe, it's effective, it's going to prevent severe infections and it will, we believe, save the provinces money," says Dr. Robert Bortolussi, chair of the Canadian Paediatric Society's infectious disease and immunization committee and a professor of pediatrics at Dalhousie University in Halifax.

l)   [From a Letter to the Editor, the *New York Times*, February 1987] In his Feb. 7 letter, Judge Bruce McM. Wright cites as historical fact the story of Thomas Jefferson's slave mistress, Sally Hemmings. It is simply ridiculous that this patent lie should still be seen in print. Its origin is almost as old as our Republic.

On July 14, 1798, the Federalist Congress passed the Sedition Act, which made publishing anything false or scandalous against the Government a crime. In May of 1800, James T. Callender, a Scottish immigrant and pamphleteer, went on trial in Richmond for violation of that act.

Callender was a pathetic creature, an alcoholic and hypochondriac, who never seemed able to extricate himself from debt. Jefferson had befriended him a few years earlier and had advanced him funds to enable him to continue his writing. At his trial . . . Callender was convicted and sentenced to nine months in prison and fined $200.

When Jefferson became President in 1801, he pardoned Callender. Since Callender had already completed his prison term, the effect of this was to refund his fine and clear his name. When Callender received his money three months later, he had grown bitter against Jefferson and his party for the delay and the time he had spent in prison. He decided to chastise the President and succeeded beyond even his expectations.

In September 1802 in the *Richmond Recorder*, he published the story of Sally Hemmings, the slave mistress of the President. Callender cited no support for the story, saying merely that it was "well known." He subsequently changed elements of the story repeatedly to bring them into line with the facts of Jefferson's life. Several times he changed the version of how the affair began, and the number of children supposedly produced by it. To those who knew Jefferson's high moral standards and devotion to his dead wife's memory, the story was laughable.

... I find it incredible that a story that all reputable historians, led by Jefferson's able biographer Dumas Malone, have discredited for years should still find its way into print. . . . Without the strictest accuracy, history is worthless.

m) [Adapted from a letter to the Editor, the *New York Times*, March 1982] As a true American, I wish to speak for what is near and dear to the hearts of Americans. I wish to speak against what is as foreign to these shores as communism, socialism, totalitarianism, and other foreign "ism's," except of course Americanism. I speak of the Administration's "medicare bill," better known as "socialized medicine."

Socialized medicine would commit us to the complete takeover by government of everything traditionally reserved for the individual. As the late Senator Robert A. Taft—a true American—warned, "if we are going to give medical care free to all people, why not provide them with free transportation, free housing, free food and clothing, all at the expense of the taxpayer. . . . Socialization is just a question of degree, and we cannot move much further in that direction unless we do wish a completely socialist state."

If medicare is sound, then a government-sponsored, -financed, and controlled program is sound for every aspect of our life. But this principle must be rejected. As Americans, freedom must be our watchword. And since freedom means no control, no regulation, no restraint, government programs like medicare are quite contrary to the American concept of freedom.

Unlike pseudo-Americans who want to socialize this country, I believe that socialized medicine would be an insult to true Americans. For true Americans don't want handouts. They want to stand on their own feet. They're willing to meet their obligations. They're willing to work and pay for their medical bills. As convincing proof of this, the AMA has advertised that it will give medical care to anyone who wants it, and practically no one responds to these ads.

We need only look at England to see what effects socialized medicine would have here—to see how it would lower the quality of medical care. For as Dr Lull of the AMA reminds us, the record in Great Britain shows that governmentally dominated medical systems burden doctors with red tape and paper work, thus robbing them of valuable time needed for careful diagnosis and treatment of patients. Not to mention all the freeloaders, hypochondriacs, and malingerers, who daily crowd the hospitals and doctors' offices and thus take away valuable beds and time from those who are really sick. In other words, socialized medicine is not only unnecessary but it would also be undesirable.

It should be obvious that it would not accomplish the utopia claimed for it. Indeed, what proof do we have that it would make everyone healthy overnight? Since there is no conclusive proof, we can only conclude that it would be a dismal failure.

n) [Another extract from Martin Luther King's "Letter from a Birmingham jail," defending his decision to go to Alabama where he was arrested] But more basically,

I am in Birmingham because injustice is here. Just as the prophets of the eighth century BC left their villages and carried their "thus saith the Lord" far beyond the boundaries of their home towns, and just as the Apostle Paul left his village of Tarsus and carried the gospel of Jesus Christ to the far corners of the Greco-Roman world, so am I compelled to carry the gospel of freedom beyond my own home town. Like Paul, I must constantly respond to the Macedonian call for aid.

o) The attached photograph is of a North Florida billboard posted during the 2011 House of Representatives election. It criticizes Representative Allen Boyd, a member of the "Blue Dog" coalition made up of Democratic members of the House of Representatives who identify themselves as moderates (Nancy Pelosi, the former Speaker of the House and the leader of the House Democrats at the time was very unpopular in Florida at the time). [Image retrieved from: www.lappdog.net]

A VOTE FOR CONGRESSMAN **ALLEN BOYD**   IS A VOTE FOR SPEAKER **NANCY PELOSI**

www.lappdog.net

© Doug Barkley

Illustration 12.1

p) [In 2007 a dispute arose in Britain between two cultural figures, Terry Eagleton and Martin Amis, over what Amis may or may not have said about British Muslims. The following is from a letter to the Editor, Amis wrote to the *Guardian* newspaper, 12 October 2007.]

Terry Eagleton inhabits a parallel universe of groaning and blundering factoids. His Comment piece of October 10 (Rebuking obnoxious views is not just a personality kink) begins: "In an essay called The Age of Horrorism . . . the novelist Martin Amis advocated a deliberate programme of harassing the Muslim community in Britain.". . .

I was not "advocating" anything. I was conversationally describing an urge—an urge that soon wore off. And I hereby declare that "harassing the Muslim community in Britain" would be neither moral nor efficacious. Professor Eagleton is making a habit of this kind of thing. A marooned ideologue, he has submitted to an unworthy combination of venom and sloth. Can I ask him, in a collegial spirit, to shut up about it?

q) [This is another excerpt from a Letter to the Editor, *The Globe and Mail*, 12 July 2010, referring to Margaret Somerville's article "Life's essence, bought and sold" that was part of exercise **11M**] Ms. Somerville's views are unscientific. Numerous peer-reviewed studies demonstrate that children born of anonymously donated eggs or sperm are of normal mental health—equal to the population at large. She simply ignores these studies, cites a few anecdotes, and preaches that it is "unethical" for egg and sperm donors to remain anonymous. A less idiosyncratic, more scholarly examination of the evidence leads to exactly the opposite conclusion.

For more online exercises, review questions, and quizzes related to the material in this chapter, please go to www.oupcanada.com/GoodReasoning5e

ESSAYING AN ARGUMENT

> We finish our account of critical thinking with some instructions on the writing of an extended piece of argumentation. Good critical thinkers are proficient at analyzing an argument and responding to it and at writing their own argumentative essays. To this end we will:
>
> ▶ discuss the **evaluative critique**
> ▶ **discuss the argumentative essay**
> ▶ **apply the** techniques they rely on to a student essay
> ▶ illustrate the way they can be incorporated in a revision of the essay.

In this text, we have focused on the two arms of critical thinking: assessing others' reasoning and presenting reasoning of our own. When we assess another person's argument, we should evaluate the reasoning on its own terms and decide whether we are convinced of the conclusion on the grounds of that reasoning. Although we may consider its context, we should not go beyond the reasoning or add anything to it. When we note hidden premises and assumptions, we should be simply recognizing what is already there (albeit in an implicit way).

After the evaluation, as we organize our critical remarks and *respond*, we will probably go beyond the original argument and bring in other considerations, emphasizing what the arguer has overlooked. We may suggest reasoning that would remedy problems we have found. An evaluative critique, then, is an argumentative response that incorporates both the features of our evaluation and our own insights.

The other arm of critical thinking is the construction of our own arguments. The argumentative essay captures this activity in its most extensive form. Unlike the evaluative critique, the argumentative essay need not be based on any prior evaluation or response to another's reasoning. It is the form our writing takes when we are setting down the arguments that support a position we hold, engaging in original research on a controversial issue, or conducting an inquiry to arrive at a position we will then hold, perhaps by testing a few hypotheses. In its clearest form, the argumentative essay is the first of these, although the other two will often have gone into its earlier drafts.

In this chapter, we will trace the details of both the evaluative critique and the argumentative essay before illustrating these activities by means of a critique of a student essay and then the writing of a revision of that essay.

1 The Good Evaluative Critique

When preparing for and producing a good evaluative critique, there are seven steps to consider. They are:

1. writing an *overview* of the main claim and sub-claims
2. diagramming the macro-structure and micro-structure of the argument
3. assessing the *language* of the argument
4. assessing the *reasoning* of the argument
5. weighing its strengths and weaknesses
6. deciding on your *response* to the argument
7. preparing the body of your *critique*.

In the following sections, we will consider each of these steps in turn.

1. Overview

In a brief paragraph, set down the main claim that is being put forward and the sub-arguments that are offered in support of it. Also note any specific types of reasoning that have been employed. For example:

> In his article, the author is opposing any form of gun-control law because (a) such a law is essentially undemocratic and (b) it will mean innocent members of society receive criminal records. But the bulk of his argument is given to support the contention that (c) gun control is unnecessary because there is no clear connection between guns and crime. The author employs causal reasoning in support of (c). In particular, he attempts to show that any causal claim linking gun ownership to criminal activity is fallacious.

2. Macro-Structure and Micro-Structure

Depict the structure of the argument in a diagram, showing as much detail as you think is necessary. Minimally, this will involve a diagram of the macro-structure, that is, a diagram showing how the sub-arguments relate to the main claim. It might help you to assign a number or letter to each paragraph of the text with which you are working and to refer to these numbers in your diagram. A micro-structure diagram will be more detailed and will show the supporting premises for each sub-claim.

For example, in the argument referred to in the Overview above, each letter represents a sub-argument in support of the main conclusion that "Gun-control laws are not necessary." The macro-structure of the reasoning would be depicted in a simple convergent diagram:

However, each of (a), (b), and (c) could also be depicted in a micro-structure diagram, showing how the respective sub-conclusions are supported by the premises provided for (a), (b), or (c). Since we have not developed the argument in the overview, we have no details to offer here. But you can imagine, for example, a collection of linked or convergent premises supporting (a), which becomes C1 in the micro-structure. We illustrate the value of macro- and micro-structure diagrams later in the chapter.

3. Language

Some consideration of language may have arisen in the overview if you had trouble with the meaning of the main claim or one or more of the sub-claims. A complete analysis of the extended argument will include a review of its language, even if no problems may be evident.

Watch for vagueness, ambiguity, and heavily loaded language. And be especially alert to poor definitions or the failure to provide the definition of a term that is important to the outcome of the argument. The macro- and micro-structure diagrams will help you assess the importance of terms according to where they occur in the flow of the argument.

4. Reasoning

Here is the bulk of your analysis: a complete assessment of the reasoning employed that proceeds by considering the various criteria for good reasoning explained in earlier chapters of this text. This will include a general assessment of basic criteria of acceptability, relevance, and sufficiency, as well as the specific criteria associated with deductive and non-deductive argument schemes. If the arguer employs an *ad hominem,* ensure that it meets the conditions for good instances of the scheme for *ad hominem.* When you assess the reasoning, remember that your goal is to weigh the strengths and weaknesses of the argument, not simply to detect errors. In many cases you will find that it's just as important to note that the arguer has employed arguments appropriately as it is to note that they have employed arguments fallaciously.

5. Strengths and Weaknesses

Now you have amassed all the information you require to make a decision about the argument and respond to it. Stages 5–7 concern your reaction to the argument. You will want to base your decision about the argument on a balanced appreciation of its strengths and weaknesses. Set out two columns with the headings "strengths" and "weaknesses," and list under each heading the main discoveries of your analysis. Again, the diagrams will help you determine how detrimental or positive each discovery is. For example, the irrelevance to the main claim of an entire sub-argument is far more detrimental to the overall argument than the irrelevance of just one of many premises to a sub-claim. With some arguments, you may find all or most of your entries are in one column. Such cases make for an easy decision. But most ordinary arguments, when fairly assessed, have both strengths and weaknesses that have to be weighed against each other. The weighing should be done objectively. With the most difficult and balanced of arguments, you may want to note that while you may decide one way, a colleague or fellow student evaluating the same argument might decide another way.

6. Response

Having weighed the strengths and weaknesses, you must next decide both the degree to which you are persuaded by the argument and the manner of your response to it. Stage 5 allowed for a wide range of decisions about the evaluated argument. At the one extreme, the reasoning may be so weak that no reasonable person could be persuaded by it. If the argument happened to have been for a position that you were previously inclined to support, then to continue supporting it you will need to do so on the basis of quite different reasoning. At the other extreme, the reasoning may have such logical strength that if, in your response, you intend to challenge the position it advocates, you will have to counter those strengths with further, even more compelling, argumentation.

As will be clear from the above, this is the stage of evaluation (really post-evaluation) where your prior beliefs and attitudes come into play. You cannot dismiss a strong argument just because you do not like the conclusion (or the arguer!). The process of evaluation has shown you that there can often be quite good arguments advanced in support of positions that you do not support. Coming to such realizations is part of gaining maturity as a critical thinker.

You may agree with the reasoning but not the conclusion. Perhaps the reasoning, while strong, is not strong enough to override other reasons that you have for rejecting the conclusion. Those other reasons will form the core of your response. You may agree with the conclusion but find the argumentation for it weak. Strengthening that argumentation and perhaps adding to it will form the basis of your response. Again, you may allow some of the argumentation, but not all of it, and respond accordingly. Or you may allow most of the argumentation but insist that it really supports a reworded claim. As you can see, there are many possible responses between the extremes of complete rejection and agreement. What is important is that your decision is fairly based on both the strengths and the weaknesses and that you take account of these in your critique.

7. Critique

Criticism is simply the use of critical judgement. It does not have to be negative, although it often carries that connotation. Where a written critique is required, you should write it making use of the six steps we have already discussed. Acknowledge both strengths and weaknesses. Use the weaknesses against the arguer in cases where you disagree, and look for ways to remedy or avoid weaknesses where you agree with the arguer's position. Promote the strengths and add to them where you agree, and look to counter them where you disagree. Your critique is where you develop your own extensive argument, and so this is the stage at which the evaluative critique can benefit from many of the considerations that contribute to a good argumentative essay, which we will turn to in the following section.

THE COMPONENTS OF CRITIQUE

1. overview of the main claim and sub-claims
2. macro-structure and micro-structure
3. language
4. reasoning
5. weighing strengths and weaknesses
6. decision
7. the body of the critique

EXERCISE 13A

Following the seven stages outlined in this section, write an evaluative critique for each of the following:

a) [In the following, a member of the Quebec bar responds to the decision that language (and in particular, facility in both official languages) is not a primary criterion in appointing Supreme Court judges. Letter to the Editor, to *The Globe and Mail*, 14 July 2010] There seems to be concern over the great legal minds we'd be depriving Canada of if we made reasonable fluency in French a requirement for someone to rise to the highest court in the land. What's really troubling is the lack of concern shown for the people—one quarter of this country's population—whose life will be affected by decisions made by unilingual judges.

The judicial exercise is profoundly human in nature. The fact that the interpretation of certain laws has changed over time, even though the text itself hasn't, is a strong reminder of that humanity. A person who doesn't speak a language with some fluency can't even start to appreciate the social, economic and factual context behind a case that person has to judge. I'd trade a great legal mind for another great legal mind who actually understands me.

b) [A.J. Ayer, in *Language, truth and logic*, Dover Publications, 1952] If the conclusion that a god exists is to be demonstrably certain, then these premises [from which it follows] must be certain. . . . But we know that no empirical proposition can ever be anything more than probable. It is only "a priori" propositions that are logically certain. But we cannot deduce the existence of god from an "a priori" proposition. For we know that the reason why "a priori" propositions are certain is that they are tautologies [statements that are necessarily true]. And from a set of tautologies nothing but a further tautology can be validly deduced. It follows that there is no possibility of demonstrating the existence of god.

c) [During a debate on gun control, one gun owner reacted to a report that "more guns means more suicide" with the following argument, in a Letter to the Editor, the *Peterborough Examiner*, March 1995] According to Dr Isaac Safinosky, who presented the Clarke Institute of Psychiatry paper to the American Association of Suicidology, in countries where the suicide rate is rising, control of inflation by the government is the main cause. This creates increased unemployment. As a consequence, he said, "Society becomes demoralized, so even the employed start to worry, causing people to stop buying. In recent times, inflation has been seen as the major economic threat to society. Monetarist policies have deliberately raised interest rates to cool the economy and reduce inflationary growth; the resulting loss of jobs is seen as a necessary evil in order to bring down wages and prices. Suicide increase in young persons in such countries appears to be the unfortunate concomitant of these policies."

This study points the finger directly at those people who are blaming us. The economic policies of the government . . . [are] the major cause of the rising rate of suicide.

d) [From http://anneburlinson.hubpages.com/hub/Divorce-Always-a-Bad-Thing]
Divorce: Always a bad thing? By Anne Burlinson
I'm a Catholic and I believe that any marriage is worth saving. But I'm also a pragmatic and I have even recommended a couple of friends to go ahead with their decision to divorce their partners. That is because I believe divorce is *not always* bad.

Worst case scenario for a divorce is spousal abuse. Sure, the couple can go to see a counsellor on that matter. In many cases, however, it is probably safer for the abused spouse to just leave. Here, divorce isn't such a bad thing. It might even save one's life.

Then there is the irreparable difference, unresolved by marriage counselling. When the couples don't even talk to each other anymore or can't stand each other anymore perhaps to the point of only wanting to hurt each other's feelings, divorce seems to be the best strategy.

What about children? That's the hardest factor in deciding to divorce. Children do thrive better when their parents are together. I remain, however, a little bit skeptical, especially considering the possible short- and long-term emotional and social effects on children when their parents can't stand each other anymore. Isn't it the children's right, too, to experience that their parents are happy individuals unrestrained by their marital statuses? And don't children thrive well when their parents are happy even when separated?

In sum, no, divorce is not *always* bad. There are circumstances where the benefits of divorce exceed its cost. This is, however, not an excuse to make divorce as the feasible exit strategy when things go awry in a marriage. There are ways to resolve dilemmas or problems in any marriage. It only takes courage, patience, and perseverance, and the desire to save the marriage.

e)   [From "Faith should harness art's appeal," by Jennie Hogan, www.guardian.
co.uk, July 12, 2010]
Visitor numbers at art galleries are soaring, whilst church attendance dwindles to
dangerous levels . . . Despite the centrality of faith in the art of centuries past,
religious themes within contemporary art are fading fast. At Chelsea College of
Art & Design, where I work as chaplain, God is dead. As students in their studios
aspire to join the avant garde there is only a faint desire to look back at works in
which the Christian tradition is central. . . . Could it be then that art is replacing
religion? The Tate's Turbine Hall, into which visitors flock, could be recreating
the awe and excitement that great cathedrals and churches once provided . . . .

The Reformation damaged the natural connection between art and faith but
some places are making serious attempts to heal it. . . . St Paul's Cathedral may
not attract the same numbers as Tate Modern, but the UK's most famous church
has recently been commissioning work from prominent artists. Antony Gormley
created Flare II, a shimmering, almost abstract form which revolves mysteriously
below Wren's geometric staircase. Bill Viola is creating video installations for two
altarpieces. Some commissioned works are explicitly religious but many others are
not. Clearly, the dean and chapter are keen to explore faith though art. It is refresh-
ing to see new work being created for this spectacular space. Taking up the tradition
of enabling great art to flourish in places of worship might not only get more people
through the doors but may also help to bring the two once unquestionably united
elements back together again. If the Tate is fast becoming the 21st century's monumental cathedral, why not arrange art in places where the atmosphere is already
heightened by the accumulation of centuries of prayer and reflection?

Tate Modern's success should not be dismissed as new entertainment for
the masses. The aim of art is to reveal, inspire and question. It is a tragedy that
many do not know or cannot accept that belief shares these aims. As many lose
their grasp of the narratives of God's grandeur, the church should ditch any fear
of the contemporary art scene and make a place for it in hallowed spaces. Faith
may begin to look interesting once again.

f)   [Robert T. Pennock, in Tower of Babel: The Evidence against the New Creationism,
MIT Press, 1999, p. 153] Look around today and you can see for yourself that most
of the organisms you come across are not making it into the fossil record. It takes a
rather special combination of physical factors—usually those of swamps or estuar-
ies where remains can be buried in sediment, be compacted and, if lucky, remain
undisturbed for millions of years—for the bones or imprints of an organism to achieve
a measure of immortality in stone. To then become part of the scientific body of
evidence, they have to erode in such a way as not to be destroyed, and then found
by someone who recognizes their importance. Furthermore, from what we know of
evolutionary mechanisms, speciation events are likely to occur in isolated populations, and competition will quickly eliminate the less fit of closely similar forms. Both
processes make it even more unlikely that there will be a smooth, continuous fossil
record of intermediaries. Thus, it is not at all surprising that there are "missing links"
in the fossil record, and this is not good evidence against evolutionary transmutation.

g) [Margaret Somerville, in *The Ethical Canary: Science, Society and the Human Spirit*, Penguin Books, 2000, p. 69] . . . creating multiple embryos from the same embryo damages respect for human life itself—even if it does not contravene respect for any one human individual—and for the transmission of human life. It turns a genetically unique living being of human origin into just an object and one that is replicable in multiple copies. It changes the transmission of human life from a mystery to a manufacturing process. It fails to recognize that we are not free to treat life in any way that we see fit, that we do not own life. Rather, we have life and, most importantly, life has us. Recognizing that we owe obligations to life can provide a basis on which to establish respect for life in a secular society. This recognition means that we must ask, "What must we not do because to do it would contravene respect for human life itself?" I believe that one answer to this question is the use of human embryos for human therapeutic cloning. This cloning can, therefore, be regarded as inherently wrong.

h) [Ian Wilmut, in *The Second Creation: Dolly and the Age of Biological Control*, by Ian Wilmut, Keith Campbell, and Colin Tudge. Farrar, Straus and Giroux, 2000, pp. 284–5] In the days and weeks that followed Dolly's birth, many a commentator raised this possibility [of cloning crazed dictators] as one of several "worst-case scenarios," hence the battalion of Hitlers on the cover of *Der Spiegel*. But a cloned dictator would not replicate the original any more than a cloned genius would. It has often been suggested that Hitler might have become a perfectly innocuous landscape painter if only the Vienna Academy of Fine Arts had accepted him as a student before World War I, and we might reasonably hope that the Hitler clone would be luckier in his choice of university.

A genetic nuclear clone of Hitler would not necessarily strive to create a Fourth Reich. This would be most unlikely. If he inherited his clone father's oratorical powers, he might as soon be a school-teacher—or a priest, which was one of Hitler's own boyhood ambitions. If he was fond of dogs, he might become a vet. Of course, the clone's genetic inheritance would set limits on his achievements. Richer postwar nutrition would most likely ensure that a Hitler clone would be taller than the original, but still, he would never shine at basketball, or trouble the Olympic scorers in the high jump. Unless he grew a poky mustache and smeared his hair across his forehead, few would spot the resemblance to his famous father. The Führer's cloned offspring would surely disappoint their clone pater no end.

The cartoonists' vision of an instant battalion of Hitlers is further nonsense. Clones like Dolly may be produced from adult cells, but they begin their lives as one-cell embryos and then develop at the same rate as others of their kind. Adolf Hitler was 44 years old when he became dictator of Germany and 50 at the outbreak of World War II. It would take just as long to produce the doppelgänger as it did to shape the original, and by that time the political moment that brought the first Hitler to power would be well and truly past, as indeed is the case.

2   The Good Argumentative Essay

There are five aspects of good argumentative essay writing that you should consider in constructing an extended argument of your own. They are:

1. scope
2. clarity
3. structure,
4. argumentation
5. objectivity.

1. Scope

Before you begin writing, you should have a clear idea of the thesis or claim you are advancing and the way you intend to defend it. Defining the scope of an argument is a matter of establishing manageable boundaries for your reasoning. Given the evidence that you have amassed for your sub-conclusions, what is the main claim you might reasonably be able to defend? And how can you express that claim without promising too much or so little that the argument becomes trivial?

To answer these questions, you need to have a clear idea of your intentions and your audience. You will need to have thought through the issue, looked at it from different perspectives (including the opposing viewpoint), and done as much research as your judgement tells you the situation requires.

Be clear about the context of your argument and its most important feature—your *audience*. Are you writing to reinforce the views of a *sympathetic* audience, as when you present an internal paper in a work situation? Are you writing for a *neutral* audience who is predisposed neither to agree nor to disagree but who is open to be persuaded, as when you prepare a paper for an academic jury like a course instructor? Or are you writing for a *hostile* audience of opponents that is predisposed to the opposite position to your own, as in the case of a controversial public debate on a contentious social issue? Think carefully about the audience you will be addressing and decide what information you can assume they have (that is, what will count as shared knowledge for that audience) and how their beliefs and values will lead them to react to what you say.

Given that the hostile audience is the most demanding one to write for, it should be the default audience when you are unsure who you will be addressing, as when your argument is to appear in a public forum or in future contexts that you cannot control.

With your position clear in your own mind and your audience established, you can set down your main claim. State this in an opening paragraph in which you also outline the principal sub-claims that you will advance to support it. Some people like to hold their main point until the end of their argumentative essay, keeping the audience in suspense and building to a climax. This has rhetorical effectiveness and may work for an accomplished and experienced arguer. It would not work for our purposes because it is important for our audience to know our intentions from the outset so that they can appraise the support for our position as it develops. They can only appreciate the relevance of each point as it arises and admire our arguing technique if they are aware from the outset of the claim for which we are arguing.

Given the essay form of the argumentative essay, there is a temptation to *discuss* the topic rather than argue a claim related to it. Avoid this tendency by adopting the language of argumentation in your opening paragraph. For example: "In the following I will argue . . ."; or "My conclusion is . . ."; or "The claim I intend to support is . . .".

The following are examples of introductory paragraphs that define the scope by presenting a clear conclusion and explaining how it will be supported.

> Advances in medical technology have given rise to new issues that concern society. One of these, perhaps the chief, is human-embryo experimentation. Critics insist this must not be permitted because the consequences may be too horrendous to handle. While I share such concerns, I will argue that, on balance, human-embryo experimentation should be permitted prior to the fourteenth day after fertilization. I will support this with the following sub-claims: (1) prior to the fourteenth day, the human embryo is not a person; and (2) only persons are morally significant; (3) the benefits of human-embryo experimentation far outweigh the negative aspects.
>
> *
>
> In his *Civilization and Its Discontents*, Sigmund Freud argues that humans are inherently aggressive. I wish to take issue with this viewpoint and will support the claim that humans are inherently good. To this end, I will argue (1) that Freud's conclusion is an overgeneralization based on a selective sample of cases and (2) that recent studies of children show that aggressive behaviour is learned, not innate.

On reading your introductory paragraph, no one should be in any doubt about what it is you are arguing. You are also giving notice of how your argument is going to be structured, which will aid you in your writing as much as it helps your readers.

2. Clarity

In order to communicate your intentions clearly, you need to think about *how* you are saying things as much as about what it is you are saying. What may be clear to you may not be so clear to your readers, and you should take time to consider this. In earlier chapters, we have seen how vague or illegitimately biased language can hurt an otherwise sound argument. When writing an argumentative essay, we need to be particularly careful about the way we state claims. One common problem is the tendency to overstate a claim, that is, to claim more than we can support. Often, this can be avoided simply by qualifying our statements. Consider the following pairs of claims:

A There are a number of reasons why we should not manipulate the human gene pool.

B The human gene pool should never be manipulated.

A Freud's examples are rarely convincing.

B None of Freud's examples is convincing.

A   It seems likely that wearing helmets while cycling will save lives.
B   Clearly, wearing helmets while cycling will save lives.

In each case, statement B is much stronger than statement A. But this is not a positive sense of "stronger than," because in each case a greater onus is placed on the arguer who must support statement B. It is more reasonable to expect that we can provide persuasive evidence for the qualified statements in A. When you put down a claim, ask yourself: "Can I support this, or should I modify it first?"

Another thing to consider is whether you have adequately defined the key terms you are using. Central to the arguments expressed in the introductory paragraphs on medical technology and Freud, above, are the terms "human embryo" and "aggressiveness." You have the obligation to define such terms, because it is likely that the entire extended argument will depend on how your audience understands them. Such definitions should come as early in the argument as possible, perhaps immediately after the introductory paragraph. It is possible for an otherwise clear argumentative essay to leave readers quite unsure about the central terms on which it depends.

3. Structure

A well-structured argumentative essay is an effective vehicle for the ideas it conveys. Develop your points in a logical order in terms of both strength and dependency. In other words, (1) begin with your strongest point or sub-argument; and (2) where points depend on one another, establish them in an order that shows that dependency and makes sense to the reader.

Beginning with your strongest and most plausible point will capture the reader's attention as well as his or her conviction. If you succeed in creating a solid foundation for the acceptance of your position, you can build subsequent arguments on it. Starting with your strongest point *for* your claim should not mean that your argument will weaken as it develops. Later arguments that deal with points *against* your claim, or that anticipate and meet objections to what you are saying, may be among the stronger points you will make overall, giving balance and completeness to your reasoning.

For example, in arguing that circuses are undesirable because they mistreat animals, the following claim could be advanced:

C1 =   Circuses put animals in unnatural environments and require them to do unnatural things.

Such a claim could be supported by premises that indicate the natural habitats and behaviours of circus animals and further common-knowledge premises indicating the performance-focused circus environment of such animals. But this argument depends upon a key claim that the argument assumes:

C2 =   What is natural is good, and what is unnatural is bad/undesirable.

C2 and its supporting evidence should precede C1 or at least be conjoined with it. For C2 to be introduced a page or so later, with other sub-arguments intervening, would be a structural weakness, since the flow of the argumentation would then not be sequential.

While no one would expect you to include a diagram even of the macro-structure, it is a good idea to plot this out for yourself and keep it by your side for reference while you are writing. This will allow you to take advantage of all the benefits of the diagramming technique. You will see how well your argument fits together, how easy (or hard) it is to detect the logical structure, and where support is lacking or overly dependent on one idea. If you have difficulty diagramming your own argument, you can expect someone else to have trouble seeing the connections.

4. Argumentation

Our purpose in writing an argumentative essay is to convince an audience of our conclusion, or to reinforce the conviction they already hold. If we are to succeed in this, our argument must be strong.

The bulk of this text has dealt with assessing various types of argument. At this point, therefore, we shall simply restate some of the basic principles set forth elsewhere insofar as those principles apply to the writing of the argumentative essay:

- Make sure that your premises are statements that are distinct and separate from your conclusion.
- Ensure that each premise offered in support of a claim, together with the other reasons, increases the acceptability of that claim.
- Ensure that issues are correctly recognized and directly addressed and that any version of an opposing argument has been fairly represented.
- Back your claims with as many relevant reasons as necessary to persuade your audience.
- Ensure that all your statements, including premises and conclusions, are consistent with each other.
- Do not rely on hidden components: make your assumptions explicit and defend them where necessary.

5. Objectivity

Besides communicating a sense of fairness and balanced judgement, objectivity in the argumentative essay covers two points.

These points concern the views of your opponents. We have all seen overtly one-sided arguments, where all the attention is devoted to *directly* promoting the position held. After all, you might say, the whole point has been to argue for one's position. But in many, if not most issues, there is an opposing point of view with its own considerations. An *indirect* way to further support your case is to consider some of the strongest points of your opponents and show how they can be dealt with or outweighed by your own points. This adds an atmosphere of objectivity to your argument because, if you do it fairly, it shows that you have thought about both sides of the issue and are prepared to recognize the stronger counter-claims.

Naturally, there is a danger of straw-reasoning here. You must only attribute to the opposing viewpoint arguments that you know exist on that side, and you should support that knowledge in some way. It is up to you to judge which are your opponents' stronger arguments. If you choose those that are obviously weaker and respond to them, or if you attribute to the opposing viewpoint arguments that no one actually holds, then the whole process backfires. Rather than demonstrating objectivity, your argument will appear to the discerning reader to lack objectivity altogether and to be guilty of misrepresentation.

After you have addressed the known arguments of the opposing point of view, a second way to exhibit objectivity is to consider what someone of that persuasion might say in response to what you have specifically said. That is, anticipate objections to your own points. In this way, you can demonstrate objectivity by showing that you are prepared to consider criticisms of your own ideas and that you are able to look at your arguments from a different perspective. Quite often, such a reading will enable you to detect flaws in your arguments and lead you to make constructive revisions.

Even once you are satisfied with what you have argued, you will still see places where objections might be raised. It is important to note these in your essay: "Someone might respond to this point by arguing that. . . ." You can then counter the objection with a reasonable response. Identifying likely objections—again, without making false attributions—and answering those anticipated objections will add further indirect support to your position.

THE COMPONENTS OF GOOD ARGUMENTATIVE ESSAYS

1. scope
2. clarity
3. structure
4. argumentation
5. objectivity.

EXERCISE 13B

Think about one of the following topics. Diagram the structure of a macro argument that would express your position on the topic. Next, develop this argument by elaborating micro arguments:

a) the use of attack advertisements in political campaigns
b) the existence of intelligent life elsewhere in the universe
c) the obligation of wealthier nations to help poorer nations
d) the rights of groups to receive compensation for historical wrongs
e) global warming
f) miracles
g) the importance of the United Nations in maintaining peace in the world.

3   A Student's Paper

For easy reference in discussing the following paper, each sentence is labelled with a letter, signifying the paragraph, and a digit, signifying the sentence within a given paragraph. Thus "C" identifies a particular paragraph and "C3" the third sentence in that paragraph. The issue in question is the merits and demerits of human embryonic stem cell research. This topic is hotly debated in contemporary societies. Some countries, like Canada, have only recently enacted legislation to govern part of the practice. Other countries are still debating questions before deciding how they will proceed. So there are many arguments out there on both sides of the debate.

Human Embryonic Stem Cell Research

(A1) Human embryonic stem cell research (HESCR) is quite a difficult subject. (A2) Different people have different reactions. (A3) But everyone agrees that it is important. (A4) Society should think very carefully about restricting it.

(B1) HESCR involves extracting cells from embryos at an early stage of their development. (B2) The purpose is to improve the lives of many people.

(C1) The main reason for this is that the benefits of HESCR greatly outnumber the costs. (C2) HESCR can lead to all kinds of health advantages. (C3) We can treat major illnesses, like Alzheimer's. (C4) And avoid birth defects.

(D1) We should always do what we can to promote any benefits in society. (D2) HESR is science put to good use. (D3) Medical technologies are intended to save lives. (D4) These embryos will die anyway.

(E1) Another reason to support this is that no persons will be harmed. (E2) Persons have consciousness and talk. (E3) Embryos are not persons.

(F1) People opposed to HESCR do so for one reason. (F2) They wrongly believe its advantages can be better got with adult stem cells. (F3) This is a bad analogy between two different kinds of things. (F4) Adult stem cells are not the answer. (F5) Also, embryos are already available. (F6) Doesn't it make sense to not waste what is there?

(G1) The costs of diseases like Alzheimer's are increasing as more people age. (G2) Society cannot afford to carry increased costs. (G3) The economic argument for HESCR is strong.

(H1) In conclusion, there are no good reasons to restrict human embryonic stem cell research. (H2) When sensible people think, about it they agree and their opinion should count.

Critique

There are several positive things that can be said about this paper. The main claim is relatively clear: embryonic stem cell research should not be restricted. Some attempt is made in paragraph B to define the key idea. Furthermore, the writer has organized the essay neatly around several sub-points, devoting a brief paragraph to each. Also, an attempt is made in paragraph F to deal with the position of those who oppose human embryonic stem cell research. Nevertheless, there is room for improvement on each feature of a good argumentative essay, as a detailed evaluation will indicate.

Overview

In this essay, the writer argues that there are good reasons in favour of human embryonic stem cell research and that society should permit it. To this end, the arguer claims (a) that there are important benefits to society from human embryonic stem cell research and that (b) this overrides any ethical costs that might be associated with the technology. Also, (c) using adult stem cells is not a better option. Finally, (d) there are economic costs to consider that human embryonic stem cell research can help address.

The arguer uses a disanalogy in paragraph F. In addressing the possible use of adult stem cells, the writer implies that these are not sufficiently analogous to embryonic cells for the purposes involved.

Structure

We can represent this argument with both the macro- and micro-structure diagrams. Doing so reveals which statements and paragraphs contribute directly to the argument and which do not. We will approach the structure paragraph by paragraph.

Paragraph A *should* have the main conclusion in it. If so, A4 is the only clear candidate. The first two statements report in a general way facts about the issue. A3, depending on its meaning, seems to undermine the need for real argumentation since, if everyone did agree, the matter would not be controversial. A4, on the other hand, is a claim that could, and should, be argued. We will come back to it when we look at paragraph H.

Paragraph B is definitional. It attempts to clarify the key concept. We will consider this under "language."

Paragraph C is the first clear sub-argument. C1 gives the main reason for "this," which is presumably the main claim. Human embryonic stem cell research has benefits that exceed the costs, because it can lead to health advantages (C2). C3 and C4 then give some of the advantages at issue. So the micro diagram of paragraph C can be read as follows:

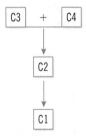

There are two things to note about paragraph D. First, it contains unsupported independent assertions. These are crucial claims to the outcome of the argument, especially D4. Second, D1 has been presupposed by C1. D1 asserts the *general* claim that we should always act to promote any benefits. C1 asserts the *specific* claim that human embryonic stem cell research has benefits. If D1 is accepted, then it serves as support for C1. So, in terms of the argument's structure, D1 is logically prior to C1 and should have been presented (together with an attempt to establish it) before C1. The micro-structure of paragraph D simply consists of D1 leading in the direction of C1, and D2, D3, and D4 giving separate support to the main claim.

The three statements of paragraph E deal with the question of whether embryos are persons. E1 asserts that persons will not be harmed, with the other two statements combined to support this.

Paragraph F deals with an opposing argument that adult stem cells are a better option for research. F4 asserts the author's denial of this. The reason for this denial lies apparently in the author's view that the opposing viewpoint depends on a bad analogy (F2 and F3). F5 shifts attention to the ready availability of embryos for stem cell research, with support for this hidden in the rhetorical question of F6. The micro diagram of paragraph F reads as follows:

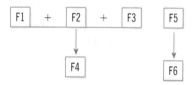

Paragraph G introduces a consideration of the economic cost to society of not using embryonic stem cells. G3 expresses the author's claim, while G1 and G2 combine as support for it:

In paragraph H, we are brought back to the question of the main conclusion. H1 expresses a very strong claim that there are no good reasons to restrict human embryonic stem cell research. From reading through the whole argument, it seems wise to understand the main conclusion as a hidden one, to the effect that "Human embryonic stem cell research should be permitted." There is no question that the student is arguing for this, although nowhere is it expressly stated. Such a hidden main conclusion captures the sentiment of both A4 and H1. But it also weakens the effect of H1. If we take H1 as the main conclusion, much of the reasoning will not support it. In fact, we will invoke the principle of charity again here and see H1 as the conclusion to only the first argument in paragraph F. This is because H1 asserts there are, in conclusion, no good reasons *against* human embryonic stem cell research and paragraph F had allowed only one reason for people opposing it.

On the other hand, H2 relates to the earlier statement in A3 in that the writer sees popular opinion supporting the use of human embryos. H2, unlike A3, is expressed as if it is intended as support for the main conclusion: "their opinion should count."

If we understand paragraph H this way, we arrive at the macro-structure of the argument:

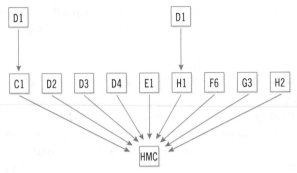

Language

You should have already noted several problems with the language in this argument. We had difficulty identifying the main claim. There are also several statements that are vague, which can be understood only by relying on their context. Even A4 that we saw contributing to the hidden main claim could be read to say that society *should* restrict this kind of research, which is the opposite of what we have taken the main point to be. It is the context that has clarified matters for us.

While most of the language is neutral in its tone, the reference to "sensible" people in H2 introduces an unnecessary bias. The assumption here is that sensible people will agree with the author.

The definition in paragraph B, while lacking in detail, is adequate to the student's purpose. It illustrates how "human embryonic stem cell research" is to be understood with respect to the concerns raised here. It is not a technical definition and would not suffice in other contexts, but it is important that some attempt has been made to explain the key term. The same positive judgement cannot be extended to another important definition—that of "person" in E2. This is quite inadequate as a definition of the concept in question, and is open to serious counter-argument in terms of other characteristic that might better capture the meaning of "person," some of which might be extended to the embryo. At the very least, what E2 provides is only a partial definition of a concept important to this debate.

We had to interpret C1 as referring to the main conclusion, as presenting the arguer's main reason for the overall position. Here we used the context to resolve the question of vagueness surrounding "this" and its referent.

One other thing worth mentioning concerns F6. This involves a rhetorical question that masks an assertion. Including F6 as a sub-conclusion involves recognizing that assertion. As a practice, the use of rhetorical questions should be avoided because the audience may miss entirely the statement that is being made.

Reasoning

We will look first at the macro-structure of the argument and consider the sub-arguments as the need arises.

We have taken the hidden main conclusion to be that human embryonic stem cell research should be permitted. Most of the claims given in support of this are relevant to it. If the benefits to society are as substantial as claimed, then C1 and the linked premises D2–D4 increase our reasons for holding the HMC. Likewise, if embryos are not persons then this removes one concern we might have, and E4 can be judged relevant. H1 certainly increases the case for the HMC, if there are no good reasons for restricting human embryonic stem cell research. Again, F6, G3, and H2 all provide relevant considerations for the HMC. Thus, the argument exhibits the general strength of internal relevance of its sub-claims to the HMC.

Where serious concerns arise is when we start to consider whether those claims are acceptable in themselves or adequately supported. Some of these are difficult to decide about. Many people would accept D1 as expressing a part of the shared values of many audiences. But if we assume a hostile audience for this argument, then both C1 and D1 could be questioned, at least to the extent of requiring further reasons for accepting them. Someone who believes strongly in the sanctity of embryonic life may not accept C1, or even D1, and such beliefs can fairly be attributed to the hostile audience for this argument. Given this, it would be wise for the arguer to address the sanctity question as involving a cost that trumps any other benefits.

D3 is another statement with which many would agree: this is a goal of much medical technology. But *is* this science put to good use, as D2 asserts? This would seem to be the very thing that is at issue here, and so D2 may be seen to beg the question. Even a sympathetic audience should be bothered by this. D4 is also unacceptable as it stands, requiring some explanatory argumentation that indicates the source of the embryos to be used and what happens to these embryos otherwise.

The sub-argument for E1 introduces the controversial topic of harm. Given the limited nature of the definition of "person" in E2, and the straight assertion of E3, this is an entire sub-argument that fails to meet its dialectical obligations. Opponents might equally offer definitions of "person" according to which an embryo would qualify. The reasons provided in the premises are relevant to E1, but both E2 and E3 are questionable.

The sub-argument leading to H1 is also a concern. H1 claims there are no good reasons to restrict human embryonic stem cell research. If correct, it provides very strong evidence for the HMC. But only one reason against the research has been considered. While F4 is relevant to H1, it is not sufficient for it, in part because H1 is worded so strongly. The acceptability of F1 becomes important to this sub-argument. We have no reason to accept that there is only one reason for opposing human embryonic stem cell research, and any exposure to the issue will have told us that this is not the case. In fact, in our consideration of C1 and D1, as well as E2 and E3, we have already recognized at least one other. So F1 is contradicted by what we know, and thus it is unacceptable. The one reason given is the disanalogy argument suggested by F3. But the arguer has failed to give any evaluation of the suggested bad analogy or supported the disanalogy. F2 and F3, while relevant to F4, do not provide sufficient support for it, and so F4 cannot be accepted. This renders ineffective an important sub-argument and reveals the arguer's appearance of objectivity to be quite the opposite.

The author expresses in F6 a belief that it is better not to waste embryos where possible. F5 provides relevant support for this. But again, F5 itself needs to be clarified.

G3, while a very controversial reason, does stand up to scrutiny. G1 reports a common state of affairs, and G2 expresses a value that even a hostile audience is likely to share. Together they provide adequate support for G3. But G3 will be subject to a serious counter-argument just because it is controversial to weigh such costs against embryonic lives.

H2, on the other hand, stands alone. Like A3, it purports to express a general sentiment. But the assertion that "most people" support the idea of human embryonic stem cell research requires the backing of a recognized poll or survey before we will have reason to accept it.

The final thing to note here, under the condition of sufficiency, is that the arguer fails to anticipate objections to the claims and assumptions being made here. Chief among these is the strength of the potential objection about personhood or, more limited, the human nature of the embryo. That is, to what degree does membership in the human family give an entity some special status, one that might justify protection against competing claims? There may well be great potential benefits to be derived from research on embryonic cells, but if it comes at a cost of harm to what we understand as human, then the cost may be too high. This is an objection that deserves to be anticipated, as any research on the topic would indicate. This would be a likely place for a critic to begin to develop a counter-argument.

Strengths and Weaknesses

We might summarize the strengths and weaknesses of the paper as follows:

Strengths	Weaknesses
• good internal relevance of sub-claims to HMC	• a number of points of vagueness and an inadequate definition
• attempts to define key term	• key sub-argument E is questionable
• acceptable sub-argument G3	• sub-argument F for H1 is unacceptable
	• sub-argument to F6 is questionable
	• H2 requires statistical support
	• insufficient evidence for HMC

On balance, we can see that there are reasons to reject this argument as it stands. This is not due to the longer list of weaknesses but to the more detrimental nature of some of those weaknesses. In spite of being characterized by strong internal relevance, the argument has too many claims that cannot be accepted or whose acceptability cannot be determined. The appearance of objectivity is lost owing to the inadequacy of the sub-argument to H1. On examination, we see that the arguer has not really considered what is at stake in the opposing viewpoint. The problematic nature of these claims, together with that of F6, means that there is not sufficient evidence for the HMC, and the argument is unpersuasive.

Many of these flaws, however, are of a kind that might be remedied. While the sub-argument H1 rests on the misconception in F1 and would have to be replaced or substantially rewritten, the sub-arguments to C1 (and D1), F6, and H2 could all conceivably be strengthened.

In the light of this critique, the student's draft clearly needs a good deal of polishing. Taking note of our comments, we will rework the argumentative essay we have been analyzing. We are not suggesting that what follows is how the student would rewrite the essay. This is our rewriting of the argument, and in many respects it is more than would be expected in an introductory course on argument. But we also have an obligation to discharge: having critiqued the paper, we submit our own version, which we invite you to critique. Usually, a rewrite like this would pass through several drafts. In this case, you will see only the final draft, but in your own revisions you should be aware that rewriting is a progressive job that may require a number of revisions. In proposing the following revision, we must also emphasize that other possible versions could successfully amend the draft with which we began.

Revision

Human Embryonic Stem Cell Research

In 2004, The Canadian Parliament enacted the Assisted Human Reproduction Act (AHRA),[1] controlling activities involving reproductive technologies and requiring them to be licensed. While the AHRA covers the derivation of embryonic stem cell lines, it does not cover their secondary use, and a debate over this issue continues. It is prohibited to produce in vitro embryos for any purpose other than the development of a human being. But the process produces embryo numbers surplus to this end, and so the question remains what might ethically be done with those surplus embryos? Do we have an obligation to use them for the good of society if embryonic stem cell research can offer such benefits?

We hold that we do have such an obligation and therefore we should use human embryonic stem cells in research aimed at alleviating diseases that afflict many members of our society. We will argue (a) that human embryonic stem cell research (HESCR) offers benefits to members of society suffering from diseases, and also to future members insofar as it may provide the knowledge to eliminate many birth defects, and on these terms there is a moral obligation to provide such benefits; (b) that the embryo does not have any status relevant to prohibiting this research: it is not a person, nor is it a member of the human family in any way that counts; and finally (c) that the alternative of adult stem cells that is proposed by many opponents of HESCR is not able to provide the benefits that HESCR promises.

By "human embryonic stem cell research" we are referring to a set of procedures using early embryos made surplus by in vitro fertilization practices (and not embryos produced solely with the intent of research), and where these embryos are at a stage of development prior to 14 days and the onset of the "primitive streak."

(a)

The principal reason for conducting HESCR is the enormous benefits it promises for society. Where there is the possibility—even likelihood—of significant breakthroughs in the treatment of major diseases, then we have an obligation to support such research in the absence of any countervailing concern of equal or greater weight. That is the case here. The list of diseases that might be addressed through this research include Parkinson's, Alzheimer's, spinal cord injuries, diseases involving damage to internal organs, and even some types of cancer.[2] These diseases affect large numbers of people and come at a significant cost to society, both in monetary and psychological terms. HESCR can also be directed to improving our understanding of the ways in which early embryos develop, in order to reverse problems and prevent certain birth defects.

These benefits come at the "cost" of destroying some embryos that are surplus to the needs of fertilization. The practice has been to freeze the embryos for future use by the "parents," but far too many embryos are produced than could be used for this purpose. Instead of allowing these embryos to deteriorate, we can employ them in research that promises to benefit others. And given the extent of those benefits, we should do so. As long as the "parents" of those embryos give non-coerced permission for their use, there is nothing that should prevent their use.

(b)

The arguments above could be seen to assume that the human embryo does not have a moral status equal to those who would benefit from the research, and we need to address this more explicitly. There are many ways in which we might understand "persons." Most of these involve some set of capacities. These might be as rudimentary as being aware of one's environment, or as complex as projecting oneself into the future and organizing one's actions to bring about that future. Language, reasoning, and so forth, are also said to be involved. It is clear that an early embryo does not possess any of these capacities. Thus, on these terms it could not be an actual person. And insofar as an early embryo can still divide in the twining process, it is difficult to see how it could even be judged *a* potential person.

We should also consider whether the early embryo is a member of the human family. This language introduces images that fuel the emotions often seen in this debate. Families are important to us. But what can it mean for an early embryo to belong to such a family? This vagueness needs to be addressed. Insofar as an embryo is not a person, its status reduces to its composition. It is comprised of human material. In fact, the cells of the early embryo, due to their totipotent nature, can divide and become any parts of a later human. On these terms, the embryo "belongs" to what is human as much as any related material does, including, for example, the placenta that is destroyed after birth. We do treat human materials with respect, as we see in the practices regulating the disposal of the dead. But we can continue to treat embryos with respect—recognizing the contribution being made to human good—while still conducting the research in question.

Moreover, at this stage in their development these embryos cannot suffer. In Canada, the limit placed on the use of human embryos is far short of the 14-day limit introduced in other jurisdictions.[3] That higher limit is the point at which the "primitive streak" appears. This develops into the spinal column and is needed for any pain to be experienced. Entities that have not developed to this point cannot suffer.

(c)

Opponents to HESCR (and there are many of them[4]) insist that the destruction of human embryos is unnecessary because the same benefits might be achieved by using adult stem cells. But there are several reasons for not preferring this alternative. Embryonic stem cells are easier to isolate and grow *ex vivo* than adult stem cell. And embryonic stem cells have greater plasticity, allowing them to be used in the treatment of a wider range of diseases. Moreover, adult stem cells can contain DNA abnormalities caused by toxins and sunlight, thus making them poorly suited for most treatments. And when adult stem cells are intended for treatment of the donor, then genetic disorders in that donor can render the treatments ineffective. There may well be some uses to which adult stem cells could be put, and research should continue in this area. But the early promise claimed for them has not been converted into concrete achievements, and embryonic stem cells continue to have the greater application and to promise the wider benefits.

In conclusion, there are several strong reasons for using human embryonic stem cells in research aimed at alleviating diseases that afflict many members of our society. Polls indicate wide public support for such research, at least in some countries.[5] Some people remain concerned about the morality of using early embryos in research, but we should be more struck by the consequences of not doing so. When we have the opportunity to do so much good, it would be wrong not to proceed.

Notes

1   Details of the AHRA can be found at www.ahrc-pac.gc.ca.

2   Snow, N.E. (2005). Ed. *Stem Cell Research*. Notre Dame, IN: University of Notre Dame Press;
    Bagley, R.G. & B.A. Teicher (2009). Eds. *Stem Cells and Cancer*. New York: Humana Press.

3   This was the limit introduced by British legislation that has influenced other jurisdictions and the
    debates elsewhere, including Germany. The British legislation followed recommendations from the
    "Warnock Report" (*Report of the Committee of Enquiry into Human Fertilisation and Embryology*,
    London, 1984). See also, Glover, J. (1989) *Fertility & the Family: The Glover Report on Reproductive
    Technologies to the European Commission*. London: Fourth Estate.

4   See Somerville, M. (2000). *The Ethical Canary: Science, Society and the Human Spirit*. Toronto:
    Penguin Books Canada; and Spaemann, R. (2006) *Persons: The Difference between "Someone" and
    "Something."* Oxford: Oxford University Press.

5   A 2007 poll reported by Angus Reid found 61 per cent of Americans supporting HESCR (www.
    angus-reid.com/polls).

4   Conclusion

Human embryonic stem cell research is a highly controversial and often divisive issue, but it is just the kind of issue that demands clear, critical thinking. We hope you will recognize the benefits of the skills we have discussed throughout this text when you work on issues such as this. Since this is a topic that raises many complex issues, we recognize that good arguments can be constructed for a point of view that opposes the one that has been advocated in our rewrite. It is the interaction between these opposing arguments that, in the long run, is most likely to bring a reasonable resolution to this debate.

Good reasoning is not, however, limited to our thinking about difficult issues. It permeates all corners of our lives, clarifying our ideas and enriching our experiences. We wish you the best in your own encounters with arguments, both those you construct and those you evaluate. We hope you will continue to build on the skills discussed here—something that can be accomplished through practice—and that you will value your development as a critical thinker. Good reasoning is often difficult, but it always matters!

5   Summary

This final chapter in our account of good reasoning draws on all that has gone before in identifying the elements that should go into a good argumentative critique and a good argumentative essay. Our principal interest here is the argumentative essay, which we construct after a full evaluation has been made of the argumentation on an issue or in an argumentative exchange. The components of a good argumentative essay include scope; clarity; structure; argumentation; and objectivity. We recall what we have said earlier about each of these and discuss how they can be used together to construct good arguments. We illustrate the account with two essays, one from a student, and a revision of our own, on the topic of Human Embryonic Stem Cell Research.

MAJOR EXERCISE 13M

1. Diagram our revised essay, and write an evaluative critique of it.

2. Research and write an evaluative essay that supports the opposite position to that argued in the revision.

3. Select a topic from the list below, or propose a controversial topic for approval by your instructor. Research it and reflect on it, and then write an argumentative essay (about four double-spaced pages in length, or 1,000 words). Assume a universal audience.

   a) gun control, in the wake of a recent mass killing (such as that in Norway, July 2011)
   b) therapeutic cloning
   c) banks' obligations to compensate for losses in the recent financial crisis
   d) the morality of zoos
   e) United Nations' peacekeeping
   f) affirmative action for men in job categories where they are under-represented (social work, nursing, primary school teaching)
   g) genetically modified food
   h) DNA testing in criminal cases
   i) universal medicare
   j) immigration policies
   k) Canada's legalization of same-sex marriage

 For more online exercises, review questions, and quizzes related to the material in this chapter, please go to www.oupcanada.com/GoodReasoning5e

SYLLOGISMS: CLASSIFYING ARGUMENTS

Chapter 3 distinguished between the acceptability of an argument's premises and its validity. This chapter continues that discussion of deductive validity for those interested in the subject. Some deductive arguments make claims about different categories, others about the relationships that exist between propositions. This appendix discusses the first kind of deductive validity and the corresponding kind of argument: the categorical syllogism. The focus is on the reasoning involved in such schemes, not the acceptability of the premises. Here, we present:

▶ categorical statements
▶ immediate inferences
▶ categorical arguments
▶ tests for validity using Venn diagrams.

This appendix discusses categorical reasoning, which encompasses deductive arguments about classes. We will make no attempt to address such reasoning in the complex ways that characterize contemporary formal logic. That is a topic for a different kind of text. Our goal is more modest but also more pertinent to an understanding of ordinary-language reasoning.

To help you understand and evaluate the arguments about classes that occur within such reasoning, we will introduce you to categorical syllogisms, to the argument schemes that characterize them, and to some useful ways in which you can diagram and judge (deductive) validity in such arguments.

Consider the following statements:

All wars are very expensive. All very expensive enterprises put a strain on the economy.

If someone sees these two statements, they are likely to bring them together and draw the conclusion that "All wars put a strain on the economy." Many advertisers depend on this kind of reasoning when planning their campaigns. An advertisement is more effective if potential customers can be expected to see the hidden conclusion and draw it out for themselves.

Consider the following slogan:

> Domino's Pizza gets there sooner, and anything that gets there sooner has to be better.

This can be recast as:

> All Domino's Pizzas are things that get there sooner.
> All things that get there sooner have to be better.

From these two statements, the advertiser expects us to draw the hidden conclusion "All Domino's Pizzas are things that have to be better." The amount of money invested in such advertising demonstrates the extent to which advertisers trust us to draw such conclusions. In the process, they demonstrate their trust in the deductive process.

You may have noticed that each of our examples includes, when the hidden components are recognized, three statements, and each statement expresses a relationship between two categories or classes of things. "Domino's Pizzas" constitute a class of things, as do "things that get there sooner." All **categorical syllogisms** express relationships between three classes of things. The statements in such arguments are called **categorical statements**. In the next section, we will examine the various types of categorical statements that can make up syllogisms. Later, we will explore the syllogism itself and ways it can be tested for validity. We will introduce a simple method for testing deductive validity by means of **Venn diagrams**.

1   Categorical Statements

Categorical statements are subject-predicate statements expressing relationships between classes of things. In the statement "All crows are black," "crows" is the subject and "blackness" is the predicate that is applied to the subject. Categorical statements always include a *subject class* (crows) and a *predicate class* (black things). The subjects and predicates are always expressed as classes of things. This is particularly important to remember about the predicate class, because it may not be expressed in a way that makes this obvious. In the statement "Domino's Pizza gets there sooner," "Domino's Pizza" is the subject class. Since "gets there sooner" cannot be described as a class, we express the predicate class as "*things* that get there sooner."

Pure Forms

There are four distinct types of categorical statement. We will consider the **pure form** of each and then consider some of their common variations in ordinary language. In presenting the pure forms, we will use the letter "S" to represent the subject class of any categorical statement and the letter "P" to represent the predicate class. We can then formulate the four types of categorical statement as follows:

1. **All S are P.** We call this a universal affirmative statement, or **UA**, since it affirms something about all members of S. In a **UA** statement, the *entire* membership of the subject class is *included within* the predicate class. "All police officers are public servants" is a **UA** statement.

2. **No S are P.** We call this a universal negative statement, or **UN**, since it denies something about all members of S. In a **UN** statement, the *entire* membership of the subject class is *excluded from* the predicate class. "No children are senators" is a **UN** statement.

3. **Some S are P.** We call this a particular affirmative statement, or **PA**, since it affirms something about only a portion of the membership of S. In a **PA** statement, at least one member of the subject class is *included within* the predicate class. "Some animals are carnivores" is a **PA** statement.

4. **Some S are not P.** We call this a particular negative statement, or **PN**, since it denies something about only a portion of the membership of S. In a **PN** statement, at least one member of the subject class is *excluded from* the predicate class. "Some people are not actors" is a **PN** statement.

These are the four "pure forms" of categorical statements. All statements expressing class relationships are logically equivalent to one or another of these forms. Hereafter we shall refer to the four forms by the letters **UA**, **UN**, **PA**, and **PN**. When interpreting these forms, there are three points that you should keep in mind. First, we must be careful to distinguish between the statement that *excludes* some S from the class of P and the statement that *includes* some S within the class of non-P. Thus, "Some S are not P" is read as a **PN** statement, while "Some S are non-P" is read as a **PA** statement. "Some penguins are not monogamous" is read as a **PN** statement, while "Some penguins are non-monogamous" is read as a **PA** statement.

Second, persons, things, and places designated by proper names, such as the President, Space Shuttle Atlantis, and Belgium, as well as defined groups such as "these cows," or "the players on the field at the moment," or "that bus" (said while pointing to a bus) should all be interpreted as referring to an entire class. Statements in which they are subjects will, therefore, be expressed as universal statements. If you think about it, this makes sense, for proper names are names of classes with only one member and statements with limited phrases denoting the subject term are intended to be universal. Thus "Belgium is a member of the European Economic Union" is a **UA** statement, and "No players on the field at the moment are Native Americans" is a **UN** statement.

Finally, note that a **UN** statement is *not* properly expressed as "All S are not P," because such a statement is ambiguous. It could mean that "*all* S are *excluded* from the class of P," in which case no S are P. On the other hand, it could mean that it is *not* the case that *all* S are *included* in the class of P, in which case some S are not P. Consider the statement "All TV evangelists are not frauds." Does the speaker mean that *all* TV evangelists are excluded from the class of frauds? Or does the speaker exclude only some TV evangelists from the class of frauds? The first alternative would be expressed as the **UN** statement "No TV evangelists are frauds." The second interpretation is the **PN** statement "Some TV evangelists are not frauds."

Since you should be charitable and not attribute to a writer a stronger claim than may have been intended, you should interpret statements of the "All S are not P" variety as **PN** statements unless you know that the classes of things denoted by S and P are logically exclusive. "All triangles are not four-sided figures" is an instance of this exception. It must be interpreted as a **UN** statement because we know that no triangle can, by definition, be a four-sided figure.

Common Variations

We have already seen some of the variations that express categorical relationships. Here are some (but only some) further variations of the pure forms:

UA (Universal Affirmative)
All astronauts are intelligent people.

- Astronauts are intelligent.
- Every astronaut is an intelligent person.
- Anyone who is an astronaut must be intelligent.
- None but intelligent people are astronauts.
- Only intelligent people are astronauts.
- No astronauts are unintelligent people.

UN (Universal Negative)
No astronauts are cowards.

- No one who is an astronaut can be a coward.
- No cowards are astronauts.
- No one who is a coward can be an astronaut.
- All cowards are non-astronauts.
- If X is an astronaut, X is not a coward.

PA (Particular Affirmative)
Some women are priests.

- At least one woman is a priest.
- Most women are priests.
- A few women are priests.
- There are some women who are priests.
- Several women are priests.
- Some women are not non-priests.

PN (Particular Negative)
Some women are not priests.

- Many women are not priests.
- Most women are not priests.

- Few women are priests.
- All women are not priests.
- Not all women are priests.

These variations do not exhaust all the possibilities. In dealing with particular propositions, it is also important to recognize that though we read "many," "few," and "most" as meaning "some," the reverse is not the case. If you have a proposition referring to "some x," you cannot assume that it means "many" or "most" unless the context indicates as much. In syllogistic reasoning, "one," "few," "many," and "most" are treated as equivalent to "some." A more powerful logic might distinguish between these "quantifiers," but that would require a more sophisticated treatment of categories than the one that we are introducing here.

As you read through the next sections of this chapter, you will see how some of the more peculiar variations are equivalent to the pure forms. When you must decide which pure form you have, ask yourself what relationship between classes is intended. Is the intent of the statement to include or exclude? Is it referring to the entire subject class or only a portion of it? Rather than trying to decide what form a statement is, it is often helpful to eliminate the forms that it is not until you arrive at the form that it must be.

One error that is so common that it should be noted here involves statements that begin with "Only." There is a temptation to render "Only intelligent people are astronauts" as "All intelligent people are astronauts." This is wrong. While the statement involved is a **UA** statement, the effect of the "only" is to reverse the classes, giving us "All astronauts are intelligent people." To see that this must be so, consider that *only* students at your institution go to the lectures you go to (there are *similar* lectures elsewhere but not the *same* lectures with the same instructor, etc.); however, it would be quite wrong to say that *all* students at your institution are going to the lectures you go to. What can be said is that all students attending these lectures are students at your institution.

Until you become practised at recognizing pure forms, you might want to employ the following three-step process for arriving at them. Take the statement "Busy people are never at home when you want them."

Step 1: Determine the classes involved.
["Busy people"] are never [at home when you want them = "people who are at home when you want them"].

Step 2: Determine whether the statement is affirming (including) or negating (excluding).
"Busy people" are *never* = excluded from "people who are at home when you want them."

Step 3: Determine whether the statement is universal or particular.
No "Busy people" are "People who are at home when you want them." **UN**

EXERCISE   **A1**

Classify the following statements as **UA, UN, PA**, or **PN**, and express each in its "pure form." Be sure to express both the subject and predicate terms as classes with members.

> **EXAMPLE**: A few scientists deny global warming.
> Step 1:   A few [scientists] [deny global warming = deniers of global warming].
> Step 2:   A few scientists are deniers of global warming.
> Step 3:   Some scientists are deniers of global warming. **PA**

a)* Most dentists have a six-digit income.

b)* Dinosaurs are extinct.

c)* Most people are not prepared to pay higher taxes.

d) No one who has paid attention should be confused.

e) None of my sons is greedy.

f) Laws are made to be broken.

g)* Only the lonely know the way I feel tonight.

h) A few students in this class wish they weren't.

i) There are some extremely wealthy people who pay no income tax.

j) Many wealthy people do not pay income tax.

k) People who live in glass houses shouldn't throw stones.

l) Stephen is far from being fastidious.

m)* New York is in New York.

n)* None but the courageous will survive.

o) People should be prohibited from using cell phones while operating a motor vehicle.

p) Many children of planned pregnancies turn out to be battered children.

q) The vast majority of murders are crimes of passion.

r) All that glitters is not gold.

s) A few students own Volvos.

t) Those who support the North American Free Trade Agreement (NAFTA) see it as a recipe for economic prosperity.

u)* Under no circumstances should the courts deal leniently with people who drive vehicles while inebriated.

v) Several renowned physicists are religious mystics.

w)* Those cars parked on the street whose permits have expired will be towed away.

x) Lotteries breed avarice.

y) Whatever will be will be.

z) Some logicians are not mathematicians.

2   Immediate Inferences

In learning to understand the pure forms, it helps to appreciate the basic relationships between them. You will have to rely on such an understanding when preparing some syllogisms for testing. The relationships between the four forms are usually called immediate inferences. This does not mean that they are immediately obvious to everyone but that no "mediate" (i.e. middle, or in-between) term is involved.

In syllogistic logic, the following is the traditional "square of opposition":

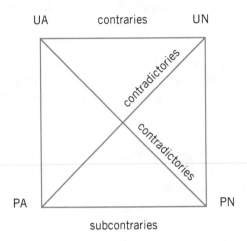

This square allows us to ascertain quickly what must be the case when various kinds of categorical statements are accepted as true or false.

From the square, we can see that the **UA** and **UN** statements are contraries. This means that they cannot both be true but can both be false and would both be false whenever **PA** and **PN** are both true. The **PA** and **PN** statements are, on the other hand, "subcontraries" and *cannot* both be false, though they are both true whenever the corresponding **UA** and **UN** statements are both false. In addition, the **UA** statement implies the corresponding **PA** statement, and a **UN** statement implies the corresponding **PN** statement. In contrast, one cannot infer either the **UA** from the **PA** nor the **UN** from the **PN**.

In identifying these and other relationships between different kinds of categorical statements, the square of opposition helps define a variety of deductively valid argument schemes. In saying that a **UA** statement implies a **PA** statement, we are, for example, saying that the following argument scheme is deductively valid (i.e. that the conclusion must be true if the premise is true):

UA, therefore **PA**.

More generally, we might define this scheme as:

All S are P. Therefore, some S are P.

This scheme indicates that anyone who accepts the premise "All S are P" must accept the conclusion "Some S are P." An instance of this scheme is the following argument:

All the readers of this page are learning syllogistic logic.
Therefore, some readers of this page are learning syllogistic logic.

If you substitute other classes for S and P in our definition of the argument scheme, you will see that this scheme defines an indefinite number of deductively valid categorical

arguments. We will not formally define all the argument schemes implied by the traditional square of opposition, but you should be able to recognize a variety of schemes
that it legitimates.

Contradiction

Another immediate inference you can expect to apply to categorical syllogisms is that
of *contradiction.*

Contradiction tells you what statement must be true if a given statement is false
and what statement must be false if a given statement is true. Two statements are "contradictories" if they cannot both be true and cannot both be false, but one of them
must be true and the other false.

You might initially suppose that the contradictory of a **UA** statement is a **UN** statement, but we have already seen that they are contraries rather than contradictories
because it is possible for them both to be false. If you examine the square of opposition,
you will see that a relationship of contradiction exists not between **UA** and **UN** but
between **UA** and **PN**, and **UN** and **PA**.

When it is true that "All astronauts are intelligent," it must be false that "Some astronauts are not intelligent." The corresponding argument scheme could be defined as:

> **UA**, therefore not **PN**

Or, more generally, as:

> All S are P. Therefore it is not true that some S are not P.

Likewise, contradiction tells us that if we accept that "Some astronauts are not intelligent," then we must accept that "All astronauts are intelligent" is false. The same
relationship holds between **UN** and **PA** statements. When we accept it as true that "No
astronauts are cowards," then we must accept that it is false that "Some astronauts are
cowards." And if we accept that "Some astronauts are cowards," then we must accept
that "No astronauts are cowards" is false.

Obversion

A further immediate inference is called obversion. Since a syllogism has three statements expressing relationships between only three classes of things or terms, then the
existence of more than three terms means that we do not have a syllogism that can
be tested. But sometimes what looks like more than three terms may be reducible to
three because the additional terms are alternatives for one or more of the other terms.
Obversion is the tool we use to make such reductions. This works when the additional
terms are complementaries of one or more of the other terms. The class of "dogs"
has as its complementary class "non-dogs." If "dogs" is the subject class S, then the
complementary class is written as "non-S." Everything in the world can be divided
into its class and complementary class: "presidents" and "non-presidents," "things that
are amusing," and "things that are non-amusing" etc. Because we often speak loosely

in ordinary language, we may be prepared to take liberties and translate, for example, "dull people" and "interesting people" as complementary classes (though strictly speaking, the complementary class of "dull people" is "non-dull people").

We have already seen that "No astronauts are non-intelligent" is a common variation of "All astronauts are intelligent." This is because each is the obverse of the other. They mean the same thing; when we obvert a statement we do not change its meaning. To obvert, you need to:

1. Change the statement from negative to affirmative or from affirmative to negative. That is, if it is a **UA**, make it a **UN**, and vice versa; if it is a **PA**, make it a **PN**, and vice versa.
2. Replace the predicate term with its complement.

For each of the pure forms, obversion works as follows:

	Given		*Obverse*
UA	All S are P.	**UN**	No S are non-P.
UN	No S are P.	**UA**	All S are non-P.
PA	Some S are P.	**PN**	Some S are not non-P.
PN	Some S are not P.	**PA**	Some S are non-P.

Conversion

Conversion allows you to switch the position of the S and P terms. In fact, that is how you convert: exchange the position of the S and P.

But conversion is possible only with **UN** and **PA** statements. The converses of **UA** and **PN** statements are not logically equivalent. The **UN** statement converts easily because both classes are being excluded from *each other*. Conversion in this case can be expressed as the argument scheme:

No S are P. Therefore, no P are S.

If we accept "No astronauts are cowards," it follows that we must also accept that "No cowards are astronauts." Likewise, if we accept that "Some women are priests," then the converse, "Some priests are women," is something we must also accept.

The **UA** statement does not convert in this way. While "All astronauts are intelligent" may be the case, we would not want to say "All intelligent people are astronauts." However, the reversal of the terms is possible in a *limited* sense. That is, if we accept that "All astronauts are intelligent," we must accept that "Some intelligent people are astronauts." So the converse of a **UA** statement is a **PA** statement.

No such qualification is possible with **PN** statements. While "Some animals are not dogs" is true, we cannot accept the converse, "Some dogs are not animals." The converse of the **PN** statement is not its logical equivalent. In other words, the **PN** does not convert.

Conversion works as follows:

	Given		Converse
UA	All S are P.	**PA**	Some P are S (by limitation).
UN	No S are P.	**UN**	No P are S.
PA	Some S are P.	**PA**	Some P are S.
PN	Some S are not P.	**X**	(i.e. no conversion is possible.)

Contraposition

A final immediate inference is contraposition. With conversion, the original and the modified statements are logically equivalent in the cases of **UN** and **PA** statements. With contraposition, it is with the **UA** and **PN** statements that this is the case. This is so because contraposition is the result of obverting, then converting, and then obverting once again.

The result of these operations for each of the four forms can be shown as follows:

Given	Obverse	Converse of obverse	Obverse of converted obverse (contrapositive)
UA	**UN**	**UN**	**UA**
All S are P.	No S are non-P.	No non-P are S.	All non-P are non-S.
UN	**UA**	**PA**	**PN**
No S are P.	All S are non-P.	Some non-P are S.	Some non-P are not non-S.
PA	**PN**	—	—
Some S are P.	Some S are not non-P.	—	—
PN	**PA**	**PA**	**PN**
Some S are not P.	Some S are non-P.	Some non-P are S.	Some non-P are not non-S.

The **PA** cannot be contraposed because its obverse, a **PN** statement, cannot be converted. The **UN** statement is subject to contraposition with limitation, since its obverse is a **UA** statement that, upon conversion, becomes a **PA**. While contrapositives strike many people as cumbersome, reflection will show you that "All non-intelligent people are non-astronauts" is simply an alternative, if unusual, way of saying that "All astronauts are intelligent."

EXERCISE   A2

1. Define all the argument schemes that are justified by conversion. For each of the schemes defined, give three sample arguments that are instances of each scheme. (Show how the sample arguments are instances of the scheme by indicating the substitutions for S and P required in each case.) For three of the sample arguments you give, show how they could be expressed in a manner that is not a direct use of the pure forms of categorical statements.

2. Provide at least two immediate inferences for each of the following:

> **EXAMPLE:** Some farmers are subsidized.
> 1. Some subsidized people are farmers.
> 2. It is false that no farmers are subsidized people.

a)* Only ticket holders will be admitted.
b)* Many New Yorkers vacation in Florida.
c)   No non-famous people are listed in *Who's Who.*
d)   Some areas of North America are not populated.
e)   It is not true that all hard workers are successful people.
f)   Not all play areas are supervised.
g)* Many donors to the club are non-users.
h)   No non-citizens are refused legal assistance.
i)   The Meadowlake circus is unpopular with animal lovers.
j)   It is false to say that some illegal acts are moral.
k)   If you haven't paid your fees, you cannot attend class.

3   Categorical Syllogisms

A categorical syllogism consists of three and only three categorical statements that relate three (and only three) classes of things. More precisely, a categorical syllogism is an argument consisting of three categorical statements related in such a way that two of them, having one class-term in common, entail a third categorical statement relating the other two class-terms.

This may seem a convoluted definition, but it is not difficult to understand what it means in practice. Consider one of our earlier syllogisms:

> All wars are very expensive. Very expensive enterprises put a strain on the economy. Therefore, all wars put a strain on the economy.

Each statement is a **UA** statement. The first two are the premises of the argument; the last one is the conclusion. These three statements relate three classes of things, namely: "wars," "very expensive enterprises," and "enterprises that put a strain on the economy." Each of these classes appears twice in the syllogism. Each of the classes in the conclusion ("wars," "enterprises that put a strain on the economy") appears in a different premise. The remaining class ("very expensive enterprises") appears once in each premise. Depending on the particular positions the classes occupy in a syllogism, the syllogism will be deductively valid or invalid.

Up to this point, we have used S and P to represent the subject and predicate terms for categorical statements. Now we will restrict the use of S and P to the terms that function as the subject and predicate of the conclusion of the syllogism, and we will introduce a third symbol, M, to represent the third class:

S =   subject of the conclusion
P =   predicate of the conclusion
M =   class common to both premises, or "middle" term

Consistent with this convention, we would identify S, P, and M in the above syllogism as follows:

S =   wars
P =   enterprises that put a strain on the economy
M =   very expensive enterprises

This identification of the meanings of S, P, and M we call the *legend*. Note again that each symbol represents a *class* of things and is always expressed in those terms.

The syllogism with which we are working can now be shown to have the following "symbolic scheme," where the line beneath the second premise separates the premises from the conclusion:

All S are M		S **UA** M
All M are P	or	M **UA** P
All S are P		S **UA** P

Preparing Syllogisms for Testing

The question whether a syllogism is *deductively valid* is a question about its *structure*. We are interested in whether the conclusion follows necessarily from the premises. At this stage, we will not worry whether the premises are acceptable (and will, in this way, ignore the first criterion for strong arguments). This in part explains why you may see quite bizarre examples offered as instances of deductively valid syllogisms. The following is a case in point:

All dogs are highly educated creatures. All highly educated creatures enjoy synchronized swimming. Therefore, all dogs enjoy synchronized swimming.

These statements are ridiculous, but as they are represented here, they constitute a deductively valid syllogism. Indeed, this argument has exactly the same *scheme* as the previous argument about "wars," "enterprises that put a strain on the economy," and "very expensive enterprises." That is, it is also of the form:

All S are M
All M are P

All S are P

We have already seen that the conclusion of a deductively valid argument follows necessarily from the premises. We would be committed to a contradictory position if we accepted the premises but rejected the conclusion. But deductive validity must not be confused with premise acceptability. They are quite separate concepts. Here, our concern is the difference between syllogistic arguments that are deductively valid and those that are invalid. In such a context, you must try not to be distracted by questions about the acceptability of an argument's premises. Translating the syllogisms into their "symbolic schema" will help us to concentrate solely on validity.

In preparing to test syllogisms for deductive validity, we need to (1) identify the types of categorical statements included in the syllogism; (2) define S, P, and M in a legend; and then (3) diagram the argument in the manner we have already noted. It is important to begin with the conclusion of the argument, because S and P can be identified by assigning them to the terms of the conclusion. The middle term, M, can *never* appear in the conclusion.

Consider an example:

> The use of physical discipline towards children is known to encourage aggressive tendencies. Aggressive behaviour results in difficulty for the child later in life. Therefore, physical discipline is not good for children. (*Child Development*, 2nd edition, 1991)

As you gain more experience working with syllogisms, you will be increasingly able to recognize examples like this as arguments that relate classes of things. Since we are dealing with ordinary language, we need to make decisions about different phrases and terms that can be interpreted as equivalent. One might compare these decisions to the kinds of decisions we make in diagramming many ordinary arguments that are expressed unclearly. In this particular argument, the conclusion is easily identified by the indicator "therefore." It is followed by the statement "physical discipline is not good for children."

This tells us that the conclusion relates two classes of things: "acts of physical discipline" and "things that are good for children." We can see that it does so by *excluding* the classes from each other. So the conclusion is either a **UN** or a **PN** statement. Since there is no qualifier to suggest that only some acts of physical discipline are intended, we interpret it as a **UN**. In its categorical form, the conclusion reads: "No acts of physical discipline are things that are good for children." Once we recognize this, we can assign S and P to the subject and predicate of this conclusion:

S =   acts of physical discipline
P =   things that are good for children

The middle term, M, is the term that both premises have in common. To recognize it, we need to determine the premises and cast them in their categorical form. The first of the two remaining statements clearly includes the S term. It tells us that acts of physical discipline (towards children) are things that encourage aggressive tendencies. "Things that encourage aggressive tendencies" is, then, a candidate for our M class. To decide on this, we would have to interpret the remaining sentence ("Aggressive behaviour results in difficulty for the child later in life") as one that relates the potential M class with P. Assuming that experiencing difficulty in later life is not good for children, we can interpret the ordinary-language statement in the argument as "No things that encourage aggressive tendencies are things that are good for children."

This confirms our hypothesis that:

M = things that encourage aggressive behaviour

Now that we have a full legend and understand the terms of the argument, we can rewrite it in categorical form as:

All acts of physical discipline are things that encourage aggressive behaviour. No things that encourage aggressive behaviour are things that are good for children. Therefore, no acts of physical discipline are things that are good for children.

All S are M
No M are P
_____
No S are P

If we had been unsure how to phrase the second premise, we could have derived it as the hidden premise required to get from the first premise to the conclusion. Having cast the argument in its categorical form, you can use the legend to check that it now has the same meaning as the original formulation.

Any syllogism can be translated into categorical form following this procedure. The critical step is the initial one of identifying the conclusion and thereby defining S and P.

EXERCISE   A3

Prepare the following syllogisms for testing, identifying S, P, and M:

EXAMPLE: All members of the United Nations are expected to meet their obligations with respect to peacekeeping. Since the United States is a member of the United Nations, it must therefore meet its peacekeeping obligation.

All members of the United Nations are nations expected to meet their peacekeeping obligations. The United States is a member of the United Nations. Therefore: The United States is a nation expected to meet its peacekeeping obligations.

S = the United States
P = nations expected to meet their peacekeeping obligations
M = members of the United Nations

All M are P
All S are M
_____
All S are P

a) Nobody with a history of heart disease should take up jogging, because jogging is a strenuous form of exercise, and no one with a history of heart disease should engage in strenuous forms of exercise.

b) Some professional clowns have personality disorders, and some people with personality disorders are deeply depressed. So some professional clowns are deeply depressed.

c)* For a vegetable to be considered fresh, it must have been harvested within the last 48 hours. These beans were picked just last night. So they should certainly be considered fresh.

d) Only healthy people can join the army, and so people suffering from debilitating illnesses cannot join the army, since they are not healthy.

e) Some polls have been skewed by unrepresentative samples. But any poll like that cannot be trusted. So some polls are untrustworthy.

f) Get-rich-quick schemes that exploit the gullible are unpopular. But some of them actually work. So, some things that actually work are not popular.

4   Venn Diagrams

We now turn our attention to tests for determining deductive validity or invalidity. Remember that if the syllogism is a deductively valid one, the truth of the premises will guarantee the truth of the conclusion. Consider again our earlier syllogism:

All wars are very expensive enterprises. All very expensive enterprises are enterprises that put a strain on the economy. Therefore, all wars are enterprises that put a strain on the economy.

We can see that if every member of the class of wars belongs to the class of very expensive enterprises (Premise 1) and every member of the class of very expensive enterprises belongs to the class of enterprises that put a strain on the economy (Premise 2), then it *must* be the case that every member of the class of wars belongs to the class of enterprises that put a strain on the economy, which is what the conclusion tells us. In short, we can see that this is a deductively valid syllogism. Accepting the premises and denying the conclusion will put us in a contradictory position.

To recognize validity is easy with simple arguments, but there are some arguments that seem deductively valid when they are invalid. Consider the next example:

All people who oppose the trade bill are people with conservative values. Smith has conservative values. Therefore, Smith opposes the trade bill.

This argument has a superficial appeal to it; it seems right (even more so if we substitute for Smith the name of a well-known conservative). But as we will see when we test the argument, the conclusion is not guaranteed by the premises and could be rejected by someone who accepted the premises. When it comes to validity and invalidity, we want more than just ways to recognize it: we want to have ways to explain it, ways to make it clear to an audience (which might simply be ourselves).

A more exacting method of testing syllogisms visually portrays the structure of categorical statements. This method is called Venn diagramming, named after the British logician John Venn. Most of the syllogisms you encounter can be tested using this method.

Venn diagrams use circles to depict the relationships between the classes of things represented by S, P, and M. Each circle represents one of these classes. The intersecting, or overlapping, parts of the circles represent the individuals the classes have in common. We shade those portions of circles that our statements tell us are "empty." If our statement tells us that "no sheep are investment bankers," then the overlapping part of two circles, representing "sheep" and "investment bankers," is considered empty and is therefore shaded. When we are told that some members of a class either are or are not members of another class, we use X to represent this on the diagram. If our statement is "some sheep are investment bankers," we place an X in the overlapping part of our two circles. These points can be illustrated by using two circles to depict each of the four pure forms of categorical statement.

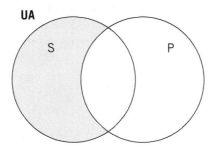

All S are P, so we shade all the circle representing S that is not included in P. This indicates that any portion of S outside of P is "empty," i.e. that there is nothing in the class of S that is not also a part of the class of P. This is what the UA statement tells us.

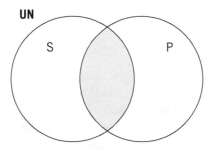

No S are P, so we shade the intersection between the circles representing S and P to show that this area is empty because there is nothing that is both an S and a P.

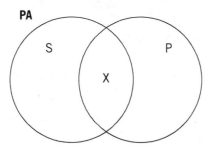

Some S are P, so we put an **X** in the intersection between the circles representing S and P to show that at least one member of the class of S is also P.

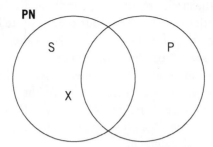

Some S are not P, so we put an **X** in the area of the circle representing S that does not intersect the circle representing P to show that at least one member of S is not P.

A Venn diagram has three circles representing the three classes involved in the syllogism.

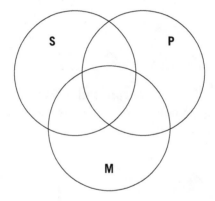

The statements of the syllogism tell us how the classes stand in relation to each other, and as we represent these statements on the three-circle diagram, we can look to see whether the premises guarantee the conclusion. In the case of a deductively valid syllogism, once the premises have been represented on the diagram, the conclusion should be *already there*. This is because the conclusion of a deductively valid argument is so strongly implied by the premises that it must, in effect, be accepted as soon as one accepts these premises. This is what a Venn diagram illustrating a deductively valid argument shows. The test for deductive validity using Venn diagrams is expressed as follows: if, after representing the premises, the conclusion is already represented on the diagram, then the argument is *deductively valid*; if the conclusion is not already represented, the argument is *deductively invalid*.

We will begin illustrating this by confirming our judgment of an earlier argument:

All wars are very expensive enterprises. All very expensive enterprises are enterprises that put a strain on the economy. Therefore, all wars are enterprises that put a strain on the economy.

This argument has the legend:	and the scheme:
S = wars	All S are M
P = enterprises that put a strain on the economy	All M are P
M = very expensive enterprises	All S are P

Each is a **UA** statement, so this is a relatively straightforward example:

P1 is represented.
All S are M.

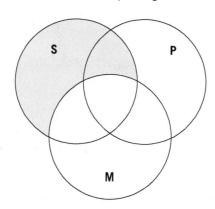

P2 is represented.
All M are P.

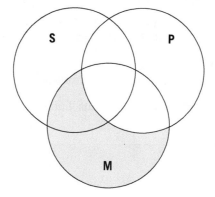

C is represented.
All S are P.

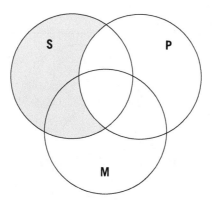

Next, we put P1 and P2 together on a Venn diagram:

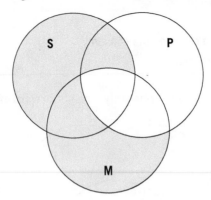

Now, as our test, we look to see whether the conclusion, "All S are P," is also represented on this diagram. And it is. The area of S that is outside of P is completely shaded, indicating that it is empty and that, indeed, "All S are P." It does not matter that other parts of the diagram are shaded; this shows that there was more information in the premises than in the conclusion. What is important is that the conclusion is contained within the premises, and so, if the premises are correct, the conclusion must also be true. So this syllogism is a *deductively valid* argument. It has a deductively valid scheme or structure, and *any* syllogism of the same scheme will also be deductively valid.

Now we will consider the second example, which is another relatively simple syllogism:

All people who oppose the trade bill are people with conservative values. Smith has conservative values. Smith opposes the trade bill.

This is another argument with all **UA** statements, but its scheme is different from that of the previous syllogism:

Legend	Scheme
S = Smith	All P are M
P = people who oppose the trade bill	All S are M
M = people with conservative values	All S are P

P1
All P are M.

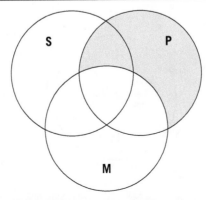

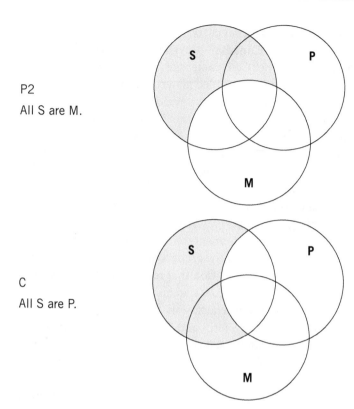

P2
All S are M.

C
All S are P.

We put P1 and P2 together on a Venn diagram:

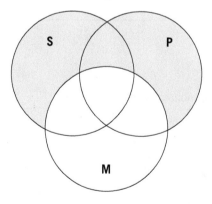

This time, we find the conclusion, "All S are P," is not already represented on the diagram. The area where S and M intersect, which is outside of P, should be shaded, but it is not. This means that one can accept the premises and not accept the conclusion and, therefore, the conclusion does not follow necessarily from the premises. It follows that the syllogism is *deductively invalid*.

Having shown simple examples of a deductively valid and a deductively invalid syllogism, we can turn to more complex examples. The following example comes from the Conservative Party of Canada and concerns one of their so-called "attack ads" against the then leader of the Liberal opposition party, Stéphane Dion. The advertisement in question, "Not a leader," ran on Canadian television in January of 2007 and could be found on the Conservative Party of Canada website (www.conservative.ca [visited 27 January 2007]). The Conservatives drew video material from an earlier Liberal Party convention at which Dion was chosen as leader over close rival Michael Ignatieff. Part of the video shows Ignatieff challenging Dion for not "getting it done" when the party had been the government and Dion had been one of its ministers. Dion responds, "Do you think it's easy to make priorities?" The advertisement concludes, "Leaders set priorities. Leaders get things done. Stéphane Dion is not a leader."

The advertisement makes several claims about leaders. In fact, the term or class arises in each of the three statements. So we will need to make some adjustment to identify three terms here. The main claim excludes Stéphane Dion from the class of leaders. It is a **UN** statement. The other two statements tell us what leaders do: they set priorities and get things done. Without altering the arguers' meaning, we can reasonably recast these statements into a single proposition that reads: "Leaders are people who get things done and set priorities." This is a **UA** statement.

Our procedure requires us to begin with the conclusion, and this gives us "Stéphane Dion," a class with only one member, as the S term and "leaders" as the P term. The premise we have relates the P term with what must then be our middle term: "people who get things done and set priorities." The hidden premise would need to relate the S and M terms, and from the context of the video, with the exchange between Dion and Ignatieff, we can see exactly how this is intended: "Stéphane Dion is not a person who gets things done and sets priorities." This is another **UN** statement. Testing this syllogism will tell us whether the writers connected their terms wisely.

Legend	Scheme
S = Stéphane Dion	All P are M
P = leaders	No S are M
M = people who get things done and set priorities	No S are P

P1
All P are M

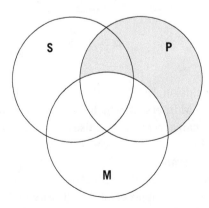

P2
No S are M.

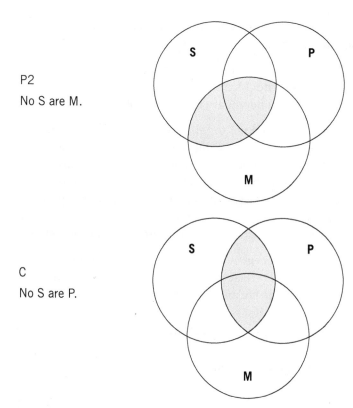

C
No S are P.

We put P1 and P2 together in a Venn diagram:

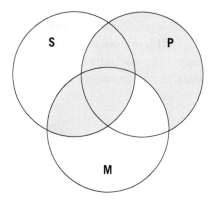

If the syllogism is deductively valid, the conclusion ("No S are P") will already be on the diagram. And it is. The entire area in which S and P intersect is shaded, showing it to be an empty class. As a deductively valid argument, it satisfies one of our two criteria for strong arguments. Of course, a final decision on whether this is a good argument will depend on the acceptability of the premises, particularly how we define "leader."

The next example is taken from an article in *The Globe and Mail* (17 March 1987, p. A1). The article reported on the rejection of public-service AIDS announcements by a committee that screens commercials for private broadcasters in Canada. The committee's reasoning included the following:

> Most (3 out of 4) public-service AIDS announcements urging the use of condoms condone casual sex. Therefore: Most (3 out of 4) public-service AIDS announcements urging the use of condoms are not acceptable for broadcast.

Since these statements refer to "most" and not to "all," we can identify them as particular statements. The first statement (a premise) includes some public-service AIDS announcements within the class of announcements that condone casual sex. It is a **PA** statement. The conclusion, identified by the indicator "therefore," excludes those announcements from the class of announcements suitable for broadcasting. It is a **PN** statement. With this example, we will proceed first to assign S, P, and M (we have enough information to do so) and then decide on how to express the hidden premise.

> Some public-service AIDS announcements urging the use of condoms are announcements condoning casual sex. Therefore: Some public-service announcements urging the use of condoms are not announcements acceptable for broadcast.

Legend	Scheme
S = public-service AIDS announcements urging the use of condoms	
P = announcements acceptable for broadcast	Some S are M
M = announcements condoning casual sex	Some S are not P

The hidden premise must involve a relationship between M and P. What does someone using the expressed reasoning in this argument believe about M and P? It seems likely that they believe the two classes to be mutually exclusive of each other. No announcements acceptable for broadcast are announcements condoning casual sex, and vice versa. Either way, it is a **UN** statement:

No M are P *or* No P are M.
(Does it make a difference which way we write this?)

P1
No M are P.

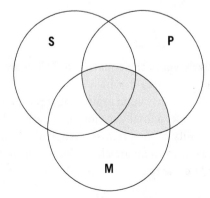

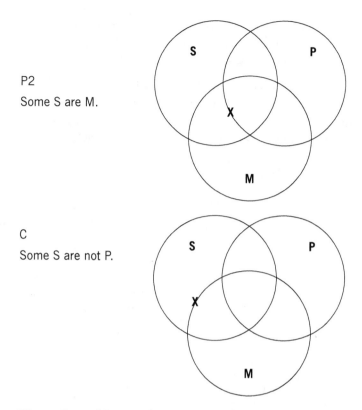

P2
Some S are M.

C
Some S are not P.

We put P1 and P2 together in a Venn diagram. Notice that when we have a statement that is universal and one that is particular, we always put the universal statement on the diagram first. This is because we often have a choice as to where to place the **X** of a particular statement. If we show the universal statement first, then its shaded area tells us where any **X** cannot go and thus where it must go.

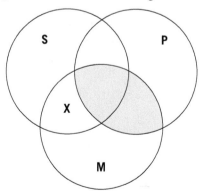

Is there an **X** anywhere in S outside of P, as the conclusion requires? Yes, there is. The argument is valid (as would be the case if we had rendered P1, "No M are P," as its converse, "No P are M").

One further example should suffice in illustrating the complexities of the Venn diagram method of testing:

Some medical professionals are not supporters of euthanasia, and some supporters of euthanasia are liberals. From this it follows that it is false to say that all medical professionals are liberals.

"It follows that . . ." introduces the conclusion from which we may identify S and P, and M is the class common to the two premises. The conclusion tells us that a **UA** statement ("All medical professionals are liberals") is false. If this is the case, its contradictory statement must be true, and the contradictory of a **UA** statement is a **PN** statement. Now our syllogism is revealed as comprising three particular statements, and we can proceed to the legend and to setting out its form.

Some medical professionals are not supporters of euthanasia. Some supporters of euthanasia are liberals. Therefore: Some medical professionals are not liberals.

Legend	Scheme
S = medical professionals	Some S are not M
P = liberals	Some M are P
M =supporters of euthanasia	Some S are not P

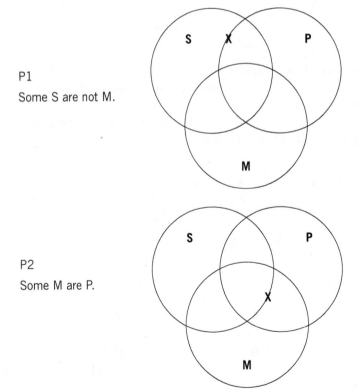

P1
Some S are not M.

P2
Some M are P.

C
Some S are not P.

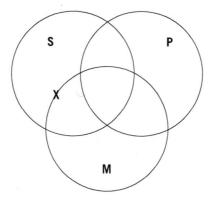

We put P1 and P2 together in a Venn diagram:

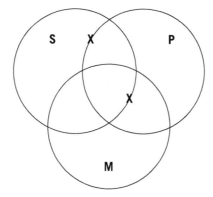

Since there are no universal premises, there are no empty (shaded) areas. So we do not know whether the **X** of P1 should go in the areas of S outside or inside of P. Consequently, we put it on the line. Likewise with P2, we do not know whether the M that is a P is also S, so we put it on the line. Now, for the argument to be valid there should be an **X** in the area of S that is outside of P. But we cannot be sure of this: the **X** is on the line. Thus, this syllogism is invalid because the premises do not guarantee the conclusion. One can accept the premises without accepting the conclusion.

This example shows one of the drawbacks of the Venn diagram method. It has worked well with our other examples, but the possibility of error arises when we are unsure where to place the **X** for particular statements. What we have provided in this appendix is sufficient to introduce the syllogism and equip you for most everyday arguments that involve relationships between classes of things.

MAJOR EXERCISE **AM**

1.   For each of the following syllogisms:
   i)   identify S, P, and M in a legend;
   ii)   provide its scheme; and
   iii) determine its validity using the Venn diagram method.

EXAMPLE: You will agree that all husbands are married and that no wives are husbands. Surely it follows that no wives are married.

Legend	Scheme
S = wives	All M are P
P = married people	No S are M
M = husbands	No S are P

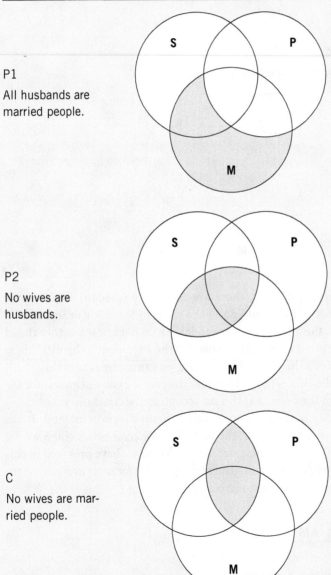

P1
All husbands are married people.

P2
No wives are husbands.

C
No wives are married people.

We put P1 and P2 together in a Venn diagram:

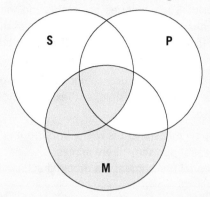

The intersection between S and P is not completely shaded. Therefore, the conclusion is not contained in the premises, and this argument is invalid.

a)*   Some cats aren't pests, but all cats are pets, so no pets are pests.

b)*   All buildings over 50 feet tall are in violation of the new city bylaw, and the bank building is over 50 feet tall. Therefore, it is in violation of the bylaw.

c)   No one who fails this course can major in psychology, and all psychology majors are assured a good career, so no one who fails this course is assured a good career.

d)   Only courses that involve disciplined thought provide good training for law. And since most philosophy courses involve disciplined thought, they must provide a good training for law.

e)   All women are mortal. Hypatia is a woman. Therefore, Hypatia is mortal.

f)   Some habits are not harmful, and some vices are not habits, so some vices are not harmful.

g)   From measuring the footprints, we are convinced that the murderer is a man who wears size nine shoes. That description fits Jim, so he must be the murderer.

h)   It is simply not true, as many people suppose, that all professors of political science are socialists. I am convinced of this because, first, it is false to say that no political science professors are money-grubbers, and, second, it is certainly true that no socialists are money-grubbers.

i)   No courteous people are rumour-mongers, and all discourteous people lack friends. Clearly it must be the case that no rumour-mongers have friends.

j)   Not all people who are irrational are illogical, since nobody who is illogical is confused, but many irrational people are confused.

k)   To make love is to engage in battle! This must be true because it takes two to stage a fight, and it also takes two to make love.

l)   Your ideas are immaterial. But whatever is immaterial does not matter. Therefore, your ideas do not matter.

m)   [From http://skepdic.com/pseudosc.html (visited 5 December 2004)] Some pseudo-scientific theories are based upon an authoritative text rather than observation or empirical investigation. Creationists, for example, make observations only to confirm infallible dogmas, not to discover the truth about the natural world. Such theories are static and lead to no new scientific discoveries or enhancement of our understanding of the natural world.

n) [Adapted from Ian Wilmut's *After Dolly*, 2006] Embryos don't have parents. Children have parents, and embryos are not children.

2. Wherever possible, supply the hidden component that would make the following syllogisms complete or valid if possible, and exhibit validity (or invalidity) by the Venn diagram method.

> **EXAMPLE:** Capital punishment is wrong because it is itself a crime.
> All acts of capital punishment are crimes.
> All acts of capital punishment are wrongful acts.

Legend	Scheme
S = acts of capital punishment	[. . .]
P = wrongful acts	All S are M
M = crimes	All S are P

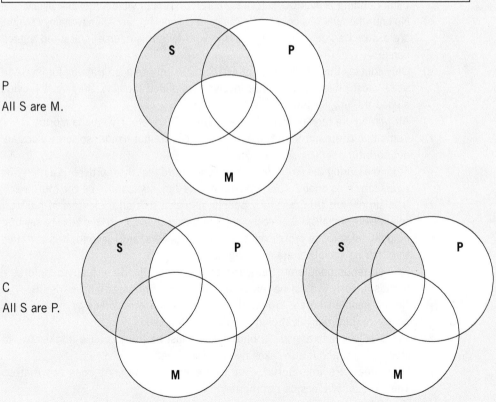

P
All S are M.

C
All S are P.

For the conclusion to be contained in the diagram (indicating validity), all of S outside of P must be shaded. The hidden premise must express a relationship between M and P, and the only possible statement that would fit these two requirements is: All M are P.

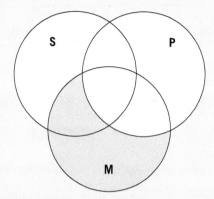

a)* No person who values integrity will go into politics, because the realities of political life force people to compromise their principles.

b) Some scientists are climate sceptics. But no one who has seriously reviewed the evidence is a climate sceptic.

c) [From *The Globe and Mail*, 12 May 1988] Most students can afford to pay more for tuition because most students make between $4000 and $6000 each summer.

d) It's not the case that all media stories are reliable, because many media reports from foreign news agencies are unreliable.

e) Some of the things parapsychologists tell us about are outlandish, because they utterly contradict the laws of nature.

f) [From The Canadian Press, 8 May 2002: A backbench MP called on the Prime Minister to declare a free vote on controversial legislation governing new reproductive and genetic technologies] "This bill touches on a moral issue, and that is, when does human life begin?" he said. "All moral votes are free votes."

g) [Adapted from *Time* magazine, 13 January 2003, p. 32] You can't conduct a reasoned debate about complex moral issues in a context that is controlled by quacks, clowns, and money. But in the case of cloning, that's what you have—quacks, clowns, and money.

h) A platypus is a mammal because the young feed on milk produced in the mother's mammary glands. It also has fur, is warm-blooded and breathes through lungs, like other mammals.

3. In each case, construct a valid syllogism by supplying premises for the following conclusions. Prove the validity of your syllogism with a Venn diagram.

    EXAMPLE: All Picasso paintings are costly.

Legend	Scheme
S = Picasso paintings	All M are P
P = costly things	All S are M
M = items prized by the world's leading art collectors	All S are P

a)* This syllogism is valid.
b)   Most trade books are not worth the paper they are printed on.
c)* No one does wrong voluntarily.
d)   Only cool-headed people will prosper.
e)   Some heavy smokers die of causes other than lung cancer.
f)   Human colonization of the outer planets is currently beyond our capabilities.
g)   All non-union members are non-employees.
h)   You will not get a better deal on a new car than at Dave's Motors.

 For more online exercises, review questions, and quizzes related to the material in this chapter, please go to www.oupcanada.com/GoodReasoning5e

PROPOSITIONAL LOGIC I

Strong arguments are valid arguments with acceptable premises. This appendix looks at cases of deductive validity, which depend on relationships expressed by words like "if," "then," "and," "or," and "not." In the process we:

▶ introduce propositional logic
▶ distinguish the different kinds of propositions these arguments contain
▶ demonstrate a way to represent the logical structure of propositions
▶ provide examples of simple propositional arguments
▶ present a way to prove that a propositional argument is valid.

In this and the following appendix, we introduce "propositional logic," though we make no attempt to provide a detailed account of it. In presenting some selected aspects of propositional logic, we ignore many features of it that are of secondary interest in ordinary-language reasoning. Our goal is a modest account of propositional logic that can help you understand ordinary reasoning by introducing you to some basic argument schemes and the rigorous step-by-step arguments associated with proofs of one kind or another. If the material in these appendices piques your curiosity, we recommend a course in formal logic.

1   Simple and Complex Propositions

The method of syllogistic logic can be used to assess whether arguments that involve relations between different classes are deductively valid or invalid. Here, we introduce other methods that can be applied to arguments understood in terms of the relations between different propositions.

A proposition *affirms that something is the case*. Each of the following sentences presents a proposition:

• Nuclear war is the most disastrous calamity imaginable.
• It will continue to snow for the next 24 hours.

- The mail has been delivered.
- I will report your actions to the Dean.
- Zeus and Hera head the Olympian family of gods.
- Kellogg's is committed to providing foods of outstanding quality.
- You were reading her email last night.

The propositions expressed by these sentences can be expressed in other ways as well. The proposition "It will continue to snow for the next 24 hours" might be expressed as the sentence "The snow will continue until this time tomorrow." In some contexts, one might make fine distinctions between sentences that have slightly different meanings, but we shall treat them as expressions of the same proposition.

Propositional arguments depend on a distinction between *complex* and *simple* (sometimes called "atomic") propositions. Complex propositions are formed by combining simple propositions with "connectives." If we combine two of the propositions we have already listed with the connective "If . . . then . . .," this may produce the complex proposition "*If* you were reading her email last night, *then* I will report your actions to the dean." This type of proposition is called a "conditional." Using the same two propositions and the connective "and," we can construct the complex proposition "You were reading her email last night, *and* I will report your actions to the dean." This kind of proposition is called a conjunction.

In analyzing syllogisms, we represented arguments in ways that allowed us to set out some of the essential features of their premises and conclusions. In dealing with propositional arguments, we can begin to illustrate the logical structure of propositions by letting lowercase letters stand for simple propositions. As an aid to your memory, you may pick a letter that you can associate with a key word or particular proposition, as in the following examples:

m = The <u>m</u>ail has been delivered.
c = You will enjoy your course in <u>c</u>ritical thinking.
n = <u>N</u>uclear war is a terrifying possibility.
h = You were reading <u>h</u>er email.
d = I'm going to report you to the <u>D</u>ean.

Definitions of this sort will form a legend we use when we represent propositional arguments in symbolic form. In order to complete our representation, we will combine our symbols for our simple propositions with symbols for our logical connectors. Using the legend above and the symbol "&" to represent conjunctions, we can, for example, represent the sentence "You were reading her email, and I'm going to report you to the dean" as h & d.

In describing propositional logic arguments (and propositional schemes of argument), we will sometimes use the capital letters X, Y, Z, W. They stand for any proposition, simple or complex. X could, for example, stand for the proposition h, or the proposition (h & d), or any of the complex propositions we will introduce. These "variables" (so called because they have a variable rather than a set meaning) will allow us to more easily define the schemes of argument that characterize valid propositional arguments.

Negations

In symbolizing the complex propositions that occur in propositional arguments, we will recognize four kinds of complex propositions and the four connectives that make them possible. A **negation** is a proposition that denies another proposition. Consider an example. The GNU Project is an attempt to develop copyright-free software for general use. Because the software it has developed (Linux systems) is Unix-like but not Unix, those working on the project coined the name "GNU," which stands for "GNU's Not Unix." The acronym GNU thus represents a negation (the proposition, "GNU is not Unix"). Like other negations, it denies another proposition, in this case the proposition "GNU is Unix."

In propositional logic, we use the "tilde," the symbol ~, to represent negations. If we let g = GNU is Unix, we can represent the negation "GNU is not Unix" as $\sim g$. For any proposition X, $\sim(X)$ is its negation, which can be read as "X is not the case" or, more simply, "Not X." If we can drop the brackets without confusion, then we will write the negation $\sim(X)$ as $\sim X$.

Negations may be expressed in many different ways in ordinary language. Former American president Richard Nixon was famous for declaring, in the midst of the Watergate affair, "I am not a crook." If we let c = Richard Nixon is a crook, then we can represent his declaration as $\sim c$. Strictly speaking, this is the proposition "Richard Nixon is not a crook." He is able to express it in a different way because he can use the personal pronoun "I" to refer to himself. One might express the same negation in a variety of other ways that include the sentences "It's not true that I'm a crook" (spoken by Richard Nixon) and "Those who say that Richard Nixon is a crook are mistaken." Typically, negations are expressed with a variety of words that include "no," "never," "nothing," "can't," "nowhere," and sometimes with the prefix "un-" (as in "She is unmotivated," which is equivalent to "She is not motivated"). Each instance of these words must be assessed in its own context, but we can generally represent them as instances of the propositional logic $\sim$.

Double Negations

You have probably heard someone complaining about the use of double negatives in ordinary language. Often, in an effort to try and emphasize the negative tone of an assertion, speakers will put an extra negative into their statements. An example of this is the statement "I *don't* need help from *nobody*." Using double negatives was considered correct in Shakespeare's time, but it is frowned upon today, especially in essay writing.

Double negatives can be confusing because the negation of a negation is an affirmation. $\sim X$ is the statement "Not X," and $\sim \sim X$ is the statement "Not Not X." If we spell it out completely, the latter proposition is the claim that "It is not the case that it is not the case that X," which is equivalent to the claim "It is the case that X." If we negate the claim ~c, where c = Richard Nixon is a crook, then the result is ~ ~c. It could be expressed as the proposition "It is not true that Richard Nixon is not a crook," but we shall instead represent it as the (equivalent) proposition "Richard Nixon is a crook."

In a fully developed system of propositional logic, the rule **double negation** allows one to move between the propositions X and ~ $\sim X$, but we will instead treat X as the negation of ~X. This is what we do in ordinary language, where we negate an affirmation by adding a negative and a negative by stating a positive. If I wish to negate your claim that "Green Day is not a talented band," for example, I do so by asserting that "Green Day *is* a talented band," not by asserting that "It is not the case that Green Day is not a talented band."

Conjunctions

Conjunctions have the form X & Y, where X and Y can be any propositions, and the symbol "&" represents the word "and." Each of the two components of a conjunction is called a "conjunct." The conjunction X & Y states that both X and Y are true. In accepting a conjunction, we accept that this is so.

When we deal with claims in ordinary language, we will treat any proposition that claims that two or more propositions are true as a conjunction. The following conjunctions are taken from the website for MapQuest, a map finder on the Web:

- MapQuest is easy to use and offers the most comprehensive coverage of the globe.
- MapQuest.com generates the majority of all Internet mapping page views, licenses its technologies to thousands of business partners and is linked to by hundreds of thousands of other websites.
- Through the MapQuest.com site and our business partners, we serve up more than 400 million maps and more than 60 million sets of driving directions every month.

The first two of these conjunctions are easy to represent. If we adopt the legend:

e = MapQuest is easy to use.
c = MapQuest offers the most comprehensive coverage of the globe.
m = MapQuest.com generates the majority of all Internet mapping page views.
l = MapQuest licenses its technologies to thousands of business partners.
w = MapQuest is linked to by hundreds of thousands of other Web sites.

then we can represent the first two of our conjunctions as e & c and m & l & w.

Our remaining example is more complex, for it contains two "ands" that must be treated differently. The first "and" is not a conjunction in the sense in which we use the term in propositional logic, for it is not an "and" that is used to conjoin two propositions (rather, it is used to link the two subjects of the proposition—MapQuest and its business partners). In contrast the second "and" does conjoin two propositions. So we can represent the sentence as s & d, where:

> s = Through the MapQuest.com site and our business partners, we serve up more than 400 million maps every month.
>
> d = Through the MapQuest.com site and our business partners, we serve up more than 60 million sets of driving directions every month.

In ordinary language, propositions may be conjoined in a variety of ways: by the use of semicolons, by the use of connector words like "but," "too," "although," and "also," or by combining their subjects or predicates. The following sentences are, for example, all instances of the conjunction a & s, where: a = Lewis Carroll wrote *Alice in Wonderland* and s = Lewis Carroll wrote *Symbolic Logic*:

- Carroll wrote *Alice in Wonderland*; Carroll wrote *Symbolic Logic*.
- Lewis Carroll wrote *Alice in Wonderland* and *Symbolic Logic*.
- Lewis Carroll wrote *Alice in Wonderland* but also *Symbolic Logic*.
- Though Carroll wrote *Alice in Wonderland*, he wrote *Symbolic Logic* too.

All of the conjuncts in the examples of conjunction we have considered thus far are simple propositions. In other cases, conjuncts may be complex propositions. The conjuncts in the conjunction a & $\sim s$ are, for example, a simple proposition (a) and a complex proposition that is a negation ($\sim s$). Using the definitions of a and s above, a & $\sim s$ can be understood as the sentence "Lewis Carroll wrote *Alice in Wonderland*, but he did not write *Symbolic Logic*."

EXERCISE   B1

1. Using the legend provided, translate the following propositional logic sentences into English:

   m = Mars is a planet we should explore.
   w = There is water on Mars.
   e = Every living thing needs water.
   s = Space is the final frontier.
   v = Venus is a planet worth exploring.

   a)* m
   b) $\sim w$
   c) s & v
   d)* $\sim(s$ & $v)$
   e) s & $\sim m$
   f) m & $\sim v$
   g) v & $\sim m$
   h) s & $\sim v$; therefore $\sim v$
   i) $\sim(m$ & $v)$; therefore $\sim m$
   j) w & $\sim s$ & $\sim m$ & $\sim v$
   k) $\sim(m$ & $v)$; v; therefore $\sim m$

2. Using the letters indicated to represent simple propositions, represent the following in propositional logic symbols:

   a) You will not become a famous writer, but you will be a published author. *f*, (*p*)
   b)* She's mistaken when she says that Lee Mun Wah didn't produce the film *The Color of Fear*. (*c*)
   c) He is not an untalented guitarist. (*t*)
   d) [Former US Vice President Al Gore, commenting on a new environmental bill in Canada, 29 April 2007] The Conservatives' new environmental platform is a complete and total fraud and is designed to mislead the Canadian people. (*n, c, t, d*)
   e) The referee didn't allow no cheating. (*r*)
   f)* You should try Shredded Wheat with cold milk and with hot milk. (*c, h*)
   g) [Judith Wallerstein, in *Mother Jones* magazine, July/August 1995] It isn't true that divorce is different for a poor child than it is for a rich child in its emotional content . . . (*d*)

2 Disjunctions and Conditionals

A **disjunction** is a complex proposition that has the form "*X or Y*." We call the component propositions, *X* and *Y*, the "disjuncts" of the disjunction. We will use the symbol *V* (called "vel") to represent disjunctions in propositional logic. For any *X* and any *Y*, the disjunction *X or Y* can be represented as *X V Y*. We understand a disjunction as the claim that at least one, and perhaps both, of its disjuncts are true. For that reason, the most precise way to understand *X V Y* in ordinary language is as the proposition that "*X and/or Y*."

The 2006 documentary film *Who Killed the Electric Car?* examines the invention, commercialization, and destruction of the battery electric vehicle in the United States in the middle 1990s. It considers a number of stakeholders who were arguably responsible for ending the promising advent of electric cars. We can represent the disjunction that underlies the film as:

a V o V u V s V b V c V h

where:

   a = Automobile manufacturers killed the electric car.
   o = The oil industry killed the electric car.
   u = The US government killed the electric car.
   s = The State of California killed the electric car.
   b = The limited range of batteries killed the electric car.
   c = Consumers killed the electric car.
   h = Alternative hydrogen cell technology killed the electric car.

In answer to the question the title of the film poses, the film considers each of these disjuncts to determine which of them are true.

In ordinary language, we often indicate a disjunction by inserting "or" or a series of "ors" in the subject or predicate portion of a sentence. In such cases, a disjunction may have more than two disjuncts. Consider the following two statements:

Jan or Fred or Kaitlin or Monica or Samari will play the piano tonight.
Fred will play piano or drums or guitar or clarinet or xylophone.

Each of these statements is a disjunction with five disjuncts. We can represent the second as *p V d V g V c V x* if we let:

p = Fred will play piano.
d = Fred will play drums.
g = Fred will play guitar.
c = Fred will play clarinet.
x = Fred will play xylophone.

Exclusive Disjunctions

We call the disjunctions we have noted inclusive disjunctions because they incorporate the possibility that their disjuncts are all true. That is why *X V Y* can be understood as the claim that "*X* and/or *Y*."

When an ordinary-language statement of the form "*X* or *Y*" excludes the possibility that both *X* and *Y* are true, we call it an "exclusive" disjunction. Consider a menu that tells you that you may have "soup or salad" with your meal. Here the "or" functions as an exclusive disjunction. The restaurant is not telling you that you can have soup and/or salad but that you can have one or the other.

In such circumstances, the context makes it clear that a disjunction expresses the proposition that one *but not both* of its disjuncts is true. In order to represent this kind of disjunction in propositional logic symbols, we make this exclusion explicit and render an exclusive disjunction as a proposition of the form *(X V Y) & ~(X & Y)*. If we let *s* = You can have soup and *a* = You can have salad, then we can represent the disjunction on the menu as *(s V a) & ~(s & a)*.

Another example of an exclusive disjunction is the following statement, made in conjunction with a television advertisement for Ultramatic beds:

You will be completely satisfied or we will happily refund your money.

If *s* = You will be completely satisfied and *r* = We will happily refund your money, then the statement can be represented as the exclusive disjunction *(s V r) & ~(s & r)*. In this case, we need to represent the disjunction in this way because it is clear that the company is guaranteeing that one, and only one, of *s* and *r* is true. If you are completely satisfied, it follows that you cannot expect that your money will be refunded.

When representing exclusive disjunctions we will sometimes use the symbol *V*. For the purposes of convenience, the statement *X V Y* simply functions as an abbreviation for the statement "*(X V Y) & ~(X & Y)*."

Conditionals

A **conditional** is a complex proposition that has the form "If X, then Y." We call X the "antecedent" of the conditional and Y its "consequent." In symbolizing propositions, we will represent conditionals as statements that have the form $X \to Y$ (you may read this statement as "If X, then Y" or as "X arrow Y"). As this kind of symbolism visually suggests, a conditional states what is true if a certain condition (the antecedent) is or was the case.

We included a good example of a conditional in our earlier exercises on bias (Chapter 2). It was the following statement printed on a "prize envelope" received in the mail:

If you reply in time and win, we'll say . . .
LEO GROARKE, YOU'VE MADE THE FINAL CUT—YOU'RE ONE OF TEN LUCKY PRIZE WINNERS GUARANTEED UP TO $11,000,000!

This is a good example of slanting by distortion. Quite literally, the arguer has distorted the size of the two parts of the proposition. They have done so because they want the reader (in this case, Leo Groarke) to think that he has made the final cut and is one of 10 lucky prize-winners guaranteed. The qualification in the fine print means, however, that the statement is a conditional rather than a simple affirmation. In this case, the antecedent of the conditional is the conjunction "you reply in time and win." We can represent this conditional as *(r & w) → s*, where r = You reply in time, w = You win, and s = We'll say, Leo Groarke, you've made the final cut—you're one of 10 lucky prize winners guaranteed up to $11,000,000. In view of this, the authors of the sentence can claim, if they are questioned, that the sentence is not just the statement s but the conditional *(r & w) → s*, which says only that s is true if r and w are.

Though "If . . . , then . . ." is a common way of expressing conditionals in ordinary language, many statements express conditionals in other ways. Former Atlanta Braves shortstop Jeff Blauser's remark (reported in *The Sporting News*) that "If somebody wants to hit me [with a pitch], he's doing me a favor" is naturally represented as $h \to f$, where h = Somebody wants to hit me with a pitch and f = He's doing me a favor. The same conditional could, however, be expressed in many different ways, which include the following:

- Someone is doing me a favor if he wants to hit me with a pitch.
- Someone is doing me a favor when he tries to hit me with a pitch.
- Someone who tries to hit me with a pitch is doing me a favor.
- By trying to hit me with a pitch, someone is doing me a favor.

All of these sentences can be represented as the proposition $h \to f$. You need to recognize ordinary-language conditionals by asking whether they can reasonably be represented by an "If . . . , then . . ." statement.

Like conjunctions and disjunctions, conditionals may have components that are complex statements and may be included in other complex propositions. The first example we provided, the proposition *(r & w) → s*, is a conditional that has a conjunction as its antecedent. Another example that illustrates these complexities is the statement "Contemporary thinkers are interesting, but Socrates is the greatest philosopher of all time, and you will find ancient accounts of him a good read if you like to see an active mind at work." If we let:

c = Contemporary thinkers are interesting.
s = Socrates is the greatest philosopher of all time.
y = You will find ancient accounts of him a good read.
l = You like to see an active mind at work.

then we can represent this proposition as:

c & s & $(l \rightarrow y)$

You should note that the brackets we use in symbolizing this proposition are needed to ensure that its meaning is clear. If we wrote c & s & $l \rightarrow y$, then the statement could be read as c & $((s$ & $l) \rightarrow y)$, which means something different. We shall have more to say about the use of brackets in propositional logic statements shortly, but first we will ask you to do some exercises, which should make you more comfortable with propositional logic symbols and the basic forms of propositional logic statements.

SIMPLE AND COMPLEX PROPOSITIONS

- **Simple statements** are statements that express a proposition that is not a negation, conjunction, disjunction, or conditional. Simple propositions are represented as lowercase letters of the alphabet.
- *Negations* deny some other proposition. They are represented as ~X, where X is the proposition that is negated.
- *Conjunctions* assert that two or more propositions (its "conjuncts") are true. They are represented as X & Y.
- *Disjunctions* assert that one or more of a number of propositions (its "disjuncts") are true. They are represented as X V Y.
- *Conditionals* are propositions that assert that some proposition (its "consequent") is true if some other proposition (its "antecedent") is true. They are represented as X → Y.

EXERCISE   B2

1. Using the legend provided, translate the following propositional logic sentences into English:

    m = The mystical is a recurrent theme in all cultures.
    w = Western mysticism is similar to Eastern mysticism.
    e = Every kind of mysticism acknowledges the irrational.
    s = We should embrace mysticism.
    v = We should openly acknowledge the irrational.

a)* m

b) $\sim w$

c) $s \& v$

d)* $m \lor v$

e) $v \rightarrow \sim m$

f) $(s \& \sim e) \rightarrow \sim v$

g)* $(s \& e \& m) \rightarrow v$

h) $\sim m \& s$

i) $(s \rightarrow v) \& (v \rightarrow s)$

j) $(v \lor m) \rightarrow s$

k) $m \lor \sim v$

l) $w \& \sim s \& \sim m \& \sim v$

m) $\sim m \& \sim v$

n) $\sim(m \lor s)$

o) $s; s \lor v;$ *therefore* $\sim v$

p) $\sim(m \& s), m;$ *therefore* $\sim s$

q) $v \rightarrow \sim m, v;$ *therefore* $\sim m$

r) $(s \& \sim e) \rightarrow \sim v; v;$ *therefore* $e \lor \sim s$

2. Using the letters indicated to represent simple propositions, represent the following as propositional logic statements. (When you come across exclusive disjunctions, make sure you represent them as such.)

a)   You will become a famous writer, or at least a published author. *f, (p)*

b)* Early to bed and early to rise makes a man healthy, wealthy, and wise (*b, r, h, w, i*).

c)   [From a box of Kellogg's Frosted Flakes] If it doesn't say KELLOGG'S on the box, it's not KELLOGG'S in the box. (*o, i*)

d)   [From the same box] If this product in any way falls below the high standards you've come to expect from KELLOGG'S, please send your comments and both top flaps to: Consumer Affairs, KELLOGG INC. (*f, s*)

e)   [A comment on the Welsh Llanelli rugby team] "Now's the time if we are to ever achieve our ultimate ambition—the European rugby championship." (*n, u*)

f)* If we let *c* = Richard Nixon is a crook, then *~c* represents Richard Nixon's famous statement "I am not a crook." (*l, r*)

g)* We define a "valid argument" as an argument in which the conclusion follows necessarily from the premises. (*v, n*)

h)   An argument is invalid if it is possible for the premises to be true and the conclusion false. (*i, p*)

i)* [From a box of Shredded Wheat] You should try Shredded Wheat with cold milk or with hot milk. (*c, h*)

j)   [From *The Economist* magazine, August 1995] If they do not set these [sugar and peanut] programmes on a path to oblivion, any idea that these Republicans deserve the adjective "free market" can be dispensed with, once and for all. (*s, p, f*)

k)   [From an advertisement in *Mother Jones* magazine, July–August 1995] If you want to burn up to 79 per cent more calories, WalkFit is your answer. (*b, w*)

l)* [Tucker Carlson of the Heritage Foundation, in a letter to *Mother Jones* magazine, July/August 1995] "Safe neighborhoods are organized." (*s, o*)

3   Translation

The process of depicting ordinary propositions in the symbols of propositional logic can be seen as a kind of "translation." Especially since propositional logic is a very simple formal logic, and our concern is a very general account of it that can be applied to ordinary statements, the translations that we will use are often approximations, though they capture the sense of the original statements well enough to allow us to investigate their role in propositional arguments.

We have already introduced the basic principles of translation, but some aspects of the process merit further comment, especially as a failure to appreciate them often leads to problems in translation. To underscore the key aspects of translation, we suggest you heed the following "10 rules" of good translation. If you let them guide your translations, you should have no difficulty translating ordinary sentences and arguments into the appropriate propositional logic symbols.

1. Use lowercase letters to represent simple propositions. This rule of translation may seem obvious, but students often represent complex propositions, most commonly negations, as simple propositions. Remember that it is a mistake to let m = Marcus Aurelius was *not* a good emperor, for this is a negation. The proper way to translate it is by letting m = Marcus Aurelius was a good emperor and by representing it as ~m.

2. Use brackets to avoid ambiguity. In earlier chapters, we emphasized that it is important to avoid ambiguity in our own arguments and to recognize ambiguity when it occurs in the reasoning of other arguers. In translating sentences into propositional logic symbols, it is important to use brackets to avoid possible ambiguities when symbolizing particular propositions. The statement $a \rightarrow b \vee c$ is ambiguous because it can be interpreted as the proposition $(a \rightarrow b) \vee c$ or as the proposition $a \rightarrow (b \vee c)$. Because these two propositions mean different things, you must make it clear which you intend when you are translating.

3. Do not confuse indicator words with connectives. Remember that words like "because" and "therefore" are logical indicators that arguers use to identify their premises and conclusions. In such cases, they are logical terms, but they are not propositional logic connectors and cannot, therefore, be represented as propositional logic symbols. In propositional arguments, they tell us what propositions are premises and conclusions. Propositional logic symbols can then be used to translate these premises and conclusions.

4. Distinguish "if" and "only if." In most ordinary conditionals, the statement that follows the connector word "if" is the antecedent. An important exception to this rule occurs when conditionals use the connector words "only if." In this case, the statement that follows "only if" is the consequent. The statement "X only if Y" is, therefore, properly represented as the proposition $X \rightarrow Y$.

You can see why this is the case by considering the conditional "You can join the air force only if you are 18." It would be a mistake to interpret this proposition as the claim that you can join the air force if you are 18, for this is only one of the requirements (other requirements include good physical health, the passing of entrance exams, and so on). As it is sometimes put, "*X* only if *Y*" states that *Y* is a necessary— but not sufficient—condition for *X*. Because *X* could not, in such circumstances, occur if *Y* is not true, this is a circumstance in which $X \rightarrow Y$ but need not be a circumstance in which $Y \rightarrow X$.

5. Treat biconditionals as conjunctions with conditional conjuncts. In an ordinary conditional, the implication goes one way: the antecedent implies the consequent. In a biconditional, the implication goes both ways: the antecedent implies the consequent, and the consequent implies the antecedent. "If you win the $6 million lotto, you'll be rich'" is a conditional because the consequent ("you'll be rich") does not imply the antecedent ("you win the $6 million lotto"): it does not rule out the possibility that you might become rich in other ways (by receiving $14 million in inheritance, for example). In contrast, one presents a biconditional if one explains the word "bachelor" by saying, "You are a bachelor if you are an unmarried man," for this is a case in which the consequent ("You are a bachelor") does imply the antecedent ("You are an unmarried man").

Biconditionals are a way to express definitions or other equivalences. Logicians often represent biconditionals as statements with the connecting words "if and only if," but in ordinary language they are more likely to be expressed as conditionals, though the context makes it clear that this is a situation in which the antecedent and the consequent of a conditional are being forwarded as equivalent.

In propositional logic, biconditionals have the form $(X \rightarrow Y) \& (Y \rightarrow X)$. The informal definition "An alchemist is the medieval version of the modern chemist" may be rendered as the biconditional $(a \rightarrow m) \& (m \rightarrow a)$, where:

a = a person is an alchemist.
m = a person is the medieval version of the modern chemist.

6. Treat "unless" statements as conditionals. In ordinary language, the connector word "unless" precedes an antecedent that is (implicitly) negated. The sentence "I'll go unless she does" is the conditional "If she doesn't go, I'll go." The sentence "Your kite won't fly unless there's a breeze" is the conditional "If there is no breeze, then your kite won't fly." This means that sentences of the form "*Y* unless *X*" are recognized as conditionals of the form $\sim X \rightarrow Y$.

7. Translate sentences that express the same proposition in the same way. In diagramming arguments, we have already seen that the same premise or conclusion is often stated in different ways. In diagramming, we replace these variations with one definition of a premise or conclusion so that we can work with a clear statement of the argument. In translating sentences into propositional logic, we must similarly recognize that a particular proposition may be expressed in different ways. If s = She got the highest mark in the math exam, then s will also serve as the translation of the sentence "No one did as well as she did." If d = She's on the dean's list, then $s \rightarrow d$ represents both the statement "If she got the highest mark on the math exam, she's on the dean's list" and the statement "She's on the dean's list if it is true that she got the highest mark on the math exam."

8. Translate logical connectors literally if you can. When ordinary sentences use propositional logic connector words, translate them literally whenever it is clear that the words are used in the same way that connectors are used in propositional logic. If Sherlock Holmes says that "Either Cecil Jones or Margaret Midgley is the guilty party," this should be translated as $c \ V \ m$, where:

c = Cecil Jones is the guilty party.
m = Margaret Midgley is the guilty party.

The statement $c \ V \ m$ implies that "If Cecil Jones isn't the guilty party, then Margaret Midgley is." This is an inference that we can prove valid in propositional logic, but it would be incorrect to represent Holmes's statement as $\sim c \rightarrow m$. That is something that is implied by what he said, but it is not what he said.

9. Ignore variations that do not affect the validity of an argument. When you are translating propositional logic arguments, many minor variations will not matter. If there is no obvious way to determine what will and will not matter beforehand, you must simply look at a particular argument and ask yourself what matters to a conclusion and an inference.

Consider the argument "As the American Anti-Vivisection Society maintains, experiments on animals are justified only if animals feel no pain. As this is certainly mistaken, animal experiments are unjustified." The general thrust of this argument can be captured by adopting the following legend:

j = Experiments on animals are justified.
p = Animals feel pain.
     $j \rightarrow p, \sim p,$ therefore $\sim j$

This representation of the argument leaves out some aspects of the argument. Notably, it leaves out the reference to the American Anti-Vivisection Society in the first sentence of the argument and does not capture the full strength of the second premise, which claims that the proposition that animals feel pain is not only true but "certain." In a more sophisticated treatment of this argument, and in a more sophisticated formal logic, these further aspects could be recognized. In working with the limited resources available in propositional logic, however, a rough analogue of the argument must suffice. While this is not the best of all possible situations, it is useful nonetheless, for it can still be used to show that the reasoning in the argument is valid.

10. Check your translation by translating back to ordinary English. If you are unsure of your translation of an ordinary-language sentence or argument, you can check it by translating it back into ordinary English. The result should be a clear instance of the proposition or argument you began with.

Translating Arguments

If you follow our 10 translation rules, you should have no difficulty translating ordinary sentences into propositional logic symbols. Once you know how to translate sentences, you will also know how to translate whole arguments, for this requires only that we use the rules to translate the argument's premises and conclusion.

Consider the following argument:

> If Samantha moves her rook, James will place her in check with his pawn. If she moves her knight, he'll place her in check with his queen. Those are the only moves open to her, so James's pawn or knight will have her in check in one move.

We can translate this argument into propositional logic symbols as follows:

r = Samantha moves her rook.
k = Samantha moves her knight.
p = James will place her in check by moving his pawn.
q = James will place her in check with his queen.

$$r \rightarrow p, \ k \rightarrow q, \ r \lor k, \ \textit{therefore } p \lor q$$

In creating this translation, you will see that we applied the 10 rules for translation to each of the argument's premises and conclusion. In translating the premise "Those are the only moves open to her" as $r \lor k$, we have, for example, implicitly relied on Rule 7, which tells us to treat different ways of expressing a proposition in the same way. We have recognized that this premise is, even though it does not employ the word "or," a way of expressing a disjunction and needs to be represented in this way.

TEN RULES FOR GOOD TRANSLATION

1. Use lowercase letters to represent simple propositions.
2. Use brackets to avoid ambiguity.
3. Do not confuse indicator words with connector words.
4. Distinguish "if" and "only if."
5. Treat biconditionals as conjunctions with conditional conjuncts.
6. Treat "unless" statements as conditionals.
7. Translate sentences that express the same proposition in the same way.
8. Translate logical connectors literally if you can.
9. Ignore variations that do not affect the validity of an argument.
10. Check your translation by translating back to ordinary English.

EXERCISE B3

1. Translate the following sentences into propositional logic form using the letters indicated:

    a) If that's Louis, we're in for trouble. If not, we're home free. (*l, t*)
    b) If Angela and Karl frequent the place, then it's no place I want to go. (*a, k, g*)
    c) Either you straighten up and get your act together or you're out of here. (*s, a, o*)
    d) If you want a good time, go to British Columbia or to California. (*g, b, c*)
    e)* If you have multimedia skills or have worked on video, you can apply for the job. (*m, v, j*)
    f) It's a good wine but not a great wine. (*a, g*)
    g) If the greenhouse effect continues to evolve as predicted, the crocuses will bloom in March. (*g, c*)
    h) If there are any boycotts of the Olympics, the games will lose their credibility. (*b, c*)
    i)* Either I'm paranoid or you are out to get me. (*p, o*)
    j)* They're lying when they say they weren't there. (*t*)
    k) North Korea will disarm if and only if South Korea disarms. (*n, s*)
    l)* Only those who can stand a lot of pain can get a Ph.D. (*s, p*)
    m) The murder can't have been committed by both the chauffeur and the butler. (*c, b*)
    n) Whenever it rains, there are dark clouds in the sky. (*r, d*)
    o) If you go to town, then you'll see the remains of the car on your right side if you turn right on Dundas Street. (*g, r, d*)
    p) If he'll buy the chair if I up the price to four hundred dollars, then we'll know that he's guilty and we'll arrest him. (*b, u, g, a*)
    q)* I'm not interested in that car unless it is in mint condition. (*i, m*)
    r) When it rains there are clouds in the sky, and when it doesn't the sky is clear unless the pollution gets too bad. (*r, c, p*)
    s) I'll go only if Joan goes too. (*g, j*)
    t) If you have a headache, it's because you drank too much last night, and I can't feel sorry for you when you drink too much. (*h, d, s*)

2. Decide whether the following statements express simple conditionals or biconditionals, and put each into symbols using the letters given:

    a)* [Boyle's Law] The pressure of a gas varies with its volume at a constant temperature. (*p, v, t*)
    b)* An individual is still alive as long as an EEG records brain signals. (*a, s*)
    c) You may become a Catholic priest only if you are male. (*p, m*)
    d) A figure is a triangle whenever it has only three sides. (*t, i*)
    e)* Metal does not expand unless it is heated. (*e, h*)
    f)* Abortion is murder if and only if the fertilized ovum is a person. (*m, p*)
    g) Whenever it rains, he's in a bad mood. (*r, b*)
    h) If there are any more boycotts of the Olympics, the games will have to be cancelled. (*b, c*)

3. Translate the following sentences into propositional logic symbols. Create your own legend.

   a) [From the *Literary Review of Canada*, November 2002] Both the US and Great Britain, but not Canada, had anti-terrorist statutes in place before 11 September.

   b) [From a report on the future of footballer Ozalan Alpay, who played for Aston Villa, www.ananova.com, 13 January 2003] "If I'm still here in the next two or three weeks, I will play for the reserve team."

   c) [From the same report] Villa needs to give him a more realistic value—or he will be stuck at Villa Park until the summer.

   d) [From the QuickTime Pro website, 14 January 2003] Whether you use a Macintosh or Windows-based pc, you can harness the power of QuickTime Pro for media authoring and playback of high-quality audio and video.

   e) [From the MapQuest website] Consumers . . . can easily access millions of locations around the world, obtain detailed maps and accurate driving directions, locate places of interest, customize road trip plans, and create, save, download or email personalized maps.

   f)* [Paul Friedman, the public-address announcer at Wrigley Field, in *The Sporting News*] "One thing I've learned is that if you make a mistake, if you say it with a deep enough voice, you can get away with it."

4. Translate the following propositional logic arguments into propositional logic forms using the letters indicated:

   a) According to the law, she's guilty only if she committed the crime and committed it intentionally. She did commit the crime, but unintentionally, so she's not guilty. (*g, c, i*)

   b) Either you've offended him or he dislikes you. It has to be the latter, for I can't imagine you offending him. (*o, l*)

   c) The Americans or the Germans or the Russians will win the most medals at next year's Olympics. But I've heard that the Russian team is in disarray, and if that's true, they won't do well enough to win. Neither will the Americans. I've concluded that the Germans will win the most medals. (*a, g, r, d*)

   d) If he moves his rook, she'll move her bishop. And if she moves her bishop, he'll be forced to move his king. And if he does that, it's checkmate in 10 moves. So it's checkmate in 10 moves if he moves his rook. (*r, b, k, c*)

   e)* In order to avoid the intricacies of such theories, we will rely on our earlier remark that the objective of an argument is to convince an audience. If this is so, then it is sufficient for our purposes that the premises of a good argument be accepted as true by both us and our audience. (*o, s*)

   f) It should be clear that this new argument is valid, for it is obviously possible for its two premises to be true when its conclusion is false, and if this is true then the argument is invalid. (*v, t*)

   g)* The Conservatives will win the election if Liberal support declines in urban ridings. But there's no chance that Liberal support is going to decline in urban ridings. (*w, d*)

   h) You have a problem with your hardware or your software. If it's your software, only Scott can fix it. If there's a problem with your hardware, only Deb can help. Either way, it will cost you a bundle. So it's going to cost you a bundle. (*h, y, s, d, b*)

4   Propositional Schemes and Proofs

In learning how to represent arguments in propositional logic symbols, you have learned how to represent propositional schemes of argument—for implicit in the translation of any argument is some propositional logic scheme, which defines a class of arguments that follow a similar pattern of reasoning. Consider, to take an example, the following argument:

> If Jim left, he's gone to Ira's, and if he's gone to Ira's, they're watching *Survivor* again, so they're watching *Survivor* again if Jim has left.

If we let l = Jim has left, i = He's gone to Ira's, and s = They're watching *Survivor* again, then this argument can be properly represented as an argument of the form $l \rightarrow i$, $i \rightarrow s$, so $l \rightarrow s$. But of course this is not the only argument of this form. There is a large (indeed, infinite) class of arguments that conforms to this scheme. By defining l, i, and s in different ways, we could easily concoct further examples of arguments that are included in this class. (As an exercise, you may want to define l, i, and s in three different ways, noting the three different arguments that result.)

Once we recognize that we identify some general scheme of argument whenever we translate an argument into propositional logic symbols, we can further our analysis of propositional arguments by identifying valid propositional logic schemes. Arguments that conform to these schemes can then be recognized as deductively valid arguments. We can prove that a particular argument is valid by translating it into propositional logic symbols and by showing that it is a variant of a valid scheme, or that one can use valid schemes to deduce its conclusion from its premises. To this end, we will proceed by identifying valid schemes of argument that are associated with each of the propositional logic connectives.

Conjunctions

The two valid schemes of conjunctive argument we will recognize are the most obviously valid propositional arguments, so it is useful to begin with them. The first scheme is **conjunction elimination**, or '&E' for short; the second is **conjunction introduction**, or "&I" for short.

These two rules can be defined as follows:

&E: X & Y, *therefore X (or Y)*
&I: X, Y, *therefore X & Y*

Both of these schemes are commonly assumed in ordinary reasoning. Both are deductively valid. In the first case, the truth of a conjunction implies that each of its conjuncts must be true, for this is precisely what it asserts. In the second case, the truth of two propositions implies the truth of a conjunction that conjoins them, for it must be true if they are true.

Consider the novel *Arcadia*. Its cover records that the author is Jim Crace. The blurb on the back cover notes that "He is the author of *Continent . . .* and *The Gift of*

Stones." If we let *a* = Jim Crace is the author of the novel *Arcadia*, *c* = Jim Crace is the author of *Continent*, and *g* = He is the author of *The Gift of Stones*, then this implies that *a*, and that *c* & *g*. Having noted that this is so, we may employ the schemes &I and &E if someone asks us about Jim Crace's works. If someone asks us what Jim Crace has written, we may deduce an answer in the following step-by-step way:

1.	*a*	P (for "premise," known from the front cover of *Arcadia*)
2.	*c & g*	P (premise, known from the blurb on the back cover)
3.	*a & c & g*	1, 2, &I

This is a very simple propositional logic *proof.* It begins with premises and uses valid propositional schemes of argument (often called "rules of inference") to arrive, in a step-by-step fashion, at a conclusion. Each of the numbered steps includes a proposition, the insertion of which is assumed or derived in a way that is precisely specified on the right. In this case, the first two propositions, 1 and 2, are assumed on the grounds that they are provided as premises. The insertion of the third is justified by applying the argument scheme &I to propositions 1 and 2.

We implicitly follow the chain of reasoning outlined in our proof when someone asks us what books Jim Crace wrote, and we reason from what we find on the cover of *Arcadia* to the conclusion that "He wrote *Arcadia, Continent,* and *The Gift of Stones.*" Reasoning about such questions may also employ the scheme &E. Having read that *c* & *g* is true, we may, for example, answer the question whether Jim Crace wrote *The Gift of Stones* by reasoning as follows:

1.	*c & g*	P
2.	*g*	1, &E

This is another simple propositional logic proof. In this case, the proof has one premise, *c & g*, and one other proposition that is inferred from it by applying the rule &E.

The argument schemes &I and &E can be used to justify inferences that involve conjunctions of any size. The following is, for example, a propositional logic proof that uses repeated instances of the scheme &I to establish a conjunction with four conjuncts:

1.	*j*	P
2.	*m*	P
3.	*p*	P
4.	*a*	P
5.	*j & m*	1, 2, &I
6.	*j & m & p*	5, 3, &I
7.	*j & m & p & a*	6, 4, &I

We have not defined the meaning of the premises in this proof. Instead, we have left this meaning open and used our proof to demonstrate that one can validly move from these premises to the conclusion that *j* & *m* & *p* & *a*, no matter how these simple propositions are defined. We know that this is so because our conclusion (and each of our intermediate conclusions) has been derived by applying a valid scheme of argument (in this case, &I).

Disjunctions

In developing our propositional logic, we will add to &I and &E one scheme of argument that can be used to construct valid disjunctive arguments. It is called **disjunction elimination** and will be symbolized as "**VE.**" We define VE as follows:

VE: X V Y (or Y V X), ~X, *therefore Y*

This is a valid inference, because the claim that a disjunction is true and one of its disjuncts false leads inevitably to the conclusion that the remaining disjunct must be true (for the disjunction asserts that at least one of them is true).

Consider the reasoning of an overconfident professor, Dave, who scans his class and sees several students yawning. We might easily imagine him reasoning as follows: "Either my students are bored or they are tired because they partied late last night. But this is one of the most interesting lectures I've ever given. It must have been some party!"

If we let b = The class is bored with my lecture and t = The students are tired because they partied late last night, then we can prove that this is a valid chain of reasoning as follows:

1. $b \lor t$ P
2. ~b P
3. t 1, 2, VE

It is important to remember that this proof—and any propositional logic proof—only shows that a particular chain of reasoning is (deductively) valid. It does not prove that an argument must be a strong argument, because that requires both validity and acceptable premises. In this case, students in the class may want to argue that the argument is weak because the premises (that there are only two possible explanations of the students' yawning and that they cannot be bored) are not acceptable.

The scheme VE can be applied to exclusive as well as inclusive disjunctions. Suppose you are unhappy with the Ultramatic bed you bought under the condition that "You will be completely satisfied, or we will happily refund your money." We have already seen that the statement can be represented as the exclusive disjunction s V r, or, more completely, as *(s V r) & ~(s & r)*, where s = You will be completely satisfied and r = We will happily refund your money. When you go to return the bed and collect a refund, you will have used this claim as a basis for the conclusion that your money should be happily returned. We can prove the validity of this reasoning as follows:

1. $(s \lor r) \& \sim(s \& r)$ P (the initial guarantee)
2. ~s P (your response to your experience with the bed)
3. $s \lor r$ 1, &E
4. r 3, 2, VE

It is worth noting that the propositional scheme of argument VE does not allow you to move directly from propositions 1 and 2 to *r*. This is because proposition 1 is, strictly speaking, a conjunction (a conjunction that *contains* a disjunction but is not itself a disjunction) and the scheme VE is applicable only to disjunctions. In using schemes, always remember that you must use them in the precise way they have been defined. In this case, this limitation does not present a significant problem, because we can isolate the disjunction in proposition 1 by using the rule &E and can then apply the scheme VE. It is by moves of this sort that we can simplify propositions and isolate their elements and in this way work toward a conclusion in a propositional logic proof.

Conditionals

Our propositional logic will include two basic schemes of argument that employ conditionals. They are called **Affirming the Antecedent**, or "**AA**," and **Denying the Consequent**, or "**DC**." (Traditionally, these rules are known as *modus ponens* and *modus tollens*.) These two schemes can be defined as follows:

> **AA**: $X \rightarrow Y$, X, *therefore Y*
> **DC**: $X \rightarrow Y$, $\sim Y$, *therefore* $\sim X$

You should see that both these schemes are deductively valid. A conditional and its antecedent must imply its consequent, for the conditional states that its consequent is true in these specific circumstances. Arguments that match the scheme DC are also valid, for the antecedent of a true conditional cannot be true if the consequent is false, since its truth would (by the scheme AA) imply that the consequent was true.

Consider the following remark by a Chinese commentator on China's move to become a leader in the development of cloning technology (reported in *Wired* magazine, January 2003, p. 121):

> We have a huge population and a one-child policy. Why would you think about making people in a laboratory?

To unravel the argument in these remarks, we need to recognize that the question in this quotation is a rhetorical question. The author of the remark is not genuinely asking the question but is suggesting that it *doesn't* make sense to think about making people in a laboratory given the first claim—that China has a huge population and a one-child policy. We can represent the implicit argument as follows:

> *h* = China has a huge population and a one-child policy.
> *s* = It makes sense for China to think about making people in a
>   laboratory.
> *h* $\rightarrow$ $\sim s$, *h, therefore* $\sim s$

Because this is a simple instance of the argument scheme AA, we can prove the validity of this reasoning as follows:

1. $h \rightarrow {\sim}s$ P
2. h P
3. ${\sim}s$ 1, 2, AA

Every time we use the scheme AA in a propositional logic proof, we state the line numbers for the lines where the relevant conditional and its antecedent appear.

We can illustrate the scheme DC with an example from the 2011 Canadian election. One of the central arguments in the election was the Conservatives' claim that voters should vote for them as the only way to avoid an unconstitutional government made up of a coalition of Liberals, the Bloc Quebecois, and the NDP. In the wake of Prime Minister Harper's repeated claims to this effect, some claimed that he was not genuine, and gave as evidence his remarks and action in the past. Consider the following report from the *Vancouver Sun* (22 April 2011):

> It's a question that moved this week to the heart of the 2011 federal election: Can a second-place party in a minority Parliament legitimately form a government? In a CBC interview aired Thursday, Conservative leader Stephen Harper offered an unequivocal answer—No—and suggested any such move by his rival parties to form a "coalition" in a divided, post-election House of Commons would spark a debate over "constitutional law."
>
> But in another televised interview in 1997—when he was trying to chart a path to bring Canada's conservatives to power in a Liberal-dominated Parliament—Harper's answer to the same question was a resounding yes.

In propositional terms, one might summarize the argument criticizing Harper that this evidence produced as follows:

g = Harper genuinely believes that a coalition government is unconstitutional.
c = Harper claimed otherwise in a televised interview in 1997.
    $g \rightarrow {\sim}c$, c, *therefore* ${\sim}g$

If we let $X = g$, and $Y = {\sim}c$, then we can see that this is a clear instance of the DC scheme ($X \rightarrow Y$, ${\sim}Y$, *therefore* ${\sim}X$). It illustrates the point that the antecedent and consequent in the conditional in the scheme can be simple or complex proposition.

We take our second example from a Letter to the Editor, *The Globe and Mail* in 1987, when the Canadian dollar was trading significantly below the American dollar, a situation that led to much debate over the question whether this was a good or bad thing:

> The prize for the most erroneous statement of the week should be shared by economist John Crispo and journalist Jennifer Lewington. Both of them claim that the present value of the Canadian dollar [$0.68 US] gives our exporters an advantage of 30 per cent or more in the US market.
>
> Nothing could be further from the truth. That would be true only if prices and costs had risen by the same amount in both countries. In fact, between

1970 and 1986, the price index of GNP rose 28 per cent more in Canada than it did in the United States.

If we let:

e = Economist John Crispo is correct.

j = Journalist Jennifer Lewington is correct.

a = The value of the Canadian dollar gives Canadian exporters an advantage of 30 per cent or more in the US.

s = Prices and costs rise by the same amount in both countries.

then the letter's argument can be translated as $e \rightarrow a$; $j \rightarrow a$; $a \rightarrow s$; ~s; *therefore* ~e & ~j. Having determined that the argument has this structure, we can prove its validity as follows:

1. $e \rightarrow a$ P
2. $j \rightarrow a$ P
3. $a \rightarrow s$ P
4. ~s P
5. ~a 3, 4, DC
6. ~j 2, 5, DC
7. ~e 1, 5, DC
8. ~e & ~j 7, 6, &I

In using the schemes AA and DC, keep in mind that the antecedent of a conditional may be a complex rather than a simple proposition. Affirming an antecedent may, in such a case, mean affirming a conjunction, a negation, a disjunction, or a conditional. Denying a consequent may mean denying a proposition of this form. If the conditional one is working with is $(t$ & $h) \rightarrow$ ~$(q$ V $r)$, then one must affirm the antecedent by affirming $(t$ & $h)$ or deny the consequent by denying ~$(q$ V $r)$. In the latter case, this requires that we assert $(q$ V $r)$.

The argument scheme DC is prominent in scientific reasoning, where it is used when a theory is rejected by showing that it implies experimental results that are not corroborated. A good historical example is the refutation of "phlogiston theory" by Lavoisier in 1775 mentioned in Chapter 10. According to phlogiston theory, combustion is a process in which a substance called "phlogiston" departs from a burning substance. This implies that a substance will lose weight if it combusts (since it has lost phlogiston), but Lavoisier demonstrated that this consequence does not hold in the case of mercury. If we let:

p = Phlogiston theory is correct.

w = Mercury will weigh less after combustion.

then we can construct a proof of Lavoisier's reasoning as follows:

1. $p \rightarrow w$ P (on the basis of the theory)
2. $\sim w$ P (established by experiment)
3. $\sim p$ 1, 2, DC

In this case, we have a strong argument, for this proves that the argument is valid and it is also the case that both premises are acceptable—the first because it is a clear consequence of phlogiston theory, the second because it is proved by Lavoisier's experiments.

Conditional Fallacies

In contrast to AA and DC, the alternatives affirming the consequent and denying the antecedent ("AC" and "DA") are not necessarily valid. You need, therefore, to ensure that you do not confuse them with AA and DC.

The problems with AC and DA can be illustrated with the following conditional:
If you are the host of a popular TV show, then you impressed someone.

This conditional is one that we can reasonably accept as true, for the producers of a popular TV show are not likely to hire you as host unless you've impressed them or someone who works with them. Once we accept the conditional, we can reasonably conclude that you impressed someone if we can establish that you're the host of a popular TV show. This is an instance of AA that illustrates the kind of inference it allows.

Suppose, however, that we accept the conditional and its consequent: i.e. that you impressed someone. In such a context, it should be obvious that one cannot validly conclude that you must be the host of a popular television show (!). For similar reasons, one cannot use the negation of the antecedent—i.e. the claim that you are not a popular television show host—to validly conclude that you have not impressed someone. In both cases, you may have impressed someone in ways that have nothing to do with hosting a popular television show (by doing something that is rewarded with a medal of bravery, for example). It follows that the consequent of our conditional does not imply the antecedent and that the negation of the antecedent does not imply the negation of the consequent.

Biconditionals

The arguments AC and DA are not valid, but similar-looking inferences are valid in the case of biconditionals.

Consider the argument:
This figure is a trapezoid only if it is a quadrilateral with two parallel sides. And it has two parallel sides, a and b, and is a quadrilateral, so it's a trapezoid.

If we let t = This figure is a trapezoid and q = It is a quadrilateral with two parallel sides, then this might seem to be the following case of AC:

$t \rightarrow q$, q, therefore t

Instead of concluding that this is an invalid argument that is an instance of AC, we can more plausibly conclude that this is an incorrect way of representing the argument, because there is another way to interpret it—for though the conditional with which we began may at first glance seem to be a simple conditional that uses the connector "only if," it is actually a biconditional. We can see this by recognizing that the conditional in the argument is a definition of "trapezoid" that can best be represented as the proposition $(t \rightarrow q) \mathrel{\&} (q \rightarrow t)$, for it is true that a figure is a quadrilateral with two parallel sides if it is a trapezoid and that it is a trapezoid if it is a quadrilateral with two parallel sides.

Once we recognize our conditional as a biconditional, we need to represent our argument as: $(t \rightarrow q) \mathrel{\&} (q \rightarrow t)$, q, *therefore t*. And this argument can be proved valid as follows, by invoking propositional logic argument schemes we have already introduced:

1.	$(t \rightarrow q) \mathrel{\&} (q \rightarrow t)$	P
2.	q	P
3.	$q \rightarrow t$	1, &E
4.	t	3, 2, AA

Once we recognize biconditionals and translate them properly into propositional logic symbols, they are relatively easy to work with, for we can use the argument scheme &E to isolate the different conditionals they contain. Once we have done this, we can usually employ conditional argument schemes like AA and DC.

Conditional Series

The last propositional scheme of argument we will introduce here is called **conditional series**, or "**CS**." It can be defined as follows:

CS: X→Y, Y→Z, *therefore* X→Z

CS is a rule that allows us to reduce two conditionals to one conditional that consists of the antecedent of the first conditional and the consequent of the second. This is a valid inference, because the antecedent of a conditional implies not only its consequent but also any further consequent that is entailed by this first consequent. If it is true both that "If Hitler had attacked Britain two months earlier, he would have won the Battle of Britain" and that "If he had won the Battle of Britain, he would have won World War II," then CS allows us to conclude that "If Hitler had attacked Britain two months earlier, he would have won World War II."

More formally, we can demonstrate the validity of this inference by letting:

t = Hitler attacked Britain two months earlier.
s = Hitler would have won the Battle of Britain.
w = Hitler would have won World War II.

and by constructing the following proof:

1. $t \rightarrow s$ P
2. $s \rightarrow w$ P
3. $t \rightarrow w$ 1, 2, CS

As you will observe in the exercises ahead, it is often useful to employ CS in conjunction with conditional rules of inference like AA and DC.

The scheme CS completes our discussion of the most basic schemes of argument that we will include within our introduction to propositional logic. You will find a summary of these rules in a box at the end of this appendix. You may use it as a convenient guide as you begin to construct propositional proofs, but you should learn the schemes well enough to make this unnecessary. The better you know the schemes, the easier it will be to construct the chains of inference that proofs depend on.

Constructing Simple Proofs

Equipped with the argument schemes we have outlined and the ability to translate ordinary sentences into standard propositional logic forms, you should be ready to construct simple proofs that demonstrate the validity of propositional arguments. For those who initially find proofs difficult, we offer the following tips for good proof construction:

1. Remember that good proofs depend on good translations. If you do not translate an argument into propositional symbols properly, your proof (however ingenious it is) cannot prove that an argument is valid, for in that case your proof is dealing with a different argument than the one that you began with. To avoid this, be sure that you translate an argument carefully. In translating argument components, follow the guidelines we introduced in the earlier sections of this chapter. If you know that an argument is valid but cannot construct a proof, check your translation. The problem may be in the translation rather than in your proof.

2. Base your strategy on an argument's premises or conclusion. The validity of an extended argument may be difficult to see. If you are unsure how to proceed, limit your attention to one step at a time. A propositional logic proof proceeds by dividing a larger argument into a series of smaller steps defined by propositional logic argument schemes.

You may find it useful to begin by asking what follows from the stated premises. To determine this, you can derive what you can from an argument's premises and see where this takes you. If a premise is a conjunction, you can isolate each conjunct. If one premise is a conditional and another its antecedent, then AA can be used to derive the consequent. Ask yourself what argument schemes are invited by the premises. After you have established this, you can ask what follows from the propositions you are able to deduce.

Keep track of the premises you have used. In most of the propositional arguments in this book, the conclusion depends on all of the premises. It is probably the premises you have not yet employed that will be the key to progressing with your proof.

Alternatively, you may plan your strategy by considering the conclusion. What kind of proposition is it? What argument scheme is likely to justify it? If it is a conjunction, you may need to use the argument scheme &I. That will require you to isolate each conjunction. How can this be done? In this way, you can think back from your conclusion until you see a way to arrive at your premises and can then construct your proof accordingly.

PROPOSITIONAL SCHEMES OF ARGUMENT

&E	X & Y (or Y & X), *therefore* X
&I	X, Y, *therefore* X & Y
VE	X V Y (or Y V X), ~X, *therefore* Y
AA	X → Y, X, *therefore* Y
DC	X → Y, ~Y, *therefore* ~X
CS	X → Y, Y → Z, *therefore* X → Z

EXERCISE   B4

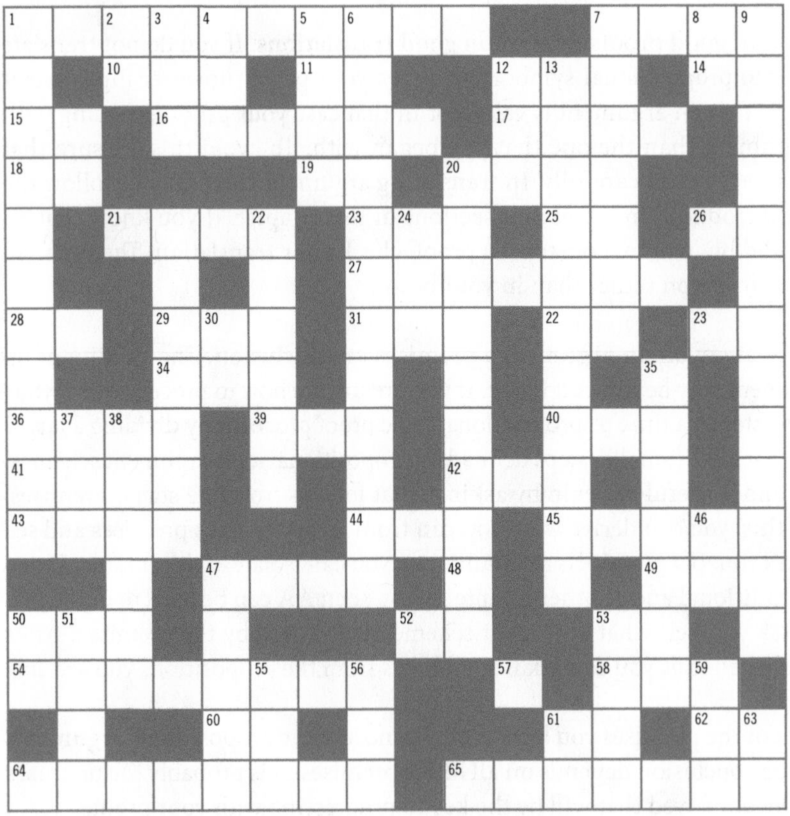

Illustration B1   "Schemes of argument crossword"

Leo Groarke

CLUES ACROSS

1. What follows from premises.
7. Booby _____.
10. If g = It's a girl, then $\sim g$ = It's a _____.
11. If p = Paul goes out, c = Chris goes out, m = Mary goes out, then $m \rightarrow$ *(p & c)* and $\sim c$ imply that Mary is _____.
12. "Lion" is equivalent to "_____."
14. If you have a Ph.D., you are a _____.
15. If x = yes, then $\sim x$ = _____.
16. $\sim$*(a & b)* _____s *a & b.*
17. _____ Fitzgerald, singer.
18. If x, then y, $\sim y$, so $\sim x$.
19. Man's title.
20. _____ of rope.
21. Sounds like our disjunctive connector.
25. Same as 61 down.
26. First word of a proverb equivalent to $h \rightarrow e$, where h = You're human.
27. _____ the antecedent.
28. The principles of identity tell us to treat "that is" as interchangeable with this abbreviation.
29. If m = Catch me, then $c \rightarrow m$ is a common saying if c = you _____.
31. If d = The stock market has its downs, then $\sim d$ is the statement that the stock market has its _____.
32. Short for Nova Scotia.
33. *(a $\rightarrow$ b) & (b $\rightarrow$ a)* is a _____ conditional.
34. In a race between two individuals, it is a false dilemma to say that one or the other will win, for it may be a _____.
36. Degree _____.
39. Word used to form negations.
40. We've discussed conditionals and biconditionals, but not _____ conditionals.
41. Food for Lassie.
42. The laws of thought apply _____ versally.
43. _____ Uris, famous author.
44. The proposition *a & b* can be false in three ways. How many ways are there for it to be true?
45. $t \rightarrow m$, t = You go to a theatre, m = You may go to a _____.
47. "*b* when *a*" is equivalent to "If *a*, _____ *b*."

48. ~*(x & ~x)* is an instance of the principle of _____-contradiction.

49. *s* → *m*, *s* = She's a Member of the Legislative Assembly, *m* = She's an _____.

50. First word of a biblical saying equivalent to *a* → *b*, where *b* = shall be given.

52. Abbreviation for light.

53. *m V a*, where *m* = a form of meditation and *a* = advertising abbreviation.

54. Half of *x V y*.

57. See 57 down.

58. A rule in propositional logic: Assume *x*, derive *y* & ~*y*, conclude ~*x*.

60. If we treated AA as a rule of elimination, its abbreviation would be this.

61. _____5, British agency.

62. *a V i*, where *a* = abbreviation for "pound," *i* = first initials of an American president.

64. Apply the rule &E to *f* & *d*, where *f* and *d* are the names of two great logicians, Frege and DeMorgan.

65. Argument building block.

CLUES DOWN

1. "If . . . then" statement.

2. Latin for "note well."

3. *a* & *b*.

4. Sounds, but is not, equivalent to a dishonest practice.

5. If *t* = Go to Thailand, and *e* = You like exotic places, and it is true that *e* and *e* → *t*, then you should go here.

6. Some propositional rules of inference—e.g. &I—are rules of _____.

7. Denying the consequent is traditionally called modus _____.

8. The next chapter discusses *reductio* _____ *absurdum*.

9. The topic of this chapter is _____ logic.

12. Let *g* = Leo, *c* = Chris, and *l* = Linda, and apply VE twice to the following: *g V c V l*, ~*c*, ~*l*.

13. *a* & *b*, *therefore b* is a case of an _____.

20. *b*, in *a* → *b*.

22. A word traditionally associated with AA.

24. Short for a Democrat's opposite.

30. Logic plays an important role in _____ research.

35. A rule yet to be introduced: *X V Y*, *X* → *Z*, *Y* → *Z*, *therefore Z*.

37. French equivalent to "island."

38. Famous baby doctor, Star Trek personality.

46. Grand _____ Opry.

47. The law of the excluded middle says statements can be true or false but not _____ or more false.

50. One of the forms of argument discussed in later chapters of this text is called _____ *hominem*.

51. Trigonometric function.

53. One might awkwardly say that &E _____s a conjunction.

55. A verb that implies repeated use of equivalent propositions.

56. The number of rules of inference introduced in this chapter, plus four.

57. First letter of the abbreviation of the rule used to derive a consequent.

59. *h* & *p* & *j*, where *h* = Hirt, *p* = Pacino, and *j* = Jolson.

61. If *m* = The culprit is me, *y* = The culprit is you, and *s* = The culprit is someone else, and *y* → *r*, *r* → *m*, *s* → (*s* & *m*), then we can be sure that one culprit is _____.

63. Hamlet asks whether he should x V ~x, where x = _____.

MAJOR EXERCISE   BM

1. Fill in the missing steps in the following proofs. Each "?" indicates a missing step. All the premises are identified.

a)* 1. *a* → *b*   P
    2. *a*   P
    3. ?   ?

b) 1. *c* → *d*   P
    2. *c* → *e*   P
    3. *c*   P
    4. ?   ?, AA
    5. *e*   2, 3, AA
    6. ?   4, 5, &I

c)* 1. (*e or d*) & P
    2. ~*d*   P
    3. ?   ??
    4. *e*   ??
    5. ?   ??
    6. *e* & 4, 5, &I

d) 1. *p* → *s*   P
    2. *r* → *p*   P
    3. *f* → *r*   ??
    4. ?   P
    5. *r*   ?, 4, AA
    6. *p*   2, 5, AA
    7. ?   1, 6, AA

e) 1. $m \rightarrow n$ P
   2. $n \rightarrow o$ P
   3. $m \,\&\, r$ P
   4. m 3, ?
   5. n 1, 4, ?
   6. o ???

f) 1. $a \,\&\, {\sim}c$ P
   2. $c \lor e$ P
   3. ${\sim}c$???
   4. ?   2, 3, ?

g)* 1. $a \rightarrow d$ P
   2. $d \rightarrow e$ P
   3. $a \,\&\, b$ P
   4. a ???
   5. ?   1, 4, AA
   6. ?   ???
   7. $a \,\&\, e$ 4, 6, ?

h) 1. $(t \,\&\, h) \rightarrow {\sim}c$?
   2. t P
   3. $h \,\&\, i$ P
   4. h 3, ?
   5. $t \,\&\, h$??
   6. ${\sim}c$??, AA

i) 1. $e \lor P$
   2. $a \rightarrow {\sim}P$
   3. $a \,\&\, b$?
   4. a 3, ?
   5. ?   4, 2, AA
   6. e ??

j) 1. $c \lor q$?
   2. $e \lor {\sim}q$ P
   3. $f \lor {\sim}e$ P
   4. ${\sim}P$
   5. ${\sim}e$ 3, 4, ?
   6. ${\sim}q$??
   7. ?   1, ??

2. Let a = Andrea had a high grade-point average last term, b = Brian did, c = Catharine did, d = David did, and e = Evan did. Translate the following propositional logic arguments from propositional logic symbols into ordinary English, adapting the wording as desirable. After you do the translation, construct a proof that proves the argument valid.

a) $b \rightarrow c, c \rightarrow d, d \rightarrow e, b$, therefore e

b)* $b \rightarrow c, a \rightarrow b, d \rightarrow a, \sim c$, therefore $\sim d$

c) $a \& b, b \& c$, therefore $a \& c$

d) $b \rightarrow c, c \rightarrow d, \sim d, a$, therefore $a \& \sim b$

e)* $a \rightarrow (b \& c), c \rightarrow e, a$, therefore $a \& e$

f) $b \& \sim c, c \vee d, d \rightarrow a$, therefore a

g) $a \rightarrow (b \& \sim c), c$ or d, a, therefore d

3.   Using the letters given, translate the following arguments into propositional logic, and prove them valid. In some cases, you will need to recognize hidden premises.

a)   If you cut off the top of a triangle with a line that is parallel with its base, you get a quadrilateral with two parallel sides. If a figure is a quadrilateral with two parallel sides, it is a trapezoid. So if you cut off the top of a triangle with a line that is parallel with its base, then you have a trapezoid. (*c*, *q*, *t*)

b)   [Pliny the Elder, *Natural History*, 7.50, arguing against astrology] If astrology is true, then our fates must be the same if we are born at the same time. But many people born at the same moment have entirely different fates. (*a*, *f*)

c)   [Galileo's reasoning on the solar system] If the planetary system is not heliocentric, Venus will not show phases. But Venus does show phases. So the planetary system is heliocentric. (*h*, *v*)

d)   Kaitlin can't be guilty, for she didn't act suspiciously, and that's how someone acts when she is guilty. (*g*, *s*)

e)   If each man had a definite set of rules of conduct by which he regulated his life, he would be no better than a machine. We're not machines, so there are no such rules. (*d*, *b*)

f)   [From an advertisement in *The Economist* magazine, August 1995] If you are looking for a bank committed to a straight-forward approach to helping you protect your wealth, consider Bank Julius Baer. (*l*, *b*)

g)*   If the government minister is not honest, she is not to be trusted, and if she's not to be trusted, she should not hold a government post and should be sent back to her law firm. But I know that the minister is not honest, so she should return to her law firm. (*h*, *t*, *g*, *r*)

h)*   As a patriot, I can tell you what attitude you should have to this great nation: love it or leave it! Clearly you don't love it, so why don't you leave? (*l*, *g*)

i)   [From a letter to *The Record*, 25 February 1995] The only negative aspect of being a No supporter in the Quebec referendum is finding oneself alongside Brian Mulroney. If keeping Canada together means accepting the company of Mulroney, then maybe we had better rethink our positions. (*k*, *a*)

j)   [Part of the ancient philosopher Timon's directions on how one can be happy] If one wants to be happy, one must pay attention to three connected questions: first, what are things like by nature, second, how should we be disposed towards things, and third, what will be the outcome of this disposition? (*h*, *n*, *d*, *o*)

4.   Construct a proof proving that if a biconditional $(a \rightarrow b) \& (b \rightarrow a)$ is true and b is false, then a is false.

5. Translate the following arguments into propositional logic symbols using the letters indicated. Construct a proof of their validity.

a)* [Zen Master Dogen in *Dogen*, by Yuho Yokoi] You should listen to the Zen master's teaching without trying to make it conform to your own self-centred viewpoint; otherwise, you will be unable to understand what he is saying. (*l, a*)

b) She's going to the Christmas party only if she has the night off work. And she has the night off work only if David can replace her. But David can replace her only if he doesn't have an exam the next day, and he does. So she isn't going to the Christmas party. (*g, n, d, e*)

c) Humans are mammals, and whales, dolphins, and elephants are mammals, so humans and whales are mammals. (*h, w, d, e*)

d)* In order to avoid the intricacies of such theories, we will rely on our earlier remark that the objective of an argument is to convince an audience. If this is so, then it is sufficient for our purposes that the premises of a good argument be accepted as true by our audience. (*o, s*)

e) It should be clear that this new argument is invalid, for it is obviously possible for its two premises to be true while its conclusion is false, and if this is true then the argument is invalid. (*t, v*)

f)* The Liberals will win the election if and only if their leader is attractive to voters in rural ridings. But rural voters will never support a Liberal leader. (*l, a*)

g) There's a problem. It's a problem with your hardware or your software. If it's your software, Deborah can fix it. If there's a problem with your hardware, Scott can help. But I don't think it's a problem with your software, so Scott can help. (*p, h, s, r, d*)

h) Either you've offended Alex or he simply dislikes you. It must be the latter, for I can't imagine you offending Alex. (*o, l*)

i)* Americans or Germans or Russians will win the most medals at next year's Olympics, but the Russians will not do well enough to win and the Germans will not do well enough to win, so the Americans will win the most medals. (*a, g, r*)

6. Translate into propositional logic symbols and prove valid the following arguments. Use the letters in parentheses to represent your simple propositions. Recognize hidden argument components where necessary.

a)* [Adapted from a cartoon by Jules Feiffer, 16 April 1972] We do not want anarchy. When criminals are not punished, the result is rising crime—in a word, anarchy. When corporations don't break the law, the result is falling stocks—in a word, anarchy. So we should punish criminals and support corporate crime! (*a, p, b*)

b) If capital punishment does not deter capital crimes, it is not justified, and if it's not justified, it should not be a part of criminal law and should be abolished everywhere. Capital punishment does not, however, deter capital crimes, so it should be abolished everywhere. (*c, j, l, e*)

c)* If you're so smart, why aren't you rich? (*s, r*)

d) Rumour had it that Sam Stone or a look-alike was having dinner at The Steak House. When Tom asked whether he had made a reservation and had showed up on time, the hostess replied affirmatively. "In that case," said Tom, "the person having dinner can't possibly be Sam Stone." (*s, l, r, t*)

e) If the Rev. Jerry Falwell evaluates his ministry by the money it makes, then he is serving mammon, not God. Now the newspapers reported a complaint by him that his ministry has probably lost $1 million, maybe closer to $2 million, in revenues over the past month as a result of infighting at PTL. If he complains in that way, he is evaluating his ministry by the money it makes. (*e, m, g, c*)

f) [REAL Women is a Canadian organization promoting some of the traditional women's roles] If you belong to REAL Women, you believe in its ideals. But if you believe in its ideals, you believe that men should be our leaders. If you believe that men should be our leaders, you must believe that REAL Women should not lead us. But if you believe that REAL Women shouldn't lead us, you don't really believe in REAL Women. So if you believe in REAL Women, you don't! (*r, i, m, l*)

g)* Zsa Zsa Gabor, who recently got married for the eighth time, gave her age as 54. If that's true, she was only five when she entered and won the Miss Hungary beauty title in 1933. (*z, f*)

h) [Adapted from an argument in Trudy Govier's *A Practical Study of Argument*, 1997, p. 214] Elephants have been known to bury their dead. But they would do so only if they have a concept of their own species and understand what death means. If they understand what death means, they have a capacity for abstraction, and if they have a capacity for abstraction, they can think. Yet you admit that elephants have no moral rights only if they can't think, so elephants have moral rights. (*b, c, u, a, t, m*)

7. Construct two proofs of the following propositional logic argument, one that uses the rule CS and one that does not.

> Campbell was mayor for the shortest time in the city's history, but it wasn't his fault if his party didn't fully support him. The party didn't fully support him if its president did not support him, so it wasn't his fault. (*c, f, s, p*)

8. Translate the following arguments into propositional logic symbols, and prove them valid. Define your own simple propositions.

a)* She can't have many friends if she doesn't respect them. If she doesn't allow them to be themselves, she does not respect them. If she objects to the clothes people wear, she doesn't allow them to be themselves. And she does object to people's clothes. So she can't have many friends.

b) Robbery or vengeance was the motive for the crime. But the victim had money in her pockets, and the motive could not have been robbery if this was so. Clearly, it was a crime of vengeance.

c)   Napoleon can be criticized if he usurped power that did not properly belong to him. If there were no laws that justified his rise to power, he usurped power improperly. But there were no laws of this sort. So Napoleon can be criticized.

d)   If we extend further credit on the Jacobs account, he will feel obliged to accept our bid on the next project. We can count on a larger profit if he feels obliged to accept our bid on the next project. But counting on a larger profit will allow us to improve our financial forecast. So we can improve our financial forecast by extending further credit on the Jacobs account.

For more online exercises, review questions, and quizzes related to the material in this chapter, please go to www.oupcanada.com/GoodReasoning5e

PROPOSITIONAL LOGIC II

Appendix 2 introduced some basic propositional schemes of argument. In this third appendix, we take this further by introducing more complex propositional schemes:

▶ conditional proofs;
▶ *reductio ad absurdum* arguments;
▶ reasoning by dilemma; and
▶ "De Morgan's Laws."

Appendix 2 introduced propositional logic connectives and some simple argument schemes that you can use in propositional logic proofs. In this appendix, we introduce more complex schemes that can help us capture important aspects of day-to-day discussion and debates. By adding them, we will make our propositional logic a system of argument that more closely approximates the kinds of reasoning that characterize ordinary thinking.

1 Conditional Proofs

The rules AA and DC may be described as instances of conditional "elimination." They allow us to use a conditional to establish the truth of its consequent or the falsity of its antecedent. In the process, we "eliminate'" the conditional and replace it with a related proposition. The scheme "conditional proof," or "→P," is a scheme of conditional "introduction" that we use when we want prove a conditional. Because we frequently argue for conditionals in ordinary reasoning, →P captures an important argumentative strategy that characterizes ordinary reasoning.

To see how →P works, consider how we might attempt to prove a conditional in the context of an ordinary conversation. Imagine that a group of us are arguing about municipal politics, about what should happen to an old industrial site (a "brownfield") in the core of the city where we live. Someone says the city should turn the site into parkland. Suppose someone answers, "No, the city will be better off if they rezone the land and divide it into residential lots." How can one defend and establish this conditional? One can imagine the conversation continuing as follows:

> Just think about it. The city will be better off if they rezone the land and divide it into residential lots. For suppose they do. The property value will increase dramatically if the land is rezoned and divided into residential lots, so the value of the property will increase dramatically. In those circumstances, private developers will be willing to pay for the development of the property, and the city won't have to pay the cost. And the city will be better off if it doesn't have to pay the cost.

This extended argument consists primarily of claims about what would be the case if the antecedent of the proposed conditional were true—i.e. if the city did rezone the land and divide it into residential lots. In arguing in this way, the arguer has adopted the argument scheme →P.

The structure of this argument can be illustrated if we adopt the following legend:

r = The city rezones the land.
d = The city divides the land into residential lots.
i = The value of the property will increase dramatically.
p = Private developers will be willing to pay for the development of the property.
c = The city will pay the cost.
b = The city will be better off.

Using this translation scheme, we can sketch our sample argument as follows:

Conclusion: $(r \ \& \ d) \rightarrow b$
   For suppose $(r \ \& \ d)$
   We know $(r \ \& \ d) \rightarrow i$
      So i
   But $i \rightarrow p$
      So p
   But $p \rightarrow \sim c$
      So $\sim c$
   And $\sim c \rightarrow b$
      So b
   Therefore $(r \ \& \ d) \rightarrow b$

You may see that this argument contains a sub-argument that is based on the supposition that $(r \ \& \ d)$ is true. This supposition is used as a temporary premise that the arguer assumes in order to deduce what would be true if $(r \ \& \ d)$ were true. On the basis of this assumption, the propositions i, p, $\sim c$, and then b are deduced. This allows the arguer to conclude that b is true if $(r \ \& \ d)$ is true, i.e. that $(r \ \& \ d) \rightarrow b$.

In arguing in this way, the arguer has constructed a conditional proof. It is a "conditional" proof for two reasons—because the proof of *b* is conditional on the supposition that *(r & d)* and because it is ultimately used to prove the conditional *(r & d)* → *b*. Within a propositional logic proof, we prove the validity of arguments like this by defining the argument scheme →P as follows:

→**P**: X (S/→P), . . . Y, *therefore* X → Y

This definition can be read as follows: Take any *X* as a supposition for a conditional proof (S/→P), deduce any proposition *Y*, and conclude that *X* → *Y*. Within a proof, we justify the line with *X* by writing "S/→P" and the line with *X* → *Y* by writing "*x-y*, →P," where *x* is the number of the line where *X* is introduced and *y* is the number of the line where *Y* occurs.

Using the legend we have already identified, our first example of a conditional proof can be proved as follows:

1. (r & d) → i   P
2. *i* → *p*   P
3. p → ~c   P
4. ~c → b   P
5. *r & d*   S/→P
6. *i*   1, 5, AA
7. *p*   2, 6, AA
8. ~*c*   3, 7, AA
9. *b*   4, 8, AA
10. (r & d) → b   5–9, →P

You are already familiar with informal instances of such reasoning, for we construct conditional proofs whenever we assume a proposition "for the sake of argument" in order to show what follows from it.

In order to ensure that the scheme →P is not used to justify any illegitimate inference in a propositional logic proof, we will stipulate that the lines of a conditional "subproof" (the lines that extend from our conditional supposition to the consequent we deduce) must not be used elsewhere in the proof. This is a restriction that is needed to ensure that the conditional supposition is employed (explicitly or implicitly) only when we are deducing what would be the case if it were true. In our proof above, this means that the lines 3–7 cannot be employed elsewhere in the proof.

Another example can illustrate →P. Suppose that you believe (1) that we can solve the problems of the world's developing countries and still enjoy a reasonable standard of living if we develop alternative forms of energy and (2) that there will be a greater chance of lasting peace if we solve the problems of the world's developing countries. If we accept these two premises, we can use the following proof to show that there will be a greater chance of lasting peace if we develop alternative forms of energy:

a = We develop alternative forms of energy.
s = We can solve the problems of the world's developing countries.

e = We will enjoy a reasonable standard of living.

g = There will be a greater chance of lasting peace.

1. $a \rightarrow (s \, \& \, e)$ P
2. $s \rightarrow g$ P
3. a P/$\rightarrow$P
4. $s \, \& \, e$ 1, 3, AA
5. s 4, &E
6. g 2, 5, AA
7. $a \rightarrow$3–6, $\rightarrow$P

Here as elsewhere, the key to a good conditional proof is the proper use of other propositional rules of inference after we have adopted our initial conditional premise S/$\rightarrow$P.

Construct proofs of the following arguments using the rule $\rightarrow$P and whatever other rules are necessary:

a)* $a \rightarrow b$, $b \rightarrow c$, therefore $a \rightarrow c$
b) $a \rightarrow b$, therefore $\sim b \rightarrow c$
c) $a \rightarrow (b \, \& \, c)$, $b \rightarrow c$, $c \rightarrow e$, therefore $a \rightarrow e$
d) $a \rightarrow (b \lor c)$, $a \rightarrow d$, $d \rightarrow \sim c$, therefore $a \rightarrow c$
e) $a \rightarrow b$, $a \rightarrow c$, therefore $a \rightarrow (b \, \& \, c)$

2   *Reductio ad Absurdum*

The schemes of argument we have discussed so far offer evidence that implies their conclusions. One may also argue for a conclusion by offering "indirect" evidence that demonstrates that the opposing point of view is mistaken. In our logic, we will include an argument scheme that is designed to allow indirect reasoning in propositional logic proofs. We call this scheme "*reductio ad absurdum*," or "RAA" for short.

Literally, *reductio ad absurdum* means "reduction to absurdity." In keeping with this, RAA arguments attempt to establish the absurdity of a position they reject. They disprove a proposition X by assuming it ("for the sake of argument") and deriving a contradiction, a proposition of the form $Y \, \& \sim Y$. Because $Y \, \& \sim Y$ cannot be true, this allows an arguer to conclude $\sim X$ (much as DC allows us to conclude $\sim X$ from $X \rightarrow Y$ and $\sim Y$). We can define the scheme as:

RAA: X (S/RAA), . . . Y & ~Y, *therefore* ~X

This definition can be read as follows: Take any X as a supposition for a *reductio ad absurdum* (S/RAA), deduce some contradiction of the form $Y \, \& \sim Y$, and conclude that $\sim X$. Within a proof, we justify the line with X by writing "S/RAA," and the line with $\sim X$, by writing "*x–y*, RAA," where *x* is the number of the line where *X* is introduced and *y* is the number of the line where the contradiction *Y* & ~*Y* occurs.

An example may make RAA arguments more intuitive. Some of the clearest examples of *reductio ad absurdum* arguments are found in mathematical and geometric proofs, but our interest is the kinds of arguments couched in ordinary language. Consider, then, a discussion of the following regulation on grade-point averages for repeated courses, taken from the Wilfrid Laurier University undergraduate calendar (1995–6, p. 35):

> Students in degree programs may repeat courses up to a maximum of two credits. Students who repeat courses above the two credit maximum will have both attempts over the 2.00 limit count toward their GPA.

It should be apparent to you that this rule makes no sense. One might try to explain this by arguing as follows:

> The calendar makes no sense. For suppose it did. Then students cannot repeat more than two credits' worth of courses. But if they can have courses above this maximum count toward their GPA, then they can repeat more than two credits' worth of courses. But then they both can and cannot repeat more than two credits' worth of courses. And how can one make sense of that!

This is an RAA argument. It shows that a certain proposition (that this calendar makes sense) leads to a contradiction and concludes that this proposition must be false.

We can prove the validity of the proposed argument as follows:

c = The calendar makes sense.
r = Students can repeat more than two credits' worth of courses.
a = They can have courses above this maximum count toward their GPA.

1.	*c* →	P
2.	*c* → *a*	P
3.	*a* → *r*	P
4.	*c*	S/RAA
5.	~*r*	1, 4, AA
6.	*a*	2, 4, AA
7.	*r*	3, 6, AA
8.	*r* & ~*r*	7, 5, &I
9.	~*c*	4–8, RAA

Like the scheme →P, the scheme RAA can be described as a proof within a proof. In one case, the subproof deduces a consequent from an antecedent that is supposed. In the other, it deduces a contradiction from a supposition that is the negation of the conclusion. In both cases, the lines within the subproof cannot be used elsewhere in our proof. In the case of RAA, this means that the lines beginning with S/RAA and ending with *Y* & ~*Y* (lines 4–8 in our example) cannot be employed elsewhere in our proof. This stipulation ensures that the conclusions we deduce on the basis of our RAA premise are restricted to conclusions about the situation that would hold if it were true.

Our second example of an RAA argument comes from a debate over cormorants and the claim that they are birds that should be eradicated or controlled because they destroy freshwater fisheries. One contribution to the debate comes from an article entitled

"Why do we hate big, black birds?" published by Nancy Clark in *Seasons* (winter 2002, p. 5). In the course of her essay, Clark proposes a theory to account for our different attitudes to different kinds of species:

> My theory is that our views are based on how abundant or rare a species is. People prize rare items, including rare animals, and will spend a great deal of time, effort and money saving a single humpback whale, but hardly any to try to prevent thousands of frogs from being run over. . . . [D]o we admire rock doves, raccoons, and Canada geese for their resourcefulness and adaptability? No, we think they're pests. We don't seem to like species that are too successful.

Is Clark's theory correct? We cannot settle the issue in any definitive way here, but consider the following RAA argument, which uses our attitudes to pets in an argument against it:

> Suppose that Clark is right, that we like animals if and only if they are rare. That means that we like dogs if and only if they are rare. Because dogs are the most common animal we know, it follows that we don't like dogs. But we do. So much for Clark's theory.

This argument could best be understood as a syllogism, but we can also construct the following propositional logic account of it:

c = Clark's theory on our attitudes to animals is correct.
l = We like dogs.
r = Dogs are rare.

1. $c \rightarrow ((l \rightarrow r) \mathbin{\&} (r \rightarrow l))$ P
2. l P
3. $\sim r$ P
4. c S/RAA
5. $(l \rightarrow r) \mathbin{\&} (r \rightarrow l)$ 1, 4, AA
6. $l \rightarrow r$ 5, &E
7. $\sim l$ 6, 3, DC
8. $l \mathbin{\&} \sim l$ 2, 7, &I
9. $\sim c$ 4–8, RAA

RAA is an important scheme of argument, not only in propositional logic but also in ordinary argument, for it allows us to prove that some views are correct by proving that opposing views are mistaken. In debates between argumentative opponents, RAA is often the argument scheme of choice, for it allows one to undermine the views of one's opponent in a very pointed way. For this reason, RAA arguments are common in political debate.

1. Go to exercise Appendix 2M, question 2. Prove all of the arguments valid using the argument scheme RAA and whatever other rules are necessary.

2.* The following argument is adapted from a Letter to the Editor, *Time* magazine (30 April 2007). Prove it valid by *reductio ad absurdum*: If we impeached George W. Bush, he would be removed from office. But if he was removed from office, that would simply bring forth someone else more reckless. Let's not have someone more reckless!

3. Using ordinary language, construct a *reductio ad absurdum* argument for or against the claim that men with beards cannot be trusted. Translate the argument into propositional logic, and construct an RAA proof of its validity.

3   Dilemmas

In ordinary language, a "dilemma" is a situation that forces us to make a choice between alternatives we would rather avoid. In propositional logic, a "dilemma" is a scheme of argument that is founded on the two alternatives set out in a disjunction. In dilemma arguments, one does not choose between the two disjuncts in a disjunction but instead one shows what follows from the proposition that one or the other disjunction is true. We will include two kinds of dilemma arguments in our propositional logic. One is called "dilemma" (or "D" for short), the other "**dilemma to disjunction**" (or "DV"). The two schemes are defined as follows:

D: X V Y, X → Z, Y → Z, therefore Z
DV: X V Y, X → Z, Y → W, therefore Z V W

As you can see from these definitions, dilemma arguments combine a disjunction and conditionals in a way that allows us to establish some conclusion that follows even though we do not know which of the disjuncts in the disjunction is true. The validity of such arguments can be understood in terms of our earlier discussion of disjunctions and conditionals. Thus, the initial disjunction in a dilemma argument states that one of the disjuncts is true, but this implies that the antecedent of one of the associated conditionals must be true and that the same can be said of one of the consequents.

Our first example, which illustrates the scheme D, also illustrates the connection between our ordinary use of the word "dilemma" and the argument scheme that goes by the same name. Consider the following argument about public speakers, which is taken from a book written by the famous sixteenth-century philosopher Thomas Hobbes (*Principles of rhetorik*, ch. 24): "'Tis not good to be an Orator, because if he speak the truth, he shall displease Men: If he speak falsely, he shall displease God."

This is a sentence that presents the dilemma of the Orator, whose goal is to convince an audience (something that compels him to say what they would like to hear) but who is morally obligated to speak the truth (which is not what people like to hear).

Hobbes's sentence presents a dilemma argument the Orator has to face. It is indicated by the premise indicator "because" and can be translated into propositional logic and proved as follows:

i = I speak the truth.
m = I please men.
g = I please God.
s = I am in a good situation.

1.	$t \lor \sim t$	P (hidden)
2.	$t \to \sim m$	P
3.	$\sim t \to \sim g$	P
4.	$\sim m \to \sim s$	P (hidden)
5.	$\sim g \to \sim s$	P (hidden)
6.	$t \to \sim s$	2, 4, CS
7.	$\sim t \to \sim s$	3, 5, CS
8.	$\sim s$	1, 6, 7, D

Our second example of dilemma is a version of DV taken from a discussion of the suggestion that airports should use face-recognition software to guard against terrorist attack (in *Atlantic Monthly*, December 2002, p. 15). Charles C. Mann writes:

At Logan Airport, in Boston, the software would have scanned the faces of 25 million passengers last year, resulting in 170,000 false identifications. . . . The additional cost and disruption, to passengers and airlines alike, of interrogating and screening those people would be enormous. . . . One could set the criteria to reduce that number of false alarms, but then the risk of missing real terrorists would be dramatically increased—the tradeoff is unavoidable. And a security system that either fails in its principal task or causes major disruptions is not desirable.

In this case, the argument can be converted into propositional logic symbols in the following way:

f = Face-recognition software is used to minimize false alarms.
d = The additional costs and disruption of false identifications would be enormous.
i = The risk of missing real terrorists is dramatically increased.
s = Face-recognition software succeeds in its principal task.
d = Face-recognition software is desirable.

1.	$f \lor \sim f$	P (hidden)
2.	$f \to d$	P
3.	$\sim f \to i$	P

4. $i \rightarrow {\sim}s$ P
5. $(d \vee {\sim}s) \rightarrow {\sim}d$ P
5. ${\sim}f \rightarrow {\sim}s$ 3, 4, CS
6. $d \vee {\sim}s$ 1, 2, 5, DV
7. ${\sim}d$ 5, 6, AA

In this and our previous example, you may note that the disjunction that is the basis of the dilemma is a hidden premise. This is common in ordinary argument, for the dilemma strategy is so common that audiences will, in normal circumstances, immediately understand that an argument of this form is founded on an assumed disjunction.

Unacceptable Disjunctions and Dilemmas

Like the argument scheme VE, our two kinds of dilemmas are founded on disjunctions. In constructing propositional logic proofs of arguments of this sort, we are proving that they are valid. We have already seen that propositional logic does not prove that an argument is a strong argument, for this requires that an argument be valid *and* have acceptable premises. In dealing with dilemmas and VE arguments in the course of ordinary argument, this means that you must judge whether the disjunction that is the basis of the dilemma or VE is acceptable.

A disjunction is called a **false dilemma** (or, less frequently, a "false dichotomy") when it fails to exhaust all alternatives and both disjuncts may be false (because some unstated alternative is true). This is not a concern if the disjunction has the form $X \vee {\sim}X$, as in the two examples of dilemma we just discussed, for in that case X must be true or false, which means that the disjunction must be true. The same cannot be said in other kinds of cases, however, for they are founded on disjunctions that may have two false disjuncts. This is frequently the case in ordinary reasoning, where false dilemmas are featured in weak arguments that reduce complex issues to simplistic alternatives that overlook other possibilities.

Consider, to take one example, an article in *Mother Jones* magazine discussing ways of making American neighbourhoods safe. In the article, Michael Castleman develops a VE argument, beginning with the disjunction "We can control crime by reducing criminal opportunity or by addressing poverty" and arguing that we can't control crime by addressing poverty. He concludes that we must try to control crime by reducing criminal opportunity.

In propositional logic, we can represent Castleman's basic argument as follows:

c = We can control crime by reducing criminal opportunity.
p = We can control crime by addressing poverty.

1. $c \vee p$ P
2. ${\sim}p$ P
3. c 1, 2, VE

This simple proof shows that Castleman's argument is a valid argument. To determine whether it is a strong argument, it follows that we need to decide whether we should accept its premises as true. In response to Castleman's article, Marc Mauer, the assistant director of the Washington Sentencing Project, wrote the following in a letter to *Mother Jones*:

> Castleman provides some good examples about ways in which neighborhoods can come together in crime prevention efforts. But his suggestion that "reducing criminal opportunity is our best bet for controlling crime" because of the difficulty of addressing poverty . . . raises a false dichotomy.

This is a good example of a charge of false dilemma, for it suggests that Castleman's disjunction, *c V p*, overlooks other alternatives that might be true—in particular the possibility that we could control crime by adopting a mix of measures that fight poverty and control criminal opportunity. As in other cases of false dilemma, the claim is that it is a mistake to think that the alternatives presented in a disjunction are the only possibilities.

In ordinary language, we say that someone *escapes through the horns of a dilemma* when they refute a dilemma argument by rejecting the disjunction it is founded on (by claiming that it is a false dilemma). Consider the argument:

> Today's politician is placed in an impossible position. Either they vote according to their own lights or as their constituents' desire. If they vote as their constituents want, they compromise their conscience; but if they vote according to their own lights, they alienate their constituents. So either they compromise their conscience or they alienate their constituents.

This is a clear example of the scheme DV. Though we could prove it a valid argument, one might still try to escape through the horns of the disjunction it is founded on. Politicians can, one might argue, reject the either/or assumption that they have two choices: to vote according to their consciences or as their constituents want, for this overlooks the fact that they may vote in different ways at different times. They might, for example, choose to vote according to their own lights on matters of conscience but vote as the majority of their constituents want on other issues. By **"escaping between the horns" of the proposed dilemma** in this way, politicians need not compromise their conscience and will on many, if not most, issues please their constituents rather than alienate them.

A different problem arises when there are grounds for questioning the conditionals on which a dilemma argument relies. One is said to take a dilemma by the horns when one refutes it by rejecting these conditionals (or the premises they are founded on). Here again, the problem is not the validity of the argument, which is guaranteed by the scheme D or DV. The problem is premise acceptability, for the premises might be rejected.

Imagine a woman who does not believe in abortion contemplating an unwanted pregnancy. Suppose she reasons as follows:

> If I have an abortion, I'll be haunted by guilt. But if I don't, I'll ruin my career. If I'm haunted by guilt, my life will be unhappy. If I ruin my career, my life will be unhappy. So I'm going to be unhappy.

If we let:

> a = I have an abortion.
> r = My career will be ruined.
> g = I'll be haunted by guilt.
> h = My life will be happy.

then we can prove the validity of this argument as follows:

1. a V ~a   P
2. a → g   P
3. ~a → r   P
4. g → ~h   P
5. r → ~h   P
6. a → ~h   2, 4, CS
7. ~a → ~h   3, 6, CS
8. ~h   1, 6, 7, D

In this case, the disjunction that the argument relies on ("Either I'll have an abortion or I won't") is clearly true, so one cannot escape through the horns of the dilemma. It follows that the only way to refute the argument is by taking the dilemma by the horns and arguing that one of its conditionals is false, i.e. that either $a \to$ ~h is false or that ~$a \to$ ~h is false. Because the arguments over these conditionals raise very complex and very controversial issues, we won't develop this strategy in detail here. Suffice it to say that opponents on the different sides of the abortion debate are likely to take hold of different conditionals and, in this sense, different horns of the dilemma.

CRITICIZING DISJUNCTIONS AND DILEMMAS

- A *false dilemma* is a false disjunction that overlooks some alternative beyond those incorporated in its disjuncts.
- One *escapes between the horns of a dilemma* when one shows that the disjunction a dilemma relies on is a false dilemma.
- One *takes a dilemma by the horns* when one refutes it by showing that one (or both) of the conditionals it relies on is not acceptable.

EXERCISE   C3

1. Prove the following arguments valid using the scheme D or DV and whatever other rules are necessary:

    a)* a V b, a → c, b → d, therefore c V b
    b) a V b, a → c, c → e, e → f, b → c, therefore c V f
    c) a V b, ~c → ~b, a → c, therefore c
    d) a → (b & (b → c)), e → c, a V e, therefore c
    e) a V b, a → c, therefore c V b

2. Construct a proof proving the validity of the following dilemma argument. How might one escape through its horns or take it by the horns?

> If I tell my boss how I bungled the contract, I'll be fired. If he finds out from someone else, he'll fire me. Either I tell him myself or he'll find out from someone else. Woe is me!

4   De Morgan's Laws

The final scheme of propositional argument we discuss also figures prominently in ordinary reasoning. It consists of one of two forms of argument called "De Morgan's Laws" ("DeM" for short), after the nineteenth-century British logician Augustus De Morgan. There are two variants of the scheme DeM, which can be defined as follows:

DeM: $\sim(X \vee Y)$ is equivalent to $\sim X \,\&\, \sim Y$
$\sim(X \,\&\, Y)$ is equivalent to $\sim X \vee \sim Y$

The word "equivalent" in each line of this definition means that the two propositions listed can be deduced from each other. The first line tells us that $\sim X \,\&\, \sim Y$ can be deduced from $\sim(X \vee Y)$ and that $\sim(X \vee Y)$ can be deduced from $\sim X \,\&\, \sim Y$. The second tells us that $\sim(X \,\&\, Y)$ can be deduced from $\sim X \vee \sim Y$ and vice versa.

The validity of DeM should be evident. The first part of DeM tells us that the proposition "I'll go to neither Salzburg nor London" is equivalent to the proposition "I won't go to Salzburg *and* I won't go to London." More generally, a disjunction claims that one of its disjuncts is true, so the claim that it is false is equivalent to the claim that the first *and* the second is false. The second part of DeM tells us that the falsity of the claim "I will go to Salzburg and to London" is equivalent to the claim "I won't go to Salzburg *or* I won't go to London." More generally, a conjunction is untrue if and only if one of its conjuncts is false, i.e. the first *or* the second is false.

In propositional logic proofs, the rule DeM is an effective way to move from the negation of a conjunction or disjunction to an equivalent disjunction or conjunction (and vice versa). Suppose we know that you will be going to the opening of a new run of *Hair* if you can find \$50 spending money and can make it to the box office four hours before the show begins. If we subsequently discover that you didn't make the show, then De Morgan's Laws allow us to deduce that either you didn't find the \$50 or you didn't make it to the box office. We can prove this as follows:

f = You find \$50 spending money.
m = You make it to the box office four hours before the show begins.
c = You go to the opening of *Hair*.

1. $(f \,\&\, m) \rightarrow c$ P
2. $\sim c$ P
3. $\sim(f \,\&\, m)$ 1, 2, DC
4. $\sim f \vee \sim m$ 3, DeM

EXERCISE   C4

1. Let *a* = Angela goes to *Hair*, *b* = Brian goes to *Hair*, and *c* = Carla goes to *Hair*. Translate the following arguments into English and construct a proof of their validity using DeM and whatever other rules are necessary.

a)* ~(a & b), b, therefore ~a

b) ~(a V b), ~a → c, therefore c

c) ~a V ~b, c → (a & b), therefore ~c

d) ~a & ~b, therefore ~(a & c)

e) a & b, therefore ~(~a V ~b)

5   Summary: Rules of Inference

We have now introduced all the argument schemes we will include in our version of propositional logic. The complex schemes we have introduced in this appendix are listed in the summary box below. You may use this box as a convenient reference, but it is best to learn the schemes by heart.

When you construct propositional logic proofs that use complex schemes, keep in mind the guidelines for proof construction we discussed in appendix 2, for they apply to these kinds of proofs. Construct your proofs in a step-by-step manner, proceeding from your premises to your conclusion. If you are unsure of how you should proceed, you may want to develop your strategy by seeing what you can deduce from your premises or by thinking backward from the conclusion (asking yourself what kinds of schemes will be needed to prove the conclusion true). The rules RAA and →P are often helpful in difficult cases, for they allow you to introduce a supposition you can work with.

We will end by once again noting that propositional logic proofs establish the validity of particular chains of reasoning but that this is only one of the two ingredients of strong arguments. To put this in a positive way, we know that an argument that can be proved valid if propositional logic satisfies one of the criteria of strong propositional reasoning. That said, a complete assessment of a propositional argument must consider questions of premise acceptability as well as validity. In the case of dilemmas and disjunctions, that is why we have noted some common issues that arise in this regard. In working with propositional proofs and arguments, we ask you to remember that an instance of good propositional reasoning exists only when one has an argument with premises that are acceptable. If you keep this in mind, then your ability to construct such proofs can provide a good basis for the construction of good arguments.

COMPLEX PROPOSITIONAL SCHEMES

→P*   X (S/→P), . . . Y therefore X → Y

RAA*   X (S/RAA), . . . Y & ~Y therefore ~X

D   X V Y, X → Z, Y → Z therefore Z

DV   X V Y, X → Z, Y → W therefore Z V W
DeMV ~(X V Y) is equivalent to ~X & ~Y
DeM& ~(X & Y) is equivalent to ~X V ~Y

*-When using →P and RAA, the lines of the subproof cannot be used elsewhere as proof.

MAJOR EXERCISE CM

1. Translate into propositional symbols and prove the validity of the following arguments. Use the indicated letters to represent simple sentences, and use the scheme specified.

   a) [From an article on determinism—the view that we do not really choose to do what we do because our actions are caused by things beyond our control, such as heredity and environment] If a man could not do otherwise than he in fact did, then he is not responsible for his action. But if determinism is true, then the agent could not have done otherwise in any action. Therefore, if determinism is true, no one is responsible for what he does. (*d, o, r;* →)

   b) If Nick does not become a poet, he will become a social worker or a doctor. If he is a social worker or a doctor, he will be financially better off but unhappy. So Nick will be unhappy if he doesn't become a poet. (*p, s, d, f, h;* →)

   c)* You can join the air force only if you're 18, so you can't join the air force unless you're 18. (*j, e;* →)

   d) [Adapted from election material that criticized the position taken by a candidate for the Conservative Party of Canada] The Conservative candidate says that he would introduce a bill adding five years in prison to the sentence of anyone convicted of a crime committed with a gun; and that he is for fiscal restraint. So much for his credibility. A person who wants to undertake huge expenditures is not for fiscal restraint, and his penal reforms would require the expenditure of hundreds of millions of dollars for the construction and maintenance of new prisons. (*i, f, e; RAA*)

   e) It's not true that there are moral principles that apply in all cases. If that were true, it would be true that we must always return what we have borrowed. This implies that you should give a gun back if you have borrowed it for target shooting and the friend you borrowed it from has suffered a nervous breakdown and is determined to kill himself and asks for it back. But in these circumstances, it is obvious that we should not give it back. Which shows that moral principles do not apply in all cases. (*m, r, g, b, n, k, a; RAA*)

   f) [Adapted from Peter King, "Against Intolerance," in *Philosophy Now*, Winter 1994–5, pp. 23–24] The main point underlying all this, I think, is that it doesn't make sense to say that we tolerate something. If I say "I tolerate *x*" I mean both that I judge *x* to be wrong and put up with *x*. If we think *x* is wrong, it makes no sense to say that we tolerate *x*. (*s, j, p, w; D*)

   g)* The most unfair question one can ask a spouse is: "If I die, would you marry again?" It's unfair because if one says "Yes," it will be taken to mean that one is waiting for them to die; and if one says "No," that will be taken to mean that one's marriage is not a happy one! (*f, y, w, n, h; DV*)

h) If we censor pornographic films, we will be denying people the right to make their own choices, thereby causing people harm. But if we do not censor pornographic films, we run the risk of exposing society to crimes committed by those who have been influenced by such films, thereby causing people harm. It's unavoidable that some people will be harmed. (*p, m, h, c; D*)

i) Consider the Chrysler worker with a home and family. Either he tries to sell his home and seek employment elsewhere or he doesn't. If he tries to sell his home and seek employment elsewhere, he faces a substantial financial loss. If he doesn't, then he will have to live with frozen wages and guaranteed layoffs, and then he faces financial disaster. Some choice! (*s, e, f, w, g; D*)

j) [Adapted from Plato's *Apology*, 40c–41a] Death is one of two things. Either it is annihilation, and the dead have no consciousness of anything, or, as we are told, it is really a change—a migration of the soul from this place to another. Now if there is no consciousness but only (something like) a dreamless sleep, there is nothing to fear. . . . If on the other hand death is a removal from here to some other place, then all the dead are there and we should look forward to meeting them. So death is nothing to fear. (*a, c, m, f, d, l; D*)

k) The robbers didn't take the Ming vase or the Buddhist statue, and she'll be satisfied if they're here. So she'll be satisfied. (*m, b, s; DeM*)

l) I saw Maryanne in Pittsburgh on the 13th at 2 p.m., so she couldn't have been in Toronto at that time. (*p, t; DeM*)

m) A professor cannot be both a reputable scholar and a popular teacher. She is popular in the classroom, so she must have abandoned a life of reputable scholarship. (*s, t; DeM*)

n)* Jacinth pulled through without complications, but Francis has a black eye the size of a football, Kirstin has a fever of 39 degrees, and I see that Fred or Paul is in the hospital. So it is false that Fred and Paul are well. (*j, f, k, f, p; DeM*)

2. Provide a ***reductio ad absurdum*** argument for each of the following claims. Construct it in an English paragraph, and then translate your argument into propositional logic and construct a proof of its validity.

   a) Every occurrence has a cause.
   b)* Religion fulfills some deep human need.
   c) People in medieval times were wrong in thinking Earth saucer-shaped.

3. Provide *reductio ad absurdum* proofs for all the arguments in question 3 in exercise 9M.

4. For each of the dilemmas in question 1 (i.e. examples f, g, h, i, j) explain how one might escape through the horns of the dilemma or take it by the horns.

5. Prove the validity of the following arguments:

   a) (b → c), (c → b), ~b, therefore ~c
   b) (a V b) → c, ~(c V d), therefore ~a
   c)* ~(a & b), a, therefore ~b
   d)* a & b & c & d, therefore c V e

e)   ~(a or b), a V c, therefore c

f)   b → ~(c & d), ~c → e, ~d → f, therefore b → (e V f)

g)   ~(a & b), therefore a → ~b

h)   (b & c) → a, ~a, therefore ~b → c

i)   ~(a & b), ~a → c, ~b → c, therefore c

6.   Prove the validity of the following arguments. Provide your own legend.

a)   You'll get a passing or a failing grade on the exam. If you get a failing grade, then my confidence in you has been misplaced. But I'm sure my confidence has not been misplaced, so I'm sure you'll get a passing grade.

b)* If you do your homework assignments, you'll learn informal logic, and if you learn informal logic, you'll be a good reasoner. But if you're a good reasoner, you'll probably succeed in your chosen field. So you'll probably succeed in your chosen field if you do your homework assignments.

c)   I hope the prime minister can use the forthcoming Commonwealth meetings to good advantage by persuading New Zealand to alter its sporting relationships with France after the latter's nuclear tests in Tahiti. If New Zealand continues to associate with France, Pacific island nations will boycott the Commonwealth Games, and if they do that the Games will be cancelled. But if the Games are cancelled, millions of dollars spent in preparation and millions of athlete hours spent in training will go down the drain. So if New Zealand continues to associate with France, millions of dollars and millions of athlete-hours will go down the drain.

d)* [Look for the hidden conclusion] If you're a great singer, then you're Shakespeare and the moon is made out of green cheese. So there.

e)   The murder of Sir Robert was motivated by the hatred he inspired or by a calculated desire to gain his fortune. If it was a calculated crime, it must have been perpetrated by both Lord Byron and his mistress, Kate; but if it was done out of hatred, then either the butler, Robert, or Lord Byron's brother, Jonathan, did it. Now, Kate was too frightened a woman to have done it, and Jonathan has the unassailable alibi of being in Brighton on the evening of the murder. Therefore, it's obvious the butler did it.

f)   If you enjoyed both Hemingway and Faulkner, you'd like Steinbeck, but you despise Steinbeck, so you must dislike either Hemingway or Faulkner.

g)   It will rain if and only if the wind changes, but the wind will change if and only if a high pressure area moves in, and a high pressure area will move in if and only if the arctic front moves southward. It follows that it will rain if the arctic front moves southward.

h)* According to a famous story in Greek philosophy, the great sophist Protagoras agreed to give Euthalus instruction in law on the following terms: Euthalus was to pay half of the fee in advance and the remainder if and when he won his first case. After the instruction, Euthalus did not take any cases, and Protagoras grew impatient waiting for the remainder of his payment. He finally took Euthalus to court himself, arguing as follows: The court will decide either for me or against me. If it decides for me, then Euthalus must pay. If it decides against me, then

Euthalus has won his first case in court. But if he wins his first case in court, then he must pay me (for that is our agreement). So Euthalus must pay me.

i)   [Euthalus learned his logic well and replied as follows:] Protagoras is wrong, for the court will decide either for or against me. If it decides for me, then I do not have to pay. But if it decides against me, then I have lost my first case in court. But if I lose my first case in court, then I do not have to pay (for that is our agreement). So I do not have to pay.

j)   [Adapted from an article comparing books and electronic readers, in *Time* magazine, 30 April 2007] The book doesn't need charging. It never crashes. Its interface is rapidly and intuitively navigable. A piece of information technology with these benefits remains a surprisingly wise choice for conveying information even today.

k)   If the patient has a bacterial infection, she will have a fever. If she does not have a bacterial infection, then a virus is the cause of her illness. So, if she has no fever, she must be ill from a virus.

l)   Either I'll go to France or I won't. If I go, I'll have an interesting time and send you a card from Metz. If I don't go to France, I'll go to Spain and send you a card from Barcelona. But if I go to Barcelona, I'll have an interesting time, so I'll have an interesting time no matter what.

m)   [From a comment on the Virginia Tech massacre in April 2007] When you explain mass murderers in their own terms, you glamorize what they do and who they are. And when you do that, you encourage similarly minded individuals to do the same. So if you're not encouraging similarly minded individuals to be mass murderers, then you can't be explaining them in their own terms.

n)   [From the *Toronto Sun*, 10 February 1983] It is wrong to think that we can both value life and be opposed to abortion and birth control. If everyone in the world were against abortion and birth control, can you imagine the terrible poverty, the starvation, the suffering? We would literally have wall-to-wall people, the whole world would be one big slum like we see in South American countries. Life wouldn't be worth living.

o)* [Adapted from Jack Miller's science column, the *Toronto Star*, 9 June 1987, p. A14] Kepler offered the theory [that the night sky should be an unbroken canopy of starlight] . . . to disprove the then popular idea that the universe stretched forever and was filled with an infinite number of stars. If that was true, he said, then there would be so many stars that no matter which way you looked at night, you would see one. In every direction there would be a star at some distance or other. There would be no dark spaces between the spots of light, so the sky would be all light. And since the sky obviously is dark at night, the universe does not stretch out forever, or does not have an infinite number of stars in it.

p)   [From an article on Senator John Glenn in the *Manchester Guardian Weekly*, 23 October 1983] "We are not flying into that and there's no way around it," he told the small band of aides and correspondents. . . . There was no argument. . . . When one of the world's greatest pilots says it isn't safe, you don't fly.

7.   Using the information provided, deduce by means of propositional logic proofs answers to the questions asked:

a) Will someone from the humanities be appointed president of the university you plan to attend?

The president has just turned 46. She is a responsible person, but her birthday has been spoiled by a financial scandal. Now she is in trouble with the board of governors or senate. If the board of governors is unhappy, they'll fire her, and she'll go somewhere else. If she goes somewhere else, one of the vice-presidents will be appointed president. But the Vice Presidents are from the humanities. (The president is from physics.) If the senate is unhappy with the president, they'll make it impossible for her to carry out her programs, and no responsible person will stay in those conditions.

b)* Are you likely to survive?

You are at sea in a terrible storm. You can run for a lifeboat or stay where you are. If you run for it, then you will be lost at sea. If you don't run, you will be safe unless the storm continues. If the storm continues, you can survive only if you run to one of the lifeboats. If the sky is dark, the storm is likely to continue. You look up and see a dark and stormy sky.

8. Prove that the following forms of argument are valid, and provide a sample argument to illustrate the scheme in question.

a)* $(p \lor q)$ & $\sim(p$ & $q)$, p, therefore $\sim q$

b) $p \lor q$, therefore $q \lor p$

c)* $p \rightarrow q$, therefore $\sim q \rightarrow \sim p$

d) $\sim r \rightarrow p$, $\sim p$ & q, $s \rightarrow \sim r$, therefore $\sim s$

e) $(a \rightarrow b)$ & $(b \rightarrow a)$, therefore $(a$ & $b) \lor (\sim a$ & $\sim b)$

f) The law of the excluded middle [i.e. $X \lor \sim X$], from no premises.

g)* The law of non-contradiction [i.e. $\sim(X$ & $\sim X)$], from no premises.

h) p & $(q \lor r)$, therefore $(p$ & $q) \lor (p$ & $r)$

THE CASE OF THE MISSING BROTHER

A case from the files of

_____ , *Super Sleuth*

(your name)

I still remember it clearly. That day I burst into your office with the news. I was flustered, but you sat there cool and unmoved.

"Calm down," you said, "and tell me what's the matter."

"He's gone," I spluttered, "he's disappeared!"

"It happens all the time," you mused philosophically.

"But he was here just yesterday, and now he's gone—poof—like a little puff of smoke."

"Calm down," you said again. "Calm down and tell me all the details."

So it began, the case of the missing brother. You've probably had more exciting cases, but it required a tidy bit of deduction, as far as I recall . . .

So much for intro. It's up to you to solve the case. The goal is to determine what happened to Louis, the missing brother. Was he kidnapped?

Murdered? Something else? Who perpetrated the crime? What, if any, were the weapons used? And where is Louis now? To deduce the right conclusion, work your way through each day of the case file below. From the information gathered on each day, you should be able to construct a propositional proof that provides some relevant information (e.g. that "if Mary did it, revenge must have been her motive"). By the time you solve the case, you should be more comfortable constructing proofs in propositional logic.

EXAMPLE

Day 1. You discover that one of the suspects, Joe, would have done something to Louis if and only if (1) he needed a lot of money or (2) he and Louis were still rivals. Yet you discover that Joe doesn't need any money (he's rolling in it!) and that Louis and Joe are no longer rivals.

> *Let:* j = Joe is the culprit.
> m = Joe needs a lot of money.
> r = Joe and Louis are rivals.

Then we can deduce the conclusion that Joe is not the culprit:

1.	(j → (m ∨ r)) & ((m ∨ r) → j)	P
2.	~m & ~r	P
3.	~(m ∨ r)	2, DeM
4.	j → (m ∨ r)	1, &E
5.	~j	4, 3, DC

Now you're on your own.

Day 2. Louis runs a house for homeless men in Montreal. If he was working on Thursday (the day of his disappearance), he would have been serving the men dinner at 5 p.m. If he was serving dinner, then Michael and Leo (two of the homeless men) would have seen him. Michael didn't see him. [If you can't sort out what conclusion you should try to prove, then turn to the answers at the end of the book.]

Day 3. If Louis wasn't working, he must have been headed to the grocery store or have gone for a run when he left on Thursday morning. If he goes for groceries, he walks past 121 rue Frontenac, where there is a big dog chained to the post. Whenever he walks past the big dog at 121 rue Frontenac, it barks furiously. The dog did not bark on Thursday morning. [Begin your deduction with what you proved on Day 2, i.e. use it as your first premise.]

Day 4. A psychic (who's always right) says Louis is kidnapped or lost. If he's lost, he can't be in Montreal (he knows the city too well). If he's kidnapped and in Montreal, the police would have found him. They haven't. [Try an RAA.]

Day 5. I receive a note demanding a ransom of a thousand dollars. The note is either from Louis and the real kidnappers or from someone trying to make some easy money. If they wanted to make some easy money, I wouldn't have received a note asking for a thousand dollars (which will be hard to get from a poor man like myself). If it is from the real kidnappers, then they and Louis are in Quebec City. [Deduce a conjunction answering the following two questions: Is the note from the real kidnappers? and Where is Louis?]

Day 6. Checking on the suspects, you find that Mary is awfully squeamish. This tells you that she had a hand in Louis's disappearance if and only if she hired someone else to do her dirty work. If she hired someone, it would be Joe and Betty Anne, or her brother Ted. But we already know that Joe is not the culprit.

Day 7. An anonymous phone caller tells you that Louis is held captive by some strange cult called Cabala (there's more to this case than meets the eye). If she's right, Chloe will know about it, though she won't say anything. Yet if Chloe or Sam knows about it, Bud will tell you if you slip him a twenty. You slip him a twenty, and he has nothing to tell.

Day 8. Arriving in Quebec City, looking for some leads, you see Mugsy. There are three reasons why Mugsy might be here. Either he is going to mail another note, or he's helping hold Louis in Quebec City, or he's vacationing. If he's mailing another note, he's a culprit, and if he's helping hold Louis, he's a culprit. As you go to find out, Mugsy sees you and runs down an alley before you can apprehend him. He wouldn't be running away if he were vacationing.

Day 9. An anonymous phone caller tells you that the whole case is "A SP—" but he chokes, and the phone goes dead after he gets out the first three letters. No one would have killed the caller unless he was right.

Day 10. Mugsy has been reported going into an old warehouse. You sneak in the back door and along a narrow corridor. There are two doors at the end of the hall. The police have said that Louis must be held in one of these two rooms. A thick layer of dust covers the door on the left.

Day 10½. Your heart pounds, you slip your pistol out of your pocket and bust through the door. Much to your chagrin, there's no one there. [This requires a revision of the conclusion reached on Day 10. Using your new information, go back to it and prove that the police were wrong when they said that Louis must be in one of these two rooms. Use a reductio argument.]

Day 11. You turn to the other door at the back of the warehouse. It leads to the only other room in the warehouse. You know that this is the warehouse Mugsy entered, and he would have entered it only if Louis was captive here.

Day 12. The minutes seem like hours as you sneak to the door and quietly open it. You see Louis, Mary, and Mugsy sharing a bottle of good French wine, laughing at how upset I must be. If this were a serious kidnapping, they would not be laughing.

Day 13. Having discovered the whole thing is a spoof, you deduce the motive and the reason why Mary and Ted were involved when you note that either Louis or Mary wanted to fool me; that whoever wanted to fool me must have had a lot of money; that Mary and Mugsy are broke; and that if Louis wanted to fool me, Mary and Mugsy must have participated because he paid them.

Day 14. You wonder whether you should charge me the full rate, given that it was all a spoof. You believe you should get paid the full rate if you did the regular amount of work, however, so. . . .

Day 15. Not having my brother's sense of humour, and thinking that one should pay for the consequences of one's actions, I decide that I should. . . .

 For more online exercises, review questions, and quizzes related to the material in this chapter, please go to www.oupcanada.com/GoodReasoning5e

GLOSSARY OF KEY TERMS

abbreviated argument · an argument that contains hidden premises or conclusions.

acceptable premises, acceptability · premises that should (at least provisionally) be accepted by the audience to whom an argument is directed.

ad hominem **argument** · an argument that dismisses what someone says because of some feature of that person's character that shows them to be unknowledgeable, untrustworthy, or illegitimately biased.

ad populum **argument** · an argument that attempts to establish some conclusion on the basis of its popular appeal: a counter to *pro hominem* reasoning.

affirming the antecedent (AA) · the propositional logic argumentation scheme $X \rightarrow Y$, X, *therefore Y,* traditionally called "*modus ponens.*"

affirming the consequent (AC) · the fallacious argumentation scheme $X \rightarrow Y$, *Y, therefore X,* which has instances that are not deductively valid.

ambiguous · An ambiguous word or phrase has more than one specifiable meaning in the context in which it is used. (See AMPHIBOLE, SYNTACTIC AMBIGUITY, and SEMANTIC AMBIGUITY.)

amphibole · an ambiguity that results from a confusing grammatical construction (also called a "syntactic ambiguity"), as when someone says, "Last night I shot a burglar in my pyjamas," which could mean "Last night I shot a burglar who was in my pajamas," or "Last night I shot a burglar while I was in my pajamas."

analogue · one of two or more things being compared in an analogy.

antecedent · the "if" proposition in a conditional, i.e. X is the antecedent in the conditional "If X, then Y."

appeal to authority · an argument that draws part or all of its support from the say-so of an expert or authoritative source.

appeal to eyewitness testimony . an argument scheme that draws evidence from someone's observation of an event or object. For the argument to be strong, the person must be in a good position to make the observation, be free from bias, and ideally have recorded the observation.

appeal to ignorance · (See ARGUMENT FROM IGNORANCE.)

appeal to precedent · an argument that uses analogical reasoning to show that some action will set a precedent whereby other relevantly similar actions will have to be permitted or not; or that a precedent has already been set such that a further action should be allowed (or disallowed) because it is relevantly similar to what has already been allowed (or disallowed).

argument · a set of reasons ("premises") offered in support of a claim (a "conclusion"). (See EXTENDED ARGUMENT and SIMPLE ARGUMENT.)

argument against authority · an argument against an appeal to authority. A good argument against authority will point out that one of the five requirements of a good appeal to authority has not been met.

argument by analogy · an argument that draws a conclusion that one analogue has a particular feature on the basis of other analogues to which it is relevantly similar having that feature.

argument by disanalogy · a counter-argument against analogy which attempts to show that two purported analogues are not analogous. A good argument by disanalogy does so by showing that the purported analogues do not share necessary similarities or that there are relevant differences that distinguish them.

argumentative essay · the form our writing takes when we are setting down the arguments for a position we hold, engaging in original research on a controversial issue, or conducting an inquiry to arrive at a position we will then hold.

argument diagram · a drawing that clarifies the structure of an argument by isolating its premises and conclusions (defined in a legend) and connecting them with + signs to indicate "linked" premises and arrows to indicate the lines of support that are proposed between the premises and conclusions. (See also SUPPLEMENTED DIAGRAM.)

argument flag · an image or some other non-verbal speech act used to draw attention to an argument.

argument from ignorance/appeal to ignorance · an argument that draws a conclusion that something is (or is not) a certain way on the basis of the absence of evidence disconfirming (or affirming) it.

argument narrative · a report of someone's argument that conveys their premises and conclusion without citing their actual words (or images or any other key components of their argument). A narrative can be the basis of an assessment of the argument but it is important to keep in mind that the person who narrates the argument may not present it accurately.

argument scheme · a pattern of argument that can be isolated and treated as a standard for judging and constructing arguments. (See also COUNTER-SCHEME.)

audience · an individual or group to whom an argument is directed.

begging the question · a type of circularity whereby a premise assumes the truth of a conclusion that it is supposed to be supporting, thereby making the premise unacceptable as a reason for that conclusion.

belief system · the basic set of beliefs and values held by an individual or audience.

bias · an inclination or prejudice for or against some view; an illegitimate bias is a bias that illegitimately influences the ways in which we argue in support of the claims that we defend, or interferes with our ability to listen to the reasons that others advance for their own points of view. (See also CONFLICT OF INTEREST and VESTED INTEREST.)

biconditional · a conditional in which the antecedent implies the consequent and the consequent implies the antecedent. In propositional logic, a biconditional is represented as $(X \rightarrow Y) \& (Y \rightarrow X)$.

burden of proof · in an argumentative situation, an obligation to argue for one's point of view.

categorical statement · a statement that expresses a relationship of inclusion or exclusion between two classes of things. "All textbook authors are wealthy" is a categorical statement.

categorical syllogism · an argument composed of three categorical statements that express relationships between three classes of things. A conclusion is drawn about the relationship between two classes based on their independent relationships to the third class in the premises.

causal argument (general), causal reasoning · an argument that attempts to establish a general or universal causal claim of the type "*X causes Y*." (See also PARTICULAR CAUSAL REASONING.)

common knowledge · knowledge we expect to be held in common by an audience by virtue of its members sharing an intellectual environment of specific ideas.

complex proposition · in propositional logic, a proposition that is formed by combining simple propositions with a connective such as "not," "if . . . then," "and," or "or."

conclusion · the claim supported by the premises of an argument.

conclusion indicator · an expression that indicates that some statement or set of statements is the conclusion of an argument.

conditional · a statement that asserts that some statement (its "consequent") is true if some other statement (its "antecedent") is true. In propositional logic, a conditional is represented as $X \rightarrow Y$.

conditional proof ($\rightarrow$P) · the propositional logic argumentation scheme $X (S/ \rightarrow P), \ldots Y$, *therefore* $X \rightarrow Y$. In constructing a conditional proof, the lines of the sub-proof cannot be used elsewhere in a proof.

conditional series (CS) · the propositional logic argumentation scheme $X \rightarrow Y, Y \rightarrow Z$ *therefore* $X \rightarrow Z$.

confirmation bias · our tendency to favour certain things suggests that we favour arguments that confirm the biases and beliefs we already have, ignoring or dismissing evidence that contradicts them.

conflict of interest · a potential source of bias that occurs when someone, usually in a professional situation, is in a position to make a decision that might unfairly provide them with important benefits. (See also BIAS and VESTED INTEREST.)

conjunction · a statement that asserts that two or more propositions (its "conjuncts') are true. In propositional logic, a conjunction is represented as $X \& Y$.

conjunction elimination (&E) · the propositional logic argument scheme X & Y, *therefore* X (or Y).

conjunction introduction (&I) · the propositional logic argument scheme *X, Y, therefore X & Y.*

consequent · the "then" statement in a conditional, i.e. *Y* is the consequent in the conditional "If *X*, then *Y*."

constant condition · a causal factor that must be present if an event is to occur.

contextual relevance · the relevance an argument must have to the context (of debate, or issues) in which it arises.

contradiction · a relationship between two statements whereby they cannot both be true or both false: one must be true and the other false.

contraposition · an immediate inference between categorical statements that allows us to reduce the terms of a syllogism to three.

contrary · a relation between two statements whereby they cannot both be true but they could both be false.

convergent premises · in an argument, premises that are separate and distinct and offer independent evidence for a conclusion (as opposed to "linked" premises).

conversion · an immediate inference between categorical statements that allows us to reduce the terms of a syllogism to three.

correlation · a relation between two or more variables, such that when one is modified, so is the other (or others).

counter-scheme · a type of scheme that is used to criticise arguments of a particular type by showing that the premises in question are unacceptable, or that the argument is not valid. (See also ARGUMENT SCHEME.)

deductively valid argument · an argument in which the conclusion necessarily follows from the premises in the sense that it is impossible for the premises to be true and the conclusion false.

DeMorgan's laws · the propositional logic argumentation schemes DeMV (which recognizes that ~(X V Y) is equivalent to ~X & ~Y) and DeM& (which recognizes that ~(X & Y) is equivalent to ~X V ~Y).

denying the antecedent (DA) · the fallacious propositional logic argumentation scheme X→Y, ~X, therefore ~Y, which has instances that are not deductively valid.

denying the consequent (DC) · the propositional logic argumentation scheme X→Y, ~Y, therefore ~X, traditionally known as "*modus tollens.*"

diagram · see ARGUMENT DIAGRAM.

dilemma (D) · the propositional logic argumentation scheme X V Y, X→Z, Y→Z, therefore Z.

dilemma to disjunction (DV) · the propositional logic argumentation scheme X V Y, X→Z, Y→W, therefore Z V W.

disanalogy · an argument that shows two or more analogues to be relevantly dissimilar and thus not analogous.

disjunction · a statement that asserts that one or more of a number of propositions (its "disjuncts") are true. In propositional logic, a disjunction is represented as *X V Y.*

disjunction elimination (VE) · the propositional logic argument scheme *X V Y* (or *Y V X*), ~X, therefore Y.

diagram · see "argument diagram."

double negation · a negation of a negation, in propositional logic ~~X, which is equivalent to X.

emotional language · language that consists of words or phrases infused with an emotional charge.

equivocation · a fallacy that occurs when an arguer conflates two or more meanings of a term or phrase.

escaping between the horns of a dilemma · showing that the disjunction a dilemma relies on is a false dilemma. (See also TAKING A DILEMMA BY THE HORNS.)

ethotic argument · one of a variety of arguments that is based in some way on issues of character.

euphemism · an expression used to substitute a mild and indirect way of speaking for words that might seem blunt and harsh (e.g. the expression "passed away" used instead of "died").

evaluative critique · an argumentative response to an argument that incorporates both the features of our evaluation and our own insights

exclusive disjunction · a disjunction that states (or assumes) that it is not possible for both disjuncts to be true, represented as *(X V Y)* & *~(X & Y)* in propositional logic.

extended argument · an argument that has a main conclusion supported by premises, some of which are conclusions of subsidiary arguments.

extensional definition · a definition that clarifies a term by identifying members of the class of things it names.

fallacy · a mistaken argument. In terms of this text, a fallacy is an argument that fails either to meet the conditions that govern the good scheme of argument or to abide by the principles of good reasoning in some other regular way.

false dilemma · a disjunction that is false because its disjuncts fail to exhaust all alternatives (and some other potential disjunct may be true); also called a "false dichotomy."

generalization · the process of moving from specific observations about some individuals within a group to general claims about the members of the group.

guilt (and honour) by association · an argument that attributes "guilt" (or honour) to a person or group on the basis of some association that is known or thought to exist between that person or group and some other person or group of dubious (or strong) beliefs or behaviour. A conclusion is drawn on the basis of the alleged guilt or honour.

hidden conclusion · an implicit (unstated) conclusion in an argument.

hidden premise · an implicit (unstated) premise that an argument depends on.

immediate inference · one of the relations between the four pure forms of categorical statement. They are called "immediate" because there are no "mediate" inferences involved.

inclusive disjunction · a disjunction that states (or assumes) that it is possible for both disjuncts to be true, represented as $X \vee Y$ in propositional logic.

inconsistent premises · premises that cannot both (or all) be correct if they are contained within the same premise set for a specific conclusion.

inductively valid argument · an argument that is not deductively valid, which has premises that make the conclusion likely.

inference indicators · words or phrases that indicate that particular statements are premises or conclusions.

intensional definition · a definition that clarifies the meaning of a term by identifying the essential qualities that make something a member of the class of things it names, i.e. by referring to its meaning or "intension."

internal relevance · the relationship of relevance (see RELEVANCE) between the premises

of an argument and the conclusions that they are intended to support.

invalid argument · an argument that is not valid. (See also VALID ARGUMENT.)

linked premises · in an argument, premises that work as a unit, i.e. that support a conclusion only when they are conjoined. (Compare CONVERGENT PREMISES).

logical consequence · a claim that follows from a specified set of claims (i.e. that is acceptable if the claims it follows from are acceptable). The conclusion of a good argument is a logical consequence of its premises.

macro-diagram · a diagram showing the support between sub-arguments within an extended argument. (Compare MICRO-DIAGRAM.)

metaphor · a description that describes one thing as though it were another (as in "Jill is a block of ice"); in non-verbal argument, a non-verbal element that operates in this way (e.g. the pig in a cartoon that represents a politician as a pig, in order to suggest that they have been greedy).

micro-diagram · a diagram showing the detailed support for each sub-conclusion within an argument. (Compare MACRO-DIAGRAM.)

modus ponens · see AFFIRMING THE ANTECEDENT.

modus tollens · see DENYING THE CONSEQUENT.

negation · a statement that denies another statement. In propositional logic, a negation is represented as $\sim X$, where X is the proposition that is negated.

non-verbal demonstration · an argument in which non-verbal elements (music, sounds, images, aromas, etc.) are used to directly present evidence in favour of a conclusion.

non-verbal metaphor · see METAPHOR.

obversion · an immediate inference between categorical statements that allows us to reduce the terms of a syllogism to three.

opponents · in the case of any argument, those individuals who hold an opposing point of view.

particular affirmative (PA) · a pure form of categorical statement that affirms a relationship between some members of one class and another class: Some S are P.

particular causal reasoning · a type of reasoning involving particular causal claims. They usually invoke general principles, scientific claims, or some generally established theory as a basis for the particular claims. (See also CAUSAL ARGUMENT.)

particular negative (PN) · a pure form of categorical statement that negates a relationship between some members of one class and all members of another class: Some S are not P.

poll · a specific kind of generalization that draws a conclusion about some population on the basis of a sample of that population.

premise · a reason offered in support of a conclusion.

premise indicators · expressions that indicate that particular statements are the premises of an argument.

principles of communication · basic principles of interpretation that make communication possible. We use the principles of communication when we interpret arguments and other "speech acts." The principles are (1) "Assume that a speech act is intelligible," (2) "Interpret a speech act in a way that fits the context in which it occurs," and (3) "Interpret a speech act in a way that is in keeping with the meaning of its explicit elements (the words, gestures, music, etc., it explicitly contains)."

principle of proportionality · the principle that the response to a wrong that someone commits must not be out of proportion with the wrong in question. The principle implies that one must not overreact to a wrong that is committed.

pro homine **reasoning** · reasoning that appeals to someone's good character (often the counter to *ad hominem* argument).

propaganda · information, especially of a biased or misleading nature, used to promote a political cause or point of view.

propositional logic · an account of deductively valid inferences that depend on the relationships between propositions that are expressed by the propositional connectives "if," "then," "and," "or," and "not."

pure form · one of the four distinct types of categorical statement: UA, UN, PA, or PN.

questionable premise · a premise for which we lack the information to determine whether it is acceptable or unacceptable. In such cases, the arguer assumes the burden of proof to supply such information.

random sample · a sample of some group chosen in a way that gives every member of the group an equal chance of being selected to be a member of it.

red herring · an irrelevant diversion in a chain of reasoning, whereby attention is shifted to another issue and not returned to the original issue.

reductio ad absurdum (RAA) · the propositional logic argumentation scheme X (S/RAA), . . . Y & ~Y, *therefore* ~X. In constructing an RAA proof the lines of the sub-proof cannot be used elsewhere in a proof.

relevance · a measure of the relationship between an argument's premises and its conclusions. The premises of an argument are *positively* relevant to a conclusion when they make it more likely and *negatively* relevant when they make it less likely. (See also INTERNAL RELEVANCE.)

representative sample · the sample examined during the course of a generalization.

rhetorical question · a question used (for stylistic reasons) to make a statement. The question in the argument "Our Phonics Package will ensure your child does not fail grade school. Do you want your child to fail grade school? Order our Phonics Package today!" is used as a way of making the statement that "You do not want your child to fail grade school."

rules for good definitions · four rules for constructing good definitions. The *rule of equivalence* stipulates that the defining phrase should include neither more nor less than the term being defined. The *rule of essential characteristics* stipulates that the defining phrase must specify the essential features of the thing defined, i.e. the traits that are indispensable to its being what it is, rather than accidental features. The *rule of clarity* stipulates that the defining phrase must clarify the meaning of the term defined by using words that make it readily understood by the intended audience. The *rule of neutrality* stipulates that the defining phrase must avoid terms heavily charged with emotion.

scientific method · method used to establish claims in scientific reasoning, which involves the formation and testing of hypotheses.

scope · the boundaries that govern the construction of an argument: what will be covered and how. The scope establishes some of the arguer's obligations in the argument.

semantic ambiguity · ambiguity that arises because a word or phrase has more than one possible meaning.

simple argument · an argument that has (only) one conclusion supported by one or more premises.

simple statement · a statement that expresses a proposition that is not a negation, conjunction, disjunction, or conditional. In propositional logic, simple propositions are represented as lower-case letters of the alphabet.

slanting · techniques used to distort reports and arguments. One slants *by omission* when one leaves out facts and details that are not in keeping with the impression one wishes to create. One slants *by distortion* when one uses words and descriptions that exaggerate or colour the facts that one is reporting in a manner that enhances an impression one wishes to create.

slippery-slope argument · an argument that purports to show that some action, if performed (or not performed), will set of a causal chain leading to an undesirable (or desirable) consequence.

speech act · an act of communication, which may be verbal (using words) or non-verbal, or a mix of both. A remark, the writing of a sentence, a wave to a friend, a "thumbs up" gesture, the drawing of a map, etc. all count as speech acts.

straw man · an argument that deliberately or accidentally misrepresents or exaggerates a position that it then proceeds to attack.

strong argument · as opposed to a "weak argument," an argument that provides premises that are acceptable and a conclusion that follows from them.

sufficiency · the degree to which there is enough evidence in the premises of an argument to support its conclusion. Premises in an argument are sufficient when they establish that a conclusion is more likely than not.

supplemented diagram · a diagram of an argument to which has been added information about the arguer, the audience to which the argument is directed, or those who oppose this point of view. A *fully supplemented diagram* contains information on all three. (See also ARGUMENT DIAGRAM.)

symbol, symbolic reference · in a non-verbal argument, a non-verbal symbol used to refer to some idea or claim or principle (as when a cross is used to represent Christ or Christianity).

syntactic ambiguity · see AMPHIBOLE.

taking a dilemma by the horns · refuting a dilemma by showing that one (or both) of the conditionals it relies on is not acceptable. (See also ESCAPING BETWEEN THE HORNS OF A DILEMMA.)

testimony · a statement or statements drawn from the personal experience of an individual.

two-wrongs argument/two-wrongs reasoning · an argument that something that would normally be judged (or is normally judged) a wrong should be permitted because it cancels or alleviates some unfairness or injustice.

two-wrongs by analogy · a two-wrongs argument that is based on an analogous relationship between two wrongs and that appeals to a principle of fairness in treating both in the same way.

universal audience · an audience made up of reasonable people, used as a tool in judging the acceptability of premises.

universal affirmative (UA) · a pure form of categorical statement that affirms a relationship between all members of one class and another class: All S are P.

universal negative (UN) · a pure form of categorical statement that negates a relationship between all members of two classes: No S are P.

vague · A vague word or phrase has no clearly specifiable meaning.

valid argument · see DEDUCTIVELY VALID ARGUMENT and INDUCTIVELY VALID ARGUMENT.

variable condition · in the case of a cause and effect, the variable condition is the change that brings about the effect.

Venn diagram · a tool for testing the validity of categorical syllogisms.

verbal dispute · a dispute in which the disputants do not really disagree but appear to because they assign different meanings to some key term or phrase.

vested interest · a potential cause of bias that exists when an arguer will benefit in some significant way if they and other arguers see issues in a particular way. (See also BIAS and CONFLICT OF INTEREST.)

visual arguments · are arguments that convey premises and conclusions with non-verbal images one finds in drawings, photographs, films, videos, sculpture, natural objects, and so on. In most cases they combine visual and verbal cues that can be understood as argument.

weak argument · as opposed to a "strong argument," an argument that fails to provide premises that are acceptable and/or a conclusion that follows from them.

CREDITS

Grateful acknowledgment is made for permission to reprint the following:

Chapter 3

Page 55: Excerpt from a Letter to the Editor, *The Washington Times*, 6 June 2011. Courtesy Tom Harris, Executive Director of the International Climate Science Coalition.

Chapter 4

Page 101: Excerpt from *The Hidden Assassins* by Robert Wilson. © Robert Wilson 2006. Used by permission of Houghton Mifflin Harcourt Publishing Company. All Rights Reserved. Reprinted by permission of HarperCollins Publishers Ltd.

Chapter 5

Page 111: Excerpt from *Sydney Morning Herald*, 15/12/2002, "$40,000-plus for eggs of clever, pretty women" by Kate Cox.

Page 121: Advertisement for Scotiabank. Source: Scotiabank.

Page 129: Excerpt from Guerilla Girls announcement. Copyright © Guerrilla Girls, Inc. Courtesy www.guerillagirls.com

Chapter 6

Page 133: Commentary on a cartoon about Iraq. Source: Cox and Forkum, www.coxandforkum.com/archives/001089.html

Chapter 7

Page 182: Excerpt from Ronald M. Green, in "The Ethical Considerations", in "The First Human Cloned Human Embryo" by Jose B. Cibelli et al, in *Scientific American* Jan. 2002.

Page 183: Quote from Owen Gingerich. Reprinted with permission of the author.

Page 184: Quote from Steve Fuller. Source: pp. 44–5, *Dissent Over Descent*, Steve Fuller. Icon Books. Used with permission.

Page 189: Excerpt from "To stop terrorists we must know the roots of terrorism." From *The Independent*, 19 December 2008. Used with permission.

Page 195: Excerpt from Howard Zinn. Reprinted by permission from *The Progressive*, 409 E Main St, Madison WI 53703 www.progressive.org

Chapter 8

Page 202: Excerpt adapted from Research and Statistics group of the department of the solicitor general of Canada, printed in *The Globe and Mail*, 9 January 1987.

Page 223: Quote from: Daniel Polsby. © Daniel Polsby. Used with permission.

Chapter 9

Page 232: Excerpt from the study "Women like practicality in cars, men go for the looks." All rights reserved. Republication or redistribution of Thomson Reuters content, including by framing or similar means, is expressly prohibited without the prior written consent of Thomson Reuters. Thomson Reuters and its logo are registered trademarks or trademarks of the Thomson Reuters group of companies around the world. © Thomson Reuters 2011. Thomson Reuters journalists are subject to an Editorial Handbook which requires fair presentation and disclosure of relevant interests.

Page 241: Excerpt from an Angus Reid survey of British Columbia residents. 20 June 2011. Used with permission.

Page 248: Excerpt from Steven Pinker, "A History of Violence", *New Republic*, 19/03/2007.

Page 248: Excerpt from *The Globe and Mail*, 9 March 1987. Source: Reuters, originally printed in the Telegraph. 06/03/87

Page 249: Excerpt from "Gas prices up, auto deaths down," by Joan Lowy, *Associated Press*, July 11, 2008.

Page 249: Excerpt from Jess Halliday, "Study links obesity to protein in infant formula." Copyright © 2000/2012 William Reed Business Media. Reprinted with the permission of NutraIngredients-USA.com. This reprint does not constitute or imply any endorsement or sponsorship of any product, service, company or organization.

Page 250: Excerpt from "Flu pandemic not nonsense," NRC Handelsblad, 12 May, 2009. www.nrc.nl/international/opinion

Chapter 10

Page 253: Excerpt from *Detroit Free Press* (8 November 2010). Source: http://www.truman-project.org/posts/2010/11/cutting-fuel-use-important-troops-national-security

Page 268: Excerpt from "Teens with part-time jobs more likely to smoke", *Canadian Press*, 27 Sept 2007. *American Journal of Public Health*, Sept, 2007.

Page 270: Excerpt from "Obesity links found between mothers and daughters, fathers and sons", 13 July 2009, http://www.southasianobserver.com/lifestylenews.php?mid=14&cid=4019

Page 271: Excerpt from "Genes say boys will be boys and girls will be sensitive," Tim Radford, June 22, 1997. Copyright Guardian News & Media Ltd 1997.

Page 272: Excerpt from "Cinema fiction vs. physics reality: Ghosts, vampires, and zombies" by Costas J. Efthimion and Sohang Gandhi', in *Skeptical Inquirer*, August 2007.

Page: 273: Excerpt from "SARS—A clue to its origin?," Reprinted from *The Lancet*, Vol. 361 no. 9371. Chandra Wickramasinghe, Milton Wainwright, Jayant Narlikar, "SARS—A Clue to its origins?". Copyright 2003, with permission from Elsevier.

Page 275: Excerpt from *Close Encounters of the Fourth Kind* by C.D.B. Bryan. Copyright © 1995 by Courtlandt Dixon Barnes Bryan. Used by permission of Alfred A. Knopf, a division of Random House, Inc.

Chapter 11

Page 280: "The wrongfulness of euthanasia," adapted from *Intervention and Reflection: Basic Issues and Medical Ethics*, Ronald Munson, ed., Wadsworth, 1979.

Page 288: Excerpt from "His Dark Material: The unsubtle atheism of Philip Pullman's books," *Wall Street Journal*, 14 December, 2007.

Page 294: Excerpt from " 'Crude' form of protest a Maori tradition," Reprinted by permission of the author.

Chapter 12

Page 309: Excerpt from Martin Luther King's letter from Birmingham jail. Reprinted by arrangement with The Heirs to the Estate of Martin Luther King, Jr., c/o Writers House as agent for the proprietor New York, NY. Copyright 1963 Martin Luther King, Jr.; copyright renewed 1991 Coretta Scott King.

Page 321: Excerpt from Terry Eagleton, "The Pope has blood on his hands," *The Guardian*, 4 April 2005. Used with permission of the author.

Page 329: Excerpt from "On Heidegger's Nazism and Philosophy," Rockmore, Tom. © 1991, University of California Books. Used with permission.

Page 333: Excerpt from article "Skeptic's Skeptic." Reproduced with permission. Copyright © 2010 Scientific American, a division of Nature America, Inc. All rights reserved.

Page 334: Excerpt from "What has Al Gore done for world peace?" Source: *Telegraph*, 12 October 2007. © Telegraph Media Group Limited 2007.

Page 335: Excerpt from Spinwatch newsletter. Source: www.spinwatch.org.uk, 11 October 2007.

Page 338: Excerpt from Martin Luther King's letter from Birmingham jail. Reprinted by arrangement with The Heirs to the Estate of Martin Luther King, Jr., c/o Writers House as agent for the proprietor New York, NY. Copyright 1963 Martin Luther King, Jr.; copyright renewed 1991 Coretta Scott King

Chapter 13

Page 346: Excerpt from "Faith should harness art's appeal" by Jennie Hogan, 12 July 2010. Copyright Guadian News & Media Ltd 2010.

Page 347: Excerpt from p. 69 of Margaret Somerville *The Ethical Canary: Science, Society and the Human Spirit*, Penguin Books, 2000. By permission of the author.

INDEX

absurdity, reduction to, 432–5, 454
acceptability, premise, 55–6, 58, 197–9, 222, 375, 450; conditions of, 200–4
ad hominem arguments ("against the person"), 308, 318–20, 322, 330, 342, 450; abusive, 320
ad populum argument ("appeals to popularity"), 310–11, 450
advertisements, 144, 148
affirming the antecedent (AA), 414, 417, 429, 450
affirming the consequent, 264, 450
al-Ghazali, 23, 68
ambiguity, 171–2, 174, 180, 190, 342, 450; avoiding with brackets, 405; semantic, 454, 172; syntactic, 171
amphibole, 171–2, 450
analogies, 265–6, 280
analogues, 281, 450
analogy, arguments from (by), 178, 280–6, 450; counter-arguments to, 284–6
anecdotal evidence, 229–30
antecedent, 262, 402, 406, 450
antonyms, 186
"Arab Spring", 276, 291, 292
argumentation: in argumentative essays, 351; study of, 2, 5
argumentative essay, 340, 348–52, 450; addressing points of opponents, 351–2; argumentation, 351; clarity in, 349–50; objectivity, 351–2; scope, 348; structure, 350; summary of components of, 352
Argument Clinic (Monty Python skit), 1, 7, 173
argument narratives, 97–8, 451
argument, sample student paper, 353–62
arguments, 1, 2–3; abbreviated, 135, 450; assessing, 120, 351; balancing, 44–5; borderline cases, 89–91; circular, 206; criticism of, 58–9; defining, 7–9, 84, 450; definition through, 181; ethotic, 12, 307, 452; "from design", 282–4; distinguishing from non-arguments, 84–5, 92–4; drafts of, 174; dressed, 81, 94, 107, 161; evaluating

("assessing"), 52; ; without explanations, 94–6; explicitness of, 161; extended, 82, 107, 108, 110–14, 125, 209–10, 452; flaws in, 220–1; fully supplemented, 120–2; general causal, 241–5, 451; hidden components, 131, 351; on the hoof, 81, 84, 226; invalid, 453; principal, 82; revising, 220–2; simple, 7, 81, 82, 108–10, 454; steps in preparing, 127; strong, 52, 55–9, 196, 214, 222, 226, 455; sub-, 82, 107, 125, 202–3; uses of, 10; valid, 75; visual, 143, 455; weak, 11–12, 20, 52, 57, 58, 220–1, 455
Aristotle, 23, 307, 322, 323
arrows, 109, 111, 219
assent, condition of, 202
assumptions, 11, 139–40, 161
audiences, 14–20, 451; of argumentative essay, 348; different kinds of, 19–20; historical examples of, 14–19; hostile, 19, 20, 348; open, 19; specific, 19, 20; sympathetic, 19; universal, 20, 197, 200, 455
authorities, 314, 315; see also experts
authority: appeals to, 74, 75, 204, 312, 450; arguments against, 75, 322–4, 450; arguments from, 312–18; arguments given by person in position of, 313

balanced argument, 215–16
begging the question, 206–7, 451
belief systems, 10–12, 19, 20, 230, 451
bias(es), 3–5, 28–31, 451; cognitive, 28; confirmation, 4, 28, 451; conflict of interest, 34–5; detecting illegitimate, 35–41; difficult cases of illegitimate, 41–5; halo effect, 4; illegitimate, 28–30; lack of self-awareness, 4; looking for balance, 40–1; overconfidence effect, 3–4; sample, 229–30; survey opposing views, 40, 41; vested interests, 31–3, 41, 45, 122, 455
biconditionals, 406, 417–18, 451
brackets, 405
Brantford Carnegie Library, 146, 147
burden of proof, 52–4, 55, 197, 451

and, 373; conversion and, 372–3; obversion
and, 372; in Venn diagram, 379
universal instantiation, 74–5
universal negative statement (UN), 366–7, 370,
376, 455; contradiction and, 371; contraposition and, 373; conversion and, 372–3;
obversion and, 372; in Venn diagram, 379
"unless", 406

vagueness, 171–2, 174, 180, 190, 342, 455
validity, 60–4, 196, 455; deductive, 60–1, 208,
374, 452; inductive, 61–2, 208, 214, 453;
relevance and, 62–3; sufficiency and, 62–4;
testing with Venn diagrams, 378–89

value judgements, 201
variable condition, 242, 455
variables, 396–7
Venn diagrams, 378–89, 455; examples of,
380–9; testing for validity, 380
verbal dispute, 173–4, 180, 455
vested interests, 31–3, 41, 45, 122, 455

web sites: appeal to authority and, 317
words: using precisely, 168